**DO NOT REMOVE
CARDS FROM POCKET**

PERSONAL FINANCE TODAY

Roger LeRoy Miller

School of Business and
Law and Economics Center
University of Miami

PERSONAL FINANCE TODAY

West Publishing Company
St. Paul   New York   Los Angeles   San Francisco

*A study guide has been developed to assist you in mastering concepts presented in this text. The study guide reinforces concepts by presenting them in condensed, concise form. Additional illustrations and examples are also included. The study guide is available from your local bookstore under the title, **Study Guide to Accompany Personal Finance Today,** prepared by Grant J. Wells.*

PHOTOGRAPHS

All photographs taken by Carol Bernson, © *1979.*

Library of Congress Cataloging in Publication Data
Miller, Roger LeRoy.
  Personal finance today.

  Bibliography: p.
  Includes index.
  1. Finance, Personal. I. Title.
HG179.M49   332'.024   78-24517
ISBN 0-8299-0233-3

CONTENTS

5014284

PREFACE

We live in a world of inflation, marked by increasingly complex consumer products, a variety of methods for investing our savings, a burgeoning insurance industry offering us all types of new insurance; the list goes on and on. In short, the financial life of the average American consumer is becoming more complicated. The study of personal finance is designed to aid you, the student, to better understand your personal finances in this complex world. And the goal of this book is to help you maximize your happiness by knowing how to spend, save, and borrow, to mention only a few of the things involved in your financial affairs. In this text, you will find not only *de*scriptions of different financial aspects of your life but also *pre*scriptions—what you *should do* in order to attain your goals.

PRACTICAL APPLICATIONS

Personal finance is not all theory; it is practice, too. For that reason, each chapter contains a **Practical Applications** section. Most of the descriptive material about a particular subject—say, transportation in the chapter on the automobile—is presented in the first few pages of each chapter. The Practical Applications are set in different type and in two columns. In the chapter on the automobile, this section discusses purchasing an automobile, including deciding on the dealer, the type of car, the financing, whether you should buy a new or a used car, and so on. These Practical Applications sections are helpful to the practicing consumer—that is, to all of us, for we all must consume. They contain numerous lists of how to do things and where to find information—for example, what to do when your car doesn't work, where to go for the best bank account, and how to buy life insurance. You will also find several tables that you can complete to help you solve a particular problem involving your own financial affairs. For example, Chapter 5, which concerns banks and the banking system, contains a table you can fill in to compare the different costs and services offered by the different banks in your community.

OTHER PEDAGOGICAL AIDS

A number of pedagogical aids have been included to help you understand the materials presented in this text.

Glossary of Terms

Because terminology is sometimes a stumbling block for students of personal finance, important terms appear in boldface type when they are first defined in the chapter. The definition, somewhat modified, is presented again at the end of each chapter under the heading "Glossary of Terms."

Chapter Summaries

Each chapter has a point-by-point summary, consisting of the most important points from the chapter and the Practical Applications section. Students will find it helpful to review these prior to examinations.

Study Questions

Every chapter has several Study Questions. By answering these, the student will better understand the chapter text. Answers to the Study Questions appear in the *Instructor's Manual.*

Case Problems

Since one of the best ways to learn personal finance is to work through actual case problems, each chapter contains two realistic case problems the student can solve. The answers to these case problems, most of which involve numerical calculations, are found in the *Instructor's Manual.* These cases and answers were thoughtfully contributed by Professor Judy Ferris of South Dakota State University.

Selected References

For those students who wish to pursue the study of a specific topic, selected references are offered at the end of each chapter. The average student of personal finance will find these articles and books interesting and readable; no purely academic, research-oriented studies are included.

OTHER DISTINGUISHING FEATURES

We've attempted to include a number of novel, interesting, and above all, useful additions to this personal finance book that help distinguish it from its competitors. Among these are:

1. A more extensive analysis of our tax system, including unique ways individuals legally can avoid taxes;
2. A careful explanation of tax shelters, including a Practical Applications section on how to avoid taxes by forming a corporation;
3. A discussion of the true cost of owning an automobile, including the cost of the money tied up in the car, even when it is paid for in cash;
4. A list of various consumer protection agencies that students can consult about consumer problems;
5. At the beginning of the book—where it belongs—a complete explanation of inflation that helps the student understand how rising prices affect him or her and how they affect personal financial decision making;
6. An expanded section on investment, including an in-depth discussion of the stock market and alternative strategies for investing;
7. A look at the effects of the 1976 Tax Reform Act on estate planning;
8. Information on choosing a career and writing a resumé.

SUPPLEMENTS

Two important supplements—an *Instructor's Manual* and a *Study Guide*—make this personal finance book a complete package.

Instructor's Manual

Professor Carlene Creviston of Ball State University has prepared an invaluable *Instructor's Manual*, which includes the following parts:

1. Outline of the chapter
2. Additional references
3. Answers to study questions
4. Answers to case problems
5. A test bank

This *Manual* is free to all adopters.

Student Workbook

Because most students find that the more they work practical problems, the more they understand and retain personal finance principles, we

have provided a *Study Guide* by Professor Grant Wells of Ball State University. The study guide includes:
1. Crossword puzzles (to develop terminology)
2. Fill-in questions
3. True-false questions
4. An outline

ACKNOWLEDGMENTS

Many individuals helped with this major project. Among the reviewers of the various drafts of the text were:

Professor Carlene Creviston
Ball State University
Muncie, Indiana

Professor Judy Ferris
South Dakota State University
Vermillion, South Dakota

Professor Forest Harlow
East Texas State University
Commerce, Texas

Professor Carole Makela
Colorado State University
Fort Collins, Colorado

Professor Joe Marchese
Monroe Community College
Rochester, New York

Professor Russell Ogden
Eastern Michigan University
Ypsilanti, Michigan

Professor Fred Powers
University of South Florida
Tampa, Florida

Professor Jolene Scriven
Northern Illinois University
DeKalb, Illinois

Professor Syble Taylor
Fullerton College
Fullerton, California

Professor William Weller
Modesto Junior College
Modesto, California

Professor Grant Wells
Ball State University
Muncie, Indiana

A special note of thanks must be given to Dr. Keith Smith, professor of finance at the U.C.L.A. Graduate School of Management. Professor Smith, the co-author of four books on investment and an expert in that field, graciously provided first drafts of Chapters 15 and 16, including the Practical Applications sections.

In spite of all the help I received from the reviewers, none of them is in any way responsible for any remaining errors. I must take sole responsibility. And I'd like to ask concerned readers to please write me with any and all comments, criticisms, and corrections they wish to make. By learning what users like and dislike, I can improve this book so that students using it in the future will be better able to understand and manage their own personal finances.

UNIT

1

Today's Concerns

Inflation

■Rising prices affect us all. The persistent increase in the cost of living in the United States is perhaps the most obvious problem facing the consumer today. We are continually reminded by newspaper and magazine articles that today's dollar is worth only 25 percent of 1940's dollar. Since inflation is ever present and, according to most experts, will be around for many years to come, it seems an appropriate starting point in a book on personal finance. In this chapter we will examine what inflation is, how it is measured, and how it affects each of us in our simultaneous roles of consumer, taxpayer, and income earner. In the Practical Applications section we look briefly at how to protect ourselves against the ravages of inflation.

A DEFINITION OF INFLATION

First, we must have a precise definition of that phenomenon called **inflation.** We will technically define it as a *sustained* rise in some average of all prices. Notice the emphasis on the word sustained in that definition. A once-and-for-all increase in the average of all prices is not, under this definition, an inflationary phenomenon. Rather, it is just a once-and-for-all event. When the average of all prices is rising year in and year out, as it has in the United States and elsewhere for many years, truly inflation exists.

During an inflationary period, some prices rise faster than others. It is important, therefore, to distinguish clearly between a price that is rising along with all others and one that may be rising at a slower or faster rate than the average of all others. The distinction we make here is

3

between what are called absolute, or nominal, prices and relative prices. Much consumer decision making is based on relative rather than nominal prices. What the consumer is interested in is what he or she must give up in terms of other goods and services in order to get the commodity in question. For example, if all after-tax salaries rose by 100 percent and all prices did, too, would the fact that a week's groceries now cost twice as much as they did the previous year deter you from buying them? It shouldn't, because the relative price of groceries would remain the same. In this simplified example, all prices rose, including wages; essentially, nothing changed except nominal prices.

Distinguishing Between Nominal and Relative Prices

When we refer to the relative price of any item, we stress the word *relative*. What is important is how expensive one good or service is compared with, or relative to, another. The relative price of apples, for example, can be compared with the price of oranges. In deciding what and how much to buy, you generally make your decisions about one good or service based on its price compared with the price of an alternative good or service.

Let us look at a common situation today in which the prices of alternative goods seem to be rising. Here are the prices given for eight-track stereo cartridges and four-track stereo cassettes in two years:

	eight-track stereo cartridge	four-track stereo cassette	ratio of prices
Year One	$ 5.00	$5.00	1:1
Year Two	$10.00	$7.50	1:¾

What has happened to the prices from year one to year two? The prices of both cartridges and cassettes have risen, but the relative price has changed. In year one, cartridges and cassettes cost the same amount, but in year two the price of cartridges relative to cassettes has risen. Or, looked at the other way around, the price of cassettes relative to cartridges has decreased. In year one, the relative price of cartridges compared with cassettes was $5/$5, or 1:1. But in year two, the relative price of cartridges compared with cassettes was $10/$7.50, or 1:¾. The relative price of cassettes has fallen.

Perhaps you can understand why it is important to compare relative prices, particularly in an economy as prone to inflation as ours is today. Just because the price of something rises does not mean it is a poor buy. You must find out whether the price of what you are interested in has risen faster or slower than the prices of other goods you wish to purchase. In other words, you have to look at relative prices.

HOW WE MEASURE RATES OF INFLATION

We have to find some index of the average of all prices in order to make comparisons from year to year. There are a number of price indexes we can use. Here we discuss the Consumer Price Index.

Constructing the Consumer Price Index

The Consumer Price Index is designed to reflect price changes in goods and services purchased by all urban workers. (It is *not* a cost-of-living index.) It covers items purchased by individuals at both ends of the income scale ranging from persons on welfare to professionals, such as doctors and lawyers.

The CPI is an index of the prices of several thousand goods and services adjusted monthly to their frequency of sales in each retail unit. The store sample that is considered involves some 21,000 outlets. The Bureau of Labor Statistics' definition states that the index covers:

> . . .prices of everything people buy for living—food, clothing, automobiles, homes, house furnishings, household supplies, fuel, drugs, and recreational goods; fees to doctors, lawyers, beauty shops; rent, repair costs, transportation fares, public utility rates, etc. It deals with prices actually charged to consumers, including sales and excise taxes. It also includes real estate taxes in owned homes, but it does not include income or Social Security taxes.[1]

In 1978, two new consumer price indexes were published. The first is an entirely new index called The CPI for All Urban Consumers; the second is a revised index called The Revised CPI for Urban Wage Earners and Clerical Workers. The revised and the new index both reflect a modernization of statistical methods and an updating of (1) the importance assigned to different expenditure categories, (2) the sample of items priced, and (3) the sample of firms where prices are surveyed.

The *new* index represents about 80 percent of the civilian population and includes urban wage earners and clerical workers, the self-employed, professional and other salaried workers, retirees, the unemployed, and others not in the labor force. On the other hand, the *revised* index for urban wage earners and clerical workers represents only about 40 percent of the civilian population.

The most important change in these two price indexes concerns the importance given to different expenditure categories. The old CPI was based on expenditure patterns derived from a survey done in the early 1960s. The revised CPI and the new index for urban consumers are based on consumer expenditures estimated from a 1972-1973 survey. Presumably, the new indexes better reflect what consumers are actually buying today relative to what they were buying in the early 1960s.

---

[1]U.S. Department of Labor, Bureau of Labor Statistics, Supplement to Economic Indicators (Washington, D.C.: U.S. Government Printing Office, 1967).

The CPI is not a "cost-of-living" index. The Bureau of Labor Statistics is quick to point out that the CPI is really not a cost of living index. First of all, it applies only to urban wage earners. Thus, it ignores changes in prices paid by rural wage earners. Additionally, the latest CPI depends on a survey of consumer buying habits in 1972 and 1973. Our buying patterns may have changed significantly since then, particularly in light of relatively higher energy prices. Also, new products are introduced every year, and it takes a long time for such products to be included in the market basket of goods used to construct the CPI. And, finally, there are quality changes in products that cannot be taken into account in the CPI. If both the quality and price of a good go up, it is not appropriate that the CPI also rises, for the higher price is merely a reflection of the higher quality.

COMPARING CHANGES IN THE *CPI* WITH OTHER PRICE CHANGES

Now that you know what the Consumer Price Index is, it is interesting to compare how it changes along with other prices. In Exhibit 1-1, changes in the index of prices of certain consumer items, such as television sets, washing machines, and automobiles, are shown. They are also shown in the first column the Consumer Price Index for all items included in the market basket of goods. That exhibit indicates that the prices of the goods have risen less than the Consumer Price Index. That tells you that the relative prices (given in parentheses below the observed price indexes in Exhibit 1-1) of certain goods are lower today than they were fifteen years ago. This is an important distinction that you, as a wise consumer, should always make. It does not matter what the *absolute* (or observed) price level is; what matters in your purchases is the *relative* prices of those things you buy. If all other prices rose by 500 percent but the price of washing machines rose by only 100 percent, the machines would have become a good buy. Although their *absolute* price is now higher, the *relative* price is dramatically lower.

HISTORY OF PRICES

Now that we have an index to look at, consider what has happened in the United States over the last 118 years. In Exhibit 1-2, we see that the Consumer Price Index has moved erratically and has fallen at times. When prices on average are falling, we are in a period of **deflation**, defined as a sustained drop in the average of all prices. In the 1970s through the beginning of the 1980s, we have had practically the highest rates of inflation, during peacetime, in the entire history of this country.

INCOMES HAVE RESPONDED, TOO

While inflation generally is considered an evil, the fact that prices today are about 600 percent higher than they were 100 years ago does not necessarily mean we are worse off. Incomes have also risen in the

EXHIBIT 1-1.

PRICE CHANGES FOR CERTAIN CONSUMER GOODS

The first column lists the Consumer Price Index for all items that consumers bought from 1960 to 1978. A price index for televisions, washing machines, electric refrigerators, and new and used cars is given for each year. Underneath each price index is what we call the relative price index, or the price of these consumer durables relative to the price of all other goods. Our base year is 1967 for both the relative price index and for the observed price index. So you see in the row after 1967 all the indices are 100. Obviously, the observed price index for many consumer durable goods has been rising at rates less rapid than the overall Consumer Price Index. In fact, the price index for television sets remained relatively constant after 1967, while the Consumer Price Index rose 25 percent. Thus, at the end of the period, the relative price of TVs had fallen around 25 percent. (1967 = 100; relative index is given in parentheses.) Sources: U.S. Department of Labor, Bureau of Labor Statistics, Handbook of Labor Statistics, 1972; Monthly Labor Review, January 1979.

YEAR	CPI ALL ITEMS	TELEVISION SETS	ELECTRIC AUTOMATIC WASHING MACHINES	ELECTRIC REFRIGERATORS	AUTOS New	Used
1960	88.7	127.1	110.7	116.8	90.6	104.5
		(143.3)	(124.8)	(131.7)	(102.1)	(117.8)
1961	89.6	123.8	107.4	115.2	91.3	104.5
		(138.2)	(119.9)	(128.6)	(101.9)	(116.6)
1962	90.6	117.7	104.5	112.5	98.0	104.1
		(129.9)	(115.3)	(124.2)	(102.6)	(114.6)
1963	91.7	114.7	103.0	109.6	93.4	103.5
		(129.9)	(115.3)	(124.2)	(102.6)	(114.9)
1964	92.9	112.1	101.6	107.4	94.7	103.2
		(120.7)	(109.4)	(115.6)	(101.9)	(111.1)
1965	94.5	107.3	100.2	104.2	96.3	100.9
		(113.5)	(106.3)	(110.3)	(101.0)	(106.8)
1966	97.2	102.1	99.7	100.2	97.5	99.1
		(105.0)	(102.5)	(103.1)	(100.3)	(103.2)
1967	100.0	100.0	100.0	100.0	100.0	100.0
		(100.0)	(100.0)	(100.0)	(100.0)	(100.0)
1968	104.2	99.8	102.5	101.3	102.8	—
		(95.8)	(98.4)	(97.2)	(98.7)	—
1969	109.8	99.6	104.6	103.1	104.4	103.1
		(90.7)	(95.3)	(93.9)	(95.1)	(93.9)
1970	116.3	99.8	107.3	105.8	107.6	104.3
		(85.8)	(92.3)	(91.0)	(92.5)	(89.6)
1971	121.3	100.1	104.1	108.1	112.0	110.2
		(82.5)	(85.8)	(89.1)	(92.3)	(90.8)
1972	125.3	99.5	110.5	108.7	111.0	110.5
		(79.4)	(88.2)	(86.7)	(88.5)	(88.2)
1977	186.1	101.2	102.1	141.0	146.0	188.0
		(54.4)	(54.9)	(77.0)	(79.8)	(102.7)
1978	198.4	102.0	105.0	148.0	155.1	198.2
		(51.4)	(52.9)	(74.6)	(83.3)	(99.9)

United States. In Exhibit 1-3, we can see the rise in nominal per capita income in the United States for the last 30 years. If we take account of inflation—that is, subtract out inflationary increases—we come up with what is called **real per capita income,** or per capita income corrected for inflation, shown on the green line in Exhibit 1-3. It has risen, also, albeit at a much lower rate. In fact, it has actually fallen in certain years, most obviously during the Great Depression and, more recently, during the early 1970s. Whether real per capita income will continue to rise in the future is a moot point. In any event, the simple fact that we have inflation does not necessarily mean that we will no longer grow as a nation or, individually, have higher real standards of living.

What Will Happen to Prices in the Future?

If inflation continues as it has in the past, we can anticipate paying some outrageous prices in the future. In Exhibit 1-4, we show the cost of the average home over the next twenty years—if inflation continues at an average rate of 7 percent per year. In the year 2000, the average home will cost a whopping $207,028. It is important to understand inflationary effects on nominal incomes when attempting to compare incomes today with incomes in the past.

In Exhibit 1-5, we show the effects of erosion by inflation. You can see what you would need in 1979 to have the equivalent purchasing power of $10,000 take-home pay in 1950. If someone made $10,000 take-home pay in 1950, it would be equivalent to $27,738 in 1979.

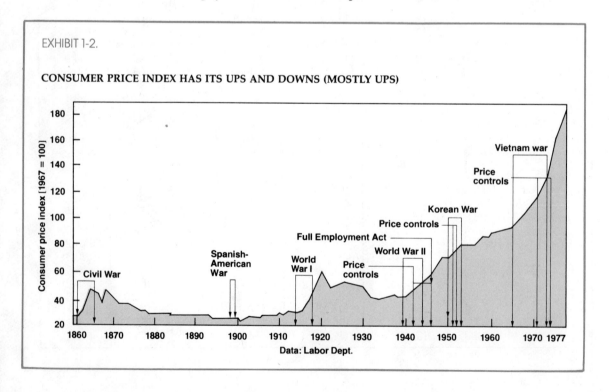

EXHIBIT 1-2.

CONSUMER PRICE INDEX HAS ITS UPS AND DOWNS (MOSTLY UPS)

Data: Labor Dept.

EXHIBIT 1-3.

RISE IN NOMINAL AND REAL PER CAPITA INCOME IN THE UNITED STATES

Per capita personal disposable income is expressed in current dollars in the green line. That is, it is not corrected for changes in the price level.
We know it has been going up steadily from 1919 until the present, except for the Great Depression when it started going downhill. The green line has been corrected for inflation. (All figures expressed in terms of 1972 dollars.) Source: Business Conditions Digest.

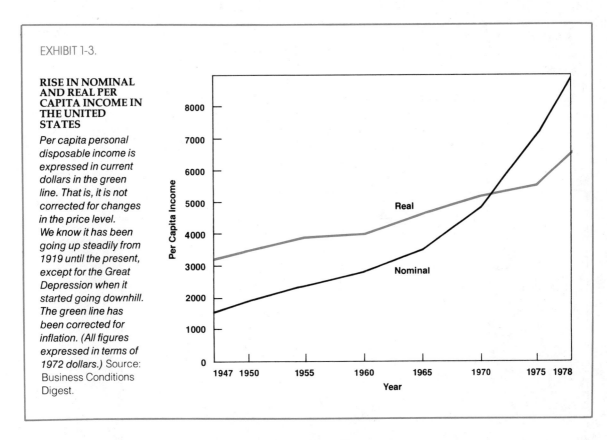

EXHIBIT 1-4.

COST OF THE AVERAGE HOME OVER THE NEXT TWENTY YEARS

If 7 Percent Annual Inflation Continues for Ten Years, the Average House Will Cost:			
1979	$50,000	1984	$70,128
1980	53,500	1985	75,037
1981	57,245	1986	80,289
1982	61,252	1987	85,909
1983	65,540	1988	91,923
		2000	207,028

HYPERINFLATION

Exhibit 1-2 showed a history of rising prices in the United States. However, we have not experienced the extremely rapid inflations of many other countries. When the rate of inflation is 50 percent a month or greater, hyperinflation exists. An example from Hungary during World War II illustrates such a situation. Assume a 1939 index of prices in Hungary of 100; by January 1946, that same price index had jumped to 5,500,000; by June 1946, the price index had jumped to

20,000,000,000,000, or 2×10^{13}. Something that cost 100 *forints* (the Hungarian monetary unit) in 1939 would have cost 5,500,000 forints in January 1946; by the end of the summer of 1946, the same item would have cost 20,000,000,000,000 forints. Imagine having to push a wheelbarrow full of money to the store just to buy a loaf of dark bread.

Certain Latin American countries currently have rates of inflation that appear "hyper" relative to those in the United States. It is not uncommon in Latin America for *annual* rates of inflation to be 100, 200, and sometimes 300 and 400 percent.

EXHIBIT 1-5.

**EFFECTS OF
EROSION ON
PURCHASING
POWER BY
INFLATION**

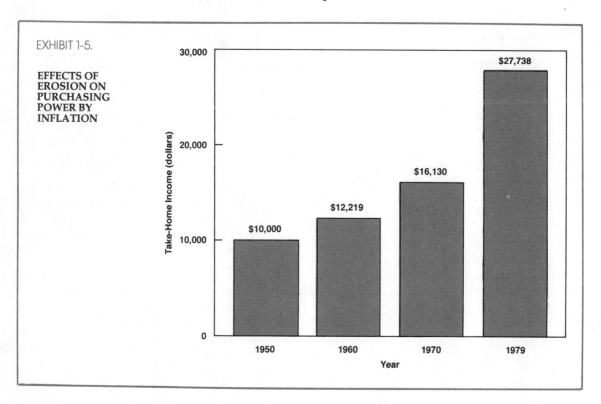

HOW INFLATION HURTS

There are many groups that get hurt by inflation. There are also many ways to get hurt. We look at both topics now.

Individuals on Fixed Incomes

The most obvious group of individuals that suffers because of inflation lives on fixed incomes. For example, a retirement income of $600 per month loses purchasing power steadily as long as there is inflation. If, over a ten-year period, the Consumer Price Index has doubled, then the purchasing power of $600 per month will be reduced to $300; the standard of living on that fixed income will be half what it was originally.

As a general rule, then, someone locked into an income stream that is fixed in nominal dollars will lose out because of inflation. But many retired individuals are not as badly off as one might think. More than 93 percent of Americans over sixty-five receive Social Security payments, which have risen faster than the rate of inflation. In fact, latest data show that while the Consumer Price Index increased 81.5 percent from 1967 to 1977, average Social Security benefits were raised 184.6 percent by Congress. Thus, Social Security recipients more than made up for the reduction in the purchasing power of dollars due to inflation.

Creditors Lose and Debtors Gain

Suppose you loan a friend $100, to be repaid one year later. Now suppose there were no inflation and none expected. You might charge your friend some "going" rate of interest for the loan—say, 5 percent. At the end of one year, you would be repaid the $100 plus $5.00 interest. If no inflation occurred during that period, the purchasing power of the money would equal the purchasing power it had at the beginning of the one-year period. On the other hand, if the Consumer Price Index unexpectedly rose by 5 percent during that one-year period, you would make no money at all on your loan. Why? Because the dollars that your friend paid back would have a purchasing power that is only 95 percent of what it was at the beginning of the period. The $100 you are paid back can only purchase $95 worth of goods. The value of your loan in purchasing power will have fallen by 5 percent; the interest you receive at 5 percent will just cover that loss in purchasing power. You will have made a real interest rate of zero percent during that period.

Consider the possibility that the rate of inflation could be even higher than the rate of interest you charge your friend. What if it had been 10 percent? That would have meant that at the end of the one-year period, in spite of the 5 percent you were paid in interest, the purchasing power of the $100 plus $5.00 interest would total less than the purchasing power of the $100 you loaned in the first place.

Thus, creditors lose and debtors gain when loans are made without an accurate prediction of how high the rate of inflation will be during the life of the loan. Had you fully anticipated that inflation would have been 5 percent, you would have asked your friend to pay you an **inflationary premium** in addition to the 5 percent interest you charged for the use of your money. We can, therefore, modify our general statement by saying that it is during periods of *unanticipated* inflation that creditors lose and debtors gain. During the 1960s and 1970s, the rate of inflation often was higher than anticipated. During those years, creditors did, on net, lose, and debtors did, on net, gain.

People who borrow money during periods of anticipated inflation are willing to pay higher interest rates because they know that the dollars they will pay back to the creditor will be "cheaper"; that is, they will have less purchasing power. If a person lends $5,000—enough to buy, say, a Buick Riviera—when prices are rising, that $5,000 may only buy a Honda Civic by the time the creditor is repaid.

Holding Cash Becomes Expensive

Most individuals carry cash in different denomination bills. Many keep checking account balances, which may average over the year to be several hundred or even several thousand dollars per month. All of us use some form of cash and/or checking account because of the convenience offered. And we all, therefore, lose value whenever there is an inflation. That is, the purchasing power of the cash in our wallets or our checking accounts falls at the rate of inflation.

Assume, for example, that you have stashed 100 one dollar bills underneath your mattress. If, after one year, the Consumer Price Index has increased 10 percent, the total purchasing power of those 100 one dollar bills will be only $95. You will have lost purchasing power value equal to the 5 percent times the amount of cash you kept on hand. In essence, then, the value of the cash we keep on hand depreciates at the rate of inflation. The only way we can avoid this type of inflationary "tax" on the cash we hold is by reducing our cash balances (and holding other, appreciating assets). But attempting to reduce our cash balances is not an easy matter. It is convenient to have a balance in our checking accounts to write checks for the things we want when we want them rather than trying to purchase everything at the beginning of a pay period, which reduces our checking account balance or the amount of cash in our wallets.

Contracts That Don't Take Account of Inflation

If you sign an agreement to work for someone over a two-year period, during which you will receive an increase at the end of one year of, say, 10 percent in your wages, you will be in quite a different position at that time if there is more inflation than you anticipated. In other words, if you get a wage increase of 10 percent and the inflation rate during the period is 20 percent, you will end up with less purchasing power than when you started the job. In an inflationary setting, it is important not to be locked into the wrong end of long-term contracts that make no allowances for higher rates of inflation than generally anticipated. The variation in the rate of inflation in the United States has been tremendous over the last fifteen years. So it would be naive to assume that there will be no further variation in the inflation rate in the next fifteen years. Thus, workers increasingly will not be tied down to long-term contracts. Or, if they are, they should demand that something be added to the contract to take account of unanticipated changes in the rate of inflation.

COST-OF-LIVING CLAUSES

If the annual rate of inflation were 1 percent, 5 percent, or 10 percent, and it stayed at that rate forever, wage contracts could allow for that fully anticipated rate. On the other hand, if the rate of inflation varies dramatically, the only way a wage contract can adjust to this variation is by the insertion of what is called a cost-of-living clause or escalator clause. This automatically raises the worker's salary to take account of the rate of inflation; and this raise is in addition to any *real* raise that is agreed upon.

Assume, for example, that you are making $10,000 a year, and your employer wants you to sign a three-year contract. Your employer offers you a guaranteed 3 percent increase in your *real* wage rate over that period. To do this, your employment contract will state that you get a cost-of-living increase every year, plus an annual 3 percent wage increase. So, if you are making $10,000 this year and the rate of inflation is 10 percent, next year you will get $10,000 plus a $1,000 cost-of-living increase, plus the 3 percent agreed-upon increase in your real income, or $330. Thus, your salary during the second year will be $11,330.

There are approximately 58 million individuals in the United States who have some sort of cost-of-living clause governing at least part of their incomes. Social Security benefits as well as federal pension payments are tied to the cost of living, as are food stamp allotments. And there are at least 8 million workers in the private sector who have employment contracts with cost-of-living clauses included.

THE EFFECTS OF INFLATION ON INCOME TAXES

Actually, inflation is beneficial for the federal government because it allows the government to collect higher income taxes without passing legislation to do so.

As we shall see in Chapter 12, we have a progressive personal income tax system. That means, the higher the income, the higher the tax rates assessed by the federal government on the additional income. Thus, if your income rises because of inflation, you pay a larger percentage of your salary in the form of taxes, since the tax rate on the additional income is higher. In Exhibit 1-6, we show the effects of a 9.4 percent increase in all prices and salaries in a one-year period. In principle, you are no better or worse off if all prices go up by the same percentage as your income. But our progressive income tax system forces you into a higher tax bracket, so you owe the government more of your income. Your real, spendable income must, therefore, fall.

The only way the government could prevent this from happening would be to increase each tax bracket. In other words, if the tax rate applied to income between $10,000 and $11,000 is 22 percent, the government could increase that $1,000 bracket according to the rate of inflation; if, in one year, the rate of inflation is 100 percent, the tax bracket increases from $10,000 to $12,000. That is, the 22 percent tax rate for federal income taxes would apply to income earned between $10,000 and $12,000. This would prevent individuals from entering higher tax brackets and, therefore, paying a larger percentage of income for taxes because of inflation.

When you buy something such as a stock listed on the New York Stock Exchange, it may increase in value. In many instances, you have to pay taxes on that increased value when you sell the stock. Part of that increased value could, however, be purely fictitious—due to inflation only. Nonetheless, the federal government still requires that you pay taxes on the *nominal,* as opposed to real, changes in the value of the stock. The government could alter this unfair increase in taxes by allowing you to correct for the change in the price level. If you bought a stock for $100 and sold it for $200 ten years later, during which time prices doubled, you would receive a zero real increase in value, and the government could then say that you owed no taxes on that gain.[2]

ANTICIPATING INFLATION

In summary, one of the best ways to avoid being hurt by inflation is to anticipate it—but not necessarily by looking at past inflation. Inflation has indeed become a permanent part of the American economic landscape. Therefore, it behooves those who can to obtain cost-of-living clauses in all contracts, so they will not be affected adversely by a change in the rate of inflation. Furthermore, the anticipation of more inflation in the future will force us to seek retirement plans that offer other than a fixed amount of dollars per month, for those fixed amounts aren't going to buy as much in the future as they buy today. We will examine several other ways to take account of inflation in the following Practical Applications section.

EXHIBIT 1-6.

9.4 PERCENT INCREASE IN ALL PRICES AND SALARIES OVER A ONE-YEAR PERIOD

Because of graduated income tax rates, even families lucky enough to get raises matching the big increase in living costs wound up losing purchasing power. Here we show how a 9.4% inflation outruns a 9.4% pay raise.

	GROSS INCOME	FEDERAL INCOME TAX	EFFECTIVE RATE	AFTER-TAX INCOME IN YEAR 1 DOLLARS
Year 1	$14,000	$1,600	11.4½	$12,400
Year 2	15,316	1,890	12.3	12,164
Year 1	20,000	3,010	15.1	16,990
Year 2	21,880	3,506	16.0	16,646
Year 1	30,000	6,020	20.1	23,980
Year 2	32,820	7,035	21.4	23,361

---

[2]The technical term for this system of increasing tax brackets is called indexing the tax system.

PRACTICAL APPLICATIONS

HOW TO PROTECT
AGAINST INFLATION

The job of protecting against inflation is not easy. In this Practical Applications section, we will look at several erroneous notions about fighting inflation and then give some general pointers on how the negative effects of inflation can be reduced—at least partially.

SHOULD YOU BUY DURING INFLATION?

Many people think that major purchases—houses, stereos, cars, and so on—should be made during periods of inflation since prices will be even higher in the future. This may or may not be true: if inflation is fully anticipated, then your basic decision about when to purchase a house or a car depends not in the least on inflation itself. Your timing of purchases should be based on your expected income, how much you want something, whether you are willing to wait, and so on. For example, say that you do not want to buy a car until next year, but you think the price is going to rise 4 percent, which has been the rate of inflation for a long time. If you buy the car this year, most likely you will borrow the money just as you would next year. Thus, for this year you will have to pay an interest rate on whatever you borrow. That interest rate will take account of the expected inflation of 4 percent, so you will be no better off buying now than waiting until next year and paying a higher price.

The key to understanding this is: if you think inflation is more or less anticipated by everybody, you are no better off buying now than waiting and paying a higher price later. As prices go up with inflation, so do incomes—often even more so. In other words, the increased price of those potential purchases may be no greater relative to your income.

Are You Better Off Owning a House During Inflation?

Many people think that, during inflation, it is better to own a house because its value will rise. This happens to have been true historically, particularly during the last decade or so. That is because the relative price of real estate has risen faster than the Consumer Price Index and, as it turns out, faster than most investments you could have made in the 1960s and 1970s. One might believe, therefore, that since investing in real estate is more advantageous than investing in just about anything else, you are better off owning a house during inflation.

But we can think of an example where this is not so. Consider buying a $30,000 house.

There is an inflation in home values of 10 percent a year. At the end of one year, you could sell that house for $33,000. Now, are you better off by owning it? Well, the *implicit cost* to you of staying in the house is the same, whether you own it or not. If someone else owned it and you were renting, you would be charged a higher rental fee. But since you own it, you, in fact, obtain an implicit rental value from having the house, and that value will go up by 10 percent. You will implicitly be paying more to live in it.

So, on the one hand, you gain; but, on the other hand, you lose in an equal amount. After all, you could sell the house for $33,000 and invest the money to get an explicit rate of return. (We assume it is also 10 percent per year.) The higher the value of the house, the higher that lost rate of return you are incurring by not selling it. It does not matter to you, actually, if you were given a house free. You are paying for the services rendered by that house, whether you like it or not, because you always have the opportunity of selling it and investing the money. You are no better off because inflation has caused the value of your house to rise, for it may have caused the value of all housing services to rise. Hence, if you sold your house, you would have to pay a higher price for anything into which you would move. (However, if the value of your house went up *faster* than the rate of inflation, you obviously will be wealthier.)

But if the *relative* cost of housing has risen, you

may decide to purchase less of it; you may decide to sell your house (which has appreciated in value), move into less expensive quarters, and do something with the money difference. The *relative* price of housing may change if you live in an area that becomes a boom town. If this is the case, you may decide that it is too expensive to live in that boom town, whether or not you own the house and no matter what you paid for it.

MINIMIZING CASH HOLDINGS

Since inflation can also be defined as the rate of reduction in the value or purchasing power of cash, the faster the rate of inflation, the more costly it is for you to hold cash in the form of dollar bills and checking account balances. Hence, one way you can fight against a rising rate of inflation is by reducing your average cash holdings. You can do this by, for example, keeping excess cash in interest-earning savings accounts (which still may not be a good deal but certainly give you a higher interest rate than zero). You can spend more time planning your expenditures so they match the receipts in your income. This way, you will not be required to carry as large an amount in your checking account or your wallet. Of course, the larger your average checking account or currency balance and the greater the rate of inflation, the more important this consideration becomes.

ADJUST YOUR INSURANCE POLICIES

Once you have figured out your insurance needs (discussed in Unit 3), be aware that your policies do not take account of inflation. You may, therefore, want to adjust your life insurance policies occasionally to allow for the decreased purchasing power implicit in the face value of those policies. Many insurance companies are now issuing "agreements for cost-of-living benefit," meaning that every year you are charged a premium to have your existing life insurance policies increased in value

according to inflation. Usually, the Consumer Price Index is used as a basis. For example, say that you have $10,000 worth of life insurance a year, which costs you $5 per $1,000; your total payment at the end of the year would be $50. Now, say that in one year the Consumer Price Index rose by 10 percent. You would get a bill from the insurance company for $5. If you agreed to pay it, this would give you a life insurance policy worth $11,000 in face value. You would still have the same real amount of protection and it would still cost the same real amount, although the nominal, or dollar, payment would increase by 10 percent because of inflation. Whenever possible, you might wish to purchase cost-of-living benefit agreements for whatever insurance you have. Or you might decide to take out more insurance every few years, to take account of inflation.

INVESTMENTS

Avoid investments that have not adapted to our inflationary times. In other words, do not put all your money into fixed-dollar income-producing investments. A good example is U.S. Savings Bonds. They have yielded, in effect, negative *real* rates of return because their stated rate of interest consistently has been *less* than the rate of inflation. (This is particularly true after you subtract the taxes you must pay on the interest earned.) Individuals who bought U.S. Savings Bonds in the past have ended up, after five or ten years, with *less* purchasing power than they gave to buy the bonds in the first place. (Of course, anyone who kept the same amount in a passbook account at a bank was even worse off because such accounts pay a lower interest rate and offer no tax advantages.)

Investments in items that will take account of inflation should at least be part of any investing strategy during an inflationary period. Real estate has been a good hedge. So has the stock market, although in the last decade it has been a poor one indeed. If, in the future, the market resumes its upward trend, it may again be an appropriate partial outlet for some of your savings and investment dollars. We will discuss the stock market in more detail in Chapter 15.

TAKING OUT LOANS

Whenever you take out any type of loan, you obviously benefit if the future inflation rate is higher than that anticipated by the creditor. But don't bet on being able to outsmart creditors. Generally, the interest rate you pay has an inflationary premium tacked onto it. In the long run and on average, this inflationary premium reflects the anticipated rate of inflation. Remember, creditors only lose and debtors only gain during periods when the inflation rate is *greater* than what was anticipated when the loans were taken out.

RETIREMENT PLANS

It is best to make certain that at least part of your retirement plan is not of the fixed-income type. Part of most people's retirement plans includes Social Security. Since Social Security is now related to changes in the cost of living, it probably will be a relatively good hedge against inflation. Other private retirement plans that you may be able to purchase should be examined in terms of their ability to anticipate inflation when you do in fact retire. Some retirement plans depend upon how well the stock market does. If the market resumes its upward trend, these plans will allow you to maintain a certain real standard of living during your retirement years in spite of the inflation rate.

YOUR SALARY

One way to make sure that you aren't caught unprepared by an unexpected rise in prices is to have a cost-of-living, or escalator, clause in your employment contract. Some employees have succeeded in bargaining for such escalator clauses on an individual basis. Unions, bargaining for a large number of employees, have been even more successful.

HOW TO COMBAT INFLATION THROUGH SMART BUYING

There are, of course, important buying techniques that one can apply all the time. During a period of inflation, these techniques become even more important. You may wish to use some or all of them every time you shop.

1. **Compare values.** Take the time to compare possible alternative ways to satisfy particular needs or desires, even within the same store.

2. **Buy for the intended use of the product or service:** Don't, for example, use high-quality wine for cooking purposes or fancy canned tomatoes for stew. Use dried milk solids for cooking rather than fresh milk.

3. **Buy basic clothing styles.** To reduce clothing budgets, stick to basic styles rather than high fashion.

4. **Buy store brands.** Private brands may cost from 10 to 60 percent less than national brands. This is true for both food and appliances. Some of Montgomery Ward's ranges are made by Tappan, and some of their other appliances are made by Westinghouse. Most of J.C. Penney's Penncrest appliances are made by Hotpoint; their power tools are made by Skil. Private-brand liquor is sold by some manufacturers to move inventory while avoiding cutting prices on their advertised brand.

5. **Do not overpay for convenience.** The price is usually high per unit of quantity provided when you buy additional convenience in the form of push-button containers, aerosol cans, buttered frozen vegetables, and so on.

6. **Buy in larger quantities and store those items if convenient.**

EXHIBIT 1-7. **KNOW WHEN TO SHOP**

JANUARY

store-wide post-holiday and
inventory sales:
small electric appliances,
drugs, toiletries, floor
coverings, rugs, furniture, toys,
books, diamonds, costume
jewelry, blankets, housewares,
luggage, radios, TVs, freezers,
stoves, refrigerators, cars,
tires, bicycles, baby carriages,
clothes dryers

FEBRUARY

final winter clearances:
sports equipment, storm
windows, washers, dryers, air
conditioners, used
automobiles, bedding

MARCH

after-Easter sales and sales of
special purchases:
ski equipment, luggage, winter
clothing, washers, dryers,
children's shoes

APRIL

after-Easter sales:
washers, dryers, outdoor
paints, garden equipment,
children's clothing, lingerie

MAY

special sales for Mother's Day
and Memorial Day:
family clothing, jewelry, paint,
wallpaper, tableware, blankets,
lingerie, camp clothing for
children

JUNE

special sales for Father's Day:
sportwear, floor coverings,
building materials, outdoor
furniture, lumber, tires, men's
wear

JULY

summer clearances, special
sales for July 4th:
sporting goods, stereo
equipment, freezers, air
conditioners, garden
equipment, storm windows,
clothes for the family, firewood

AUGUST

summer clearances:
white sales, floor coverings,
housewares, paints, furniture,
sporting goods, fans, furs,
major appliances, clothes for
the family

SEPTEMBER

special sales for Labor Day:
dishwashers, freezers, china,
paints, fabrics,
home-improvement products,
bicycles, cars, car batteries

OCTOBER

special sales for Columbus
Day:
floor coverings, lamps,
silverware, fishing equipment,
cars, men's wear, major
appliances

NOVEMBER

special sales for Veterans Day,
Thanksgiving Day:
fall clothing for the family,
fabrics, quilts, wines, liquors,
car seatcovers, bicycles

DECEMBER

special sales for
post-Christmas:
cards, giftwraps, decorations
(after Christmas), gift
certificates

7. **Take advantage of sales throughout the year.** Exhibit 1-7 gives a bargain calendar indicating when stores usually hold sales.

IN CONCLUSION

The key to protecting yourself against inflation is to realize the decline in the purchasing power of money paid you in the future. If you think through all of the contracts and commitments that you make or are going to make and include an inflationary factor, you will be ahead of the game. There is no way you can completely protect yourself against inflation in a world where inflation rates cannot be completely anticipated. If everything were written in real terms— that is, with cost-of-living, or escalator, clauses— then you wouldn't have to worry. But, because this is not the case, you should take advantage of every new inflation protector you can buy, such as cost-of-living benefit additions to your life insurance, cost-of-living or escalator clauses in your wage contracts, hybrid checking accounts in which you can earn interest on unused balances, and so on.

You can learn to adjust to inflation. You may never like it, but you can make sure that it doesn't destroy your well-being, now or in the future.

GLOSSARY OF TERMS

INFLATION A sustained rise in the average of all prices of goods and services.

ABSOLUTE, OR NOMINAL, PRICES The actual or current dollars-and-cents price of goods and services at the time of purchase.

RELATIVE PRICE The price of a good or service relative to another price or to the average of all other prices.

CONSUMER PRICE INDEX An index, constructed by the Bureau of Labor Statistics, U.S. Department of Labor, of the average price of a market basket of goods and services purchased by an urban consumer.

DEFLATION A sustained fall in the average of all prices paid by consumers for goods and services.

REAL PER CAPITA INCOME Nominal, or absolute, income of the entire country divided by the total number of individuals in the country and then corrected for any price changes.

HYPERINFLATION A situation of extreme inflation in which prices are rising at sometimes hundreds of percentage points per month.

INFLATIONARY PREMIUM The additional interest charged for taking out a loan during an inflationary period. The inflationary premium compensates the creditor for the loss in the purchasing power of the dollars lent.

COST-OF-LIVING, OR ESCALATOR, CLAUSE A clause put in contracts that corrects the sums involved for changes in the price level. A cost-of-living clause in a wage contract allows wages to rise automatically whenever, for example, the CPI rises.

CHAPTER SUMMARY

1. Inflation is the most persistent economic phenomenon that consumers have encountered in the last few decades; it is, therefore, extremely important in personal finance.

2. During inflation, it is important to distinguish between nominal and relative prices. In spite of inflation, the relative price of a number of goods, such as television sets and washing machines, has fallen.

3. The most well-known and widely used index of the average of all prices is the Consumer Price Index, compiled monthly by the Bureau of Labor Statistics.

4. Even though we have had many years of rising prices, incomes have also gone up, so the real per capita income in the United States is higher today than it ever has been. That is, we are richer in spite of inflation. The following groups of individuals are hurt by inflation: (a) individuals on fixed incomes, (b) creditors who do not fully anticipate the future rate of inflation, (c) individuals who hold currency and checking account balances, and (d) individuals who sign long-term contracts without escalator clauses.

5. Whenever inflation is fully anticipated, lenders require that borrowers pay an inflationary premium to allow for that inflation.

6. If you hold $100 for a year in cash and there is an inflation of 10 percent, you have paid an inflationary "tax" of $10. That is, your purchasing power has fallen by $10.

7. Individuals on Social Security, food stamps, and federal pension plans are covered by cost-of-living clauses. Additionally, many individuals in the private sector have these clauses in their wage contracts.

8. If inflation is fully anticipated, the decision as to when to buy is not affected by the rate or the existence of inflation.

9. If *all* prices are rising at the same rate, you may not be better off owning a house during that inflationary period. If, however, the price of housing is rising faster than all other prices, you are better off owning a home.

10. One way to minimize the effects of an inflationary tax on the cash you hold is to reduce the average amount of dollars and checking account balances throughout the year. This can be done by matching more closely your income receipts with your expenditures.

11. You can usually buy inflation-adjustment additions to any life insurance. These are called agreements-for-cost-of-living benefits.

12. Avoid investments that yield fixed dollars every year, such as U.S. Savings Bonds.

13. Taking out loans is only beneficial during a period of *unanticipated* inflation; if inflation is anticipated, creditors will tack on the appropriate inflationary premium.

14. Seek out retirement plans that will at least partially take account of future inflation.

15. Always try to have escalator clauses added to your employment contracts.

STUDY QUESTIONS

1. If the price of gasoline rises next year, is that inflation?

2. What is the difference between absolute and relative prices? How can you compute relative prices?

3. What is the difference between inflation and hyperinflation?

4. Which groups of individuals are hurt most by inflation?

5. Is it always better to be a debtor than a creditor during an inflationary period? Does it matter whether inflation is fully anticipated?

6. You have an average checking account balance over the year of $350. The Consumer Price Index has increased by 8.4 percent. How much inflationary tax did you pay?

7. If all the contracts in which you enter have escalator clauses, does it matter whether the rate of inflation is fully anticipated?

8. Analyze this statement: "Buy now and save, since prices are going up in the future."

CASE PROBLEMS

1-1 Interest on Loan Perplexes Recipient

Hugh Cameron, a junior biology major, has just come storming into the local student pleasure palace. He is ranting about his uncle, Walter, who lent him $700 to buy a car. Walter said he wouldn't make any profit on the loan, but he didn't want to lose any money either. Hugh had assured his uncle that he had nothing to worry about. He said he would sign a note and repay the money within a year. Later, Hugh signed the note without reading it. On his way back to the campus, he read his copy and was shocked to see that he would have to pay 7% interest. He thinks his uncle lied to him when he said he wouldn't be making any money on the loan.

What can you, as a student of personal finance, say to Hugh that will explain Walter's statement and the 7% interest charge?

1-2 To Move or Not to Move

Sheila Montgomery, twenty-five, an assistant production engineer for a manufacturing firm in Omaha, has been offered a transfer to the Pittsburgh plant. If she accepts the offer, she would receive a 5% salary increase to compensate for the higher cost of living in Pittsburgh, plus the company's annual 7% cost of living increase and a 3% increase in her real income. Sheila currently is earning $14,000 per year and paying 11.4% in federal income taxes. She has calculated her pre-tax income for next year at $15,400 for Omaha and $16,100 for Pittsburgh.

1. Are these figures correct? If not, what should they be?

2. If she stays in Omaha, her tax rate will be 12.4%; if she moves, it will be 13%. How much more would she pay in taxes next year on each job?

3. How will the higher tax rates affect the 3% increase in real income on each job?

4. From an economic stand-point, what should she do?

SELECTED REFERENCES

Bach, G.L., *The New Inflation: Causes, Effects and Cures.* Providence, R.I.: Brown University Press, 1973.

Brimmer, A. "Why Inflation Hits Some People Less than Others." *Nations Business,* February 1977, pp. 38-40.

"Can You Inflation-Proof Your Savings?" *Changing Times,* October 1974, pp. 7-12.

"Drive to Keep Prices from Soaring Higher." *U.S. News,* April 25, 1977, pp. 23-25.

"Galloping New Inflation of Fears," *Time,* March 14, 1977, p. 38.

Holt, Charles C., et al. *The Unemployment-Inflation Dilemma: A Manpower Solution.* Washington, D.C.: Urban Institute, 1971.

"How Govemement Itself Keeps Prices Rising." *U.S. News,* April 18, 1977, pp. 16-17.

"Plan for Fighting the Double Digits." *Time,* April 18, 1977, pp. 59-60.

Rose, Sanford, "We've Learned How to Lick Inflation," *Fortune,* September 1976, pp. 100-105.

Samuelson, P.A. "Hedging Against Inflation." *Newsweek,* May 27, 1974, p. 73.

Walinsky, L. J. "What Can We Do about Inflation?" *New Republic,* March 2, 1974, pp. 21-25.

"Why Inflation Is So Hard to Stop." *Changing Times,* April 1977, pp. 33-36.

Income, Education, and Occupation

■Managing money entails such diverse activities as budgeting, comparison shopping, saving, investing, and tax planning. But before you can engage in these activities, the money must be earned. We start this chapter with a look at income, both personal and national, to find out what causes differences in both.

There are, of course, many different reasons why some people earn a lot and others relatively little. Some people are more clever than others. Some have more artistic ability than others. Many people prefer riskier jobs at higher rates of pay than do others: if you are willing to work as a welder on top of high-rise buildings, you will probably make more money than you would as a welder with a safe, ground-floor job.

But more important, at least for those of you who are now making the investment, is your decision to go to school. That will permanently affect your command over goods and services in your role as a consumer. You may think you have never made an investment in your life, but you will soon see that you did—and not a bad one, either.

INVESTING IN YOURSELF

Few people think it strange or unfair that someone with a bachelor's degree gets paid more than someone with a grade-school diploma. In the first place, the degree holder has spent a long time acquiring specialized knowledge; in the second place, the grade-school graduate probably could do little of the work the college graduate does. And a basic fact of life is that individuals are generally paid only what they are worth to employers. Education can be considered, then, as a process of making workers more productive. Thus, you are making an investment in your-

25

self; going to school is an **investment in human capital**, as it is called. Usually, the longer you go to school, the more new skills you learn. You may become a better thinker; you generally become a more responsive person, at least in working situations. Why otherwise would employers pay more for the services of college graduates than for high-school graduates, when they could get less-educated people to work for them for less money?

Don't assume, however, that going to school will automatically guarantee you a higher income. If you specialize in a field that is of little interest to many people, the *demand* for your services is going to be small. No amount of services you could supply would induce others to hire you at high wages, because the supply and demand for different types of labor ultimately determines the individual's wages or income.

For any given specialty, the more trained you are, the more productive you will be and, therefore, the higher the demand for your services. One way to predict your future income is to analyze how productive you can be. Employers tend to pay workers their exact worth—no more, no less. Thus, anything you can do to make yourself more productive will result in a higher wage and higher total lifetime earnings.

Specialized Training

Formalized schooling is not the only way to invest in yourself; you can learn on your own by reading and practicing skills, and you can learn on the job. In fact, **on-the-job training** is one of the chief ways individuals increase their productivity. (People engaged in on-the-job training—for example, as apprentices—are usually paid more after that training is over.) However, productivity cannot occur in a vacuum. You could be very productive at something that nobody values highly. Unless you choose wisely, your area of specialization at any given time may be something that society does not value highly and for which you will be relatively poorly paid. Few people would now consider specializing in learning how to make horseshoes. But some people were doing just that right when horseshoes were no longer worth much because of the introduction of mass-produced automobiles. Needless to say, such an investment of time proved to be unwise.

Ultimately, then, investing in yourself requires careful planning. That is, you must invest in yourself in a way that increases your productive capacities in areas that are demanded by the economy. If it looks as though computer keypunch operators won't be needed in the future because of optical scanning techniques, then you certainly don't want to specialize in computer keypunching—unless you are willing to retrain in the future. Choosing an occupation that benefits you most may require some research about future demands for different types of jobs.

The Benefits of Education

While the evidence is overwhelming that an education is valuable, the idea that you must "get all the education you can" does not apply equally to everybody. And it certainly is not meaningful without qualification, because you could be acquiring formal education for the rest of your life—as some perennial students do. We can give a general rule, though: *Acquire more education as long as the expected benefits at least cover the costs.*

Exhibit 2-1 shows the **age-earnings profile** for three levels of degree holders—grade school, high school, and college. Note that the more education you get, the higher the curve is. For example, the average high-school graduate at forty years of age may be earning 40 percent more than the average grade-school graduate at forty years of age. In dollars and cents, the figures are even more impressive. Exhibit 2-2 shows the average lifetime earnings of various degree holders: college graduates obviously make more than grade-school graduates.

The Costs of Education

Our general rule has its limits, because it is, of course, more expensive to acquire more education. The main cost of going to college is *not* tuition and books; this cost ranks second, although college is not inexpensive. The main component is the cost of foregone income—that is, the **opportunity cost** of not working. In other words, had you not gone to college for four or more years, you could be working full time at some average salary. But even with all the costs of foregone earnings, tuition, and

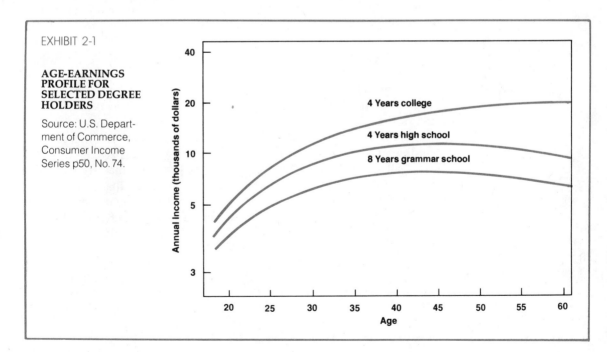

EXHIBIT 2-1

AGE-EARNINGS PROFILE FOR SELECTED DEGREE HOLDERS

Source: U.S. Department of Commerce, Consumer Income Series p50, No. 74.

4 Years college

4 Years high school

8 Years grammar school

Annual Income (thousands of dollars)

Age

EXHIBIT 2-2

AVERAGE LIFETIME EARNINGS OF SELECTED DEGREE HOLDERS

The average lifetime earnings of selected degree-holders are given in this table. The difference between eight years of grammar school and four years of college is over $500,000. These figures are averages only, and are not corrected for the timing of the income received. (Strictly speaking, these figures should be corrected [discounted] for timing, and all made comparable on a present value basis.) Source: U.S. Department of Commerce.

LEVEL OF EDUCATION	AVERAGE LIFETIME EARNINGS
8 years of grammar school	$1,381,412
4 years of high school	$1,676,314
4 years of college	$2,004,141

books, the rate of return on an education is at least as good as the rate of return on, say, the stock market and certainly higher than on money in a savings and loan association account.[1]

IS COLLEGE A MISTAKE?

In certain years, some college graduates cannot get jobs. But this hardly means that going to college was a mistake. It means only that during fluctuations in business activity, the demands for different types of college-degree holders shift. Although you may be out of a job in your area of specialization immediately after college, you still may have made the right choice.

Some of you, however, will have made the wrong choice. According to the Carnegie Commission, 300,000 to 900,000 of the 8.5 million students enrolled should not be in college. The authors of the study suggest that this large number of students attends college mainly because of social and parental pressures rather than from personal choice.[2] There are several books that support the Carnegie Commission's report, including one by Caroline Bird titled *The Case Against College* (New York: David McKay, 1975). Bird believes that going to college may well be "the dumbest investment" people can make. She contends that a bachelor's degree doesn't help obtain a job and that college training doesn't enable a graduate to earn more money or live a more satisfying life. She doesn't even believe college "broadens" students or teaches them to think.

[1]This is obviously true only for those people who were successful at college. For computation, see Gary Becker, *Human Capital: A Theoretical and Empirical Analysis, with Special Reference to Education* (New York: Columbia University Press, 1964).

[2]*More Effective Uses of Resources: An Imperative for Higher Education* (The Carnegie Commission on Higher Education, June 1972.)

What is college then? For all except about 25 percent of the students who love to learn, it is, according to Bird, "at best a social center, a youth ghetto, an aging vat, and at worst a young folks' (rhymes with old folks') home, a youth house (rhymes with poor house) or even a prison . . . a place where young adults are set apart because they are superfluous people who are of no immediate use to the economy."

The author of *The Case Against College* may be exaggerating, but she certainly has started a debate in academe. In response to the book, the executive director of the Association of Independent California Colleges and Universities, Mr. Morgan Odall, states that within three years after graduation, more than 70 percent of those who graduated from college occupy jobs they consider appropriate. And one cannot deny U.S. Census data that show college graduates earning 40 percent more than nongraduates throughout their lifetimes. Moreover, during downturns in the economy, unemployment is lowest among college graduates.

OTHER FACTORS THAT INFLUENCE PERSONAL INCOME

The amount of education one receives is not, of course, the only factor that determines the relative personal income one will earn. We can list several other important determinants of differences in income.

1. Innate Abilities and Attributes

These factors are obviously the easiest to explain and the hardest to acquire if you don't have them. Innate abilities and attributes can be strong, if not overwhelming, determinants of a person's potential productivity. Strength, good looks, coordination, mental alertness, and so on are all facets of nonacquired human capital and thus have some bearing on one's ability to earn income. If one is born without "brains," he or she has a smaller chance of "making it" in the economic world than does an individual who is born "smart." The determinants of intelligence are, of course, not a topic for economic discussion. It is no longer believed, however, that intelligence is purely innate. Some sociologists and educators think that intelligence can be changed by the environment. Nevertheless, whether a change in intelligence due to a "better" environment leads to a higher income is a debatable and untested contention.

2. Experience

Gaining additional experience at particular tasks is another way to increase one's productivity. Experience can be linked to the well-known **learning curve** that occurs when the same task is done over and over. Take an example of a person going to work on an assembly line at a factory. At first he or she is able to screw on only three bolts every two minutes; then the worker becomes more adept and can screw on four bolts in the same time plus insert a rubber guard on a bumper. After a few more weeks, yet another task can be added. Experience allows this individual to improve his or her productivity. And we would expect people with more experience to be paid more than those with less experience.

3. Training

Training is similar to experience but is more formal. Much of a person's increased productivity is due to on-the-job training. Many companies have training programs for new workers, who learn to operate machinery, fill out forms, and do other things required for the new job. On-the-job training is perhaps responsible for as much of an increase in productivity as is formal schooling.

4. Inherited Wealth

Obviously, individuals who inherit large amounts of money will be able to obtain income from that wealth that others have no chance of obtaining. Actually, inherited wealth is not a major determinant of differences in income today in the United States, although it seems to be the one that gets considerable press coverage. Witness our fascination with such wealthy families as the Rockefellers, the Kennedys, the Vanderbilts, and so on.

5. Exploitation and Discrimination

Differences in income can, in some instances, be attributed to exploitation and discrimination. Even with equal educational achievement, both in quality and quantity, certain groups often do not receive income equal to those of other groups. While professional economists still debate the degree to which differences in incomes between blacks and whites and between men and women can be attributed to the phenomenon of discrimination, none has been willing to state that discrimination doesn't enter the picture.

6. Personal Tastes

People who are partial to leisure may not be willing to work very hard. Other people may be risk takers, willing to undertake some activity in which the payoff would be enormous if they succeed but nonexistent if they fail. Thus, a person could decide to become a professional baseball pitcher, but the odds of becoming a "superstar" are extremely small. Individuals who opt for tenured government jobs may receive a steady income throughout their lives. The income of individuals willing to take more chances may, at times, be much greater than that earned in a secure government job. However, there is a big difference in the amount of risk assumed by the different groups of workers. In sum, the degree to which individuals are willing to take risks will determine, at least in part, relative differences in income.

OCCUPATIONAL INCOME DIFFERENTIALS

An important contributing factor to differences in income concerns the occupation one chooses. Exhibit 2-3 shows the median earnings by occupation for 1974, the latest complete data that are available.

Among the incomes of different occupations, the highest are earned by those in the professions of medicine, dentistry, and law. Does that mean you should immediately start studying medicine, dentistry, or law? Obviously not. For one thing, you may be wasting your time. Unless you are able to enter an accredited medical school (and, of course, graduate from it), you cannot legally practice medicine in the United States. The ratio of applicants to acceptances in most medical schools is astounding. Therefore, unless your father is a doctor or you are an outstanding student in an extremely good school, the odds are against your admission to medical training.

The same is not as true of law, however. There are numerous law schools that you can attend; you can even learn law at home by mail. Of

EXHIBIT 2-3

MEDIAN EARNINGS BY OCCUPATION AND SEX, 1974

Source: U.S. Bureau of the Census, *Current Population Reports,* Series P-60, Nos. 41, 53, 80 and 97.

	MALE	FEMALE
TOTAL	$11,835	$6,772
Professional, technical, kindred workers	14,873	9,570
Self-employed	21,501	(B)
Physicians and surgeons	25,000+	(B)
Salaried	14,661	9,600
Engineers, technical	18,230	(B)
Physicians and surgeons	24,267	(B)
Teachers, primary and secondary	12,392	9,537
Farmers and farm managers	5,459	(B)
Managers and administrators, exc. farm	15,425	8,603
Self-employed	12,795	4,175
In retail trade	11,723	4,457
Salaried	16,709	9,151
Clerical and kindred workers	11,514	6,827
Secretaries, stenographers, typists	(B)	6,955
Sales workers	12,523	5,168
In retail trade	9,125	4,734
Craft and kindred workers	12,028	6,492
Blue-collar worker supervisors	13,452	6,823
Craft workers	11,772	6,290
In construction	12,142	(B)
Private household workers	(B)	2,676
Service workers, exc. private household	8,638	5,406
Farm laborers and supervisors	5,097	(B)
Laborers, exc. farm	8,145	5,891

(B) Not computed; base less than minimum required for reliability.

course, you shouldn't base your decision solely on the high salaries of some lawyers. To obtain a law degree, you must take three additional years of training after college. This additional cost of education means that the rate of return on becoming a lawyer may be no higher than on some other occupation. Moreover, you may "starve" for a few years before you become a junior partner in a law firm: at the start of your age-earnings profile, you will receive a relatively low salary. Even doctors start their practices at low wages. So, even though the average salary for the occupation is high, you should not anticipate that your impressive amount of schooling will earn you a handsome salary right away. To see why this is not necessarily "unfair" or "unjust," we must examine more closely the typical age-earnings profile represented in Exhibit 2-1.

Look at it this way: when you begin a job, you are inexperienced and might even need on-the-job training. Your employer will not be inclined to pay you as much as he or she pays a more experienced worker who is more productive. Gradually, as you become more productive and as the number of weekly hours you work increases, so, too, does your wage rate (even corrected for inflation).

If you are like the average worker in America, you may "peak" at age forty-five to fifty-five, and then your earnings will slowly decline until retirement. Generally, older people work fewer hours per week and are less productive than middle-aged people—hence, the gradual downturn in the age-earnings profile.

MAKING THE BIG CHOICE

Now that you know something about what determines differences in incomes in the United States, you may have to face the dilemma of choosing a career and occupation. In the following Practical Applications section, we offer some pointers on where you can get information on careers, how to apply for jobs, and what to do in interviews.

HOW TO CHOOSE
AND START A CAREER

The choice of a career will determine, to a large extent, your future income. Among the determinants of income mentioned in this chapter was your chosen occupation. Note, though, that the choice of a career is not based on money alone.

APTITUDE MAY DETERMINE
YOUR CAREER

Many individuals have specific aptitudes and abilities that lend themselves to specific careers; others do not. It would be futile to choose a career as a concert violinist if you had no aptitude for music. Virtually all specialty occupations that might be labeled "glamorous" or "artistic" require special aptitude. This is also true for professional sports. Many individuals want careers in these areas but cannot and, indeed, should not seek them because they lack the appropriate aptitudes.

On the other hand, one can, with relatively little risk, try out a few of these areas. In effect, it is possible to test one's aptitude during one's youth. At this time, you can decide whether you should take the considerable risk of choosing a glamour career.

You can also consider the possibility of choosing a glamour career without necessarily attempting to be in the spotlight. If you would love to be in the theatre but realize during your second year in college that you just don't have any natural acting talent, you can still enter that profession. You might be able to train as a technician, an assistant producer, or a cameraperson.

In such careers as law, medicine, engineering, accounting, and others, aptitude is still crucial. The competition for good jobs (and even entrance to professional schools) is keen. If you are considering these careers, it would be appropriate to take aptitude tests well in advance. Most colleges and

universities have services that can, either for free or a small fee, provide you with such tests.

GETTING INFORMATION ON
AN OCCUPATION

There are at least four publications you can consult to get information on career outlooks.

1. *The Encyclopedia of Careers and Vocational Guidance* is a two-volume work published by J. G. Ferguson Company of Chicago and distributed by Doubleday & Company. These two volumes contain general information on vocational testing, interviewing, and the like. In addition, there is information on jobs and professions that do not require college training.

2. *The Occupational Outlook for College Graduates* is a publication of the U.S. Department of Labor. Annually, it surveys the job outlook for college graduates and describes each profession in terms of training required, salaries, working conditions, and the nature of the work. This publication may help you avoid choosing a career for which there will be no demand in the future.

3. *The Occupational Thesaurus* may be obtained from Everett A. Teal, Lehigh University, Bethlehem, Pennsylvania. This two-volume work lists employment areas for which college majors are qualified. There are specific job-skill categories, arranged according to demand, for different industries.

4. *The College Placement Annual* is published by the College Placement Council, Inc., P.O. Box 2263, Bethlehem, Pennsylvania. It gives job information for

college graduates and alphabetically lists all major private employers in the United States. Government agencies are also listed. A unique employment index lists employers by occupations that are needed in the region the employer serves.

WHERE TO OBTAIN MORE
JOB INFORMATION

The following are some of the places where you can obtain additional job information.

1. *College or university placement centers.* As previously mentioned, virtually every college and university has some type of placement center. For college students, this might be the first place to look for job information. Placement centers have career consultants and vocational guidance counselors, as well as facilities for providing interviews between prospective graduates and recruiters from major firms and government agencies.

2. *State employment agencies.* All fifty states have state employment offices. There are more than 1800 operating in conjunction with the U.S. Employment Service of the Department of Labor. They charge no fee and make placements in all types of jobs. Some even provide computer job matching. Many state employment offices will provide free career guidance and aptitude tests.

3. *Specialized placement services.* Employers seeking women and women seeking jobs may consult some of the various special job-matching services, including:
   a. Catalyst National Network, 14 E. 60th Street, New York, New York 10022. This organization provides listings and resumés of managerial and professional applicants.
   b. Talent Search Skills Bank, Office of Voluntary Programs, Equal Opportunity Commission, 1800 G Street N.W.; Washington, D.C. 20506. This office maintains a file on minority female applicants and their skills.
   c. National Federation of Business and Professional Women's Clubs, Inc. 2012 Massachusetts Avenue N.W., Washington, D.C. 20036. This organization operates a talent bank to help women find positions in educational institutions, private industry, and government.

4. *Help-wanted ads in newspapers and professional or trade journals.* Virtually every newspaper in the country has help-wanted ads listing vacancies for various jobs. There are also vacancies listed in trade and professional journals. Since they usually require that you apply by mail, an impressive resumé is imperative.

5. *Private employment agencies.* You can register with an agency and wait to be called or apply directly for a job that is advertised in a periodical.

   Agencies generally require you to sign a contract that obligates you to pay a fee if you are placed by the agency. These contracts must be read carefully: you may, for example, owe the agency the fee even if you are fired after one week. Agency fees run from 5 to 15 percent of annual starting salaries. In upper-income job brackets, agency fees can sometimes be 30 percent.

   For guidance on agencies in your chosen field, look at *Employment Directions,* which lists agencies by specialty in forty-nine states and five foreign countries. You can order this from the National Employment Association, 2000 K Street N.W., Washington, D.C. 20006.

PREPARING A WINNING RESUMÉ

For almost all job applications, you must submit a **resumé.** While the resumé may be enjoyable to prepare, it is far from enjoyable for the personnel officer in a corporation who must read thousands of them every year. In order, therefore, to have a competitive edge over other job seekers, it behooves you to do your best on your resumé. Remember: your resumé is an "advertisement for yourself."

Keep it Brief

Since your resumé is, in large part, bait for the interview, it need not be an entire dossier, starting out with letters of commendation from your junior-high-school principal. Nor should it list your every accomplishment, information about your outside interests (if you have them), or the backgrounds of your parents.

Presentation of Your Resumé

Your resumé should be on one or more sheets of paper, preferably high-quality rag bond. A good resumé is usually typed or printed. Remember, the appearance of a resumé is like the appearance you will make for an interview: first impressions count.

The Format of a Resumé

You needn't write a resumé as if it were an application for college. In other words, don't put the word NAME before your name; the fewer headlines, the better. But you can divide your resumé into sections, such as education, experience, publications, honors, awards, and special interests. While there is no single format for a resumé, Exhibit 2-4 gives you a preferred possibility.

Experience. On your resumé, you should list your experiences, either in reverse chronological order or according to functional headings, such as sales, teaching, or administration.

Education. In this section, list appropriate institutional degrees and certificates. Thus, if you went to college, you need not mention high school, unless it was a special kind. If you transferred to three or four different colleges, you need not list all of them, only the one from which you received your degree; doing otherwise might cause a prospective employer to think you were unstable.

Assuming that your resumé got you an interview, there are certain pointers that can improve your job chances.

HOW TO BE INTERVIEWED

Remember, the personnel officer of the company interviews many prospective employees. You must somehow convince the interviewer that you are as good as or better than anyone else who is being considered for a job. Basically, your interview should be constructed to convince the prospective employer that you will fullfil his or her needs. In order to do that, you must find out, beforehand, about the job requirements, the company, and, if possible, your prospective interviewer.

Some Pointers on Successful Interviews

Here are some suggestions for a successful interview:

1. Be on time.

2. Come with a list of your qualifications.

3. Always maintain eye contact and listen attentively.

4. Be honest and frank, but do not make derogatory comments about a previous employer.

5. Let your interviewer offer you information on benefits, salary, and agency fees (if any).

6. Decide in advance that you want the offer. It is better to have more options than less.

7. Find out what you need to learn about your potential employer as well as they about you.

8. Dress appropriately; first impressions are important.

OBTAINING INFORMATION ABOUT PROSPECTIVE COMPANIES

Prior to the interview, you should find out some facts about the company. This can be done by looking at some of the following sources:

1. *Moody's Manuals*

2. *Fitch Corporation Manuals*

3. *Thomas' Register of American Manufacturers*

4. *MacRae's Blue Book*

5. Company annual reports

SOME FINAL POINTERS ON JOB HUNTING

Remember that the key to success in job hunting is motivation. If you are motivated, you will follow some of the suggestions just mentioned. If you feel that you need more professional advice, consider seeking the services of a professional resumé writer, who is generally associated with a private employment-counseling firm. If you need help with interviews, practice with a friend or with someone who works in the placement center at your college or university. Without a doubt, serious career choice and job hunting require effort.

EXHIBIT 2-4 **A SAMPLE RESUMÉ FORM**

JOHN W. SMITH
10 Smith Street
City, State 11111

Broad based experience with responsibility for Hourly Employment, Industrial Safety and Health, Wage Administration, Compensation, Professional Employment, College Recruiting, Medical Services, Human Resources Information System, Employee Relations, and Labor Relations. Will relocate.

OBJECTIVE: Chief Responsibility for full function Personnel/Industrial Relations Department, or Major Department responsibility reporting to Chief Personnel Executive.

EXPERIENCE:
Aug 1976
To Present **Director of Industrial Relations**
Name of Employer
City, State

EXHIBIT 2-4 **CONTINUED**

Responsibilities:	Labor Relations (I.B.E.W., Teamsters, and U.A.W.)

Chief Spokesman for Contract Negotiations, Labor Agreement Administration, and Arbitration.

Apr 1974- Aug 1976	Name of Employer Division City, State

Director of Personnel (Mar 1976-Aug. 1976)

Responsibilities: Supervised wage and salary administration for Exempt and Non-Exempt employees, utilizing HAY system.

Director of Labor Relations (May 1975-Mar. 1976)

Responsibilities: Assisted waterfront management on labor relations policies and labor contract interpretation for 10,000 Production and Maintenance bargaining unit employees.

Member of contract negotiating team representing waterfront.

Manager of Personnel and Industrial Relations (Apr. 1974-May 1975)

Responsibilities: Wage and salary administration for Exempt, and Non-Exempt and Union Eligible employees.

Labor relations.

May 1972- Apr 1974	**Supervisor of Personnel Services** Name of Employer Division City, State

Responsibilities: Professional recruiting.

Administered group health programs for 1,000 salaried employees in United States and Europe.

Assisted in plant site selection.

College recruiting.

Assisted in contract negotiations with U.A.W., Rubber Workers, and Canadian Steel Workers.

RELATED ACTIVITIES:

Taught Graduate Course, Personnel Administration at George Washington University, Norfolk, Virginia, 1975.

EXHIBIT 2-4 **CONTINUED**

PROFESSIONAL ORGANIZATIONS:

    American Society for Personnel Administration

    American Society for Training and Development

    Society of Naval Architects and Marine Engineers

EDUCATION:

Jan 1973   M.A., Personnel Administration and Organizational Behavior
University of Illinois
Institute of Labor Relations
Champaign/Urbana, Illinois

June 1972   B.S., University of Illinois
Champaign/Urbana, Illinois

     Major in Communications; Minor in Economics.

PERSONAL: Age: 30 Date of Birth: June 3, 1948
Height: 6' 1" Weight: 185 lbs. Health: Excellent
Married July 1975. One child.

REFERENCES: Available on request.

Permission to reprint given by RESUMES, INCORPORATED 4009 Adams Street Independence, Missouri 64055 (800) 821-3186 (816) 373-3311

GLOSSARY OF TERMS

INVESTMENT IN HUMAN CAPITAL Any type of activity that increases your ability to earn a higher income in the future. You, the human being, are considered capital. Because education, training, and so on make you more productive, they are considered investments in yourself.

ON-THE-JOB TRAINING Training you receive by virtue of working on a job. This training can be either explicit, in the form of a training program, or implicit, in the form of more experience.

AGE-EARNINGS PROFILE The profile of how earnings change with your age. When you are young and just starting work, your earnings are low; as you get older, your earnings increase because you become more productive and work longer hours. Toward middle age, they start to decrease.

OPPORTUNITY COST   The foregone alternative that you gave up in order to do something. The opportunity cost of going to school is the income you could have made had you not gone to school but worked instead for pay.

LEARNING CURVE   The curve representing how fast you learn to do a job the more you do it. Typically, you learn to do something fast in the beginning; after a while, improvements in your ability come more slowly.

RESUMÉ   A brief summary of your education, training, honors, and so on that is given to a prospective employer.

CHAPTER SUMMARY

1. Individuals who attend college are investing in themselves because they will make higher incomes in the future.

2. Formalized schooling is only one way to invest in human capital; another way is to obtain on-the-job training. Most people who obtain such training are paid less during this training period than when they become more proficient.

3. You should acquire more education as long as the expected benefits at least cover the costs.

4. Those who hold higher-education degrees earn, on average, more than others. Thus, you can expect to be wealthier if you obtain more education.

5. Only part of the cost of education is books and tuition; the major cost is the earnings you give up while going to school. This is called an opportunity cost.

6. A number of studies and concerned individuals contend that too many people go to college. On the other hand, college graduates do earn more than nongraduates on average, and, during downturns in the economy, college graduates have the lowest unemployment rate.

7. The factors that influence personal income (besides education) are: (a) innate abilities, (b) experience, (c) training, (d) inherited wealth, (e) exploitation and discrimination, and (f) personal taste for risk.

8. There are huge differences in average salaries paid people in different occupations. Note, though, that higher-paid occupations require a longer formal and informal education period—during which salaries are low.

9. Aptitude can determine which career you pursue. It is important to determine, early in life, whether you have the appropriate aptitude for specialized careers, such as professional sports and the arts.

10. You can obtain information on occupations from *The Encyclopedia of Careers and Vocational Guidance, The Occupational Outlook for College Graduates, The Occupational Thesaurus,* and *The College Placement Annual.*

11. You can obtain further information on jobs from: (a) private employment agencies, (b) state employment agencies, (c) your local college placement centers, and (d) help-wanted ads in newspapers and professional journals.

12. A resumé is bait for an interview; therefore, it should be brief, outlining your experience and education but not your entire life history.

13. Successful interviewing requires that you follow a few rules: be on time, be honest and frank, and obtain information about the company before the interview.

STUDY QUESTIONS

1. Why is going to school an investment?

2. How does on-the-job training differ from formalized schooling? Do they both have the same effect on productivity and future wages?

3. What is an age-earnings profile?

4. What is the main cost of going to school? Is it the same for an eighteen-year old who has never had a job as it is for a thirty-five year old who decides to quit his or her job and return to school?

5. What are some of the factors that influence personal income?

6. How can you explain the fact that physicians, dentists, and lawyers are the highest-paid professionals in our country?

7. Where are some places you can obtain information on an occupation?

CASE PROBLEMS

2-1 The Resumé Opens Employment Doors

Terry Waters, a college junior, is in your personal finance class. You both intend to apply for summer jobs with a firm located 200 miles from the university. Terry has heard that the company only considers students who send resumés, so she is preparing one. Perhaps you should do the same.

2-2 College Means Losing Income to Earn More

Marietta Wycofsky, eighteen, currently works as a teller in a local bank. She earns $9000 per year, and the chances for advancement are poor. She would like to go to college and major in business management or economics and then return to the banking business. She feels the opportunities for advancement would be greater with a college degree. The current starting salary for college graduates at the bank is $12,000. Her father wants her to keep her present job. He points out that she would be giving up $36,000 in income just to go to school and that college graduates, especially women, don't make that much more money anyway. What information do you have that would help Marietta convince her father that college is the better choice for her?

SELECTED REFERENCES

Berg, Ivar E. *Education and Jobs; The Great Training Robbery*. New York: Center for Urban Education, Praeger, 1970.

Brown, Gary D. "How Type of Employment Affects Earnings Differences by Sex." *Monthly Labor Review*, July 1976, pp. 25-30.

"Career Education: A Whole New Focus for Schools." *Changing Times*, April 1974, pp. 37-39.

Carey, Max L. "Revised Occupational Projections to 1985." *Monthly Labor Review*. November 1976, pp. 10-22.

Cosgrave, Jerald P. *Career Planning: Search For a Future*. Toronto: University of Toronto Faculty of Education, 1973.

Erlick, A. C. "Youth, Education and Jobs." *Intellect*, October 1972, p. 10.

Freeman, Richard. *The Market for College-Trained Manpower: A Study in the Economics of Career Choice*. Cambridge: Harvard University Press, 1971.

Ginzberg, Eli. *Career Guidance, Who Needs It, Who Provides It*. New York: McGraw-Hill Book Company, 1971.

Gordon, Margaret S. *Higher Education and the Labor Market*. New York: McGraw-Hill, 1974.

Guzzardi, Walter, Jr. "The Uncertain Passage from College to Job." *Fortune*, January 1976, pp. 126-129ff.

Haldane, Bernhard. *Career Satisfaction and Success: A Guide to Job Freedom*. American Management Association, New York, 1974.

"How Workers Are Faring in Wage-Price Race." *U.S. News & World Report*, June 17, 1974, pp. 47-48.

Howe, H., II, and Freeman, R. B. "Does it Pay to Go to College?" *U.S. News*, January 24, 1977, pp. 59-60.

Iris, B., and Barrett, G.V. "Some Relations between Job and Life Satisfaction and Job Importance." *Journal of Applied Psychology*, August 1972, pp. 301-304.

"Jobs to Help You Pay for College." *Changing Times*, May 1977, pp. 17-20.

Johnson, L., and Johnson, R. H. "High School Preparation, Occupation and Job Satisfaction." *Vocational Guidance Quarterly*, June 1972, pp. 287-290.

Miller, Herman P. *Rich Man, Poor Man*. New York: Thomas J. Crowell Company, 1971.

Owen, John D. "Workweeks & Leisure: An Analysis of Trends, 1948-1975." *Monthly Labor Review*, August 1976, pp. 3-8.

Seixas, Suzanne. "How to Handle a Job Interview." *Money*, October 1976, pp. 55-66.

Von Hoffman, N. "What Price Education?" *Progressive*, February 1977, p. 55.

"When College Graduates Enter the Real World." *U.S. News* March 14, 1977, pp. 79-80.

Budgeting

■American consumers are rich. That is, we are rich compared with the British consumer, the Indian consumer, the Ivory Coast consumer, the Spanish consumer, or the Venezuelan consumer. The average real per capita income in the United States is considerably higher than in many other countries of the world.

But per capita income does not tell the whole story. Exhibit 3-1 shows the distribution of families in the United States at income levels ranging from poverty to extreme opulence. Most of us are somewhere in the middle: we are neither absolutely broke nor in a league with the Rockefellers.

All of us, rich or poor, have something in common: we cannot buy everything we would like to buy. This problem of scarcity is universal. All of us are faced with a limited budget, even the Shah of Iran; if he wanted to buy every jet plane in the world, he would not have enough money to do it. Since we all face this universal problem of scarce resources, we can better understand why personal money management is important for each of us, no matter what our income level.

WHY FIGURE OUT A BUDGET, OR SPENDING PLAN?

If you are at either end of the income spectrum, you may think it a waste of time to formulate a budget, which we will define as a financial plan for your future activities. Obviously if you have no income, a budget is not what you should be looking for. If you have a seemingly infinite amount of income, you may not need to formulate a budget with respect to your usual purchases. Most of us, however, lie somewhere in between.

43

TOTAL MONEY INCOME	PERCENTAGE DISTRIBUTION
UNDER $3,000	8.4
$ 3,000-$ 4,999	9.5
$ 5,000-$ 6,999	9.0
$ 7,000-$ 9,999	12.4
$10,000-$11,999	7.9
$12,000-$14,999	11.2
$15,000-$19,999	16.4
$20,000-$24,999	10.7
$25,000 and over	14.6

Since we have limited incomes, every action that involves spending part of that income means sacrificing something else. Economists term this the opportunity cost of spending. If you decide to spend more on entertainment, you have less left over for some or all of the other things in your budget. Or if you decide to spend more on transportation, you have less for other things. In other words, every spending decision you make involves an opportunity cost: you give up the opportunity of spending that income on something else.

Planning a budget and attempting to stick to it forces the issue of scarcity and opportunity cost out in the open. You cannot deny the fact that you are giving something up when you decide, for example, to take a trip to Mexico. For, if you plan it in your budget, you will realize that eventually something has to be cut from the budget. A budget, then, is a way of managing your money in a more or less systematic and rational manner. When making out a budget, you estimate future income and expenditures. It is, then, a way of planning income and spending during a particular period; you are making a forecast of the fact.

The Budget as a Control Mechanism

The budget is also a control mechanism that can help you be aware of the consequences of your decisions. A budget allows you to make explicit choices among the trade-offs that occur every time you spend money. With it, you can control undirected spending activities that ultimately may lead to unhappiness and occasionally financial disaster if the household must declare bankruptcy.

Budgets are usually planned around a pay period, perhaps a month or sometimes as short a time as a week. To be most helpful, budgets should be set up for a year at a time (allowing ample opportunity for revisions during the year). On a yearly basis, one is able to:

1. Anticipate and prepare for changes in one's financial situation.
2. Set aside money for large anticipated expenses and emergencies.
3. Plan for seasonal changes—for example, greater clothing needs in the fall or spring, higher utility bills during the winter.

HOW DOES A TYPICAL HOUSEHOLD ALLOCATE ITS INCOME?

Averages sometimes can be deceiving. But it may be instructive to see how typical households in the United States allocate their fixed incomes to the many competing demands. The U.S. Department of Labor, Bureau of Labor Statistics, has for some time obtained survey data on the spending patterns of households of various income levels. Exhibit 3-2, a pie graph, shows how an average American family spends its income. A large portion usually goes for housing services, which include utilities and maintenance. Equal to that expenditure, and sometimes even larger, is the percentage of income that goes for food. Food and housing often account for more than 50 percent of the average American

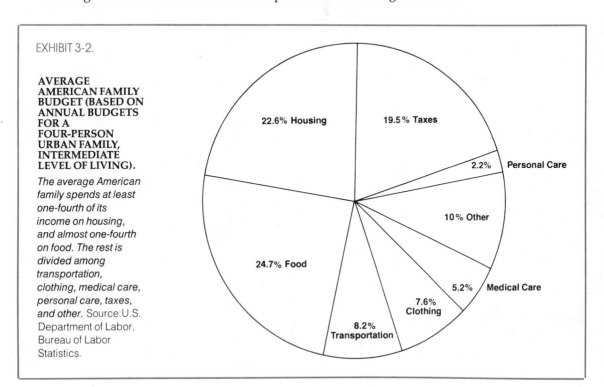

EXHIBIT 3-2.

AVERAGE AMERICAN FAMILY BUDGET (BASED ON ANNUAL BUDGETS FOR A FOUR-PERSON URBAN FAMILY, INTERMEDIATE LEVEL OF LIVING).

The average American family spends at least one-fourth of its income on housing, and almost one-fourth on food. The rest is divided among transportation, clothing, medical care, personal care, taxes, and other. Source:U.S. Department of Labor, Bureau of Labor Statistics.

22.6% Housing
19.5% Taxes
2.2% Personal Care
10% Other
24.7% Food
5.2% Medical Care
7.6% Clothing
8.2% Transportation

family's after-tax expenditures in any one year.

Clothing, personal care, and health care absorb another large part of each family's budget in the United States. Medical care itself has been taking up an increasingly large percentage of total consumption spending in the United States. (We will examine the reason for this when we study health care in detail in Chapter 10.) Taxes, unfortunately for many of us, command an ever-increasing amount of our income. For the average American, more than 40 percent of every dollar earned goes to federal, state, and local taxes. Some of those tax monies are returned in the form of transfer payments, such as Social Security benefits and unemployment compensation. But the remainder, almost 25 percent, is still a large fraction of our total income in the United States.

Budgets at Different Levels

The make-up of the various budget categories changes as we go from lower-income to higher-income spenders. Exhibit 3-3 shows the U.S. Department of Labor's estimates of what it takes to live within low,

---

EXHIBIT 3-3.

SUMMARY OF ANNUAL BUDGETS FOR A FOUR-PERSON FAMILY AT THREE LEVELS OF LIVING, URBAN UNITED STATES, AUTUMN 1977.

SOURCE: U.S. Department of Labor, Bureau of Labor Statistics, News, Washington, D.C.

COMPONENT	LOWER	INTERMEDIATE	HIGHER	ITEM AS PERCENTAGE OF TOTAL BUDGET LOWER	INTERMEDIATE	HIGHER
Total budget	$10,481	$17,106	$25,202			
Total family consumption	8,657	13,039	17,948			
Food	3,190	4,098	5,159	30%	24%	20%
Housing	2,083	4,016	6,085	20	23	24
Transportation	804	1,472	1,913	8	9	8
Clothing	828	1,182	1,730	8	7	7
Personal care	282	377	535	3	2	2
Medical care	980	985	1,027	9	6	4
Other family consumption[1]	489	909	1,499	5	5	6
Other items[2]	472	763	1,288	5	4	5
Taxes & deductions	1,352	3,303	5,965	13	19	24
Social Security & disability	632	961	985	6	6	4
Personal income taxes	720	2,342	4,980	7	14	20

[1]Other family consumption includes average costs for reading materials, recreation, tobacco products, alcoholic beverages, education, and miscellaneous expenditures.

[2]Other items include allowances for gifts and contributions, life insurance, and occupational expenses.

NOTE: Because of rounding, sums of individual items may not equal totals.

intermediate, and high budgets for a hypothetical urban family of four. (Note that these estimates say nothing about actual incomes in the United States.) Notice that, as percentages of total income, food spending falls and housing expenditures rise as income increases. That means that as our incomes go up, we spend proportionally more for housing and less for food. Housing, then, is often considered a luxury good, because people spend a larger and larger fraction of their income on it as they get richer. Food, on the other hand, has the opposite characteristic and is still considered a necessity.

We must be careful with such labels as luxury and necessity, however, because they have some subjective connotations. Just as one person's meat is often another person's poison, one person's luxury may be another person's necessity and vice versa. Most of us have difficulty determining our own values and goals, let alone deciding for other people. But that's what we do when we consider someone else's spending to be wasted on so-called luxury items or frivolous consumption. After all, we purchase "satisfaction," not the items per se. So who can judge what another's derived satisfaction is?

CITY VERSUS COUNTRY

Not only are there differences in budget allocations among low-, medium-, and high-income families, there is also a difference in typical income levels between urban and rural areas. The costs of living in cities differ from those of living in the country. And the costs of living in a large city differ from those of living in a small city. The U.S. Department of Labor has issued indexes of relative living costs in different parts of the country. In Exhibit 3-4 we show these indexes. The average of urban areas with populations in excess of 2,500 has a base index of 100. To find out what an intermediate budget would cost in a city with an index of 110, increase the total budget figure under the *Intermediate* column in Exhibit 3-3 by 10 percent. If the area you live in or wish to live in has an index in Exhibit 3-4 that is less than 100, you must reduce the corresponding budget figure in Exhibit 3-3 accordingly.

A low family budget in New York City may be the equivalent of a high family budget in Podunk, Anywhere. But, of course, people are generally paid more if they work in cities that are expensive to live in. In fact, you would not expect that moving to a city would necessarily make you better off just because you were offered a higher salary.

Of course, such a comparison is only part of the information you need to decide whether or not to move from one city to another or from the country to the city or vice versa. A move to the city means access to a variety of cultural activity that is unavailable in less-populated areas. "Specialization is a function of the size of the market," said Adam Smith, the father of modern economics. That means: the larger the city, the more specialized services you'll be able to buy. Just think how many movies, restaurants, theaters, operas, and concerts you can go to in cities of 3 million compared to cities of 3,000. Many people are willing to

EXHIBIT 3-4.

RELATIVE COST OF LIVING INDEXES FOR SELECTED CITIES (U.S. CITY AVERAGE = 100)
Source: Monthly Labor Review, May 1977.

	RELATIVE COST OF LIVING INDEX		RELATIVE COST OF LIVING INDEX
Atlanta, Georgia	99	Minneapolis-St. Paul	100
Baltimore, Maryland	102	New York, New Jersey	103
Boston, Massachusetts	102	Philadelphia, Pennsylvania-	
Chicago, Illinois-		New Jersey	101
Northwestern Indiana	97	Pittsburgh, Pennsylvania	99
Cincinnati, Ohio	100	Portland, Oregon-	
Dallas, Texas	98	Washington	98
Detroit, Michigan	99	San Diego, California	100
Honolulu, Hawaii	95	San Francisco-Oakland,	
Houston, Texas	104	California	98
Kansas City, Missouri-		Scranton, Pennsylvania	100
Kansas	98	Seattle, Washington	96
Los Angeles-Long Beach,		Washington, D.C.-	
California	98	Maryland-Virginia	100
Milwaukee, Wisconsin	98		

contend with such things as increased congestion, higher living expenses, and greater pollution and crime in order to avail themselves of numerous recreational and cultural activities. All of us would certainly like to have the benefits of big cities without paying the costs, but few of us have figured out how that can be done. Again, we live in a world of scarcity where, generally, every benefit has a cost. You have to decide whether the benefit is worth that cost.

LETTING THE COMPUTER TELL YOU WHERE YOU ARE

Recently, a number of banks and firms began offering computerized financial evaluations through the mail, along with a consumer finance course covering such subjects as budgeting, insurance, and investment. For example, Responsive Communications (RCI) of Newton, Massachusetts, markets its programs through the following banks: First National Bank of Boston, First National Bank in Dallas, Continental Illinois National Bank and Trust Company of Chicago, First National Bank of Denver, Manufacturers Hanover Trust Company in New York, and Fidelity Bank in Philadelphia. Residents not served by those banks can write directly to RCI at 430 Lexington Street, Newton, Massachusetts 02166.

For a fee ranging from twenty-five to fifty dollars, you receive six booklets with six lessons, which are followed by exams you take after reading the material. You send in the exam answers, and a computer sends back an analysis of your answers with accompanying comments. If the student has any questions, he or she may telephone the course administrator. At the end of the sixth lesson, the student is asked to complete a "computerized financial analysis" booklet, which asks about Social Security contributions, whether you have a will, whether you are retired, if you own your own home, the total of your outstanding debts, the insurance coverage you have, your assets, and so on. The information is fed into a computer and you receive a confidential analysis based on your answers. The computer has been programmed with literally thousands of paragraphs that apply to different situations. You get back approximately fifteen pages of single-spaced information, which may include how much you should be saving to send your children to college, how much life insurance you should buy, and other useful pieces of advice.

Undoubtedly, other companies and banks soon will be offering similar financial planning courses. You can write RCI for more information. Or you might wish to write COAP Planning, Inc., 21 Alberton Avenue, Alberton, New York 11507, for their computerized materials. There are also a number of other firms, catering to insurance-company investment advisors and brokers, that offer computerized individual financial presentations. Generally these services are free to customers of the insurance or brokerage companies and are used as promotional devices.

FITTING IT ALL INTO A LIFETIME PLAN

There is much talk today about early retirement and the decisions that must be made if it is to be a fulfilling period. There is also considerable talk about more leisure time and the need to purchase more leisure-related products. These matters should be considered as part of a **lifetime plan,** one that is revised periodically to take account of changing values, income, and consumption situations.

The purpose of a lifetime plan is to rationalize your behavior as a consumer—in the most fundamental sense of the word. If you specify certain values and goals for yourself and your family, you can work toward them and measure your progress. This can give you a sense of satisfaction and serenity. If, however, you are frenetic about your plans, any failure to meet them may cause grief. But if you can use your plans to mold your decisions so that no important elements of your values or goals are omitted, then, by all means, figure out where you are and where you want to be eventually. Such a method is an effective way to stimulate motivation, if motivation is what you need, and is also an effective way to accomplish things expeditiously. What follows are a few suggestions for making lifetime planning work for you.

The Mechanics of a Plan

Important to you, as a consumer, are monthly and yearly lists of goals, tasks, and ideas. The monthly list, for example, would tell you when to have scheduled maintenance on your car, when to have services performed on household appliances, what days sales are coming up at various stores, and so on. The yearly list, of course, can do the same thing but with greater scope. This list will tell you what goals you want to attain by the end of the year, what purchases you would like to make, and other such items. Such lists can help you decide the kind of savings and spending programs you must undertake in order to maximize your happiness from your income. Instead of telling yourself, "I really wish I could afford a new camera or a new stereo" you might, instead, make such a purchase part of your yearly goals and save toward it. When you work toward a goal, it is easier to make the appropriate decisions and take the appropriate actions. Your goals can be stretched to five, ten, or even fifteen years—in which case, they will be much broader and subject to revision.

Long-range planning is quite simple in concept but sometimes difficult to do, mainly because people don't always like to face the difficulties of attaining certain goals. For example, one way to increase your powers of consumption is to make more income. And one way to make more income is to become more productive in your job or to change jobs, moving to one where you are in fact more productive. That may involve attending night school, taking additional training, working on weekends, and so on. If you are aware of such requirements, then you know the cost of achieving your goal for yourself and/or your family and can determine if the cost/goal ratio is acceptable.

EMOTIONAL ASPECTS OF MONEY

In the following Practical Applications section you will see examples of possible budgets. But first, let's consider the emotional underpinnings of making and spending money. Budget making, at best, is not a picnic. And, unless emotional implications are understood by the members of the family beforehand, the process can become painful and even counterproductive. In the next few paragraphs, some of the most frequently encountered emotional problems are considered.

Breadwinners Believe They Own All the Money They Make

If there is one wage earner in the family, that person often tends to believe that he or she should control every expenditure because he or she made the money. Obvious problems, including resentment by other members of the family and what we will call retaliatory spending, frequently arise.

Retaliatory Spending

The nonworking member of a family unit may decide to spend a large sum of money on a new clothing item just to "get back" at a breadwinner who has controlled all the expenditures to date. Sometimes retaliatory spending results when the breadwinner dictates where the family lives; he or she maximizes a personal job situation without considering other family members' needs.

Status Spending

In order to achieve acceptance by one's peers, one is often tempted to spend excessively in order to maintain a desired status. Yet such status spending often contradicts one's inner set of personal values. This is a form of conspicuous consumption or attempting to "keep up with the Joneses." Status spending is often associated with the purchase of such items as new cars and expensive houses. Status spenders consistently run into credit problems by overextending themselves with too much debt.

Money As a Control Mechanism

Insecurity on the part of a particular family member may cause him or her to be overbearing in making spending decisions. This person may write checks without telling anyone else in the family, even if it means financial embarrassment for others (whose checks are then not honored by the bank). Another way to control money is to require that every family member seek a "handout" from the person in charge of the money. A budget worked out by such an individual certainly would not be respected by most family members.

PRACTICAL APPLICATIONS

HOW TO BUDGET YOUR LIMITED INCOME

Once you decide to do some positive money management, you must figure out a budget and try to stick to it. The budget, remember, is a planning tool to help you reduce undirected spending. In this Application, we will look at two different types of budgets for two different situations; one is for college students, and the other is for people not in college.

STEPS IN BUDGET MAKING

Very briefly, after the income and goals of the relevant spending unit are determined, these basic steps should be followed to create a spending plan.

1. Analyze past spending by keeping records for a month or two.

2. Determine **fixed expenses,** such as rent, and any other contractual payments that must be made—even if they come infrequently, such as insurance and taxes.

3. Determine **flexible expenses,** such as for food and clothing.

4. Balance your fixed plus flexible expenditures with your available income. If a surplus exists, you can apply it toward achieving your goals. If there is a deficit, then you must re-examine your flexible expenditures. You can also re-examine fixed expenses in view of reducing them in the future.

Note that so-called fixed expenses are only philosophically fixed in the short run. In the longer run, everything is essentially flexible, or variable. One can adjust one's fixed expenses by changing one's standard of living, if necessary.

THE IMPORTANCE OF KEEPING RECORDS

Budget making, whether you are a college student, a single person living alone, or the head of a family, will be useless if you don't keep records. The only way to make sure that you are carrying out the plans implicit in your budget is by having records to show what you are actually spending. The ultimate way to maintain records is to write everything down, but that becomes time-consuming and, therefore, costly. Another way to keep records is to write checks for everything. Records are also important in case of problems with faulty products, services, or the Internal Revenue Service. Thus, you serve at least two purposes by keeping good records.

Which Records to Keep at Home

Here are eleven types of records that you should keep at home. Not all of these records are directly related to budget making; some are for such purposes as insurable losses, lost credit cards, and the like.

1. **Income**—paycheck stubs, record of self-employment income, W-2 Forms (given to you at the end of the year by your employer(s)), 1099 Forms (indicates interest, dividends, etc., earned during the year).

2. **Most canceled checks**—keep at least one year and, in some cases, a minimum of seven years.

3. **Insurance policies**—automobile, home owners, fire, health, life, and so on.

4. **Large purchases**—all receipts and canceled checks for the following: autos, furniture, equipment, appliances, stereos, and so on. These should be kept as long as you own the item.

5. **Home improvements**—all receipts and canceled checks must be kept until you

are no longer a home owner. You can reduce taxes this way.

6. **Investment transactions**—a register of all stock transactions, confirmations of purchases and sales sent to you by brokers, and receipts.

7. **Tax-deductible items** — canceled checks and receipts for interest, taxes, contributions, business expenses, medical and dental expenses, and drugs (should be kept at least three years after tax-filing deadline).

8. **Tax returns**—copies of all returns, worksheets, and schedules to be kept three years after date of tax-filing deadline.

9. **Information on valuables**—canceled checks and receipts on art, antiques, and jewelry and appraisals of same. These records should be kept as long as you own the item, plus three years after any sale, for income-tax purposes.

10. **Credit cards**—all credit card numbers, telephone numbers and/or addresses, and/or prepaid envelopes to notify of loss or theft; update constantly.

11. **Other current documents**—warranties, loan contracts, service contracts.

Things to Keep in a Safe Deposit Box

There are a number of items that you want to keep in a safe deposit box. Although they don't specifically relate to budget making, they are part of sensible and complete record keeping.

1. **Personal documents**—birth certificates, marriage certificate, military records, naturalization papers.

2. **Securities and properties**—deed to a house, car titles, stock certificates, insurance policies, bonds.

3. **Wills**—all current wills; originals should be kept by those who will carry out the will.

4. **Inventory of personal and household items**—make complete and update in case of loss or damage. Take photographs, and perhaps make a tape-recorded inventory.

GENERAL BUDGETING

Exhibit 3-5 is a monthly general-budget form that encompasses both estimated and actual cash available and fixed and variable payments.

You will note that the savings category is located under the *Fixed Payments* heading. This is because the money in your savings account may be used to pay such fixed annual expenses as auto, fire, and life insurance, and it is necessary to plan to save in advance for these expenses.

The key to making a budget work for you is to review your figures every month to see how your monthly estimates compare to your spending.

COLLEGE STUDENT BUDGETS

There are approximately 8.5 million men and women in American universities and colleges. While many students live at home, many others live in dormitories, fraternity and sorority houses, rooming houses, and apartments. Students who live away from home must rely on themselves to make decisions about how to spend their limited incomes, whether those incomes are obtained from parents, scholarships, and/or part-time jobs.

Exhibit 3-6 presents a suggested budget form for college students. Expenses are anticipated both for the college year and for each month. College students have many expenses that other people do not, such as tuition, fees, books and supplies, and, in some cases, dues to fraternities, sororities, and

EXHIBIT 3-5. **A GENERAL WAY TO BUDGET***

CASH FORECAST, MONTH OF _____	ESTIMATED	ACTUAL
cash on hand and in checking account, end of previous period	_____	_____
savings needed for planned expenses	_____	_____
Receipts		
net pay	_____	_____
borrowed	_____	_____
interest/dividends	_____	_____
other	_____	_____
TOTAL CASH AVAILABLE DURING PERIOD	_____	_____
Fixed Payments		
mortgage or rent	_____	_____
life insurance	_____	_____
fire insurance	_____	_____
auto insurance	_____	_____
other insurance	_____	_____
savings	_____	_____
local taxes	_____	_____
loan or other debt	_____	_____
children's allowances	_____	_____
other	_____	_____
TOTAL FIXED PAYMENTS	_____	_____
Flexible Payments		
water	_____	_____
electricity	_____	_____
fuel	_____	_____
telephone	_____	_____
medical	_____	_____
household supplies	_____	_____
car	_____	_____
food	_____	_____
clothing	_____	_____
nonrecurring large payments	_____	_____
contributions, recreation, etc.	_____	_____
other	_____	_____
TOTAL FLEXIBLE PAYMENTS	_____	_____
TOTAL ALL PAYMENTS	_____	_____
Recapitulation		
total cash available	_____	_____
total payments	_____	_____
cash balance, end of period	_____	_____

*For more specific categories, see Exhibits 3-7 and 3-8.

EXHIBIT 3-6.   SUGGESTED BUDGET FORM FOR COLLEGE STUDENTS

	ANNUAL TOTAL (Estimated)	MONTH										ANNUAL TOTAL (Actual)
		9	10	11	12	1	2	3	4	5	6	
INCOME												
Current earnings												
Drawn from savings												
Gifts from parents												
Gifts from others												
Grants												
Sale of assets (i.e., used textbooks)												
Scholarships, prizes												
Tax refund												
Other												
Total												
PERSONAL EXPENSES												
Food away from "home"												
Recreation & entertainment												
Tobacco												
Personal care												
Clothing purchases												
Clothing upkeep												
Sending messages (telephone, postage)												
Receiving messages (subscriptions)												
Medical & dental												
Transportation												
Insurance (life, health, auto)												
Gifts & donations												
Loan repayments												
Taxes												
Bank charges												
Vacations												
Fraternity/Sorority												
Honorary societies, clubs												
Professional memberships												
Child care												
Pets												
Subtotal												
COLLEGE EXPENSES												
Tuition												
Fees												
Board												
Room												
Books												
Supplies												
Other												
TOTAL												

honorary and professional societies. But many students can also anticipate income that most others do not: gifts from parents and others, scholarships, and prizes. All of these must be taken into account if the budget content is to be accurate. You can, of course, alter the budget form to fit your particular situation.

It is important that all categories be arranged according to their fixed and/or flexible qualities. For example, tuition is fixed in terms of cost-per-credit-hour but flexible in terms of the number of hours you wish to take each semester.

We repeat: To make the budget work, go over it every month to see how close to your budget specifications you actually came in your spending. If you are out of touch with the realities of economics this is how you can find out—and the sooner the better. To budget is not merely to keep records, but to *plan* and to *control* as well.

Even if you have a small budget today, you might want to consider a budget-and-planning program as an investment in money-management skills for later years, when you will have more money than you need to cover basic necessities. Often the rate of return on such an investment can be high indeed.

BUDGETING FOR THE NONSTUDENT SPENDING UNIT

Those of you in family units face a slightly different situation from that of the unmarried college student. Your income generally is more predictable and less a function of the generosity of others. But your expenses are also generally much higher and involve payments on life-insurance policies, mortgages, and so on. Naturally, you would have to expect a slightly different set of classifications for your budget than does the college student. Exhibits 3-7 through 3-11 are examples of possible monthly budget sheets, which would be incorporated in a yearly expenditure tally. And this expenditure tally fits in with a lifetime plan, which you design with the other members of the spending unit and which you will change as your values, goals, and economic situation change.

Notice in the budget sheets the entries for savings. (We cover savings in more detail in Chapter 14.) Saving involves a decision *against* present consumption and *in favor* of future consumption. In other words, it is a trade-off between the present and the future. Also, you save in order to optimize your level of consumption throughout your lifetime. In other words, you save to provide for those periods when your income is very low so that your consumption— your expenditures for things you like to buy —won't have to fall drastically. Saving allows you to smooth out your consumption expenditures, even if your income is variable. We all realize that we have to save for the day when, as older people, we no longer can work. We also should save in case something happens to us when we are young that temporarily keeps us from working. Saving for a rainy day is a trite but true analysis of the act of saving. The savings umbrella allows you to keep dry during the storm. After the storm is over, you can repair that umbrella for the next time you need it.

COMPUTER BUDGETING SERVICES

Certain banks now offer monthly computerized budget accounts for a fee ranging from three to six dollars per month. One such service, called "Money Minder," is offered by the United States National Bank of Oregon (P.O. Box 3460, Portland, Oregon 97208). All such computerized systems offer major budget classifications with a specific code number that you mark on each check and deposit slip. For a higher fee, you can choose up to 1,000 individually selected income and expense categories. The monthly report will give you, at a minimum, the following information:

1. Total income and expense by category.

2. Number of items in each category.

3. Percentage of total income and expense by category for month.

4. Percentage of total income and expense

by category for that year to the month in question.

Some systems even allow you the option of budget comparisons. They will compare, for example, a fixed amount you had budgeted to a particular category compared with what you actually spent.

EXHIBIT 3-7.

SUGGESTED MONTHLY BUDGET FORM FOR FAMILY UNITS.
This form does not include fixed monthly major contractual obligations, important future expenses, or savings and investments.

Market purchases: food, beverages, sundries	$ _____
Automobile: operation, servicing, minor repairs	_____
Utility bills: electricity, fuel, water, garbage, telephone, cable TV	_____
Laundry and cleaning	_____
Clothing	_____
Incidental expenses	_____
Medical and dental expenses, prescription drugs (not covered by insurance)	_____
Adult allowances	_____
Children's allowances	_____
Family recreation: eating out, hobbies, movies, home entertainment	_____
Miscellaneous labor: babysitter, housecleaning, etc.	_____
Subscriptions: newspapers, magazines	_____
Dues: union, lodge, club (other than deducted from paycheck)	_____
Education: evening courses, school charges and fees, special lessons	_____
Charity contributions (other than deducted from paycheck)	_____
Unexpected expenses	_____
Other expenses such as gifts and pets	_____

TOTAL MONTHLY LIVING EXPENSES (Average Month) $ _____

Also, after you have used the system for at least thirteen months, you can request a previous-year comparison, which permits you to see the change from last year's totals to this year's totals for each classification. Such automated budgeting systems eliminate some of the drudgery often associated with financial planning.

Computer budgeting services from nonbank sources are also available. We give an example of the output of one such service in Exhibit 3-12. The sample budget report from Budget Control Service, Inc. (P.O. Box 105, Shelburne, Vermont 05482) shows how much John Doe spent in various categories during June 1975. The column marked *YTD* shows how much money has been spent year-to-date for each of the expense categories. The column marked *DIFF* indicates whether John Doe spent more or less for each category in June than he spent in May. The column *AVG* gives the average monthly amount spent for each category. Finally, the column marked % gives the percentage of total expenditures in each category.

A subscriber to Budget Control Service can fill out the names of up to fifty categories. These are then entered into his or her account. Each month, the subscriber enters the amounts spent in these different categories. The cost of such a budgeting system is usually two to four dollars per month after a one-time programming charge of ten to fifteen dollars is paid.

EXHIBIT 3-8.

**FIXED MONTHLY
PAYMENTS.**
*Fixed by lease,
mortgage, contract,
court order or
conscience. Does not
include fixed annual or
semi-annual payments,
such as insurance or
taxes.*

Rent or mortgage payment on home	$ _____
Auto loan payment—car no. 1	_____
Auto loan payment—car no. 2	_____
Appliance, TV, furniture loans	_____
Personal loans	_____
Other loans	_____
Credit card payments	_____
Major store installment debt	_____
Other contract debts or payments	_____
Regular contributions to others—parents, etc.	_____
Alimony or child support	_____
TOTAL FIXED MONTHLY PAYMENTS	$ _____

EXHIBIT 3-9.

IMPORTANT FUTURE EXPENSES.

Divide total of yearly expenses by twelve for average amount to be saved on each month for future big payments or purchases.

(Of course, if you are starting your budgeting on January 1st and the car insurance is due June 30th, you must have enough cash on hand by June 30th to pay the bill. If you have not yet begun saving for this expense, divide the total needed by six.)

	TAXES—FEES	INSURANCE	SHOPPING	VACATION	OTHER	TOTAL EXPENSES
JANUARY						
FEBRUARY						
MARCH						
APRIL						
MAY						
JUNE						
JULY						
AUGUST						
SEPTEMBER						
OCTOBER						
NOVEMBER						
DECEMBER						
TOTALS						

EXHIBIT 3-10.

**MONTHLY MONEY
PLANNER**

*Now you are in a
position to compare
your income with your
expenses. In the top
part of this exhibit, fill
in your average
monthly cash income.
Now use the results of
your computations
from Exhibits 3-7, 3-8,
and 3-9 to fill in your
average monthly
expenses. Now you
can compare your total
average monthly
expenses with your
total cash income for
an average month.
This gives you the
amount of income
available for savings
and investments. You
are now in a position
to complete a yearly
money planner, which
we present in Exhibit
3-11.*

INCOME

Salary and wages—(take-home pay) husband $ _____

Salary and wages—(take-home pay) wife   _____

Interest (average month)   _____

Income from securities (average month)   _____

Received from income property (average month)   _____

Other monthly income   _____

TOTAL CASH INCOME FOR AVERAGE MONTH $ _____

EXPENSES

Total monthly living expenses (from Exhibit 3-7) $ _____

Total fixed monthly payments (from Exhibit 3-8)   _____

Total future expenses—monthly average (from Exhibit 3-9)   _____

TOTAL AVERAGE MONTHLY EXPENSES $ _____

INCOME AVAILABLE FOR SAVINGS AND INVESTMENTS $ _____
(Total expenses subtracted from total income)

EXHIBIT 3-11. **YEARLY MONEY PLANNER**

It is now possible for you to fill out a total yearly money planner, based on the information you provided for Exhibits 3-7 through 3-10. At the bottom of this exhibit, we also provide spaces for you to list your savings and investments and to indicate how they change in value over a one-year period. This important information will help you plan how to increase your net worth.

MONTH	INCOME	LIVING EXPENSES	FIXED PAYMENTS	FUTURE EXPENSES	SAVINGS AND INVESTMENTS	TOTAL MONTHLY ALLOCATIONS
JANUARY						
FEBRUARY						
MARCH						
APRIL						
MAY						
JUNE						
JULY						
AUGUST						
SEPTEMBER						
OCTOBER						
NOVEMBER						
DECEMBER						
TOTALS						

SAVINGS BALANCE	NOW	END OF YEAR	INVESTMENT VALUE	NOW	END OF YEAR
Emergency fund			Savings bonds		
Education fund			Mutual funds—securities		
Special purposes			Real estate		
Other			Other		
TOTAL			TOTAL		

EXHIBIT 3-12.

**SAMPLE MONTHLY
REPORT**

SAMPLE MONTHLY REPORT

```
JOHN DOE
100 MAIN STREET
ANY TOWN, USA  99999
```

CATEGORY	JUN '75	YTD	DIFF	AVG	%
HOUSING.	180.73	1084.38	0.00	180.73	15.0
IMPROVEMENTS.	0.00	283.68	0.00	47.28	3.9
ELECTRICITY.	64.68	554.65	1.35	92.44	7.7
PHONE.	18.26	80.61	7.59	13.43	1.1
REFUSE.	5.00	26.00	1.00	4.33	0.3
SEWER & WATER.	0.00	70.00	-21.30	11.66	0.9
HOUSE MISC.	0.00	75.60	-20.60	12.60	1.0
FOOD.	333.06	1794.99	35.02	299.16	24.9
CLOTHING.	22.72	400.55	-58.73	66.75	5.5
CLEANING SUPPLIES.	17.00	81.50	0.50	13.58	1.1
HOUSEHOLD MISC.	19.71	87.97	-23.09	14.66	1.2
CLEANING AND LAUNDRY.	3.40	13.86	1.60	2.31	0.1
PERSONAL CARE.	4.00	17.51	0.85	2.91	0.2
DOCTOR.	2.50	38.50	2.50	6.41	0.5
DENTIST.	30.00	84.00	24.00	14.00	1.1
MEDICINE.	0.00	19.28	-6.22	3.21	0.2
MEDICAL MISC.	48.50	48.50	48.50	8.08	0.6
AUTO REPAIRS & MAINT.	13.56	298.85	-68.30	49.80	4.1
GAS & OIL.	44.07	137.74	-3.49	22.95	1.9
AUTO INSURANCE.	47.10	143.10	47.10	23.85	1.9
HOME INSURANCE.	0.00	151.00	0.00	25.16	2.0
PROPERTY & SCHOOL TAX.	0.00	345.60	0.00	57.60	4.8
OTHER TAX.	22.72	22.72	22.72	3.78	0.3
LICENSES.	0.00	71.50	0.00	11.91	0.9
FINANCE CHARGES.	3.40	35.78	-1.31	5.96	0.4
CLUBS & ORGANIZATIONS.	1.00	15.00	-9.00	2.50	0.2
GIFTS.	31.84	98.26	-16.42	16.37	1.3
EDUCATION.	18.00	158.00	3.00	26.33	2.1
PET CARE.	31.21	64.21	28.21	10.70	0.8
BOOKS & SUBSCRIPTIONS.	29.60	120.07	5.95	20.01	1.6
ENTERTAINMENT.	51.60	149.41	51.60	24.90	2.0
CONTRIBUTIONS.	0.00	32.00	0.00	5.33	0.4
CHILD CARE.	27.50	43.50	27.50	7.25	0.6
HOBBIES.	0.00	7.63	0.00	1.27	0.1
SPORTS & EQUIPMENT.	0.00	89.87	0.00	14.97	1.2
SPECIAL NO. 1.	45.00	286.95	0.00	47.82	3.9
SPECIAL NO. 2.	53.87	203.90	53.87	33.98	2.8
TOTALS THIS MONTH	1170.03	7236.67	134.40	1206.11	

SAMPLE MONTHLY REPORT

With permission of Budget Control Service, Inc., of Shelburne, Vermont.

GLOSSARY OF TERMS

SCARCITY The universal problem of desires exceeding means. Scarcity occurs whenever we want more than is available at a zero price.

BUDGET The financial plan of your current and future activities.

LUXURY GOOD A good for which the quantity bought and consumed increases more than in proportion to one's increase in income over time.

NECESSITY A good for which the amount spent as a percentage of total income falls as income rises.

LIFETIME PLAN A type of projection in which one outlines goals for the next five, ten, even twenty years for oneself and/or one's family. A lifetime plan is often re-evaluated and revised.

FIXED EXPENSES Expenses that occur at specified times and cannot be altered after the fact. A house payment would be considered a fixed expense, once a house is purchased or rented. A car payment would also be one.

FLEXIBLE EXPENSES Expenses that can be changed in the short run. The amount of money you spend on food is a flexible expense, because you can buy higher- or lower-quality food than you are now doing.

CHAPTER SUMMARY

1. Since we all have limited incomes, budgeting must be done either implicitly or explicitly.

2. Given our limited incomes, every action we engage in involves an opportunity cost. That is, we give up something else.

3. A budget can be a controlling mechanism to avoid financial problems and even financial disaster.

4. A budget is set up on a yearly basis and allows one to: (a) anticipate and prepare for changes in one's financial situation, (b) set aside money for large anticipated expenses, and (c) plan for seasonal changes.

5. The typical American household allocates about one-fourth of its spending to housing and one-fourth to food.

6. The greater the income a family receives, the smaller the percentage of spending that goes to food and the larger the percentage that goes to housing.

7. In comparing incomes in different parts of the country, it is necessary to correct for changes in the cost of living. This is done by looking at specific indexes of living costs in different regions and cities, compiled by the Bureau of Labor Statistics, U.S. Department of Labor.

8. It is possible for a computer to set up a budget for you and to tell you exactly where you are in the lifetime plan.

9. A lifetime plan involves setting goals for next year and five, ten, and twenty years hence and revising those goals according to changes in tastes and situations.

10. Budget making involves numerous emotional aspects and can create problems whenever: (a) one person believes he or she owns all the money made, (b) individuals engage in retaliatory spending, (c) individuals engage in status spending, or (d) money is used as a mechanism to control other members of the family spending unit.

11. Budgeting involves: (a) analyzing past spending by keeping records, (b) determining fixed expenses, (c) determining flexible expenses, and (d) balancing fixed plus flexible with available income and possibly saving the surplus.

12. Record keeping is important. These are the eleven categories of records you should keep at home: (a) income, (b) most canceled checks, (c) insurance policies, (d) large purchases, (e) home improvements, (f) investments, (g) tax-deductible items, (h) tax returns, (i) information on valuables, (j) credit cards, (k) warranties, service contracts, etc.

13. You should keep in a safe deposit box the following: (a) personal documents, (b) securities and properties, (c) wills, and (d) an inventory of personal and household items.

14. The key to making a budget work is for you to review it each month to see how closely your spending meshes with your budget projections.

15. Saving is a decision for future consumption, instead of present consumption; it is a trade-off between present and future. The more you give up today, the more you have tomorrow.

16. Computerized budgeting services provide subscribers with print-outs of numerous categories, their average spending in the past year for each category, and what they actually spent the previous month.

STUDY QUESTIONS

1. How does scarcity affect your life?

2. What is the opportunity cost of spending? How does opportunity cost relate to scarcity?

3. What percentage of the typical American family budget is spent on housing and food?

4. What happens to the percentage of total budget spent on housing as income rises for the family unit? For food? Why does this happen?

5. What are some of the most frequently encountered emotional problems relating to money and the family unit?

6. What is the difference between fixed and flexible expenses? Are fixed expenses always fixed in the long run?

7. List some of the records you should keep at home. List some of the records you should keep in a safe deposit box.

8. A budget is not merely for record-keeping purposes. What else is it used for?

CASE PROBLEMS

3-1 Budget Planning

Ralph and Alice Sutton have been married for 6 months. They have been recording their expenses, and now they want to prepare their first budget. Their combined monthly take-home pay is $1450, and they have listed the following expenses:

Monthly: food, $200; car payment, $97; school loans, $37; miscellaneous, $100; clothing, $150; recreation and dining out, $75; church and charities, $25; personal allowances, $160; rent and utilities, $320; medical, $25; telephone, $49; furniture payments, $105; gas for car, $37.

Yearly: life insurance, $180; car insurance, $360; renters insurance, $72; subscriptions to professional and personal publications, $102; newspaper, $42.

The Suttons want to save $900 for a holiday ski trip, which is 6 months away, and they also would like to save $1200 per year for investments. They have no savings account.

1. Arrange their expenditures into fixed and flexible categories, indicating the monthly expense for each item.

2. How much will they have to save each month to achieve their goals? Where could they cut their expenses to do this? (Assume that all credit payments will continue for at least 12 months.)

3-2 College Costs

Chris Mayville, 18, just graduated from high school and is trying to decide if she should accept a summer job, which would net $900, or spend the summer loafing and visiting relatives before entering the university in the fall. Her grandparents set up an endowment that will pay $2500 per year for her education, so she won't have to work during the school year. The university has sent her a list of annual expenses, and she estimates it will cost 30 dollars per month for gas if she goes home every weekend. Her parents will pay for her car insurance, but can't afford to give her any other money. Because she doesn't know what other types of expenses college students have, she has asked you, a student at the university, for help.

University expense list:

tuition	$640
fees	$145
health insurance	$20
room	$550
board	$660
books	$180

1. Prepare a budget for Chris, including estimates for flexible expenses that she hasn't included.

2. Would your budget be different if Chris were male? Explain your answer.

3. Should Chris accept the summer job offer? Explain.

SELECTED REFERENCES

Auerbach, Sylvia. *Your Money: How to Make It Stretch*. Garden City, NY: Doubleday, 1974.

Burnes, Scot. *Squeeze It Til the Eagle Grins: How to Spend, Save, and Enjoy with Your Money*. Garden City, NY: Doubleday, 1972.

"Can a Budget Really Help You Manage Your Money?" *Better Homes & Gardens*, June 1976, pp. 4-6.

Daly, M. "Family Money Management." See issues of *Better Homes & Gardens*.

Dowd, M. "Managing Money in the First Year of Marriage." *Money*, September 1973.

Madrick, Jeffrey G. "The Uncluttered Bookkeeper." *Money*, January 1973.

Margolius, Sidney. *How to Make the Most of Your Money*. New York: Appleton, Century, Crofts, 19.

Persons, Robert H., Jr. *The Practical Money Manager*. New York: Scribner's, 1974.

"Spending and Saving: Readers Tell How They Do It." *Changing Times*, November 1976, pp. 21-23.

Tahl, Helen M. *Your Family and Its Money*. New York: Houghton-Mifflin, 1973.

"When Your Budget Signals Danger." *Changing Times*, February 1977, pp. 33-35.

DEPT. 4
SMALL
CLAIMS

Consumer Protection

▰ In 1962, President John F. Kennedy sent the first consumer protection and interest program to Congress. The program specified four consumer rights:

1   The right to safety—a protection against goods that are dangerous to life or health;

2   The right to be informed—not only to discover fraud but also to make rational choices;

3   The right to choose—a restatement of the need for many firms in a competitive market and for protection by government where such competition no longer exists;

4   The right to be heard—consumers can voice their concerns when government policy decisions are being made.

To these four rights outlined by President Kennedy, most consumer representatives would add a fifth:

5   The right to redress for reasonable damages incurred when dealing in the marketplace.

Presidents Lyndon B. Johnson and Richard M. Nixon reaffirmed the consumer rights stated by President Kennedy, and the strong tide of consumer legislation at the federal level continued. In the mid-1970s, President Jimmy Carter asked for further legislation.

Passing legislation, of course, is not the end of the story. The legislation must be administered efficiently if the concept of consumer protection is to be effective. In 1964, President Johnson made a gesture in this direction when he appointed the first special presidential assistant for consumer affairs. Although this position carried no direct authority, its very existence made certain that consumer interests would have some representation at the federal policy level. In 1973, President Nixon transferred the position from the Office of the President to the Department of Health, Education, and Welfare. This transfer from the direct contact of the president appeared to some consumer activists to be a sign of weakening federal support.

In the past several years, there has been an attempt by Ralph Nader and other consumer advocates to have Congress establish an agency for consumer advocacy. The object of such an agency would be to argue the consumer's case before regulatory commissions and other agencies that affect consumer spending, lifestyles, and well-being. As of the printing of this book, all efforts at establishing such enabling legislation have failed.

STATE AND LOCAL GOVERNMENT
AND PRIVATE CONSUMER PROTECTION

Federal action is important because, once adopted, it expresses national policy. Nevertheless, such policy often is the result of prolonged activity at the state and local government levels or in the private sector of the economy. This has been especially true of consumer-protection policy. In fact, some states, localities, and private groups have gone far beyond the limits set by federal policy.

State and local governments have long been involved in setting quality and safety standards, weights and measures, and marketing standards, as well as defining the word *fraud*. Even today, enforcement of consumer-fraud statutes is left largely to state and local governments. Many areas of fraud are most commonly dealt with under criminal fraud statutes arising out of earlier criminal-fraud case decisions. And these are primarily state and local law. Furthermore, in the areas of credit, insurance, health and sanitation, and all issues dealing with contract rights, it has been primarily state governments that have enacted legislation dealing with consumer problems.

In fact, state response has sometimes greatly preceded federal response. For example, as early as 1959, both New York and California had legislation on the books to protect the rights of consumers in credit transactions. And not until Massachusetts passed the first truth-in-lending law was federal action on this important issue likely to succeed. The Federal Consumer Credit Protection Act (truth-in-lending) was passed in 1963; Massachusetts was, in effect, a pilot case for the national legislation.

The Private Sector

How does the private sector of the economy fit in with the public activities for consumer protection? Activity in the private sector of the economy has been varied and, in many cases, short-lived and somewhat ineffectual. But in some specific areas, private activities have been most important. The first of these is *product testing*. Only recently has government at any level begun to test products and reveal the results of those tests so consumers can use the information in making their own purchases. But private product-testing groups have been around for a long time. Consumers Union and Consumers' Research, Inc. exist primarily for the purpose of providing consumers with information on products.

Consumers Union *Consumer Reports* is the publication of Consumers Union, chartered in 1936 as a nonprofit organization under the laws of the State of New York. The object of Consumers Union has been to bring more useful information into the seller-buyer relationship so that consumers could buy rationally. The first issue of *Consumer Reports,* in May 1936, went to three thousand charter subscribers. They were told about the relative costs and nutritional values of breakfast cereals, the fanciful claims made for Alka Seltzer, the hazards of lead toys, and good buys in women's stockings, toilet soaps, and toothbrushes. Consumers Union's policy has always been to buy goods in the open market and bring them to the lab for testing.

Now approximately two and a half million subscribers and newsstand buyers read *Consumer Reports* every month. Consumers Union accepts no advertising in its magazine and tries to test various types of consumer products objectively. In addition, it gives advice on purchasing credit, insurance, and drugs. One of the major aspects of Consumers Union's testing involves automobiles: which are the best buys, which are safe, which have good brakes, which have safety defects, and so on. Recently, Consumers Union has published articles on ecological topics such as pesticides, phosphates in detergents, and lead in gasolines. It also strongly criticizes government agencies when they act against consumer interests.

If you decide to rely on the recommendations of *Consumer Reports,* you have to realize that it is difficult for even highly objective researchers to present purely objective results. That is not to say that you will get misinformation, but you may sometimes get emphasis on certain aspects of products that are consistent with the tastes of the researchers but not with your own. For example, recommendations about cars may give more weight to safety, gas mileage, or comfort than you personally want to give. You may opt for a different car because you prefer styling or low cost as opposed to safety. Even though the occupants of VWs face a higher probability of serious injury in an accident than do occupants of bigger cars, people continue to buy VWs, presumably because they are cheaper. But you will face this problem of acceptance with any information you obtain either free or at a price. In the last analysis, only you can make a decision, and it has to be based in part upon your personal value judgments. If you are a lazy shopper, you can probably get away with looking at *Consumer Reports* for whatever you want to buy, picking either the "best buy" or the top of the line, calling up your local dealer, and having it delivered. You may get some products you dislike, but on average, if your tastes correspond with those of the persons running Consumers Union, you will save much time searching and will probably avoid basically defective products.

Consumers' Research Magazine Consumers' Research, Inc., founded in 1929, puts out a monthly *Consumers' Research Magazine,* similar to *Consumer Reports,* with a readership of several hundred thousand. It gives product ratings, as well as ratings of motion pictures and phonograph records, and gives short editorials, just like *Consumer Reports.* No advertising income is permitted. The product testing policy of Consumers' Research often involves its borrowing test samples of large, expensive items from manufacturers who sign affidavits that the goods are typical and were selected at random. Sometimes the goods are rented—for example, typewriters—for testing. Consumers' Research often restricts its tests to brands or goods that are nationally distributed, while *Consumer Reports* sometimes tests brands that are distributed in various high-density localities. It is Consumers' Research policy to service their national and international audience rather than give any special attention to products or brands sold in specific geographical areas. Further, *Consumers' Research Magazine* does not give brand names as "best buys" as does *Consumer Reports.* Both organizations pride themselves on stressing safety and efficiency in products. Both have found potentially unsafe products long before any government agency.

Other Product Testing Groups And then there are the product-testing groups whose interest may not be directed toward consumers but whose activities produce information that consumers can use. The American Standards Association is an example of this kind of private agency. The ASA, organized in 1918, exists primarily to develop standards and testing methods that may be used by manufacturers. By setting a common level of performance, these standards and testing methods can protect manufacturers themselves against unfair competition. And, of course, they also provide protection to consumers who are buying products, the safety of which may be important. Using the standards developed by the ASA, other private laboratories or testing groups certify the efficiency and/or safety of such items as electrical and gas appliances, textiles, and many other products. In addition to product testing at the manufacturing level, a wide range of product testing is done by retailers who wish to perform a consumer service and provide themselves with a competitive advantage at the same time.

One must be aware of the significance and meaning, however, of the "seals of approval" that appear on numerous products. Here we can discuss two of the most well-known seals: the Underwriter's Laboratory, or UL, label and the *Good Housekeeping* "Seal of Approval."

Underwriter's Laboratory. Most household appliances display the UL label, and many manufacturers boast of it in their advertising. The UL label, however, only certifies that the product or appliance does not have the potential of causing fire, electric shock, or accident under normal conditions. Underwriter's Laboratory does not evaluate the actual quality of any appliance. The UL label does not mean that the product has been compared to its competitors and been proved better. Moreover, the only way the UL label can be obtained is by the manufacturer either submitting the product and paying a fee or agreeing to a specified control procedure. In order to keep the UL label, a fee must be paid every year. Some companies that decide not to pay that fee may have perfectly sound products.

Recently, the Underwriter's Laboratory has branched out into the testing of marine equipment (for example, life preservers), medical equipment (for example, adjustable hospital beds), and others. UL has also entered the area of general safety hazards. For example, it might test a particular electric coffeepot to see if the lid falls off when it is tipped, although this has nothing to do with the electrical part of the product. UL now requires manufacturers to include safety tips in the use-and-care manuals for products it approves.

Good Housekeeping seal. More than thirty-five years ago, the Federal Trade Commission required the Good Housekeeping Institute Laboratories to eliminate the terms "seal of approval." Nonetheless, for many consumers, the seal does denote approval. Good Housekeeping does not test whether a product is good or bad. Presumably, it only sees whether the product or service submitted by a manufacturer, who plans to advertise in *Good Housekeeping* magazine, measures up to all the claims made for it in the advertisement.

In principle, if the Good Housekeeping seal is on a product, the manufacturer will give you a refund or replacement if the product or performance is defective. No product is tested by the Good Housekeeping Institute Laboratories in New York City, unless there is a possibility of it being advertised in the magazine. Before a manufacturer can use this Good Housekeeping seal, it must guarantee to the magazine that the volume of advertising placed in *Good Housekeeping* is the same as that which it places in other media (or at least two columns a year).

PRIVATE AGENCIES

Probably the best-known of such private agencies is the Better Business Bureau. The National Better Business Bureau has been in existence since 1961 and has local affiliates in most, but not all, major cities and countries. The Better Business Bureau has three main purposes:

1   To provide information on products and selling practices to consumers;
2   To provide businesspeople with a source of local standard setting for acceptable business practices;
3   To provide a means for mediating grievances between consumers and sellers.

Since the Better Business Bureau has no enforcement powers, all actions must be voluntary. And since the Bureau depends on the business community for its membership, it cannot afford to antagonize those in business more than it antagonizes consumers. The weaknesses in the voluntary system were felt most strongly when the consumerism movement began to press for protection against not only the fraudulent firm but against marketing practices that were generally accepted by the business community.

But the Better Business Bureau continues to improve communication with the consumer. For example, the BBB's arbitration program has been expanding, attempting to deal more formally with the issue of consumer redress for grievances with sellers and producers of goods and services.

Although the Better Business Bureau is the oldest private agency that seeks to mediate consumer grievances, it is not the only one. As consumerism has grown, the media have been both criticized for their performance and mobilized for consumer protection. The media have been criticized for the type of advertising they carry and for their lack of interest in providing time for "countercommercials" or public-service consumer information. But newspapers and radio and TV stations have been in the forefront of attempts to help consumers who have legitimate complaints. By providing column space or air time for "consumer action," media have succeeded in obtaining results for those consumers who are able to make use of them. Affiliates of both the ABC and NBC networks have run regular consumer-report and consumer-action series, as have many independent television stations. These programs typically use publicity as a powerful weapon to resolve the consumer's grievance.

PROVIDING LEGAL ASSISTANCE

Many consumers feel that they would like to sue for improper services performed or defective products purchased. However, high legal fees often keep consumers from getting their "day in court." One alternative, which is outlined in detail in the Appendix to this chapter, is small claims court. The other option is a legal clinic.

Legal Clinics

A legal clinic is based on a group-practice concept. A group of lawyers share office space and facilities; they use paralegal personnel for routine work that doesn't involve actual law practice. They standardize their procedures and are able to reduce fees anywhere from 25 percent to 50 percent below what one would normally pay a regular attorney in a typical law firm. For a fee of ten to twenty-five dollars, lawyers in legal clinics will even teach you to help yourself in traffic or small claims courts. They will not take cases, however, requiring extensive litigation. As of 1976, there were legal clinics in Los Angeles, Phoenix, Denver, and Washington, D.C.

Prepaid Legal Service

It is now possible for some individuals, particularly in California and New York, to subscribe to a prepaid legal plan, just as they subscribe to prepaid health and automobile insurance. A subscriber to such a plan pays an annual flat fee that entitles him or her to an array of legal services. For example, Group Legal Services, Inc., in Los Angeles, charges twenty-five dollars a year. For that fee, subscribers can dial a toll-free number twenty-four hours a day for legal advice. If the problem cannot be easily resolved on the telephone, the subscriber is referred to one of 500 participating attorneys. The subscriber gets a 25 percent discount from the prevailing local rate. A pilot plan was started in New York by New York County Legal Services Corporation. Initially, it was restricted to people with incomes between $6,000 and $20,000. The membership cost was a flat fee of $100, plus $25 a year for a spouse and $10 for each child under twenty-one.

There are many ways to obtain satisfaction when you, the consumer, feel you have been wronged in the marketplace. In the following Practical Applications section, we outline the steps you should take and the agencies to which you can go for help.

PRACTICAL APPLICATIONS

HOW TO GET HELP FOR CONSUMER PROBLEMS

WHERE TO GO

Knowing when, where, and how to seek solutions to consumer problems may be as difficult as knowing how to buy. There are at least thirty-seven federal agencies involved in consumer issues and even more state, local, and private agencies with which you might have to deal. We will be concerned primarily with the problems you face when something goes wrong, rather than with how you get information before you buy a product. But even this limitation does not significantly reduce the number of agencies or organizations with which you must contend, for many of the agencies that provide information before you buy are the same ones that provide protection after you buy. And, or course, when you are concerned with complaints about products, you probably will deal with a business firm, of which there are some 12 million in the United States. Thus, if you are going to deal successfully in the marketplace and with consumer-service agencies, you will have to develop a strategy.

A STRATEGY

First you should try to figure out a strategy for resolving your grievances that does not involve an outside party. After all, it takes additional time and effort to involve someone else in your disputes with a seller. Thus, whenever you buy anything of any consequence *keep a receipt* and such relevant materials as advertisements and orders. Even before you make the purchase, put into writing everything about take-back provisions, warranties, guarantees, and so on.

Imagine that you buy something that falls apart a week later. A call to the store and a talk with the person from whom you bought it will tell you immediately whether or not you will have problems.

Many times, reputable stores will either give you an identical article in good working condition, repair the one you have, or refund your money. If the salesperson does not agree, then go to his or her superior—the manager or the owner. If you still do not get satisfaction and if you are dealing with a nationally advertised product or with a large chain store, you may want to write a complaint to the president or the chairperson of the board of the company(ies) involved.[1] Personal letters to the presidents of large companies usually get quick responses to you. Exhibit 4-1 is a sample copy of a letter that might be appropriate.

Before attempting to resolve a consumer grievance, you may have to decide how much effort you want to expend. Do you just want your money back or your own satisfaction? Or do you want to make sure that this never happens again?

Some states publish special catalogs that tell you what to do with your complaint. For example, California offers the *Complete California Consumer Catalog,* available for $1.50 from the Publications Section, P.O. Box 20191, Sacramento, California 95820. By the time you read this, other states may have published similar booklets.

START AT THE LOCAL LEVEL

If getting your money back or solving your own problem is your primary goal, then you will probably do best to work with those at the local level who are similarly concerned. First, check to see if there is a consumer-affairs agency or office in your local government. The telephone book is probably your nearest source of this information. In most major cities today, there is a Yellow Pages listing—under the entry *Consumers* – of the major public agencies that provide county or city should quickly produce information on the availability of public consumer services.

---

[1]In your local library, you can look at *The Consumer's Register of American Business* and *The Directory of Foreign Manufacturers in the U.S.* for this information.

EXHIBIT 4.1

**HOW TO LODGE
A COMPLAINT**

Your Complete Address
Date

Addressee
Company Name
Street Address
City, State   Zip Code

Dear Sir or Madam:

This letter is to inform you of my dissatisfaction with (name of product with serial number or the service performed.) Details are on the enclosed document, which I purchased (the date and location of purchase).

My complaint concerns (the reason[s] for your complaint). I believe that, in all fairness, you should (the specific action you desire for satisfaction) in order to solve this problem.

I sincerely look forward to your reply and a speedy resolution to my complaint. I will allow two weeks before considering referring this complaint to the appropriate consumer agency.

Yours truly,

Your Name

Enclosures (include copies, not originals, of all related records)

In some areas of the country, you can even lodge your consumer complaint via videotape. In Pitkin County, Colorado, a caucus of consumers concerned about a specific problem usually can obtain fifteen minutes of videotape time to present their concern. The tape is then shown on TV at a commissioners' meeting, and the commissioners' responses are videotaped. The requests and responses are then compiled into one tape, which is shown in the rural area where it originated.

If you find no local consumer agency, look under the state listings; if no listing looks promising there, call the state attorney general's office. If there is a consumer agency in the state, the attorney general's office will know. That office and such agencies always work closely, because much consumer fraud uncovered by the consumer agency is prosecuted through the attorney general's office. In Exhibit 4-2 we list the addresses of state consumer-protection agencies.

EXHIBIT 4-2.

**STATE CONSUMER
PROTECTION AGENCIES**

Alabama. Consumer Protection Office, Office of the Governor, 138 Adams Building, Montgomery 36104

Alaska. Attorney General of Alaska, Pouch "K" State Capitol, Juneau 99801

Arizona. Consumer Fraud Division, 159 State Capitol Building, Phoenix 85007

Arkansas. Consumer Protection Division, Justice Building, Little Rock 72201

California. Consumer Protection Unit, Office of the Attorney General, 600 State Bldg., Los Angeles 90012

Colorado. Office of Consumer Affairs, 112 E. 14th Avenue, Denver 80203

Connecticut. Dept. of Consumer Protection, State Office Bldg., 165 Capitol Ave., Hartford 06115

Delaware. Division of Consumer Affairs, 704 Delaware Avenue, Wilmington 19801

Florida. Division of Consumer Affairs, Dept. of Agriculture and Consumer Service, 106 W. Pensacola St., Tallahassee 32301

Georgia. Georgia Consumer Services Program, 15 Peachtree St., Room 909, Atlanta 30303

Hawaii. Director of Consumer Protection, Office of the Governor, 250 S. King St., 602 Kamamalu Bldg., Honolulu 96811

Idaho. Consumer Protection Division. State Capitol, Boise 83702

Illinois. Consumer Fraud Section, Office of the Attorney General, 134 N. LaSalle Street, Room, 204, Chicago 60602

Indiana. Office of Consumer Protection, 219 State House, Indianapolis 46204

Iowa. Consumer Protection Division, Office of the Attorney General, 220 E. 13th Court, Des Moines 50319

Kansas. Consumer Protection Division, Office of the Attorney General, State House, Topeka 66612

Kentucky. Office of the Attorney General, 309 Shelby Street, Room 109, Louisville 40601

Louisiana. Office of the Governor, Office of Consumer Protection, 1885 Wooddale Boulevard, Suite 1218, P.O. Box 44091, Capital Station, Baton Route 70804

Maine. Consumer Protection Division, Office of the Attorney General, State House, Augusta 04330

Maryland. Consumer Protection Division, Office of the Attorney General, One South Calvert Street, Baltimore 21202

Massachusetts. Consumer Protection Division, State House, Boston 02133

Michigan. Assistant Attorney General in Charge of Consumer Protection, Law Building, Lansing 48913

Minnesota. Office of Consumer Services, 5th floor, Metro Square Building, 7th & Robert, St. Paul 55101

Mississippi. Consumer Protection Division, Office of the Attorney General, State Capitol, Jackson 39201

Missouri. Consumer Protection Division, Office of the Attorney General, P.O. Box 899, Supreme Court Building, Jefferson City 65101

Montana. Consumer Protection Division, Office of County Attorney, 155 W. Granite Street, Butte 59701

Nevada. Deputy Attorney General for Consumer Affairs, Supreme Court Building, Carson City 89701

New Hampshire. Assistant Attorney General, State House Annex, Concord 03301

New Jersey. Director Division of Consumer Affairs, Room 504, 1100 Raymond Boulevard, Newark 07102

New Mexico. Consumer Protection Division, Supreme Court Bldg., Box 2246, Santa Fe 87501

New York. Consumer Frauds and Protection Bureau, 80 Centre St., New York 10013

North Carolina. Consumer Protection Division, Office of the Attorney General, P.O. Box 629, Raleigh 27602

North Dakota. Consumer Protection Division, Office of the Attorney General, State Capitol, Bis-

EXHIBIT 4-2 **CONTINUED**

marck 58501

Ohio. Administrator, Division of Consumer Protection, Department of Commerce, 275 East State St., Columbus 43215

Oklahoma. Assistant Attorney General for Consumer Protection, 112 State Capitol, Oklahoma City 73105

Oregon. Consumer Protection Division, Office of the Attorney General, 555 State Office Building, Portland 97201

Pennsylvania. Bureau of Consumer Protection, Department of Justice, 25 South Third Street, Harrisburg 17101

Rhode Island. Chief of Consumer Affairs, Rhode Island Consumers' Council, 365 Broadway, Providence 02909

South Carolina. Office of Consumer Affairs, Governor's Office, State House, Columbia 29201

South Dakota. Secretary, Dept. of Commerce and Consumer Affairs, State Capitol, Pierre 57501

Texas. Antitrust and Consumer Protection Division, Capitol Station, P.O. Box 12548, Austin 78711

Utah. Assistant Attorney General for Consumer Protection, State Capitol, Room 236, Salt Lake City 84114

Vermont. Consumer Protection Bureau, Box 981,

Burlington 05401

Virginia. Consumer Affairs, Department of Agriculture and Commerce, 8th Street Office Building, Richmond 23219

Washington. Consumer Protection and Antitrust Division, 1266 Dexter Horton Building, Seattle 98104

West Virginia. Consumer Protection Division, Department of Agriculture, Charleston 25305

Wisconsin. Director Bureau of Consumer Protection, Dept. of Agriculture, 801 W. Badger Road, Madison 53713

Wyoming. State Examiner and Administrator, Consumer Credit Code, State Supreme Court Building, Cheyenne 82001

District of Columbia. Department of Economic Development, Consumer Retail Credit Division, Room 306, 614 "H" Street, N.W., Washington 20001

Commonwealth of Puerto Rico. Director of the Consumer Services Administration, P.O. Box 13934, Santurce 00908

Virgin Islands. Consumer Services Administration, P.O. Box 831, Charlotte Amalie, St. Thomas 00801, or Vitraco Mall, Christiansted, St. Croix 00820

THE FEDERAL GOVERNMENT

If your problem concerns a product that is sold nationally or if you think your problem might affect people all over the country, you may want to go to a federal agency.

Office of Consumer Affairs

The office of Consumer Affairs, which once advised the president directly, is now within the Department of Health, Education, and Welfare. It analyzes and coordinates all federal activities on behalf of consumers, as well as conducting investigations and surveys and organizing conferences. The office also provides policy guidance to the General Services Administration in its role of making consumer-product information publicly available. The Office of Consumer Affairs is also involved in a consumer-education program.

You are encouraged to send inquiries, comments or suggestions to the director, Office of Consumer Affairs, Department of Health, Education, and Welfare, Washington, D.C. Although the agency has no power to redress grievances, the director will, if enough letters are sent about a problem, suggest government policy changes or new legislation.

Usually, though, if you think you have a grievance worth federal attention, you should contact one of the many federal agencies. It might be worth your while to send for a ten-cent booklet called *Consumer Information.* catalog number PL86, from the Superintendent of Documents, U.S. Government Printing Office, Washington, D.C. 20402.

Or you might address your complaints to one of the following agencies. When you write, direct your letters to the chairperson, the agency's name, Washington, D.C., and the appropriate zip code.

The Food and Drug Administration (5600 Fishers Lane, Rockville, MD 20857)

The Food and Drug Administration (FDA) has regional offices in many cities. In each of these offices is a person specifically charged with consumer services. Many of the FDA's 5,000 employees are technical experts working in specific fields under FDA jurisdiction. Any complaint about a food, drug, or cosmetic that you purchased should be made either to your regional office or directly to Maryland. The agency will ask for as much information as you can give them: they are particularly interested in seeing the food or drug about which you are complaining or its container.

If they believe your complaint is justified, they will have a staff member visit the firm in question to observe its production and packaging procedures. They will check the labeling on the container and the contents of the product to determine whether or not they meet all legal requirements. If you do not have the product—because you used it up or it was destroyed—you may still make your complaint. The FDA will seek additional supplies of the product on which to base its decision.

Through consumer reports, the FDA often discovers new problems developing in foods and drugs or new outbreaks of old problems. In those areas where the FDA sets and/or enforces standards, consumers can play an important role, because these standards ultimately are set for them.

Federal Trade Commission (Washington, D.C. 20580)

The FDA enforces standards of product and performance. But the Federal Trade Commission (FTC) standards are essentially those of practice—competition in the marketplace; false, misleading, and deceptive advertising by sellers to buyers; and packaging and labeling of firms engaged in nonfood sales. In recent years, the FTC has become quite demanding in its rulings on advertising practices. It has begun to require more than merely stopping the offensive practice; sometimes it requires the seller of a deceptively advertised product to make a public statement about the product's limitations.

To increase competition in the marketplace, the FTC has, in recent years, looked hard at merchandising methods long considered fair and competitive. For example, the commission has studied whether or not the control of advertising and the resultant brand loyalty of consumers can be grounds for an antitrust suit in the cereals industry. The commission has also been interested in the general effect of advertising on consumer buying habits. This is a whole new approach; previously, the commission considered only specific advertising issues and only after consumers or another seller or advertiser had complained.

The FTC has regional offices in major cities and also has consumer service representatives. It has established a special office to serve consumers and provides a wide range of informative pamphlets. If you have a complaint for the FTC, you may take it either to the regional office or to the Washington, D.C., headquarters. If it believes you have a valid complaint, the FTC will send an investigator to check with both you and the firm.

Typically, the FTC works in two ways. First, it investigates whether or not a particular seller or advertiser has violated a particular law that the agency enforces; if so, it will take action to stop the practice by the single firm. Second, the agency looks for new patterns of practice or new areas that may mislead consumers. If it finds any such patterns or areas, the FTC may act against an entire industry, rather than a single firm, to stop the practice altogether. Sometimes such investigation leads to a new interpretation of an old law; other times it leads to information upon which new legislation will be based. As with the FDA, individual consumers can play an important role in the work of the FTC, because, again, they are the people for whom this work is ultimately performed.

U.S. Department of Agriculture (Washington, D.C. 20250)

Although the U.S. Department of Agriculture (USDA) primarily provides services to farmers, it also protects consumers in important ways, notably by inspecting and grading meat and poultry. In recent years, the agency has also become a primary source of information for consumers on the best ways to spend their food dollars. The USDA does this primarily through its Cooperative Extension Service, operated in conjunction with land-grant universities throughout the United States. Any complaint you have on the grades of meat you buy or the quality of the poultry that is shipped interstate is best reported to your local health department or your local department of agriculture.

U.S. Postal Service (Washington, D.C. 20260)

This agency is responsible for investigating mail fraud, unordered merchandise, obscenity, and other mail-related problems.

Department of Housing and Urban Development (Washington, D.C. 20410)

HUD is responsible for numerous federally subsidized housing programs. If you have a related complaint, you would contact HUD's consumer-affairs coordinator.

Interstate Commerce Commission (Washington, D.C. 20523)

Any complaints you have regarding moving companies, truck shipments, or railroads can be addressed specifically to the ICC.

The Consumer Product Safety Commission (Washington, D.C. 20260)

The Consumer Product Safety Commission (CPSC) was created to do the following:

1. Protect the public against unreasonable risk of injury associated with consumer products;

2. Assist consumers in evaluating the comparative safety of consumer products;

3. Develop uniform safety standards for consumer products and minimize conflicting state and local regulations;

4. Promote research and investigation into causes and prevention of product-related deaths, illnesses, and injuries.

Not only can the CPSC set safety standards for consumer products, it also can ban the manufacture and sale of any product deemed hazardous to consumers. It has, for example, banned some adhesive sprays.

If you think there is an unsafe product on the market or if you have any questions about product hazards and safety, you may want to get in touch directly with the CPSC. Their hot-line number, (800) 638-2666, is toll free from anywhere in the United States; in Maryland it is (800) 492-2937. You can also write directly to the Consumer Product Safety Commission in Washington and explain your concern over a particular product or products.

OBTAINING MORE INFORMATION ON FEDERAL CONSUMER SERVICES

To obtain more information on the availability of federal consumer services, send for *The Guide to Federal Consumer Services* (publication number [OS]76-512), published by the Department of Health, Education, and Welfare, Office of Consumer Affairs, and available from the Superintendent of Documents, Washington, D.C. You can also subscribe to

Consumer News (Stock number 057D), which is published twice monthly by the Office of Consumer Affairs; it costs four dollars a year. And you can ask to be put on their mailing list to receive a free booklet, *Consumer Information,* which is a catalog, published quarterly, or approximately 250 selected government publications of consumer interest. Finally, you can write to the Consumer Information Center, Pueblo, Colorado 81009. If you do not know where to turn, you may wish to write to or visit a Federal Information Center. There you will find a person trained to provide information about the vast number of federal agencies and programs. In Exhibit 4-3, we list the Federal Information Centers in 37 cities.

If none of these centers is near you, you may call one of the local numbers listed in Exhibit 4-4 and ask to be connected by a toll-free tie to a Federal Information Center.

EXHIBIT 4-3.

**FEDERAL
INFORMATION
CENTERS**

ARIZONA
Phoenix
(602) 261-3313

CALIFORNIA
Los Angeles
(213) 688-3300
Federal Building
300 N. Los Angeles St.
90012
Sacramento
(916) 449-3344
Federal Building—
U.S. Courthouse
650 Capitol Mall
95814
San Diego
(714) 293-6030
202 C St. 92101
San Francisco
(415) 556-6800
Federal Building
U.S. Courthouse
450 Golden Gate Ave.
92002

COLORADO
Denver
(303) 837-3602

Federal Building
U.S. Courthouse
1961 Stout St.
80202

DISTRICT OF
COLUMBIA
Washington
(202) 755-8660
7th & D Sts. S.W.
20407

FLORIDA
Miami
(305) 350-4155
Federal Building
51 S.W. 1st Ave. 33130
St. Petersburg
(813) 893-3495
William c. Cramer
Federal Building
144 1st Ave. S. 32701

GEORGIA
Atlanta
(404) 520-6891
Federal Building
275 Peachtree St. N.E.
30303

HAWAII
Honolulu
(808) 546-8620
U.S. Post Office
Courthouse &
Customhouse
335 Merchant St. 96813

ILLINOIS
Chicago
(312) 353-4242
Everett McKinley
Dirksen Building
219 S. Dearborn St.
60604

INDIANA
Indianapolis
(317) 269-7373
Federal Building
575 N. Pennsylvania St.
46204

KENTUCKY
Louisville
(502) 582-6261
600 Federal Place
40202

LOUISIANA
New Orleans
Federal Building
(504) 589-6696
701 Loyola Ave. 70113

MARYLAND
Baltimore
(301) 962-4980
Federal Building
31 Hopkins Plaza
21201

MASSACHUSETTS
Boston
(617) 223-7121
John F. Kennedy
Federal Building
Government Center
02203

MICHIGAN
Detroit
(313) 226-7016
Federal Building
U.S. Courthouse
231 W. Lafayette St.
48226

EXHIBIT 4-3 **CONTINUED**

MINNESOTA
Minneapolis
(612) 725-2073
Federal Building
U.S. Courthouse
110 S. 4th St. 55401

MISSOURI
Kansas City
(816) 374-2466
Federal Building
601 E. 12th St. 64106
St. Louis
(314) 425-4106
Federal Building
1520 Market St.
63103

NEBRASKA
Omaha
(402) 221-3353
Federal Building
U.S. Post Office &
  Courthouse
215 N. 17th St. 68102

NEW JERSEY
Newark
(201) 645-3600

Federal Building
970 Broad St. 07102

NEW MEXICO
Albuquerque
(505) 766-3091
Federal Building
  U.S. Courthouse
500 Gold Ave., S.W.
87101

NEW YORK
Buffalo
(716) 842-5770
Federal Building
111 W. Huron St. 14202
New York
(212) 284-4461
Federal Office Building
U.S. Customs Court
26 Federal Plaza 10007

OHIO
Cincinnati
(513) 684-2801
Federal Building
550 Main St. 45202
Cleveland
(216) 522-4040

Federal Building
1240 E. 9th St. 44199

OKLAHOMA
Oklahoma City
(405) 231-4868
U.S. Post Office
building
201 N.W. 3rd St. 73102

OREGON
Portland
(503) 221-2222
1220 S.W. 3rd Ave.
97204

PENNSYLVANIA
Philadelphia
(215) 597-7042
Federal Building
600 Arch St. 19106
Pittsburgh
(412) 644-3456
Federal Building
1000 Liberty Ave.
15222

TENNESSEE
Memphis

(901) 534-3285
Clifford davis Federal
  Building
167 N. Main St. 38103

TEXAS
Fort Worth
(817) 334-3624
Fritz Garland Lanham
Federal Building
819 Taylor St. 76102
Houston
(713) 226-5711
Federal Building
U.S. Courthouse
515 Rusk Ave. 77002

UTAH
Salt Lake City
(801) 524-5353
Federal Building, U.S.
Post Office, Courthouse
125 S. State St. 84138

WASHINGTON
Seattle
(206) 442-0570
Federal Building
915 2nd Ave. 98174

EXHIBIT 4-4.

**HOW TO REACH
A FEDERAL INFORMATION
CENTER**

ALABAMA
Birmingham 322-8591
Mobile 438-4421

ARIZONA
Tucson 622-1511

ARKANSAS
Little Rock 378-6177

CALIFORNIA
San Jose 275-7422

COLORADO
Colorado Springs
471-9491
Pueblo 544-9523

CONNECTICUT
Hartford 527-2617
New Haven 624-4720

FLORIDA
Fort Lauderdale
522-8531
Jacksonville
354-4756
Tampa 229-7911
West Palm Beach
833-7566

IOWA
Des Moines 282-9091

KANSAS
Topeka 232-7229
Wichita 263-6931

MISSOURI
St. Joseph 233-8206

NEW JERSEY
Trenton 396-4400

NEW MEXICO
Santa Fe 983-7743

NEW YORK
Albany 463-4421
Rochester 546-5075
Syracuse 476-8545

NORTH CAROLINA
Charlotte 376-3600

OHIO
Akron 375-5475
Columbus 221-1014
Dayton 224-7377
Toledo 244-8525

OKLAHOMA
Tulsa 548-4193

PENNSYLVANIA
Scranton 346-7081

RHODE ISLAND
Providence 331-5565

TENNESSEE
Chattanooga
265-8231

TEXAS
Austin 472-5494
Dallas 749-2131
San Antonio
224-4471

UTAH
Ogden 399-1347

WASHINGTON
Tacoma 363-5230

WISCONSIN
Milwaukee 271-2273

CHAPTER SUMMARY

1. The first consumer program sent by President Kennedy to Congress included four consumer rights. These were the rights to: (a) safety, (b) information, (c) choice, and (d) a hearing.

2. A fifth right involves redress for reasonable damages incurred in dealing in the marketplace.

3. Most consumer legislation started at the state and local levels many years ago. Even today, enforcement of consumer fraud statutes is left largely to state and local governments.

4. The private sector has numerous product-testing organizations, including Consumers Union and Consumers' Research, Inc.

5. Another private agency is the American Standards Association, organized in 1918.

6. The Underwriter Laboratories, or UL, label certifies that the product does not have the potential of causing fire, electric shock, or accident.

7. The Good Housekeeping Seal only guarantees that if the product is defective, the manufacturer will refund or replace it.

8. The Better Business Bureau is set up to provide: (a) information on products and selling practices, (b) businesspeople with the source of localized standard setting, and (c) mediating services between consumers and sellers.

9. It is possible to obtain legal assistance through legal clinics and prepaid legal services. In both cases, the cost of legal services is less than one normally pays.

10. When you have a grievance to be settled, you should figure out a strategy and decide if you wish to involve a third party.

11. If your grievance concerns a store, start at the bottom and work your way up. Deal with the salesperson first; then his or her superior; then, if necessary, with the president or the chairperson of the board. It is possible to find out the names of the presidents of large corporations by consulting with the *Consumer's Register of American Business* and *The Directory of Foreign Manufacturers in the U.S.*

12. If you are not satisfied, you can turn to a local consumer-affairs agency or office. They can be found in the Yellow Pages under the listing *Consumers*.

13. If there is no local consumer agency, call the state attorney general's office to seek help.

14. At the federal government level, you can contact the Office of Consumer Affairs in the Department of Health, Education and Welfare; the Food and Drug Administration; the Federal Trade Commission; the U.S. Department of Agriculture; the U.S. Postal Service; the Department of Housing and Urban Development; the Interstate Commerce Commission; and finally, the Consumer Product Safety Commission.

STUDY QUESTIONS

1. What are the five consumer rights presented in this chapter?

2. Name several groups that engage in product testing.

3. What does the Underwriters Laboratory (UL) label mean when it is attached to a product?

4. What does the Good Housekeeping seal mean when it is attached to a product?

5. What is a legal clinic, and how does it differ from prepaid legal service?

6. Outline a strategy for lodging a complaint on a defective product or service.

CASE PROBLEMS

4-1   Faulty Thermostat Ignites Consumer Issue

Bill and LeAnn Bixler have been having problems with their 4-month-old dishwasher. Every other time they use it, the heat on the dry cycle becomes so intense that dishes break; and Bill has noticed that the coating on the dish racks is beginning to sag and crack. The repairperson has been to the house 3 times. Although he does take the back off the machine and fiddle with the thermostat, Bill and LeAnn get the distinct impression that he doesn't think anything is really wrong—even though they've shown him the broken dishes. The last time he was at the house, he said that he wouldn't make any more calls, although the machine was still under warranty. Last night, LeAnn put her oven thermometer in the dishwasher. When she opened the door halfway through the drying cycle, the thermometer reading was 750°F. This morning, she called the store and arranged to meet with the manager.

1. What information should the Bixlers have when they meet with the manager? What possible courses of action could they suggest that might solve the problem to their satisfaction?

2. If they are not satisfied after the meeting, what further action could they take without resorting to legal action?

4-2   A Variation on Thermostat/Consumer Theme

Rob and Karen Striana have been haggling with a local store for the past 18 months. The store had installed a new furnace in their home, and the thermostat was miswired. As a result, the compressor on the central air conditioner came on every time the furnace shut off. This went undetected for 2 weeks during a bitter Minnesota December before Rob discovered it. They notified the store, and the installer rewired the thermostat the next day. The following summer, the air conditioner would not work, and the Strianas claimed the store was responsible. The manager said that running the compressor in the winter would not harm it and refused to consider the matter. Rob and Karen persisted and interviewed three independent air conditioning experts, who all stated that cold weather operation would indeed ruin a compressor. The manager finally agreed to install a new compressor. This was done two months ago, and four days later the Strianas received an 87 dollar bill for installation labor. The manager says that he only agreed to replace the compressor, not to "donate labor, too." He also says that if they don't pay, he will turn the bill over to a collection agency. The Strianas don't want to pay the bill, because the original offer to replace the compressor indicated that there would be no cost to them.

What legal recourse would you recommend? Be specific about the procedure for your community and the costs involved.

SELECTED REFERENCES

Aaker, David A. and Day, George S. *Consumerism: Search for the Consumer Interest.* New York: The Free Press, 1974.

Campbell, S. R. "Consumer Complaints: What to Do If You Don't Get Action." *Better Homes and Gardens,* April 1974.

"Caveat Venditor; Suing in Small Claims Court; Advice of D. Matthews." *Time,* September 10, 1973, pp. 70ff.

Consumer Information in Canada: Consumer's Association of Canada, 100 Gloucester Street, Ottowa 4, Ontario, Canada.

"Consumer Is Paying Plenty." *U.S. News & World Report,* November 4, 1974.

"Consumers Are Rewriting the Rule Book." *Fortune,* March 16, 1974, p. 41.

"Consumers Aren't Angels Either." duPont Context, E. I. duPont DeNemurs & Company, Vol. II, No. 1, 1973, pp. 9-10.

Cratchit, B. "Tell Us about Small Claims Courts." *Ramparts,* September 1972, pp. 47ff.

Faber, Doris. *Enough! The Revolt of the American Consumer.* New York: Farrar, Straus, & Giroux, 1972.

Gaedeke, Ralph M. and Etcheson, Warren W. *Consumerism: Viewpoints from Business, Government, and the Public Interest.* San Francisco: Canfield Press, 1972.

"Got a Complaint? Call Your State Consumer Office." *Changing Times,* April 1975, p.

Levy, R. "Metamorphosis in the Market Place?" *Dun's Review,* February 1977, pp. 65-67.

MacDonald, S. "Sue Me, Said Mr. Kass to Mrs. Blustein; New York's Small Claims Court." *New York Times Magazine,* April 7, 1974, pp. 32ff.

Magnuson, Warren. *The Dark Side of the Marketplace,* 2d. Ed. Englewood Cliffs, NJ: Prentice-Hall, 1972.

Mead, W. B. "Help from a Consumerist Congress." *Money,* April 1975.

Nader, Ralph, Editor. *The Consumer and Corporate Accountability.* New York: Harcourt, Brace, Jovanovich, Inc., 1973.

"Needed: Peoples Courts That Work for People." *Reader's Digest,* July 1974, pp. 39-40.

Price, Howard, *et al. The California Handbook on Small Claims Courts.* Hawthorne Books, Inc., Publishers, 1972.

Schrag, Philip G. "Consumer Rights." *Columbia Forum,* Summer 1970.

Schrag, Philip G. *Counsel for the Deceived.* New York: Pantheon, 1972.

"Small Claims Courts." *Consumer Reports,* December 1973, and December 1974, pp. 383-85.

"Things Are Getting Better Faster for Consumers." *Changing Times,* February 1977, pp. 17-18.

APPENDIX A

How to Use a Small Claims Court

Do you think that your former landlord gypped you by keeping your security deposit when you moved out? Did a dry cleaner ruin or lose your clothes? Did you make a claim to your insurance company that it refused to pay? Did a company issue you a warranty on one of its products and then charge you for a repair job while it was still covered?

If you felt helpless when any of these things happened, you needn't have. To right such wrongs, you could have used the small claims court in your area. However, before you use a small claims court, you may want to exhaust some of the available alternatives, which include the consumer hot lines available in many states and cities; consumer advocates, who will take up your gripes with the appropriate people and print the results in newspaper columns; and, in some cities, radio and TV newspeople who discuss complaints over the air. We discussed some other ways you can complain and get redress of your consumer grievances in the previous Practical Application. If you still feel you need judicial help, then you might want to use a small claims court.

PROBLEMS TO ANTICIPATE

Complications can arise in any small claims court proceedings. In many states, the defendant can automatically and routinely have a case transferred to a regular civil court, where noncriminal suits are brought. In most civil courts, your efforts are worthless without an attorney. So, if a case in which you are plaintiff is transferred to the civil court, you must incur the expense of an attorney or drop the suit.

Further, a small claims judgment in your favor does not mean you will get full satisfaction for your loss. The judge may tell the defendant to pay you $100 on a $150 claim (which, of course, is still $100 more than you started with). But no matter what the defendant is told to pay you, the small claims court does not act as a collection agency. You do not always collect when you win. For example, in a 1970 study by Consumers Union, of the 62 cases the consumer plaintiff won, 13 proved uncollectable. You must realize that a defendant who does not show up in court is not likely to pay. You may be able to obtain a so-called writ of execution from the small claims court if you can show that the defendant is not paying you. But this writ of execution against the defendant's property, bank account, or wages is often ineffective.[1]

Additionally, you must realize that you probably will have to make several trips to the courthouse. If the court has no evening or Saturday sessions in your area, you will miss time from work.

HOW TO PLAN YOUR ACTION

After you find the small claims court in your area, ask the court clerk if the court can handle your kind of case. For example, some large cities have special courts to handle problems between renters and landlords. While you are at the courthouse, it is a good idea to sit in on a few cases. This will give you an idea of what to expect when your day in court arrives. Then make sure that the court has jurisdiction over the person or business you wish to sue. Usually the defendant must live, work, or do business in the court's territory. In other words, the suit must be filed in the county where the defendant does business. If you are trying to sue an out-of-town firm, you probably should go to the state government, usually the secretary of state, and find out where the summons should be sent. Remember that the small claims

---

[1]Note that even if a debt is not collectable now, it stays on the records. Thus, if the person who owes you money (because of a judgment in small claims court) acquires some assets in the future, you can activate the judgment in the future.

court is not a collection agency; if you are filing suit against a firm that is no longer in business, you will have a difficult time collecting.

Make absolutely certain that you have the correct business name and address of the company being sued. Frequently, courts require strict accuracy, and if you do not abide by that requirement, the suit is thrown out.

Once you file suit, a summons goes out to the defending party, either by registered mail or in the hands of a sheriff, bailiff, marshal, constable, or, sometimes, a private citizen. Once a company receives the summons, it may decide to resolve the issue out of court; about one-fourth of all cases for which summons are issued are settled this way. Many times, however, the defendant company may not even show up for the trial, in which case you stand a good chance of winning by default. But, as we said, it is usually difficult to collect from a defendant who doesn't come to court.

PREPARING FOR THE TRIAL

How should you prepare for trial? Obviously, if you have a personal friend who is a lawyer you can get some quick advice. In any event, you should have all necessary and pertinent receipts, canceled checks, written estimates, contracts, and any other form of documentary evidence you can show the judge. It is best to describe, on paper, the entire situation in chronological order, with supporting evidence, so you can show the judge exactly what happened. Make sure your dates are accurate; inaccurate dates would prejudice your case against you.

If you are disputing; say, a repair job, you may have to get a third party—generally someone in the same trade—as an "expert." Although it is often difficult to get people to testify against their fellow workers in the same trade, an expert may be willing to give a written statement. Sometimes this is viewed as acceptable evidence. When you are suing over disputed workmanship, try to bring the physical evidence of your claim into court. If, say, your dry cleaner shrunk a wool sweater of yours from a size fourteen to a size three, show the garment to the judge.

WHAT HAPPENS IN COURT

Generally, the judge will let you present your case in straightforward language and without the help of a lawyer. In fact, in many states, neither you nor the defendant can bring a lawyer to help. You may get the judge's decision immediately or by notice within a few weeks. In some states, you can appeal the case; but often the small claims court plaintiff does not have the right to appeal a case that is decided against him or her. Remember, whatever action you decide to take after the judgment should be weighed against the costs of that action. Your time is not free, and the worry involved in pursuing a lost case further might not be worth the potential reward of eventually winning.

If your opponent tries to settle the case out of court, make sure everything is written down in a manner that can be upheld if he or she reneges on the offer. Anything that is written should be signed by both of you and filed with the court so the agreement can, in fact, be enforced by the law. Better yet, have him or her appear with you before the judge to explain the settlement terms. Generally, if you win or if you settle out of court, you should be able to get him or her to pay for the court costs, which range from three to twenty dollars, depending on the state.

WHERE, WHAT, AND HOW MUCH?

On pages 90 and 91 in Exhibit A-1, we list small claims courts in selected states, where the court is located, the maximum amount of the suits, and other pertinent information, such as the costs to you of filing a small claims suit. Weigh the potential benefits of going to court against the potential costs. Opt for small claims court when you think you'll be better off. If, however, the potential gain to you is less than the value you place on your time and the worry and apprehension involved in facing a judge, it may be better to forget the whole thing. If, on the other hand, you are convinced that your case is valid, that you have indeed been gypped, and that the sum of money involved is not insignificant, then use the information presented in this Appendix and start the proceedings.

EXHIBIT A-1. SMALL CLAIMS COURTS CHARACTERISTICS IN RANDOMLY SELECTED STATES

| | Name And Location Of Court | Maximum Amount Of Suit | Are Lawyers Ordinarily Allowed? | Who Can Appeal? | | What Is The Initial Cost To Sue? |
				Plaintiff	Defendant	
California	Small Claims Branch of Municipal Court, Sacramento & various counties	$750	No	No	Yes	$2.00+
Colorado	Small Claims Courts, County Court, Denver	$500	No	Yes	Yes	$9.00+
District of Columbia	Small Claims Branch of Superior Court, Washington, D.C.	$750	Yes	Yes	Yes	$1.00+
Florida	Civil Division of the County Court, Miami	$2,500	Yes	Yes	Yes	$3.50+
Georgia	Small Claims Branch of Civil Court, Atlanta	$299.99	Yes	Yes	Yes	$7.00+
Illinois	Circuit Court, Springfield	$1,000	Yes	Yes	Yes	$0-$500-$11.00 $500-up-$26.00
Iowa	Small Claims Div. of Municipal Court, Des Moines	$1,000	Yes	Yes ($5.00)	Yes	$9.00+
Maine	Small Claims Div. of District Court, Augusta	$800	Yes	Yes	Yes	$5.00
Massachusetts	Small Claims Div. of Municipal Court, Boston	$400	Yes	No	No	$3.98

	Name And Location Of Court	Maximum Amount Of Suit	Are Lawyers Ordinarily Allowed?	Who Can Appeal?		What Is The Initial Cost To Sue?
				Plaintiff	Defendant	
Michigan	Small Claims Div. of District Court Lansing	$300	No	No	No	$5.00+
Minnesota	Small Claims Div. of Municipal Court, St. Paul	$1,003	Yes	Yes	Yes	$3.00
New Jersey	Small Claims Div. of District Court, Trenton	$500	Yes	Yes	Yes	$2.70+
New York	Small Claims Div. of Civil Court, New York City	$1,000	Yes	Yes	Yes	$4.48
North Carolina	Small Claims Div. of District Court, Raleigh	$500	No	Yes	Yes	$10.00
Pennsylvania	Small Claims Div. of Municipal Court, Philadelphia	$1,000	Yes	No	No	$11.00
Texas	Justice Court, Houson	$150	Yes	Yes	Yes	$7.00
Virginia	Civil Div. of District Court, Richmond	$5,000	Yes	Yes (if over $50)	Yes (if over $50)	$5.50
Washington	Small Claims Div. of Justice Court, Seattle	$300	No	No	Yes (if over $100)	$1.00
Wisconsin	Small Claims Div. of County Court, Madison	$1,000	Yes	Yes	Yes	$7.50

Borrowing
and Buying

Banks and the Banking System

■ We live in a money economy. We use currency, consisting of various denomination bills and coins, and we also use checks. In fact, of the total amount of money outstanding in the United States, some 80 percent is in checking account balances; every year about 30 billion checks are written and processed through our banking system. Understanding how that system works and what services banks can offer you is, therefore, an important aspect of your personal finance education. In this chapter, we will look at the banking system as a whole, the types of checking accounts and other services that various commercial banks offer, and the cashless society. In the Practical Applications section, we will examine how to choose a bank, how to open an account, how to write a check, how to endorse checks, and how to reconcile a checking account balance.

THE FEDERAL RESERVE SYSTEM

In the United States banking system, the monetary authority, or Federal Reserve System, determines the quantity of money in circulation. The Federal Reserve System was established in 1913 with the passage of the Federal Reserve Act under President Woodrow Wilson. According to its preamble, it was "an act to provide for the establishment of Federal Reserve banks, to furnish an elastic currency, to afford means of rediscounting commercial paper, to establish a more effective supervision of banking in the United States, and for other purposes."

Currently, the Federal Reserve System consists of twelve member Federal Reserve banks, which have twenty-five branches; a Board of Governors, consisting of seven members nominated by the president for fourteen-year terms; a Federal Open Market Committee; and other less important committees, as indicated in Exhibit 5-1.

A Clearinghouse for Checks

The Federal Reserve System has greatly simplified the clearing of checks, the method by which checks deposited in one bank are transferred to the banks on which they were written. Let us say that Mr. Smith of Chicago writes a check to the Jones family in San Francisco. When the Joneses receive the check in the mail, they deposit it in their bank. Their bank then deposits the check in the Federal Reserve Bank of San Francisco. That bank, in turn, sends it to the Federal Reserve Bank of Chicago. That Federal Reserve Bank then sends the check to Mr. Smith's bank, where the amount of the check is deducted from Mr. Smith's account. We show how this is done in Exhibit 5-2.

THE DIFFERENT TYPES OF CHECKING ACCOUNTS

Commercial banks offer at least six basic types of checking accounts, plus combinations of these six:

1 Minimum balance,
2 Free checking,
3 Analysis or transaction,
4 Activity or "per check,"
5 Package account, and
6 Overdraft account.

Minimum Balance

Minimum balance accounts give you unlimited checking at no charge per check or deposit as long as you maintain a specified balance, such as

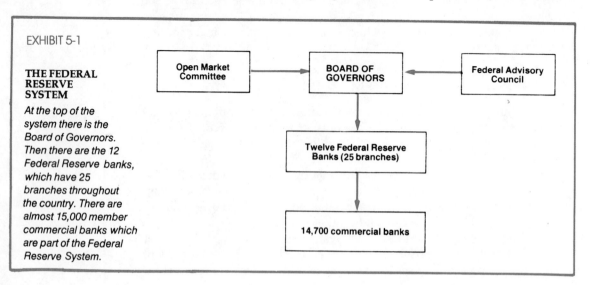

EXHIBIT 5-1

THE FEDERAL RESERVE SYSTEM

At the top of the system there is the Board of Governors. Then there are the 12 Federal Reserve banks, which have 25 branches throughout the country. There are almost 15,000 member commercial banks which are part of the Federal Reserve System.

Open Market Committee → BOARD OF GOVERNORS ← Federal Advisory Council

Twelve Federal Reserve Banks (25 branches)

14,700 commercial banks

$200, $300, or $500. Whenever the account balance falls below the specified balance in a certain month, a service charge is usually added.

There are two methods used to determine whether or not your account has been maintained above a specified minimum balance: the minimum balance method and the average balance method.

Minimum Balance Method. A service fee is based on the lowest balance on any day during the month. Thus, if you go below the specified balance even for one day, you will be charged a service charge.

Average Balance Method. Balances are computed daily, then totaled at the end of the month and divided by the number of business days in the month. If your average balance falls below the minimum required balance, you are charged a service charge. On the other hand, if

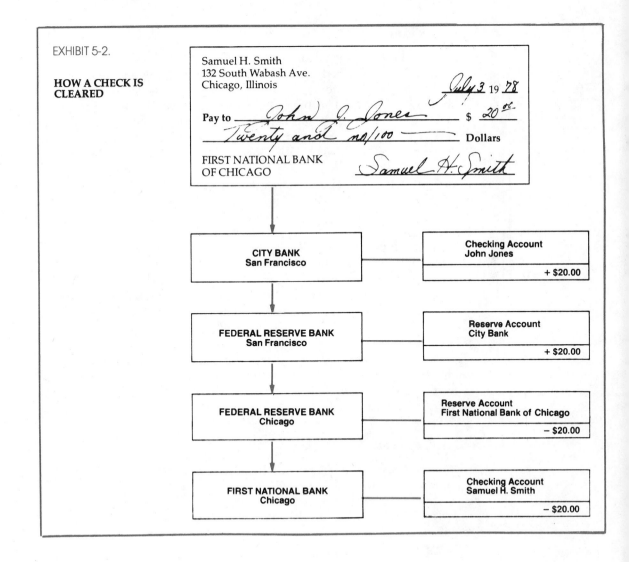

EXHIBIT 5-2.

HOW A CHECK IS CLEARED

your average balance is above the minimum, you are not charged for service, even though there may have been a number of days during which you fell below the minimum required balance. Clearly, the average balance method is better for the consumer, especially when your deposit balance fluctuates widely during the month.

Not Really a Free Account. Although minimum balance checking accounts are advertised as "free," they clearly are not. If you have to keep $500 as a minimum balance in your checking account for a one-year period, then you have lost the *potential* interest you could have earned in, say, a savings account during that time. Assume that the interest rate you could have earned in a savings account for that one-year period is 6 percent. You would have been charged implicitly, therefore, 6 percent times $500, or $30 per year, for the so-called free minimum balance checking account.

Free Checking

This account gives you unlimited checking at no charge with no strings attached—no required minimum balance, no monthly maintenance fee, and so on. At last report, the American Bankers Association estimated that only 13 percent of the nation's banks, most of them in the mid-Atlantic and New England states, offered true free checking account services. Generally, banks offer free checking only to a limited number of customers, such as elderly persons and students. Often, smaller banks will give you free checking account services in order to lure business away from the larger, more established banks.

Analysis, or Transaction, Plan

With this type of checking account, you are charged for every transaction you make, including deposits. At the end of the month, the total amount of transactions fees charged to you is reduced by credit that is based on your average balance during that month. The higher the average balance you maintain, the lower the final service charge. As an example, one plan might charge you twelve cents for each check and six cents for each deposit. On the other hand, it will give you a twenty cent credit for each $100 average balance maintained. If you average twenty checks a month plus two and a half deposits a month and maintain an average balance of $100, this analysis plan account will cost you $28.20 a year.

Activity, or "Per Check" Plan

With this type of account—often called a special checking account—your monthly fee is based on the amount of your banking activity. There are two separate charges: a flat monthly "maintenance" fee and a charge for every check written. Usually the monthly fee is fifty cents to one dollar, and the check fee is ten cents. This particular account is most suited for customers who write relatively few checks (five to ten) a month. For an individual who averages twenty checks a month, the annual cost for this account would be thirty-three dollars—if the per-month fee was seventy-five cents and the per-check fee was ten cents.

Package Plan

This combination all-in-one package has been introduced recently by many banks. You are generally charged a single monthly fee, probably three dollars. For that fee, you get something called a Blue Chip Account or a Gold Account or an Executive Account. Included are the following services:

1. Unlimited check writing.
2. Personalized checks, sometimes with your picture embossed on them or with a reproduction of a famous painting or landscape in your area.
3. Overdraft protection; if you write checks for more money than you have in your account, funds will be transferred automatically from either a credit card account or a personalized line of credit.
4. A safe deposit box.
5. Free travelers checks, cashiers checks, and money orders.
6. Sometimes preferred interest rates on personal loans.

Package accounts apparently benefit only those customers who make heavy use of virtually every type of bank service. Usually, most of the services offered by package accounts are used by very few individuals who have such accounts. Statistics show that only 50 percent of package customers actually have safe deposit boxes or use the personal-loan discount offered. Moreover, there are a number of services attached to package accounts that are offered to other customers free of charge anyway, such as free-rein lines of credit.

Overdraft Accounts

Customers who can supply satisfactory credit ratings may be able to obtain an overdraft account, in which the bank automatically lends the customer money when his or her checking account balance falls below zero. Thus, instead of refusing payment on the checks written when the balance is negative, the bank lends the customer a specified amount and deposits that into his or her account automatically. Most plans lend a minimum of $100 and add to the account in multiples of $100. Although few banks actually will loan you the exact amount of your overdraft or negative balance, you would be better off if they did because you would pay interest only on the smaller sum.

Most overdraft accounts require that you make a special deposit at regular intervals and indicate that it is to pay off the loan. Some banks automatically deduct a part of the loan from your regular checking account after you have made deposits in it later in the month. Many overdraft accounts charge a service fee every time they add to your account. Thus, the implicit interest on an overdraft account loan may be quite high.

Overdraft accounts are also known as Ready Reserve accounts and Constant Credit accounts.

RECEIVING INTEREST ON YOUR CHECKING ACCOUNT

Traditionally, commercial banks have been prohibited by law from offering interest on checking account balances. A number of mutual savings banks in New England found a way around this legal restriction by offering **negotiable orders of withdrawals,** or **NOWs.** With a NOW account, you receive interest on your balance in this supposed "savings" account, and you can write negotiable orders of withdrawal, which are equivalent to checks. Because there is a service charge of ten or fifteen cents on each check, you would not want to use a NOW account if you wrote fifty checks per month. In that situation, you would pay more in service charges than you earned in interest. Most institutions that offer NOW accounts pay 5 percent, at most, and some pay as little as 3 or 4 percent. There are, however, a number of institutions that do not charge for NOW withdrawals; these offer the best of both possible worlds— free checking plus 5 percent interest on checking account balances.

NOWs were introduced by Massachusetts savings banks in 1972. The trend toward NOW-type accounts is clearly on the upswing. All savings banks in Maryland, Indiana, and New Jersey and some in Delaware, Oregon, and Connecticut can offer NOW accounts, but only a few states are allowed to pay interest on the accounts. In Philadelphia, the Western Savings Fund Society has WOW (Western Order of Withdrawal) accounts, which require the bank to countersign a draft before it can be used as a check. There's a host of similar accounts in other banks. Additionally, credit unions are now offering their equivalent of NOW accounts. Most credit unions effectively pay over 5 percent interest on what are actually checking account balances in such accounts. It may be only a matter of time before the majority of savings banks, savings and loan associations, and similar type financial institutions will be directly competing with commercial banks with their ability to offer checking accounts.

OTHER COMMERCIAL BANK SERVICES

Commercial banks are not just places to have checking and savings accounts. Banks also provide loans, a topic we discuss in detail in Chapter 6. It would be impossible to explain all the other services banks provide, so here we will limit ourselves to an explanation of safe deposit boxes, travelers checks, certified checks, and cashier's checks.

Safe Deposit Boxes

A safe deposit, or lock, box kept under dual locks and dual keys in a specified section of a bank's vault. They are rented by customers for an annual fee that depends on the size of the box—say, ten dollars per year for a box measuring two by five by twenty-two inches. Each customer has his or her own separate key; the bank has another. In most cases, the box cannot be opened unless both keys are used.

Safe deposit boxes are useful for storing important papers, such as stock certificates, real estate deeds, and titles to such consumer durables as cars and jewelry. One disadvantage of having important papers in a safe deposit box is that, when the owner dies, the box may be immediately (albeit temporarily) sealed when the bank receives the notice of death. Sometimes it may not be reopened until a tax officer is present.

Travelers Checks

Most banks sell their customers travelers checks issued by American Express, Bank of America, Cook's, First National City Bank of New York, and so on. Travelers checks usually cost one dollar for $100 worth of checks. They are issued in denominations of $10, $20, $50, $100, and $500 (sometimes even $1,000). The individual purchaser signs each check upon its purchase and then countersigns it when cashing it. The comparison of the two signatures is proof that the person cashing the check was the original purchaser.

One of the main advantages of travelers checks is that, if they are lost or stolen, you can be reimbursed. Generally, you keep a record of the numbers of the particular checks you purchased. Then, if you lose them or they are stolen, you can contact the issuing company, such as American Express, for a rapid refund. For this reason, using travelers checks is preferable to using cash while traveling extensively.

Certified Checks

Banks will often issue a certified check at no, or nominal, charge. Such a check has been certified by the bank to the effect that there are sufficient funds to cover it when it is cashed. Actually, the cashier at your bank immediately notifies the bank's bookkeeping department to reduce the size of your checking balance by the amount of the certified check. Then the check is stamped *certified*. Many contracts frequently call for payment by check. A **certified check** is a means of assuring that the person to whom the check is made out will be guaranteed payment. There can be no "bad" check in such a circumstance.

Cashier's Checks

A **cashier's check** is actually drawn by a bank on its own order to a designated person or institution. This check is a liability of the bank itself, not of the individual who might request a certified check. You actually purchase a cashier's check by going to your bank and paying the face value of the check, which the bank then will write on itself. Usually, there is a small fee for this service. A cashier's check and a certified check serve the same purpose. A nondepositor in a bank can, however, purchase a cashier's check at a bank, but a certified check can be obtained only by a depositor in that bank. A cashier's check gives the payee absolute assurance that he or she can convert the check into cash.

WHEN A BANK WON'T HONOR A CHECK

There are many reasons why a bank may not honor a check drawn upon it. You may deposit someone else's check in your account only to have your bank return it. Some of the reasons for returning a check are shown in Exhibit 5-3.

EXHIBIT 5-3.

REASON FOR RETURNING A CHECK

Returned to _____

by PEOPLES NATIONAL BANK

☐ N.S.F.   ☐ Account closed

☐ Uncollected   ☐ Payment stopped

☐ Endorsement   ☐ Date

☐ _____

The most common reasons why a check is not honored are:

1 **Insufficient funds.** The depositor does not have enough money in his or her account to cover the check. This is usually called an overdraft. You have overdrawn your checking account if someone deposits your check and it "bounces." You usually are charged three to five dollars for each bounced check.

2 **Signature appears "different."** Banks keep a file of signatures of all depositors. If the signature on a check you write looks sufficiently different from the one on file, the check will be returned—marked "not satisfied with signature"—to whomever has deposited it.

3 **The check appears to have been altered.** Suppose you make a mistake in writing your check and then scribble a correction over the mistake. The bank may refuse to honor such a check. It is best to destroy the altered check and write another.

4   **There is no signature on the check.** It is not uncommon for checks to be mailed out without signatures on the endorsement line. These checks are almost always returned.

103
*Banks and the
Banking
System*

STALE CHECKS

A check that is more than six months old is considered "stale." Some banks will contact their depositors before they honor a stale check; however, this is not bank policy but, rather, a courtesy. Some banks will even return stale checks, indicating that they are "too old." But no law requires such action. Banks are not responsible for screening stale checks, even if they are many years old. Thus, if a customer does not want a check to be cashed when it is presented for payment, it is up to the customer to put a **stop payment** on the check—that is, an order for it not to be honored.

STOP PAYMENTS

If you wish to stop a check from being collected after you have given it to someone, you can notify the bank, which will then refuse to honor it. You might issue a stop-payment order when you think a check has been lost or stolen. Some consumers order a stop payment when they realize they have been given defective merchandise.

Many banks require that you fill out a stop-payment order after you phone them. A typical stop-payment order is shown in Exhibit 5-4.

EXHIBIT 5-4.

A TYPICAL STOP PAYMENT ORDER

TO THE FIRST NATIONAL BANK
OF SOUTH MIAMI
SOUTH MIAMI, FLORIDA

DATE OF ORDER   ACCOUNT NUMBER

Please STOP PAYMENT on my (or our) check drawn on your bank, described as follows:

NO: DATED: PAYABLE TO: AMOUNT: $

REASON: DUPLICATE ISSUED?

THIS REQUEST IS MADE WITH THE UNDERSTANDING THAT THE BANK WILL USE REASONABLE PRECAUTION IN FOLLOWING YOUR INSTRUCTION, BUT IN CONSIDERATION OF THE ACCEPTANCE OF THIS REQUEST, IT IS EXPRESSLY AGREED THAT THE BANK WILL IN NO WAY BE LIABLE IN THE EVENT THE CHECK IS PAID, IF PAID THE SAME DAY YOUR ORDER IS RECEIVED OR IF PAID BY OVERSIGHT OR INADVERTENCE OR IF BY REASON OF SUCH PAYMENT OTHER CHECKS DRAWN BY THE UNDERSIGNED ARE RETURNED FOR INSUFFICIENT FUNDS, AND THE UNDERSIGNED FURTHER AGREES TO INDEMNIFY THE BANK AGAINST ALL EXPENSES AND COSTS THAT IT MIGHT INCUR BY REASON OF REFUSING PAYMENT ON SAID CHECK

EXPIRATION DATE

IT IS HEREBY AGREED AND UNDERSTOOD THAT THIS ORDER WILL REMAIN IN EFFECT FOR A SIX-MONTH PERIOD UNLESS OTHERWISE DIRECTED AND THE BANK WILL CHARGE $5.00 FOR EACH SIX-MONTH PERIOD OR PORTION THEREOF THAT THIS ORDER IS IN EFFECT, THE BANK MAY CHARGE MY ACCOUNT WITH THIS AMOUNT

ORDER RECEIVED BY   IN PERSON   BY LETTER   SIGNATURE OF MAKER

BANK NOT LIABLE IF CHECK HAS BEEN CASHED IN THE SAME DAY THIS ORDER WAS ACCEPTED.

Most banks charge two to five dollars for each stop-payment order executed. Generally, a phone call will only stop payment on a check for fourteen days; written notice will stop payment for six months, with the possibility of a renewal of the stop-payment order. Once the stop-payment order has been issued, the tellers in the bank are requested not to pay the particular check. The stop-payment information is also put on the computer in order to reject the check if another bank presents it in the bank-clearing process. A stop payment can only be made on a regular check from a checking account; cashier's and certified checks cannot be stopped.

THE CASHLESS AND CHECKLESS SOCIETY

Some cities, such as Lincoln, Nebraska, and Macon and Atlanta, Georgia, are trying a system of cashless, checkless spending. And it seems to be working. What is it all about? And does it mean that money will be useless? No, it only means that money will take another form. Money in the form of cash—currency and checking account balances—is a means of storing purchasing power. Since our income receipts do not always match our expenditures, we generally keep some money in a checking account balance or in our wallets in order to make expenditures later each month. In the cashless, checkless society, you still would need a checking account balance on which to draw, even though you did not write a check and even though the transmission mechanism was semiautomatic at the beginning of each month. You would have to deposit your income checks in your account at the beginning of each month, just as you do now, although that, too, could be done automatically.

In those cities that allow cashless, checkless transactions, you still keep part of your wealth in the form of a checking account balance, but you use it in a semiautomatic manner. When you make a purchase in a store, you merely give the salesperson a credit card that automatically transfers money from your checking account balance to the store's balance.

The cashless, checkless society is merely a means of reducing transactions costs. Instead of you having to write monthly checks for your mortgage, phone, milk, electricity, and so on, a computer does it automatically.

The official banking term for computer money is **electronic funds transfer system,** or EFTS. There are basically three parts to an EFTS system—teller machines, point-of-sale systems, and automated clearinghouses.

Teller machines. Also called customer bank communication terminals or remote service units, these machines are located either on the bank's premises or in stores, such as supermarkets or drugstores. Automated teller machines receive deposits, dispense funds from checking or savings account, make credit card advances, and receive payments. The device is connected on-line to the bank's computers.

Point-of-sale systems. Such systems allow the consumer to transfer funds to merchants in order to make purchases. On-line terminals are located at check-out counters in the merchant's store. When a purchase is made, the customer's card is inserted into the terminal, which reads the data encoded on it. The computer at the customer's bank verifies that the card and identification code are valid and that there is enough money in the customer's account. After the purchase is made, the customer's account is debited for the amount of the purchase.

Automated clearinghouses. Such clearinghouses are similar to those that now clear checks between banks. The main difference is that the entries are made in the form of electronic signals; no checks are used. Thus, this is a replacement system, not a system for further automating the handling of paper checks. Such systems are especially useful to businesspeople for such payments as payroll, Social Security, or pension fund plans, which must be made weekly or monthly.

The automated clearinghouse is really a glorified processing system, which saves the customer time and the banks and companies money. After all, it is estimated that the banking system spends over 6.5 billion dollars annually just to process 30 billion checks. If this processing can be reduced somehow, the consumer will benefit. Since most of your fixed expenses for car payments, house payments, and the like are anticipated anyway, their being paid automatically is not going to change your routine. In the cashless, checkless society, you will get a statement at the end of every month just as you do now; in fact, you will probably always be able to find out, by phone, where your finances stand. Since we are all faced with budget constraints (we know that we cannot spend more than we make), checks and balances against overspending will have to be built into the system. And, of course, that all goes back to formulating a budget and sticking to it.

Note that there, however, are some serious consumer concerns over such a system as EFTS.

1   There is no mechanism for issuing a stop-payment order on a check when there is trouble with the seller of a good or service.
2   Fewer records are available (no canceled check as proof of payment).
3   The possibility of tampering is increased.
4   There is a loss of "float"—the time between when you write a check and when the sum of the check is deducted from your account.

Will electronic money increase financial problems in our society? Perhaps, but one basic fact remains unaltered: No matter what type of credit or money system we use, each family and each individual faces a budget constraint. If that individual or family engages in more buying—whether or not it is impulse—because of credit cards or electronic money systems, then less funds will be available to purchase other items.

PRACTICAL APPLICATIONS

HOW TO CHOOSE
AND USE A BANK

SELECTING THE RIGHT ACCOUNT FOR YOU

We have listed six different basic types of accounts and their respective characteristics. To decide which type of account is most appropriate for you, you will have to do the following:

1. Figure out how many checks you write per month. If you write less than fifteen, you are a light check writer; you are average if you write fifteen to twenty-four; and you are a frequent check writer if you average more than twenty-five.

2. Determine the average amount of money you keep in a checking account over and above what you actually use. Many individuals play it close, depositing just enough to cover the checks they are going to write. Others maintain a cushion of several hundred dollars for unforeseen expenses.

Now you can decide which plans you should consider. If you write fewer than five or six checks per month, you may be better off without a checking account. You could put your funds in a saving institution that places no limit on withdrawals but charges, say, ten cents per money order. This way you earn interest on your cash and are not charged too much for the "checks" you write.

If you regularly keep a several hundred dollar balance in your checking account, you probably will want to look for a minimum balance plan that charges nothing for checks, provided you keep a minimum balance.

By using the checklist we provide in Exhibit 5-5, you can compare the total cost of banking services, which you anticipate using in a year's time, for any specific bank.

CHOOSING THE RIGHT BANK

Choosing the bank that is best for you depends on a number of factors. For many individuals, the cost of the banking services is less important than the location of the bank itself. In fact, that is a major factor that prompts people to decide on one bank instead of another. Although, with the advent of banking by mail, some individuals rarely go to the bank to make deposits. Thus, they can base their decision on the best-priced banking services—even if the bank that offers them is not in their neighborhood or near where they work.

Convenience in terms of the banking hours is also important. If you cannot get off work during the hours a particular bank, which offers the best deal in banking services, is open, you might wish to choose another, slightly more expensive, one.

When you go shopping for banking services, use the checklist in Exhibit 5-5 to compare costs for the services you desire. Some of the miscellaneous costs won't apply to you. For example, if you never require a certified or a cashier's check, then it really doesn't matter how expensive that service is at any particular bank. Note that all of the information required to complete this check list can be obtained over the telephone.

The Best Deals

If you live or work in Massachusetts or New Hampshire, a free NOW account offered by many thrift institutions is probably the best "checking" deal around. You earn up to 5 percent on the funds you deposit, but you are not charged when you withdraw your money to pay bills, regardless of how many negotiable orders of withdrawals you write. Those NOW accounts for which you are charged ten to fifteen cents a "check" are certainly not as attractive, but they may still be a good deal—if you don't write too many checks per month. Either way, you will be earning interest on the balance in your account.

If you are a frequent check writer with normally low balances in your account, you probably will want

EXHIBIT 5-5.

CHECKLIST FOR CHECKING ACCOUNTS

	BANK 1	BANK 2
Name of bank	_____	_____
Name of officer providing information	_____	_____
Account Costs		
Minimum balance checking	_____	_____
Balance required	_____	_____
Service fee if you fall below	_____	_____
Free checking available	_____	_____
Analysis, or transaction, plan	_____	_____
Monthly maintenance fee	_____	_____
Cost per check	_____	_____
Cost per deposit	_____	_____
Credit per $100 balance	_____	_____
Activity plan	_____	_____
Monthly maintenance fee	_____	_____
Cost per check	_____	_____
Package accounts	_____	_____
Cost per month	_____	_____
Services provided	_____	_____
Overdraft account	_____	_____
Cost per overdraft	_____	_____
Automatic payment	_____	_____
NOW account	_____	_____
Balance required	_____	_____
Cost per NOW	_____	_____
Rate of interest paid	_____	_____
Check Costs (if any)		
Free personalized	_____	_____
Free nonpersonalized	_____	_____
200 personalized	_____	_____
Miscellaneous Costs		
Free two-way postage	_____	_____
Travelers checks	_____	_____

EXHIBIT 5-5 **CONTINUED**

	BANK 1	BANK 2
Certified checks	_____	_____
Cashier's checks	_____	_____
Money orders	_____	_____
Safe deposit box	_____	_____
Returned check	_____	_____
Stop payment order	_____	_____
Overdraft charge	_____	_____
Miscellaneous Services		
Notify before bouncing	_____	_____
Automatic deposit of paycheck	_____	_____
Automatic payment of recurring bills, such as mortgage payments	_____	_____

to take the time to find a truly free checking account. You can save from twenty to forty dollars a year over the cost of other plans with such accounts. It may be even worth your while to go to a bank outside your area if you write checks frequently. Banking by mail is a possibility, particularly if merchants in your area permit you to write checks over the amount of the purchase so you can always have currency available for small purchases.

OPENING AN ACCOUNT

The following simple steps are involved in opening a checking account:

1. Decide on a single or a joint account. A joint account can be opened in the name of any two people, but typically this is done for a husband and wife. Most couples open a joint account with the right of survivorship: both can draw on the account, and, if one dies, the other may continue to use that account. Usually, though, survivors must assure tax authorities that all taxes due will be paid before continuing to use that account.

2. Complete an information card that gives your occupation and employer (if working), address, telephone number, place and date of birth, and so on.

3. Sign signature cards. Your signature will appear on checks, and tellers must be able to verify whether your check has been forged. Exhibit 5-6 is an example of a signature card.

4. Decide which type of check you wish. Often banks have a variety of colors and designs to choose from.

5. Make an initial deposit, for which you will be given a receipt.

6. Use a temporary checkbook, which will have your account number on it but not your name, address, or telephone number.

HOW TO WRITE A CHECK

Writing a check is a relatively simple skill. You must make sure, however, that your check cannot

EXHIBIT 5-6.

**BANK SIGNATURE
CARD**

( ) MR.
( ) MRS.
( ) MISS
( ) DR.

INDIVIDUAL
RCA
ACCT. NO.

NAME

LOCAL ADDRESS

OTHER ADDRESS

DATE _____ SIG. OK _____ PHONE _____

FIRST NATIONAL BANK OF SOUTH MIAMI

The undersigned is opening an account in FIRST NATIONAL BANK OF SOUTH MIAMI, FLORIDA, in the above name, and hereby authorizes and directs said bank to recognize and honor the signature hereunto subscribed as the bank's authority for the payment of funds from said account; and as a condition of the acceptance of said account by the bank it is agreed that said account is opened and accepted, and shall continue to be at all times subject to all reasonable rules and regulations of said bank. It is further understood and agreed that the First National Bank of South Miami will only recognize stop payment orders on the above account for the following reasons: (1) Failure of consideration. (2) Fraud. (3) Satisfaction of Indebtedness. (4) Lost Instrument. The Bank is authorized to apply this account towards any indebtedness due the Bank from the depositor.

( ) MR.
( ) MRS.
( ) MISS
( ) DR.

JOINT
RCA
ACCT. NO.

( ) MR.
( ) MRS.
( ) MISS
( ) DR.

NAME

ADDRESS

DATE _____ PHONE _____

FIRST NATIONAL BANK OF SOUTH MIAMI

The undersigned joint depositors are opening an account in FIRST NATIONAL BANK OF SOUTH MIAMI, FLORIDA, and hereby authorize and direct said bank to recognize and honor either and/or and /or every of the signatures subscribed as the bank's authority for the payment of funds from said account; and the undersigned hereby agree each with the other and with said bank that all sums heretofore or hereafter deposited by the undersigned in said account shall be owned by the undersigned jointly, with right of survivorship, and shall be subject to payment upon the check of either or any one of the undersigned, or the survivor or survivors of them, and payment thereof to either of them upon the joint or several order of either of them shall discharge said bank from liability to either, or the heirs, executors, administrators or assigns of either. As a condition of the acceptance of said account by the bank it is agreed that said account shall at all times be subject to all reasonable rules and regulations of said bank. The account may be closed by either of the undersigned. The Bank is authorized to apply this account toward the payment of any indebtedness due the Bank from the depositor or depositors, or either of them, whether the debt is several and this account is joint, or the debt is joint and the account is several. The Bank is authorized to supply the endorsement and to place to the credit of this account, any and all checks, drafts, or other items, payable to both of the depositors jointly or to either of them severally, whether deposited by them or sent to the Bank by others for the account of either of them. It is further understood and agreed that the First National Bank of South Miami will only recognize stop payment orders on the above account for the following reasons: (1) Failure of consideration. (2) Fraud. (3) Satisfaction of Indebtedness. (4) Lost Instrument.

be altered easily. If you follow carefully the steps outlined here, this will not be possible:

1. Fill out your check stub or ledger before you write the check. This way you will always have an accurate record of the checks you wrote, your balance, the actual amount, and to whom the check was made.

2. Always fill out checks in ink, legibly and completely.

3. Complete the following items:
   a. **The date.** Enter the date when the check is actually written. Postdating a check is not advisable. The check should not be cashed until the date that appears on it but banks may slip

up and cash a check before its post-dated date. If you postdate a check in hopes of having sufficient funds to cover it, you might end up with an overdraft because of an oversight on the bank's part. So don't count on postdating to get you out of an over-draft situation.

b. **The check number.** This should be filled in if it is not printed on the check itself. Most checks do, however, have numbers printed on them serially.

c. **The payee's name.** Make sure you spell the name correctly. Be wary of making out checks to cash, since anyone can then cash them. And, if you lose them, it is the same as losing currency.

d. **The amount of check in numbers.** This is entered after the payee's name and should be written close to the dollar sign to prevent anyone else from increasing the amount. The correct way to give dollars and cents is: $15.43/100.

e. **The amount in words.** This is written in the line below the name of the payee, started as far left as possible to prevent anyone from inserting other words that would raise the amount.

f. **Your signature.** Write this on the signature line exactly as you signed your signature card.

g. Many banks have a space where you can indicate what the check is for, such as rent deposit, groceries, or whatever.

Exhibit 5-7 shows a properly made out check and one containing some common errors.

ENDORSING A CHECK

When you wish to cash or deposit a check made out to you, you must sign it on the back, usually at the extreme left end of the check. This procedure is called check endorsement. When a check has been made out to you and you wish to transfer it to someone else, you endorse it first, and then the other party endorses it. The check has then become a third-party check. The first party was the person who made it out, the second party was you, and the third party was the person to whom you endorsed it.

It is advisable never to endorse a check prior to arriving at the bank or to giving it to the person who is cashing it for you. If it is endorsed beforehand and you lose it, it will be easier for someone to cash it. There are basically four kinds of endorsements.

Endorsement in Blank

This most common type merely involves signing your name on the back of the check. This makes the check legally payable to whoever possesses it. That means that anyone can cash it. A *blank endorsement* is the name only of the payee on the check.

R. L. Miller

Special Endorsement

With endorsement, the payee endorses the name to whom the check is to be paid. For example, a *special endorsement* might read:

Pay to the order of John Doe
R. L. Miller

EXHIBIT 5-7.

**HOW TO MAKE
OUT A CHECK
PROPERLY**

ROGER LEROY MILLER   1699

November 4 19 77   63-587
670

PAY TO THE
ORDER OF *University of Miami* $ 5.65

Five and 65/100 ~~~~~ DOLLARS

First National Bank of South Miami
5750 Sunset Drive
South Miami, Fla. 33143

FOR *Books*   *Roger Miller*

**SOME COMMON
ERRORS IN MAKING
OUT A CHECK**

**Postdating is unusually
not a good idea.**

**If you lose this check, it's
like losing currency.**

**This could be easily al-
tered or added to. And it is
not complete.**

**Someone could add a
Zero to this very easily.**

ROGER LEROY MILLER   1699

January 1 19 99   63-587
670

PAY TO THE
ORDER OF *cash* $ 100

One hundred   DOLLARS

First National Bank of South Miami
5750 Sunset Drive
South Miami, Fla. 33143

FOR   *Roger Miller*

Restrictive Endorsement

This type of endorsement limits the purpose to which the check can be put. It puts a further restric-tion on a special endorsement given above. This *restrictive endorsement* may read as follows:

*Pay to the order of John Doe only
R. L. Miller*

*For deposit only
R. L. Miller*

Always endorse a check exactly as it is made out to you.

EXHIBIT 5-8.

**RECONCILING
YOUR BANK
STATEMENT .**

1. *Adjust balance in
   checkbook for
   service charge and
   other bank charges
   and credits shown
   on bank statement
   nor recorded in
   checkbook.*

2. *See that all deposits
   made by you are
   properly credited.*

3. *See that all checks
   enclosed in your
   statement are
   checks issued by
   you.*

4. *Check each paid
   check against your
   checkbook stubs.
   List all checks
   outstanding in
   space provided
   below.*

**Checks outstanding
not charged to account**

No.	$	
Total	$	

Bank balance shown
on this statement $ _____

ADD +

Deposits not credited $ _____
in this statement $ _____
                           $ _____
TOTAL $ _____

SUBTRACT
Checks outstanding $ _____

BALANCE $ _____

Should agree with your checkbook balance

Conditional Endorsement

This type of endorsement places a condition on the endorsement. Legally, the condition is not binding on the person who cashes the check. The *conditional endorsement* does, however, make further negotiation of the check impossible. It might read as follows:

> Pay to the order of John Doe when
> he completes sandblasting my
> swimming pool.
> R. L. Miller

RECONCILING YOUR BANK BALANCE

Every month you will receive a bank statement and a set of canceled checks. It is important that you reconcile your bank balance with your checkbook or set of stubs so that you: (a) know exactly how much you have in the bank, (b) can catch any mistakes the bank might have made, and (c) can find out if someone has not cashed a check that you wrote.

Since you may have written checks immediately prior to the closing date on your bank statement and the checks probably will not have been paid by the bank yet, the balance in your checkbook rarely will be exactly the same as the balance on your bank statement. Thus, you must reconcile the two by taking account of deposits you made that did not show up on your bank statement and checks you wrote that have not yet been processed.

Exhibit 5-8 shows the steps to be followed in reconciling your bank balance.

1. Sort your checks, either numerically or by date issued.

2. Deduct from your checkbook balance any service charges not previously recorded—for example, for new checks, overdraft charges, and so on.

3. Enter your bank statement balance.
   $_____

4. After adding up all the checks outstanding that are not on your bank balance statement, subtract the total of these unpaid checks from the bank balance entered above and obtain a new balance here. $_____

5. Add up any deposits you made that did not show in your bank statement and put them here. $_____

6. Add the outstanding deposits to the line above them to obtain a balance. This should be the same as your checkbook balance after service charges are deducted. $_____

Don't destroy your checks and the bank statement after you reconcile your bank balance. For income tax purposes, it is generally important to keep bank statements and canceled checks for at least three years. Some individuals keep them longer in case there is a dispute with the Internal Revenue Services over your federal income taxes.

GLOSSARY OF TERMS

NEGOTIABLE ORDERS OF WITHDRAWAL (NOWs)   The equivalent of a check written on a special type of savings account on which interest is earned on the unused balance.

CERTIFIED CHECK   A check for which the bank has certified that sufficient funds are available to cover it when it is cashed.

CASHIER'S CHECK   A check drawn on the bank by its own order to a designated person or institution. A cashier's check is paid for before it is obtained.

STOP PAYMENT   An order issued by the payer to a bank not to honor a particular check when it is presented for payment.

ELECTRONIC FUNDS TRANSFER SYSTEM (EFTS)   A system of transfering money with electronic or magnetic signals.

CHECK ENDORSEMENT   The way in which you sign over a check to be cashed or deposited. The endorsement is found on the blank side of a check and is written or stamped by the person to whom the check was made payable, as well as any subsequent parties to whom it was endorsed.

CHAPTER SUMMARY

1. The Federal Reserve System is the monetary authority in the United States. It consists of twelve member Federal Reserve Banks with twenty-five branches, a Board of Governors, and a Federal Open Market Committee.

2. The Federal Reserve System is the main clearing-house for checks in the United States.

3. There are at least six different types of checking accounts: (a) minimum balance, (b) free checking, (c) analysis, or transaction, plan, (d) activity, or per check, plan, (e) package, and (f) overdraft.

4. "Free" accounts are not really free, because you must keep a specified balance in the bank. That balance does not earn interest; therefore, you give up the interest you could have earned had you kept that balance in a savings account that offered interest.

5. It is possible in some states to receive interest on your checking account balance if you obtain Negotiable Orders of Withdrawal (NOW) from special mutual savings banks.

6. Commercial banks offer, among others, the following services in addition to checking accounts: (a) safe deposit boxes, (b) travelers checks, (c) certified checks, and (d) cashier's checks.

7. A cashier's check differs from a certified check in that the former is actually drawn on the bank that writes it.

8. Checks will not be honored if: (a) an account is closed, (b) the check has been altered, (c) there are insufficient funds, (d) the signature is not present or is incomplete. There are other reasons, also, why a check may be returned.

9. A check that is six months old or older is considered "stale." Many banks will contact the writer of a stale check before they honor it.

10. Stop payments can be made to prevent honoring a particular check.

11. In the cashless society, electronic funds transfer systems (EFTS) are used. These consist of: (a) teller machines, (b) point-of-sale systems, and (c) automatic clearinghouses.

12. Some of the consumer concerns over EFTS are that: (a) fewer records are available, (b) the threat to lack of privacy is increased, and (c) it is difficult to issue a stop payment order.

13. Before you decide what the best checking account is for you, you must determine how many checks you write per month and what your average checking account balance is. Then you can use the checklist in Exhibit 5-5 to select a checking account.

14. One of the best deals is a free NOW account offered currently by some thrift institutions in New England and elsewhere.

15. When you open an account, you must: (a) fill out an information card, (b) sign signature cards, (c) make an initial deposit, (d) decide which type of check you wish, and (e) determine whether you want a joint or single account.

16. It is important to fill out a check properly. That means including: (a) the date, (b) the check number, (c) the payee's name, (d) the amount of the check in numbers, (e) the amount of the check spelled out, and (f) your signature.

17. There are at least four types of check endorsements: (a) blank, (b) special, (c) restrictive, and (d) conditional.

STUDY QUESTIONS

1. What is the difference between the average balance method of computing a monthly checking account fee and the minimum balance method?

2. What is an overdraft account?

3. What is a NOW account?

4. What is the difference between a certified check and a cashier's check?

5. What is the method by which you can stop payment on a check that you have already signed and given or sent to someone?

6. Will an electronic funds transfer system eliminate money in our society?

7. Will an electronic funds transfer system make budget making more difficult?

8. What is the difference between an endorsement in blank and a restrictive endorsement on a check?

CASE PROBLEMS

5-1 Balancing the Bank Statement

Sharon Williams opened her checking account at the First National Bank a month ago and has just received her first bank statement, which shows a balance of $217.86. This morning she deposited $73 and purchased groceries for $31. Her checkbook balance is $182.52. On the bank statement, she notes a service charge of $2.00 and a deduction of $4.75 for printed checks. Four checks ($8.16, $15, $25.57 and $35.36) have not yet been cashed. Reconcile the balances. How much does she actually have?

5-2 Choosing the "Best" Checking Account Plan

Mark Stein, twenty-two, a management trainee in Cleveland, has decided to open a checking account. He keeps his cash reserves in a 6% savings account and will transfer money to the checking account as needed. He will keep a $100 "cushion" in the account, but if a minimum balance is required, he will keep it on deposit. Mark plans to make two deposits and write eight checks each month. Which plan should he select? If he writes twenty-five checks each month, which would you recommend?

Plan 1—minimum balance: requires a minimum balance of $300. If the balance falls below $300, a $1.50 service charge is assessed. Checks cost $2.50 per 100.

Plan 2—analysis plan: the charge is 12¢ per check and 6¢ per deposit. A 20¢ credit is given for each $100 average balance. Checks cost $1.00 per 100.

Plan 3—a monthly fee of 50¢ plus 10¢ for each check. Checks cost 25¢ per 100.

SELECTED REFERENCES

"A Guide to Bank Services." *Consumer Reports*, January 1975, pp. 32-38.
"Are Those Bank Services in a Package a Good Buy?" *Changing Times*, March 1976, p. 14.
"Checkpoints on Checking Accounts." *Changing Times*, September 1974, p. 14.
"Electronic Banking: A Retreat from the Cashless Society." *Business Week*, April 1977, pp. 80-90.
Rose, Sanford. "Checkless Banking Is Bound to Come." *Fortune*, June 1977, pp. 118-21ff.
"The Ins and Outs of Safe Deposit Boxes." *Money*, April 1977, p. 112.

*

Carte Blanche.
WELCOME

AMERICAN EXPRESS
Cards
Welcome

**DINERS CLUB
INTERNATIONAL**

Thank you - call again

master charge.
THE INTERBANK CARD.

Amoco Torch Club
International Credit Card
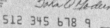
512 345 678 9   DC

JOHN Q MODERN

Credit and Borrowing

■ Debt has been a problem in the United States since its colonial beginnings. In fact, The Society for the Amelioration of the Condition of Debtors was formed by a group of New York businessmen shortly before the American Revolution. Today, the overextended American is still with us. He or she is not the type of person you might think. Instead of a ghetto dweller in a disadvantaged situation (who has a hard time getting credit anyway), the overextended American is more accurately portrayed as a blue-collar worker who makes $1,100 a month, typically with a spouse and two or more children. His or her indebtedness (excluding the home mortgage) is in the neighborhood of $4,000 to $5,000. While he or she might be what people call "credit drunk," a compulsive buyer, more realistically this individual is simply an average American who gradually sank into debt.

BANKRUPTCIES

Bankruptcies are on the rise. Every year, almost a quarter of a million Americans seek refuge from what they consider to be excessive debts in personal bankruptcy proceedings. The Constitution allows Congress "to establish an uniform Rule of Naturalization, and uniform Laws on the subject of Bankruptcies throughout the United States." So we have Chapter XIII of the Federal Bankruptcy Act to help us out. In 1960, there were less than 100,000 personal, nonbusiness bankruptcies. By 1970, there were almost 180,000, and by 1978, the estimate was 210,000. Just because someone files for bankruptcy does not mean his or her life is ruined. Many of those who have gone through bankruptcy proceedings start using credit again; one estimate is that 80 percent of those who file for bankruptcy use credit and are in debt trouble again within five years. No wonder, then, that the amount of debt outstanding in the United States keeps rising.

THE INDEBTED SOCIETY

At least 50 percent of all Americans have outstanding installment debt at any given time. In 1977, the median debt for families with installment debt was almost $2,000. For families of adults under forty-five years of age with no children, 25 percent had $3,500 or more of outstanding debts. Exhibit 6-1 shows the total amount of aggregate, or economywide, private debt in the United States during the past years. It has risen to more than one trillion dollars and is expected to rise even more. Of course, part of this is due to inflation and part to a growing population. For a better perspective, check the bottom line in Exhibit 6-1, which gives the inflation-corrected per capita debt in the United States.

We break down the total credit outstanding into categories in Exhibit 6-2. Today, installment debt repayment takes almost 15 percent of disposable personal income.

WHY BORROW?

The reason most of us borrow is very simple. Say, for example, you want to buy an automobile. Now, you are not buying an automobile per

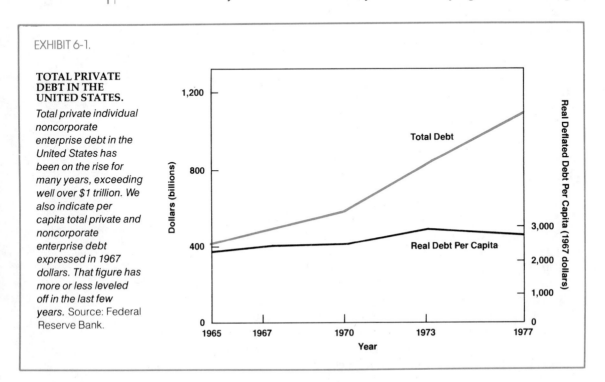

EXHIBIT 6-1.

TOTAL PRIVATE DEBT IN THE UNITED STATES.

Total private individual noncorporate enterprise debt in the United States has been on the rise for many years, exceeding well over $1 trillion. We also indicate per capita total private and noncorporate enterprise debt expressed in 1967 dollars. That figure has more or less leveled off in the last few years. Source: Federal Reserve Bank.

se but the *services* from that automobile for each day, week, month, and year you will own it. In fact, what is really important to you is the cost per-service-flow per-period. In other words, what does it cost you per month to operate that Ford, as compared with that VW or Toyota? What will it cost you per month or per year to buy a new car instead of keeping your old one? Cars are sometimes called **consumer durables,** as are houses, TVs, stereos, and other goods that last a relatively long time. You do not consume them immediately; rather, you consume the services from the durables over a period of time.

Now, when you go to the movies, you consume that movie during the hour and a half or two you are there, and you pay for it when you

EXHIBIT 6-2.

CREDIT BREAKDOWN

	BILLIONS OF DOLLARS	PERCENT OF TOTAL
TOTAL CREDIT (NONMORTGAGE) OUTSTANDING	216.3	100
BY TYPE OF HOLDER		
Commercial Banks	105.7	48.9
Finance Companies	44.1	20.4
Credit Unions	37.2	17.2
Retailers	20.1	9.3
Other	9.2	4.2
BY TYPE OF CREDIT		
Auto	78.0	36.1
Mobile Home	15.0	6.9
Home Improvement	13.0	6.0
Revolving Credit (Credit Cards)	18.0	8.3
All Other	92.3	42.7

consume it. When you go out to dinner, you eat a meal, pay for it on the spot, and that is the end of it. When you consume things and pay for them at the same time, you are synchronizing the payment for the good or service with the rate at which you consume it. This, then, is a reason for borrowing: *You want to synchronize the payments for the services you are consuming from a consumer durable, such as an automobile, with the services themselves.* Therefore, you do not feel obliged to pay for the car with cash because you will be using it over a certain number of years. So you decide to purchase the automobile on credit. You decide, in other words, to borrow. *When you borrow, then, you synchronize your cash outlay to correspond more or less with the* service flow *from the good.*

DON'T BE FOOLED BY SAVINGS AND LOAN ADS

An astute savings and loan association once ran an ad in some national magazines. The ad pointed out that if you were to save for thirty-six months and buy a $5,000 car with the savings, you would have had to save only $4,600, the rest being made up by the interest you received over the three years. On the other hand, the ad pointed out, if you bought the car immediately and paid for it over thirty-six months, not only would you not receive interest on your savings, but you would have to pay a finance charge on the installment debt. Thus, the total price of the car might be $5,800, considerably more than $4,600. The conclusion, according to the savings and loan association: It is better to save now and buy later than to buy now and go into debt.

Is anything wrong with the reasoning in that ad? Yes, it omitted a crucial point: During the three years in which you saved, you would not be enjoying the services of the car or of the other goods you could buy. Most people do not want to wait that long. They would prefer to have the services of the car immediately and pay the finance charges in order to do so.

The finance charge is a payment for using someone else's money so that you can consume and that other person—the saver—cannot. You have decided that the implicit utility you get per service flow of whatever you buy is greater than the interest payments due your creditor in order to get the total amount of money to buy the goods now. No moral judgment need be passed here; it is simply a question of comparing costs and benefits. The benefit of borrowing is having purchasing power today; the cost is whatever you have to pay in finance charges, which may be 18 percent a year or more. Obviously, if the cost were zero, you would borrow as much as you could. Then you could buy everything you wanted today and pay back whatever you owed when you felt like it.

SOURCES OF CREDIT

There are numerous sources of credit. The following are a few of the more frequently used.

Commercial Banks

The most obvious place to go for credit is a commercial bank. Today, the personal loan departments of commercial banks make almost 60 percent of all loans for automobile purchases and almost one-third of all loans for other consumer goods. Banks often assume considerable personal debt because the place of purchase—for example, a car dealer—makes an arrangement whereby the bank takes over the loan.

Sales Finance Companies

Sales finance companies buy installment credit from retail merchants; this way, retailers sell the risk involved in loaning money. For example, a finance company may take over the title to the car you bought. It collects a monthly or weekly payment from you and hands over the title to the car when you have finished the payments. Finance companies supply almost 30 percent of all automobile credit and account for about 35 percent of all personal loans. An example of this type of finance company is General Motors Acceptance Corporation (GMAC).

Consumer Finance Companies

Consumer finance companies are loan companies that make small loans to consumers at relatively high rates of interest. These are the loan companies you hear advertised on radio and TV. They are the largest source of installment cash loans—that is, loans that consumers obtain for purposes other than direct purchase of durable goods. There are perhaps 25,000 licensed consumer finance offices in America today. Some examples are Household Finance Corporation (HFC) and Beneficial Finance.

Credit Unions

Credit unions are consumer cooperative agencies that are chartered by various states and the federal government. You must be a member of a credit union in order to use it. Teachers generally have their own credit unions, as do workers in large unions or companies. Credit unions account for about 13 percent of all consumer installment credit.

Loans on Your Life Insurance

If you have a life insurance policy with a cash (as opposed to face) value (whole or straight life, usually), then you may be able to obtain a relatively low-cost loan on your life insurance policy. (Various life insurance policies will be discussed in Chapter 9.) Usually you pay something less than 10 percent for a loan on the value of your policy. You cannot be turned down for a loan from your insurance company, and no questions are asked about the use of the money (because you're borrowing your own). Your credit rating has nothing to do with whether or not you get the loan. You can take as long as you wish to repay. In fact, you need not repay at all if you choose. However, whenever the policy becomes payable, either because it matures or its owner dies, any outstanding loan plus interest is deducted from the amount of the insurance claim that the company must pay. Hence, any loan you take out reduces your insurance protection.

Credit Cards

Today, more than 50 percent of all families have at least one nongasoline credit card, and fully 25 percent have three or more. You are probably familiar with the most widely known of these—American Express, Master Charge, VISA (BankAmericard), Diners Club, Carte Blanche, and Chargex. About 6,000 banks now offer Master Charge, and 4,000 offer VISA. Not everyone uses credit cards for credit; some consumers prefer credit cards for recordkeeping and convenience reasons. Many cardholders pay *all* balances due each month, thereby avoiding finance charges and gaining, in effect, an interest-free loan during the "float" period.

Oil Company Cards

Approximately one-half of adults carry one or more oil company credit cards. These are offered by Exxon, Shell, Texaco, and most other major (and even minor) oil companies in the United States.

Airline and Auto Rental Cards

Many major airlines offer credit cards that can be used to charge airline travel tickets and other accommodations for which reservations were made when air travel tickets were purchased. Most major auto rental companies, such as Hertz, Avis, Budget, and National, have their own credit cards, which usually cover only auto rentals.

Retail Stores

An increasingly large number of retail outlets offer some form of credit to their customers. Virtually all major department stores—Sears Roebuck and Co., J.C. Penney Co., Marshall Field, Montgomery Ward and Co.—offer several types of credit arrangements to customers. These stores provide store credit cards, which are similar to Master Charge and VISA.

Other Sources

Savings and loan associations sometimes give loans for other than home purchases. "Loan sharks", who loan money at interest rates that greatly exceed legal limits, exist in many large cities. Loan sharks usually will loan money to individuals who cannot otherwise obtain it because they lack sufficient collateral and/or a good credit record. Friends and relatives can often be a source of credit, but the cost of borrowing from them may be very high in psychological terms. Pawn shops are a source of credit to some individuals, who use the pawned items as a type of collateral.

NONCREDIT CARDS—PAY CASH AND PAY LESS

The merchant who accepts a credit card generally has to pay the credit card company a fee of up to 8 percent. Moreover, the merchant doesn't get the money for the item until the credit slips are turned in and processed. Thus, if you pay cash, you save the merchant money. And there is a way in which some of that savings is passed on to you.

The Fair Credit Billing Act, which went into effect in October 1975, allows merchants to give customers up to a 5 percent discount for paying cash. These merchants are not, however, obliged to grant such discounts. Before this legislation was enacted, merchants risked losing a credit card company contract if they offered such cash discounts. In fact, Consumers Union brought suit against the American Express Company, which prohibited merchants using its charge facilities to offer cash discounts.

There are even "cash" cards you can obtain now, which, when shown to member merchants, allow you to obtain a "cash" discount. In the mid-1970s, there were at least three cash card companies—Equity Club International, Savers Clubs of America, United International Club, Inc.—with a total membership of about half a million.

WHAT IT COSTS TO BORROW

You are all aware that borrowing costs money. But why must you pay to borrow? Because someone else is giving up purchasing power, or command over goods and services today. When other people give up command over goods and services today, they must be compensated, and they are usually compensated with what we call *interest*. Ask yourself if you would be willing to loan, say, $100 to your friend, with the understanding that the loan will be paid back in ten years—but with *no* interest. Would you do it, even if you were sure of getting the money back? Probably not. While your friend spent the $100, you would have to sacrifice what it would have bought for you. Most people will not make this sacrifice for no reward.

INFLATION AND INTEREST RATES

There is a definite relationship between rising prices and high interest rates. When prices rise, interest rates will have an inflationary premium tacked onto them. Suppose, for example, that you are a banker who has been loaning money at 5 percent a year for the last twenty years, during which time there has been no inflation. That 5 percent interest you have been charging is the *real* rate of interest you are receiving. It just covers your costs and gives you a normal profit for your lending activities. Now prices are rising at 5 percent a year, and you expect they will rise at that rate indefinitely. If someone asks to borrow money, how much would you want to loan at the 5 percent rate of interest you have always charged?

Imagine that someone wants to borrow $1,000 for a year. At the end of the year, with an inflation rate of 5 percent, the actual purchasing power of that $1,000 paid back to you will be only $950. If you only ask for 5 percent, or fifty dollars in interest payments, you will just be compensated for the erosive effect of inflation on the value of the money you lent. You will, therefore, want to tack on an inflationary premium to the real interest rate you had been charging when there was no inflation and none was anticipated. Hence, in periods of fully anticipated inflation, we find, on average, the inflationary premium tacked on everywhere. It is not surprising, then, that during an inflationary period when prices are rising at 5 percent a year, interest rates would be 10 percent, as illustrated in Exhibit 6-3.

Inflationary premiums have focused attention on the problem of usury laws. There have always been restrictions on interest rates, both for the lender and the borrower. Yet everyone seems to think that moneylenders have some unique monopolistic power over others in the economy. Indeed, moneylenders have been condemned so long that dominant ethnic groups have historically shunned the profession, leaving it to minority groups. During the Middle Ages, the Catholic Church made laws against *usury,* or the lending of money at "unreasonable" rates.

THE WHY AND WHERE OF USURY LAWS

Today, many states have laws against charging borrowers interest rates that exceed a specified limit. The persistence of legislation affecting the lending of money makes it clear that a widespread suspicion about the moneylender still lingers. Many individuals favor limiting the amount of interest that can be charged on a consumer loan. However, since no action is cost-free, you should be aware of both the benefits and the costs of usury laws.

EXHIBIT 6-3. **THE "REAL" RATE OF INTEREST**

The rate of interest you are paying on a $100 loan for one year	10%
The rate of inflation (loss in value of money) this year	5%
The difference between the rate of interest you are paying and the loss in the value of dollars you will pay back	5%

So 5 percent is the real rate of interest you pay when you are charged 10 percent on a loan and the rate of inflation is 5 percent.

Selling credit is no different from selling anything else. If usury laws are valid, then so are government controls on every single price in the economy. Let's look at some of the unpredicted effects of the usury laws that went into effect in the state of Washington.

Washington State Usury Laws—An Example

Prior to 1968 in the state of Washington, interest on consumer loans from the credit card companies—BankAmericard and Master Charge, and so on—as well as on revolving credit loans from the big stores— Sears and others—were generally 18 percent per year, or 1.5 percent per month. Many consumer advocates and concerned citizens felt that, because this rate of interest was so high, poor people could not afford credit. At that time, for example, commercial bank loans to some customers were going for as low as 9 percent. Poor people, who obviously could not get bank loans at that low interest rate, supposedly were being discriminated against and had to forego the benefits of "buying on time." A movement was begun to pass legislation against such usurious interest rates. In 1968, a motion was put on the ballot to set the maximum legal interest on consumer loans at 12 percent instead of 18 percent. It was felt that lowering the interest rate would benefit those who could not afford the higher rate. The measure passed, and all the credit card companies and stores in the state were forced to lower their rates to 1 percent per month, or 12 percent per year.

What results would you predict? Obviously, cheaper credit. But it turned out that this credit was not necessarily given to people whom the formulators of this new law had in mind. Two professors, John J. Wheatley and Guy G. Gordon, did a study[1] of the effects of the law a year after it became operative. Their main conclusion was startling: Low-income people, who are marginal credit risks, seem to have suffered most from the enactment of the law because of the general tightening of credit.

What, in fact, had creditors done? They raised some prices, adjusted their credit practices and merchandise assortment, and raised charges or instituted new charges on other services, all in an effort to make up the lost revenues from their credit accounts. Both before and after the legal maximum limit was put on interest rates, there was a tremendous amount of competition for consumers' credit dollars. According to one study of the profits of credit institutions, the price being charged did not lead to above-normal profits; that is, the price reflected only the costs of providing credit plus some normal rate of return or profit to the companies. (The results of the study by Wheatley and Gordon confirm this supposition.) Creditors had to make up the lost revenues somehow. One way was to raise prices. Another way, of course, was to eliminate risky debtors.

---

[1]"Regulating the Price of Consumer Credit," *Journal of Marketing*, Volume 35, October 1971, pp. 21-28.

A further study by R.F. Sauter and O.C. Walker, Jr.[2] shows that "the largest proportion of retailers expect to react to interest ceilings by becoming more selective in granting credit." This reaction demonstrates the retailers' desire to reduce costs and increase profits. Who is burdened by this reaction? Obviously, low-income and other "marginal" customers who are forced to forego credit purchases and turn to more costly sources of funds, such as small-loan companies, loan sharks, and pawnbrokers.[3]

Ways To Raise Interest Rates

A number of banks have started charging implicitly higher interest rates without actually changing the stated interest rate. New York CitiBank, a major issuer of Master Charge cards, began charging card holders a fee of fifty cents during those months in which the accounts were paid in full and for which no interest was charged. (This charge was finally dropped in 1978.) Some banks in Minnesota and West Virginia are charging an annual fee for the VISA cards they issue. New billing procedures have been instituted by still other banks, in which the finance charges begin on the day each purchase is posted to the account rather than on the monthly billing date. And, finally, some banks have reduced the number of days they permit for credit card accounts to be paid in full without being charged interest. Seattle First National Bank, for example, reduced the time period from twenty-five to twenty-one days.

TRUTH-IN-LENDING

The Truth-in-Lending Act, which is Title I of the Consumer Credit Protection Act of 1968, is essentially a disclosure law. Most kinds of installment debt now must be properly labeled so that the consumer knows exactly what he or she is paying. The bill had a long history. Former Senator Paul Douglas had introduced a similar bill in the 86th, 87th, and 88th Congresses; he called his bill "A Disclosure of Finance Charges in Connection with the Extension of Credit." The testimony and exhibits presented at the hearings before the Senate Committee on Banking and Currency in 1960, 1961, and 1963 filled nearly 4,000 pages; hearings in 1967 added another 1,200 pages. Because lending institutions, retailers, and their trade associations strongly opposed these bills, they were

---

[2]"Retailers' Reactions to Interest Limitation Laws—Additional Evidence," *Journal of Marketing*, Volume 36, April 1972, pp. 58-61.

[3]The evidence continues to support this contention. A study by Donald F. Greer— "Rate Ceilings and Loan Turn-Downs" (*Journal of Finance*, December 1975, pp. 1376-83)—suggests that the impact of low-rate ceilings falls heavily on marginal credit risks who rely on consumer finance companies for credit. Using a sample of forty-eight states, Greer found that a larger percentage of those who requested credit were rejected in those states that had low legal rate ceilings on interest rates compared with other states.

blocked for many years. When President Johnson signed the Act, he stated succinctly, "As a matter of fair play to the consumer, the cost of credit should be disclosed fully, simply, and clearly."

How does a 5¾ percent discount rate compare to a 6 percent add-on rate? Is one percent per month on the unpaid balance a better deal than either of the two above? And what are finder's fees, points, and service charges? These kinds of questions, couched in terms typically used to describe credit plans prior to the enactment of Truth-in-Lending, provide an obvious reason for the legislation. Prior to 1969, the majority of consumers were unable to understand credit terminology or the many methods used for rate calculations. Therefore, they were poorly equipped to make intelligent comparisons among types of credit plans or among competitors.

The Congressional purpose of the Act is "to insure a meaningful disclosure of credit terms so that the consumer will be able to compare more readily the various credit terms available to him and avoid the uninformed use of credit." The Act attempts to accomplish this purpose in several ways. It requires that all the various terms used to describe the dollar cost of credit, such as interest, points, and so on, be described and disclosed under one common label, finance charge. Likewise, it abolishes all the various terms previously used to describe the cost of credit in percentage terms, such as discount rates, add-ons, and the like, and prescribes a uniform method of computation of a single rate known as the annual percentage rate (APR). (We will see, however, that there are still problems with computing this rate.)

The Truth-in-Lending Act does not cover credit extended to corporations, trusts, governments, and partnerships; to private loans among friends and families; or to loans for business purposes. The extension of credit must be for $25,000 or less, unless it is secured by real property, such as in a typical home mortgage with no dollar limit.

The Truth-in-Lending Act also grants the consumer/borrower a right of rescission (cancellation) for certain credit contracts. Section 125 of the Act gives the consumer three business days to rescind a credit transaction that results or may result in a lien on his or her home or on any real property that is used or expected to be used as his or her principal residence. The right of rescission is designed to allow additional time to reconsider using the residence as security for credit. However, this right of rescission does not apply to first mortgages on homes. Exhibit 6-4 shows a typical "cooling off" contract.

The Truth-in-Lending Act also regulates the advertising of consumer credit. One of the primary purposes of the Act's advertising requirements is to eliminate "come-on" credit ads. For example, if any one important credit term is mentioned in an advertisement—down payment or monthly payment—all other important terms also must be stated.

A 1970 amendment to the Act provides federal regulations on the use of credit cards. This amendment prohibits the unsolicited distribution of new credit cards and establishes a maximum fifty dollar limit on liability for the unauthorized use of such cards. That is, the owner of a lost or stolen card that has been used illegally by another person cannot be made liable to pay more than fifty dollars on its illegal purchases. The owner has the responsibility of notifying the credit card company of the loss or theft. The companies often provide self-addressed, stamped cards to speed this notification.

ENFORCEMENT

A relatively novel scheme of administrative enforcement has been created, whereby the Federal Reserve Board is given broad authority to write and administer regulations implementing the Truth-in-Lending Act. The Board's regulations are spread among nine federal agencies. Generally, those federal agencies with pre-existing supervisory author-

---

EXHIBIT 6-4. **NOTICE OF CANCELLATION**

(enter date of transaction)

_____
(date)

You may cancel this transaction, without any penalty or obligation, within 3 business days from the above date.

If you cancel, any property traded in, any payments made by you under the contract or sale, and any negotiable instrument executed by you will be returned within 10 business days following receipt by the seller of your cancellation notice, and any security interest arising out of the transaction will be canceled.

If you cancel, you must make available to the seller at your residence, in substantially as good condition as when received, any goods delivered to you under this contract or sale; or you may, if you wish, comply with the instructions of the seller regarding the return shipment of the goods at the seller's expense and risk.

If you do make the goods available to the seller and the seller does not pick them up within 20 days of the date of your notice of cancellation, you may retain or dispose of the goods without any further obligation. If you fail to make the goods available to the seller, or if you agree to return the goods to the seller and fail to do so, then you remain liable for performance of all obligations under the contract.

To cancel this transaction, mail or deliver a signed and dated copy of this cancellation notice or any other written notice, or send a telegram, to

_____
(name of seller)

at _____ not later than midnight of_____
(address of seller's place of business)   (date)

I hereby cancel this transaction.

_____   _____
(date)   (buyer's signature)

ity over a particular group of creditors were also given Truth-in-Lending enforcement responsibility over them. For example, the National Credit Union Administration is responsible for federally chartered credit unions, and the Federal Home Loan Bank Board is responsible for federally chartered savings and loan institutions. Other enforcers include the Comptroller of the Currency, the Federal Deposit Insurance Corporation, the Department of Agriculture, the Civil Aeronautics Board, and the Interstate Commerce Commission. Enforcement of all remaining creditors not covered by the above agencies falls to the Federal Trade Commission. The FTC shoulders most of the federal enforcement effort. In fact, it estimates that its responsibility extends to nearly one million creditors, including all retail creditors and finance companies.

Obviously, the FTC would have great difficulty enforcing the Act against *all* local retailers throughout the nation. Hence, the Truth-in-Lending Act provides that any state enacting legislation similar to Truth-in-Lending and providing for "adequate" enforcement may apply to the Federal Reserve Board for an exemption from the federal act and thereby obtain authority to enforce its own statutes instead.

REVOLVING CREDIT

When the Truth-in-Lending Act was applied to revolving credit contracts, a battle was waged in Congress. Revolving credit, or open-ended credit, is a growing part of total consumer credit. Many department stores allow revolving charge accounts, which have three main characteristics:

1   The customer may pay the balance in full or in installments.

2   The creditor permits the customer to make purchases (or loans) at irregular intervals, usually by means of a credit card.

3   The creditor usually computes the finance charge on the *outstanding* balance.

The last aspect of an open-ended credit account has bothered consumers and caused trouble for the Truth-in-Lending Act. Creditors used the following different techniques to compute finance charges on revolving credit accounts:

1   **Previous balance method:** Here the creditor computes a finance charge on the previous month's balance, even if it has been paid.

2   **Average daily balance:** The finance charge is applied to the sum of the actual amounts outstanding each day during the billing period divided by the number of days in that period. Payments are credited on the exact date of payment.

3   **Adjusted balance method:** Finance charges are assessed on the balance after deducting payments and credits.

4   **Past-due balance:** No finance charge is assessed if full payment is received within a certain period, such as twenty-five days after the closing date of the last statement.

It is, therefore, important to know which method is used in assessing the finance charge you pay, because the different methods can result in finance charges that vary enormously. Exhibit 6-5 shows the differences among the previous balance method, the adjusted balance method, and the average daily balance method. The same monthly finance charge of 1 percent results in three different annual rates of finance charged, depending on which computational method is used by the creditor. The Truth-in-Lending Act requires that all revolving credit contracts and monthly bills state the "nominal annual percentage rate," which equals twelve times the monthly rate. However, the nominal rate does not tell you the effective, or actual, annual rate. Retailers were given a further concession in one provision in the Truth-in-Lending Act that permits them to exclude, from the disclosure of finance charges, a certain minimum monthly charge on small, unpaid revolving account balances.

EXHIBIT 6-5.

DIFFERING RESULTANT FINANCE CHARGES

METHOD	OPENING BALANCE	PAYMENTS	MONTHLY FINANCE CHARGE	ACTUAL FINANCE CHARGE	ACTUAL MONTHLY RATE	ACTUAL ANNUAL RATE
Previous Balance Method	$300	$100	1%	.01 x $300 = $3	1½%	18%
Adjusted Balance Method	$300	$100	1%	.01 x $200 = $2	1%	12%
Average Daily Balance	$300	$100	1%	.01 x $250 = $2.5	1.25%	15%

Because the Truth-in-Lending Act does not actually give protection, only information, it is a disclosure act. But information can be valuable protection. It allows you, a consumer looking for credit, to shop around, to see exactly what you are paying, and to know exactly what you are committed to.

Exhibit 6-6 shows a typical disclosure statement. The Truth-in-Lending Act requires that an accurate assessment of the annual percentage rate be given; you should look at this (circled here) when you compare the prices of credit offered by various dealers and companies. In addition, you may want to look at the finance charge, which is the total number of dollars you pay, either directly or in the form of deferred

EXHIBIT 6-6.

**A TYPICAL
DISCLOSURE
STATEMENT**

ACCOUNT
NUMBER

SEARS, ROEBUCK AND CO.
DISCLOSURE STATEMENT

Sales Check No._____   Date _____ 19____

DESCRIPTION OF MERCHANDISE

☐ Easy Payment Plan

☐ Modernizing Credit Plan

OFFICE USE ONLY (Code 4 Sales)	
NO. OF MONTHS	MONTHLY PAYMENT

CASH PRICE			
CASH DOWN PAYMENT			
UNPAID BALANCE OF CASH PRICE - AMOUNT FINANCED			
FINANCE CHARGE			
DEFERRED PAYMENT PRICE			
TOTAL OF PAYMENTS — THIS SALE			

This purchase is payable in installments pursuant to my Sears Easy Payment Plan—Modernizing Credit Plan Retail Installment Contract and Security Agreement.

Beginning _____ , I will pay $ _____ per month for _____ months and a final monthly payment of $ _____ until the amount financed and the finance charge for this purchase are fully paid.

If the **FINANCE CHARGE** exceeds **$5.00**, the **ANNUAL PERCENTAGE RATE** is _____ %

In accordance with my Sears Easy Payment Plan-Modernizing Credit Plan Retail Installment Contract and Security Agreement, a subsequent purchase may change the number and amount of my monthly payments, the amount of the Finance Charge and the Annual Percentage Rate of this purchase. Any such change will appear on my next monthly billing statement.

A copy of my sales check is attached hereto and incorporated by reference. Ownership of the merchandise described in such attached sales check remains in Sears until paid for in full.

If I pay in full in advance, any unearned finance charge will be rebated under the Rule of 78, after deducting a charge of $5.00.

11078-202 (F11363 WW) Rev. 12/72

payments on a purchase, to borrow the money. These total finance charges include all the so-called carrying charges that are sometimes tacked on to a retail installment contract, plus such things as once-and-for-all "set up" charges (a fee for the paper work) and credit life insurance. These all contribute to your cost of having purchasing power today instead of waiting; of having command over goods and services right now; and of taking that command away from someone else. Your annual percentage interest rate, expressed as a percentage of the total amount borrowed, may be alarmingly high.

ELIMINATING CREDIT DISCRIMINATION

Since October 1975, the Equal Credit Opportunity Act has made it illegal to discriminate on the basis of sex and marital status in the granting of credit. Regulations pursuant to the Act, issued by the Federal Reserve Board, prohibit:

1   Demanding information on the credit applicant's childbearing intentions or birth control practices.
2   Requiring cosignatures on loans when such requirements do not apply to all qualified applicants.
3   Denying credit solely on the basis of sex or marital status.
4   Terminating or changing the conditions of credit solely on the basis of a change in marital status.
5   Ignoring alimony and child support payments as regular income in assessing the credit worthiness of the applicant.

Basically, the Equal Credit Opportunity Act reaffirms a woman's right to keep credit in her own name, rather than that of her husband or her former husband. Women who wish to establish their credit history are advised to do the following:

1   Open separate checking and savings accounts.
2   Start an active credit history, assuming you qualify for and can afford it.
3   Open a charge account at a retail store. When applying, list only your own salary, not that of your spouse.
4   Require credit account grantors and credit bureaus to report credit information in your own name, not your spouse's.
5   Apply for a bank credit card and use it wisely.
6   Finally, take out a small bank or credit union loan and repay it on time. Even if you don't need it, this would expedite establishing your own credit reliability.

PROBLEMS WITH INSTALLMENT CONTRACTS

Individuals who sign installment contracts when they purchase furniture, appliances, and the like often find themselves in a bind. In many cases, the merchant who sells an item on an installment contract promptly resells that contract to a finance company. This type of plan is known as the holder-in-due-course doctrine. Until recently, the holder in such a doctrine was entitled to continue to collect payments on that product—even if it was defective because he or she was not the original seller. When the holder-in-due-course doctrine applied, you could not stop payment because of dissatisfaction with the product.

A new Federal Trade Commission regulation on credit buying now gives consumers (as opposed to commercial buyers) a defense against this practice. Installment contracts must prominently note that "the holder of this consumer-credit contract is subject to all claims and defenses which the debtor could assert against the seller." Imagine that you bought a set of encyclopedias from a door-to-door salesperson. You agree to a specified monthly payment for a certain number of years and sign on the dotted line. When the encyclopedias are delivered, you are satisfied with your purchase. Four months later, however, the binding is falling apart on half of them. You obviously have purchased a faulty product. According to the recent FTC rule, the finance company that possesses the installment contract on which you are paying is just as responsible for the faulty encyclopedias as is the original seller.

Note that credit cards are not covered under the new FTC ruling. However, they are covered under the Fair Credit Billing Act, which eliminates the holder-in-due-course doctrine in credit card transactions of more than fifty dollars and within 100 miles of the card holder's home.

THE FAIR CREDIT BILLING ACT

The Fair Credit Billing Act became effective in October 1975. Under the rules of that act, you can withhold payment until a dispute over a faulty product that you purchased and paid for by credit card is resolved. It is up to the credit card issuer, such as American Express or Master Charge, to intervene and attempt a settlement between you and the seller. You do not have unlimited rights to stop payment. You must exercise a good-faith effort to get satisfaction from the seller before you do so. But the rules seem to favor the consumer. You don't even have to notify the credit card company that you are cutting off payment. You just wait for the company to act. However, it is advisable to let the company know what you are doing. Ultimately, you can be sued by the credit card company if no agreement is reached.

Several other rules were established by the Fair Credit Billing Act. When you suspect an error in your bill, the card company must investigate and suspend payments until it does so. You simply write the card company within sixty days of getting the bill, briefly explaining the circumstances and why you think there is an error. It is a good idea to include copies (not the originals) of the sales slips at issue. Under the law, the company must acknowledge your letter within thirty days and resolve the dispute within ninety days of receiving your letter. During that period, you don't have to pay the amount in dispute or any minimum payments on that amount. And, further, your creditor cannot charge you finance charges during that period for unpaid balances in dispute. It can't even close your account. If it turns out that there was no error, the creditor can then attempt to collect finance charges.

PRACTICAL APPLICATIONS

HOW TO COPE WITH
THE CREDIT MAZE

WHEN SHOULD YOU BORROW?

Some personal finance books give you cut-and-dried formulas for when and how much you should borrow. It is not unusual to find a financial adviser telling consumers that they should borrow only for major purchases. Just about everyone who buys a house automatically assumes that it is respectable to borrow, for few of us are in a position to pay the full cost of a house in one amount. Since we know that the housing services we consume per month represent a very small part of the total price (because houses last so long), it seems unwise to spend all that cash. So we take out a mortgage. The same holds for cars, especially new ones. A car is such a large expense that few of us consider paying cash for it; in fact, 71 percent of all new automobiles are purchased on credit.

But what about other items? Is it financially wise to buy a stereo on credit? Some financial advisers say yes, and some say no. Is it all right to buy furniture on credit? Again, yes and no. Of course, for clothes and food, most financial advisers are adamant about the desirability of paying cash.

A Dollar Is a Dollar Is a Dollar

When you think about it, the reasoning behind such firm rules is pretty shaky. Gertrude Stein once wrote that "a rose is a rose is a rose," and so, too, a dollar is a dollar is a dollar. Does it matter what you say each dollar is going to buy? Certainly you can't earmark each one. If you make $100 a week and spend $10 for clothes, $50 for food and lodging, and the rest on entertainment, do you know which dollar you used for "essentials"—food, lodging, and clothes—and which you used for the "nonessential"—entertainment? Obviously you don't, because you can't tell one dollar from another.

Does it matter if you say you are going to use credit to buy your clothes and pay cash for your entertainment? Obviously not. What is important is to decide what percentage of your anticipated income you are willing to set aside for fixed payments to repay loans. You should care about the total commitment made to creditors, making sure you have not overcommitted yourself. Exhibit 6-7 is an example of what may be "safe" for you.

Values Count, Too

Value judgments enter in, too. Some people consider certain types of consumption activities frivolous and feel you should never borrow money to engage in them. But it is difficult to determine which activities are frivolous and which are not. *You* may deem it absolutely essential for your mental health to spend a large part of your income on entertainment. Someone else may say that you are wasting your money, that entertainment is frivolous consumption that does not justify borrowing. Likewise, some people find it so "essential" to take vacations that they may be willing to go into debt to do so. This activity may not be frivolous to them, but to an outsider it may appear to be.

Thus, if we judge each other's behavior, we can never tell whether the other's purchases are superfluous or not. Nor can we tell whether the other is borrowing for the "right" kinds of things or not. Again, what is important is that the total amount of indebtedness relative to a person's income not be excessive. An individual or a family is always faced with a scarcity constraint. What happens in the future depends on what you do today. Excessive borrowing, for whatever reason, cannot lead to long-run financial success and stability. One's financial chickens eventually come home to roost.

In any event, you will always face a maximum amount of indebtedness allowed by creditors. And they have fairly simple rules for determining what your borrowing capacity is. Remember, however, that reliance on lending agencies to limit your borrowing is a mistake: you, the lendee, should be re-

EXHIBIT 6-7.

**DETERMINING A
SAFE DEBT LOAD**

ITEM	AMOUNT
Car payment	$
Installment dept (department stores, etc.)	
1.	
2.	
3.	
4.	
Loan payments due	
1.	
2.	
3.	
4.	
Others	
1.	
2.	
Overdue accounts (e.g. phone, electricity, etc.)_____	
TOTAL OUTSTANDING	$

Having thereby determined your short-term debt load, you are in a position to determine whether you want to extend it. Below are two methods by which you might decide:

METHOD #1

10% of monthly income (after) taxes) _____

multiply by 18 _____

SAFE DEBT LOAD RESULTS (principal *plus* interest) _____

METHOD #2

Indicate your annual income after taxes _____

Subtract your annual expenditures on housing, food, and clothing _____

Divide by 3

SAFE DEBT LOAD RESULTS _____

sponsible for your own limits. Creditors check your credit worthiness to protect themselves, not you.

WHAT IS THE MAXIMUM YOU *CAN* BORROW?

If you go to a bank or a credit company and ask for a loan, the loan officer probably will require you to fill out a form on which you list your **liabilities** and your **assets.** This enables the credit officer to estimate your **net worth.** Exhibit 6-8 shows, in simplified terms, how to calculate your net worth. Exhibit 6-9 shows the kind of form you would fill out for a bank loan application. You must list all your assets—whatever you own—and all your liabilities—whatever you owe. The difference is

---

EXHIBIT 6-8.   **DETERMINING YOUR NET WORTH**

ESTIMATED AMOUNTS, END OF THIS YEAR

ASSETS
    House (including furniture)—market value   _____
    Car(s)—resale value   _____
    Life insurance cash value   _____
    Bonds, securities—market value   _____
    Cash on hand, in checking and savings accounts   _____
    Other (for example, stereo, cameras, land, etc. at market value)   _____
TOTAL ASSETS   _____

LIABILITIES
    Mortgage   _____
    Loans   _____
    Other   _____
    TOTAL LIABILITIES   _____

NET WORTH   **December 31, 19____**   _____

An annual net worth statement may help you and/or your family to keep track of financial progress from year to year. Essentially, your net worth is an indication of how much wealth you actually own. We generally find that young people have low net worths—or even negative net worths: that is, they owe more than they own—because they are anticipating having higher income in the future. As individuals and families get further down the road, their net worth increases steadily only to start falling again, usually, when retirement age approaches and the income flow slows down or stops completely, thereby forcing the retired person or couple to draw on past accumulated savings. The above very simplified statement of family net worth can be easily filled out. Just make sure that you include all of your assets and all of your liabilities. Assets are anything that you own, and liabilities are anything that you owe.

EXHIBIT 6-9.   TYPICAL NET WORTH STATEMENT

(Personal Financial Statement) .... **OFFICE**

Name ....   **Address** ....

Business ....   **City** ....   **Zip** ....
Social Security Numbers:
Borrower: ....   **Spouse:** ....   **Statement as of:** ....

ASSETS				LIABILITIES			
Cash on hand and in banks.............				Notes payable banks:			
U. S. Government Securities—Schedule 1..........				Secured			
Stocks and Bonds—Schedule 1..................				Unsecured			
Accounts receivable				Notes payable other............			
Notes receivable				Accounts and bills payable........			
Cash surrender value life insurance...........				Accrued taxes and interest............			
Face Value $.......				Mortgages payable on real estate—Schedule 2...			
Real estate—Schedule 2.........							
Automobiles				Security Agreements			
Other assets—itemize				Other debts—itemize			
....				....			
....				....			
....				....			
....				....			
....				Total liabilities			
....				Net worth			
TOTAL ASSETS				TOTAL LIABILITIES AND NET WORTH....			

SOURCE OF INCOME				GENERAL INFORMATION
Salary				Married (name of spouse) ....
Bonus and commissions............				Single ....
Dividends				Number of children...
Real estate income............				Other dependents ....
Other income				Are any assets pledged?..............
....				Defendant in any suits or legal actions? ....
....				Personal bank accounts carried at...............
....				Life Insurance - face amount, company, beneficiaries......
....				....
TOTAL				

DO YOU HAVE A WILL? YES____ NO____

CONTINGENT LIABILITIES

Endorser or comaker...
Legal claims ....
Federal Income Taxes:
  1. Do you owe any Federal Tax for years prior to the current year?   Yes ☐ No ☐ Amount $.................
  2. Are there any unpaid Federal Tax Assessments outstanding against you? Yes ☐ No ☐ Amount $.................
Other ....

your net worth. Obviously, if your net worth is negative, you will have difficulty getting a loan from anyone, unless you can show that your expected income in the immediate future will be extremely large.

You still do not know what your maximum credit limit is. That, of course, depends on the loan officer's assessment of your financial position. This will be a function of your net worth, your income, your relative indebtedness, and how "regular" your situation is. Regularity can mean different things to different people, but, in general, it means the following:

1. You have been working regularly for a long period and, therefore, have been receiving regular income.

2. Your family situation is stable.

3. You have regularly paid off your debts on time.

Or your credit worthiness can be measured by the three C's that loan officers use as a guide to lending:

1. Capacity to pay back;

2. Character; and

3. Capital or collateral that you own.

Loan officers may appear to discriminate against people with unstable living situations—that is, those who have unstable jobs and unstable family situations. That may or may not be true, depending on your definition of discrimination. But you can be sure that a loan officer is supposed to make decisions that maximize the profits for his or her company. At the going interest rate, he or she may decide to eliminate people who are high risks. Loans will be refused to people with records that indicate they will not pay off their debts as easily or regularly as those who seem more stable. If you are a credit buyer with an unstable living situation, you may persuade a loan officer not to refuse you by candidly

discussing your problems with him or her and producing a past record of loan repayments that was stable in spite of your unstable situation. Or, alternatively, you could offer to pay a higher interest rate or go to a finance company that will charge you more to compensate for the added risk. You may still be refused credit because of a bad credit rating. Once, there was little you could do about this, but now a new federal law gives you some recourse.

WHAT TO DO WHEN YOU ARE REFUSED CREDIT

The Fair Credit Reporting Act (Title VI of the 1968 Consumer Credit Protection Act) was passed in 1970 and went into effect in 1971. Under this new law, you have recourse when a credit investigating agency gives you a bad rating. Now, the company that refuses to give you credit because of a bad credit rating must give you the name and address of the credit investigating agency it used. The same holds true for an insurance company when you are refused insurance.

The 1971 Act attempts to insure that credit reporting agencies supply information that is equitable and fair to the consumer. The problems that led to passage of the Act were the reporting of incorrect, misleading, or incomplete information, as well as one-sided versions of disputed claims. In addition, many people were concerned about the invasion of privacy involved in the distribution of such reports to those lacking a legitimate business need for them. These reports often contained material about a person's general reputation, personal characteristics or lifestyle, and character.

The Act applies not only to the usual credit bureaus and investigating concerns, but also to finance companies and banks that routinely give out credit information other than that which is developed from their own transactions.

Under the rules of the new law, a credit bureau must disclose to you the "nature and substance of all information" included under your name in its files.

You also have the right to be told the sources of almost all that information. If you discover that the credit bureau has incomplete, misleading, or false information, the Fair Credit Reporting Act requires that the bureau reinvestigate any disputed information "within a reasonable period of time." Of course, the credit bureau is not necessarily going to do it, but you do have the law on your side and can go to court over the issue. In addition, at your request, the credit bureau must send to those companies that received a credit report in the last six months a notice of the elimination of any false information from your credit record. See Exhibit 6-10 for a summary of what can be done.

Even if you have not been rejected for credit, you still have the right to go to a credit bureau and find out what your file contains—perhaps for a nom-inal fee. You also have the right to ask the credit bureau to delete, correct, or investigate items you believe to be fallacious or inaccurate. The credit bureau then has the legal right to charge you for the time it spends correcting any mistakes. Also, the Fair Credit Reporting Act specifically forbids credit bureaus from distributing any adverse information that is more than seven years old. But there are important exceptions. Bankruptcy information can be sent out to your prospective creditors for a full fourteen years. And there is no time limit on any information for loans or life insurance policies of $50,000 or more or for a job application with an annual salary of $20,000 or more. That means that adverse information may be kept in your file and used indefinitely for these purposes.

EXHIBIT 6-10.

WHAT YOU CAN DO TO PROTECT YOURSELF AGAINST UNFAIR REPORTS.

If you are trying to get insurance, credit or a job, you may be subjected to a personal investigation. Under the Fair Credit Reporting Act of 1971–

☐ The company asking for the investigations is supposed to let you know you are being investigated.

☐ You can demand the name and address of the firm hired to do the investigating.

☐ You can demand that the investigating company tell you what its report contains—except for medical information used to determine your eligibility for life insurance.

☐ You cannot require the investigators to reveal the names of neighbors or friends who supplied information.

If the investigation turns up derogatory or inaccurate material, you can—

☐ Demand a recheck.

☐ Require the investigators to take out of your file anything that is inaccurate.

☐ Require them to insert your version of the facts, if the facts remain in dispute.

☐ Sue the investigating firm for damages if negligence on its part resulted in violation of the law which caused you some economic loss —failure to get a job, loss of credit or insurance, or even great personal embarrassment.

☐ Require the company to cease reporting adverse information after it is 7 years old—with the exception of a bankruptcy, which can remain in the file for 14 years.

Problems with the Act

Critics of the 1971 Act have been numerous, and various proposals have been sent to Congress to amend the statute and increase its effectiveness. One of the main criticisms is that consumers cannot obtain a copy of the credit reports or have actual physical access to the files. Moreover, many critics contend that consumers who have asked for information from these agencies have been subjected to evasion, delaying tactics, or exorbitant charges. Many other consumers believe they are not receiving all the information in their files.

The credit reporting agencies have opposed any legislation that would give consumers direct access to the agency files. They argue that they would no longer have any sources of confidential information. Moreover, there would be a substantial increase in the costs of providing accurate credit reports. Some credit bureaus, such as TRW, Inc. give written reports, but in most companies, all the information is on computers. It would be difficult, if not impossible, to give individuals physical access to their own files, although print-outs can sometimes be obtained.

SHOPPING FOR CREDIT

Once you have decided that you want to buy some credit—that is, you want to get some goods now and pay for them later—you should shop around. The Truth-in-Lending Act, which requires a full statement of the annual interest rate charged, makes such shopping easier these days. This is certainly true if you are comparing, say, revolving credit accounts: if the actual annual interest charge (APR) for one is 22½ percent, you know this is not as good a deal as another one at 18 percent.

Things to Watch For

Acceleration clauses. You must be careful when you look at loan agreements because all have various contingency clauses written into them, which may or may not affect you. For example, if

you sign a credit agreement with an **acceleration clause**—meaning that all the debt becomes due immediately if you, the borrower, fail to meet any single payment on the debt—you probably could not pay such a large sum. Obviously, if you could not meet a payment on the debt because you lacked the money, you certainly would be unable to pay off the whole loan at once. The addition of an acceleration clause in a credit agreement increases the probability that whatever you bought on credit will be repossessed.[4]

Add-on clauses. You also want to be aware of what is called an **add-on clause** in installment contracts, particularly when you go shopping for furniture and appliances. An add-on clause essentially makes earlier purchases security for the more recent purchase. Let's say that you buy furniture for your living room from a particular store on an installment contract. Six months later, you decide that you want new furniture for a bedroom. You return to the same store and also buy the bedroom furniture on an installment contract. If there is an add-on clause and you default on the installment contract for the bedroom furniture, you not only can lose that furniture but all the items you purchased for the living room, even if you have paid for that furniture after making the second purchase.

Garnishment. It is also possible for a court order to allow a creditor to attach, or seize, part of your property. Your bank account may be attached and used to discharge any debts. Or your wages may be **garnished.** That is, if a judgment is made against you, your employer is required to withhold wages to pay a creditor. (If this happens often, you may find it hard to keep your job or get another.)

The Federal Garnishment Law, effective July 1, 1970, is part of the Consumer Credit Protection Act.

---

[4]Since loans with an acceleration clause usually can be obtained at relatively lower interest rates, they may still be a good deal for people who rarely or never default on loan payments.

It limits the portion of an employee's wages that can be garnished. Garnishment can be no more than the lesser of the following:

1. Twenty-five percent of take-home pay; or

2. The amount by which take-home pay is in excess of thirty times the federal minimum hourly wage, which is scheduled to be $2.90 an hour in 1979, $3.15 an hour in 1980, and $3.40 an hour in 1981. (It could be raised more, however.)

The Act prohibits firms from firing an employee because of a wage garnishment.

Balloon clause. Balloon clauses are defined as terms of an installment loan contract that require, after a period of time, a specific payment more than twice the normal installment payment. For example, a contract may indicate that $100 a month is due for eleven months, then a single payment in the twelfth month of $600. If the signer of the contract does not have that amount of money available when it is due in the twelfth month, he or she either has to refinance or, possibly, lose the item purchased on credit.

The Rule of 78

Suppose you took out a loan for twelve months and wanted to pay it back after five months. The bank or finance company normally would use what is called the rule of 78 to calculate what you owe in terms of the percentage of the total year's interest that would have been earned, had you carried out the full contractual agreement.

If you pay off the loan after one month, then, based on the rule of 78, you will have to pay your creditor 12/78ths of the year's total interest. This is equivalent to 15.38 percent of one year's interest owed. On the other hand, the exact proportional amount of interest that you would have paid on such an installment contract for one month would equal 1/12th the year's total interest, or 8.33 percent. Notice the penalty for such an early repayment: you pay almost double the interest for that one-month loan than is stated in the installment contract.

If you keep the loan for two months and then repay it, you end up having to pay $\frac{12+11}{78}$, or 23/78ths of the total year's interest. Again, the comparison is that the 2/78ths equals 29.49 percent, and 2/12ths equals 16.67 percent. You almost double the effective amount of interest that you pay over what you would have paid had you kept the loan outstanding. In sum, then, using this rule of 78 to calculate early repayment results in the lender obtaining more than a strictly prorated distribution of interest.

The rule of 78 becomes the rule of whatever the sum of the digits is involved for the number of equal installment payments for which you have contracted. For example, if you are making an early repayment on a two-year loan with twenty-four equal installments, you would use the rule of 312. If you repaid the loan after one month, you would owe 24/312ths of the total amount of interest that would have been paid over a two-year period (since there are twenty-four monthly installments). That means you would pay 7.69 percent of the total as opposed to the pro rata distribution of interest that would equal 1/24th, or 4.17 percent.

Lenders do not have to calculate what you owe in this step-by-step manner because they use prepared tables. The method used to prepare the tables, however, is similar to the process just described.

If you wish to figure out what it would cost you to borrow $1,000 for any specified period of time, look at Exhibit 6-11. Here we show different specified annual percentage rates for different time periods.

FIGURING OUT THE INTEREST RATE YOU ARE PAYING

There is a relatively simple formula to give you the approximate annual percentage rate you are actually paying on a consumer installment loan. The formula is as follows: $i = \dfrac{2 \cdot t \cdot C}{P(n+1)}$

where:

i = annual simple interest rate in decimal form;

t = how many times a year you have to pay (for example, fifty-two if weekly, twelve if monthly);

C = actual dollar cost of borrowing (finance charge);

P = the net amount borrowed;

n = the total number of payments.

Let's take an example. Assume that you apply for a loan of $100. The finance company will give it to you for a service fee of ten dollars for a one-year period, to be repaid in twelve monthly installments. Although you are told that you are only paying ten percent interest, that is not really so. Let's put those numbers into our simple formula above. The net amount you are receiving is $100, so

P = $100
C = $10
t = 12
n = 12

The formula becomes

$$i = \dfrac{2 \cdot 12 \cdot \$10}{\$100\,(12+1)} = 18.46\%$$

If it was a discount loan, you would only receive $90, and the formula would look like this:

$$i = \dfrac{2 \times 12 \times \$10}{\$90\,(12+1)} = 20.5\%$$

Interest Rate and Taxes

To calculate the actual interest you will pay, you must take into account not only inflation but also the taxes you save by borrowing. All interest payments

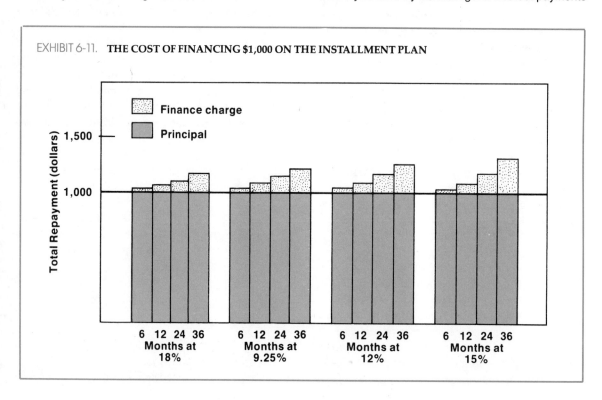

EXHIBIT 6-11. **THE COST OF FINANCING $1,000 ON THE INSTALLMENT PLAN**

and finance charges are usually tax deductible (if you fill out a "long" form and itemize your deductions). Every dollar of interest payments you make reduces the income on which you pay taxes by one dollar. That means that your tax savings would be twenty cents on each dollar if you are in the 20 percent tax bracket; if you are paying an interest rate of 10 percent and your taxable income bracket is 20 percent, the after-tax interest payment you are actually paying is only 8 percent. Obviously, the higher your tax bracket, the less it really costs you to borrow. See Exhibit 6-12 for an example.

Where Should You Go for a Loan?

Some kinds of asset purchases tell you immediately where you should go for a loan. If you are buying a house, you obviously don't go to your local small-loan company. You go to a savings and loan association, a commercial bank, or a mortgage trust company, or you sign a contract with the seller of the house. The real estate agent usually helps the buyer of a house secure a loan. The easiest way to shop around is to call various savings and loan associations to see what interest rates they are charging or visit those that won't reveal that information over the telephone. In the Practical Applications in Chapter 7, we discuss in more detail what you should look out for when you borrow money for a house.

You probably will not go to a small-loan company to borrow for a car either. Rather, you would go to a credit union or a commercial bank, where car loans cost less. The interest rate for new cars is usually lower than for a used car. Why? Because the car is used as collateral, and a new car is generally easier to resell than a used car, although this may not be true with pollution control equipment on new cars. You should note also that if you buy a car that is technically "brand new"—that is, you would be the first owner—but you purchase it after next year's models are in the showroom, the lending agency may consider the car to be used and charge the higher interest rate.

If you want to borrow money to purchase smaller items, a credit union loan might be cheapest. And the next best deal would be credit card companies, of which Master Charge and VISA (BankAmericard) are the best known.

The key to selecting the best credit deal is to treat credit as a good or service; use the same shopping techniques for purchasing credit that you would use to purchase any other item. Your having spent time to find the best deal for a car doesn't mean that your shopping should stop there. You

---

EXHIBIT 6-12.

ACTUAL INTEREST PAID AFTER TAX DEDUCTION

1. Assume your tax rate is 20 percent, that is, you must pay Uncle Sam 20¢ of the (last) dollars you earn.

2. Interest payments are tax deductible.

3. You borrow $100 at 10 percent, that is, you pay $10 interest.

4. But when calculating your taxes you get to deduct that $10 from your income *before* you compute your taxes owed.

5. Hence, what you do not have to pay Uncle Sam is
.20 × $10.00 = $2.00

6. Your actual interest payment for that $100 loan is therefore $10 − $2 (in tax savings) = $8.00, or 8 percent (instead of 10 percent).

may not be getting the best deal possible if you buy the credit for the car from the dealership or its affiliate. You may do better at your local commercial bank. But you can't predict: you have to compare.

LOAN CONSOLIDATION IS NOT FREE

You often hear ads for companies that "want to help you help yourself." They propose to consolidate all your debts into one fixed monthly payment, which will be smaller than the total of what you are paying now to all of your creditors. Don't be taken in by this. Usually, you won't pay a smaller interest rate by consolidating your debts than you would pay if you handled them separately. Remember, you have already incurred any setup charges involved in taking out the various earlier lines of credit that you want consolidated. Credit companies do nothing for free. Like any other company, they will not render you any service unless they make a profit on it. So, if you let a credit company pay off all your existing debts and then lend you the total amount that they paid, you will have to incur the setup charge for that.[5]

Now, it may be more *convenient* for you to have all your loans consolidated into one. Then you have to write only one check a month instead of many. But this service won't be handed to you without charge. You may, in fact, have a smaller monthly charge, but it will be for more months. And, ultimately, you will pay higher finance charges for the whole consolidation package and, thus, a higher total payment. If you dislike record keeping and check writing, you may want to incur this additional cost (and additional debt) by taking a loan consolidation. As long as you realize that nobody gives you

anything for free, you can make a rational choice. Loan consolidation is not going to pull you out of financial trouble. The only way out of such trouble is either to make a higher income or cut back on your current consumption so you can pay off your debts more easily. You could, of course, sell some of your assets to pay off your debts, too.

DANGER SIGNALS

If you observe any of the following, you are in danger of having overextended your debt.

1. You consistently postpone paying your bills or paying any given bill on a rotation basis.

2. You begin to hear from your creditors.

3. You have no savings or not enough to tide you over a financial upset.

4. You have little or no idea what your living expenses are.

5. You use a lot of credit, having charge accounts all over town and several credit cards in your wallet, and you pay only the monthly minimum on each account.

6. You do not know how much your debts total.

HOW TO KEEP FROM GOING UNDER

You can do certain things to prevent yourself and your family from getting into deeper financial trouble. Some of the following common-sense actions will be of special help.

1. Itemize your debts in detail, making sure you note current balance, monthly payments, and dates when payments are due.

2. List the family's total monthly net income that can be counted on every month.

---

[5]Sometimes debt consolidation may save you some money. If, for example, you consolidate all your revolving credit accounts, which charge you 18 percent, into one 12 percent credit union loan, you will be better off (assuming there are no early-payment penalty charges on the revolving credit accounts).

3. Subtract your monthly living expenses from your net income. Don't include the payments on debts you already have. The result will be the income you would be able to spend if you had no debts. Now subtract the monthly payments you are committed to making on all your debts. If you come out with a minus figure, you are obviously living beyond your means. If you come out with a very small positive figure, you still may be living beyond your means.

4. If you think you are, in fact, living beyond your means, you must inform your family that the money situation is tight. Tell them that you and every other spender in the family unit will have to cut expenses, such as those on recreation, food, and transportation.

DEBT COUNSELING

If you have gotten into financial trouble by overextending yourself, you may wish to consult a nonprofit organization that works with people in serious debt. Such work is generally called credit or debt counseling. For example, there is a Financial Crisis Clinic at Long Beach State University in California, which is part of the program in financial counseling under the auspices of the home economics department. You may wish to consult the home economics or business department or school of your local college or university to find out if a similar program is available in your area.

There might be a local office of the Consumer Credit Counseling Service in your area. This is a nonprofit organization that may be financed partly by the United Way and partly by a rebate from creditors. You usually are not charged for using the service, unless you make long-distance telephone calls. These centers, located throughout the country, have trained counselors who will analyze your situation. None of the offices will assume complete control of your finances, but they will help you deal with your creditors.

Talking Things Over with Them

A counselor might draw up a budget and ask you to stick to it and refrain from further use of credit. You might be asked to send a certain amount of money each month, which is then parceled out to creditors. If a Consumer Credit Counseling Service does not think it can help you, a counselor will refer you to another agency.

Other Steps You Can Take

If you only have one or two major bills that you cannot pay, you can talk to your creditors directly. Usually, they will be willing to extend your account. If you are a member of a credit union or have access to one, you might consider a consolidation loan at a lower interest rate than the average of what you are paying on several installment contracts.

The most drastic step you can take is to declare personal bankruptcy. During a true bankruptcy proceeding, you may not need a lawyer. Not all your assets will be taken, such as pensions, insurance proceeds, veterans' benefits, and Social Security. Depending on the state, you may be able to keep your home, if you are head of the household, and $1,000 of your personal property. On the other hand, some debts that you must continue paying are: (1) back taxes, (2) child support, and (3) any secured claim debts—that is, those for which you put up collateral. Basically, personal bankruptcy absolves you of unsecured debts, such as store charge accounts and finance company loans.

An alternative to personal bankruptcy is to apply for a Chapter XIII plan, which means that you propose to pay your creditors a certain percentage of the debts over a certain time period. If a majority of your creditors approve, the court can put the plan into effect. However, consumers are warned against attempting a Chapter XIII plan without the help of a lawyer. The Consumer Credit Counseling Service office can give assistance on this point.

Basically, most credit problems result from the lack of a financial plan. While such influences as credit advertising, credit selling, and other credit-oriented techniques tend to push families into using credit excessively, you, the consumer, ultimately are the one who signs on the dotted line. If you have a sound financial plan, perhaps along the lines outlined in Chapter 3, advertising or fast talk will not tempt you to overextend yourself financially.

GLOSSARY OF TERMS

BANKRUPTCY A condition of such indebtedness that legal provisions are made that entitle a person's creditors to have his or her assets administered for their benefit. One can declare bankruptcy when liabilities greatly exceed assets, and there is little hope of the situation improving.

CONSUMER DURABLES Goods that last a considerable period of time—for example, stereos, television sets, and cars.

SERVICE FLOW The flow of benefits received from an item that has been purchased or made. Consumer durables generally give a service flow that lasts several years. For example, the service flow from a stereo may be a certain amount of satisfaction received from it every year for its five-year life.

FINANCE CHARGE The total amount of charges that a borrower must pay in order to receive a loan. They include interest, service charges, insurance charges, and so on.

ANNUAL PERCENTAGE RATE (APR) The actual amount of finance charge expressed as a percentage of the loan outstanding over a year.

RIGHT OF RESCISSION The right to withdraw from a signed contract or agreement. For example, before you sign an agreement to buy a set of encyclopedias, you may want to obtain the right of rescission during a three-day period.

REVOLVING CREDIT Basically, an open credit account at, say, a department store. You have the right to pay the balance in full or in installments. Purchases or loans can be made at irregular intervals by use of a credit card, and usually the finance charge is computed on the outstanding unpaid balance.

PREVIOUS BALANCE METHOD A method of computing interest owed in which the finance charge is assessed on the previous month's balance, even if it has been paid.

AVERAGE DAILY BALANCE   A method of computing a finance charge in which it is applied to some of the actual amounts outstanding each day during the billing period divided by the number of days in that period.

ADJUSTED BALANCE METHOD   A method in which finance charges are assessed on the balance after deducting payments and credits.

PAST DUE BALANCE   No finance charge is assessed if full payment is received within a certain period, usually twenty-five days after the closing date of the statement.

HOLDER-IN-DUE-COURSE DOCTRINE   The last person actually holding the loan contract you sign is owed that money even if the product you purchased was defective.

LIABILITIES   Something for which one is responsible according to law or equity, especially pecuniary debts or obligations. The term also refers to the amounts of debts owned.

ASSETS   The entire property of a person, association, corporation, or estate that is applicable or subject to the payment of his or her or its debts; the items on a balance sheet showing the book value of property owned; or the value of property owned.

NET WORTH   The difference between your assets and your liabilities, or what you are actually worth. If your liabilities exceed your assets, your net worth is negative.

ACCELERATION CLAUSE   A clause contained in numerous credit agreements whereby, if one payment is missed, the entire unpaid balance becomes due, or the due date is accelerated to the immediate future.

ADD-ON CLAUSE   If this clause is put into an installment loan contract, your early purchases become security for your new purchases.

GARNISHMENT   A system by which your wages are attached in a credit deficiency judgment against you. For example, 25 percent of your wages may have to go to your creditors in a garnishment action.

BALLOON CLAUSE   A requirement in a loan contract that means a large payment, at least more than twice the size of any other one, is due after a certain number of periodic payments.

RULE OF 78   A method of computation for early repayment of an installment loan. This rule specifically applies to a twelve-month loan with twelve equal installments. The sum of one through twelve equals 78. Prepayment after one month of the entire loan will require that 12/78 be paid in interest. This is higher than a pro rata share, which would equal 1/12 of the total interest owed.

CHAPTER SUMMARY

1. Aggregate debt and per capita debt in the United States are increasing.

2. We borrow, at least in part, to match up the payments we make with the service flow we receive from the consumer durables we buy. In other words, borrowing is the synchronization of cash outlay with the service flow from the good.

3. There are numerous sources of credit, including: (a) commercial banks, (b) sales finance companies, (c) consumer finance companies, (d) credit unions, (e) credit cards, (f) oil company cards, (g) airline and auto rental cards, and (h) retail stores.

4. Additionally, there are savings and loan associations, pawn shops, and loan sharks.

5. In some cases, it is possible to obtain a discount if you pay in cash in a store where credit cards are usually used.

6. One can borrow from one's life insurance policy under certain circumstances.

7. The cost of borrowing is interest. Interest will include an inflationary premium to allow for expected inflation in the future.

8. Usury laws limit the maximum rate that lenders can charge borrowers. In many cases, the effect of a usury law is to limit the amount of credit available to lower-income individuals. Moreover, it is possible for lenders to get around usury laws and actually charge a higher-than-legal interest rate.

9. The Truth-in-Lending Act of 1968 requires that all costs of a loan be included in one finance charge and that it be calculated as an annual percentage rate on the loan.

10. Consumers have the right of rescission for certain credit contracts. This allows them to cancel, several days after signing, an installment loan contract for goods to be purchased.

11. Revolving credit involves making purchases irregularly and obtaining loans for those purchases and then paying off the total amount, either all at once or in installments. The interest rate charged depends on the method used for computing the balance owed.

12. The Equal Credit Opportunity Act attempts to outlaw various methods of discriminating against individuals because of sex and marital status.

13. Borrowing makes you decide how much your total debt outstanding should be. You can use one of the two methods given in Exhibit 6-7 for determining a safe debt load.

14. The maximum you can borrow is a function of your: (a) capacity to pay back, (b) character, (c) capital, or collateral.

15. The Fair Credit Reporting Act, which went into effect in 1971, allows you to investigate your credit ratings if you think they are unreasonable.

16. You must consider the consequences of the following when you shop for credit: (a) acceleration clauses, (b) add-on clauses, (c) garnishment agreements, (d) balloon clauses.

17. If you prepay a loan, you will be subject to the Rule of 78 which requires that you pay a more-than-proportionate share of the interest owed—that is, more than if you had adhered to the original payment schedule.

18. As of the late 1970s, all interest was tax deductible. Thus, if you itemize your tax return, the actual interest you pay is equal to the nominal interest minus the tax savings you obtain.

19. Generally, loan consolidation is more expensive than keeping all your loans outstanding. Only when, say, a credit union offers to consolidate your loans at a lower average interest rate will you be better off.

20. Consumer credit counseling services in your area will help you resolve your credit problems.

21. One alternative is to declare personal bankruptcy.

STUDY QUESTIONS

1. Why do you think the aggregate amount of debt in the United States has been growing so much? Does it have anything to do with increased incomes? Increased population? Increased price level?

2. What is the difference between credit and debt?

3. The interest rate charged by different lenders varies tremendously. Does this mean that some of them have a monopoly? If not, how can you account for the differences?

4. Does it seem fair that those who pay cash pay the same price as those who use a credit card?

5. Can you think of some very specific reasons why you would ever want to borrow money? Or ever have?

6. Is it better to save and buy? Or to buy and go into debt?

7. Do you think it is appropriate that interest rates be regulated? If your answer is yes, how does the regulation of interest rates differ from the regulation of other prices in our economy?

8. During a number of years in this decade, the rate of inflation exceeded the rate of interest that some borrowers had to pay on their loans. What does that mean about the real rate of interest those borrowers were paying?

9. Do you think the Truth-in-Lending Act has been effective? Why?

10. Can consumers figure out how they are actually being charged for their credit? What information would be helpful in addition to that which now exists?

11. If you are charged a setup fee in addition to some annual percentage rate to borrow money from a credit card company, should that setup charge be included as part of the total finance charge? Would this raise or lower the annual percentage rate of interest?

12. What is the right of rescission? What does it have to do with a "cooling off" period?

13. Distinguish among these four methods of computing interest on open-ended credit accounts: (a)previous balance, (b) average daily balance, (c) adjusted balance, and (d) past-due balance. Which is the cheapest?

14. What are your assets? What are your liabilities? What is the difference between your assets and liabilities? Can that difference be negative?

CASE PROBLEMS

6-1 The Eternal Question: Cash or Credit?

Bill and Jane Bonney want to replace their major household appliances and move the ones they now have to their lake cabin. They could buy a refrigerator, range, washer, and dryer for $1500 on credit, with monthly payments of $139.50 for one year. Or they could save for one year and pay cash. They are in a 25% marginal tax bracket, their savings account pays 5½% interest, and inflation is estimated at 7% for the next year.

1. Compute the dollar cost of credit and the APR.

2. What would be the total dollar cost due to credit buying versus saving and paying cash? (Assume an average savings balance of $750.)

3. What would be the cash price of the appliances in one year?

4. From a financial standpoint, should they buy now or save and buy in one year?

5. What other factors should be considered before they decide?

6-2 Selecting a Loan Source

Amanda Weaver is a twenty-five year old registered dietitian at Mercy Hospital. She has been saving $100 per month during the fifteen months she has been at Mercy and now plans to buy a $3770 Mazda "hatchback." The dealer will give her $270 for her 1970 Ford, which will leave a balance of $2000 to be financed. Amanda is considering two sources of credit:

A. An installment loan requiring 24 monthly payments with the Westwood Bank. The interest rate is 8% add-on, and Amanda would use the money she usually puts into her savings account to repay the loan.

B. A loan from the Mercy Employees Credit Union at 10% annual interest with the amount to be repaid in one payment at the end of two years. If Amanda selects this option, she would deposit her $100 per month in her 6% savings account and use this money to pay off the note in two years.

1. Determine the finance charges, APR, and monthly payments on the Westwood Bank loan.

2. Determine the finance charges, APR, and amount of the single payment on the credit union loan.

3. Which source would you recommend and why? (Assume an average savings account balance of $600 the first year and $1800 the second year.)

SELECTED REFERENCES

Annual Report to Congress on Truth in Lending. Board of Governors of the Federal Reserve System (latest edition).

Be Wise: Consumers' Quick Credit Guide. Washington, D.C.: U.S. Department of Agriculture, Government Printing Office, September 1972.

Buying on Time. New York State Banking Department, 2 World Trade Center, New York, New York 10047 (latest edition).

Chapman, J. "Women's Access to Credit." *Challenge,* January/February 1975.

"Check Out Your Credit Rating." *Better Homes & Gardens,* May 1977, pp. 240-245.

Cobleigh, Ira U. *What Everybody Should Know About Credit Before Buying or Borrowing Again.* New York: Simon & Schuster, 1975.

"Hooked on Credit and Out of Control." *Changing Times,* February 1977, p. 34.

Kaplan, Lawrence J., and Malteis, Salvatore. "The Economics of Loansharking." *American Journal of Economics and Sociology* 27 (1968).

Main, J. "Who's a Good Credit Risk? Credit-Scoring Systems." *Reader's Digest,* May 1977, p. 197.

Meyer, Jerome I. *Wipe Out Your Debts and Make a Fresh Start.* New York: Chancellor Press, 1973.

Meyer, Martin J. *How to Turn Plastic into Gold.* Lynnbrook, N.Y.: Farnsworth Publishing, 1974.

Nelson, P. "Giving Yourself Credit; Four Easy Steps to Establish Your Financial Identity." *McCalls,* March 1977, p. 106.

Russell, Thomas. *Economics of Bank Credit Cards.* New York: Praeger, 1975.

"When Your Budget Signals Danger." *Changing Times,* February 1977, pp. 33-35.

Housing

■ If you happen to be an Eskimo living in the Yukon Territory, putting a roof over your head is complicated but not impossible: you build an igloo. If you live in the bush country of Tanzania, putting a roof over your head takes time, but eventually your thatch hut will be completed. If you were a pioneer settling down on some cleared land in the Old West, putting a roof over your head would have meant building a log cabin.

Today, by way of contrast, if you are Mr. and Mrs. Superwealthy, putting a new roof over your head may involve $30,000 in architect's fees, $100,000 for a plot of land (not too small, of course), and perhaps another $200,000 for quite a nice house. Then again, if you are the average American, you can have a three-bedroom house with 1,300 square feet of floor space, which, with its land, has a market value of $60,230 in 1978.

Shelter is a necessity, even for the poorest people, but the various types of housing that people "need" vary drastically from region to region and person to person. The variety of houses one can purchase seems almost infinite. And the price range that one could consider is also vast. Housing is like clothes or food: once we pass a certain minimum level, the rest depends on our tastes and preferences. And our tastes and preferences must coincide with our limited budgets.

Early Americans probably had as many fanciful ideas about how they would like to live as we have. But today, some of us—in fact, most of us—live like kings compared with earlier Americans. Why? Because we are considerably richer. Each year for the last 150 years, our real incomes have increased at about 1.5 percent per capita. And we have spent an increasing proportion of our budgets on housing services,

155

mainly because most of us like to cater to our fancies. We like the good life, and that includes a home suited to our particular needs.

THE HOUSING INDUSTRY

Almost 70 percent of all households in the United States own their own homes. In almost any year, more than 1 million new houses are being built. In a typical year, between 3.5 and 5 million families buy a house. Americans also spend billions of dollars every year for home additions, improvements, maintenance, and so on. The number of houses in the United States, as depicted in Exhibit 7-1, has been rising at the rate of about 2.5 percent a year for the last twenty-five years.

However, these figures can be deceptive. A truer picture of our circumstances might emerge from measuring how many additional services we get from the rising housing stock. Building another 1 million one-bedroom apartments is one thing; building 1 million four-bedroom houses is quite another. We buy or rent houses or mobile homes or apartments for the services they yield, just as we buy clothes or cars or other goods that last. When we buy a house, we expect to reap an implicit rate of return in the form of housing services over a number of years; thus, it is important not to confuse the existing stock of housing and the *flow* of services from that stock.

What we are buying is not the house itself but how much pleasure we get from living in it. And that pleasure is a function of its size, the

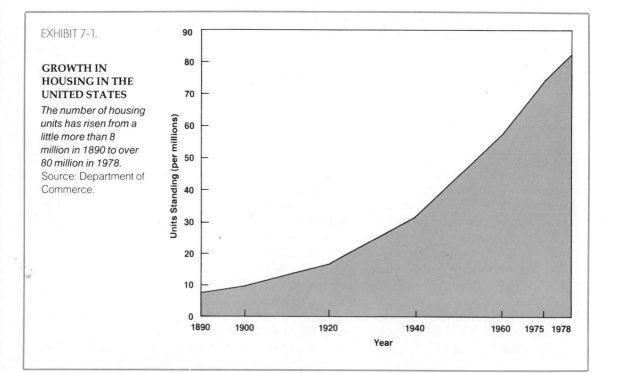

EXHIBIT 7-1.

**GROWTH IN
HOUSING IN THE
UNITED STATES**

*The number of housing
units has risen from a
little more than 8
million in 1890 to over
80 million in 1978.*
Source: Department of
Commerce.

conveniences it offers, the view, the neighborhood, and everything else that contributes to our happiness when we are home. We try to derive from our homes the greatest amount of utility or services possible. It is important to realize, then, that when we buy a $75,000 house, we are getting a larger flow of services per month than if we had bought a $30,000 house.

TYPES OF HOUSING

We mentioned before that it is important to distinguish among the different housing services currently available. Everyone is familiar with single-family dwellings, but fewer people are as familiar with multiple-family dwellings, such as duplexes, high-rise apartments, and so-called tenements. Additionally, in the United States we have seen an increase in condominiums, cooperatives, and mobile homes.

Many mobile homes are being built today. Basically, the cost-per-service-flow from mobile homes is considerably lower than from regular dwellings. One reason is that mobile homes are built by different rules and construction techniques than are required for regular houses.

Cooperative Housing

In a building of cooperative apartments, each dweller owns a pro rata (proportionate) share of a nonprofit corporation that holds a legal right to that building. Each member of a cooperative does the following:

1. Leases the individual unit he or she occupies.
2. Accepts financial responsibility for his or her own payments and accepts responsibility for increases in assessments if one or more members fails to make a payment.
3. Pays a monthly assessment to cover maintenance, service, taxes, and mortgage for the entire building.
4. Votes to elect a board of directors.
5. Obtains approval from the corporation before remodeling, selling, renting, or changing his or her unit.

Co-ops themselves are nonprofit corporations and are, therefore, owned and operated solely for the benefit of the members. The Federal Housing Authority estimates that the costs of living in cooperative apartments are about 20 percent less than renting comparable apartments from a private landlord. It is interesting to speculate about this 20 percent differential. Perhaps it exists because maintenance costs are lower in a co-op, where the owner/members take better care of their apartments than renters would. The fact that co-ops are nonprofit organizations and other apartments are profit-making ventures definitely contributes to the 20 percent price differential. Also, fuller occupancy and lower turnover contributes to lower operating costs. And, as we will explain, owner/members can claim income-tax deductions not available to renters.

Members in cooperative units have a right to sell their particular unit when they decide to move. They recoup any difference between what they owe on their mortgage and the resale price of their unit. In general, the co-op organization itself has the first option to buy an apartment that is for sale. In most cases, if the apartment is to be sold to a nonmember, the members of the cooperative must approve the sale.

Condominiums

In a **condominium,** the dweller has the legal title to the unit he or she owns. In addition, a condominium owner usually:

1 Has joint ownership interest in the common areas and facilities of the building or complex, such as swimming pools, tennis courts, and so on.

2 Arranges his or her own mortgage and pays taxes individually on his or her unit.

3 Makes separate payments for building maintenance and services.

4 Does not accept financial responsibility for other people's units or their share of the overall operating expenses.

5 Votes to elect a board of managers that supervises the property.

6 Has the right to refinance, sell, or remodel (with limitations) his or her own unit.

Advantages and Disadvantages of Condos

Some housing experts contend that, because condominiums have certain advantages over cooperative units, we will see a continued growth in condominiums relative to co-ops. In many situations, owners who want to sell their condominium apartments are under fewer restrictions than are the owners of co-op units. The condominium can be sold without the approval of a board of directors. If the owner of a condominium unit defaults on a payment, it only affects the mortgage. In the case of a cooperative unit, any owner who defaults causes the other co-op members to contribute an amount to cover what has been defaulted. Condominium owners usually are free to rent or lease their units to anyone.

All of the various tax advantages of owning a home apply to condominiums and cooperatives. Basically, all local taxes and interest on the mortgage for the prorated share in the cooperative and the entire share for the condominium unit are deductible from income before taxes are paid. Because this benefit is not directly available to renters, it is one of the reasons why many people prefer to own condominiums or join a cooperative instead of renting an apartment.

There are possible disadvantages to owning a condominium. There have been numerous scandals about poor construction of certain condominiums, particularly in resort areas. In the past, condominium owners found that their management fees often exceeded the value of the services rendered. And a number of apartments have been turned into condominiums inappropriately: that is, they really were not suitable for individual ownership.

Mobile Homes

Exhibit 7-2 shows the increase in mobile-home construction since 1970. Mobile homes are one of the most popular forms of low-income housing in the United States today. One reason why is that some states tax them

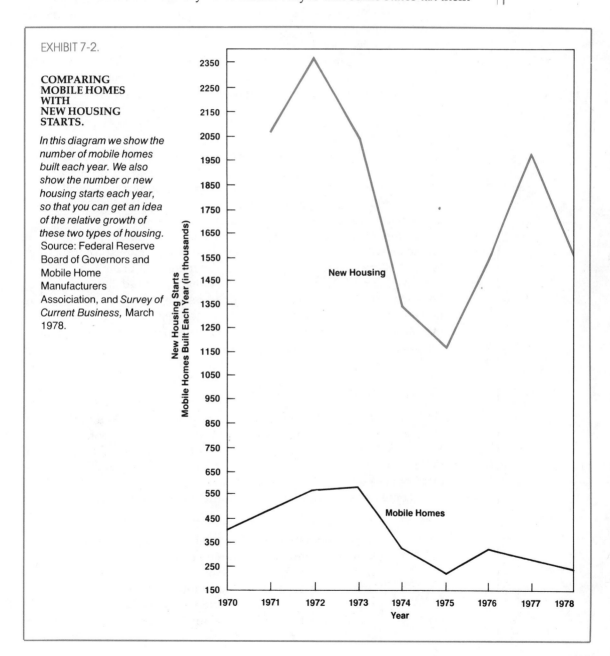

EXHIBIT 7-2.

COMPARING MOBILE HOMES WITH NEW HOUSING STARTS.

In this diagram we show the number of mobile homes built each year. We also show the number or new housing starts each year, so that you can get an idea of the relative growth of these two types of housing. Source: Federal Reserve Board of Governors and Mobile Home Manufacturers Assoiciation, and *Survey of Current Business,* March 1978.

New Housing Starts
Mobile Homes Built Each Year (in thousands)

New Housing

Mobile Homes

Year

as vehicles instead of as homes. Another reason is that you may get more housing services per dollar spent, since mobile homes are often built on an assembly line by nonunion labor and without restrictive building codes. That means that alternative, less-costly building techniques can be used. The state of California, however, has been compelled to regulate the way mobile homes are built.

The Department of Housing and Urban Development (HUD) finally passed nationwide standards that mobile home manufacturers must meet. These standards control the thickness of insulation, the air tightness of the structure, and so on. It is estimated that the new standards will raise mobile home costs from $500 to $1,500 per unit. Not everyone necessarily desired these new standards. Individuals buying homes in areas where the climate is temperate are not enthusiastic about paying extra money to ensure that their mobile home is more air-tight.

Two Other Types of Houses

Two other types of individually owned housing units are townhouses (sometimes called row houses) and modular homes. The former, a regular house with a front and backyard, shares common side walls. The obvious advantage of a townhouse is economy, for its construction permits savings on the costs of land, insulation, windows, foundation, roofs, and walls. Some townhouses are sold as condominiums. Two problems with such housing units are lack of adequate soundproofing, because of the shared walls, and the close proximity of neighbors.

Modular homes consist of factory-manufactured living-unit sections that can be arranged in various ways. The two types of modular units are "wet" and "dry." The former include plumbing, baths, heating, and kitchen equipment; the latter consist of living, dining, and sleeping rooms only.

RENTING A PLACE TO LIVE

Until fairly recently, it was common for renters to be looked down upon as people unable to manage their money correctly. The proof, of course, was a lack of home ownership. But this attitude has been changing, and today many people rent apartments or houses by choice, even though they could easily buy their own homes.

There are several reasons why individuals chose to rent instead of buy:

1 Greater mobility is possible than if one owns a home.
2 No down payment or (usually) credit check is required. (But there may be a damage deposit.)
3 Renters are spared the maintenance tasks and physical property depreciation that home owners face.
4 The exact cost of purchasing housing services can be figured easily for the period of the lease.

5   Property values are not a worry because you don't own the property.
6   Spending on home improvements is low or nonexistent.
7   There is little need to estimate carefully your future housing needs in terms of the size of your family.
8   Before investing in a house in a new community, you can rent and familiarize yourself with your new surroundings.
9   Common recreation facilities may be insured.
10 Interest is not lost on investment of your savings.
11 There is no liability of ownership.

Many apartments are rented on a month-to-month basis, with the rent paid in advance; the renter or tenant automatically gets the right to live in the apartment for the next month. In this type of tenant/landlord relationship, the contract may be terminated on thirty days' written notice. Given the proper thirty-day notice, the rent can be raised at any time, or the tenant can be asked to leave. There are advantages and disadvantages to this short-term contract. On one hand, renters can move when they wish without giving notice long in advance. On the other hand, there is the uncertainty of possibly being asked to leave on short notice or of finding the rent raised sooner than had been anticipated.

Alternatively, renters may obtain a lease, a long-term contract binding both landlord and tenant to specified terms. The lease, which is usually for one year, generally requires one month's rent in advance and, perhaps, one month's rent as a cleaning deposit.

As with any contract, you should be aware of all provisions of a lease which tend to protect landlords more than tenants. We examine this topic in Appendix B.

THE ADVANTAGES OF BUYING RATHER THAN RENTING

We have pointed out some of the advantages of renting as opposed to buying a place to live. Here we briefly list the advantages of buying a housing unit.

1   Allows you freedom of use: you can remodel or alter your home any way you wish.
2   Offers an investment option that, historically, has been a good hedge against inflation, particularly in the last decade.
3   Causes you to save because part of your monthly payments create equity in the housing unit.
4   Provides tax benefits: you can deduct interest payments and property taxes from income before paying federal (and state) income taxes.
5   Helps you save taxes by means of "do-it-yourself" upkeep.

Saving Money by Doing It Yourself

The last point is sufficiently misunderstood to warrant an explanation. The best way to understand it is to consider a numerical example. Suppose that your house needs repainting. You get a number of bids for the labor, and the average is $2,000. How much do you have to earn to get $2,000 *after taxes?* That, of course, depends on your marginal tax rate. If your marginal tax rate is, say, 50 percent, then you would have to earn $4,000 in order to have $2,000 to pay someone to paint your house. If you decided to paint it yourself, you would, in effect, be working for yourself but not declaring the income you earned—that is, the $2,000 worth of services that you performed rather than paying someone else to do them. So, instead of spending your time working to earn $4,000, of which $2,000 goes to Uncle Sam and $2,000 to the house painter, you paint the house yourself and avoid any taxes at all; as yet, the Internal Revenue Service does not require you to estimate the market value of do-it-yourself services performed around the house.

THE TAX GAME

Did you know that if you buy a house and borrow the money to pay for it, all the interest you pay to the bank can be deducted from your income before you pay taxes?[1] All property taxes are deductible, too. This may not mean much if you are not in a high tax bracket, but it will make a big difference when you get into a higher one.

For example, suppose you buy a $30,000 house and are somehow able to borrow the entire $30,000. Let's say that you paid $3,000 interest every year on that $30,000. You would be able to deduct that $3,000 from your income before you paid taxes on it. If you were in the 20 percent tax bracket, you would get a tax savings of $600. But if you were in the 70 percent bracket, you would get a tax savings of $2,100; the interest on your loan would, in effect, only cost you $900, which is relatively inexpensive. Now you know why people in higher income-tax brackets generally buy houses instead of renting.

This tax policy is an implicit subsidy to the housing industry and to all home owners who have any taxable income. The Joint Economic Committee figured out that the implicit subsidy was costing the U.S. Treasury $2.6 billion a year.[2] The benefit from this implicit subsidy is directly proportional to your marginal tax bracket, which is, of course, directly proportional to how much you make. Since poor people make little money, they are not in a higher marginal tax bracket. Thus, even if they deduct all their interest payments for their housing, the implicit tax savings will be little, if anything. Obviously, this interest rate subsidy to home owners has not been very helpful to lower-income people.

---

[1] Actually, interest payments can only be deducted if you use the long-form 1040, which we discuss in Chapter 12, to file your income taxes.

[2] Joint Economic Committee, "The Economics of Federal Subsidy Programs" (Washington, D.C.: U.S. Government Printing Office, 1972).

Taxes and housing are related in still another way. If you buy a house for $20,000 and sell it ten years later for $30,000, you have made $10,000. And, generally, you would be taxed on that sum, for it is a capital gain. However, if you buy another house that costs the same or more within a year (or have a new one built within eighteen months), you pay no capital-gains taxes for this transaction. Incidentally, capital-gains tax rates are generally lower than normal personal-income-tax rates.

MORTGAGES

Unless you are really cash rich, you will have to pay for a good part of your house with a mortgage, which is a loan that a bank or trust company makes on a house. In some states, you hold the title to the house; in others, the mortgagee does. In nine states and the District of Columbia, a special arrangement is made whereby the borrower (mortgagor) deeds the property to a trustee, a third party, on behalf of the lender (mortgagee). The trustee then deeds the property back to the borrower when the loan is repaid. If the payments are not made, the trustee can deed the property to the lender or dispose of it by an auction, depending on the state's law. As the mortgagor, you make payments on the mortgage until it is paid. More than 90 percent of all people who buy homes do so with a mortgage loan.

Sources of Mortgages

There are basically four sources of mortgage money, the most common being savings and loan associations, which account for almost 50 percent of all home loans made. The second most common are mortgage companies, which account for around 20 percent. Commercial banks are next. And mutual savings banks make some mortgage loans, particularly in the East. There is a whole category we will call "other," which includes pension funds, mortgage pools, insurance companies, mortgage investment trusts, and state and local credit agencies. Only under special circumstances can you get a mortgage loan from one of these institutions.

THE KINDS OF MORTGAGES

There are basically three kinds of mortgages. Although you may not be eligible for all of them, each is available from the same sources: commercial banks, savings banks, mortgage companies, savings and loan associations, and insurance companies.

Conventional Mortgages

Most conventional mortgages run for twenty to thirty years. However, in recent years, savings and loan associations have been reluctant to write mortgages for thirty years, and, in fact, some of them are charging higher interest rates for mortgages that last so long. Naturally, the rate of interest charged is determined by conditions in the money market (but also subject to state usury laws, which we discussed in Chapter 6). Interest rates in the past few years have been at, or close to, record highs. This should not, however, be a surprise when you consider the high inflation rates of recent years. The mortgagee's interest rate must allow for any expected loss in the purchasing power of the dollars that will be paid back to it in the future.

With a conventional mortgage loan, the money that the lender risks is secured only by the value of the mortgaged property and the financial integrity of the borrower. To protect the investment from the start, the conventional lender, such as a savings and loan association, ordinarily requires the down payment of 5 to 35 percent of the value of the property. Some private mortgage insurers will protect lenders against loss on at least part of the loan. When such extra security is provided, the lender may go to a higher loan figure. The borrower, of course, pays the cost of the insurance. If you make a very large down payment, lowering the risk of lending, the lender may be willing to grant you a slightly lower interest rate, perhaps a fraction of a percent below the prevailing local rate.

Conventional loans can be arranged on just about any terms satisfactory to both parties. Because different lenders favor different arrangements, it pays to shop around. And since most borrowers pay off their mortgages well before maturity (after nine years), it is wise to look for liberal conditions on prepayment to limit the penalty if you wish to prepay.

Veterans Administration Mortgages

These loans can be obtained only by qualified veterans or their spouses or widows. The interest rate charged is administered rather than determined strictly by the forces of supply and demand in the money market. The VA loan is guaranteed rather than insured. That is, the government simply promises that, on an approved loan, it will repay up to a certain amount—say, $17,500—or a certain percent—say, 60 percent. The borrower has no insurance premium to pay.

Nothing-down loans are possible under the VA program, often for amounts of $70,000 for up to thirty years. However, you cannot get a loan on a VA-financed house for more than the VA appraisal of its current market value nor for longer than the VA estimate of its remaining economic life. All VA loans can be prepaid without penalty.

The Veterans Administration makes some mortgage loans directly to veterans, usually to those in rural areas where lenders are not making guaranteed loans. In all other circumstances, a would-be borrower goes to the usual supply of mortgage money, such as a savings and loan association, a mutual savings bank, commercial banks or mortgage companies. It is particularly useful to check with the bank, savings and loan, or mutual savings bank where you happen to be a saver or a depositor; such institutions probably will be more accommodating to you when you seek a VA loan.

FHA Mortgages

The Federal Housing Administration issues insurance covering the entire amount of an **FHA loan.** This security enables qualified borrowers to obtain a much more generous loan, in relation to the value of the property, than they could obtain with an uninsured loan. Of course, to the borrower, a bigger loan means a smaller down payment.

Generally, it is possible to borrow 97 percent of the first $25,000 of the appraised value of an approved house you intend to live in yourself, plus 90 percent of the next $10,000 and 80 percent of the rest, up to $45,000. The maximum interest rate that can be charged usually has been below current market interest rates. But a 1/2 percent premium for the insurance and a 1 percent origination fee (for the work of drawing up the papers) are also permitted. The loan can be for as long as thirty-five years, not to exceed three-fourths of what the FHA estimates is the remaining economic life of the dwelling. There are no penalties for prepayment.

You apply for an FHA insured mortgage loan just as you would for any other loan. The lender, be it a savings and loan association, mortgage company, or commercial bank, will supply you with the necessary forms and help you complete them. If that lender is willing to make the loan, the application to the FHA insuring office will be submitted for processing. This may be quite time-consuming. The FHA staff will analyze the transaction (including your qualifications as a mortgagee), the estimated value of the property, and so on. While the FHA has no arbitrary rules regarding age or income, these factors are considered for their possible effect on your ability to repay the loan over the period of the mortgage.

The FHA also sponsors a subsidy program for low- and moderate-income families. In this program, down payments can be as low as several hundred dollars and interest as low as a couple of percentage points.

The big difference between FHA loans and so-called conventional loans is that the FHA interest is not determined strictly by market conditions but is set at an arbitrary rate by the Secretary of Housing and Urban Development. Usually, the secretary tries to fix a rate well below the lowest prevailing market rate. However, this practice has been associated with the "point" system.

What About Points?

Sometimes you may be asked to pay **discount points.** The point system is a device to raise the effective interest rate you pay on a mortgage. It is employed whenever there are restrictions on the legal interest rate that can be charged on the mortgage loan. You may think this is unfair. But if you are faced with the possibility of either paying the discount points or not getting the loan at all, you may decide to pay the implicitly higher interest rate.

A point is a charge of 1 percent of the loan. This charge may be assessed against the buyer or the seller or both. To see how a discount point system works, imagine that you have to pay four discount points on a $25,000 loan: that means you get a loan of $25,000 minus 4 percent of $25,000, or only $24,000. However, you pay interest on the full $25,000. Obviously, the interest rate you pay on $25,000 understates the actual interest you pay, because you get only $24,000. Some states have laws against discount points, and the FHA and VA have restrictions on buyers paying points. They are charged to the seller but are, in reality, passed on to the borrower in the form of a higher price on the housing unit.

ALTERNATIVE MORTGAGE ARRANGEMENTS

In the late 1970s, a number of more flexible payment arrangements were established for home buyers. In Exhibit 7-3, we describe five different types of mortgages: (1) graduated payment, (2) variable rate, (3) roll-over, (4) price-level adjusted, and (5) reverse annuity. At the bottom of that exhibit is an example of monthly payments for a standard mortgage, as well as payments under the provisions of a variable interest rate mortgage, a five-year roll-over mortgage, and two types of graduated payment mortgages. Obviously, we cannot show an example of a price-level adjusted mortgage, where the outstanding balance and monthly payments change according to fluctuations in the price level, because we don't know what the price level will be in the next few years.

HOUSES DON'T LAST FOREVER

Remember, when you buy a house, you aren't buying the house for itself but for the services it yields. And in order to get a constant level of services from a house, you must maintain it. Houses frequently need repairs, and repairs can sometimes be expensive. The average increases in the wages of craftspersons are among the highest in the nation. The same is true for the wages of people who fix sprinkler systems, clogged drains, leaking roofs, and broken furnaces. Since the maintenance expenses on a house can be extremely important, you should figure out how much it will cost to maintain any house you consider buying. A house with a large front and/or back lawn and much shrubbery will have high grounds-maintenance costs. You or someone in your family could do the work, or you could hire a gardener. In either case, you pay more for your housing services.

All maintenance costs should be included in the costs per year of owning a house. After all, you are buying a service flow for, say, a year at a time. And you should not ignore some of the important costs of obtaining those services.

SELECTING WHERE YOU WANT TO LIVE

Even before you start looking for the kind of house you want to buy, you must first decide where you want to live. The following is a list of the most important variables you must consider.

EXHIBIT 7-3. **FIVE KINDS OF MORTGAGES**

TYPE OF MORTGAGE AND HOW IT WORKS	PROS AND CONS	WHO BENEFITS
Graduated payment mortgage. Monthly payments are arranged to start out low but get bigger later, perhaps in a series of steps at specified intervals. The term of the loan and the interest rate remain unchanged.	The main object is to make buying easier in the beginning. Initial payments have to be balanced by larger payments later. One disadvantage: Possible "negative amortization" in the early years, which means that for a time your debt grows instead of diminishing.	Mainly first-time home buyers, who have a hard time becoming homeowners but can reasonably look forward to higher earnings that will enable them to afford the bigger payments coming later.
Variable rate mortgage. Instead of a fixed interest rate, this loan carries an interest rate that may change within limits—up or down—from time to time during the life of the loan, reflecting changes in market rates for money.	Because the size of the payments you'll have to make in the future is uncertain, this loan is a bit of a gamble. If money rates go down in the future, your payments will go down. But if rates go up, so will your payments.	Helps lenders keep their flow of funds in step with changing conditions, and this in turn could make home loans easier to come by when money is tight. You may get fractionally lower interest at first or other inducements to make future uncertainties more palatable.
Rollover mortgage. The rate of interest is fixed and the size of the monthly payment is fixed, but the whole loan—including principal, rate of interest and term—is renegotiated, or rolled over, at stated intervals, usually every five years.	If interest rates go up, you can expect to be charged more when you renegotiate. But you'll also have opportunity to adjust other aspects of the loan, such as term and principal. Or you can pay off the outstanding balance without penalty. Renegotiation is guaranteed.	Lenders, for the same reason variable rate loans are good for them. Benefits to borrowers are as shown for variable rate loans, with this plus: Periodic renegotiation gives you a chance to rejigger the loan to suit your changing needs without all the expense of refinancing.
Price-level adjusted mortgage. The interest rate remains fixed, but the outstanding balance and monthly payments change according to fluctuations in a specified price index.	If interest cost is your big worry, this plan at least ties down the percentage rate. All else remains uncertain, including how much you'll have to pay in toto and each month.	If this plan gets you a loan when you can get one no other way, then it helps you. Otherwise it mainly helps lenders. Not likely to become popular with borrowers.
Reverse annuity mortgage. You take out a loan secured by the accumulated equity in your house. The money is used to purchase an annuity that provides monthly income to you. You continue to live in the house. Its sale pays off the loan.	This is not a plan for putting money *into* a house. It's a plan for taking money *out*. It converts an existing frozen asset into current income that you can use without giving up your house.	Homeowners, principally older and retired people who have paid for or substantially paid for their homes but need additional current income to live on.

EXHIBIT 7-3 **CONTINUED ON NEXT PAGE**

EXHIBIT 7-3 **CONTINUED**

A STANDARD MORTGAGE WITH FOUR ALTERNATIVES
Here are figures for a 30-year, 9% loan for $30,000.

MONTHLY PAYMENTS	Standard Mortgage	Variable Interest	Five-year Rollover	Graduated Payments Five-year, 7½% Increase	Graduated Payments Ten-year, 3% Increase
year 1	$241	$241	$241	$182	$200
2	241	252	241	196	206
3	241	263	241	211	212
4	241	273	241	226	219
5	241	284	241	244	226
6	241	294	292	262	233
11	241	294	292	262	270

OUTSTANDING BALANCE					
year 1	$29,795	$29,795	$29,795	$30,533	$30,304
2	29,570	29,592	29,570	30,945	30,562
3	29,326	29,389	29,326	31,212	30,765
4	29,057	29,184	29,057	31,306	30,908
5	28,764	28,976	28,764	31,197	30,983
10	26,828	27,618	27,416	29,098	29,975

TOTAL PAID					
year 1	$ 2,896	$ 2,896	$ 2,896	$ 2,188	$ 2,408
2	5,793	5,922	5,793	4,540	4,888
3	8,690	9,075	8,690	7,070	7,443
4	11,586	12,356	11,586	9,788	10,075
5	14,483	15,764	14,483	12,710	12,785
10	28,969	33,435	32,026	28,419	27,607
30	86,900	104,122	102,197	91,254	92,335

Adapted from *Changing Times*, May 1978, pp. 21-22.

1 *Relationship to work:* Is the area you are looking at near or far from your work? If distant, is there good transportation—by bus, train, or via a highway that isn't congested when you go to work? Can you afford the transportation costs? The farther away from a city's work center, the cheaper the land will be, all other things remaining constant. But you make up the difference in this price of land by having to spend more time, which has a value, and more money for transportation.

2 *Property taxes:* Find out what the average assessment is in the area you are considering. This is an important out-of-pocket cost to remember when calculating your housing needs relative to your means. What are the trends in tax rates? What services do taxes provide?

3   *Schools for your family:* If you think the area schools are not going to be suitable, you will probably be dissatisfied with the educational opportunities available. And you may wind up spending money for private education. Talk with the teachers, the principal, and other parents at the neighborhood schools. Question the philosophy behind the teaching techniques. If it differs from yours, you may not want to live in that area or, at least, send your children to neighborhood schools.

4   *Shopping:* How close will your house be to the kinds of stores you use? Will you have to pay for parking every time you shop? Generally, the farther away a house is from a shopping area, the lower will be the value of the land, all other things held constant. But you will make up the difference in extra time and expense transporting yourself to the shopping centers.

5   *Air quality:* Is the area polluted or clean? Is it close to factories or close to a scenic wonder? The site value of the land may depend on the level of pollution, but you may place a much higher value on clean air than do the rest of the consumers in the housing market. If you have special respiratory problems, you definitely will be willing to pay more for an environment with unpolluted air.

6   *Noise pollution:* How close is the area to an airport? Will one be built or expanded nearby? Can you hear an expressway or freeway during rush hour? Can you hear traffic from a second-story bedroom but not from a living room? Will anything else cause disturbing noises?

7   *Crime:* Check with real estate agents in different sections of town, the police department, neighbors, and statistics from the police department's annual reports. Usually, the police are obliged by law to give you those statistics. You can also check the deductible clause in home owners' insurance for an indication of theft in the area.

8   *The neighborhood:* What kind of neighbors will you have? Are they people with the same lifestyle as yours? Will you feel comfortable at home? If you have children, do other people in the area have any the same age? If not, will that present problems?

9   *Zoning and development:* Are nearby undeveloped areas zoned for industry, housing, apartments? Is there going to be further development in the area? All these things should be checked out, either with a responsible real estate agent or by yourself.

MAKING THE MOVE

Ours is a mobile society. One in five families in the United States move once every year; among people twenty-five to thirty-four years old who have gone to college, almost 38 percent move every year. The average

American moves twelve times in his or her lifetime.

The decision to move often is based on a desire to change location, to go to a place with a better school system, to be in a different climate. Sometimes a move is related to a job commitment. Whatever the reason, you doubtless have too many personal possessions to be moved in your car. Either you rent a truck or you hire a professional mover. Even in the best of circumstances and with the best movers to help you, moving is a chore.

The next Practical Application offers some pointers about choosing a moving company and preparing for the move. One must include in the cost of a move the time and energy that will be expended. All costs taken together must be considered before a final decision concerning relocation is made. Professional moves are expensive, but the do-it-yourself prices are not low either, especially if you rent a truck that only gets five to eight miles per gallon of gasoline. If the move is a long one and if another vehicle must be driven, the expenses mount quickly.

PRACTICAL APPLICATIONS

HOW TO BUY HOUSING

The American dream usually includes home ownership. Let us assume that you share that dream. When you go to buy a house, you should figure out how much you can safely spend.

HOW MUCH CAN YOU AFFORD?

It is easy to get carried away when buying housing services. A desirable house may mean many unanticipated financial obligations and headaches. To make a sound decision, you should first calculate the level of your *dependable* monthly income for, say, the first third of all the mortgage payments due on a house. If you happen to be making more money than usual this year, it is best not to count on that as permanent income. Be conservative. This particularly applies to moonlighting jobs, and families where the spouse has only recently gone to work.

Next, you must figure out prospective monthly housing expenses, including mortgage payments, insurance premiums, taxes, costs of maintenance and repair, heating, air conditioning, electricity, telephone, water, sewage, and other services. Your mortgage payments may be higher than you think. Exhibit 7-4 gives estimates of monthly payments on different sized mortgages. It shows how much per month you would have to pay on a mortgage per $1,000 borrowed. If you borrowed, for example, $30,000 at 10 percent interest on a twenty-five year loan, it would cost you 30 times $9.09, or $272.70 monthly. Remember, this is in addition to the amount you would be paying on the loan. In addition, you would pay insurance and taxes. Exhibit 7-5 is a chart you can fill out for a guide.

Only rarely can you finance 100 percent of the cost of the house. You may have to pay one-fifth of

EXHIBIT 7-4.

MONTHLY PRINCIPAL AND INTEREST PAYMENTS PER $1000

If you borrow $35,000 for 30 years at 9-1/2 percent, it will cost you 35 x $8.41, or $294.35 per month for 30 years for principal and interest.

Interest Rate	LENGTH OF MORTGAGE		
	20 Years	25 Years	30 Years
7.5 %	$8.06	$7.39	$7.00
7.75	8.21	7.56	7.17
8.0	8.37	7.72	7.34
8.25	8.53	7.89	7.52
8.5	8.68	8.06	7.69
8.75	8.84	8.23	7.87
9.0	9.00	8.40	8.05
9.25	9.16	8.57	8.23
9.5	9.33	8.74	8.41
9.75	9.49	8.92	8.60
10.0	9.66	9.09	8.78
10.25	9.82	9.27	8.97
10.5	9.99	9.45	9.15
10.75	10.16	9.63	9.34
11.0	10.33	9.81	9.53

EXHIBIT 7-5.

**HOUSING
EXPENSES**

HOUSING EXPENSES PER MONTH	CURRENT	FUTURE
Mortgage payments	_____	_____
Property taxes	_____	_____
Insurance	_____	_____
Heat	_____	_____
Gas, electricity, water & phone, sewage	_____	_____
Yard care, trash pick-up, etc.	_____	_____
A savings fund for repairs, remodeling & maintenance	_____	_____
Other	_____	_____
Total	_____	_____

the purchase price as a down payment. In addition, there are closing costs, which we discuss shortly. Exhibit 7-6 gives rules for estimating how much housing you can afford. It tells you, for example, that the purchase price divided by your annual income should be 2 or less. Another helpful rule of thumb is that you should not spend more than one-fourth of your take-home pay for monthly housing payments. These are only rough rules, but they do serve as a guide. If you buy a $40,000 house on a yearly income of $8,000, you are asking for trouble: after housing expenses, food, and transportation, you will have little money left over.

New Versus Used

As with the purchase of almost any goods that last a long time, you can choose between an older house and a new house. New ones are advertised in the home section of your Sunday newspaper. In some years, as many as 2 million new housing units

are built in the United States. Perhaps an older unit makes more sense for you than a new one. Of course, you must be more careful about future maintenance with an older home, but using an inspection service ahead of time can alleviate that problem. Older houses usually are on property that is already landscaped. And often they provide more space for the same money as a new house.

WHEN TO USE A REAL ESTATE BROKER

You can start a housing search by looking in the classified section of a newspaper. This entails much time, telephoning, and driving to see houses that interest you. But if you are looking casually for a house, this may be the best way to do it: generally, you will save a real estate broker's commission if the people advertising are selling the house themselves. However, the majority of ads are placed by real estate companies, so, ultimately, you pay the brokerage fee even if you find the house through the newspaper.

If you decide to use a broker, call several, tell them what you want, and have them show you a few houses. You will soon find out how serious each broker is about working with you. You will also find out whether he or she understands your tastes and preferences in searching for a house. If you know individuals in the area who have used brokers, find out which have given satisfactory service. It will help if you have a good idea what your housing needs are, what you specifically do and do not want.

What Does a Broker Do?

Among their many functions, brokers provide buyers and sellers of houses with information. Information, remember, is a costly resource, particularly with such a nonstandard product as a house. Every house is different from every other, and it is difficult to get buyers and sellers together for such products.

The broker, then, saves you information costs by conducting the search procedure for you and for the seller. He or she is a specialist in matching up the wants of buyers with the supplies of sellers.

How Much Will You Pay?

For selling a house, most brokers charge a fixed fee (commission) that is paid, at least nominally, by the seller. But don't be fooled about how fixed this fee is. When houses are selling slowly, you can bargain with a broker over a house you think you want to buy. You can stipulate, for example, that you will buy the house if a refrigerator, stove, or other accessory is supplied. In a good market, the seller can do the same thing. That is, the seller will agree to pay the fixed commission, but over a seven year period: this means, in effect, that the commission will be worth less to the broker and cost less to the seller of the house.

EXHIBIT 7-6.

A GUIDE TO HOW MUCH HOUSING CAN YOU AFFORD

Most savings and loan association loan officers will use the rules alongside to determine how much housing you can afford. Rule 1 states that the purchase price of the house should not exceed 2 times your yearly gross income. Rule 2 states that your monthly mortgage payment should be no more than 25 percent of your total monthly income. Rule 3 states that all of your debt payments combined, including your mortgage payment, should not exceed one-third of your monthly income. And Rule 4 indicates that most savings and loan associations will not loan you more than 95 percent of the purchase price of your house. And generally, the maximum is closer to 80 percent, and in some cases, even as low as 65 percent. Source: The United States Saving and Loan League.

1. $$\frac{\text{PRICE}}{\text{GROSS INCOME}} < 2.0 \text{ (1.5 might be safer)}$$

2. $$\frac{\text{MORTGAGE PAYMENT}}{\text{MONTHLY INCOME}} < 25\%$$

3. $$\frac{\text{ALL DEBT SERVICE}}{\text{MONTHLY INCOME}} < 33\%$$

4. $$\frac{\text{LOAN AMOUNT}}{\text{VALUE}} < 95\% \text{ (usually around 80\%)}$$

Brokers can do more than help you find the house you want. They can also help you arrange for the financing, make sure that the papers are in order, and even bargain for you.

BEFORE YOU SIGN ANYTHING

Before you sign anything, make sure you are getting a house that is structurally sound. Pay an expert to go over everything in the house that could cause problems—wiring, frame, plumbing, sewage, and so on. Often, this costs $25 or $50, but for more expensive houses you will have to pay $100 to $200. This is money well invested—unless you can figure out what can go wrong with the house just by looking at it yourself. Look under *Building Inspection Service* or *Home Inspection Service* in the Yellow Pages. Again, such services sell the same thing a broker sells—information. Such information can save you hundreds, if not thousands, of dollars in repairs. Often, if a building inspector discovers structural faults in a house, you can have the seller of the house pay for the repairs even after you move in. Or this can be a bargaining point: the agreed-upon price can be reduced by the amount of the repair costs.

HOW TO BARGAIN

Most Americans are unaccustomed to bargaining because goods and services are sold at set prices, which are rarely lowered. But the **asking price** of a house is generally not the final sale price. If you are unaccustomed to bargaining and feel uncomfortable doing it, you can let a real estate broker do it for you.

To get a general idea of how much profit the seller is trying to make, find out what was paid for the house previously. Look at the deed to the house, which is a public document and can be examined at the office of the county clerk or county registrar of deeds. Or you can find out what the house cost the seller by looking at the federal tax stamps affixed to

the deed when the ownership was transferred. The stamps cost $1.10 for every $1,000; thus, if a deed has $33 worth of stamps, the owner paid $30,000 for the house.

Many times sellers do not expect to get the price they are asking on their houses. They set a price that they think may be, say, 5 or 10 percent more than what they will receive. It is up to you to find out how far they will go in discounting that list price. You can start by asking the real estate broker whether the price is "firm." Since the broker's commission is a percentage of the sale price, the higher that price, the more the broker benefits—but not if it means waiting months or years for a sale. The broker's desire to get that commission as soon as possible is an incentive to arrange a mutually agreeable price that will close the deal. Incidentally, it is realistic to assume that the broker works for the seller and represents the seller's interests rather than the buyer's.

You may want to bargain, for example, on a $35,000 list price for, say, $32,000 plus the refrigerator, freezer, washer, and dryer already in the house. You should not accept the list price just because you think you want the house. While that price may be the lowest you can get it for, it may not be. You will only know if you bargain. And if you are unwilling to do so yourself, ask your broker to. The broker ultimately may decide to take a lower (implicit) commission rate in order to seal the deal, the first stage of which is signing a written **earnest, or binder, agreement.**

WHAT HAPPENS WHEN YOU DECIDE TO BUY?

Generally, when you decide to buy a house, you make an offer, in writing, and you put up a deposit, often called earnest money. The earnest agreement binder, usually good for twenty-four hours, details your exact offering price for the house and lists anything that is not normally included with a house but will be included in this deal, such as appliances.

Within twenty-four hours, the seller of the house either accepts or rejects the earnest agreement, or binder. If the seller accepts and you try to back down, the earnest money you put up (which may be several thousand dollars) is, legally, no longer yours. But sometimes you can get it back, even when you decide against the house after signing the agreement.

In any earnest agreement, it is, therefore, advisable to add an escape clause, especially if you are unsure about getting financing. Include a statement such as "This earnest agreement is contingent upon the buyer's obtaining financing from a bank for XXX thousand dollars." Remember, the earnest agreement (called an *offer* in California) is *your* proposal. Put in what *you* want. Let the seller change it, then you review it.

If the earnest, or binder, agreement is accepted, a contract of sale is drawn. This is sometimes called a sales contract, a conditional sales contract, or a purchase contract. Usually the signing of a contract of sale is accompanied by a deposit, which may be 10 percent of the purchase price paid to the seller. Often the buyer merely adds to the existing earnest money to bring it up to that desired amount.

The deposit may be put into an **escrow account** or a trusteed savings account that earns interest from the time it is paid to the seller until the buyer takes possession of the house. When any substantial sum is involved, it is, of course, advantageous to the buyer to have the deposit put into a trusteed savings account with the interest accruing to the buyer rather than the seller. This is particularly advantageous if there is a long time lag between the signing of the sales contract and the actual date of possession of the house.

Closing Costs

Exhibit 7-7 indicates the typical closing costs on a $60,000 house. Generally, closing costs are 3 or 4 percent of the total purchase price and is money that you must produce in addition to your down payment. That means you must have cash for closing costs.

Exhibit 7-8 shows a form you can use to figure the costs involved in buying a house.

THE REAL ESTATE SETTLEMENT PROCEDURES ACT

A recent law requires that all closing costs be specifically outlined to you before you buy a home. The 1976 revisions of the Real Estate Settlement Procedures Act make these stipulations about buying a house and borrowing money to pay for it:

1. Within three business days after you apply for a mortgage loan, the lender must send you a booklet, prepared by the U.S. Department of Housing and Urban Development, that outlines your rights and explains settlement procedures and costs.

2. The lender must give you an estimate of most of the settlement costs within that three-day period.

3. The lender must clearly identify individuals or firms that he or she may require you to use for legal or other services, including title insurance and search.

4. If your loan is approved, the lender must provide you with a truth-in-lending statement that shows the annual percentage rate on the mortgage loan.

5. Lenders, title insurors, and others involved in the real estate transaction cannot pay kickbacks for referring business to them.

For further details about RESPA regulations, you may write the Assistant Secretary for Consumer Affairs and Regulatory Functions, Real Estate Practices Division, Department of Housing and Urban Development, Room 4100, Washington, D.C. 20410.

EXHIBIT 7-7.

**TYPICAL CLOSING COSTS ON
A $60,000 HOME**

*The service or setup charge on a
mortgage usually varies from 1-1/2
to 2-1/2 percent, the lower figure
being applied to a loan that is 75 to
80 percent of the purchase price of
a house. If, for example, on a
$60,000 house, you put a down
payment of 20 percent, or $12,000,
you would have to pay a setup or
service charge of 1-1/2 percent of
$48,000 or $720. Title insurance
would average $200. A recording
fee would be another $6, and vari-
ous other things added in would
make the total closing costs 3 to 4
percent of the value of the house, or,
for a $60,000 house, about $1,800 to
$2,400.*

Service Charge:	on 75 or 80% loan = 1½% on 90 or 95% loan = 2 to 2½%
Title Insurance:	average $200
Recording Fee:	about $6
Fire Insurance:	about ¼% of sale price
The bank also collects the taxes on the house	
Credit Report:	$10 to $15
Appraisal Fee:	VA-FHA = $50 Other $75 to $100
TOTAL CLOSING COSTS:	3 to 4% of house value

SEARCH AND TITLE INSURANCE

When you purchase something as large as a house, you must be sure that you really own it, that no one with a prior claim can dispute your title to the land and structure. Any of the four following methods of search can inform you if you have title, free and clear, to the property.

1. *An abstract.* Usually a lawyer or title guarantee company will trace the history of the ownership of the property. The resulting document, called an abstract, will indicate whether any claims are still outstanding. Note, however, that the abstract, no matter how lengthy it is, does not guarantee that you have the title. Nonetheless, if the search has been careful, it provides reassurance.

2. *Certificates of title.* In some areas of the country, this is used instead of an abstract. An attorney merely certifies that all the records affecting the property have been examined, and, in the opinion of the attorney, there are no claims on it. Note, however, that the attorney is not guaranteeing his or her opinion and cannot be liable if some obscure claim does arise in the future.

3. *Torrens certificate.* This certificate, issued by a governmental unit, gives evidence of title to real property. It is used mainly in large cities. You can get it more quickly and it is usually safer than an abstract or certificate of title. An official recorder or registrar issues a certificate stating ownership and allowing anyone who has prior claim on the real property to sue. If no suit develops, then a court will order the registrar to record the title in your name; a certificate to this effect will be issued.

EXHIBIT 7-8.

AN ESTIMATE OF COST AND CASH REQUIREMENTS FOR PURCHASING A HOUSE

Loan Amount $_____   Purchase Price $_____

ESTIMATED COSTS

Service Charge $_____

Title Insurance   _____

Recording Fee   _____

Due Seller for _____ Taxes   _____

Fire Insurance Premium   _____

Interest from _____ to _____   _____

Tax Registration   _____

Allowed Toward _____ Taxes   _____

Assessments   _____

Credit Report   _____

Escrow Fee   _____

Appraisal Fee   _____

TOTAL $_____ *

ESTIMATED CASH REQUIREMENTS

Down Payment $_____

Estimated Costs $_____

Subtotal $_____

Less Earnest Money $_____

TOTAL $_____

ESTIMATED MONTHLY PAYMENT AT ____% FOR ____ YEARS

Principal & Interest $_____

Taxes   _____

Insurance   _____

Mortgage Life Insurance   _____

Mortgage Disability Insurance   _____

TOTAL $_____

*Plus Reimbursement to Seller for Unused Fuel Oil

4. *Title insurance.* A title guarantee company will search extensively through the records pertaining to the property you wish to buy. When it is satisfied that there are no prior claims to that property, it will write a title insurance policy for the lender and/or for you, the new owner. The insurance policy guarantees that if any defects arise in the title, the title company itself will defend for the owner and pay all legal expenses involved.

If the property you are purchasing is already covered by a title policy, you might be eligible for a reduced rate on the one you want to take out. Ask for a reissue, the lower rate of which will only apply to the original face value of the old policy. The regular rate will apply to the difference between what you are paying for the house and the original value.

Note that title insurance may sound better than it actually is. Generally, it does not cover government actions that could restrict use of ownership of the property you just bought. Often, title insurance excludes mechanics liens not recorded with the proper official agency when the policy was issued. In other words, if work was done on the house and not paid for by the former owner, it is possible, even with title insurance, that you must pay for that work. You should always ask the seller for a copy of paid bills for any obviously recent repairs or additions to the home.

SHOPPING FOR A MORTGAGE

If you are like most individuals, you will look for a mortgage when you decide to buy a house. And it's a good idea to shop around. Note that for every 1/2 of 1 percent that you reduce the interest rate on your mortgage, you will save $4.08 a year per $1,000 of mortgage. Thus, on a thirty-year $30,000 mortgage, you would save a total of $3,672 over the thirty-year period.

The larger your down payment, the better your chances of getting a lower rate. So you can reduce mortgage costs by making as large a down payment as possible. But then you can't earn explicit interest on all the money tied up in your house.

The shorter the term that you make your mortgage, the lower will be your overall interest payments and, generally, the greater your ability to receive a preferred interest rate. Try, therefore, to make the payment period as short as possible while keeping your monthly mortgage payments manageable.

When you shop for a mortgage, you should know the language of the mortgage trade.

1. *Prepayment privilege.* The mortgage can be prepaid, without penalty, before the maturity date. You might want to prepay later on if interest rates in the economy fall below what you are actually paying or if you move. You would pay the mortgage off by refinancing it at a lower interest charge.

2. *Package mortgage.* This mortgage covers the cost of all household equipment, as well as the house itself. You might try to get one if you do not have the cash to buy furniture and you think you can get a lower interest charge through a mortgage company than through other credit sources. (Some finance experts advise against this because you pay interest on the money for the equipment long after you have used it to its maximum.)

3. *Open-end mortgage.* This mortgage allows you to borrow more money in the future without rewriting the mortgage. With an open-end mortgage, you can add on to the house or repair it and have the mortgage company pay these bills. The mortgage company then charges you a larger monthly payment or increases the life span of your loan.

PREPAYING INSURANCE AND TAXES

Most mortgage sellers require the mortgagor—that is, the home owner—to prepay taxes and insurance as part of the monthly payments. Say that a savings and loan association is the mortgagee: a special reserve account is set up within the savings and loan association, and the cost of your home insurance and taxes are paid from it every year. This way the mortgagee does not have to worry about foreclosure on the house because of unpaid taxes or problems if the house burns down and is not insured.[3]

Appraising the Replacement Cost of Your House

You may wish, or be required by the lender, to use the services of a professional appraiser to get an accurate replacement value of your house. Rather than paying from $50 to $200 for an appraiser to do this, you can use the services of companies such as GAB Business Services, Inc., 1101 State Road, Princeton, New Jersey 08540 (telephone (800) 621-2306). You can write or call for a GAB Valurate, which you complete and return with a check for $9.95. You will get back an appraisal based on your local labor-materials cost. American Appraisal Associates, Inc., of Milwaukee, Wisconsin, provides a similar service but only through certain insurance agents. You might ask your local insurance agent to help appraise your house, or a local home builder might be able to assist you.

COPING WITH REPAIRS

One way to avoid having to make many repairs is to keep your property well maintained. But this, of course, takes time and money. It is often useful to

---

[3]Incidentally, the special reserve account into which you pay each month usually does not earn interest. Rather, the holder of that account uses it in a way that will earn interest for the mortgaging institution.

keep a list of repair people whom you know are honest and give high-quality service. Perhaps you can join a local organization that can simplify your repair problems by reducing information costs. The American Homeowners Association (AHA), organized in Milwaukee in 1969, has spread to at least six other states. Members pay between ten and twenty dollars a year to cover emergency repair calls. The first half-hour of such work is free, and everything else costs straight-time rates—that is, with no overtime pay. The AHA is responsible for assigning workers they consider competent.

Also available is a prepaid repair and maintenance program called Palace Guard, a service of the American Homeowners Association. It is similar to a life or casualty protection policy, except that it covers major equipment in your house, such as central heating and cooling systems, sheet metal duct work, electrical and plumbing systems, plumbing fixtures, hot water heaters, water softeners, and built-in appliances, including oven, range, dishwasher, and garbage disposal. Basically, you pay an annual set fee for this service. Information on the American Homeowners Association can be obtained from 5301 West Burleigh Street, Milwaukee, Wisconsin 53210. Local divisions of the American Homeowners Association administer the Palace Guard program and can give you full details.

Buying Repair Insurance

An increasing number of home buyers purchase warranties or insurance against defects in the home. These contracts protect new owners against such things as defective plumbing and wiring and, sometimes, appliance, roofing, and structural defects. Some plans give protection against major structural defects for up to ten years. Such warranties, available to buyers of *new* homes for some time, are issued through builders affiliated with the National Association of Home Builders.

Now, buyers of *used* homes can obtain similar coverage for anywhere from $150 to $300 per year. One of the largest warranty providers is American

Home Shield Corporation based in Dublin, California. More than 2,000 agents offer its program in California, New Jersey, and Florida and, perhaps by the time you read this, in Arizona and Texas. The basic yearly fee is around $200; however, home owners must pay a $20 fee for each service call. Certified Homes Corporation, based in Columbia, Maryland, offers warranties in sixteen major areas (mainly in the Northeast). It gives an eighteen-month contract but only for homes found in good condition after the inspection. It is estimated that 2 million used homes will be covered by such warranties by the end of the 1970s.

MAKING THE MOVE

If you are moving from one part of the country to another, you can employ the services of moving consultants. But, generally, this is useful only if you are in an upper-income bracket. Otherwise, your time may be worth less than a moving consultant's time.

Although the government regulates movers, you cannot be certain of a guaranteed move. The following new regulations apply to the moving industry:

1. The price estimates must be based on the moving company's actual physical inspection of whatever you ask it to move.

2. Well in advance of the actual moving day, a mover must give you, the consumer, an *Order for Service,* which states the estimated price of the move and the mutually agreed upon pick-up and delivery dates.

3. The moving van must come on the promised day. The company can be fined up to $500 if it fails to do so.

4. The shipment must be delivered and all services performed on payment of the estimated amount, plus no more than an additional 10 percent in case of an underestimate. You have fifteen working days to pay anything you owe the company above 110 percent of what they estimated in writing.

How to Pick a Mover

Picking a mover is tricky. Surveys of people's reactions to different movers show that, even within the same moving company, the quality of service varies greatly. The level of complaints seems to be about the same for each of the largest firms: North American Van, United, Bekins, Allied, and Arrow Mayflower. You should get two or three estimates made of your moving task. But don't be fooled into giving the job to the company with the lowest estimate: The ICC has made sure that the industry charges about the same price for weight and mileage.

Don't Cut Time Corners

Don't postpone your move to the last minute. Make sure that the movers come a few days before you must vacate your house. Sometimes movers fail to come to your old house on time, and that may spell disaster if you are supposed to leave the same day the mover comes.

Appliances

You must pay extra to have appliances prepared for moving. Call your regular repair services and have them do it. Also have them explain, in writing, what must be done to restore things to service later.

Watch Out!

As the movers load your belongings, check a copy of the inventory form to find out how they describe the condition of your furniture. A series of code letters indicate scratched, marred, gouged, cracked, soiled, and so on. If you think the movers' description is exaggerated, make sure it is changed immediately. If the description of damage to your furniture is overstated, you will have no recourse for a damage payment if your belongings are damaged in transit. Since a full 25 percent of all moves end in some dispute over damages, this is a critical point.

The ICC suggests that you personally observe the weighing of the empty truck, its loading, reweighing, and unloading. You should also personally check off, on your inventory sheet, the items as they are unloaded. When your furniture is finally delivered, be there. Don't sign an inventory sheet, no matter what the driver says, until you've had the time to check for damage and loss.

Having your goods moved by a firm that is fully insured and/or bonded doesn't mean a thing. Unless otherwise arranged, any carrier's liability for your goods damaged in transit is limited to sixty cents a pound. If a $400 portable color TV, weighing sixty pounds is completely destroyed, the carrier is only liable up to sixty cents times sixty pounds, or thirty-six dollars. But there are two ways to get more adequate protection:

1. Do not set a specific value on your goods. The mover's maximum liability becomes $1.25 multiplied by the weight of the shipment; thus, a 4,000 pound shipment would have a $5,000 maximum liability. You get the full value up to the maximum for anything damaged or lost, minus depreciation.

2. Insure the actual dollar value of your goods. This protection costs 50 cents per $100 of value.

Making a Claim

There's a good chance you will want to make a claim for lost, broken, or damaged items. Generally, there is a claims bureau in your town that will send someone to your home to estimate damage or to take things to be repaired. A 1972 ICC rule stipulates that the van line on an interstate move is "absolutely responsible for all acts or omissions" of its agents. If you fail to get satisfaction, call the nearest ICC office. If that fails also, write the director of the Bureau of Operations, Interstate Commerce Commission, Washington, D.C. 20423. If you think you have been badly abused, you may want to go to small claims court, which we described in Appendix A.

An Alternative

If you have the time and some friends to help and you want to save some money and avoid problems with movers, you can rent a truck and move yourself. The one-way rental rate across the United States is quite reasonable. Remember, though, you must count the time and fatigue costs of this particular moving method. Since the cost of moving yourself is directly related to the income you forego or the implicit value you put on the leisure time lost, you may find moving yourself is the most economical way. Students who do not have summer jobs, for example, have a very low opportunity cost and, therefore, may wish to move themselves. On the other hand, if you are a high-income executive, it wouldn't make sense for you to spend two weeks driving a truck across the United States in order to save moving expenses, for you would sacrifice considerable income.

Problems with Do-It-Yourself Moving

If you decide to move yourself, be aware of a number of problems:

1. If you have no experience loading a truck and distributing the weight evenly in a vehicle, the trailer may jackknife causing considerable damage. Therefore, you must place large, heavy items on the bottom and fill open spaces with small items. It is best to strap down all items.

2. Be careful of back strain, a frequent result of moving heavy items.

3. Be wary of inexperienced helpers.

4. Realize that, unless you make sure your insurance is in effect, you will not be insured during the move.

5. Consider other costs — motels, babysitters — of moving yourself.

GLOSSARY OF TERMS

COOPERATIVE APARTMENTS Each dweller owns a proportionate share of a nonprofit corporation that holds legal rights to the building.

CONDOMINIUM The owner has legal title to the apartment and joint ownership interest in the common areas and facilities in the building.

MOBILE HOMES Homes that are built on an assembly line and transported to a specific location, usually a mobile home park, from which they are rarely, if ever, moved.

TOWNHOUSE A unit, with a front and back yard, that shares common side walls.

MODULAR HOMES A factory-manufactured living unit, the sections of which can be arranged in various ways.

LEASE Usually a long-term rental contract for a home, apartment, car, or other durables.

EQUITY The difference between what is owed on, for example, a home and what is the resale value. If the home is worth $100,000 and the bank is still owed $70,000, the equity is $30,000.

MARGINAL TAX RATE The tax rate applied to the last dollars earned. It is the tax rate that must be paid on additional income.

MARGINAL TAX BRACKET The last bracket of income to which the marginal tax rate applies.

CAPITAL GAIN The difference between the buying and selling price of an asset.

MORTGAGE A loan for which a dwelling unit is used as security, or collateral.

CONVENTIONAL MORTGAGE A loan, made for a dwelling, that usually runs for twenty to thirty years and requires equal payments throughout the years, generally monthly.

VA LOANS Loans administered by the Veterans Administration to qualified veterans or their spouses or widows. Such loans are guaranteed; the lender does not have to worry about default.

FHA LOANS A mortgage insured by the Federal Housing Administration.

DISCOUNT POINTS A device used to raise the effective interest rate paid on a loan. A point is a charge of 1 percent; each discount point is subtracted from the amount of the loan to give a net loan figure, even though the interest rate is charged on the total amount of the loan prior to the deduction of interest points.

ASKING PRICE   The price at which a home is put on the market for sale.

EARNEST, OR BINDER, AGREEMENT   An agreement you sign when you make an offer for a house. Usually it is good for twenty-four hours, during which time the owner of the house must accept or reject your offer. If it is accepted, you are committed to the purchase and can, under most circumstances, lose your earnest agreement money if you back down.

ESCROW ACCOUNT   An account into which earnest money or a deposit or down payment is put. Once the money is put into an escrow account, it is no longer under the control of the buyer. But title to the property of the house does not pass to the buyer until all the agreements in the sale contract are fulfilled.

CHAPTER SUMMARY

1. There are numerous types of housing units, including cooperatives, condominiums, duplexes, apartments, mobile homes, townhouses, and modular homes.

2. The owner of a cooperative apartment: (a) leases the unit; (b) has financial responsibility for his or her own payments plus those other owners miss; (c) is assessed a monthly fee to cover maintenance, services, taxes, and mortgage; and (d) votes to elect a board of directors.

3. A condominium owner: (a) owns the unit, (b) has joint ownership interest in the common areas, (c) arranges for his or her own mortgage and pays taxes individually, (d) makes separate payments for building maintenance, and (e) votes to elect a board of managers.

4. Mobile homes often are purchased today because their initial price is lower than other housing types. They are built on an assembly-line basis, often using lower-priced nonunion labor.

5. The advantages of renting are: (a) greater mobility, (b) no down payment, (c) no maintenance and depreciation, (d) no worries about changes in property values, and (e) no liability of ownership.

6. The advantages of buying are: (a) freedom of use, (b) a possible investment, (c) tax benefits.

7. "Doing it yourself" reduces taxes because you don't first have to earn money on which you pay taxes in order to pay for the services rendered. Rather you do them yourself. The government does not tax you on the value of the services performed.

8. Interest paid on a mortgage and taxes for a home are both tax deductible.

9. There is no guarantee that investment in a home will yield an above-normal rate of return.

10. There are four sources of mortgage money: savings and loan associations, mortgage companies, commercial banks, and mutual savings banks. Additionally, there are insurance companies and mortgage pools.

11. There are three kinds of mortgages: conventional, Veterans Administration (VA), and Federal Housing Administration (FHA).

12. When discount points are applied to a mortgage, the implicit interest rate is raised; the points are to raise interest rates above some legal ceiling.

13. A variable-interest-rate mortgage is attractive to mortgage-granting institutions in a period of dramatically changing rates of interest. They don't have to worry about losing money when interest rates rise unexpectedly.

14. Deciding where you want to live depends on: (a) the area's relationship to your work, (b) property taxes, (c) schools, (d) shopping availability, (e) air quality, (f) noise pollution, (g) crime, (h) the neighborhood, and (i) zoning and development.

15. When shopping for a house, you must determine how much you can afford. This requires estimating your dependable after-tax income for at least one-third of the mortgage and estimating housing expenses per month.

16. A general rule of thumb is that you should not buy a house whose price is greater than one-and-one-half to two times your gross yearly income.

17. A real estate broker provides you with information about available houses.

18. The broker receives a commission for selling the house. That commission can be negotiated, at least implicitly, by the seller asking that the commission be paid over a certain number of years. Further, the buyer can negotiate that commission by telling the broker that he or she will buy the house only if the broker provides, say, a new refrigerator or a new stove.

19. The asking price of a house generally differs from the final sales price. A broker can help you bargain.

20. Once the decision is made to purchase a house, the prospective buyer usually signs an earnest, or binder, agreement. This is sometimes called an offer or conditional sales contract. If the owner agrees to the earnest agreement within twenty-four hours, it usually becomes binding.

21. It is usually advisable to have a building inspection service examine a house before an earnest agreement is signed.

22. Closing costs may account for 3 to 4 percent of the total purchase price of a home.

23. Title insurance is recommended when an older home is being purchased and is often required by the mortgagee (lender). A lawyer's abstract or certificate of title may be sufficient when the house is relatively new or has had only one or two owners.

24. It is possible to reduce title insurance costs by having the original title insurance reissued and merely adding to it if the value of the house has increased.

25. Picking a mover is not an easy job, particularly since no one company seems to have a sterling national reputation. Do not pick movers on the basis of which one gives the lowest estimate. Rates are regulated, so they will all charge the same ultimately.

26. Be careful about how movers evaluate the condition of your household items as they put them into the van.

27. An alternative to using a mover is doing it yourself. However, this may present a number of problems, including the amount of time involved, the cost of one-way rental of a truck, and the possibility of physical injury.

STUDY QUESTIONS

1. Does $46,000 sound like a lot to spend on a house? What is the average price of a new home today?

2. What are the advantages of buying versus renting a house? Can you be guaranteed that the home will always appreciate in value?

3. Do the tax advantages of owning a home benefit everyone equally?

4. If you buy a house for $40,000 in 1979 and sell it for $50,000 in 1985, do you come out ahead? (Be careful: What about inflation?)

5. What are the differences among conventional, VA, and FHA mortgages?

6. How do you compute discount points on a mortgage?

7. Why would mortgage companies require you to prepay insurance and taxes?

8. How do you build up equity in a house?

9. When you "do it yourself," how are you saving money?

10. What is a capital gain?

11. What is the single most important determinant of land value?

CASE PROBLEMS

7-1 Is a House Financially Feasible?

Walt and Mary Jensen, a couple in their late twenties, currently are renting an unfurnished two-bedroom apartment for $350 per month, with an additional $62 for utilities and parking and $5 for renters insurance. They have found a house they can buy for $40,000, with a 20% down payment and a twenty-five year, 9½% mortgage. Closing costs are estimated at $1400. Property taxes are $1080, and insurance is $180 per year. Monthly operating and maintenance costs are estimated at $125.

The Jensens have a combined income of $23,000 per year, with take-home pay of $1400 per month. They are in a 27% tax bracket, pay $125 per month on an installment contract (twelve payments left), and have $9700 in savings.

1. Can the Jensens afford to buy the house? Support your answer with data.

2. Walt and Mary think their monthly costs would be less the first year if they buy the house. Do you agree? (Assume $3040 mortgage interest the first year.)

3. How much will they have left in savings to pay for moving expenses?

7-2 Financing a New Home

Bonnie and Clyde Barker have been married for five years and live with their twin sons Jess and James in a small, two-bedroom older home. They plan to sell their home and buy a newer four-bedroom home for $44,500. They will realize $6000 from the sale of the house and also have $5200 in savings they can use for the down payment plus closing costs of $1780 on their new home. Bonnie has been working full time as a music teacher but has been laid off due to recent cutbacks in funds. Next fall she will be attending the local university part time to earn her masters degree in music therapy. Clyde is a podiatrist in the local medical clinic. He is buying into the medical group, so his gross income will be $17,500 ($15,120 after taxes) for the next three years and then can be expected to increase quite rapidly. The Barkers have been shopping for financing and have three alternatives to choose from:

   a. 10% down payment with a twenty-five-year mortgage at 9¾%;
   b. 20% down with a twenty-five-year mortgage at 9¼%; or
   c. 20% down with a twenty-year graduated payment mortgage at 9½%. The payments for the first five years will be interest only.

1. Which plan will have the lowest monthly payment? The highest?

2. Can they afford the house? What would you recommend and why?

Aaron, Henry J. *Shelters and Subsidies: Who Benefits From Federal Housing Policies?* Washington, D.C.: The Brookings Institution, 1972.

"Buy or Rent a Home?" *U.S. News & World Report,* April 25, 1977, p. 86.

Davis, Joseph C. *Buying Your House: A Complete Guide to Inspection and Evaluation.* New York: Emerson, 1975.

Gray, Genevieve. *Condominiums: How to Buy, Sell, and Live in Them.* New York: Funk & Wagnalls, 1975.

Gross, P. "How to Home in on a Place to Live." *House & Garden,* January 1977, p. 54.

Home Buyers Checklist, National Home Buyers and Home Owners Association, 1225 19th Street N.W., Washington, D.C. 20036 (latest edition).

"How to Avoid the Ten Biggest Home-Buying Traps." *Consumer Bulletin,* August 1969.

Mager, Byron J. *How to Buy a House.* New York: Lyle Stuart, 1965.

Perl, Lila. *The House You Want* New York: David McKay Co., 1965.

APPENDIX B

HOW TO RENT A PLACE TO LIVE

If you decide to rent, you face at least four problems:

1. Obtaining information on rental units available.

2. Making sure you get the right rental unit for you.

3. Making sure the contract or lease is "appropriate."

4. Knowing how to register valid complaints after you have rented the housing unit.

INFORMATION ABOUT RENTAL UNITS

There are basically four sources of information about available rental units:

1. Ads in the local newspapers.

2. Listing agencies.

3. Signs in front of apartment buildings and homes for rent.

4. Friends and acquaintances.

A source of information that people are not always familiar with is rental information agencies, which go by such names as Rentex, Apartment Hunt, and so on. After paying a fee (usually twenty, thirty, or fifty dollars), you have the right to an unlimited number of searches through the files of the agency. In principle, these files are up-to-date and provide information that will save you time and fruitless inspections of unsuitable apartments. For example, if you definitely want to keep a pet in your apartment, you can eliminate many vacant rental units because the files will indicate those that do not allow pets on the premises. The same goes for young children; many apartments do not allow them. Consumers' experiences with rental listing agencies vary. Some report that the listings are up-to-date and accurate. Others contend that the listings are inaccurate and dated.

A number of rental listing agencies practice a form of "bait and switch." They will put an ad for an extremely advantageous rental unit in the classified sections of local newspapers. When you call the agency, you are told that you must pay an advance fee for an "exclusive" list of available houses and apartments. When you request the address of the "too-good-to-be-true" rental unit listed in the newspaper, you will be told that that one has been rented, "but we have lots of other listings." Unlike real estate brokers, who receive a commission *after* they have found you a place to live, rental listing agencies don't refund their fees if you don't find a place to rent through their listings. It is not surprising that the New York Better Business Bureau issued a press release a few years ago indicating that "all advance fee rental agencies [are] not in the public interest."

MAKING THE RIGHT CHOICE

When looking for a rental unit, it is helpful to carry a check list to make comparisons. That way, you won't sign a lease on an apartment or house only to discover later that the rental unit lacks an essential feature.

Exhibit B-1 is a partial recommended check list. You can add any important factors you desire.

THE THORNY PROBLEM OF SECURITY DEPOSITS

It is virtually impossible these days to rent any type of housing unit without leaving a "refundable" security deposit, usually equal to one month's rent. This deposit is supposed to be returned to you if you leave the apartment in an "appropriate" condition. Landlords argue that they need security deposits because they often find damage.

Most states do not have laws regulating security deposits. You can look at deposits in one of two ways. You can assume that you are not going to get it back and divide the number of months you will live in the rental unit into the security deposit to determine the surcharge you are actually paying per month. Or, you can attempt, from the beginning, to have a strong case in favor of getting the money back. To do that, consider the following:

1. Go through the apartment with the landlord the day you move in, marking down every single indication of wear and damage. Sign a copy of your findings and have the landlord sign it, too. Better yet, have it notarized. In some cases, you might want to live in the apartment a few days to find out what is amiss. This is particularly true if you have rented a furnished apartment or house.

2. Retain copies of all bills for improvements, repairs, and/or cleaning you have had done as evidence that you maintained the unit well.

3. Take fairly detailed snapshots showing the condition of the apartment when you moved in and when you leave.

4. If the building you live in is sold, obtain a letter from the former owner explaining who has the security deposit money.

5. Find out what the checking-out regulations are. If they require that the apartment be "broom cleaned," sweep the apartment and then show it to the superintendent or manager.

6. Find out the protections assured by state law.

7. If you do all of the above, you will be ready to go to court if your deposit is not refunded. If you are obviously prepared to do so, most landlords will return your security deposit.

MAKING SURE THE LEASE IS OKAY

Most **standard form leases** seem to favor the landlord. There are a number of clauses that you may want to excise.

Clauses to Cross Out

Confession of judgment. If your lease has this provision, your landlord's lawyer has the legal right to go to court and plead guilty for you in the event that the landlord thinks his rights have been violated—that is, the property has been damaged or the terms of the lease have not been honored. If you sign a lease with a confession-of-judgment provision, you are admitting guilt before committing any act. Such a clause is, in fact, illegal in some states.

Waiver of tort liability. If this provision is in your lease, you have given up in advance the right to sue the landlord should you suffer injury or damage because of your landlord's negligence.

Arbitrary clauses. Certain arbitrary clauses give the landlord the right to cancel the lease because of "dissatisfaction" with your behavior. Other

EXHIBIT B-1. **A RENTAL CHECK LIST**

	APARTMENT A	APARTMENT B	APARTMENT C	APARTMENT D
Monthly rent (including utilities, recreational fees, etc.)				
Amount of security or cleaning deposit				
Are pets allowed?				
Is there a manager or superintendent on the premises at all times?				
Garbage disposal facilities?				
Laundry equipment available on the premises?				
Is the laundry room safe?				
When can the laundry room be used?				
Is there a lobby?				
Is there a doorman?				
Will you have direct access to your unit?				
Is there an elevator? What is its condition?				
Is the apartment close to public transportation?				
Is it close to food stores?				

EXHIBIT B-1 **CONTINUED ON NEXT PAGE**

	APARTMENT A	APARTMENT B	APARTMENT C	APARTMENT D
Entertainment?				
Other shopping?				
Are there sufficient electrical outlets?				
Are carpets and drapes included?				
Is there enough closet space?				
Are there safe and clearly marked fire exits?				
Will the tenants be compatible with you?				
Others				

clauses include: (1) forbidding immoral behavior, (2) forbidding hanging pictures on the wall, (3) forbidding overnight guests (this is usually done by requiring that the apartment can be occupied only by the tenant and members of the tenant's immediate family), (4) forbidding subleasing, (5) allowing the landlord to cancel the lease and holding you liable for rent for the balance of the lease if you are one day late, (6) allowing the landlord to enter your apartment when you are not there (except in case of emergency), (7) making you liable for all repairs, (8) making you obey rules that have not yet been written, (9) stating that you agree that the premises are "fine" as they are.

Clauses to Add to Your Lease

1. If the person renting the unit says that it comes with dishwasher, disposal unit, air conditioner or other equipment, see that these items are listed in the lease.

2. If you have been promised the use of a recreation room, gymnasium, parking lot, swimming pool, and so on, make sure that the lease says so specifically. Also, have it indicate whether or not you must pay extra for the use of those facilities.

3. If the landlord has promised to have the apartment painted, have this indicated in the lease, along with the promised date. If you wish to choose the color, state that in the lease also.

4. In certain cases, you may be able to negotiate a right to premature cancellation if you are transferred to another location. Usually, however, you must negotiate the amount you pay the landlord for exercising this privilege. Ideally, this will be less than the security deposit.

5. Any fixtures, shelves, furnishing, and so on that you install should become your property when you leave the premises.

How to Handle Trouble with Your Landlord

If you believe that you have been unfairly treated by your landlord, there are several steps you can take.

1. Explicitly indicate to your landlord what your grievance is, such as the daytime temperature in your apartment is fifty-five degrees or you have a stopped-up sewage system, a leaking toilet, a refrigerator whose freezing compartment doesn't work.

2. If you get no satisfaction, type several copies of the complaint list. Mail one to your landlord; one to the housing agency or renter's office in your area; and one to the housing inspector, if one comes. Keep one for yourself. If there is an organized tenants' group in your area, send one to it, too. You can find out where these organizations are by writing the National Tenants Organization, 425 Thirteenth Street N.W., Washington, D.C. 20005.

3. Whenever you contact the agency that administers the housing code in your area, request a visit from a housing inspector, who will certify the validity of your complaint.

Withholding Rent

If your complaints are serious enough, you may have, in some states, the legal right to withhold part or all of your rent. Approximately half the states in the union allow the tenant to deduct repairs from the rent and provide for not paying any rent when the dwelling is "unlivable." Many states also have procedures for legal rent strikes. If you repair and deduct from your rent the cost of repairs, there may be a limit to how much money can be deducted. In many states, the limit is one-half a month's rent or $100, whichever is greater. In Massachusetts, the limit is two months' rent; in New Jersey, there is no fixed maximum.

GLOSSARY OF TERMS

Security Deposit: A deposit—usually one month's rent—that must be given to the landlord. Also called a cleaning deposit, it is, in principle, refundable.

Standard Form Lease: A printed lease used by landlords in a particular geographic area. It will have standard clauses, such as confession of judgment and waiver of tort liability.

The Automobile

EIGHT

■The twentieth century might aptly be called the Age of the Automobile. The automobile has indeed become a pervasive part of American life. The trend began modestly at the turn of the century, when a few courageous souls drove around in Stutz Bearcats, Hupmobiles, and Model T's. Then Henry Ford developed low-cost mass-production techniques to turn out his $870 "Tin Lizzies." Today, toward the end of the 1970s, fully 88 percent of all American families own cars. The trend toward multiple-car families is also continuing, as Exhibit 8-1 shows; today, one-third of all families in the United States have two vehicles in their driveways.

WE SPEND A LOT ON CARS

In the United States today, there are close to 110 million cars. The number of new cars manufactured every year sometimes exceeds 11 million. Money spent on purchasing automobiles, on automobile repairs, and on other related expenses accounts for 12 percent of total income in the United States. The automobile industry itself is huge. One out of every six people in the United States has a job related to automobiles, whether it be as a factory worker in Detroit or as an employee of a company making spare parts or servicing cars. The famous statement, "Whatever is good for General Motors is good for America," could well be based on the sheer numbers involved in automobile-related employment.

THE RISING COST OF NEW CARS

Exhibit 8-2 shows what has happened in nineteen years to the nominal cost of a typical new car. Even when we correct for inflation, we still see

193

that the average real price has risen in the last decade. There are at least two reasons why car prices relative to other prices have risen; they involve additional safety equipment and pollution abatement devices.

We Are Buying More Safety

In 1962, Ralph Nader wrote *Unsafe At Any Speed*. With the publication of that book, he and others launched a campaign to require that cars be

---

EXHIBIT 8-1. **TREND IN MULTIPLE CAR OWNERSHIP**

The trend in multiple car ownership is continuing upward. In 1957, only 13 percent of families in the U.S. had two or more cars, whereas in 1972, the figure reached almost 30 percent. Source: 1971-72 *Survey of Consumers*, Lewis Mandell, George Katona, James N. Morgan, Jay Schmiedeskamp, Contributions to Behavioral Economics (Institute for Social Research, The University of Michigan: Ann Arbor) 1973. Later years are estimated.

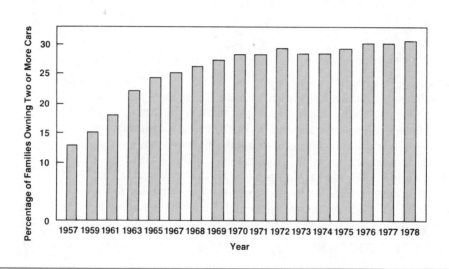

EXHIBIT 8-2.   **NOMINAL COST OF A TYPICAL NEW CAR**

1978	$5,600
1977	5,250
1972	4,000
1970	3,800
1968	3,690
1966	3,500
1964	3,400
1962	3,250
1960	3,200

built to protect the occupants. Congress responded, and the result was the Motor Vehicle Safety Act of 1966, the basis of most current safety requirements on automobiles.

Some of the requirements imposed on car manufacturers by the National Highway Traffic Safety Administration are:

1 Dual braking systems;
2 Nonprotruding interior appliances;
3 Over-the-shoulder safety belts in the front seat;
4 Head restraints on all front seats;
5 Seat-belt warning systems and ignition interlocks;
6 Collapsible, impact-absorbing arm rests; and
7 Impact-absorbing instrument panels.

Most, if not all, of the required safety equipment on a new car add to the cost of each car's production. It may only cost an additional fifteen dollars per car to move the gas tank from under the trunk to behind the back seat (in order to reduce the number of injuries or deaths by fires). But when you add that fifteen dollars to the additional cost of all of the other safety requirements, the total is significant. In other words, we are driving safer cars today, and we are paying considerably more for them.

Pollution Abatement Costs Money, Too

Cars emit pollution. Some states and the federal government have legislated maximum pollution limits on internal combustion engines. In order to satisfy these legislated limits, car manufacturers have had to install pollution abatement devices, redesign engines, and do numerous other things in order to meet the requirements. The costs of research and development, as well as the actual per unit cost of pollution abatement devices, are passed on to you, the consumer. This, then, is another reason why the relative price of cars has risen in the last decade, before which virtually no such devices were required.

THE PRIVATE COSTS OF DRIVING

The price of a new or used car is only one aspect of the total cost to you, the purchaser. There are at least five other private costs you must consider before purchasing a particular car. They are: (1) interest payments, (2) depreciation, (3) gasoline, (4) repairs, and (5) insurance.

Interest

If you were able to borrow all the money to buy a $5,000 car (this is highly unlikely), then you would know explicitly the interest you would pay for the loan on the car. Your creditor would give you an explicit statement of the average percentage finance charge. You could then calculate the dollars per year that you would spend on interest.

Actually, though, whether or not you borrow the money for the car, you will implicitly be paying interest on its value. Consider, for example, the possibility of your having the entire $5,000 purchase price in cash. You pay the seller of the car and now own it outright. Does that mean that you are paying zero interest? The answer is no. You are giving up the opportunity of earning interest on that $5,000. You could have, alternatively, put the $5,000 in a savings and loan association and earned, say, 6 percent per year. Thus, the *implicit* interest cost to you of the automobile is the interest you could earn on the money tied up in the car. Actually, since the resale value of the car will drop steadily, the interest that you forego will be based on a smaller and smaller figure. In the second year you own the car, its resale value may only be, say, $3,000, in which case, you are giving up the opportunity to earn interest on $3,000 rather than $5,000.

In technical language, you face an opportunity cost of continuing to possess a car, whether or not you have borrowed the money. The greater the resale value of the car and the higher the rate of interest you could earn in, say, a savings and loan association, the greater will be this opportunity cost of continuing to own the car—regardless of whether or not you bought the car on credit.

Depreciation

Virtually all consumer durable goods, such as automobiles, washers, dryers, and stereos, depreciate. **Depreciation** is defined as the reduction in market, or resale, value of a durable good over a period of time. Actually, we can distinguish here between the almost instantaneous depreciation a car suffers when it is purchased and the depreciation more closely linked with the amount of time you keep the vehicle.

Cost of acquisition. When you sign on the dotted line for an automobile, you immediately incur what we call the **cost of acquisition.** That cost is equal to the difference between the price you paid for the automobile and its *immediate* resale value. Usually, if not always, it is virtually impossible to turn around and sell a car for exactly the price you paid for it. It is difficult to find someone else with exactly the same tastes and income you have who wants a car at that moment. Thus, to get someone else to purchase exactly the car you bought, you would have to offer it at a discount—hence, the difference between the price you paid and the immediate resale price. Once you sign on the dotted line and take legal possession of the car, you incur the cost of acquisition, and there's nothing you can do about it.

Normal depreciation. If you decide to keep a car after you have bought it, its market value will decrease slowly for two reasons. First, newer models, more sought after by the buying public, will become available. And, second, the car will deteriorate physically. The greatest percentage of depreciation is in the first year of ownership. Then the percentage rate of depreciation gradually declines. When you keep a car for one more year after owning it for, say, eight years, the reduction in its market value may be only a few percentage points.

EXHIBIT 8-3. **DEPRECIATION RATE OF CARS**

	1ST YEAR	2ND YEAR	3RD YEAR	4TH YEAR	5TH YEAR
Standard	75.1%	59.7%	46.6%	37.0%	30.0%
Compact	86.0%	73.0%	61.5%	51.0%	41.0%
Subcompact	88.0%	77.0%	66.0%	55.3%	45.0%

Here we show what happens to the market value of three types of cars kept for five years. For example, a standard car has an average resale value, one year after purchase, of only 75.1 percent of its original price; by the fifth year, it has a resale value of only 30 percent of its purchase price. Thus, the depreciation is approximately 25 percent the first year. Over five years, the car depreciates in value 70 percent. U.S. Department of Transportation, Federal Highway Administration

Exhibit 8-3 shows the U.S. Department of Transportation's estimates of the rate of depreciation of automobiles. As you can see, the more expensive the car, the greater the rate of depreciation in the first few years. Thus, a subcompact depreciates at a slower rate than a large luxury car. And the percentage rate of depreciation of certain specialty cars, such as high-priced Ferraris and Lamberghinis, is even more pronounced.

Gasoline

Gasoline is a major cost of operating an automobile. Because it is consumed whenever a car is driven, the cost of gasoline for running an automobile varies directly with the rate of use.

As gasoline becomes more expensive, individuals have sought to reduce its consumption. This can be done by purchasing lighter, less-powerful automobiles; scheduling more frequent tune-ups; and driving at slower speeds. The U.S. Department of Transportation has studied the effect of speed on fuel consumption rates. Their findings can be seen in Exhibit 8-4. Note, for example, that, on average, driving at seventy miles an hour increases the consumption of gasoline by over 30 percent compared with driving at fifty miles an hour.

Repair Costs

Repairs are an important part of the total cost of driving. Since there are so many cars on the highway, it is not surprising that the automobile repair industry is immense. There are at least 100,000 garages in the United States, as well as 200,000 gas stations that also give repair service. The labor costs for auto repairs have increased rapidly in the last few years. Exhibit 8-5 shows what has happened to average hourly earnings of automotive mechanics from 1961 through 1978. From 1961 to 1978,

EXHIBIT 8-4.

EFFECT OF SPEED ON FUEL CONSUMPTION RATES
SOURCE: U.S. Department of Transportation, Federal Highway Administration, *The Effect of Speed on Automobile Consumption Rates,* October 1973.

TEST CAR NUMBER AND WEIGHT		MILES PER GALLON AT DIFFERENT SPEEDS					PERCENT INCREASE OR DECREASE IN GASOLINE CONSUMPTION CAUSED BY INCREASE IN SPEED				
	(lbs.)	30	40	50	60	70	30 to 40	40 to 50	50 to 60	60 to 70	50 to 70
1	(4,880)	17.12	17.20	16.11	14.92	13.13	—0.05	6.76	7.97	13.63	22.70
2	(3,500)	19.30	18.89	17.29	15.67	13.32	2.17	9.25	10.34	17.64	29.80
2A	(3,500)	21.33	21.33	18.94	17.40	15.36	—0.01	12.64	8.85	13.28	23.31
3	(3,540)	23.67	24.59	20.46	14.83	13.42	—3.74	22.67	37.96	8.96	52.46
4	(3,975)	18.25	20.00	16.32	15.77	13.61	—8.75	22.55	3.49	15.87	19.91
5	(2,450)	31.45	35.19	33.05	30.78	22.82	—10.63	6.47	7.37	34.88	44.83
6	(3,820)	22.88	19.41	20.28	17.78	14.88	17.88	—4.29	14.06	19.49	36.29
7	(3,990)	15.61	14.89	16.98	13.67	11.08	4.84	—12.31	24.21	23.38	53.25
8	(2,050)	24.79	27.22	26.80	24.11	n.a.	—8.93	1.57	11.16	n.a.	n.a.
9	(2,290)	21.55	20.07	19.11	17.83	16.72	7.37	5.02	7.18	6.64	14.29
10	(2,400)	22.72	21.94	22.22	21.08	17.21	3.56	—0.13	5.41	22.49	29.11
11	(5,250)	18.33	19.28	15.62	14.22	12.74	—4.93	23.43	9.85	11.62	22.61
12	(4,530)	20.33	20.00	17.50	16.17	14.86	1.65	14.29	8.23	8.82	17.77
Average (unweighted)		21.05	21.07	19.49	17.51	14.93	0.00	8.11	11.31	17.28	30.53

EXHIBIT 8-5.

AVERAGE EARNING OF AUTO MECHANICS
SOURCE: Bureau of Labor Statistics

1961	$2.69	1970	$4.01
1962	2.80	1971	4.39
1963	2.91	1972	4.83
1964	3.01	1973	5.21
1965	3.11	1974	5.65
1966	3.23	1975	5.94
1967	3.36	1976	6.21
1968	3.54	1977	6.95
1969	3.76	1978	7.13

average wages for automotive mechanics increased 265 percent; during that same time period, the Consumer Price Index increased only 220 percent. In total, we spend $18 billion a year on automobile repairs.

Some consumer economists believe that preventive maintenance avoids large repair bills. This is true, but you must consider the maintenance costs themselves. In the long run, it may be cheaper not to keep your car in perfect condition but, rather, to let some things (other than brakes, tires, and safety-related parts) wear out and then replace them or to trade in your car every few years. Some state governments buy fleets of cars, which they don't service at all for a year, and then trade them in. This seems to be cheaper than trying to maintain the cars and, as the price of repair services rises, will become still cheaper by comparison.

Thus, you have two choices: either buy a car you expect to keep only for a short period of time, or buy a car with a reputation for low service requirements. The yearly April issue of *Consumer Reports,* for example, reports its readers' experiences with the repair needs of different makes and years of cars. This is an important aid when you try to assess the annual cost of operating an automobile.

Insurance

Automobile insurance is an important cost of driving. Average insurance rates have risen dramatically in the last decade, far outstripping inflation. One reason insurance companies claim they must continually raise rates is that juries are giving larger and larger awards to victims of automobile accidents.

THE TOTAL COST OF DRIVING—AN EXAMPLE

We have just outlined five costs of driving. Now let's work through a numerical example to make these costs more meaningful. Consider the possibility of purchasing a standard car for $5,000 plus tax, which we'll assume is 10 percent of the purchase price. (There is a federal excise tax on the purchase of new automobiles, as well as state and, sometimes, city sales taxes.) Let's further assume that the car is purchased with cash, so that all the interest lost is implicit rather than explicit. The car will be driven 10,000 miles the first year. It gets twenty miles per gallon, and gas is selling for seventy cents per gallon.

Here are the costs for one year's operation:
1 *Taxes* = 10 percent of $5,000 = $500[1]
2 *Gasoline* = 10,000 miles ÷ 20 miles per gallon = 500 gallons; 500 gallons × 70¢ per gallon = $350
3 *Repairs.* Since the car will be under warranty, we will assume that only tune-ups are necessary, and the cost is $125.

---

[1]These taxes are usually deductible for the purposes of figuring federal income taxes. Therefore, their net, or actual, cost is somewhat lower.

4   *Insurance.* We'll assume that insurance is $400.
5   *Cost of acquisition.* For a $5,000 car, we'll assume that the difference between purchase price and immediate resale would be $750.
6   *Interest foregone.* The interest foregone will be calculated on the basis of what the car could be sold for immediately after its purchase, or $5,000 − $750 = $4,250. If we assume that you could get 6 percent in a savings and loan association, the interest cost of continued possession for the first year is $255.
7   *Depreciation.* In Exhibit 8-3, we showed that the first year's depreciation for a standard car is 25 percent. 25 percent × $5,000 = $1,250. We have already taken account of what the U.S. Department of Transportation considers first year depreciation when we calculated the cost of acquisition at $750. Thus, the remainder will be the true first year's depreciation. So 25 percent × $5,000 = $1,250 − $750 = $500.
8   *The grand total* is $2,880.

That means that, for the first year of ownership of this $5,000 standard car, you will pay $2,880, or 28.8¢ a mile.

SHOULD YOU BUY A NEW OR USED CAR?

Most of us, when we consider purchasing transportation, are tempted to buy something new. There are certainly good reasons for buying a new car instead of a used one. A new car has never been touched by someone else so you don't have to worry about how it was treated by a previous owner. A new car may be safer, it may run more smoothly, it may be more stylish, and so on, although these aspects are not as subject to annual changes as they once were. On the other hand, new cars don't always run as well as used cars; to some buyers, they don't always look as nice; and they may not always be as comfortable. Knowing this, you still may choose a new car—simply because you like new things. Remember, though, that a new, full-sized domestic car may automatically depreciate about $1,000 when you take it off the dealer's showroom floor.

Sometimes you get the benefit of a warranty when you buy a new car. American Motors, for example, had the following warranty for its 1978 automobiles: Twelve months or 12,000 miles on the complete car, from windshield wiper blades to complete engine overhaul if needed. An example of this can be seen in Exhibit 8-6. Volkswagen has a warranty that gives you 12,000 miles (or one year) on servicing any parts that might need replacement, plus a total of two years or 24,000 miles on the internal parts of the engine and transmission. What's more, Volkswagen will tow you to the nearest dealer or give you a rental car if yours must be kept overnight for any warranty repair.

A recurring question is: Is it better to buy a new car every year or so or to buy and hold a car for, say, ten years, until it has no significant resale value. A few years ago, the U.S. Department of Transportation conducted a study in order to answer this question.

Researchers looked at the actual costs of depreciation, insurance, maintenance, and so on for a 1970 full-sized, "big-three" (Ford, General Motors, Chrysler) four-door sedan equipped with V-8 engine and automatic transmission. They compared buying a car and keeping it for ten years with buying a new car every year or every two or three years. After a certain number of years, the older car often became a second car in a two-car family and was driven fewer miles. The study showed that to buy a new car every other year would cost you $4,000 more over a ten-year period than keeping one for ten years. The study concluded

EXHIBIT 8-6.

SAMPLE NEW-CAR WARRANTY

1978 AMC Full 12-Month/12,000-Mile* New Car Warranty

When you buy a new 1978 AMC car from an AMC dealer, American Motors Corporation** guarantees to you that for 12 months or 12,000* miles from the date of delivery or first use, whichever comes first, it will, except for tires, pay for the repair or replacement of any part it supplies which proves defective in material or workmanship.

All we require is that the car be properly maintained and cared for under normal use and service in the fifty United States or Canada and that guarantee repairs or replacements be made by an AMC dealer.

No other express warranty is given or authorized by American Motors. American Motors shall not be liable for loss of use of vehicle, loss of time, inconvenience or other incidental or consequential damages. Some states and provinces do not allow limitation or exclusion of incidental or consequential damages so the above exclusion and limitation may not apply to you. This warranty gives you specific legal rights and you may also have other rights which vary from state to state or province to province.

* In Canada (20,000 km)
** In Canada: American Motors (Canada) Limited

that, at least in this case, it was cheaper to buy and hold.

Unfortunately, this conclusion is only a starting point for you in making your own decision about whether to buy a new car or not. If you hold a car for ten years and even keep it in good condition, you have not purchased the same kind of transportation services you would have if you bought a new car every other year. If cars become safer every year, you don't have the benefit of new safety features. This is probably less important now since most basic features have been required for some time. But what if you had bought a car before dual brakes and safety laminated glass were required? You would be driving a much different piece of machinery than if you had traded in your car every two years and received the benefits of the new safety features.

You also lose the psychological benefit of enjoying that new-car feeling. This aspect of new car ownership is nebulous and hard to quantify; it might mean much to you or very little.

However, with pollution equipment now required on new cars, the decision whether or not to buy one is even more complicated. Some automotive engineers maintain that 1971 or 1972 was the last good year to buy a car; since then, pollution equipment has made the engine so expensive to run that you're better off not buying a new car.

But that trend seems to have reversed itself recently. Gas mileage for newer cars is better than it was a few years ago. In deciding whether or not to keep an older car, one must, therefore, also take into account the reduced gas mileage of some older cars compared with their newer models. A new VW might get thirty miles to a gallon compared to one ten years old that gets only seventeen miles to a gallon. Depending on how much you drive, these different rates of gas consumption could mean saving—or spending—a considerable sum each year.

THE FINANCIAL BENEFITS OF LEASING A CAR

Many individuals no longer buy new cars. Rather, they lease one from a new car dealer for a two- to four-year period. In some cases, leasing for three years is cheaper than buying and selling or trading in the average car. Hertz Corporation Car Leasing Division contends that, in California, over 60 percent of all new cars are leased or rented. Nationally, one in every four cars is now leased, compared with one in twenty-five fifteen years ago. In a typical thirty-six-month closed-end lease, you pay a specified monthly figure for the use of the car. You care for the car as if it were yours. At the end of three years, you return it to the leasing company. In many larger cities, the auto insurance included in your leasing agreement is implicitly sold to you at a lower rate than if you had bought it on your own for a privately purchased car.

For many individuals, an important advantage of leasing a car is the convenience of accounting for the business use of a car. If you use your car, for example, 50 percent of the time for business, you simply figure that 50 percent of your annual lease cost is deductible from your income before you pay taxes.

Alternatives to the Automobile

Because the relative cost of driving has increased so much, many individuals are trying to cut down on transportation expenses in several ways.

1 Since it costs more to own a car during the first year of its operation than in later years, people are keeping cars longer than they used to. Therefore, the average age of automobiles on the highway has risen in the last decade.

2 There has been a dramatic increase in the use of motorcycles, mobilettes, and bicycles since the relative price of new (and used) cars has risen. These forms of transportation have a lower initial expense and lower operating expenses. There are disadvantages to them, however. All three are less safe than cars. All expose the rider to the elements. And they all limit the driver's ability to transport several people at once.

3 Individuals have found new ways to organize car pools. Some employers have provided a mini-bus vehicle to an employee who is willing to drive back and forth to work with at least seven other passengers. The employee can, for a small fee, use the van as a personal car after work. Municipal governments have encouraged car pools by giving priority to them in special lanes on the highway. A number of toll bridges charge less to cars in which three or more people are riding. The Federal Highway Commission did a study on the savings possible from car pooling; Exhibit 8-7 shows some of their findings.

EXHIBIT 8-7.   **CAR POOL SAVINGS—1977**

Home to Work	Annual Round Trip Cost and Savings	Subcompact (Pinto, Datsun, Vega, VW, Colt)	Compact (Nova, Dart Maverick, Pacer)	Standard (Matador, Cutlass, LTD, Caprice)
20 MILES (40 MILES ROUND TRIP)	**COST OF DRIVING TO WORK ALONE**	**$982**	**$1,177**	**$1,561**
	SAVINGS PER PERSON IN:			
	2-person carpool	$449	$ 545	$ 734
	3-person carpool	585	712	963
	4-person carpool	645	796	1,077
	5-person carpool	693	845	1,145

Source: For a complete report on the car pool study, write to the Department of Transportation, Federal Highway Administration, Washington, D.C. 20590.

EXHIBIT 8-8.   **PRICE COMPARISON CHART**

	Car #1	Car #2	Car #3	Car #4
List Price				
OPTIONS Power Steering, Brakes				
Automatic Transmission				
Non-Standard Engine				
Air Conditioning				
Rear Window De-Fogger				
Special Radio/Tape Deck				
Limited Slip Differential				
White Wall Tires				
Tinted Glass				
Vinyl Roof				
Tires—Radial, Oversized, or Snow				
Speed Control				
Fuel Economy Indicator				
Other				
Freight Charges				
Federal Excise Tax				
Dealer Service Charge				
State Sales Tax				
State Registration and Licensing Fees				
Total Cost				
Subtract Trade-in or Down Payment				
Total Amount to be paid to Dealer				

HOW TO PURCHASE AN AUTOMOBILE

IF YOU DECIDE TO BUY A NEW CAR

If you decide to buy a new car, you must determine where to buy it, which one to buy, and what options or accessories to purchase.

The Dealer

1. **Location.** Where to buy it depends on a number of factors, one of the most important being how far the dealer is from your job or home. After all, you must take the car in for servicing. And a new car, no matter how good it is, is going to have at least a few problems in the beginning. If you value time and convenience highly, you will be better off if you can leave your car at the dealer and walk to work or back home.

2. **Dealer service facilities and personnel.** To find out about the dealer's service facilities and personnel, ask specific questions about them. How does the dealer expedite service for customers? What are the size and reputation of the service department? How long is service work guaranteed—thirty days, ninety days, or not at all? What electronic diagnostic equipment does the shop have? Are there provisions for replacement transportation while your car is in service? When is the service department open?

3. **Dealer reputation.** Talk to others who have bought from the dealer and have used the service department. Or, better yet, take your present car in for servicing and see what you think of the service department.

4. **The deal offered.** Obviously the deal offered is of utmost importance in all the preceding considerations. You may, however, be willing to pay a slightly higher price to a specific dealer whom you like and who has a good reputation for service. Other aspects of the deal are discussed later in this Practical Applications section.

DECIDING ON THE TYPE OF CAR

Deciding which new car to buy depends, at least in part, on how much money you want to spend. You should figure out the exact yearly out-of-pocket costs you will incur for different price ranges and then decide which one you are willing to pay for. Remember, as you go up the ladder of car prices, you aren't buying more safety or speed, only styling, prestige, and so on. Be aware of the price you are paying for these qualities.

You should also be aware of the various operating costs of the cars you consider. Compacts are cheaper to run than full-sized cars. But they hold fewer people comfortably and less baggage, and they provide less protection in case of a crash.

What options you should buy also depends upon your taste relative to your income. Some options make sense, even if you think you don't want them. It would be ridiculous to buy a Cadillac with a stick shift: when you tried to sell it, you'd find few people who would want to buy it. Likewise, large cars without power steering and power brakes are hard to sell—and very hard to drive and park while you own them.

Tires are an important feature of any car and something on which you probably won't want to compromise. Radial tires seem to offer the most protection and are sometimes the longest lasting. Today, many new cars come with radials; if the car of your choice comes without them, you should consider trading in the standard tires for radials. Another accessory you may want to consider is a rear-window defogger; most cars now have them as standard equipment.

Exhibit 8-8 on page 204 is a comparison chart you can fill in to determine the actual cost of four different types of cars with different options.

GETTING THE BEST DEAL ON A NEW CAR

The differences in prices for the same car with the same accessories depend on the dealer from whom you buy and on your bargaining skills. Generally, however, the differences in prices for the same car will never be great, particularly for the lower-priced subcompacts and compacts. Thus, it won't be worth your while to go to twenty-five dealers to bargain on a particular car. In fact, one study showed that, after checking three dealers, the probability of getting a better deal was small.

You can obtain dealer cost information and a list price on all cars and options from auto guides sold at newsstands, in the December issues of *Changing Times* magazine, and in some paperback books, such as Edmund's and Car/Puter's *AutoFacts*. The annual April issue of *Consumer Reports* is also helpful. Or you can fill out a form on which you list a particular car and all the options you want to buy and send it to Car/Puter International, Inc., 1603 Bushwick Avenue, Brooklyn, New York 11207. For ten dollars you will receive a computer print-out showing dealer cost and list price for that car with all its options. Dealer markups vary from 17 to 25 percent, depending on whether the car is a subcompact, compact, intermediate, or full-size model; luxury cars, such as Cadillacs and Lincoln Continentals, have a markup of 25 percent. By markup, we mean the difference between what the dealer pays for a car and what the dealer asks for a car.

Shopping by Phone

Although many dealers refuse to reveal prices over the telephone and others will only tell the sticker price, there are some, especially foreign-car dealers, who will tell you exactly the final cost. In fact, if you are assertive enough over the telephone, sometimes you can negotiate a deal without ever visiting the showroom. Consider the following tactic. Call the dealer and ask to speak to a salesperson. Immediately indicate that you were just disappointed by a competing dealer who had "low balled" you: you had been quoted one price and then the salesperson upped that figure just as you were about to close the deal. Telling the salesperson this over the phone alerts him or her that you have shopped around, are serious, and won't settle for higher than the stated price. When the salesperson suggests a particular figure for the car you want with the options you want, ask him or her if that is the best possible deal. In many cases, the salesperson will offer you a lower price just to get you into the showroom.

Things to Watch For

Once you reach an agreement with the salesperson, make sure that the exact car and optional equipment you want are listed plainly on the order and that that order is countersigned by someone in authority, such as the sales manager of the dealership. Also, have at least the following four things listed on the order:

1. There will be no increase in price; the price shown at the bottom of the order is the total price to be paid on delivery.

2. There will be no reappraisal of your trade-in.

3. There will be no substitutions of nonfactory equipment for anything that you order on the car.

4. The car will be delivered at a specific time—or reasonably close to it.

Finally, make sure that you don't fall for a "switch." For example, several days after you place your order, a salesperson might call to tell you that the factory is jammed up with orders and that it will take you longer to get your car. The salesperson then might say that another dealership has an identical car—with a few extra options—for about $320 more. In such cases, the salesperson may just be trying to force you to buy a more expensive car. Another ploy is for the dealer to install several options on your car before you take possession. You will be told that they were on the car when the dealer received it and that you will have to pay an extra $200 or $300 if you want that car.

Using a Buying Service

If you want to skip all the haggling and frustrations associated with bargaining for a new car, you may wish to use a buying service. Such a service offers the car for $125 to $500 above factory cost, depending on the basic price and the size of the car. You buy the car from a regular dealer but at a guaranteed price. Warranties, rebates, and service are the same. One such car buying service is United Auto Brokers, which is a subsidiary of Car/Puter International, Inc. Most cars can be ordered for $125 over dealer's cost.

Critics of car buying services contend that, because the buyer does not usually select the dealer,

the service after the sale may be less dependable, more inconvenient, and more costly than had the car buyer personally chosen the dealer.

TRADING IN YOUR WHEELS

When you trade in your old car, you can be fairly certain you will get no more than the standard trade-in price listed by the National Automobile Dealers Association in its *Offical Used Car Guide,* or "blue book." It's advisable for you to look up this information yourself.

It is generally a good idea to bargain on your trade-in after you have completed the new car purchase with the dealer. This way you will avoid what is called the "high ball" gimmick, in which the salesperson quotes you a trade-in price for your used car that exceeds, by $200, $300, or even $500, its blue book value. Although you might think you are getting a bargain, the additional price you receive for your trade-in will be included somewhere else in the price of the new car. You can assume that you will get the wholesale price of your old car as a trade-in if the car is in good condition. You can attempt to sell the used

EXHIBIT 8-9. **WHAT YOUR CAR LOAN WILL COST PER $1,000 BORROWED**

Annual Percentage Interest	ONE YEAR		TWO YEARS		THREE YEARS		FOUR YEARS	
	Monthly Payment	Total Finance Charge	Monthly Payment	Total Finance Charge	Monthly Payment	Total Finance Charge	Monthly Payment	Total Finance Charge
9	$87	$50	$46	$ 97	$32	$145	$25	$195
10	88	55	46	107	32	162	25	218
11	88	61	47	119	33	179	26	241
12	89	66	47	130	33	196	26	264
13	89	72	48	141	34	213	27	288
14	90	78	48	152	34	231	27	312

NOTE: Figures rounded to nearest dollar

car yourself, but then you must incur the time and money costs of doing so.

IF YOU BUY A USED CAR

If you decide to buy a used car, you must be especially careful about the condition of the vehicle. You might have an independent mechanic check the used car before you commit yourself to buying it. You may be charged for this, just as you will be charged by a building inspector who checks out a house you want to buy. But you are buying information from the mechanic that may save you hundreds of dollars in the future. The mechanic may point out that a transmission is about to fail, that the gaskets leak, and so on.

You may wish to take the car to a diagnostic center, which will charge you from fifteen to fifty dollars to analyze electronically all major aspects of the car you intend to buy. Generally, these centers don't do repair work, but they can usually indicate what it will cost to have the used car repaired, if necessary.

Another way to insure yourself against major repair expenses is to work with used car dealers who have ninety-day written warranties on their products. Sometimes you must pay for such a warranty; sometimes its price is included in the price of the used car. You are buying a type of insurance that costs you a little in the beginning but reduces the probability that you will pay a great deal in the future. Occasionally, a used car may still be covered by the manufacturer's one-year, 12,000-mile or two-year, 24,000-mile warranty. Because such a car is worth more to you, the potential purchaser, than those without warranties, you will be willing to pay more.

You can check yourself whether a used car has been in a major accident. Look for mismatched colors in the paint and for ripples, bumps, and grainy surfaces on the body. These will indicate extensive repainting and, therefore, extensive repairs. Such discoveries may not dissuade you from buying the car, but they should persuade you to have an inde-

pendent mechanic look it over.

There are numerous methods of examining a prospective used car purchase. These can be found in the section on buying a used car in any annual *Consumer Reports Buying Guide,* which gives more than a dozen on-the-lot tests and eight to ten driving tests you can do yourself. It also tells you what specific repair jobs will cost. However, since nothing can duplicate a shop test by a good mechanic, this step is highly recommended, unless the deal includes an extremely good warranty. You might also be able to get a helpful brochure from your local consumer affairs office. If you are purchasing a used car from a dealer, ask the dealer for the name and address of the car's previous owner; then ask this person about possible problems, defects, or advantages of the car.

FINANCING THAT PURCHASE

A new or used car is usually such a major purchase that at least part of it will be financed by credit. Don't automatically accept the credit the dealer offers when you decide to buy a car. Shop around for credit, just as you shop around for anything else. You may get a much better deal from your credit union or your local bank. Fortunately for you, the Truth-in-Lending Act of 1968 requires every lender to disclose the total finance charge you will pay and the actual annual interest rate to be paid. Thus, the credit offered by the dealer can be compared to the credit offered by competing sources, such as banks and finance companies. Remember, in many cases, if you default on your car payment, the car can be repossessed. In some states, finance companies can take your car away from you without a judicial hearing. Don't buy a more expensive car than you know you can afford. If the car is repossessed, you are bound to lose.

Where to Borrow for a Car

You can go to insurance companies, loan companies, banks and savings institutions, credit unions, and auto dealers themselves. Generally, credit unions offer the most beneficial rates on automobile loans; if you are a member of one, or can become a member without much trouble and expense, find out what you will be charged there.

After the auto dealers themselves, banks are the most commonly used source of financing automobiles. What your local banker will charge depends on your credit rating, the amount of down payment or trade-in value on the car you are buying, and the general state of the economy.

You may wish to look to auto insurance companies, which sometimes issue car loans. They may do this through a bank or through their own subsidiaries. To find out, call your auto insurance agent.

You will pay the highest annual percentage fee for an auto loan through a small-loan company or a car dealer.

What Length of Loan to Take Out

Many consumer experts recommend that automobile loans be taken out for the shortest time period possible, pointing out that you pay a relatively high interest charge when you take out a three- or four-year car loan. On a typical $4,100 loan, you pay, on average, $8.37 a month in additional interest in order to reduce your payments by $52 a month. Additionally, you end up paying a hefty balance when you trade in your car before the end of four years.

Does that mean that you shouldn't take out a four-year auto loan? Not necessarily. But if you think you would be uncomfortable with a debt outstanding for four years, you may want to opt for a shorter time period. However, by doing so, you must use more of your discretionary funds to pay off the automobile loan each month; thus you will have less to spend on other items during that period. It costs more to keep an auto loan outstanding longer because you are using someone else's money for a longer period. If you think you can borrow at a lower rate using something other than the automobile as collateral, then it would be more costly to take out a four-year auto loan. As with all borrowing decisions, you must balance the benefits of having more cash available for

other purchases against the increased interest cost for borrowing more or for borrowing for a longer period of time. You can figure your actual borrowing cost in Exhibit 8-9 on page 207.

GETTING GOOD REPAIRS

Every car owner is faced with the problem of car repairs. Finding a good repair shop or an honest mechanic may be difficult in your area. There are currently two private programs—one for mechanics and one for garages—being developed to certify reliable workmanship on cars.

Certifying Mechanics

The National Institute for Automotive Service Excellence began certifying mechanics in 1972. In order to be certified by the institute, a mechanic must pass a written examination and have at least two years experience in the area being tested. There are now over 94,000 certified automotive mechanics in one or more of eight categories, including automatic transmission, manual transmission and rear axle, front-end brakes, electrical system, engine repair, heating and air conditioning, and engine tune-up. Additionally, there are about 17,200 mechanics who have mastered all eight tests and have been certified as "general mechanics" by the institute. If you are interested in seeking the services of a certified mechanic, you can write to the National Institute for Automotive Service Excellence, 1825 K Street N.W., Washington, D.C. 20006. For $1.95, they will direct you to certified mechanics in your area.

Certifying Garages

The American Automobile Association has begun a program to certify reliable garages and service stations. So far, the program is relatively small, but eventually it may become as extensive as the program for certifying mechanics. The garages must meet American Automobile Association requirements for covering scope of service, customer service, equipment, number of persons on the premises, and so on. Once a garage is certified, it must offer members of the American Automobile Association a written estimate of work to be performed. The garage must also make available any replaced parts after repairs are completed and guarantee its work for ninety days, or 4,000 miles, whichever comes first. Furthermore, each participating garage has agreed in writing to accept AAA's decision on any complaint registered by a member of that organization.

MAKING SURE YOU AREN'T CHEATED

A number of ruses are used by unscrupulous car mechanics. One is replacement of ball joints in the front suspension. These parts do wear out, but they are fairly sturdy, and some movement is acceptable. An unscrupulous mechanic may put your car on a hoist, turn the wheel to the side, and wiggle it to make it appear that the ball joint (in the steering system) is about to jump from the socket. Before you have the ball joints replaced, get the opinion of another mechanic; you may not need that repair job. The same "wiggle" test is often used by mechanics for the idler arm, which is a short piece of metal in the lower steering mechanism of the car. Some mechanics may try to sell you new piston rings because you have a smoking exhaust, but that may not be the solution. Finally, if you repeatedly need to add automatic transmission fluid, it doesn't necessarily mean you need a new transmission or a complete overhaul. Rather, it may mean you need a new modulator valve in the transmission, which can be replaced for less than twenty-five dollars.

WHEN YOU HAVE A NEW-CAR PROBLEM, AUTOCAP MAY HELP

AUTOCAP was formed to help resolve problems consumers have with dealers and repairpeople. Say, for example, that you live in Connecticut and are dissatisfied with the car you just bought from a dealer. You call the AUTOCAP toll-free number (1-800-492-2276 in this case) and register your complaint. AUTOCAP then sends you a form on which you describe your problem. When you return the form to AUTOCAP headquarters in West Hartford, the dealer involved is notified by mail and urged to work out the problem with you, the customer. If this fails, the matter goes before an AUTOCAP panel, consisting of four dealers and three public members, for arbitration.

It's easier to arrive at a "just" settlement when a dealer and a customer can agree. Obviously, the panel is not a court of last resort; it has no enforcement powers and relies on dealer cooperation to handle complaints satisfactorily. But, according to a Connecticut dealer and panel head, Richard D. Wagner, dealer cooperation has been excellent: only two dealers balked at AUTOCAP's proposed settlement in the first year of operation.

When Things Get Sticky

When the going gets sticky on a matter of warranty or car performance, AUTOCAP goes directly to factory representatives. So far, manufacturers have cooperated completely. But if you, the customer, feel that you weren't treated fairly by AUTOCAP, you can still go to your state motor vehicle department or take private legal action. The following automobile dealer organizations currently are operating AUTOCAP under sponsorship of the National Automobile Dealers Association:

Kentucky Automobile Dealers Association, P.O. Box 498, Frankfort 40601.

Metropolitan Denver Automobile Dealers Association, 70 West 6th Ave., Denver 80122.

Automotive Trade Association of National Capital Area, 8401 Connecticut Ave., Chevy Chase, Md. 20015.

Central Florida Dealer Association, 1350 Orange Ave., Winter Park, Fla. 32789.

Idaho Automobile Dealers Association, 2230 Main St., Boise 83706.

Greater Louisville Automobile Dealers Association, 332 W. Broadway, Louisville 40202.

Cleveland Automobile Dealers Association, 310 Lakeside Ave., West, Cleveland 44113.

Oklahoma Automobile Dealers Association, 1601 City National Bank Tower, Oklahoma City, 73102.

Oregon Automobile Dealers Association, P.O. Box 14460, Portland 97214.

Utah Automobile Dealers Association, Newhouse Hotel, Salt Lake City 84101.

Louisiana Automobile Dealers Association, 201 Lafayette St., Baton Rouge 70821.

Indianapolis Automobile Trade Association, 822 North Illinois, Indianapolis 46204.

Connecticut Automotive Trade Association, 18 N. Main St., West Hartford 06103.

The four largest domestic automobile producers have offices for customer complaints if dealers are unable or unwilling to resolve problems with your car. You can write to or call the following offices directly:

1. American Motors Corporation, Owner Relations Manager, 14250 Plymouth Road, Detroit, Michigan 48232.

2. Chrysler Corporation, Your Man in Detroit, Box 1086, Detroit, Michigan 48231.

3. Ford Customer Service Division, Owner Relations Department, Park Lane Tower West, 1 Park Lane Boulevard, Deerborne, Michigan 48126.

4. General Motors Corporation, Owner Relations Manager, 3044 West Grand Boulevard, Detroit, Michigan 48202.

If you wish to find out about a possible safety defect in an older car, you can call the Auto Safety Hotline at the National Highway Traffic Administration in Washington, D.C. (800-424-9393). The hotline facilitates the exchange of information about auto safety defects between the public and the government. By reporting problems you have had with certain cars, you help other consumers. And you can find out about defects in a car you might own or wish to own. The hotline operator can tell you if a used car you are considering purchasing has ever been included in a recall campaign by the manufacturer.

GLOSSARY OF TERMS

PRIVATE COST   The cost that an individual incurs.

DEPRECIATION   The reduction in the market value of an asset, such as an automobile.

COST OF ACQUISITION   The difference between the purchase price of the asset, such as an automobile, and its *immediate* resale value.

CHAPTER SUMMARY

1. Today cars are safer than they used to be. Dual braking systems, over-the-shoulder safety belts, head restraints, seat-belt warning systems, and so on raise the price of a new car.

2. Pollution abatement equipment in cars also raises the price.

3. The cost of driving includes interest payments, depreciation, gasoline, repairs, and insurance.

4. The interest on a car purchase exists whether or not a loan is taken out. If the car is paid for in cash, the interest is implicit; it is equal to the opportunity cost—what the money could earn in a savings and loan association—of the purchase price.

5. Depreciation during the first year of a car's life is a function of the physical reduction in the car's value over the year plus the reduction in value due to obsolescence.

6. The cost of acquisition is paid for as soon as one is legally committed to purchasing the car.

7. Normal depreciation on a car results from its physical depreciation, as well as the fact that consumers prefer newer to older cars.

8. It is cheaper to buy and hold rather than to buy and sell a car every year. Note, though, that you are consuming a different product when you keep a car for a long time.

9. For some individuals, leasing a car is financially beneficial, particularly if the car is used for business purposes.

10. As new automobiles have become more expensive, consumers have kept cars longer and increased their use of such alternatives as motorcycles, bicycles, and mobilettes.

11. Choosing a car dealer depends on: (a) location, (b) service facilities and personnel, (c) reputation, and (d) the deal offered.

12. Searching for the best deal does not require going to every dealer in town. Books, such as Car/Puter's *Auto Facts*, indicate the list price of all cars and the price of their options. Dealer markup varies from 17 to 25 percent, depending on the size of the car. The luxury models have markups of 25 percent.

13. When you order a new car, make sure that: (a) there can be no increase in price, (b) there can be no reappraisal of your trade-in, (c) there can be no substitutes of nonfactory equipment for ordered options, and (d) the car will be delivered at a specific time.

14. You can use a buying service, such as United Auto Brokers, to obtain a car for about $125 over dealer cost.

15. Preferred options for a new car are radial tires, rear window defrosters, disc brakes, and other safety equipment.

16. Find out the wholesale trade-in value of your used car by looking at the official *Used Car Guide* (the "blue book") put out by the National Automobile Dealers Association.

17. When you buy a used car, it is advisable to take it first to an automobile diagnostic center for a complete "checkup."

18. Find out the repair record of used cars in the April issues of *Consumer Reports* magazine.

19. One way to locate a reliable mechanic is to ask others about their car-repair experiences.

20. AUTOCAP is available in many states to adjudicate disputes between consumers with car problems and car dealers.

21. You can also write to AMC, Chrysler, Ford, and GM to express complaints about specific cars.

22. The financing of automobiles should be considered a separate purchase and not necessarily arranged through the dealer. Go to your credit union or bank to find the best deal.

23. It is not necessarily inadvisable to take out a four-year car loan, even if you decide to trade in the car before then. But your outstanding debt load will, of course, be greater than it would otherwise. Also, you may be able to get cheaper credit when it isn't tied to your depreciating car.

STUDY QUESTIONS

1. Why does the cost of new cars keep rising?

2. If you pay cash for a car, do you incur any interest costs? (What about the implicit interest you could have earned on the purchase price?)

3. What is the cost of acquisition, and how does it differ from depreciation?

4. The cost of acquisition of a new car is quite high, particularly on the larger models. Why do some people buy new cars instead of used ones?

5. What are some of the benefits of not buying a new car every couple of years?

6. Car pools save on gas. What are some other benefits? What are some of the costs of car pooling?

7. Which is more important when deciding where to buy a new car—the dealer's location or the dealer's reputation? What about the deal offered?

8. What is meant by the "blue book" price of a used car?

9. Does it make sense to take out a four-year loan on a car that you plan to trade in after three years?

CASE PROBLEMS

8-1 Which Wagon Will It Be?

Roger and René Sandness are high-school teachers living in a metropolitan suburb. They commute thirty-five miles daily during the school year, and, in the summer, they and their daughter, Helen, age nine, spend two months camping and visiting friends and relatives. Their three-year-old Mercury station wagon, which they purchased new for $5900, averages thirteen miles per gallon. They drive 18,000 miles per year. During the next year the Mercury will need four new radial tires ($73 each) plus other maintenance and repairs estimated at $300. License and insurance will be $365 and depreciation, $566.

They could trade in the Mercury for $3100, and, with cash from their 6% savings account, buy a smaller twenty-two mpg Chevrolet Malibu wagon for $5700 plus 9% tax. Repairs and maintenance not covered by warranty are estimated at $100, insurance and license at $420, and gas costs 71¢ per gallon.

1. What will be the cost of owning each car during the next year?

2. What would you recommend that they do, given both the economics of the situation and their lifestyle?

8-2 Another Dimension to the Wagon Debate

After much discussion, the Sandnesses found another alternative. If they keep the Mercury and use it only for longer camping trips, they would increase the mpg to sixteen. They could then purchase a ten-month-old Horizon demonstrator from the local dealer for $3000 plus 9% tax. They estimate they would drive this car 12,000 miles annually and get thirty mpg combined city and highway mileage. They would pay cash for the car. Repairs, maintenance, license, and insurance are estimated at $250, and second year depreciation at $480.

1. What would be the total cost of operating the two cars for the first year?

2. Given the economics of the situation and their lifestyle, which car should they buy?

SELECTED REFERENCES

Aerospace Education Foundation, *The Safe Driving Handbook*. New York, Grossett & Dunlap Publishers, 1970.

"Buying a Used Car." *Changing Times,* January 1975, pp. 25-28.

Cost of Operating an Automobile. Washington, D.C.: U.S. Government Printing Office, 1978.

"How Much Does Auto Upkeep Really Cost?" *Better Homes & Gardens,* August 1976, pp. 28ff.

How to Buy a Used Car. Consumers Union, 1972.

Nader, Ralph. *Unsafe at Any Speed: The Designed-in Dangers of the American Automobile*. New York: Grossman Publishers, 1965.

Porter, John Paul, Ed., et al. *The Time-Life Book of the Family Car*. Time-Life Books, 1973.

Tendell, Robert. *New Era Car Book and Auto Survival Guide*. New York: Holt, Reinhart, & Winston, 1975.

"Used Car Dealers: How They Operate." *Changing Times,* September 1972.

Weathersbee, Christopher. *Intelligent Consumer: How to Buy Food, Clothes, Cars, Houses*. New York: E.P. Dutton & Company, 1973.

"Will It Pay to Fix Up Your Old Car?" *Changing Times,* June 1972.

Insurance

Life Insurance

■ Security is important for most families. In fact, psychologists contend that the average American wants security more than just about anything else in his or her life. Some of the major deterrents to *financial* security and the ways that Americans provide for these hazards are:

1   *Illness:* health and medical insurance, an emergency savings account, Medicare and Medicaid, disability insurance.
2   *Accidents:* accident insurance, a savings account, state workers' compensation, Social Security, aid to the disabled, veterans' benefits.
3   *Unemployment:* a savings fund for such an emergency, unemployment compensation.
4   *Old age:* private retirement pension plans, savings and investments, annuities, Social Security old age insurance.
5   *Premature death:* survivors' insurance under the Social Security Act, life insurance, workers' compensation, savings and investments, accident insurance.
6   *Desertion, divorce, and so forth:* savings, investments, aid to families with dependent children, education of spouse.
7   *Unexpected, catastrophic expenses:* health insurance, property insurance, liability insurance.

The responsibility for providing family economic security may be assumed by the family, relatives of the family, charitable institutions, employers, and/or the government. Historically, financial security was provided primarily by the first three, but now employers and the government are extending this kind of protection.

PREMATURE DEATHS

The mortality rate in the United States and elsewhere has been declining for many years. Fewer people are suffering from fatal diseases than they used to and are living longer, as can be seen in Exhibit 9-1. Nonetheless, many do die before their retirement years. In 1978, 301,224 males and females between the ages of 25 to 55 died. In many cases, a premature death means financial hardship for surviving dependents. This is true whether a man or a woman dies. When a woman who has been responsible for a household and children dies, those responsibilities must be assumed by others. This can bring financial hardship to a family unit. The same is more obviously true when a male wage earner dies. Both cases call for financial protection against the burden imposed by such a premature death, which is one reason there is an extremely large life insurance industry in the United States.

SELLING LIFE INSURANCE

The life insurance industry in the United States has grown dramatically to meet the needs of concerned family members. In 1900, there were a mere eighty-four life insurance companies selling some 14 million policies with a total face value of only $7.5 billion. By the beginning of the 1960s, there were some 1,441 companies selling 282 million policies, with an average face value of $10,200 of life insurance per family. By the beginning of the 1970s, there were 1,800 companies. In 1978, the average insured American family had $37,000 in life insurance. More than 90 percent of all wife-husband families have life insurance, which represents 85 percent of the assets that males leave at their deaths.

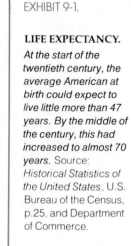

EXHIBIT 9-1.

LIFE EXPECTANCY.
At the start of the twentieth century, the average American at birth could expect to live little more than 47 years. By the middle of the century, this had increased to almost 70 years. Source: *Historical Statistics of the United States*, U.S. Bureau of the Census, p.25, and Department of Commerce.

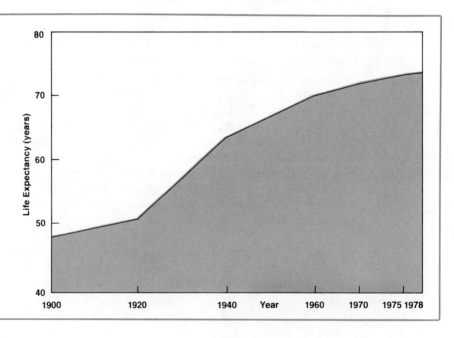

HISTORY OF LIFE INSURANCE

Some historians believe that the first recorded life insurance policy was written in June 1536 in London's Old Drury Ale House. A group of marine underwriters agreed to insure the life of William Gybbons for the grand sum of $2,000. For an eighty dollar premium, this coverage was obtained—unfortunately for the underwriters, as Gybbons died a few days before the policy was to expire. And so it was that life insurance became a sideline for marine underwriters. In 1692, the Society for the Equitable Assurance of Lives and Survivorship began issuing policies covering a person for his or her lifetime. Old Equitable, as it became known, exists today. In North America, the first corporation to insure lives was the Presbyterian Ministers' Fund, started in Philadelphia in 1759. By 1800, there were only 160 life insurance policies in force in the United States. After the Civil War, the industry began to flourish.

LIFE INSURANCE PRINCIPLES

Life insurance is like any other type of insurance: if the risk is spread among a large enough number of people, the premiums will be small compared to the coverage offered. In any particular age group, only a small number will die in any one year. If a large percentage of this age group pays premiums to a life insurance company in exchange for a benefit payment in case of premature death, there will be a sufficient amount of money to pay off the survivors.

Given a long enough time for collection of data about the group and the particular disaster—in this case, premature death—insurance companies can predict with great accuracy the total number of premature deaths in any one year. Thus, they can estimate the total payout they will incur if they insure the group. And they can predict the rates for each member of the group in order to meet this payout, plus a profit for the company.

DIFFERENT TYPES OF LIFE INSURANCE

The insurance principles just outlined are simple to grasp, but the variety of insurance programs you can purchase is wide and complex. In this chapter, we outline the basic types of life insurance policies. The Practical Applications section offers some ideas to help you determine your own life insurance needs and some recommendations about the appropriate type of insurance for you.

Basically, there are two types of life insurance—**term and whole life.** But there is a variety of others we will discuss; Exhibit 9-2 illustrates the different types of insurance plans. Note, though, that these are schematic diagrams and do not represent actuarial accuracy. Term insurance offers "pure" protection. Whole life—also called straight life, ordinary life, or cash-value insurance—combines protection with a cash surrender value.

Term Insurance

Premiums for term insurance, unlike those for whole life, commonly increase at the end of each term (such as every five years), if you wish to keep the same face value on your insurance policy. The increased premium reflects the rising probability of death as age increases. Thus, it will cost you relatively little to buy term when you are twenty-five years old. But, by the time you are sixty, your premiums will have risen dramatically. However, by that time you probably won't want as much term insurance because your children will be well on the way to financial independence, your spouse will have a shorter life expectancy (statistically speaking), and you, presumably, will have other financial resources for any dependents you still have. Thus, you can reduce the premium burden by reducing the amount of insurance carried to protect your family.

EXHIBIT 9-2

SUMMARY OF INSURANCE PLAN

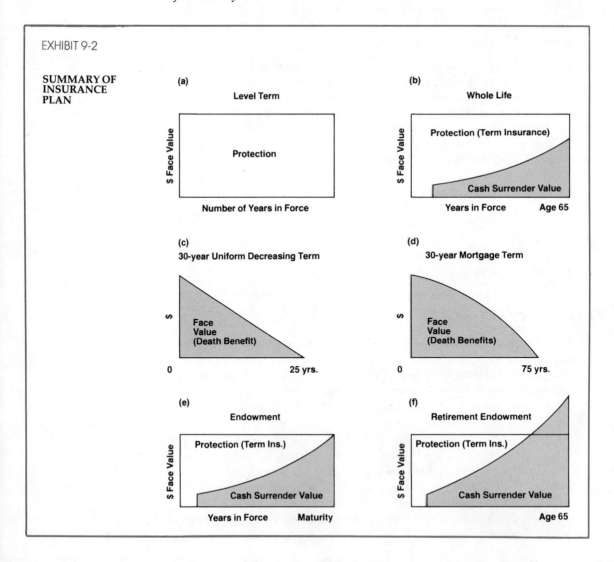

Decreasing term. Families often choose **decreasing term insurance,** which has a level premium but a decreasing face value. Since the *face* value of the policy decreases the same way the amount owed on a mortgage decreases, such policies are often called **home protection plans.** If one is taken out that has a face value equal to the amount of a home mortgage, the home can be paid off with the proceeds should the insured die at any point during the life of the mortgage.

Actually, if you want a policy that covers exactly what is left on a mortgage, you must purchase a mortgage term insurance policy. Such a policy decreases in uneven dollar amounts, which exactly keep pace with the reduction in the principle balance due on your home mortgage. In the early years of a home mortgage, a large percentage of the monthly payments are for interest. Therefore, the reduction in the amount you owe is small. The face value on the mortgage term insurance policy also falls relatively less rapidly in the early years. Because of this feature, a mortgage term insurance policy will be somewhat more expensive than a uniform annual decreasing term policy.

Renewability. Standard term insurance is often labeled one-year term or five-year term because those are the intervals, or terms, between premium increases. Other terms are also available. A term policy is called *renewable* if the coverage can be continued at the end of each period merely by paying the increased premium and without having a medical examination. The **renewability** feature must, of necessity, add to the cost of the policy; but if you wish to preserve your insurability despite changes in your health, you would want to pay the extra costs for this feature. Term policies are commonly renewable until the policy holder reaches retirement age (usually sixty-five or seventy) when all coverage stops. When the policy holder retires, no net financial loss would be suffered by his or her dependents upon his or her death anyway. Therefore, the policy holder no longer needs insurance; once the policy holder stops working, his or her dependents no longer run the *financial* risk of his or her ''premature'' death.

In one sense, the premiums for any term policy are constant for the life of the policy. But since most term policies are written with a one-year or five-year ''life,'' the constancy of premium isn't too meaningful. The premium is truly constant throughout a long period of time only with decreasing term insurance, in which the face value falls every year. Even then, the ''unit'' cost—the premium per dollar protection—goes up.

Convertibility. Often riders can be attached to term policies that permit you to convert the policy into other than term insurance without having a medical examination. You pay for this additional feature, however. If you have a convertible term policy, you can convert it into whole life without any problems. You might want to convert in order to continue your coverage after you pass sixty-five or seventy or if you believe your poorer health in the future will prevent renewal of an otherwise nonrenewable policy. After converting the policy, you would pay whole life premiums based on your age at the time of conversion. Most insurance experts believe that **convertibility** and renewability should be purchased because they provide flexibility at a reasonable additional cost. Exhibit 9-3 shows the costs of $50,000 of one-year renewable term insurance for a thirty-five-year-old male. If this man keeps $50,000 of term insurance until age sixty-five, he will pay a total of $17,893. He will have no cash value in the policy, as he would in a whole life policy.

Whole Life Insurance

Whole life insurance accounts for perhaps half the total value of all life insurance in force in the United States. The average payoff value of such policies is around $15,000. Life insurance salespeople almost always will try to sell you a whole life policy because it is usually more profitable for them and their companies.

Premiums. Whole life premiums generally remain at the same level throughout the life of a policy. As a result, the policy holder pays more than is necessary to cover the insurance company's risk in the early years and less than would be necessary to cover the company's risk in later

EXHIBIT 9-3.

A TYPICAL $50,000 YEARLY RENEWABLE TERM POLICY FOR A MALE, AGE 35.	YEAR	ANNUAL PREMIUM
	1	$ 165.50
	2	172.50
	3	181.00
	4	192.00
	5	204.50
	6	219.00
	7	235.00
	8	252.00
	9	270.50
	10	290.50
	11	312.50
	12	339.00
	13	368.00
	14	400.00
	15	435.00
	16	473.50
	17	515.50
	18	560.50
	19	609.50
	20	642.50
	20 Year Total	$ 6,838.50
	Total At Age 65	$17,893.00
	(30 annual premiums)	

years. Exhibit 9-4 gives an example of a $10,000 ordinary life insurance policy with an annual level premium of $222.70 for a thirty-five-year-old male. In the first year, $205.50 of the $222.70 goes to the insurance company to cover insurance costs and $17.20 goes to the cash surrender

EXHIBIT 9-4.

COMPOSITION OF CASH SURRENDER FUND AND OPERATING CHANGES IN 20-YEAR ORDINARY LIFE PREMIUMS

$10,000 ORDINARY LIFE
DIVIDENDS[1] TO PURCHASE PAID-UP ADDITIONS
ANNUAL PREMIUM: $222.70   MALE AGE: 35

Year	Deposit To Cash Surrender Fund	Deposit To Insurance	Total Cash Surrender Fund
1	$ 17.20	$205.50	$ 17.20
2	179.71	42.99	196.91
3	190.43	32.27	387.34
4	201.97	20.73	589.31
5	213.47	9.23	802.78
6	225.43	2.73−	1028.21
7	237.14	14.44−	1265.35
8	250.35	27.65−	1515.70
9	262.61	39.91−	1778.31
10	275.17	52.47−	2053.48
11	270.17	47.47−	2323.65
12	282.60	59.90−	2606.25
13	294.64	71.94−	2900.89
14	306.82	84.12−	3207.71
15	320.64	97.94−	3528.35
16	333.21	110.51−	3861.56
17	346.11	123.41−	4207.67
18	360.95	138.25−	4568.62
19	376.12	153.42−	4944.74
20	391.60	168.90−	5336.34

SUMMARY

	20th Year	At Age 65
TOTAL CASH SURRENDER FUND	$5608.97[2]	$10,566.83[2]
TOTAL DEPOSITS	$4454.00	$ 6,681.00
NET GAIN	$1154.97−	$ 3,885.83−

[1]*Dividends are neither estimates nor guarantees but are based on the current dividend scale.*
[2]*Includes terminal dividend.*

fund for the purchaser of the policy. By the sixth year, the deposit to the cash surrender fund is greater than the level annual premium and stays greater throughout the life of this particular policy. You can see in the summary of this policy that by the twentieth year—when our policy holder is fifty-five years old—there is a cash value in that policy of $5608.97, which "cost" $4454. The cash value aspect of this policy, then, is $1154.97; at the end of twenty years, the policy represents a type of "savings account."

Owners of whole life policies often take comfort in the fact that their premiums are level and, therefore, represent one of the few costs that don't rise with inflation. (However, the real value of the policy, as well as the premiums, declines as the buying power of a dollar falls.) True, the cost is relatively high to begin with, but it gets no higher. The exact level of premiums you would pay for a $10,000 ordinary life insurance policy, as represented in Exhibit 9-4 depends on your age when you buy the policy. The younger you are, the less it will be, because the company expects to collect more years of premiums from you. The older you are, the greater it is.

Compared with term insurance, whole life is relatively more costly because it is a form of financial investment as well as an insurance protection. The investment feature is known as its "cash value." In Exhibit 9-4, the cash value at the end of twenty years exceeded $5,000 and, when the policy holder was sixty-five, actually exceeded the face value of the policy. You can cancel a whole life policy at any time and be paid the amount of its cash value. Individuals sometimes "cash in" a whole life policy when they retire. The cash value can be taken out either as a lump sum or in installments called annuities, which we'll discuss later. These are the so-called **living benefits** of a whole life policy.

Living Benefits. Living benefits are the opposite of **death benefits**. The death benefit of a life insurance policy is obviously the face value of the insurance you have purchased. The living benefit, on the other hand, provides the possibility of converting an ordinary policy to some sort of lump sum payment or stream of retirement income. In any one year, up to 60 percent of all insurance company payments are in the form of living benefits.

Note that the level premium for a whole life policy is paid throughout the life of the policy holder until age ninety-five or one hundred.

Borrowing on your cash value. One feature of a whole life insurance policy is that you can borrow on its cash value whenever you want. The interest rate on such loans is relatively favorable (as it should be, since you're borrowing your own money). It depends on the contract and the age of the policy. However, if you should die while the loan is outstanding, the sum paid to your beneficiary is reduced by the amount of the loan plus interest. In any event, the borrowing power given you in the cash value of a whole life insurance policy can be considered a type of cushion against financial emergencies. If you ever have to drop a whole life insurance policy because you are unable to pay the premiums or because you need its cash value, you will give up the insurance protection.

When You Reach Retirement Age

When you retire, you can discontinue premium payments on a whole life policy and choose one of the following living benefit programs:

1 Protection for the rest of your life but at a lower face value.
2 Full protection but for a definite number of years in the future (extended term insurance).
3 A cash settlement that returns whatever savings and dividends (cash surrender fund) that have not been used to pay off the insurance company for excessive costs incurred for your particular age group.
4 A whole life policy converted into an annuity, whereby you receive a specified amount of income each year for a certain number of years or for the rest of your life.

Death Benefits

In most life insurance policies, you specify a beneficiary, who receives the death benefits of that policy. If you bought a $10,000 ordinary life policy and have not borrowed any money on it, your beneficiary will receive $10,000 when you die. However, there are certain options for settling a life insurance policy. Before you purchase any policy, discuss the available settlement terms with the underwriter of that insurance. There are generally four option settlement plans from which to choose:

Plan 1: Lump sum payment.

Plan 2: The face value of the insurance policy is retained by the insurance company, but a small interest payment is made to the beneficiary for a certain number of years or for life. At the end of the specified period, the principal (face value) is then paid according to the terms in the contract.

Plan 3: The face value is paid to the beneficiary in the form of installments, either annually, semiannually, quarterly, or monthly. The company makes regular payments of equal amounts until the fund is depleted. Meanwhile, the company pays interest on the money remaining to be paid out. There are two options here. Each payment is for a specific amount, with payments spread out over a specific time period. If each payment is made for a specific amount, the length of time during which the payments will be made depends on:

1 The amount of income payment.
2 The face value of the policy.
3 The rate of interest guaranteed on the policy.

If payments are spread out over a given time period, the amount of each payment depends on:

1 The number of years the income is to be paid.
2 The face value of your policy.
3 The rate of interest guaranteed on the policy.

Plan 4: Regular life income is paid to the beneficiary. The insurance company guarantees a specific number of payments or payments that will total the face value of the policy. If, however, the beneficiary dies before the guaranteed payments have been made, the remainder goes to the estate of the beneficiary or as directed in the contract. This is sometimes called an annuity plan.

In sum, whole, straight, or ordinary life insurance gives you insurance plus a cash surrender fund and, hence, the possibility of retirement income, as illustrated in Exhibit 9-5. You can, of course, buy term insurance at a lower cost than whole life. You can invest the difference in your own saving and retirement plans and perhaps be better off, especially if you get a higher rate of return on your savings than the insurance company offers and do not die prematurely. The latest research suggests that whole life can be a sensible long-term investment for those who otherwise could expect their own investments to earn only about 4 percent *after taxes.* But if you can make 5 percent or more after taxes on your own investments, whole life may not be the type of policy for you.

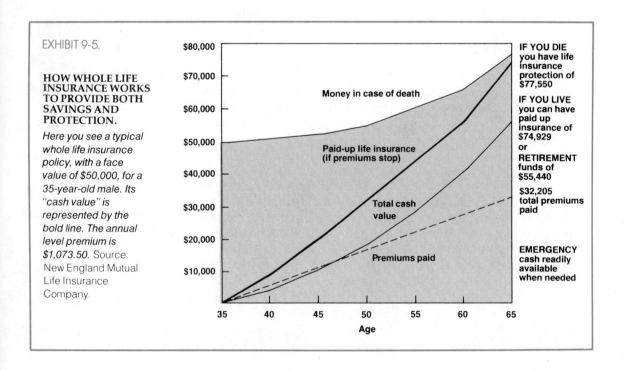

EXHIBIT 9-5.

HOW WHOLE LIFE INSURANCE WORKS TO PROVIDE BOTH SAVINGS AND PROTECTION.

Here you see a typical whole life insurance policy, with a face value of $50,000, for a 35-year-old male. Its "cash value" is represented by the bold line. The annual level premium is $1,073.50. Source: New England Mutual Life Insurance Company.

Money in case of death

Paid-up life insurance (if premiums stop)

Total cash value

Premiums paid

IF YOU DIE
you have life insurance protection of $77,550

IF YOU LIVE
you can have paid up insurance of $74,929
or
RETIREMENT funds of $55,440

$32,205
total premiums paid

EMERGENCY cash readily available when needed

Age

Limited Payment Whole Life

Limited payment is whole life insurance that is payable only at the death of the insured; the premiums are payable only for a stated number of years or until the insured reaches a certain age, such as sixty or sixty-five. The insurance is called limited because payments are limited to ten, twenty, twenty-five, or thirty years: if you took out a twenty-year **limited payment whole life** policy, you would have to pay premiums for twenty years, after which the entire policy would be paid up. Regular whole life premiums, on the other hand, are paid until you, the insured, dies. Obviously, the premium rate is considerably higher for this type of policy than for an ordinary life policy, because it is fully paid up at a much earlier date.

Generally, for any fixed amount that you spend on insurance, limited payment life policies provide less protection when you are young than either whole life or term insurance does. Limited payment life insurance might be appropriate if you expect to have a very short career at a high income level, such as a professional athlete or a rock star does. For others, it is usually not advisable, although there are some exceptions.

Endowment insurance

An **endowment policy** offers a combination of temporary life insurance and a rapidly increasing cash surrender fund. It can be considered both a term insurance policy and a growing savings account. If at any time during the specified life of the policy—usually anywhere from ten to thirty years—the policy holder dies, his or her beneficiaries receive the full face value, as with any other life insurance policy. The special feature of the endowment policy is that, at the end of its maturity, the living benefit is also equal to the face value. If the policy holder lives to the end of the period, he or she may collect.

Individuals who purchase endowment policies usually wish to have a specific number of dollars for a specific purpose at a desired time in the future. Endowment policies have been used, for example, to set up children's college funds. They are a poor way of accomplishing that objective, however, because they yield a low rate of return.

Because an endowment policy builds up a cash value equal to its face value by the end of the specified time period, the premiums on such a policy are even higher than on limited payment whole life.

Retirement Endowment Policies

Such policies are designed specifically to accumulate funds for retirement. The difference between a regular endowment policy and a **retirement endowment policy** is that you continue paying into the latter policy even after the cash surrender value has exceeded the face value of the policy. For example, your cash surrender value may equal, say, $30,000 by the time you reach age sixty, but you will continue to pay premiums until age sixty-five. If you die before age sixty-five, your beneficiaries would receive the face value of the policy, plus any excess cash surrender value. In essence, after the cash surrender value equals the face value, you are making pure investment.

TYPES OF INSURANCE COMPANIES AND THEIR POLICIES

There are basically two types of insurance companies—stock and mutual. These companies generally issue two types of policies—participating and nonparticipating.

Stock Insurance Companies

A **stock insurance company** is owned by the stockholders, who take the risk of losses and are entitled to any profit. Stock companies sell life insurance at guaranteed premium rates, which are kept as low as possible because of competition. If they are set too low, the stockholders take a loss; if they are more than sufficient, the stockholders obtain a profit.

Mutual Insurance Companies

A **mutual insurance company** is a cooperative association established by individuals to insure their own lives. There are no stockholders. General mutual company rates are set high enough to cover all contingencies.

Types of Policies

Participating Policies. Since a mutual company must take account of all cost increases during the year, it generally sets rates that will cover all anticipated costs plus any extraordinary ones. At the end of the year, it will figure what its costs actually were and refund its participating members—those who are insured—a pro rata share of the difference. This refund, generally called a dividend, is a partial return of your insurance premium. The premium charged you by a mutual company offering a **participating policy** generally (but not always) is an overstatement of your actual net cost per year, because you get a refund or dividend at the end of the year.

Nonparticipating Policies. Stock companies generally issue **nonparticipating policies.** You receive no refund or dividend at the end of the year; thus, the premiums you pay represent the actual cost of your policy.

COMPARING NONPARTICIPATING WHOLE LIFE AND TERM POLICIES

It is interesting to see a numerical comparison of two nonparticipating policies—one whole life, the other term—when we invest the difference between the premiums of the lower priced term policy in a savings account yielding 5 percent compound interest before taxes. In this comparison, by the editors of U.S. News & World Report Books, the individual is assumed to be a thirty-five-year-old man. He can purchase $10,000 of whole life for an annual premium of $191.10 or five-year renewable term for an annual premium of $64.50. The difference ($126.60) is put annually into a savings account, which compounds at 5 percent a year. Exhibit 9-6 shows that the term insurance policy plus a savings account yielding 5 percent will always provide more cash value than a whole life policy.

But what about federal and state income taxes? Cash value increments in a whole life insurance policy are relatively tax-free; thus, at the end of twenty years, when this individual surrenders his whole life policy, there would be virtually no income tax to pay. On the other hand, the interest earned on the savings would have been taxed each year.* The amount of the reduction and the available savings would, of course, depend on the individual's marginal tax bracket. The higher the marginal tax bracket, the less beneficial it is to buy term insurance and put the difference into a savings account.

OTHER LIFE INSURANCE POLICIES

In addition to life insurance that you buy as an individual, you also may be eligible for certain other types of life insurance policies which generally are offered at more attractive rates.

EXHIBIT 9-6.

CASH IN WHOLE LIFE POLICY VERSUS CASH IN SAVINGS ACCOUNT.

The table compares cash values in a $10,000 nonparticipating whole life policy with deposits in a bank (at 5 percent compounded interest before taxes) made with savings derived from buying $10,000 of 5-year nonparticipating renewable term insurance. The total of decreasing term and increasing savings always is $10,000.

END OF YEAR	CASH SURRENDER VALUE IN $10,000 WHOLE-LIFE POLICY	IN SAVINGS FUND WHILE CARRYING TERM INSURANCE
1	none	$ 133
2	none	272
3	$ 160	420
5	480	740
10	1,370	1,633
15	2,350	2,703
20	3,420	4,027

Note: All figures to nearest dollar.

Reprinted from the book How to Buy Insurance and Save Money. Copyright 1975 U.S. News & World Report Inc., Washington, D.C. 20037.

*Note, however, that our hypothetical consumer could get slightly over 6 percent on a tax-postponed Series E savings bond in which taxes only have to be paid when the bond is cashed. Also, it is possible to obtain 8.06 percent on a tax-deferred individual retirement annuity from a bank or savings and loan association.

Group Insurance

Group insurance is usually term insurance written under a master policy that is issued to either a sponsoring association or an employer. Some types of group insurance currently are offered to employees of universities and large businesses, to members of recreational and professional associations, and the like. Per $1000 of protection, the cost of group insurance is generally lower than individually obtained insurance for two main reasons—lower selling costs and lower bookkeeping costs. The selling costs are lower because the employer or sponsoring group does all the selling; thus, the selling agents receive lower commissions. And the bookkeeping costs are lower because, again, the employer or the association may do all the paperwork. Generally, no medical examination is required for members of the group, unless they want to take out an unusually large amount of group insurance. Today there are perhaps 400,000 master group life insurance policies outstanding in the United States.

Industrial Insurance

This type of insurance involves weekly premiums, usually costing ten, twenty, or fifty cents, which are collected at the home by an insurance agent. The insurance agent visits the home and writes a receipt for these small sums. Industrial insurance policies are written for small face values, usually $500 or no more than $1000. There are 65 million industrial policies in force today. The average death payment is, of course, small, so the percentage of the total amount of life insurance in force is small.

Savings Bank Insurance

As of the late 1970s, only three states offered savings bank insurance: New York, Connecticut, and Massachusetts. You must either live or work in those states in order to purchase the insurance. The rates are quite low because, again, there are lower selling costs. You go directly to the savings bank to buy the insurance. Sometimes savings bank life insurance gives you a better deal than other forms of life insurance. But, of course, you don't get the benefit of pertinent information that salespeople from other commercial companies can provide.

Credit Life Insurance

If you take out a loan, you may be forced to buy insurance, in the amount of the loan, on your life. The reason is simple: without such insurance, the creditor may have trouble collecting if you die with part of the loan outstanding. But if the creditor is named the beneficiary in the life insurance policy you take out as part of the loan, then that creditor is assured payment of any remaining amounts due. Today there are almost 100 million credit life insurance policies outstanding. The average amount per policy is small, perhaps $1300.

One must be careful with credit life insurance because a creditor may, in fact, force you unnecessarily to take out insurance. It is not a legal requirement. Check to see that the rate you actually are paying is commensurate with other group policy rates. If it isn't, then the difference you pay should be added to the total finance charge in order for you to figure out the true percentage rate of interest you are paying on the loan.

SOME SPECIALIZED INSURANCE POLICIES

Among the special life insurance policies offered by a variety of companies are combination plans, which combine different types of insurance, and variable life insurance policies.

Family Plan

This insurance plan combines some term insurance and some whole life insurance. Under the family plan, every member of the family has some insurance; even newborns are automatically covered so many days after birth. There is usually whole life on the insured or named (usually the breadwinner) and term on all other family members.

Family Income Plan

This combination term insurance and whole life insurance policy is designed to provide supplemental income to the family should the breadwinner die prematurely. If, in a typical twenty-year family income policy plan, the policy holder dies, his or her beneficiary might receive $10 per month for each $1,000 of the policy during the balance of the twenty years after the policy was taken out. Then, at the end of the twentieth year, the beneficiary would receive the face value of the policy, either in a lump sum or in monthly installments. A variation on this policy is called the family maintenance plan. With such a plan, the monthly payments continue for a full twenty-year period *after* the insured dies.

Extra Protection Policy

This policy also combines term and whole life insurance in double, triple, and even quadruple amounts. A triple protection policy, for example, gives, for each $1,000 of whole life insurance, $2,000 of term insurance. The term insurance usually continues until age sixty or sixty-five and then expires; however, the whole life portion of the policy remains in force. Insurance experts point out that these policies give less protection for the extra premium dollar than the family policies just described. The extra protection continues for a longer time period, though.

Variable Life Insurance

A number of companies are now offering policies in which the death benefit is based on the performance of the stocks in the insurance company's portfolio. Thus, the better the market performs over the life of the policy, the more cash the beneficiary will receive. If the stock market performs as it has historically, then **variable life insurance** seems like a pretty safe bet. However, if it does less well (as it has in the past decade), it is not as good as a regular whole life policy. Usually such policies have a minimum face value. Alternatively, you can have the minimum benefit increased by at least 3 percent each year for, say, fifteen years. Of course, you must pay higher premiums for such an expanded policy.

Modified Life Policies

Modified life policies are generally sold to newly married couples or to young professional people just starting new careers. For the first three to five years, the premiums are low. Then they increase. The first three or five years' premiums are below the mortality tables, so the later ones must be above. In the trade, these plans are called Mod 3 and Mod 5.

OPTIONS AND CLAUSES

There are numerous clauses and options that can be added to whole life and term insurance policies. Among them are the following:

1. *Guaranteed insurability option.* This option is sold with whole life policies; it allows the policy holder to purchase additional insurance at specified ages and amounts without having to meet medical qualifications.

2. *Automatic premium loan option.* With this provision, the insuror will automatically pay any premium that is not paid when due. The premium then becomes a loan against the cash value of the policy. This option continues until a total of the automatic loans equals the cash value; then the policy is terminated.

3. *Convertibility.* This clause or option applied to term insurance policies allows you to switch the policy to whole life or endowment at standard premium rates, regardless of any change in your health.

4. *Accidental death; double, or triple indemnity.* An additional sum is paid to your beneficiary if you die as the result of an accident. It usually doubles or triples the face amount of the policy and, therefore, is called double or triple indemnity.

5. *Incontestability.* Most policies have a clause that denies the company the right to challenge statements made in your application after two years if you should die. Thus, even if you made false statements, the company cannot nullify the policy after a stated period.

6   *Suicide exclusion clause.* Most life insurance policies will not pay off for death by suicide if it occurs during a stated period, usually the first year or two of the contract. The suicide clause states that the insurance company will return the premiums paid in case of suicide during this period.

5
Life Insurance

PRACTICAL APPLICATIONS

HOW TO MEET YOUR INSURANCE NEEDS

Before you figure out how much insurance you should buy, what type it should be, and where you should get it, first think about who should be insured in your family. You must take into account Social Security benefits. Then you should consider the actual economic (or financial) dependency that others have on a particular member of a spending unit. If you are a single college student, for example, it is usually not recommended that you have any life insurance. By the same token, it is usually pointless for a family to insure its children (unless the children contribute a substantial amount to the family income). Should one of them die, the family's earning power usually will not be affected. This is not necessarily true for a homemaker, however, who frequently contributes explicitly to the family earnings by working outside the home, as well as implicitly by servicing the family. For this reason, the family unit may want to take out an insurance policy on the homemaker's life. The wage earner(s) should, of course, be the one(s) with the most insurance because, if he or she dies prematurely, the spending unit will suffer the greatest loss.

NAMING A BENEFICIARY

For any insurance policy you buy, you should name one or more beneficiaries. You may retain the right to change the beneficiary later if you wish to do so.

In most policies, you can name a primary beneficiary. For example, a spouse may name his or her mate as primary beneficiary and their children as contingent beneficiaries. Thus, if the primary beneficiary dies before the insured, then the contingent beneficiaries will collect whatever is due upon the insured's death. One can include future children as contingent beneficiaries by stating so when the policy is purchased. You can go one step further and indicate how a deceased's contingent beneficiary's share should be distributed—either to his or her children or divided equally among his or her brothers and sisters, who are also contingent beneficiaries.

SOME INSURANCE BUYING RULES

Insurance is another item competing for your consumer dollar, as is a new bicycle, a new car, or another house. When you buy life insurance, you obtain a certain amount of satisfaction in knowing that your dependents will be somewhat financially secure should you die prematurely. Note, however, that there are other possible uses of these same funds that also yield satisfaction; thus, there is no standard formula that indicates exactly how much insurance is best for you. But these four suggestions may help you decide:

1. Identify the major risks that you and your family reasonably face; insure them according to the *potential* loss they could produce.

2. Insure big losses, not small ones.

3. Never buy any type of insurance policy until you have compared the costs and terms of coverage of at least two, and perhaps more, companies. Check a company's performance in *Best's Guide to Insurance Companies.*

4. Limit your losses and control your risks through preventive measures.

ARE YOU UNDERINSURED?

If anyone depends on you for even part of his or her livelihood, you may well be underinsured. If, however, you are young and unmarried or married to someone who also contributes explicitly to the family income, then you may not need much (if any) life insurance. If, however, you are married and have children and/or a spouse who depends on you for at least part of his or her income, then you probably should have some form of life insurance. But you should also realize that Social Security could fulfill all your protection needs, assuming you are covered by Social Security.

In this Practical Applications section, we'll make an assumption that you should make when trying to figure out your insurance needs: should you die now, your dependents will need money immediately. How much would be left for your dependents, in what form, and over what period? This is not an easy thing to figure out, so plan on taking some time. You may want to work it out with an insurance agent, but you can probably do it yourself.

HOW TO FIGURE OUT YOUR FAMILY'S LIFE INSURANCE NEEDS

Financial counselors at the First National City Bank in New York (Citibank) have devised a new method to figure out your insurance needs. Citibank's insurance specialists have calculated that a family can maintain its standard of living with an after-tax income that is 75 percent of what that income was before the breadwinner's death. Citibank believes that if a family has less than 60 percent of the pre-death level of after-tax income, its living standard will be lowered considerably. In Exhibit 9-7, the **net income replacement** columns are labeled 75 percent and 60 percent; these are the target net after-tax income replacement levels that insurance should provide. "The Multiples of Salary" Chart tells you how many times your current *gross* salary you should own in life insurance to provide either 75 or 60 percent of your current after-tax income to your family, should you die. The chart assumes that your family will also receive Social Security benefits. In devising the chart, Citibank's staff assumed that insurance proceeds would be invested to produce (after inflation) a rate of return of 5 percent a year. Moreover, it is assumed that the principal from the insurance policy would be gradually consumed; by the time of

the surviving spouse's death, it would disappear.

Assume, for example, that your spouse is twenty-five years old and you wish to provide him or her with 60 percent of your after-tax income, should you die. If your gross earnings are $9,000 a year, you must have three times that worth of life insurance, or $27,000 worth. This figure may seem low, but it takes account of a higher Social Security benefit that a younger spouse would obtain until the children reach eighteen (or twenty-two if they are full-time students.) Note that the table is for a family of four; the figures would have to be modified for different numbers of dependents.

WHAT TYPE SHOULD YOU BUY?

Of the life insurance plans already discussed—term, whole life, limited payment whole life, and endowment—all but term insurance include some element of cash surrender value. With term, you are buying "pure" insurance; with the others, you are investing and getting a rate of return. Your decision whether to buy term insurance or to buy term plus using some form of savings will determine the payments you must make to the insurance company. The cheapest way to buy insurance is, of course, to buy term: you buy only protection. If you already have a satisfactory savings program, you may not wish to save additional sums with an insurance company.

Consumers Union points out, as do several other research organizations, that if purchasing whole life insurance is compared with buying term and investing the difference—that is, the difference between the whole life premium and the lower term premium—the combination of term and other investments will yield more money at the end of any period. A critic of this conclusion, Herbert S. Denenberg, former Pennsylvania Insurance Commissioner, contends that this comparison is true only if you get approximately a 6 percent rate of return (over a long period of time) on savings you invest yourself. He contends that, if you can get only 4 percent, you're better off buying whole life.[1]

Insurance salespeople generally urge you to buy whole life rather than term insurance. They say that whole life is a bargain or even "free" because you eventually get back much or all of your money. They use the cash value aspect of whole life to tout its desirability over term insurance. Since term has no cash value, salespeople may say that buying it is "just throwing money down the drain." This "down the drain" argument often ignores the fact that the term premiums are lower than whole life premiums in the early years (and the sales commission lower for term insurance). For a man twenty-five years old, whole life premiums in the early years may cost three to four times more than term premiums.

[1]Herbert S. Denenberg, "Consumers Union: No Help For Insurance Shoppers," *Business and Society Review,* No. 6 (Summer 1973), pp. 107-8.

EXHIBIT 9-7. **THE MULTIPLES OF SALARY CHART (FOR NET INCOME REPLACEMENT)**
Reproduced by courtesy of Consumer Views *Vol. VII, No. 7, July 1976 published by Citibank, N.A., 399 Park Avenue, N.Y., NY 10022*

	PRESENT AGE OF SPOUSE							
YOUR PRESENT GROSS EARNINGS	25 Years*		35 Years*		45 Years*		55 Years†	
	75%	60%	75%	60%	75%	60%	75%	60%
$ 7,500	4.0	3.0	5.5	4.0	7.5	5.5	6.5	4.5
9,000	4.0	3.0	5.5	4.0	7.5	5.5	6.5	4.5
15,000	4.5	3.0	6.5	4.5	8.0	6.0	7.0	5.5
23,500	6.5	4.5	8.0	5.5	8.5	6.5	7.5	5.5
30,000	7.5	5.0	8.0	6.0	8.5	6.5	7.0	5.5
40,000	7.5	5.0	8.0	6.0	8.0	6.0	7.0	5.5
65,000	7.5	5.5	7.5	6.0	7.5	6.0	6.5	5.0

*Assuming federal income taxes for a family of four (two children). There are four exemptions and the standard—or 15% itemized—deductions. State and local taxes are disregarded.
†Assuming you have only two exemptions. (Any children are now grown.)

To calculate the amount of life insurance needed for either net replacement level, multiply your present gross salary by the number under that level.

If your gross income or spouse's age fall between the figures shown, take an average between the multiples for nearest salaries and ages.

Social Security benefits will be part of both levels.

If personal liquid assets (savings, predictable inheritance, retirement plan, invest- ment, etc.) equal one year of gross salary or less, use them as part of the fund for the small-emergency reserve and final expenses. If they equal *more* than one year, subtract that extra amount from the insurance needed to replace income.

People with no personal assets who can't afford the 75% level might try for at least 60%. The average family would then face some lowering in level of living but wouldn't be financially devastated.

Disadvantages of Term Insurance

The rate per dollar of term protection in a pure term policy is higher than the rate per dollar of term protection in a whole life or endowment policy. The reason for this difference is the mortality experience on term insurance. A prospective policy holder who is in relatively poor health will usually select an insurance plan with the lowest premium outlay. Additionally, term insurance turns out to be expensive because there is a relatively high sales expense (often called the "loading"). This sales expense, included in the premium, covers overhead expenses of the insurance companies. It constitutes a greater portion of the lower premium rate on a term policy. Thus, a term policy can, in fact, involve the lowest premium outlay but still be relatively expensive per unit of protection.

SOME SPECIAL CONSIDERATIONS

Buying whole life insurance is a way of forcing yourself to save because part of each premium goes to a savings plan. The lower rate of return on savings in an insurance company is compensated for by the fact that you have savings you otherwise would lack because you have little will power.

As another argument for whole life over term, some insurance agents point out that individuals in extremely high income brackets may be better off buying whole life insurance, borrowing on it to pay the premiums, and deducting the interest payments on the "loan" from their income so that taxes need not be paid.

A permanent or whole life insurance policy contract is essentially a piece of property with certain unique characteristics. Under current law, a permanent insurance plan can accumulate income, tax free: dividends as well as interest on cash value are not taxable as current income. Essentially, then, you get a higher return than is actually shown in your life insurance saving plan because you don't pay a tax on the savings you accumulate. With a regular savings account, you must pay federal and sometimes state income tax on its interest earnings.

Furthermore, death benefits on ordinary or straight life insurance policies usually go to age 100. Except in very rare cases, therefore, there always will be a death benefit.

SHOPPING AROUND FOR INSURANCE

Obviously, it is unwise to buy insurance from the first salesperson who knocks on your door. Since large sums of money may be involved, it is advisable to investigate several plans. Seek out a knowledgeable insurance salesperson who represents a large number of companies and who can explain the complexities of each program in simple language. Ask the salesperson to give you the average annual costs per $1,000 of, say, five-year renewable term insurance. With such assistance, you are well on your way to being able to pick the right company to insure you.

A good source of information on comparative life insurance costs is a series of studies in the January through March 1974 issues of *Consumer Reports.* Consumers Union presents the basic facts on the types of policies available and compares different companies in a sophisticated index. The **interest-adjusted relative index** takes account of dividends, interest, and earnings on the policies. Not everyone can buy insurance from some of the companies listed. For example, only teachers and staff members in schools, universities, and educational or scientific institutions can buy insurance from Teachers Insurance and Annuity Association of America, one of the least expensive insurance policies available. If you work or live in Massachusetts, New York, or Connecticut, you can take advantage of extremely low-cost five-year renewable term insurance available from the mutual savings banks.

LIFE INSURANCE SOLD ON CAMPUS

Insurance agents have become familiar figures on many campuses, and college students are contacted four to six times a year by these agents. The insurance agent approaches a premium-paying problem of the poor student by offering to finance, on credit, the first annual premium and even the second with a loan to be paid off perhaps five years later. This. student policy holder typically signs a policy assignment form, which makes the insurance company the first beneficiary if the student dies. Thus, the insurance company will make sure that it can collect the unpaid premium and interest. But generally, most college students don't need life insurance because they don't have dependents.

SOME WAYS TO CUT LIFE INSURANCE COSTS

1. Don't carry insurance on children. Either save the premiums or use them to buy additional term insurance for yourself.

2. Consider term as opposed to whole life insurance.

3. If you don't smoke and/or don't drink, look for insurance companies that give discounts to nonsmokers and/or nondrinkers. (But still compare rates with other companies.) See if you fit into a preferred risk category.

4. Attempt to buy insurance on group plans through your employer or any organization of which you are a member.

5. Pay your premiums annually instead of quarterly or monthly.

6. If you have a participating policy, don't let your dividends or refunds accumulate on deposit with the insurance company at a lower rate than the money could earn in, say, a savings and loan institution.

EXHIBIT 9-8.   **COST-OF-LIVING STATEMENT**

HERE IS IMPORTANT INFORMATION...
about "Cost of Living" insurance available to you in connection with TIAA Policy No.

(1) For the year beginning October 28, 1977, you have $114,010 as the contractual amount of insurance under this policy.

(2) During the period used to measure cost-of-living changes for this policy, the Consumer Price Index increased by 40%, making $45,630 of insurance available to you for the coming year in addition to the contractual amount. The year's premium for this Cost of Living insurance is shown in the Notice above.

The Cost of Living insurance is offered without medical examination in return for the premium due on the date shown above. You can have this insurance by simply sending TIAA the Notice above and your check for the premium. If you do *not* want the additional insurance, just disregard the Notice. This will automatically eliminate any future offers of Cost of Living Insurance in connection with this policy, as explained on the reverse side.

Keep this part for your records. See reverse side for explanations.

DON'T FORGET INFLATION

The first chapter of this book dealt with the continuing problem of inflation, and the necessity of taking account of inflation when determining life insurance needs was mentioned. This means that the policy holder must reevaluate his or her insurance needs every few years to take account of cost-of-living increases that have occurred.

Alternatively, it is possible to purchase or contract for automatic cost-of-living increases in a policy's face value. Exhibit 9-8 shows a cost-of-living statement from the Teachers Insurance and Annuity Association. If the term insurance policy holder signs up for this feature, he or she is automatically billed for the increased coverage every year. If the bill is paid on time, the cost-of-living "rider" continues in force for another year.

GLOSSARY OF TERMS

TERM INSURANCE   Life insurance for a specified term (period of time) that has only a death benefit.

WHOLE LIFE INSURANCE   Also called cash value, straight, and ordinary life insurance. It has both death and living benefits. One builds cash surrender value in the policy.

DECREASING TERM INSURANCE   Term insurance in which a fixed premium is paid and the face value of the policy falls throughout its life of, say, twenty years.

HOME PROTECTION POLICY   A type of decreasing term insurance that mirrors the decline in the principal owed on a home mortgage.

RENEWABILITY   A clause in a term insurance policy that guarantees it can be renewed without the insured passing a medical exam.

CONVERTIBILITY   A clause in a term insurance policy that gives the insured the option of switching to whole, or straight, life insurance.

LIVING BENEFITS   The benefits derived from the cash surrender fund in a whole life insurance policy.

DEATH BENEFITS   The face value of any insurance policy that is paid to the beneficiary upon the death of the insured.

LIMITED PAYMENT WHOLE LIFE   A whole life policy payable only at the death of the insured. The premiums are paid for a stated number of years or until the insured reaches a certain age, such as sixty or sixty-five.

ENDOWMENT POLICY   A policy that combines temporary life insurance and a rapidly increasing cash surrender value.

RETIREMENT ENDOWMENT POLICY   Similar to an endowment policy, but you continue paying into the policy even after the cash surrender value has exceeded the face value of that policy.

STOCK INSURANCE COMPANY   An insurance company owned by stockholders, who take the risks of any loss and are entitled to a pro rata share of profit.

MUTUAL INSURANCE COMPANY   A cooperative association without stockholders.

PARTICIPATING POLICY   A policy in a mutual insurance company in which you become a participant and are given, therefore, a pro rata return on your premium commensurate with any excess of premiums over payouts and expenses of the company.

NONPARTICIPATING POLICY   The type of policy that a stock insurance company usually offers. The premiums you pay represent the full and actual cost of the policy.

GROUP INSURANCE   Term insurance written under a master policy and offered to members of a particular group.

INDUSTRIAL INSURANCE   Insurance involving weekly premiums collected at the policy holder's home by an insurance agent. The policies usually have a very small death benefit.

SAVINGS BANK INSURANCE   Insurance offered by savings banks in New York, Connecticut, and Massachusetts.

CREDIT LIFE INSURANCE   Insurance that is taken out when you make a loan. The beneficiary is whoever extends the loan.

VARIABLE LIFE INSURANCE   Payment of the death benefit or the living benefit is based on the performance of the stock market, which is where the cash surrender fund is invested.

NET INCOME REPLACEMENT   The replacement level that will guarantee your family a specific percentage of your present living standard. If the net replacement ratio you choose is 60 percent, then your family will live at 60 percent of the level they were living at when you were alive.

INTEREST-ADJUSTED RELATIVE INDEX   An index used to compare the cost of whole life insurance. It takes account of the rate of return earned on the cash surrender fund for whole life policies.

CHAPTER SUMMARY

1. The major hazards to financial security are: (a) illness, (b) accident, (c) unemployment, (d) old age, (e) premature death, (f) desertion and divorce, and (g) unexpected catastrophic expenses.

2. The basic types of life insurance are term and whole life. In the latter, a cash surrender fund is built.

3. With decreasing term insurance, or a home protection policy, premiums remain level while coverage decreases. This resembles a mortgage, whose principal decreases over time.

4. Desirable clauses in term insurance contracts are renewability and convertibility, both of which cost extra.

5. More than half the insurance in force in the United States is whole life insurance.

6. Premiums on a whole life policy remain the same throughout the policy; thus, you pay more than is necessary to cover the insurance company's risk in the early years and less than would be necessary in the later years. You build up a cash surrender fund, which is given to you whenever you wish.

7. You can borrow on the cash surrender fund, usually at lower interest rates than you can obtain elsewhere, basically because you are borrowing your own money.

8. When you retire, you can discontinue premium payments on a whole life policy and choose one of the following living benefit programs: (a) protection for the rest of your life with a lower face value, (b) full protection for a definite number of years, (c) a cash settlement, or (d) conversion of your whole life policy into an annuity.

9. Death benefits can be paid to your beneficiaries several ways: (a) a lump sum payment, (b) interest payments on the cash surrender value paid to the beneficiary for a number of years and then the principal paid to the children or other beneficiaries, (c) face value of the policy paid to the beneficiary in installments, or (d) a lifetime income, or annuity, paid to the beneficiary.

10. Limited payment whole life insurance might be appropriate for someone making a larger income than he or she anticipated earning in, say, ten, fifteen, or twenty years.

11. An endowment policy offers the most savings of any whole life insurance policy. In particular, a retirement endowment policy allows you to keep investing even after the cash surrender fund exceeds the face value of the policy (its death benefit).

12. It is often financially advantageous to buy term insurance rather than whole insurance. The difference in the premiums can be invested to yield a higher rate of return than the cash surrender fund left with an insurance company for a whole life policy.

13. There are numerous specialized insurance plans, including the family plan, family income plan, family maintenance plan, and modified life policies.

14. Not everyone in a family necessarily should be insured. It seems appropriate to insure only those who contribute to the family income.

15. You should name both primary and contingent beneficiaries.

16. Insurance is like any other good or service; one decides to buy it the way one decides to buy another car, a boat, a house, or a bicycle.

17. Before deciding how much insurance to buy, you should identify major risks and do some comparison shopping.

18. To figure out your family's insurance needs, use Exhibit 9-7, which was prepared by the economists at Citibank in New York.

19. Most industry experts agree that term insurance should form the basis of most people's life insurance policies. On the other hand, if you need a forced savings plan, then whole life insurance would be the answer, even though the rate of return to the cash surrender fund may be less than is possible through other investment outlets.

20. One should shop around for life insurance. The interest-adjusted relative index of different life insurance companies is presented in the January, February, and March 1974 issues of *Consumer Reports*.

21 It is advisable to purchase cost-of-living riders to all term insurance policies.

STUDY QUESTIONS

1. List and explain the most frequent financial needs that must be satisfied after the death of the family breadwinner.

2. What is the difference between term insurance and whole life insurance?

3. What are the advantages and disadvantages of term insurance?

4. What is the cash surrender fund for a whole life insurance policy?

5. What is the difference between a primary and a secondary beneficiary? Why is it essential to designate such beneficiaries for a life insurance policy?

6. What is an incontestability clause in a life insurance contract?

7. What is the difference between a stock life insurance company and a mutual life insurance company?

8. How would you figure out your life insurance needs?

9. Why shouldn't children be insured?

CASE PROBLEMS

9-1 Life Insurance: Luxury or Necessity?

Frank Ferguson, twenty-five, works in a nonprofit nursery school in a community on an Indian reservation in western South Dakota. He and his wife, Laurie, and their two children, ages two and four, live in a rented trailer. Frank earns $7800 a year. He often worries about what would happen to Laurie and the children if he should die. He feels that he is too poor to afford life insurance, as their budget would only allow them to spend five dollars a month on it.

1. Do you think he can afford insurance?

2. If so, what kind and how much should he have?

9-2 Deciding Between Term and Whole Life Insurance

Ken and Donna Mayfield are a couple in their late twenties. They have two children, ages six and nine. Ken, a purchasing agent for a Kansas City manufacturing firm, earns $32,500 per year. They have a $46,000 mortgage and are making credit payments on two cars, furniture, and various other items, including last year's vacation, for a total debt load of $10,950. None of their debts is covered by insurance. They have never missed a credit payment but seem to be unable to put anything into savings. (The down payment on their house came from insurance proceeds realized when Ken's father died.) Ken has a $25,000 group insurance policy provided by his employer. During a financial seminar sponsored by the company, the instructor strongly urged the employees with young families to purchase additional term insurance, instead of whole life, and to invest the premium difference. Ken agrees he needs more insurance but doesn't know how much.

1. What amount of insurance should Ken have?

2. Which type of policy would you recommend?

SELECTED REFERENCES

"A Guide to Life Insurance." *Consumer Reports,* January, February, and March, 1974, Parts I, II, & III.

Belth, Joseph M. *Life Insurance: A Consumer's Handbook.* Bloomington, IN: Indiana University Press, 1973.

"Campus Life Insurance at Best a Delusion, at Worst a Snare." *Consumer Reports,* March 1977, pp. 168-71.

Denenberg, Herbert S. "Insurance in the Age of the Consumer." *Best's Review,* April 1970,

Denenberg, Herbert S. *The Insurance Trap: Unfair at any Rate* Racine, WI: Western Publishing Company, 1972.

Denenberg, Herbert S. *The Shopper's Guide to Life Insurance* Harrisburg, PA: Pennsylvania Insurance Department, April 1972.

Greene, Mark R. and Swadener, Paul. *Insurance Insights.* Cincinnati, OH: Southwestern Publishing Co., 1974.

"Insurance Salesmen Admit Unethical Practices on Campuses." *Consumer Newsweekly,* March 21, 1977.

"Life Insurance: How It Can Help You Build a Nest Egg." *Better Homes & Gardens,* March 1975,

"Life Insurance: What You'd Better Know Before You Buy." *Changing Times,* March 1977, pp. 36-40.

Mehr, Robert I. *Life Insurance: Theory and Practice.* Dallas: Business Publications, 1977.

Oehlbeck, J. Tracy. *Consumer's Guide to Life Insurance.* Elmhurst, NY: Pyramid Press, 1975.

Health Care and Insurance

■ For years, the lack of adequate health care for large segments of our population has been criticized by presidents, members of Congress, lay people, and even doctors. There have been many suggested solutions to our health care problems, some of which have been enacted in the form of Medicare and Medicaid. But even before those programs went into effect, members of Congress were demanding more comprehensive medical care insurance.

In dealing with the problems of inadequate medical care, concerned legislators and citizens noticed the spiraling costs of obtaining available medical care. Exhibit 10-1 shows the Consumer Price Index and the price indexes of various health care services, the latter having risen considerably faster than the overall CPI. Thus, not only is health care more expensive than it was, but its *relative* price is rising; it is more expensive in relation to other services than it once was.

HEALTH CARE EXPENDITURES

The expenditures for medical care in the United States have increased dramatically in the last four or five decades. We spent only $4 billion on medical care in 1929; we increased our spending to $40 billion by 1965; and it is well over $150 billion today. In 1929, expenditures on medical care represented 4 percent of total national spending, but today's expenditures represent nearly 10 percent. We can say, therefore, that as real incomes rise, Americans demand not just more medical care but proportionally more than the rise in incomes.

247

WHY DOES MEDICAL CARE COST SO MUCH?

No one expects medical care to be free. But many people wonder why medical care costs have risen faster than all other costs. We can give several reasons why this is happening. The first concerns the increases in demand brought about by government programs.

When Medicare Started

Prior to Medicare—medical care for the aged—Congressional estimates of what the program would cost were many times less than the actual cost proved to be. That's because the demand for medical services responds to the price charged. When Medicare was instituted, the actual price of health care services to many people was lowered drastically. In some cases, the price was reduced to zero. As the price fell, the quantity demanded rose, and the available supply of medical care services was taxed beyond capacity. The only thing that could change was the price, and it changed radically. Hospital room charges have skyrocketed since the imposition of Medicare. But Medicare is not the only reason medical prices have soared.

Insurance Plans

More than 80 million Americans are covered by some form of private medical insurance, most of which pays a certain part of hospital expenses. The problem is, insurance rarely covers outpatient service.

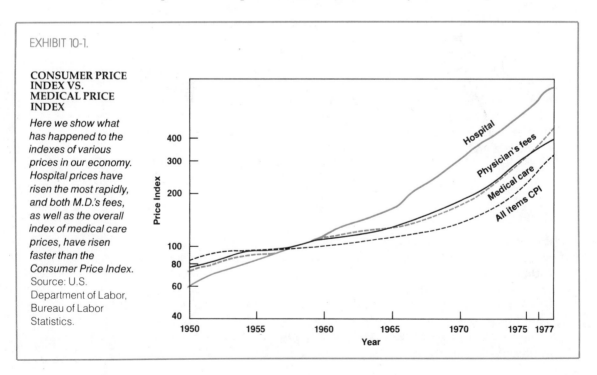

EXHIBIT 10-1.

CONSUMER PRICE INDEX VS. MEDICAL PRICE INDEX

Here we show what has happened to the indexes of various prices in our economy. Hospital prices have risen the most rapidly, and both M.D.'s fees, as well as the overall index of medical care prices, have risen faster than the Consumer Price Index. Source: U.S. Department of Labor, Bureau of Labor Statistics.

Rather, it covers only inpatient service. Individuals covered by medical insurance are, therefore, impelled to go to the hospital to be taken care of by their doctors. And doctors have an incentive to send them to hospitals in order to collect the insurance payments. They know, of course, that fewer patients would be willing to have the services performed in doctors' offices, where they would not be covered by insurance. Additionally, insurance plans generally have little control over the number of tests and examinations performed on patients. Hospitals have an incentive to use the most complex techniques possible. And doctors order them, knowing that a large percentage of the costs are reimbursed by insurance companies. Patients covered by insurance do not pay the *direct* costs of the medical care they receive in a hospital. Hence, they demand much more than they otherwise would. This increase in quantity demanded causes hospital expenses to rise, all other things held constant.

Higher Quality Service

There is an increased sophistication in the medical field, with many new areas of diagnosis, surgery, drug treatment, physical therapy, and so on. With all these specializations, Americans are demanding better health care, which, in turn, costs more. This increased specialization has fostered the need to visit two or more specialized doctors rather than one, as in the past. This, of course, raises the cost of medical care. Additionally, patients receive better services than before. Many hospitals now have complete staffing around the clock and use more sophisticated equipment. All this costs more.

Higher Malpractice Insurance Costs

Individuals are suing their doctors and hospitals more now than ever before. Because juries are awarding larger amounts, malpractice insurance costs are rising alarmingly. For example, in 1972, Baylor University Medical Center in Dallas paid $11,000 for malpractice insurance; in 1976, the bill was to be $1.5 million. In 1974, Mount Sinai Hospital Medical Center in Chicago paid $281,000 for $6 million in malpractice insurance; in 1976, the same insurance companies wanted $3 million to provide the $6 million in coverage. Had the hospital paid the premium sought by the insurance companies, the daily cost of malpractice insurance to the patient would have gone from seven dollars to twenty-two dollars.

A number of hospitals have stopped paying regular insurance companies for such coverage. Instead, they are self-insuring: that is, they set aside a certain sum of money each month in a reserve account to cover claims against them in malpractice lawsuits. Unfortunately, this means that some hospitals could conceivably go out of business if a former patient won an extraordinarily large malpractice suit. Hospitals also protect themselves from malpractice suits by ordering excessive testing and prolonged stays in intensive care units after surgery. This also increases medical care costs.

Some concerned individuals have suggested that the government should offer malpractice insurance to hospitals. This would mean that hospitals could then force the general taxpayer to cover their mistakes. There may be further solutions to the malpractice insurance issue, but today it remains a problem.

HIGHER PRICES LEAD TO SELF TREATMENT

There are two ways to obtain medical help: one is self-diagnosis and self-treatment; the other is reliance on the medical care industry. If the price of a physician's diagnosis and treatment goes up, then one might expect that the quantity demanded would fall. Reliance on self-diagnosis and self-treatment would increase. People would decide to go to doctors only after their symptoms became alarming. Perhaps the increase in quality and, therefore, the price of doctors' services would produce a decrease in the total quantity of medical care utilized because physicians would be consulted less often. Moreover, some people might forego the services of a licensed physician in favor of some alternative method, such as that offered by naturopaths or faith healers. When the services of licensed physicians become more costly, the demand for substitute services from chiropractors, midwives, naturopaths, and so on increases.

There is, of course, a real danger when consumers ignore treatment or engage in extensive self-treatment. Numerous over-the-counter medicines are available, and many are quite powerful. There is a growing tendency to be quite casual about self-prescription, even to the point of overusing patent medicines. It's one thing for a doctor to tell you to take three aspirin every four hours and something else altogether for you to make that decision yourself; laypeople often are unaware of possible side effects of particular medicines. This problem becomes acute when children see adults taking medicines for almost every physical and emotional complaint. The result of a child taking adult drugs may be dangerous and even fatal. Recent advertisements for over-the-counter medications have been accompanied by the warning, "Use only as directed." This is an attempt to counter the serious health hazards presented by self-prescription.

DRUGS, DRUGS, DRUGS

Drug regulation is a difficult task. Consumers spend more than $9 billion for drugs a year, of which about $4 billion are sold only by prescription. More than 90 percent of the prescriptions today are for drugs that did not exist thirty years ago.

The ethical (prescription) drug industry has always presented a problem to regulators and consumers alike. The information problems are sometimes insurmountable. Even the drug companies often don't know the effectiveness, or the side effects, of a drug. Doctors rarely have, or take the time to get, exact information on all the drugs they use. And, in the past, drug companies have not always carefully screened the drugs they sold. The largest regulator of drugs in the United States is the federal Food and Drug Administration, established by the Food, Drug, and Cosmetic Act of 1938, which replaced the Pure Food and Drug Act of 1906 signed by President Theodore Roosevelt.

What the FDA Does

Since the 1962 Kefauver-Harris Amendment to the 1938 Act, the FDA has issued detailed procedures that a drug company must follow before it receives approval for a new product. The steps may take years to complete before the company can market its new drug.

The Benefits and Costs of FDA Requirements

If aspirin was subjected to the current FDA requirements for drug certification, it would fail to pass. That's because no one knows exactly why it works, but it is known to produce side effects if too many are taken. Certainly aspirin would be a prescription drug if it were under current rulings. Do you think aspirin should be dispensed only by prescription? Do you think it should be taken off the market because no one knows how it works? Did you know that taking too much aspirin can result in duodenal ulcers and kidney dysfunction? If you believe it should be taken off the market, then you will agree with the spirit of the 1962 Kefauver-Harris Amendment.

A few years ago, Dr. Sam Peltzman, a University of Chicago economics professor, did a study on the costs resulting from the 1962 FDA amendment. He found that the entry rate of new drugs into the market had slowed considerably:

> The 1962 Drug Amendment sought to reduce consumer waste on ineffective drugs. This goal appears to have been attained, but the costs in the process seem clearly to have outweighed the benefits. It was shown [in the study] that the amendments have produced a substantial decline in drug innovation since 1962.
>
> The net effect of the amendment on consumers, then, is comparable to their being taxed something between 5 and 10 percent on their . . . drug purchases.[1]

As with all legislation, consumers should weigh the costs against the benefits. The benefits of preventing certain drugs from entering the market are that no one suffers the side effects. The costs are those mentioned by Dr. Peltzman, who believes such costs outweigh the benefits. You may interpret his data differently.

---

[1]Sam Peltzman, "An Evaluation of Consumer Protection Legislation: The 1962 Drug Amendments," *Journal of Political Economy,* Vol. 81, No. 5 (September/October 1973), pp. 1089-90.

Restrictions in Pharmaceutical Sales

Did you know that only 5 percent of prescriptions are compounded by the pharmacist? The druggist fills the other 95 percent by dropping pills into bottles and/or merely typing the patient's and doctor's names and dosage instructions on a label, which is then pasted on a bottle supplied by the manufacturer.

Why do drugs cost so much? One reason is that price competition among druggists has been restricted: it is not considered "ethical" to advertise prescription drug prices. Thirty-seven states prohibited drug price advertising for many years. In many cases, druggists won't reveal over the phone the charges for filling a prescription or their prescription costs. But some states now require that prices be given over the phone.

Pharmacy practices came to light in 1972 when the federal Price Commission considered requiring retailers to display base prices of the best-selling drugs. The American Pharmaceutical Association claimed this would be a police-state method of controlling prices. Unfortunately for consumers, the Price Commission backed down and did not require the posting of prices. Instead, pharmacies were told they could provide consumers with the standard list of wholesale drug prices and the store's professional fee or markup for filling a prescription.(Some states now require posting the top 100 drug prices.)

In 1976, *Money* magazine priced three of the ten most prescribed drugs in four stores in five cities. *Money* found as much as a 406 percent difference in the price for a given drug. The results were as follows (price on a per-pill basis):

Drug	Lowest Price	Highest Price	Spread
Valium (5 mg.)	8.9¢	23.2¢	161%
Darvon Compound-65	7.6¢	19.8¢	161%
Tetracycline (250 mg.)	4.9¢	24.8¢	406%

In 1967, the American Medical Association conducted a study in Chicago that revealed a 1,200 percent price differential for exactly the same drug. No wonder the U.S. Justice Department concluded:

> Differentials such as these can only exist when they are unknown to potential customers; for a given choice, most consumers would refuse to pay 10 or 12 times the going price for a drug available elsewhere. The cost to the public of the lack of price competition is enormous.

The Supreme Court Intervenes

In 1976, the U.S. Supreme Court handed down a landmark case for consumers. A consumer activist, Lynn Jordan of Virginia, decided a Virginia law banning prescription-drug price advertising was unfair. She and the consumer council she headed in the Virginia AFL-CIO sued and won.[2] It was ruled unconstitutional for states to forbid pharmacies

---

[2]*Virginia State Board of Pharmacies* v. *The Virginia Citizens Consumer Council* – 74-895.

to advertise prices for prescription drugs, even though state or pharmacy board regulations prohibit it. According to Justice Harry H. Blackmun, "Advertising, however tasteless and excessive it sometimes may seem, is nonetheless dissemination of information as to who is producing and selling what product for what reason and at what price." If consumers are to make more intelligent marketplace decisions, they need the "free flow of commercial information," according to Blackmun and the Court.

Even before the Supreme Court decision, some states had gone further and actually required the posting of drug prices. Since January 1, 1974, New York State pharmacists must post the price and name of the 150 most frequently prescribed drugs. Since 1971, Boston has required the posting of the 100 most frequently prescribed drugs and their prices. California, Minnesota, New Hampshire, and Texas have followed suit.

Generic Versus Brand Name Drugs

Prescriptions for drugs can either be written in terms of the drug's generic name or its brand or trademark name. The price of a drug that isn't trademarked is much less. Because only about 10 percent of all new drug prescriptions are written with the generic name of the drug, the consumer pays more. Why do doctors often prescribe expensive brand name drugs? Perhaps they become accustomed to certain drugs and automatically prescribe them; some believe that physicians are "wooed" by drug companies. A druggist is required to make no substitution when filling out a prescription that mentions a brand name. However, a study of a penicillin drug called Ampicillin, its generic name, showed that even though 53 percent of the prescriptions had that name on them, 98 percent of them were filled by the druggist with major brand names. The brand name price is usually two to four times more expensive than the lowest generic price, and it can be as much as thirty times more.

The FDA believes strongly that there is no significant difference in quality between the generic and brand name products tested. But strong proponents of brand name drugs believe they are more effective than generic drugs. They measure effectiveness by the amount of active medication that is absorbed from the intestine into the bloodstream.

A number of consumer groups and consumer advocates strongly supported a bill introduced in the Senate by Senator Gaylord Nelson of Wisconsin in 1973. Had that bill passed, pharmacists would have been required to use the generic drug if the generic name was on the prescription. Some advocates, such as Consumers Union, want to eliminate completely the use of brand names for drugs.

ALTERNATIVE HEALTH CARE SYSTEMS

The traditional health care system has been based on the standard "fee for service" between doctor and private patient. But in recent decades, alternatives to this system have developed. Among these are group health, Health Maintenance Organizations (HMOs), and national health insurance.

Group Health

Group health service is basically a hospital where doctors work for a salary, not for a fee. You become a member of a group health care plan by paying a specific fee determined by the number of members in your family. After prepaying, you receive all group health services, except for certain drugs, without charge. In some plans, you can select your doctors from among those on the staff; in others you cannot. Group health plans stress preventive medicine in their practice.

Some of the better-known group health plans are the Kaiser Foundation Health Plan, the Ross-Loos Medical Group of Los Angeles, the Community Health Association of Detroit, the Health Insurance Plan of Greater New York, and the Group Health Cooperative of Puget Sound.

Most of these prepaid group plans provide their members all services out of the plan's own resources. If, however, a specialist who is not on the group plan's staff is required, he or she is hired on a fee basis.

The Pros and Cons of Group Health. According to a report of the National Advisory Commission on Health Manpower, the quality of many group health plans equaled the medical care available in most communities. And members' medical care costs were at least 20 to 30 percent less than those obtained elsewhere. Cost is controlled mainly by eliminating unnecessary health care, particularly hospitalization. That's because partner doctors generally get a year-end bonus, depending on the difference between total revenues and total costs. Doctors, therefore, have an incentive to prevent illnesses before they become serious enough to require hospitalization. It is not unusual, then, to find highly computerized testing services, which check out fifty to one hundred possible medical ills and make a permanent medical history of each patient.

Detractors of group health care maintain that since the doctors are essentially profit sharers, they will stint on needed hospitalization. Moreover, many patients complain about the impossibility of seeing the same doctor consistently. There also may be long waits for certain medical procedures.

HMOs

Toward the end of 1974, many Americans were asked by their employers whether they wanted to drop group health insurance in favor of prepaid medical care. Those employees who chose that particular option became members of what the government calls an HMO, or Health Maintenance Organization.

HMOs run the range from group practice setups—similar to clinics, with such extras as specialists, affiliated hospitals, and

dentists—to individual practice foundations, in which doctors continue
to practice in their own offices but take HMO patients in exchange for a
share of the premium.

Employees were given this opportunity to switch from group
health to prepaid medical care by a provision in the Health Maintenance
Organization Act signed by President Nixon in December 1973. Under
the law, any company with twenty-five or more employees and some
sort of group health insurance plan must negotiate a group HMO contract and offer it to employees—provided there is a qualified HMO in
the area and only if the employer is first contacted by an HMO orga-
nizer. The legislation requires HMOs to accept individual members as
well as groups of employees.

The list of basic services that must be covered by the monthly
premium includes: hospital and physical care, including maternity;
x-rays and laboratory tests; psychiatric treatment; emergency care; preventive health services, including regular checkups; birth control services; alcoholism and drug abuse treatment; and, for children only, dental
checkups and eye examinations.

Obviously, this coverage is more extensive than typical health insurance programs. Thus, HMO premiums range from at least five dollars a month more than a very good health insurance program up to
thirty dollars or more than some group health plans.

Proponents of HMO legislation point out that the higher premium
cost is more than made up in savings in out-of-pocket medical expenses.
Why? Because HMOs save considerable money on hospitalization,
largely by treating people in the doctors' offices instead of in the hospital.

Problems with HMOs. The 1973 law proved to be unrealistic, however. By 1976, only 12 of the 181 prepaid health groups in the United
States qualified as HMOs. The huge Kaiser Foundation Health Plan,
which was the model of the law, didn't even qualify, and it has 3 million
subscribers. Critics of the 1973 law point out that Congress required
HMOs to offer so many medical services that the cost would be too high,
thus preventing HMOs from competing with traditional health insurance plans. Moreover, the law requires that HMOs open membership
rolls to all prospects for thirty days a year. According to critics, that
would leave HMOs with a disproportionate number of chronically ill
and elderly patients.

National Health Insurance

National health insurance is not a different way to provide medical
services, but it pays for them in a different way. Government-provided
insurance for everyone won't alleviate the supply problem in medical
care. Its chief benefit will be to ensure that whatever medical services an
individual obtains will be paid for somehow. A national health insurance plan essentially benefits those people who are sick more often than

those who are not, unless it is based on preventive health care.

As of this writing, national health insurance is not yet a reality. While Nixon was president, he proposed a Comprehensive Health Insurance Plan (CHIP); the leading alternative to Nixon's plan was identified with Senator Edward M. Kennedy. Nixon wanted to build on the existing system, with private insurance companies maintaining their current role. Employees were to be offered private health insurance by their employers, who would pay 75 percent of the premium. On the other hand, Kennedy's National Health Security Act would have been, in its original form, a completely public program, financed by employer and employee payments to a trust fund and modeled on the Social Security system. The Kennedy plan would offer much broader coverage than the Nixon plan.

Among other national medical plans proposed in the last few years are the Long-Ribicoff Plan, the AMA Plan, and the Ford Administration Plan.

A few years ago, Consumers Union presented what it considered to be the five minimum goals any national health plan must meet.

1   Everyone's health care needs should be covered, and the entire population should be included within the system.
2   There should be no connection between the patient's income and the extent or quality of care dispensed by doctors, hospitals, and others.
3   The plan should be financed progressively and in a manner open to public scrutiny.
4   The plan should provide incentives for efficiency, control over the cost and quality of services, and encouragement of alternative or innovative systems of delivering health care.
5   The administrators of the program should be accountable to the public, and consumers should have a voice in the administration.[3]

One aspect of national health insurance that many of its proponents often ignore involves consumers' response to the different insurance plans. Economists point out that Medicare caused the quantity of medical care demanded to increase dramatically and thus drove up costs. Studies show that private insurance causes medical care costs to increase because of increased demand for more frequent and more sophisticated treatment. If such studies are correct, we can predict that any national health insurance plan that doesn't require individuals to pay direct expenses for medical care will encourage more individuals to demand more medical care more often. We can't say whether this is good or bad. We only can say it is a possible result of a truly comprehensive national health insurance scheme.

---

[3] *Consumer Reports*, February 1975, pp. 119-22.

THE TYPES OF PREPAID MEDICAL INSURANCE

The following are some categories of medical service for which health insurance can be purchased. No doubt there are other categories for special situations.

Hospital Expenses

Experts believe that more than 90 percent of all people in the United States are now protected under some voluntary program(s) that covers at least part of the medical care costs arising from illness or accidents. Hospital expense protection provides benefits toward full or partial payment of room, board, and services any time you are in a hospital. Usually it covers use of the operating room, laboratories, x-rays, medicines, and incidental care. Exhibit 10-2 shows a typical payment pattern for hospital expenses under a health insurance policy. Almost all insurance companies that issue any sort of total health insurance package will issue hospital expense insurance.

Surgical Insurance

Almost everyone with some sort of hospital insurance also has surgical insurance, which pays for the services of a surgeon. Generally, there is a fee schedule, such as in Exhibit 10-3, that fixes the maximum amount. Any excess over the stipulated maximum must be paid either by another type of insurance policy or by the patient. Since the higher the maximum limits for surgery, the higher the cost of the insurance, you must decide what risk you want to take.

EXHIBIT 10-2.

TYPICAL HOSPITAL PAYMENTS UNDER A TYPICAL INSURANCE PLAN

HOSPITAL SERVICES	TOTAL HOSPITAL CHARGES	AMOUNT PAID BY INSURANCE COMPANY
Room and board 31 days at $85 per day	$2,635	$2,025
X rays, laboratory work, medicines, etc.	800	400
Use of operating room, recovery room, cast, dressings, etc.	150	150
Physicians' fees	600	220
TOTALS	$4,185	$2,795

Regular Medical Protection

This type of protection pays for visits to the doctor's office as well as all x-ray, diagnostic, and laboratory expenses related to such visits. Generally, there is a maximum number of calls allowable for each sickness and also a one-call deductible. In many cases, when your family is covered under your medical insurance policy, only you, the subscriber, are covered under regular medical insurance provisions: your spouse and children are covered only in case of accidents. Regular medical protection plans usually pay only for visits to the doctor or for you as an inpatient in a hospital.

Major Medical

This insurance covers virtually all types of medical care, such as hospital room and board, surgical expenses, administration of anesthesia, x-rays, nursing care, drugs, and the like. It is the single most important kind of health insurance for the consumer to carry.

Major medical insurance coverage does not provide for a fixed schedule of limits for each of these expenses as do the policies just discussed. Rather, major medical covers a fixed percentage of all expenses, even though with some policies there are limits imposed for private nursing, extended care, hospital room and board, and outpatient psychiatric treatment. Major medical insurance is generally bought through a group contract offered by an employer, but it can be purchased as an individual policy. The contract will include a single lifetime maximum for each person covered. The limits range from $5,000 to $1 million. The lifetime limits normally restore themselves by a fixed amount per year if there is what is called an automatic restoration clause.

Major medical insurance is often cheaper if you also have one of the basic policies previously described. You can, however, buy it alone.

EXHIBIT 10-3. **SURGICAL INSURANCE BENEFITS**

Appendectomy	$ 375	Fracture, closed reduction of femur	$ 390
Gall bladder removal	580	Fracture, closed reduction of rib	75
Hernia repair	340	Brain tumor	2,900
Tonsillectomy	200	Intervertebral disc removal	924
Thyroid removal	600	Kidney removal	628
Benign tumor	210	Eardrum incision	36
Prostate gland removal	380	Boil, incision	19

Dental Insurance

While few insurance policies cover dental work, such coverage is becoming an increasingly important part of all health insurance policies. Because it is generally provided only on a group basis, if you are not part of a group (such as a large company, government agency, labor union, etc.), you may be unable to buy it.

There has been a dramatic rise in the number of people with dental expense protection. In 1967, 2.3 million people were covered under dental insurance plans; by 1976, some 25 million people were protected by them. The largest providers of such protection were private insurance companies, which insured 18 million people under regular dental plans. Blue Cross/Blue Shield covered some 2.6 million individuals; the remainder were covered by Dental Service Corporation and union welfare funds.

Most dental insurance is a standard prepayment plan that covers usually 80 percent of the cost of treatment after some sort of deductible, such as $50 or $100. There is a fairly low maximum that can be paid in any one year, usually $600 to $1,000. Exhibit 10-4 shows the fixed allowances for different dental treatments.

MEDICARE

The Medicare program, effective July 1, 1966, was an addition to the Social Security Act and has been amended a number of times. In 1978, 25 million people were eligible for the hospital insurance provided under the Medicare program. Insurance companies and Blue Cross/Blue Shield participate in the Medicare program as fiscal intermediaries for the government. Medicaid, effective January 1, l966, is slightly different from Medicare. Under Title 19 of the Social Security Act, states may expand, with federal matching funds, their public assistance to people, regardless of age, whose income is insufficient to pay for health care.

Medicare consists of two parts. Part A is a compulsory hospitalization insurance that is financed by contributions from employees and employers. Part B is a voluntary medical insurance program designed to

---

EXHIBIT 10-4. **TYPICAL DENTAL INSURANCE BENEFITS**

Cleaning	$ 14	Removable space maintainer	$ 69
X-ray	22	Anesthesia	24
Extraction	13	Crowns, porcelain	126
Silicate filling	17	Maxillary dentures	243

help pay for physicians' services and some medical services and supplies not covered by the hospital part of Medicare. It is financed by monthly premiums shared equally by those who choose this protection and the federal government.

Medicare Part A

The hospital insurance plan pays most of the cost of service in a hospital or extended care facility for eligible people sixty-five years or older.[4] They receive the cost of nursing services, a semiprivate room, meals, inpatient drugs and supplies, laboratory tests, x-ray and other radiology services, use of appliances and equipment, and medical social services. There is, however, a hospital deductible amount that is "intended to make the Medicare beneficiary responsible for expenses equivalent to the average costs of one hospital day." As of 1978, this deductible was $144 per hospital benefit period (defined as a period of illness not interrupted for more than sixty days). In other words, if a patient is ill for eighteen days, then well for forty-five days, and then ill again (that is, requiring hospitalization or confinement to a nursing home or other extended-care facility), the first and second illnesses would have occurred in the same benefit period. If the person were well for seventy-five days, then the new hospitalization would constitute another benefit period and again be subject to the $144 hospital deductible amount.

Under this program, any illness must commence with a hospital stay of at least three days if extended-care facilities are to be covered. After the hospital stay, any referral to an extended-care facility must commence within fourteen days (except where a problem arises regarding space availability, etc.). If nursing care does not begin within fourteen days, it is not covered under Medicare. And Medicare recipients are subject to later deductible amounts depending on the length of illness:

1   First sixty days: all specified benefits are covered except the $144 deductible.
2   Days sixty-one to ninety: the same items are covered, but the deductible becomes $36 per day.
3   After ninety days: recipients are entitled to what Social Security calls their "lifetime reserve" of sixty days additional coverage, with a $72 per day deductible.

This "lifetime reserve" can only be used once during the recipient's lifetime. If one illness requires 105 days of confinement in a hospital or

---

[4]Under the 1972 amendments to the Social Security Act, individuals under the age of sixty-five are extended Medicare coverage if they require hemodialysis or renal transplantation for chronic renal disease and currently are fully insured or entitled to monthly Social Security benefits or if they are the spouses or dependent children of such insured or entitled individuals. Medicare protection is also extended to people eighteen years and over who are receiving Social Security or Railroad Retirement monthly benefits based on disability and who have been entitled to such benefits for at least twenty-four consecutive months.

extended-care facility, a subsequent illness would only have a remaining 45 days under that lifetime reserve; it does not "renew" itself, as do the other periods of coverage, with subsequent benefit periods.

Hospital insurance pays for all covered services in an extended-care facility for the first twenty days of such services in each benefit period and all but $18 per day for up to eighty more days in the same benefit period. Of course, the following provisions must be met: you are in medical need of such care, you have met the requirements just indicated (at least three days' hospital stay and admittance to an extended-care facility within fourteen days of hospital discharge), and you are admitted for further treatment of the same condition for which you were treated in the hospital.

Subsequent to either a hospital stay or a covered nursing facility stay, you may be eligible for home health benefits—including occupational therapy, part-time services of home health aides, medical social services, and medical supplies and appliances—for as many as 100 home health visits.

All the benefits of Part A require treatment in participating health care facilities; most facilities do participate. And the law further specifies that the various dollar amounts charged to recipients, such as the $144 deductible and daily amounts, are subject to annual review. By the time you read this, the figures may have changed substantially. Under no circumstances does Part A cover doctor's services. But Part B does.

Medicare Part B

This supplementary medical insurance plan will help pay for the cost of doctors' services, as well as other medical costs, if you are over sixty-five and a participant. There is a charge, however, which was $8.20 in 1978. And you must sign up as soon as you become eligible. If you sign up later (as you can *once* any year between January 1 and March 31), you pay a penalty fee of 10 percent for each year you were eligible but not enrolled.

Essentially, the federal government pays half the cost of this medical insurance, and you, as beneficiary, pay the other half. The amount you pay is reviewed annually to insure that it is in line with current medical costs. Recently, however, changes in the law provided that your monthly payments cannot increase beyond the percentage increase in general Social Security benefits. So the government eventually may pay more than half the coverage.

The medical insurance program helps pay for the following:

1 Doctors' fees in a hospital, office, or home for surgery and other services.
2 Home visits.
3 X-rays, surgical dressing, diagnostic services.
4 Drugs administered by a doctor or nurse as part of treatment.
5 Doctors' services for lab, x-rays, and other services. (These are covered 100 percent if you are a bed patient in a hospital

and covered as other benefits if you are not.)

6   Limited services of chiropractors, ambulances, some physical therapists (with a payment limitation), and the services of certain practitioners, such as Christian Scientists and naturopaths.

Under no circumstances does the supplementary medical insurance under Medicare pay the full costs of any of these services (with the single exception of doctors' lab and x-ray services). First, there is a sixty dollar deductible every year. After that, you pay 20 percent, and the insurance plan pays 80 percent, just as with major medical insurance. And the medical insurance does not cover routine checkups, vision or hearing examinations, glasses or hearing aids, immunizations, routine dental care, self-administered prescription drugs, or the first three pints of blood received in any given year.

INSURING YOUR INCOME STREAM

For many individuals, the thought of being unable to make an income is indeed frightening. It is possible to insure against the loss of income by buying what is called disability insurance, or salary continuation insurance. If you have such protection, you will be assured a certain amount of income, even if you are partially or fully (depending on the policy) incapacitated. For example, if a plumber has an auto accident and can no longer use his or her hands, then a disability insurance policy would make up at least part of the lost income. Approximately 65 million Americans have some form of short-term disability insurance.

Rates vary with the occupation of the individual. Professional people, such as doctors and lawyers, pay a lower premium than people in more hazardous occupations.

Most disability policies offer payment when a policy holder loses earnings because of sickness or because of an accident. The length of time one is paid for being disabled because of an accident is usually longer than when one is disabled due to sickness.

Homemaker's Disability Insurance

One of the most recent changes in disability insurance is its availability for homemakers who manage household and family affairs full-time. Their value to the family can be measured in terms of what it would cost to replace their services—housekeeping, babysitting, cooking, and so on. As of 1976, there were at least four companies selling homemaker's disability insurance—Aid Association for Lutherans form ADA (available to Lutherans only), Mutual of Omaha's form 3760M, Ohio State Life Insurance Company's form A-1650, and World Insurance Company's form A6503. Ohio State's coverage is available only as a rider to a husband's disability policy with the same company. Annual premiums depend on the age of the homemaker and the length of the waiting period.

For a typical policy on a thirty-five-year-old homemaker that would pay $200 a month for two years, the premium would cost approximately $100 annually.

The Maximum Payments Possible

Because insurance companies believe you will have an incentive to remain unemployable after your disability or illness is cured, it is difficult, if not impossible, to insure your income for more than 50 to 65 percent of your normal earnings. This is a problem lawyers call "moral hazard." If your earnings were replaced 100 percent, then you, the insured, might not feel compelled to return to work after an accident.

Life insurance riders. You may be able to purchase salary continuation insurance as a rider to your life insurance policy. Such a rider will usually offer a $10 a month disability income benefit for each $1,000 face value of your life insurance policy.

PRACTICAL APPLICATIONS

HOW TO REDUCE
HEALTH CARE COSTS

There is no way that you can eliminate completely the costs of medical care. However, you can insure yourself against at least extraordinary costs and, if you see fit, against all normal medical care expenditures throughout the year. In this Application, we will give the pros and cons of different types of medical insurance coverage and explain how Medicare and Medicaid affect you.

KEEPING HEALTHY

One of the best protections against excessive medical costs is a consistent, comprehensive program of physical fitness. All of us know what we *should* do, but many of us let ourselves become run down, hypertensive, overweight, and so on. To avoid extensive medical care, doctors recommend the following:

1.   **Good diet.** This means getting all the minimum amounts of nutrients regularly and in the right quantity so you don't become either overweight or underweight. Good diet does not require a high income; people with low incomes can obtain a nutritious diet if they are willing to sacrifice variety.

2.   **Adequate exercise.** Medical experts are convinced that if you exercise, you feel better, sleep better, and are less prone to serious cardiovascular illnesses. Again, this doesn't require money. For example, walking and jogging are free.

3.   **Moderation with foreign substances.** There is less agreement on this point than on the others, but most experts believe you should not abuse your mind and body with such drugs as nicotine, alcohol, hal-

lucinogens, "uppers," "downers," and the like. They also advise against relying on patent medicines; hypochondria can lead to overusing medicines that eventually may cause serious bodily damage.

WHERE TO GO FOR HEALTH INSURANCE

A variety of organizations sell health insurance. The largest are Blue Cross and Blue Shield; the next largest are the commercial insurance companies. In addition, there are labor union plans, community organization plans, and consumer cooperatives, as well as group health plans, one of which may be available in your area.

Blue Cross and Blue Shield

Formed in 1929 by a group of Dallas school teachers, Blue Cross had a membership of over 500,000 by 1938. Today, about 84 million members participate in almost eighty Blue Cross plans.

Blue Shield was established in 1946 by the coordinators of the Associated Medical Care Plans. Originally sponsored by the AMA, Blue Shield is sometimes known as the Doctors Plan because subscribers can choose their doctors. While Blue Cross is concerned primarily with hospital insurance, Blue Shield is concerned with surgical and general medical.

Of all those who have any kind of insurance for hospital care, over 43 percent participate in one of the many autonomous Blue Cross plans. Many Blue Cross group policies offer a 120-day plan that gives full hospital protection for 120 days in a semiprivate room. Obviously, you save money if you can participate in a group Blue Cross plan. If you are not already aware of the possibility of joining a group plan, ask your employer, your fraternal organization, or any other group in which you participate. You can also buy individual coverage.

Many people take out Blue Shield as well as Blue Cross because Blue Shield covers the cost of doctors' services. Blue Shield plans contract with participating doctors to accept payment according to a preplanned fee schedule. If you select a doctor who doesn't participate in the plan, Blue Shield gives you a cash payment up to a set amount on a given fee schedule; you then make your own financial arrangements with that doctor. You can anticipate paying a monthly amount of between thirty and fifty dollars for family coverage, particularly if you are involved in a combination Blue Cross/Blue Shield arrangement.

In addition to Blue Cross/Blue Shield, there are almost 1,000 nonaffiliated health insurance plans from which to choose. All are independent of Blue Cross/Blue Shield and commercial insurance companies. However, these plans cover only 5 percent of all persons receiving health care insurance. Among the most significant independent organizations are the various group health plans already discussed.

IMPORTANT ASPECTS OF THE INSURANCE POLICIES YOU BUY

You must understand three important aspects of insurance policies in order to pick the right coverage. All three determine the price you pay for your health insurance. They involve the amount of deductible, waiting periods, and coinsurance.

The Deductible

The cost of any major medical policy is, in large part, a function of the deductible you choose. The larger the amount of medical expenses per year that won't be covered by a major medical policy, the smaller your premium will be, all other things remaining the same. Exhibit 10-5 shows how premiums decrease as the deductible increases. When you go from a deductible of $100 per year to a deductible of $1,000, the premium is halved, and the coverage limit in our example increases by 67 percent.

Clearly, then, you can reduce your health insur-ance premiums by picking a larger deductible. On the other hand, the larger the deductible, the more out-of-pocket expenses you must pay each year for medical bills. The decision depends on your financial capacity to assume risk and your evaluation of your and/or your family's needs during any given year. If you are a relatively healthy person and have no dependents, you may wish to have a very large deductible because you are really only concerned about large medical expenses. If, on the other hand, you have several children who are predisposed to minor illnesses, it may be better for you to have a smaller deductible in spite of the higher annual premium and the lower coverage limits for that higher premium. If, however, you pay the premiums on yourself, you generally will find that a high deductible (say, $500) makes the best use of your hard-earned premium dollars.

Waiting Period

When we discussed disability, or salary continuation, insurance in the last chapter, we didn't specify how premiums could be reduced or, alternatively, how the amount of disability income can be increased for the same premium. Basically, the longer you agree to wait, after being unable to work, before you request disability income payments, the lower your premium. Typical waiting periods are 15, 30, 90, and 180 days. Exhibit 10-6 shows the hypothetical increased amount of disability income that can be purchased for a $125 annual premium for a twenty-two-year-old male. If you are willing to wait 180 days instead of 15, the amount of disability income almost doubles for that same premium.

You might wish to pick the level of disability income you think would be necessary to keep you and your family in an acceptable standard of living (taking account of your employer's sick-leave benefits). Then determine how many liquid funds you would have available if you were temporarily or permanently unable to work. Pick the longest waiting

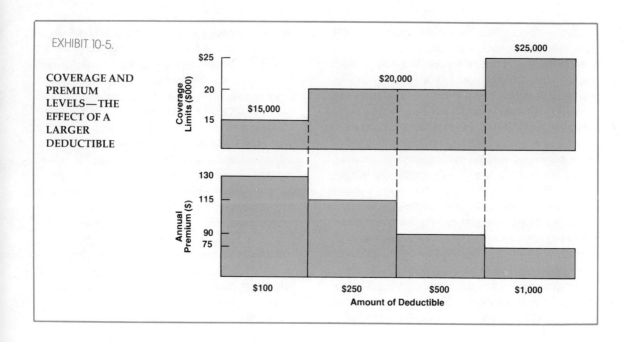

EXHIBIT 10-5.

COVERAGE AND PREMIUM LEVELS—THE EFFECT OF A LARGER DEDUCTIBLE

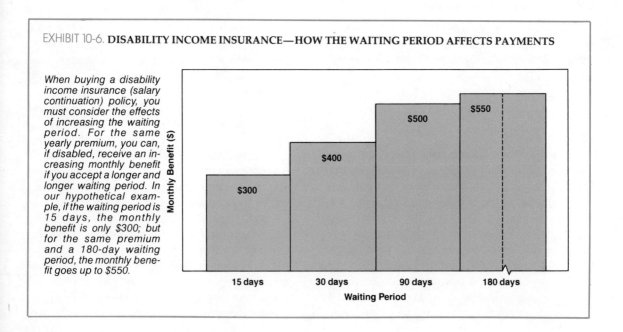

EXHIBIT 10-6. **DISABILITY INCOME INSURANCE—HOW THE WAITING PERIOD AFFECTS PAYMENTS**

When buying a disability income insurance (salary continuation) policy, you must consider the effects of increasing the waiting period. For the same yearly premium, you can, if disabled, receive an increasing monthly benefit if you accept a longer and longer waiting period. In our hypothetical example, if the waiting period is 15 days, the monthly benefit is only $300; but for the same premium and a 180-day waiting period, the monthly benefit goes up to $550.

period possible within those two constraints to determine the lowest premium for the desired level of disability benefits. Again, as with the deductible in major medical insurance, the longer the waiting period you choose, the more risk you assume.

Coinsurance

Most major medical policies, as well as a large number of other types of insurance policies, have a coinsurance structure. For example, a major medical policy may pay you, after the deductible, only 80 percent of all of your medical expenses for a single illness up to your lifetime maximum. You are, in effect, taking upon yourself the payment of 20 percent of that bill after the deductible. You become a coinsuror, along with the insurance company.

But even though you pay part of your bill when there is a coinsurance clause in any type of medical plan, you might still be better off with such insurance, especially in times of rapidly rising medical costs. If you are covered by a fixed schedule of rates, you end up paying a larger and larger difference if those rates don't rise as fast as medical costs do. Coinsurance, on the other hand, means that you only pay a certain percentage—say, 20 percent—of the rising medical rates; the insurance company pays the rest.

COVERING THE GAPS IN MEDICARE INSURANCE

Medicare is paying less and less of total medical bills for older people. But there is an entire group of insurance policies called Medigap that serves as supplemental insurance to fill some, but never all, of the gaps in Medicare's coverage. Annual premiums range from about $75 a year to over $300, depending on the extent of benefits. Blue Cross/Blue Shield sell Medigap policies, as do some insurance companies and associations for retired persons, such as the National Council of Senior Citizens and the American Association of Retired Persons, in conjunction with the National Retired Teachers Association. When comparing Medigap policies, one should question at least three aspects of the coverage:

1. Does the policy provide for payment of all or a percentage of all actual charges by Medicare? If not, then the policy is a fixed one and may not cover the bills not met by Medicare.

2. How many of Medicare's gaps does the policy fill? For example, does it cover the Medicare deductibles for hospital stay and medical bills? Does it cover the coinsurance the recipient must pay? Does it cover long-term care in nursing homes and out-of-hospital prescription drugs?

3. What is the exclusion for pre-existing illnesses? If it is six months, the policy obviously is more advantageous than if it is a year.

SOME FINAL POINTERS

1. Find out more information about staying healthy. Develop rules and follow them.

2. Have a family physician diagnose your complaints and refer you to a specialist *if* one is needed.

3. When looking for a doctor, get several names from a local hospital or medical society. Phone the doctor and ask for a summary of fees and methods of practice.

4. Pick your doctor before you get sick.

5. If you have a choice, pick your hospital. Avoid being admitted on a Friday if your problem won't be dealt with until Monday and there's no real reason for you to be there.

6. See if tests before surgery can be done on an outpatient basis to avoid unnecessary room and board charges.

7. Explore the alternative of walk-in

surgery, where minor operations are done without a hospital stay.

8. Cut prescription costs by asking your doctor to specify the generic name of the drug. If you cannot read the prescription, ask him to print it on a separate sheet of paper.

9. Shop around for prescription drug prices. Many pharmacists will now give prices over the telephone. If you are going to be using a medicine over a long period of time, buy it in larger quantities if it retains its quality.

10. Make sure your insurance coverage is adequate and all members of your family are covered.

11. If possible, opt for a policy with a larger deductible, particularly if you and your family do not have numerous minor illnesses.

12. Obtain group protection, as opposed to individual or family policies, if you can.

13. If you, instead of your employer, pay your own premiums, pay quarterly or annually rather than monthly.

14. Occasionally compare your health insurance policy with alternatives to see if you're still getting the best deal.

15. If your doctor or specialist tells you that you need elective surgery, always consult at least one other specialist for an opinion.

16. Read some of the more recent books on medical care, such as *The Medicine Show,* issued by the editors of *Consumer Reports,* and *The Consumer's Guide to Successful Surgery* by Dr. Seymour Isenberg and Dr. L. M. Elting (New York: St. Martins Press).

17. Take a look at a publication of the Washington Center for the Study of Services titled *Washington Consumers' Health Checkbook.* It's available from Suite 303, 1910 K Street N.W., Washington, D.C. 20006.

GLOSSARY OF TERMS

MEDICARE   A federal system for the payment of health care services to the aged. The funds are derived from taxes.

OUTPATIENT SERVICES   The services of doctors and/or hospitals that don't require the individual to be a registered patient in the hospital.

INPATIENT SERVICES   Services rendered to an individual by doctors and/or a hospital while the patient remains in the hospital for at least one night.

MALPRACTICE INSURANCE   Insurance carried by doctors (and lawyers and other professionals) to cover lawsuits against them for improper practice of their profession.

NATUROPATH   A practitioner of a system for treating disease. He or she emphasizes assistance to nature and uses natural medicinal substances and physical means, such as manipulation and electrical treatment.

GENERIC NAME   The general overall name applied to a particular drug, as opposed to the brand name.

GROUP HEALTH SERVICE   A hospital that offers virtually all medical services and to which individuals subscribe or prepay for each year of membership.

HEALTH MAINTENANCE ORGANIZATION (HMO)   A prepaid medical plan to which employees in certain areas can subscribe. HMOs can either be group practice or individual practice; with the latter, the individual doctor obtains a share of the HMO premium for servicing its members.

NATIONAL HEALTH INSURANCE   A proposed scheme by which the federal government (taxpayers) would provide some or all of medical care insurance payments.

MAJOR MEDICAL INSURANCE   Insurance that covers a certain portion of medical expenses after a specified deductible.

DISABILITY, OR SALARY CONTINUATION, INSURANCE   A type of insurance that provides for payment of lost income due to disability caused by sickness or an accident.

DEDUCTIBLE   The amount of medical expenses you must incur before your insurance becomes effective. The larger the deductible, the smaller the premium for any given coverage.

WAITING PERIOD   The period during which an insurance policy is not in effect and during which you will be paid nothing from the policy. This particularly applies to disability income payments. For example, if there is a waiting period of thirty days under such a policy, you must be disabled thirty days before a payment is made to you for loss of earnings.

COINSURANCE   A provision in a medical insurance policy requiring you to pay part of your medical expenses. For example, with a major medical policy that provides for 80 percent of expenses after a deductible, you are the coinsurer to the tune of 20 percent of those expenses.

CHAPTER SUMMARY

1. Medical care expenditures have been rising. They now constitute over 10 percent of the gross national product. They have risen because of (a) Medicare (increased demand), (b) insurance schemes, (c) higher quality service, and (d) higher malpractice insurance costs.

2. The increase in the relative price of medical care has caused many people to treat their own ailments and to seek cheaper alternatives, such as naturopaths.

3. The Food and Drug Administration regulates the ethical drug industry. Some of its regulations have reduced the number of new drugs introduced into the marketplace.

4. Restrictions on advertising and prices for ethical drugs have allowed druggists to overcharge consumers for many years. Competition requires that information now be made available.

5. It is possible to obtain a drug at a lower price if its generic name, rather than its trade or brand name, is used.

6. Alternative health care delivery systems include group health insurance and health maintenance organizations.

7. No national health insurance plan will be free. Someone must pay for the medical care services provided.

8. Disability, or salary continuation, insurance is often appropriate for someone who would be burdened financially by temporary or permanent loss of job earning abilities.

9. Homemakers can now obtain disability insurance from limited sources at a modest cost.

10. Prepaid medical insurance includes coverage for (a) hospital expenses, (b) surgical expenses, (c) regular medical costs, (d) major medical expenses, and (e) dental expenses.

11. Medicare which consists of parts A and B, covers many of the medical expenses incurred by older people.

12. One way to reduce medical care costs is to keep healthy by means of (a) a good diet, (b) adequate exercise, and (c) moderate use of foreign substances.

13. The largest private health insurance organization is Blue Cross/Blue Shield. There are a number of other commercial insurance companies, such as Aetna and Traveler's.

14. The larger the deductible in a major medical policy, the lower the premium or the greater the maximum limit for the same premium. You would want a larger deductible if you and your family were relatively healthy and didn't require numerous visits to the doctor.

15. In a disability, or salary continuation, insurance policy, the longer the waiting period, the smaller the premium—or, for the same premium, the greater the potential benefit payment if disabled.

16. Many health insurance policies require you to be a coinsurer because they only pay a certain percentage, such as 80 percent, of all expenses over the deductible.

17. A Medigap policy from Blue Cross/Blue Shield, the National Council of Senior Citizens, or the American Association of Retired Persons covers the gaps in Medicare insurance.

CASE PROBLEMS

10-1 Two Health Plans: Same Cost, Different Coverage

Martha Jane Canary, forty-seven, has worked as a cab driver since the death of her husband a year ago. She earns $8400 a year, which is ample for her needs. She has $3200 in savings and no debts. She feels she does need health insurance to protect her in case of some physical calamity. She is presently considering two different plans:

Plan A—Hospital and surgical policy. The policy pays up to $75 per day for room and board for 120 days, with a $150 deductible clause. Surgical costs for any one year are covered up to $2000. The cost is $275 a year.

Plan B—Major medical. This policy has a $750 deductible clause, with 80/20 coinsurance up to $10,000. The company will pay 100% of the next $30,000. The cost is $275 per year.

Which plan should Martha Jane select? Why?

10-2   The High Cost of Skiing

Paul Adams, a forty-seven-year-old restaurant manager from Denver, was skiing at Aspen when he and a tree had a serious difference of opinion. Paul broke his left leg, left arm, and three ribs; punctured a lung; and contracted pneumonia from exposure to the cold. He had surgery and spent three weeks in the hospital and another seven weeks at home. Fortunately, he had a ninety-day disability policy that paid $240 a week and a major medical plan with $750 deductible and 80/20 coinsurance. The total hospital and surgical bill was $4500.

1. How much did Paul collect on his disability policy?

2. How much did Paul have to pay on his medical bill?

SELECTED REFERENCES

"As Health Costs Soar...Needed: A New Direction for Our Medical System." Interview with Walter J. McNerney, President, Blue Cross Association in *U.S. News & World Report*, March 28, 1977.

First Facts About Drugs, FDA Fact Sheet 1712-0122. Washington, D.C.: Consumer Product Information, 1970.

Fuchs, Victor R. *Health, Economics, and Social Choice*. New York: Basic Books, 1975.

Gwinup, Grant. *Energetics*. New York: Bantam Books, 1972.

"Hidden Costs of Drug Safety; FDA's Regulations Effect on Drug Industry Research Projects." *Business Week*, February 21, 1977, p. 80.

Kennedy, Edward M. *In Critical Condition: The Crisis in America's Health Care*. New York: Simon & Schuster, 1973.

Krizay, John, and Wilson, A. *The Patient as Consumer-Health Care Financing in the United States*. Lexington, Mass.: Lexington Books, 1974.

Lamberg, L. "Your Doctor's Prescription: Is It Greek to You?" U.S. News, February 14, 1977, pp. 47-48.

Property and Liability Insurance

■ Everyone with assets is exposed to a variety of possible financial losses. For example, if you own a physical structure, such as a house, it could be robbed, destroyed in a hurricane, or leveled by fire. If you own personal property, such as a stereo, it could be stolen. If you own a car, it could be wrecked in a collision. In order to prevent financial losses should such things happen, people normally take out property insurance. In this chapter, we will examine how you can insure your home, your car, and other personal belongings.

If someone slips on the doormat in front of your house, you may be sued. If you cause an accident in which someone else is injured, you also may be sued. In such instances, you may be held liable for the injuries sustained by someone else. That's why you may wish to carry liability insurance, which is available with your homeowner's insurance policy and your automobile insurance policy and is available separately in special policies. We will also discuss liability insurance in this chapter.

THE PROPERTY YOU CAN INSURE

Basically, you can insure anything you own that has a determinable value, except land. In other words, most insurance companies will insure property that, if damaged, lost, or stolen, will cause you financial loss. Therefore, you can't insure your best friend's car—even if you ride in it occasionally—because you have no monetary interest in this property.

If it's difficult to determine the value of property you own, an insurance company may be unwilling to insure it. For example, if you own a rare book that you believe is worth $3,000, you may find it dif-

273

ficult to obtain insurance for that amount. The same holds for manuscripts, family heirlooms, collections of unusual items, and so on. Furthermore, even if you do obtain insurance, the annual cost of it may be high and the amount the insurance company pays if the articles are lost or damaged may be much smaller than you think they are worth. Additionally, if the risk of loss of a piece of property is deemed too great, an insurance company won't insure it. It is difficult, for example, to insure certain types of sports cars in certain cities because the risk of theft is so high. It is difficult for many students on college campuses to obtain insurance on their personal property because the incidence of theft has been high in these areas in certain cities.

But there are countless other items that can be insured: your home and attached structures, such as a garage or a tool shed, shrubs, trees, and plants around the house; any personal property on the premises and away from the premises under certain circumstances; other people's property on the premises (usually up to a certain amount); your car and the items inside it; and many more.

KEEPING A PERSONAL PROPERTY INVENTORY

One of the first things to do if you decide to insure personal property is to take a complete inventory. Exhibit 11-1 is a sample household inventory sheet for the kitchen-breakfast area. The inventory contains space for the name of the article, a description, the purchase date, original price, and insured value. You should keep with your household inventory any receipts and repair bills relating to important items. Some people even take a complete photographic inventory. With all appliances and costly equipment, it is advisable to record serial and model numbers, too.

Market Value

If your insured property is lost or stolen, you generally won't receive the replacement cost. It is possible to buy replacement cost policies, but they are more expensive than the usual personal property policy usually attached to your homeowner's insurance policy. In any event, you will often be paid only the market value, or fully depreciated value, of the lost property. Say, for example, that you bought a sound movie camera for $400. Two years later, it is stolen out of your house. Most insurance companies will depreciate it by 10 percent each year for five years; thereafter, they will give you 50 percent of the purchase price. In this particular example, the insurance company will pay $400 minus 20 percent of $400, or only $320.

In times of inflation, the replacement value may greatly exceed the purchase price, so even though you are paid, in this case, 80 percent of the purchase price, you may not be receiving anywhere near 80 percent of the replacement cost. In principle, then, the insurance company is supposed to pay you the market value when it pays the depreciated

EXHIBIT 11-1.   **HOUSEHOLD INVENTORY**

KITCHEN/BREAKFAST AREA

Article	Description	Purchase Date	Original Price	Insured Value
Flooring				
Curtains				
Shades				
Lighting fixtures				
Tables				
Chairs				
Cabinets				
Flatware				
Dishes				
Glassware				
Cooking utensils				
Appliances				

value of your lost or stolen items. In an inflationary setting, however, this isn't the case. The insurance company's depreciated value of your items may be significantly less than their market value. Some insurance companies are starting to take account of inflation, so this may not be a problem in the future.

YOUR LIABILITY EXPOSURE

Every time you drive a car, you expose yourself to a law suit—if you're found negligent in an accident. Every time you engage in a sport where someone else could be injured, you expose yourself to a law suit for negligent action. In other words, you have many liability exposures. Even if you believe you will never act negligently, you still expose yourself to liability because a judge or a jury may decide otherwise. Liability law suits can be expensive and legal fees even more so. Therefore, you seek liability insurance in order to protect yourself and your family from losses resulting from liability exposure.

Negligence

The legal definition of negligence is neither straightforward nor consistent. The definition has changed through the years: today's negligent action would not have been so defined a hundred years ago. We are now held more accountable for our actions as they affect others than we were in the past. In general, you are negligent when your behavior does not correspond to what a person would do under normal conditions with normal experiences. The law says that, to be negligent, you must act differently than "the reasonable man" would. Furthermore, if you are accused of negligence, it often must be proved that you had a responsibility to be more careful to the person accusing you.

How Can You Defend a Liability Suit?

When you are accused of being negligent, you do have defenses. One of them is called the assumption of risk defense. If, say, a friend volunteers to accompany you on a hike in the mountains, you are relieved of any assumption of risk for that person's safety. If your friend slips and falls on the hike, he or she can't sue you for negligence merely because you were the one who suggested the hike.

Another defense is called defense of contributory negligence. You are sued but contend that the plaintiff (the person suing you) acted in a negligent manner. If a visitor at your house slips and breaks an ankle on your porch, you may use the defense of contributory negligence if that individual was drunk at the time. You may, however, be subjected to comparative negligent statutes: a judge or jury may agree that the visitor was drunk and contributed to 50 percent of the negligence, but you contributed to the other 50 percent by not having adequate light on your porch. Thus, you would have to pay 50 percent of the stipulated damages.

THE PRINCIPLE OF INDEMNITY

Insurance companies generally don't want to compensate you any more than you have actually suffered in financial losses. Thus, the **principle of indemnity** states that the insured may not be compensated for an amount that exceeds economic loss. Most liability and property insurance contracts are based upon this principle, of which there are several related concepts:

1 Actual cash value,
2 Insurable interest,
3 Subrogation, and
4 Other insurance.

Actual Cash Value

The principle of indemnity limits the amount you may collect to the actual cash value of the property insured. Actual cash value is most commonly defined as replacement cost less depreciation. We have already mentioned the problems with estimating replacement cost in times of inflation. Replacement cost may exceed purchase cost, but depreciation schedules are often applied to the actual purchase price rather than the current purchase price. In any event, under the principle of indemnity, the insurance company is not obligated to pay more than the true replacement cost minus depreciation, which is, in effect, the market value of the item insured.

Insurable Interest

Remember, you can't insure your friend's car because you have no insurable interest in it. In order to insure, you must stand to lose something if property is destroyed. And what you stand to lose must be more than a feeling of loss. If you could insure other people's property, you would have an incentive to let their property be damaged or destroyed because you would always be paid. Or imagine that you own a building on which you have full coverage insurance. You sell the building but forget to cancel your insurance policy on which you are still paying premiums. If the building is destroyed by fire, will the insurance company pay you because you have a policy in force? No, not under the principle of indemnity: you have suffered no economic loss because you no longer have insurable interest in the property.

The Right of Subrogation

The **right of subrogation** allows your insurance company to request reimbursement from whoever may have caused the loss on which it paid. Alternatively, the right of subrogation allows your insurance company to collect from the negligent person's insurance company. Suppose that your car is wrecked in an auto accident, and the issue of negligence is not clear-cut. Your insurance company may indeed pay to have your car fixed. But then it can, under the right of subrogation, attempt to collect from the other person's insurance company if it is proved that the other person was negligent. Once you receive payment from your insurance company, you subrogate (transfer) your right to sue the other company. You cannot, in other words, collect once from your insurance company and once from the other person's.

Other Insurance Clauses

Suppose that you have medical insurance on your automobile policy and health insurance offered by your employer. You are injured in a car accident, and your total medical bills amount to $2,000. But you cannot be reimbursed simultaneously by your group health insurance policy and by your automobile insurance policy. Why? Because most insurance policies have an "other insurance" clause stating that any person with more than one insurance policy on property or health cannot collect more than the total economic, or financial, loss sustained. Here's another example. You take out fire insurance on your house from two different companies, with each policy having a face value of $50,000. Should the house burn down, you won't be paid $100,000 if the replacement value of the house is only $50,000. Each insurance company will pay you a pro rata share of the loss—in this case, 50 percent.

COINSURANCE CLAUSES

Many property insurance contracts require that the policy holder buy insurance equal in amount to a certain percentage of the replacement value of the property. Whenever a policy holder complies with this requirement, the policy holder will be reimbursed for all losses, dollar for dollar, up to the policy limit. We give a numerical example of this later on.

TYPES OF HOME, PROPERTY, AND LIABILITY INSURANCE POLICIES

There are basically two types of insurance policies for a home—standard fire insurance policies and homeowner's policies.

Standard Fire Insurance Policy

The **standard fire insurance policy** protects the homeowner against fire and lightning, plus damage from smoke and water caused by the fire and the fire department. If you pay a little more, the coverage can be extended to protect you against damages caused by hail, windstorms, explosions, and so on. You can also add personal theft and a comprehensive liability policy.

Homeowner's Policy

The homeowner's policy provides protection against a number of risks under a single policy, allowing you to save over what you would pay if you bought each protection separately. In addition to a standard fire policy, you can obtain liability coverage.

There are basically two types of homeowner's policy coverage:

1   *Property coverage.* This includes garage, house, and other private buildings on your lot; personal possessions and property, either at home or while you are traveling or at work; and additional living expenses that would be paid to you if you couldn't live in your home because of a fire or some other peril.

2   *Liability coverage.* Basically, this is for personal liability in case someone is injured on your property, or you damage someone else's property and are at fault, or you injure someone else off your premises when you aren't in your automobile.

Similar to liability coverage is coverage for medical payments for injury to others who are on your property and for the property of others that you or a member of your family damages.

Forms of Homeowner's Policies. There are basically five forms of home and condominium owners' policies. Exhibit 11-2 describes each type. The basic form covers eleven perils, or risks; the broad form covers eighteen perils, or risks; and, finally, the comprehensive form covers those eighteen perils or risks, and all other perils.

Renters Take Out Insurance, Too

Homeowners aren't the only ones who can get an insurance policy to cover loss through fire, theft, and the like. Landlords or owners of apartment buildings are liable for property damage and for injuries occurring in common areas, such as lobbies or hallways. But renters are responsible for protecting the inside of their dwellings, as well as being liable for accidents that occur there. Renter's insurance, called residence contents broad form (HO-4), is a homeowner's policy that covers personal possessions against the eighteen risks described in Exhibit 11-2. It includes additional living expenses and liability coverage.

Before you choose a rental policy, make a detailed inventory of your possessions. Decide on the coverage you want and then do some comparison shopping. A general policy for, say, $5,000 of property insurance and $50,000 of liability coverage probably will cost less than $100 a year, depending on location. If you are in a high crime area and can't find available commercial insurance, you can apply through the Federal Crime Insurance Program and the Fair Access to Insurance Requirements (FAIR) Plan. The former covers loss by burglary; the latter covers fire, vandalism, and windstorms. Neither plan gives you liability coverage. Ask a commercial insurance agent in your area where you can

EXHIBIT 11-2.

GUIDE TO PACKAGE POLICIES FOR HOMEOWNERS

These are the principal features of the standard types of Homeowners insurance policies.

The amount of insurance provided for specific categories, such as personal property and comprehensive personal liability, can usually be increased by paying an additional premium.

The special limits of liability refer to the maximum amounts the policy will pay for the types of property listed in the notes. Usually, jewelry, furs, boats and other items subject to special limits have to be insured separately to obtain greater coverage. Adapted from New Jersey Insurance Department, *A Shopper's Guide to Homeowners Insurance*, 1977.

	BASIC FORM HOMEOWNERS HO-1	BROAD FORM HOMEOWNERS HO-2	SPECIAL FORM HOMEOWNERS HO-3	COMPREHENSIVE FORM HOMEOWNERS HO-5	HO-6 (FOR CONDOMINIUM OWNERS)
PERILS COVERED (see key below)	perils 1-11	perils 1-18	perils 1-18 on personal property except glass breakage; all risks, except those specifically excluded, on buildings	all risks except those specifically excluded	perils 1-18 except glass breakage
STANDARD AMOUNT OF INSURANCE ON: house, attached structures	based on property value; minimum $8,000	based on property value; minimum $8,000	based on property value; minimum $8,000	based on property value; minimum $15,000	$1,000 on owner's additions and alterations to unit
detached structures	10% of amount of insurance on house	10% of amount of insurance on house	10% of amount of insurance on house	10% of amount of insurance on house	no coverage

trees, shrubs, and plants	5% of amount of insurance on house; $250 maximum per item	5% of amount of insurance on house; $250 maximum per item	5% of amount of insurance on house; $250 maximum per item	5% of amount of insurance on house; $250 maximum per item	5% of amount of insurance on house; $250 maximum per item	10% of personal property insurance; $250 maximum per item
personal property on premises	50% of insurance on house	50% of insurance on house	50% of insurance on house	50% of insurance on house	50% of insurance on house	based on value of property; minimum $4,000
personal property away from premises	10% of personal property insurance (minimum $1,000)	10% of personal property insurance (minimum $1,000)	10% of personal property insurance (minimum $1,000)	50% of insurance on house	50% of insurance on house	10% of personal property insurance (minimum $1,000)
additional living expense	10% of insurance on house	20% of insurance on house	20% of insurance on house	20% of insurance on house	20% of insurance on house	40% of personal property insurance
SPECIAL LIMITS OF LIABILITY*	standard	standard	standard	standard	standard	standard

KEY TO PERILS COVERED:

1. fire, lightning
2. damage to property removed from premises endangered by fire
3. windstorm, hail
4. explosion
5. riots
6. damage by aircraft
7. damage by vehicles not owned or operated by people covered by policy
8. damage from smoke
9. vandalism, malicious mischief
10. glass breakage
11. theft
12. falling objects
13. weight of ice, snow, sleet
14. collapse of building or any part of building
15. bursting, cracking, burning, or bulging of a steam or hot water heating system, or of appliances for heating water
16. leakage or overflow of water or steam from a plumbing, heating or air-conditioning system
17. freezing of plumbing, heating and air-conditioning systems and domestic appliances
18. injury to electrical appliances, devices, fixtures and wiring (excluding tubes, transistors and similar electronic components) from short circuits or other accidentally generated currents

*Special limits of liability: Money, bullion, numismatic property, bank notes–$100; securities, bills, deeds, tickets, etc.–$500; manuscripts–$1,000; jewelry, furs–$500 for theft; boats, including trailers and equipment–$500; trailers–$500.

obtain information on policies available through these programs, or write HUD, Washington, D.C., for an informative booklet.

Adding a Personal Articles Floater Policy

You may wish to pay a slightly higher premium to insure specific personal articles—for example, cameras, musical instruments, works of art, jewelry, and other valuables. This would be done by adding a personal property or articles floater to your homeowner's policy. You will be asked to submit a list of those things you wish covered and some affidavits giving their current market value. When you insure under such a floater, you have provided all risk insurance and, therefore, can omit the covered property from your fire and theft policies.

Personal Effects Floater Policy

You can take out a personal effects floater policy to cover personal items when you are traveling. In most cases, a personal effects floater is not necessary because your regular homeowner's insurance covers you. Because this floater only covers the articles when they are taken off your property, you need separate insurance for them when they are on your property. The policy does not cover theft from an unattended automobile, unless there is evidence of a forced entry. And even when there is evidence of a forced entry, the company's liability generally is limited to 10 percent of the amount of insurance and to not more than $250 for all property in any one loss. You can, however, remove this restriction from the policy by paying an additional premium.

Flood Insurance

Even a comprehensive form insurance policy does not cover floods. If you live in an area that may be flooded because of hurricanes and/or other natural disasters, it is advisable to purchase federally subsidized flood insurance. Your insurance agent will be able to tell you if you live in an area designated eligible by the Federal Insurance Administrator of the U.S. Department of Housing and Urban Development.

HOW MUCH INSURANCE SHOULD YOU HAVE?

As a general rule, you should have 80 percent of the total value of the house insured—that is, 80 percent of its replacement value. If you have at least that much coverage, you can collect the full replacement cost, not the depreciated value, of any damaged real property (up to the limits of the policy). Say, for example, that your ten-year-old roof is damaged in a fire. It costs you $2,500 to replace it. If you have at least 80 percent coverage on your house, your insurance company must pay you the full amount of the roof damage. But if your house is covered for less than 80 percent of replacement, you will get less: you will be paid only that portion of the loss equal to the amount of insurance in force divided by 80 percent of replacement cost of the entire house times the loss on the roof.

Now imagine that you have a house with a replacement value of $50,000. Eighty percent of $50,000 is $40,000, but you don't have a $40,000 insurance policy. Rather, you only have insurance equal to $30,000. To find out what your insurance company pays, you multiply the amount of loss for your roof in the preceding example ($2,500) by the amount of insurance in force over $40,000 (80 percent of total replacement value). Thus, your insurance company will pay

$$\$2,500 \times \frac{\$30,000}{\$40,000} = \$1,875.$$

If you'd had $40,000 worth of insurance coverage, you would have received the full $2,500 to replace the roof.

You need not insure your house for the full replacement value for two reasons. First, the land has a value that wouldn't be destroyed in a fire or flood. Second, even if the house burns down, the foundation, sidewalks, driveway, and so on still remain. Remember, though, if you live in a house you bought many years ago, the cost of replacement may be much more than you think. Construction costs have increased enormously lately. So make sure your insurance keeps pace with them. You may want to arrange with your insurance company to increase the value of your insurance 10 percent every year or two to keep pace with construction cost increases.

The insurance industry is regulated, and every state has its own insurance commissioner who judges the rates charged by various companies. Because there is significant competition within the industry, different prices often are charged for the same amount of insurance. But prices alone can be misleading because different insurance companies offer different qualities of service. One company may be less willing to pay off claims than another. One may have an insurance adjustor at your house immediately if you have an accident, while another may never send one and let you do the adjusting yourself.

AUTOMOBILE INSURANCE

In any one year, 45,000 to 55,000 Americans die in automobile accidents, and as many as 2 million receive disabling injuries. It has been estimated that the economic loss to society from automobile accidents exceeds $30 billion a year. Society also pays all police and court costs. Finally, there is a loss in the productive capacity of the nation. Fortunately, individuals can, to a certain extent, insure themselves against the major portion of the private losses. This is done through life, health, and automobile insurance. Now we will look at the automobile insurance industry, no-fault auto insurance, and the actual policies offered by various companies. In the Practical Applications section, we offer some tips on how to shop for car insurance.

THE AUTOMOBILE INSURANCE INDUSTRY

In May 1974, President Nixon wired the National Governors Conference that no-fault auto insurance was "an idea whose time has come." The president added, though, that the place for no-fault action is at the state, not the federal, level. Labor and consumer groups, however, were dissatisfied with the pace of state action and the lobbying tactics of no-fault opponents. Therefore, pressure was brought upon Congress to institute a federal plan. Supporters of such a plan indicate that eventually it will save motorists $1 billion a year in auto insurance premiums.

Under a no-fault insurance system, your insurance company does not have to decide whose fault the accident was before payments are made for medical expenses resulting from the accident. In a traditional liability-based fault system, it must be determined who caused an accident. The insuror of the party deemed "at fault" then pays the bills—medical, lost earnings, pain and suffering, and automobile repairs—of the injured party.

No-fault insurance is not a new idea. Almost all other types of insurance are already no-fault. For example, when you own life insurance, the life insurance company pays without asking about fault (unless you die by suicide). The same is true of fire, homeowner's, and health and accident insurance. If you break an ankle and are covered under a medical plan, the insuror does not ask whose fault it was before your medical bills are paid.

Original proponents of no-fault auto insurance believed it soon would be adopted by all states in the union; however, by 1977, only sixteen states had converted to pure no-fault: Colorado, Connecticut, Florida, Georgia, Hawaii, Kansas, Kentucky, Massachusetts, Michigan, Minnesota, Nevada, New Jersey, New York, North Dakota, Pennsylvania, and Utah. Another eight states had passed some modified form of no-fault automobile insurance. In most no-fault states, the no-fault laws apply only to bodily injuries. Property damage claims still are settled by standard liability and collision sections of automobile insurance policies.

If you live in a state with no-fault insurance, you still can sue the other party in case of an automobile accident. Generally, you must satisfy certain "threshold" criteria before you are allowed to sue for pain and suffering, inconvenience, lost wages, and deprivation of the company of a spouse. The medical threshold level ranges from a few hundred dollars up to two thousand dollars in the sixteen no-fault states. In other states, you must suffer serious injury or permanent disfigurement before being allowed to sue.

Reducing Legal Fees

Originators of the no-fault system pointed out that only forty-four cents of each premium dollar went toward paying the injured parties in an automobile accident. Much of the remaining fifty-six cents of each premium dollar went to the cost of litigation—to lawyers. Proponents of no-fault reason that such a system should reduce dramatically the amount of needless expenditures on legal fees, particularly when minor injuries are involved.

Has the reduction in legal expenses lowered premiums in no-fault states? The data are not all in, and a preliminary survey among the twenty-four states with some form of no-fault insurance didn't produce a definite conclusion. From 1970 to 1976, premiums rose less in fifteen of those twenty-four states than in all the remaining states without no-fault; thus, no-fault seems to have a slight edge in terms of keeping premiums down. This, of course, is not sufficient evidence to claim total success for the new type of auto insurance.

GETTING AN ADEQUATE AMOUNT OF INSURANCE

The second most important step when buying an automobile is obtaining adequate automobile insurance. Of the many kinds of insurance coverage available, the most crucial is liability insurance.

Property Damage and Bodily Injury Liability Coverage

This insurance covers bodily injury liability and property damage. **Liability** limits are usually described by a series of three numbers, such as 25/50/5; this means the policy will pay a maximum of $25,000 for bodily injury to one person and $50,000 to more than one person, and a maximum of $5,000 for property damage in one accident. Most insurance companies offer liability up to $300,000 and sometimes $500,000. The cost of additional liability limits is relatively small, as can be seen in Exhibit 11-3. You should consider taking out a much larger limit than you ordinarily would expect to need, because personal injury suits against drivers proved negligent are sometimes astronomical. Sometimes, dependents of automobile accident victims have successfully sued for $1 million. Exhibit 11-4 shows minimum insurance coverage required by state laws.

Individuals who are dissatisfied with the maximum liability limits offered by regular automobile insurance coverage can purchase a separate amount of coverage under an **umbrella policy.** Umbrella limits sometimes go as high as $5 million. They also cover personal liability in excess of homeowner's liability limits.

Medical Payment Coverage

Medical payments on an auto insurance policy cover hospital and medical bills and, sometimes, funeral expenses. Usually you can buy $2,000 to $5,000 per person for around $10 or $15 a year. This insurance protects all the passengers in your car when you are driving.

Physical Damage Coverage

Collision. This insurance covers damage to your own car in any type of collision. Usually, it is not advisable to purchase full collision coverage (otherwise known as **zero deductible**). The price per year is quite high because it is likely that small, but costly, repair jobs will be required each year. Most people take out $50 or $100 deductible coverage, which costs about one-fourth the price of zero deductible.

Comprehensive. This insurance covers for loss; damage; and destruction by fire, hurricane, hail, and vandalism. It is separate from collision insurance. Full comprehensive insurance is quite expensive. Again, $50 or $100 deductible is usually preferable.

Uninsured Motorist Coverage

This coverage insures the driver and passengers against injury caused by any driver without insurance or by a hit-and-run driver. Certain states require that it be in all insurance policies sold to drivers.

Accidental Death Benefits

Sometimes called **double indemnity,** this provides a lump sum to named beneficiaries if the policy holder dies in an automobile accident. It generally costs very little, but it may not be necessary if you have a sufficient amount of life insurance.

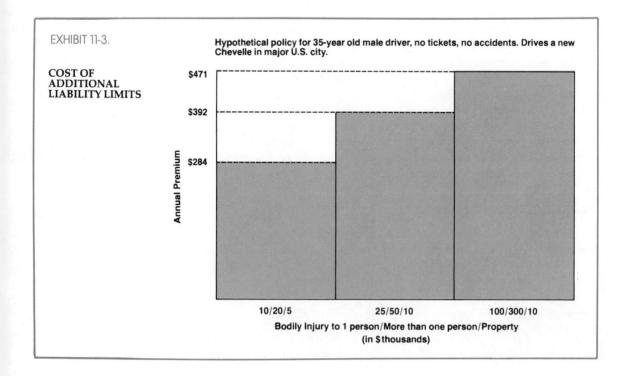

EXHIBIT 11-3.

Hypothetical policy for 35-year old male driver, no tickets, no accidents. Drives a new Chevelle in major U.S. city.

COST OF ADDITIONAL LIABILITY LIMITS

Annual Premium

$471

$392

$284

10/20/5 25/50/10 100/300/10

Bodily Injury to 1 person/More than one person/Property (in $thousands)

EXHIBIT 11-4.

MINIMUM INSURANCE COVERAGE REQUIRED TO MEET FINANCIAL RESPONSIBILITY LAWS BY STATE

Amounts shown as listed in "Best's Recommended Insurance Attorneys." 1974-1975 Edition. There may have been changes in some states since these data were published. For latest information, check your own state department of motor vehicles, or your auto insurance agent.

AMOUNTS IN THOUSANDS

State	Injury to Any One Person	Injuries in One Accident, to All Persons	Damage to Property	State	Injury to Any One Person	Injuries in One Accident, to All Persons	Damage to Property
Alabama	$10	$20	$ 5	Montana	$10	$20	$ 5
Alaska	15	30	5	Nebraska	15	30	10
Arizona	15	30	10	Nevada	15	30	5
Arkansas	10	20	5				
California	15	30	5	New Hampshire	20	40	5
				New Jersey	15	30	5
Colorado	10	30	5	New Mexico	10	20	5
Connecticut	20	40	5	New York	10	20	5
Delaware	10	20	5	North Carolina	15	30	5
District of Columbia	10	20	5				
Florida	10	20	5	North Dakota	10	20	5
				Ohio	12.5	25	7.5
Georgia	10	20	5	Oklahoma	5	10	5
Hawaii	10	20	5	Oregon	10	20	5
Idaho	10	20	5	Pennsylvania	10	20	5
Illinois	10	20	5				
Indiana	15	30	10	Rhode Island	10	20	5
				South Carolina	10	20	5
Iowa	10	20	5	South Dakota	15	30	10
Kansas	15	30	5	Tennessee	10	20	5
Kentucky	10	20	5	Texas	10	20	5
Louisiana	5	10	1				
Maine	20	40	10	Utah	15	30	5
				Vermont	10	20	5
Maryland	20	40	5	Virginia	20	40	5
Massachusetts	5	10	5	Washington	15	30	5
Michigan	20	40	5				
Minnesota	10	20	5	West Virginia	10	20	5
Mississippi	10	20	5	Wisconsin	15	30	5
Missouri	10	20	2	Wyoming	10	20	5

PRACTICAL APPLICATIONS

HOW TO SHOP FOR INSURANCE

Shopping for automobile insurance may be easier than shopping for a car. You might check first with your local credit union. Or, if you are a member of certain organizations, there might be special insurance sources available to you. Sometimes companies get special rates for their employees. If you are a government employee, you sometimes can get special types of automobile insurance. When comparing insurance companies, you should look at the service they give. You can shop for insurance by figuring out the exact coverage you want—including liability, uninsured motorist, medical, collision, comprehensive, and perhaps towing—with the specific limits you want. Then you can get a written statement from several insurance companies' agents. Insurance premiums can vary by 90 percent or more, depending on what company you select.

The insurance agent you work with is also important. If one in your area has the reputation of being fair and knowledgeable, you can feel confident with his or her suggestions. Here, again, reliable information is part of the package. (You may also be buying "clout"—the ability to get your claim settled—if you are dealing with a company agent rather than a broker for many different companies.)

TYPES OF AUTOMOBILE INSURANCE POLICIES

There are basically two types of policies, family and special. When you ask for an insurance quote, you generally will be quoted for a **family automobile policy.** This includes liability, comprehensive, collision, uninsured motorist, and medical in the amount you specify. A cheaper, but more restricted, type is called **special automobile policy.** (It is also called a single limit policy.) It is restricted to better-than-average drivers and combines bodily injury and property damage liability, accidental death, and uninsured motorist protection. Instead of awarding separate amounts on those items, a lump sum maximum is given per accident. If that maximum is, say, $100,000, then total compensation of any one person, to a group of people, or for property damage will not exceed $100,000. In some cases under a special policy, medical payment insurance only pays the difference between what the medical bill is and what your health insurance pays. In other words, you cannot collect more than the full amount from both policies. Finally, under a special policy, you purchase collision and comprehensive insurance separately. Also, you may be able to get safe driver policies, reductions if you have taken driver training, and so on. All these possibilities should be discussed with prospective insurance agents. Exhibit 11-5 helps you compare insurance policies.

Choosing Higher Deductibles

To repeat: the lower the deductible for collision coverage, the higher the insurance costs. If you opt for a much higher deductible—say, $250—your auto insurance costs drop dramatically. Exhibit 11-6 shows the absolute and percentage reduction in the cost of a typical collision policy. If you are a careful driver and rarely have minor traffic accidents or have available funds to pay for minor accident costs, you should consider the possibility of having a higher deductible in your policy.

DIFFERENT GROUPS PAY DIFFERENT RATES

Automobile insurance companies consistently differentiate among different classes of drivers. Why? Because the probability of an accident occurring is different for different classes. Competition among the various insurance companies has forced them to find out which classes of drivers are safer than others and offer those classes lower rates. For example, because statistics indicate that single males sixteen to twenty-five years old have the high-

EXHIBIT 11-5.

COMPARING AUTO INSURANCE COMPANIES

KIND OF COVERAGE	LIMITS DESIRED	PREMIUM COST COMPANY		
		A	B	C
Liability:				
Bodily injury	$ __ /person, $ __ /accident	___	___	___
Property damage	$ __ /accident	___	___	___
Physical damage:		___	___	___
Compensation for total lost	blue book wholesale price	___	___	___
Collision	$ __ /deductible	___	___	___
Medical payments	$ __ /person	___	___	___
Uninsured motorists	$ __ /person, $ __ /accident	___	___	___
Accidental death benefits		___	___	___
Towing		___	___	___
Comprehensive	$ __ /deductible	___	___	___
Other		___	___	___
Annual Total		___	___	___

est accident record among all drivers, they pay a much higher price for auto insurance. And because statistics indicate that women drivers have fewer accidents than male drivers, on average, women often pay lower insurance rates than men. Young drivers are clearly hardest hit by this system of differentiated rates.

Rates depend on coverage

Insurance rates depend on the extent of coverage. A wide range of coverages can be purchased, from the very minimum to huge policies that will cover most suits brought against you if you are involved in a car accident.

PROBLEMS OF INSURING YOUNG DRIVERS

As parents of teenagers know, it is extremely expensive to insure a young driver, particularly if that driver is a male. But there are ways to reduce such auto insurance expenses. One way is to limit the son's or daughter's driving time; "occasional use" is defined by most insurance companies as using the car less than 50 percent of the time. If the young driver uses the car for going out on weekends or, occasionally to school, the lower rate applies. However, if the car is driven to school every day, then the lower rate does not apply. Some companies give discounts if the driver has a grade average of B or better in school. And there are discounts for compact and subcompact cars. A drivers education course also will qualify some students for a premium discount.

TIPS ON LOWERING AUTOMOBILE INSURANCE PREMIUMS

1. Don't buy unnecessary coverage, such as collision insurance on an older car. For example, if you have a five-year-old car whose blue book value is relatively low, you may not want collision insurance; you never collect more than blue book value, and damage may be more than the car is worth.

2. See if a special policy, rather than a more expensive family automobile insurance policy, is suitable for your needs.

3. Avoid high-performance or expensive cars for which auto insurance is more expensive.

4. Take a higher deductible on collision and comprehensive insurance. Remember, the higher the deductible, the lower the premium.

5. See if you qualify for a discount for not smoking, not drinking, belonging to a car pool, having an accident-free record for the past three years or more, having a car with heavy bumpers or a passive restraint system, driving a compact car, or limiting annual mileage.

6. Don't use your car for work if you can obtain other transportation.

7. Don't duplicate insurance. If you have a comprehensive health and accident insurance policy, then you don't need medical payments in your automobile insurance plan (unless you often have nonfamily passengers).

8. Pay your insurance premium for the full period rather than in installments.

9. Any time your situation changes, notify your company. Do this when your estimated yearly mileage drops, when you join a car pool, or when a driver of your car moves away from home.

IF INSURANCE IS REFUSED OR COVERAGE IS CANCELED

You might be refused liability coverage by an automobile insurance company because of, say, a bad driving record. You then become what is called an **assigned risk.** Should this happen, you must first certify that you have attempted, within the past sixty days, to obtain insurance in the state in which you reside. A pool of insurance companies (or sometimes the state) will then assign you to a specific company in the pool for a period of three years. After three years, you can apply for reassignment, provided you are still unable to purchase insurance outside the pool.

If you are an assigned risk, you can only purchase the legal minimum amount of insurance in your state. In most cases, you will pay a much higher premium for the same amount of coverage than would someone who is not an assigned risk.

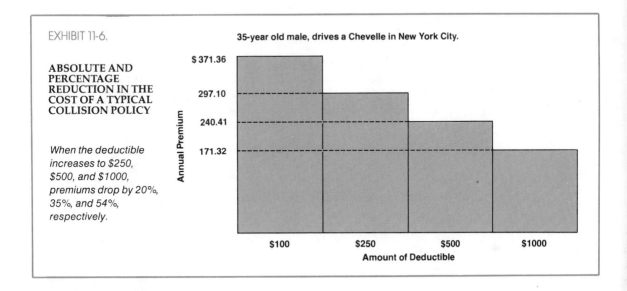

EXHIBIT 11-6.

**ABSOLUTE AND
PERCENTAGE
REDUCTION IN THE
COST OF A TYPICAL
COLLISION POLICY**

*When the deductible
increases to $250,
$500, and $1000,
premiums drop by 20%,
35%, and 54%,
respectively.*

35-year old male, drives a Chevelle in New York City.

Annual Premium

$ 371.36

297.10

240.41

171.32

$100 $250 $500 $1000

Amount of Deductible

GLOSSARY OF TERMS

MARKET VALUE Replacement value of an asset minus depreciation.

PRINCIPLE OF INDEMNITY The insured may not be compensated by an insurance company for more than his or her economic, or financial, loss.

SUBROGATION The right of an insurance company to force you to transfer your right to sue another party. If you collect from your insurance company on an automobile accident, you must transfer the right to sue the other person to your insurance company.

STANDARD FIRE INSURANCE POLICY A standard insurance policy that homeowners purchase to protect against fire and lightning, plus damage from water and smoke caused by fire and the fire department. This coverage can be extended to cover damage caused by hail, storms, wind, and explosions. In some cases, you can also add personal theft and a comprehensive liability policy.

HOMEOWNERS' POLICY This insurance policy protects you against a number of risks under a single policy and is less expensive than a number of separate policies.

BASIC FORM Also called HO-1, this standard homeowners' insurance policy covers eleven risks, including fire, lightning, riots, damage by aircraft, and theft.

BROAD FORM   Also called HO-2, this policy covers eighteen risks.

COMPREHENSIVE FORM   Also called HO-5, this homeowners' insurance policy covers virtually all risks except glass breakage and flooding and offers a higher amount of protection on personal property away from your premises and on certain detached structures.

RESIDENCE CONTENTS BROAD FORM   This HO-4 insurance policy covers the personal possessions of renters.

NO-FAULT AUTO INSURANCE   A system of automobile insurance liability in which each insured's insurance company automatically pays for collision damages, a certain amount of medical bills, and, in some cases, a certain amount for pain, suffering, and lost wages, up to a maximum, regardless of who is at fault.

LIABILITY INSURANCE   Insurance that covers suits against the insured for such damages as injury or death to other drivers or passengers, property damage, and the like. It is insurance for those damages for which the driver can be held liable.

UMBRELLA POLICY   A supplemental insurance policy that can extend normal automobile (and personal) liability limits to $1 million or more for a relatively small premium.

ZERO DEDUCTIBLE   In the collision part of an automobile insurance policy, this provision means that the insured pays nothing for any repair to damage on the car due to an accident caused by the insured. Zero deductible is, of course, more expensive than, say, a $50 or $100 deductible policy.

COMPREHENSIVE   Coverage in an automobile insurance policy for loss or damage to the automobile due to fire, theft, vandalism, and so on.

DOUBLE INDEMNITY   Also called an accidental death benefit, this provides a lump sum to named beneficiaries should you die in an automobile accident.

FAMILY AUTOMOBILE POLICY   An automobile insurance policy that includes liability, comprehensive, collision, uninsured motorist, and medical.

SPECIAL AUTOMOBILE POLICY   A policy restricted to better-than-average drivers, it combines bodily injury and property damage liability, accidental death, and uninsured motorist protection in one lump-sum maximum.

ASSIGNED RISK   A person seeking automobile insurance who has been refused coverage. That person is assigned to an insurance company that is a member of the assigned risk pool in that person's state.

CHAPTER SUMMARY

1. The owner of assets suffers financial loss if those assets are damaged, lost, or stolen.

2. The first step in insuring one's personal property is to take a complete inventory, listing all items, their model and serial numbers, original cost, and year purchased. It is advisable to take snapshots of important items. And it is important to retain receipts.

3. Whenever you engage in an activity, you expose yourself to liability suits in which someone else can claim that you were negligent or caused pain, suffering, or financial loss.

4. Liability insurance takes account of such potential losses.

5. Liability suits can be defended on the basis of assumption of risk and contributory negligence. In some cases, however, a judge or jury will rule comparative negligence and assess you a percentage of total damages owed if the plaintiff was not 100 percent responsible for causing the accident.

6. The principle of indemnity assures insurance companies that they will not pay more than the financial loss you suffer. Thus, you must have an insurable interest in the property you insure. You cannot be compensated for more than the actual cash value (market value) of the property. You must allow the insurance company to sue the offending party if your insurance company pays you for damages you suffered. Finally, you normally cannot collect from several insurance companies for the same loss; each will pay a pro rata share so that the total compensation equals the actual loss.

7. Many property insurance contracts require that you buy insurance with a limit equal to a certain percentage of the actual replacement value of the insured property. Once you do, all losses will be paid at full replacement cost up to the limit of your policy.

8. There are many types of homeowners' insurance policies, numbered HO-1 through HO-6. HO-1 is called the basic form homeowners'. HO-2 is the broad form, HO-3 the special form, HO-4 the residence contents broad form (for renters), HO-5 a comprehensive form, and HO-6 is for condominium owners.

9. In most states, there are minimum liability insurance limits pertaining to bodily injury and property damage.

10. One can purchase large increases in liability insurance limits for a modest amount.

11. Additionally, automobile insurance policies include medical payments coverage, collision coverage, comprehensive, and uninsured motorists coverage, as well as the possibility of accidental death benefits.

12. Family and special (single limit) are the two types of car insurance policies you can purchase.

13. One way to reduce your automobile insurance is to choose a higher deductible for collision coverage. A zero deductible is extremely expensive.

14. If you are refused insurance because of a poor driving record, you may have to purchase coverage from a company in a so-called assigned risk pool. Premium payments will be higher than they are for the average motorist.

STUDY QUESTIONS

1. Explain the principle of indemnity. How does insured interest relate to this principle?

2. Why can't you generally collect from several insurance companies for the same loss, the total amount of which exceeds the actual economic loss?

3. How does the right of subrogation help lower your insurance costs?

4. You have a house with a replacement cost of $50,000. You insure it for $28,000. One entire room is destroyed. Its replacement cost is $10,000. How much will the insurance pay toward replacement?

5. What is the difference between replacement cost coverage and actual cash value coverage? For which would you expect to pay more?

6. Why is there sometimes a difference between the amount an insurance company pays for a loss on personal property and the actual cash, or market, value?

7. What type of insurance policy should you buy in order to insure an expensive camera?

8. If something is stolen from your car, which insurance coverage is necessary for compensation?

9. What is the difference between automobile collision insurance and automobile comprehensive insurance?

10. Why is it inadvisable to have a zero deductible on automobile insurance?

11. What is no-fault insurance? What are the pros and cons?

12. Why do different groups of individuals pay different rates for the same amount of automobile insurance?

13. Under what conditions would it be preferable not to carry comprehensive and collision insurance for your car?

14. What is the difference between a family automobile policy and a special, or single limit, automobile policy?

11-1 Property Damage Plagues Pals

The Hatfields and the McCoys were good friends who had purchased adjoining summer cabins on a lake in upstate New York. Each cabin was valued at a replacement cost of $18,000. The Hatfields purchased a HO-1 policy with a face value of $18,000, and the McCoys, an HO-2 policy with a face value of $15,000. During the winter of 1978, a thirty-six-inch snowfall caused the roof on each cabin to collapse. The repairs were estimated to be $7000 for each cabin.

1. How much did the Hatfields collect?

2. How much did the McCoys collect?

11-2 Collision Claims Can Cost Plenty

Jerry Satterlee, a systems engineer; his wife Gwen, an attorney; and their three children were driving home to San Diego from Disneyland when a car drove onto the freeway from an off-ramp at an excessive rate of speed. As a result of the collision, Jerry was killed, Gwen and the three children were injured, and their $13,000 Cadillac was completely destroyed. Carole Clutz, the driver of the other car, escaped with minor cuts and bruises and $2300 damage to her car. Carole had the minimum insurance coverage required by California law and $300 deductible collision coverage.

Gwen sued Carole for $15,000 in her own name, for $15,000 in the names of each of her three children, and for $13,000, the replacement value of the car. After a brief deliberation, the jury decided in Gwen's favor.

1. How much did the insurance company pay the surviving Satterlees?

2. How much did the company pay Carole for the damages to her car?

3. How much did Carole have to pay as a result of the accident?

SELECTED REFERENCES

A Family Guide to Property and Liability Insurance. New York: Insurance Information Institute, 1973.

"Auto Insurance Companies Offer Cost-Cutting Advice to Motorists." *Consumer Newsweek,* November 15, 1976, p.

Consumer Action Auto Insurance Guide. San Francisco Consumer Action, 26 Seventh Street, San Francisco, CA 94103.

Denenberg, Herbert S., et al. *Risk and Insurance,* Second Edition. Englewood Cliffs, NJ: Prentice-Hall, 1974.

Every Ten Minutes. New York: Insurance Information Institute, 1974.

"Filing a Home Insurance Claim? You May Be in for a Shock." *U.S. News & World Report,* February 21, 1977, pp. 77-78.

"How to Cut Your Insurance Costs and Still Be Safe." *Better Homes & Gardens,* April 1977, pp. 86ff.

Taxes

INTERNAL
REVENUE
SERVICE
TAX ASSISTANCE→

U.S. TREASURY DEPARTMENT
INTERNAL REVENUE SERVICE

GENERAL TAX INFORMATION

PAYMENTS ON DELINQUENT ACCOUNT

FORMS DISTRIBUTION

DEPARTING ALIEN CLEARANCES

CASHIER

← ROOM 1002

HOURS
MON. FRI. 8:00 A.M. 4:30 P.M.

Our Tax System

■ Governments provide a multitude of goods and services. They generally provide national defenses, a court system, police, fire fighters, schools, libraries, and numerous other programs that help specific groups. To do·so, governments must be financed by the citizens they serve. You currently pay for government services with about 40 percent of every dollar you make. Much of that is returned to you in the form of transfers, such as Social Security, unemployment compensation, and the like, but at least 24 percent are direct expenditures by governments. Obviously, government is big business. The disposition of federal dollars is shown in Exhibit 12-1. Now let's look at various methods of taxation and some of the principles behind them.

THE WHYS AND WHERES OF TAXATION

Governments—federal, state, and local—have various methods of taxation at their disposal. The best known is the federal personal income tax, which generates fully 44 percent of all revenues collected by Uncle Sam. At the state and local levels, where personal income taxes are not as common, property taxes constitute the bulk of the taxes collected. In addition to these taxes are corporate income taxes, sales taxes, excise taxes, inheritance taxes, and gift taxes.

PRINCIPLES OF TAXATION

Naturally, everyone would prefer a tax that someone else pays. Since we all think that way, no tax could be invented that everyone would favor. Economists and philosophers have come up with alternative justifica-

299

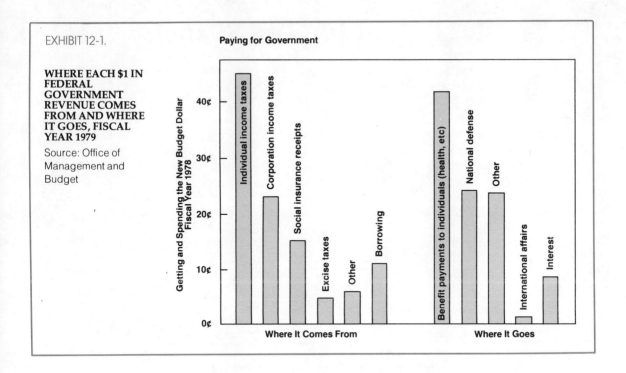

EXHIBIT 12-1.

Paying for Government

WHERE EACH $1 IN FEDERAL GOVERNMENT REVENUE COMES FROM AND WHERE IT GOES, FISCAL YEAR 1979

Source: Office of Management and Budget

Getting and Spending the New Budget Dollar Fiscal Year 1978

Where It Comes From — Individual income taxes, Corporation income taxes, Social insurance receipts, Excise taxes, Other, Borrowing

Where It Goes — Benefit payments to individuals (health, etc), National defense, Other, International affairs, Interest

tions for different ways of taxing. The three most-often discussed principles of taxation are: (a) benefit, (b) ability to pay, and (c) sacrifice.

The Benefit Principle

One widely accepted doctrine of taxation is the **benefit principle,** which says people should be taxed in proportion to the benefits they receive from government services. The more they benefit, the more they should pay; if they benefit little, they should pay little. An example of an application of the benefit principle is taxes that pay for police protection, roads, and bridges. In the first case, a person pays a higher property tax, part of which is used to finance the police department; but the person with more property to protect benefits more from police protection. Taxes on gasoline often are used to finance roads, so the more people use roads, the more taxes they pay. A tax on the specific use of a toll bridge is a direct example of the application of the benefit principle.

This principle of taxation has problems in application, however. First of all, how do we determine the value people place on the goods and services the government provides? Can we ask them? If people think that others will pay their way, they will claim that they receive no value from government services. For example, some people are unwilling to pay for national defense because they believe it is of no value to them. Hence, the **free rider problem;** many individuals would be free riders if they thought they could get away with it. If you think everyone else will pay for what you want, then you'll gladly let them do so. This problem is schematized in Exhibit 12-2. How much national defense will you benefit from if you agree to pay along with everyone else? $90,000,000,100. How much will there be if you don't pay but everyone else does? Ninety billion dollars. If you think everyone else will pay, wouldn't you be tempted to get a free ride?

One way out of this dilemma is to assume that the higher a person's income, the more services he or she receives, and, therefore, the more value he or she gets from goods and services provided by the government. If we assume that people receive increases in government services that are *proportional* to their incomes, then we can use this benefit doctrine to justify proportional taxation.

Proportional Taxation. With this system of taxation, taxpayers pay a fixed percentage of every dollar of income. When their income goes up, their taxes go up. If the proportional tax rate is 20 percent, you pay twenty cents in taxes from every dollar you earn. If you earn $1,000, you pay $200 in taxes; if you earn $1 million, you pay $200,000 in taxes.

Progressive Taxation. If a tax is progressive, the more you earn, the more you pay in taxes—as with the proportional system. But, in addition, the *percentage* taken out of each additional dollar earned goes up. In terms of marginal and average, we can describe progressiveness as a system by which the marginal tax rate goes up.[1] So does the average tax rate but not as much. In the example illustrated in Exhibit 12-3, the first $100 of income is taxed at 10 percent, the next $100 at 20 percent, and the third $100 at 30 percent. The average rate is always equal to or less than

---

[1] We discussed marginal tax rates in Chapter 7—the tax benefits of home ownership.

EXHIBIT 12-2.

SCOREBOARD FOR NATIONAL DEFENSE

The free rider is the one who will gladly let everyone else pay for him or her. If you don't pay your share of national defense but everyone else does pay, there will still be $90 billion available for the country's defense. Whether you pay or not seems to make little difference.

	If you pay	If you do not pay
If everyone else pays	$90,000,000,100	$90,000,000,000
If no one else pays	$100	$0

the marginal rate with a progressive taxation system. With a proportional system, the marginal tax rate is always the same, and it equals the average tax rate. Our federal personal income tax system is an example of a progressive system.

Can the benefit principle of taxation be used to justify progressiveness? Yes, it can. The only additional assumptions needed are: (a) the *value* people obtain from increased goods and services provided by the government rises faster than their income, and/or (b) the *amount* of government goods and services received increases faster than income. The benefit principle alone, without one of these two assumptions, cannot be used to justify progressive taxation.

Regressive Taxation. This is the opposite of progressive taxation. A regressive tax system takes away a smaller and smaller additional percentage as income rises. The marginal rate falls and is usually below the average rate. As an example, imagine that all revenues of the government were obtained from a 99 percent tax on food. Since we know that the percentage of income spent on food falls as the total income rises, we also know that the percentage of total income that would be paid in taxes under such a system also would fall as income rises.

Social Security taxes are a good example of a regressive system. The individual contributor pays 6.05 percent on income up to some maximum level; in 1978, for example, that maximum was $17,700. A person making twice that amount—$35,400—pays exactly the same Social Security taxes; thus, that person's average tax rate for Social Security falls to half of 6.05 percent, or only 3.025 percent. As income goes up after the cut-off point, the average Social Security tax falls.

The three systems—proportional, progressive, and regressive—are compared in Exhibit 12-4.

EXHIBIT 12-3.

A PROGRESSIVE TAX SYSTEM.

The percentage of tax taken out of each additional dollar earned goes up; that is, the marginal tax rate increases progressively.

INCOME	MARGINAL RATE	TAX	AVERAGE RATE
100	10%	$10	$\dfrac{\$10}{\$100} = 10\%$
200	20%	$10 + $20 = $30	$\dfrac{\$30}{\$200} = 15\%$
300	30%	$10 + $20 + $30 = $60	$\dfrac{\$60}{\$300} = 20\%$

EXHIBIT 12-4.

THREE DIFFERENT TYPES OF TAXING SYSTEMS.

In this exhibit, we can see that with the proportional tax system, no matter what an individual's income level, the marginal tax rate and the average tax rate remain the same. With a progressive system, as the individual's income goes up from, in our example, $10,000 to $20,000 to $30,000, a higher and higher marginal tax rate is applied. The average tax rate therefore increases from 10% to 20%. Finally, with a regressive system, a lower and lower marginal tax rate is applied, and the average tax rate is seen to decrease in our example from 30% down to 20%.

HYPOTHETICAL INDIVIDUALS:
Individual A, $10,000 of taxable income
Individual B, $20,000 of taxable income
Individual C, $30,000 of taxable income

A PROPORTIONAL SYSTEM:
The proportional tax rate is 20 percent applied to all taxable income.

	Taxes Paid	Average Tax Rate
Individual A	$.2 \times \$10,000 = \$2,000$	$\dfrac{\$2,000}{\$10,000} = 20\%$
Individual B	$.2 \times \$20,000 = \$4,000$	$\dfrac{\$4,000}{\$20,000} = 20\%$
Individual C	$.2 \times \$30,000 = \$6,000$	$\dfrac{\$6,000}{\$30,000} = 20\%$

A PROGRESSIVE SYSTEM
Marginal tax rates in brackets are as follows: 10 percent on first $10,000, 20 percent on second $10,000, 30 percent on third $10,000.

	Taxes Paid	Average Tax Rate
Individual A	$.10 \times \$10,000 = \$1,000$	$\dfrac{\$1,000}{\$10,000} = 10\%$
Individual B	$.10 \times \$10,000 = \$1,000$ $.20 \times \$10,000 = \$2,000$ TOTAL $3,000$	$\dfrac{\$3,000}{\$20,000} = 15\%$
Individual C	$.10 \times \$10,000 = \$1,000$ $.20 \times \$10,000 = \$2,000$ $.30 \times \$10,000 = \$3,000$ TOTAL $6,000$	$\dfrac{\$6,000}{\$30,000} = 20\%$

A REGRESSIVE SYSTEM:
Our example has the following marginal tax rates in designated tax brackets: 30% on the first $10,000, 20% on the second $10,000, and 10% on the third $10,000.

	Taxes Paid	Average Tax Rate
Individual A	$.30 \times \$10,000 = \$3,000$	$\dfrac{\$3,000}{\$10,000} = 30\%$
Individual B	$.30 \times \$10,000 = \$3,000$ $.20 \times \$10,000 = \$2,000$ TOTAL $5,000$	$\dfrac{\$5,000}{\$20,000} = 25\%$
Individual C	$.30 \times \$10,000 = \$3,000$ $.20 \times \$10,000 = \$2,000$ $.10 \times \$10,000 = \$1,000$ TOTAL $6,000$	$\dfrac{\$6,000}{\$30,000} = 20\%$

The Ability-to-Pay Doctrine

The second principle of taxation concerns people's ability to pay: those who are able to pay more taxes *should* pay more taxes. Obviously, people who make more money should generally be able to pay higher taxes. But do we make them pay taxes that parallel their income (a proportional system)? Do we make them pay taxes at a higher rate (a progressive system)? Or do we make them pay more taxes but at a rate that isn't in proportion to their income (a regressive system)? To answer these questions, we must decide whether their ability to pay rises faster than, in proportion to, or slower than their income. Whatever assumption we make determines whether we use a progressive, proportional, or regressive tax system. The ability-to-pay doctrine would suggest progressiveness—but only if we assume that ability to pay rises more rapidly than income.

The Sacrifice Doctrine

The third principle of taxation holds that the sacrifice people make to pay their taxes should be equitable. It is generally assumed that the sacrifices people make to pay taxes become smaller as their incomes become larger. A millionaire paying a $100 tax surely sacrifices less than a person who only earns $1,000 a year. The pleasure the millionaire gives up for that $100 is less than the pleasure the other person gives up for that amount. Again, we face the problem of determining how fast satisfaction from income rises as income itself rises, and this involves a value judgment. If the satisfaction from income rises at a rate that is more than, equal to, or less than in proportion to income, we will end up justifying a system of progressive, proportional, or regressive taxes, respectively.

STATE AND LOCAL TAXES

State and local governments raise revenues through a variety of taxes, the most well-known being sales and property taxes. In addition, there are at least forty states with some form of income tax.

Property Tax

In most areas, the property tax is used to pay for local school systems; libraries; specific city, county, and government activities, such as sewer treatment systems; and so on. There is usually a predetermined formula that allocates revenues obtained through the property tax to the various uses.

How the Property Tax Is Computed. Property taxes are computed on the basis of the assessed or appraised value of one's property (usually the individual's home) and the tax rate in effect. This tax rate is also called millage because property taxes usually are expressed in mills; a mill is one-tenth of one cent. Thus, if the property tax rate is ten mills, the taxpayer owes, for an assessed property value of $50,000, the following:

$$10 \text{ mills} \times 0.001 \times \$50,000 = \$500$$

Usually, assessed value is not equal to market, or resale, value. Thus, a house that could be sold for $50,000 may have, for the purposes of property taxes, an assessed value of only $30,000. Assessed value, which is often given as a percentage of market value, is usually legislated in each locality.

Criticisms of the Property Tax. The property tax may be one of the most disliked of all taxes. It is criticized because:

1   The ability-to-pay principle is not followed.
2   It appears inequitable because property of equal value is not on the tax rolls at equal assessments.
3   It is generally regressive because more valuable property seems to be assessed at a lower percentage of its market value than is less valuable property.
4   It is a costly tax to administer.

State and Local Income Taxes

Exhibit 12-5 shows that there is a great variation in the amount of income taxes collected by the various states and cities. States increasingly tie their income taxes to the federal government's income taxes. This saves the states money and makes it easier for the taxpayer because a simplified state income tax form, based on the federal form, can be completed.

Sales Taxes

The most ubiquitous state and local tax is the sales tax. Rates vary from 3 to 8 percent for the state's share; in some localities, cities tack on another 1, 2, or 3 percentage points. Thus, in New York City, for example, the combined state and local sales tax is a whopping 10 percent. It is not surprising that more and more New Yorkers are buying products outside the state or by mail order. Exhibit 12-6 shows figures for sales taxes in various parts of the country.

An important sales tax that generally is given special consideration is the one applied to the sale of tobacco and liquor. In fact, most of the variation in the price of liquor results from the differential rates of taxation by various states on this product.

THE FEDERAL TAX SYSTEM

We pay a large number of federal taxes to support our federal government. They include, but are not limited to, the following:

EXHIBIT 12-5. **AVERAGE STATE AND LOCAL TAXES PAID (RANKED STATE BY STATE)**

*The amount of income taxes collected by the state governments varies enormously. A number of states –such as
Connecticut, South Dakota, Tennessee, Texas, Utah, Washington, and Wyoming –have no income tax at all.
Those states collecting the most state income taxes are Alaska, California, Delaware, the District of Columbia,
Hawaii, Idaho, Minnesota, Massachusetts, Montana, New York, Oregon, Virginia, and Wisconsin.* Source:
Information Please Almanac, 1978, pp. 691-92.

ADJUSTED GROSS INCOME

	$10,000– 15,000	$15,000– 20,000	$20,000– 25,000	$25,000– 35,000	$35,000– 50,000	$50,000– 100,000
Alabama	$ 784 (40)	$1,082 (39)	$1,346 (40)	$1,723 (38)	$2,151 (41)	$3,392 (41)
Alaska	1,054 (20)	1,284 (27)	1,657 (24)	2,018 (27)	2,876 (25)	4,418 (25)
Arizona	952 (24)	1,240 (30)	1,541 (30)	1,876 (33)	3,140 (17)	4,258 (29)
Arkansas	778 (41)	999 (43)	1,408 (36)	1,740 (36)	3,044 (21)	4,770 (19)
California	1,179 (11)	1,559 (11)	1,926 (10)	2,533 (10)	4,075 (6)	7,340 (3)
Colorado	1,112 (16)	1,490 (13)	1,824 (14)	2,353 (15)	3,081 (19)	4,794 (16)
Connecticut	1,218 (9)	1,442 (16)	1,711 (20)	2,082 (24)	2,699 (31)	4,447 (23)
Delaware	930 (25)	1,425 (18)	1,796 (17)	2,422 (13)	3,708 (9)	7,178 (4)
Dist. of Columbia	1,069 (18)	1,431 (17)	1,901 (11)	2,646 (8)	3,651 (10)	6,131 (7)
Florida	649 (46)	811 (47)	929 (47)	1,244 (46)	1,879 (43)	2,600 (44)
Georgia	834 (38)	1,135 (35)	1,550 (29)	2,082 (25)	2,896 (23)	4,697 (21)
Hawaii	1,164 (13)	1,571 (10)	1,985 (7)	2,661 (6)	3,602 (11)	6,124 (8)
Idaho	895 (32)	1,308 (25)	1,645 (25)	2,309 (17)	3,356 (14)	4,879 (15)
Illinois	1,082 (17)	1,358 (20)	1,686 (22)	2,021 (26)	2,690 (32)	3,824 (37)
Indiana	862 (35)	1,103 (37)	1,358 (39)	1,652 (40)	2,160 (40)	3,204 (43)
Iowa	999 (22)	1,335 (22)	1,715 (19)	2,185 (22)	2,892 (24)	4,333 (26)
Kansas	914 (28)	1,184 (31)	1,452 (34)	1,883 (32)	2,312 (38)	3,921 (34)
Kentucky	1,125 (15)	1,452 (15)	1,797 (16)	2,216 (19)	2,760 (29)	4,266 (28)
Louisiana	505 (51)	664 (51)	853 (50)	1,105 (49)	1,429 (47)	2,458 (47)
Maine	992 (23)	1,251 (29)	1,558 (28)	1,948 (29)	2,744 (30)	4,302 (27)
Maryland	1,305 (5)	1,739 (6)	2,165 (5)	2,885 (5)	4,025 (7)	5,931 (10)
Massachusetts	1,550 (1)	1,995 (2)	2,334 (3)	3,160 (3)	4,205 (5)	6,522 (6)
Michigan	1,244 (7)	1,631 (8)	1,988 (6)	2,546 (9)	3,357 (13)	4,950 (14)
Minnesota	1,414 (3)	1,865 (4)	2,304 (4)	3,054 (4)	4,622 (3)	7,116 (5)
Mississippi	743 (42)	1,068 (41)	1,369 (37)	1,717 (39)	2,650 (33)	3,626 (39)
Missouri	899 (30)	1,263 (28)	1,485 (32)	1,967 (28)	2,517 (36)	3,683 (38)
Montana	883 (33)	1,333 (23)	1,583 (27)	2,127 (23)	2,812 (28)	4,734 (20)
Nebraska	835 (37)	1,121 (36)	1,457 (33)	1,623 (42)	2,046 (42)	3,826 (36)
Nevada	691 (44)	879 (46)	965 (46)	1,236 (47)	1,425 (48)	2,198 (48)
New Hampshire	1,062 (19)	1,374 (19)	1,599 (26)	1,643 (41)	2,301 (39)	3,434 (40)
New Jersey	1,245 (6)	1,636 (7)	1,895 (12)	2,408 (14)	3,441 (12)	4,586 (22)
New Mexico	721 (43)	1,038 (42)	1,304 (42)	1,773 (35)	2,478 (37)	4,181 (30)
New York	1,474 (2)	2,032 (1)	2,573 (1)	3,505 (1)	5,512 (1)	9,867 (1)
North Carolina	928 (26)	1,287 (26)	1,673 (23)	2,351 (16)	3,233 (15)	5,244 (13)
North Dakota	835 (36)	1,179 (32)	1,522 (31)	1,940 (30)	2,951 (22)	4,418 (24)
Ohio	820 (39)	1,093 (38)	1,362 (38)	1,815 (34)	2,562 (35)	4,157 (31)
Oklahoma	658 (45)	908 (45)	1,210 (44)	1,732 (37)	2,620 (34)	3,910 (35)

EXHIBIT 12-5 **CONTINUED**

ADJUSTED GROSS INCOME

	$10,000- 15,000	$15,000- 20,000	$20,000- 25,000	$25,000- 35,000	$35,000- 50,000	$50,000- 100,000
Oregon	1,202 (10)	1,546 (12)	1,977 (8)	2,653 (7)	4,283 (4)	5,923 (11)
Pennsylvania	1,160 (14)	1,479 (14)	1,805 (15)	2,193 (21)	2,824 (27)	4,002 (33)
Rhode Island	1,221 (8)	1,624 (9)	1,861 (13)	2,479 (12)	3,155 (16)	5,681 (12)
South Carolina	869 (34)	1,165 (33)	1,426 (35)	1,927 (31)	3,136 (18)	4,773 (18)
South Dakota	911 (29)	1,068 (40)	1,268 (43)	1,423 (44)	1,751 (46)	2,472 (46)
Tennessee	576 (49)	802 (48)	906 (49)	1,059 (50)	1,345 (50)	2,083 (49)
Texas	606 (48)	782 (49)	918 (48)	1,117 (48)	1,410 (49)	1,807 (50)
Utah	1,003 (21)	1,309 (24)	1,699 (21)	2,197 (20)	2,828 (26)	4,075 (32)
Vermont	1,164 (12)	1,740 (5)	1,939 (9)	2,482 (11)	3,856 (8)	5,938 (9)
Virginia	926 (27)	1,351 (21)	1,729 (18)	2,230 (18)	3,066 (20)	4,782 (17)
Washington	895 (31)	1,141 (34)	1,320 (41)	1,462 (43)	1,802 (45)	2,517 (45)
West Virginia	641 (47)	965 (44)	1,188 (45)	1,419 (45)	1,867 (44)	3,286 (42)
Wisconsin	1,353 (4)	1,888 (3)	2,388 (2)	3,185 (2)	4,717 (2)	7,849 (2)
Wyoming	545 (50)	708 (50)	779 (51)	958 (51)	1,066 (51)	1,398 (51)
U.S. AVERAGE	**$1,069**	**$1,446**	**$1,795**	**$2,342**	**$3,340**	**$5,271**

Source: *Internal Revenue Service*

EXHIBIT 12-6.

SALES TAX RATES IN VARIOUS STATES —AUGUST 1977

STATE	% RATE	STATE	% RATE	STATE	% RATE
Alabama	4	Kentucky	5	Ohio	4
Arizona	4	Louisiana	3	Oklahoma	2
Arkansas	3	Maine	5	Pennsylvania	6
California	4.75	Maryland	5	Rhode Island	6
Colorado	3	Massachusetts	5	South Carolina	4
Connecticut	7	Michigan	4	South Dakota	4
D.C.	5	Minnesota	4	Tennessee	4.5
Florida	4	Mississippi	5	Texas	4
Georgia	4.5	Missouri	3.125	Utah	4
Hawaii	4	Nebraska	3	Vermont	3
Idaho	3	Nevada	3	Virginia	4
Illinois	4	New Jersey	5	Washington	4.6
Indiana	4	New Mexico	4	West Virginia	3
Iowa	3	New York	4	Wisconsin	4
Kansas	3	North Carolina	3	Wyoming	3
		North Dakota	3		

Source: *Information Please Almanac, 1978.*

NOTE: Local and county taxes, if any, are additional. Alaska, Delaware, Montana, New Hampshire and Oregon have no statewide sales and use taxes.

1   Personal income taxes
2   Corporate income taxes
3   Social Security taxes
4   Excise taxes
5   Estate and gift taxes.

In the remainder of this chapter, we will look at corporate and excise taxes and concentrate on the personal federal income tax. Social Security taxes are discussed in Chapter 19 and estate and gift taxes are discussed in Chapter 20.

The Corporate Income Tax

Corporate income taxes account for more than 16 percent of all federal taxes collected. Corporations are generally taxed on the difference between their total revenues, or receipts, and expenses. In 1901, the corporate tax rate amounted to a mere 1 percent of corporate profits, with the first $5,000 a year being exempted. By 1932, this exemption had disappeared, and the rate had jumped to 13.755 percent. The Revenue Act of 1978 made corporate taxes be as follows: 17% on up to $25,000; 20% on $25,000 to $50,000; 30% on $50,000 to $75,000; 40% on $75,000 to $100,000; and 46% on any corporate profits over $100,000.

Excise Taxes

The excise tax is somewhat similar to a sales tax. The federal government places excise taxes on a large number of services and goods, such as liquor, gasoline, tobacco, automobiles, airline tickets, long distance telephone calls, and jewelry. A sales tax generally is applied to all purchases of goods, whereas an excise tax applies only to specifically named items, such as those just mentioned. Federal excise taxes raise less than seven cents out of every dollar of federal government revenues.

THE FEDERAL PERSONAL INCOME TAX

The federal personal income tax is the most important of all federal taxes. Exhibit 12-7 shows that it accounts for more than 45 percent of all federal revenues. At the beginning of the 1920s, a little more than 20 percent of federal revenues were accounted for by individual income taxes.

Exhibit 12-8 shows the progressive nature of our federal personal income tax system; the different tax brackets, with their respective marginal and average tax rates, are indicated. A **tax bracket** is the range of income that is subject to a specific percentage tax rate. For example, in Exhibit 12-8 the tax bracket for taxable income between $5,000 and $10,000 is subjected to a 17 percent marginal tax rate on any dollars earned between $5,000 and $10,000 per year.

How Taxes Are Collected

There are basically two ways in which the federal government collects personal income taxes: withholding and estimated tax payments.

Withholding. Since January 1, 1943, all employers have been required to withhold a certain portion of virtually all employees' wages for federal income tax purposes. Such a withholding scheme assures the federal government that taxes will be paid. Presumably, it also simplifies things for the taxpayer, who doesn't have to set aside the required money owed at the end of the year to the federal government. (The taxpayer does, however, give up the interest he or she could have earned on these tax payment dollars.)

Each person starting to work files a Withholding Tax Exemption Certificate (W-4), which is shown in Exhibit 12-9. It contains a statement about the number of exemptions a person is allowed. For example, if you are a single person working for someone else, the number of exemptions you normally would be entitled to is one—for yourself. You can, under certain circumstances, take more exemptions. The more exemptions you claim on your W-4 form, the less your employer is required to withhold from your weekly or monthly pay check.

At the end of each year, employers are required to give employees copies of what is called a W-2 form, which is also shown in Exhibit 12-9. This shows the amount of income earned by the employee, Social Security contributions, and the amount of taxes withheld by the employer for the year.

EXHIBIT 12-7.

PERCENTAGE OF FEDERAL TAXES ACCOUNTED FOR BY PERSONAL INCOME TAXES

During the Depression, individual income taxes accounted for less than 20 percent of federal revenues. Now, however, individual income taxes account for almost 45 percent of federal revenues. The importance of the personal income tax has increased. Source: U.S. Department of Treasury.

FISCAL YEAR	PERCENT OF FEDERAL REVENUES ACCOUNTED FOR BY PERSONAL INCOME TAXES
1927	25.7%
1932	19.0
1936	16.7
1940	15.5
1944	39.5
1950	40.7
1955	45.1
1960	45.6
1965	43.8
1969	44.9
1971	43.0
1974	42.3
1976	44.6
1977	45.1

EXHIBIT 12-8.

FEDERAL PERSONAL INCOME TAX FOR A CHILDLESS COUPLE, 1978

Here we show the different income brackets and the marginal tax rates along with the average tax rates. As you can see, the marginal tax rates go up to a maximum of 70 percent. However, if income qualifies as being "earned," the maximum is 50 percent. All wages are considered earned income, but interest on bonds or dividends from stocks is not.

NET INCOME BEFORE EXEMPTIONS (BUT AFTER DEDUCTIONS)		PERSONAL INCOME TAX	AVERAGE TAX RATE, PERCENT	MARGINAL TAX RATE, PERCENT
Below $	1,500	$ 0	0	0
	2,000	70	3.5	14
	3,000	215	7.2	15
	4,000	370	9.2	16
	5,000	535	10.7	17
	10,000	1,490	14.9	22
	20,000	3,960	19.8	28
	50,000	16,310	32.6	50
	100,000	44,280	44.3	60
	200,000	109,945	55.0	69
	400,000	249,930	62.5	70
	1,000,000	669,930	67.0	70
	10,000,000	6,969,930	69.7	70

Employers not only take out money for federal income taxes; they also take out Social Security taxes, or FICA (for Federal Insurance Contributions Act). The employer assesses the Social Security tax on all income up to some cut-off point, which in 1979 was $22,900. After that, the employee no longer has to pay Social Security taxes. Each time an individual goes to work for a new employer during any one year, that new employer will assess Social Security taxes up to the maximum income. At the end of the year, however, any overpayment on Social Security is either refunded or applied to federal income taxes owed. Social Security is treated in detail in Chapter 19.

Making Estimated Tax Payments. The federal government also collects personal income taxes by having individuals make estimated tax payments. Whenever an individual believes that he or she will not have enough withholding taken out of his or her salary, an estimated tax payment must be made on a quarterly basis. This might occur, for example, if you had a regular job but also were receiving large payments from stocks left you by a deceased relative. The income from those stocks in the form of dividends is taxable; but since it isn't salary, nothing is withheld from that money.

Under such situations, you would fill out a form 1040ES (shown in Exhibit 12-9) on or before April 15th of each year. On this form, you would indicate your expected income and your expected tax for that year. Whenever your expected taxes due are forty dollars more than

EXHIBIT 12-9.

Form **W-4**
(Rev. May 1977)
Department of the Treasury
Internal Revenue Service

Employee's Withholding Allowance Certificate
(Use for Wages Paid After May 31, 1977)
This certificate is for income tax withholding purposes only. It will remain in effect until you change it. If you claim exemption from withholding, you will have to file a new certificate on or before April 30 of next year.

Type or print your full name		Your social security number

Home address (number and street or rural route)	Marital Status	☐ Single ☐ Married ☐ Married, but withhold at higher Single rate **Note:** *If married, but legally separated, or spouse is a nonresident alien, check the single block.*
City or town, State, and ZIP code		

1 Total number of allowances you are claiming . . . .
2 Additional amount, if any, you want deducted from each pay (if your employer agrees) . . . . $
3 I claim exemption from withholding (see instructions). Enter "Exempt" . . . .

Under the penalties of perjury, I certify that the number of withholding exemptions and allowances claimed on this certificate does not exceed the number to which I am entitled. If claiming exemption from withholding, I certify that I incurred no liability for Federal income tax for last year and that I anticipate that I will incur no liability for Federal income tax for this year.

Signature ▶ .... Date ▶ ...., 19 ....

-------------------------------- Detach along this line --------------------------------

▲ *Give the top part of this form to your employer; keep the lower part for your records and information* ▲

Instructions

The explanatory material below will help you determine your correct number of withholding allowances, and will assist you in completing the Form W-4 at the top of this page.

Avoid Overwithholding or Underwithholding

By claiming the number of withholding allowances you are entitled to, you can fit the amount of tax withheld from your wages to your tax liability. In addition to the allowances for personal exemptions to be claimed in item (a), be sure to claim any additional allowances you are entitled to in item (b), "Special withholding allowance," and item (c), "Allowance(s) for credit(s) and/or deduction(s)." While you may claim these allowances on Form W-4 for withholding purposes, you may not claim them under "Exemptions" on

ing additional withholding allowances based on itemized deductions, check the worksheet on the back to see that you are claiming the proper number of allowances.

How Many Withholding Allowances May You Claim?

Use the schedule below to determine the number of allowances you may claim for tax withholding purposes. In determining the number, keep in mind these points: if you are single and hold more than one job, you may not claim the same allowances with more than one employer at the same time; or, if you are married and both you and your spouse are employed, you may not both claim the same allowances with your employers at the same time. A nonresident alien, other than a resident of Canada, Mexico, or Puerto Rico, may claim only one personal allowance.

will be withheld if you are covered by the Federal Insurance Contributions Act.

You must revoke this exemption (1) within 10 days from the time you anticipate you will incur income tax liability for the year or (2) on or before December 1 if you anticipate you will incur Federal income tax liability for the next year. If you want to stop or are required to revoke this exemption, you must file a new Form W-4 with your employer showing the number of withholding allowances you are entitled to claim. This certificate for exemption from withholding will expire on April 30 of next year unless a new Form W-4 is filed before that date.

The Following Information is Provided in Accordance with the Privacy Act of 1974

The Internal Revenue Code requires

			Wage and Tax Statement 19		
	For Official Use Only		▷ Type or print EMPLOYER'S name, address, ZIP code and Federal identifying number.		Copy A For Internal Revenue Service Center

	Employee's social security number	1 Federal income tax withheld	2 Wages, tips, and other compensation	3 FICA employee tax withheld	4 Total FICA wages
21 ☐					
Name ▶	Type or print Employee's name, address, and ZIP code below. (Name must aline with arrow)		5 Was employee covered by a qualified pension plan, etc.?	6 *	7 *

* See instructions on back of Copy D.

Form **W-2**   See instructions on Form W-3 and back of Copy D   Department of the Treasury—Internal Revenue Service

EXHIBIT 12-9 **CONTINUED**

| Form **1040-ES** Department of the Treasury Internal Revenue Service | **Estimated Tax Declaration–Voucher for Individuals—19** (To be used for making declaration and payment) | **Voucher 1** (Calendar Year—Due April 17, 19   ) |

*A. Estimated tax for the year ending _____ (month and year)

$ _____

B. Overpayment from last year credited to estimated tax for this year

$ _____

1 Amount of this installment . . . ▶ $ _____
2 Amount of overpayment credit from last year (all or part) applied to this installment (see Instruction 9) . . ▶
3 Amount of this installment payment (subtract line 2 from line 1) . . . . ▶ $ _____

File this original declaration–voucher even if line 3 is zero.

Sign here ▶

Your Signature

Spouse's signature (if joint declaration)

If fiscal year taxpayer, see Instruction 11.

* Do not file this declaration–voucher if your total estimated tax for the year is less than $100.00.

Return this voucher with check or money order payable to the Internal Revenue Service. For where to file your declaration–voucher, see Instruction 4.

Please type or print

Your social security number | Spouse's number, if joint declaration

First name and middle initial (of both spouses if joint declaration) | Last name

Address (Number and street)

City, State, and ZIP code

---

your expected taxes paid over the year, you must fill out this form. Additionally, you must fill out this form if your expected non-wage income *not* subject to withholding tax is more than $500. There are, in addition, other rules governing the completion of the 1040ES. After you make your declaration, you must make quarterly tax payments on April 15, June 15, September 15, and January 15. At the end of the year, the sum of your quarterly payments of estimated taxes owed, plus whatever has been withheld (minus any overpayment of Social Security) must be within 20 percent of your actual taxes owed. Otherwise, a penalty is assessed for underpayment—except under certain circumstances. For example, there is no penalty, even if you underpay by more than 20 percent, if the total taxes paid during the year were at least equal to the total taxes paid the previous year. There are other loopholes that can save you from making an underpayment penalty.

What Is Considered Income?

Since the federal personal income tax is applied to income, taxable income must be defined. According to the Internal Revenue Service, taxable income is virtually all income that is not legally exempted from taxation. The major categories of such income are:

1 Wages, salaries, bonuses, commissions, tips, and other compensations
2 Interest
3 Dividends (in excess of $100 per taxpayer)
4 Rents and royalties
5 Profits from a business or profession

6   Income from partnerships and trust funds
7   Gambling winnings
8   Alimony
9   Profits realized from the sale of assets, such as stocks and bonds.

There are also types of income that are not considered such by the IRS. These income categories, most of which relate to the proceeds from insurance policies, include:

1   Accident and health insurance proceeds (under $5200 annually)
2   Death payments to survivors of armed forces personnel who died during active duty
3   Workers' compensation payments
4   Disability pension payments
5   Social Security benefits and payments
6   Veterans' disability compensation benefits
7   Life insurance proceeds
8   G.I. education benefits.

There is an even longer list of special categories, which include such things as Peace Corps travel and living allowances, Pulitzer Prize money, and an Armed Forces trailer-moving allowance. For a complete list, you can refer to Publication #17, *Your Federal Income Tax—For Individuals,* which is available free from any IRS office in your area.

Capital Gains

A **capital gain** is the difference between the buying and selling price of a capital asset, such as a stock, a bond, jewelry, and furs. If you buy a share of Silver Syndicate Mining stock for thirteen dollars and are fortunate enough to sell it for sixty-seven dollars, the capital gain is fifty-four dollars. The capital gain is computed after brokerage fees, commissions, and incidental transaction costs are deducted from your so-called profit.

A **capital loss** is the opposite of a capital gain. Long-term capital gains and losses occur if the asset was held for at least one year. Any asset held for less than one year and sold at a loss or a gain involves a short-term capital loss or gain. There is an advantageous tax rate applied to long-term capital gains. Basically, if you hold an asset for one year or more and make a capital gain, your tax rate is only 0.4 of your regular marginal tax rate. Thus, you can't pay more than 20% taxes on long-term capital gains (since passage of the 1978 Revenue Act).[2]

Consider an example. You bought ten shares of XYZ stock at $100 per share; thus, you paid $1,000. Two years later, you sold them and received (after paying a selling commission) $3,000. Your long-term capital gain, therefore, is $2,000. Assume that you are in the 50 percent

---

[2]Note, though, that so-called minimum taxes used to raise capital gains rates to higher than the specified rates. There was also an alternative tax for some individuals that had a 25 percent maximum on gains up to $50,000.

tax bracket. The capital gain taxes owed would be 0.4 of 50 percent, or 20 percent, multiplied by $2,000. Uncle Sam would collect $400 from your $2,000 gain.

Gross and Adjusted Gross Income

The IRS uses what it calls gross and adjusted gross income on most of the standard forms that taxpayers complete.

Gross Income. Gross income is defined as all gains, profits, and income derived from wages; salaries; personal service compensation; and professional, vocational, business, commerce, trade, or sales work dealing in personal services or property. It also includes dividends, rent, interest, and so on. In effect, it is all income not explicitly exempted by the law.

Adjusted Gross Income. Adjusted gross income is defined as gross income minus legitimate business expenses and losses. To derive adjusted gross income, you can deduct from gross income the following:

1. Necessary expenses for obtaining rent and royalty income
2. Business expenses except common ones, such as the cost of driving to and from work
3. Moving expenses, if your new job site is at least thirty-five miles further from your old residence than the former job site (this is subject to a maximum)
4. Alimony paid
5. Individual Retirement Account payments
6. Employees' reimbursed expenses
7. Expenses incurred for travel, room, and board while away from home in connection with employment or owning a business
8. Self-employed retirement plan payments
9. Long-term capital gain deduction
10. Interest forfeited on premature withdrawals from time savings accounts.

For most people, gross income and adjusted gross income are the same because their income consists entirely of wages and salaries.

Deductions

Deductions are expenses that may be subtracted from one's gross income or adjusted gross income. Only those items that specifically are provided in tax laws or regulations can be used as deductions. The list used to derive adjusted gross income represents a set of deductions. In addition to those listed are other broad categories, such as interest expenses, state and local taxes, contributions, property and casualty losses, a certain amount of medical and dental expenses, and so on. In the following Practical Application, we offer a more complete list of those deductions and describe how they help reduce your taxes.

Zero bracket amount. Rather than itemizing deductions, it is possible to take what is called the zero bracket amount (formerly called the standard deduction). The zero bracket amount is a type of blanket deduction and is so named because a zero tax rate is applied to this amount of the taxpayer's income. Single people and heads of households get a $2,300 zero bracket amount; married people filing joint returns get $3,400. Finally, married people filing separate returns get a zero bracket amount of $1,700.

You have the choice of either itemizing your deductions or using the zero bracket amount. Your decision is not, however, irrevocable. If, after filing your income taxes, you find that you made the wrong choice, you may recompute your taxes owed and claim a refund for the difference.

SOME RELATED ASPECTS OF OUR FEDERAL TAX SYSTEM

To understand completely our federal tax system, you would have to read many thousands of pages of text. In this section, we will cover only a few more topics—income splitting, income averaging, and the minimum tax.

Income Splitting

Income splitting is the process by which income can be shifted from an individual in a high marginal tax bracket to one in a lower tax bracket. When one spouse earns considerably more than the other, a married couple can split its income by filing a joint return.

There are other ways to split income. One can, for example, make a gift to a child of an income-producing asset, such as a savings certificate. The income from the savings certificate is taxable to the child who, in all likelihood, will earn so little income that no taxes will be owed. That income can be amassed over a period of years in order to provide a college education for the child.

Income Averaging

Look back at Exhibit 12-8. Consider two individuals who over a two-year period both made a total of $20,000. Individual #1, however, made it at the rate of $10,000 a year, whereas individual #2 earned nothing the first year and $20,000 the second year. As the exhibit indicates, individual #1 would pay an average tax rate of almost 15 percent; individual #2, however, would pay an average tax rate of almost 20 percent. Why? Because of the progressive nature of our federal personal income tax system. The second individual would be subjected to a maximum 28 percent marginal tax rate, whereas the first individual would be subjected to only 22 percent marginal rates.

In order to avoid this inequity and help taxpayers reduce their tax burden, the IRS allows income averaging. There are certain rules that must be followed, however, in order to be eligible for it. To determine if you are:

1   Add up your taxable incomes for the previous four years (excluding the present year).
2   Multiply that amount by .3.
3   Add $3,000.
4   If this year's taxable income is larger than the final amount, you are eligible for income averaging. Exhibit 12-10 shows how this saves tax dollars.

An obvious example of a person who would want to use income averaging is someone who had worked for several years and then decided to return to school full-time. Suppose that you are this person and that you have a certain amount of part-time income even while you are a full-time student. Your yearly income, though, will be significantly less than it was in the prior taxable years. Thus, you are a prime candidate for income averaging.

The Minimum Tax

The Tax Reform Acts of 1969 and 1976 attempted to shore up what were considered excessive tax revenue losses due to preferential income—that is, income that was either nontaxable or taxed at lower rates. Capital gains, remember, generally are taxed at a lower rate than other income. But now it is virtually impossible for individuals to escape federal taxation completely. If all their income is preferential income from, say, tax-exempt sources, they still will have to pay a minimum tax.

Basically, a minimum income tax is 15 percent. It is levied on the total value of tax preference income when it exceeds $10,000 (or one-half of regular income taxes due for that year, whichever is greater).

CAN WE IMPROVE OUR TAX SYSTEM?

Anyone who has tried to fill out a federal income tax form knows that our tax system is complicated. When one president's life-long valet asked him to help out with his taxes, the president could not. It was too complicated to figure out. It is estimated that, in terms of time, the cost of filling out forms is somewhere between $3 and $6 billion a year! Enormous sums are also spent to have accountants and lawyers complete the forms. One reason our tax system is complicated and expensive is that special-interest groups seek benefits for themselves and further entangle our tax laws.

One reason special-interest groups attempt to get special legislation to reduce their tax burden is the high progressive income tax rates. The higher the rate you pay, the greater the incentive you have to find a loophole or, as a member of a group of like-minded people, to influence tax legislation to benefit your group. If all taxes were only 2 percent, nobody would try very hard to find loopholes. But if you're in the 70 percent tax bracket, it is worthwhile to find one: every dollar of income declared nontaxable nets you seventy cents in cash, because that's the tax you don't have to pay.

EXHIBIT 12-10

SCHEDULE G
(Form 1040)
Department of the Treasury
Internal Revenue Service

Income Averaging
▶ See Instructions on pages 3 and 4.
▶ Attach to Form 1040.

19

Name(s) as shown on Form 1040 | Your social security number

Base Period Income and Adjustments

	(a) 1st preceding base period year 19	(b) 2d preceding base period year 19	(c) 3rd preceding base period year 19	(d) 4th preceding base period year 19
1 Taxable income				
2 Income earned outside of the United States or within U.S. possessions and excluded under sections 911 and 931				
3 If you checked, on {2 or 5 enter $3,200} in your 1977 Form {1 or 4 enter $2,200} each 1040, box {3 enter $1,600} column .				
4 Base period income (add lines 1, 2 and 3). If less than zero, enter zero				

Computation of Averageable Income

5 Taxable income for _____ from Schedule TC (Form 1040), Part I, line 3 . . . **5**

6 Certain amounts received by owner-employees subject to a penalty under section 72(m)(5) **6**

7 Subtract line 6 from line 5 . . . . **7**

8 Excess community income **8**

9 Adjusted taxable income (subtract line 8 from line 7). If less than zero, enter zero **9**

10 30% of the sum of line 4, columns (a) through (d) **10**

11 Averageable income (subtract line 10 from line 9) **11**

Complete the remaining parts of this form only if line 11 is more than $3,000. If $3,000 or less, you do not qualify for income averaging. Do not fill in rest of form.   **G**

Computation of Tax

12 Amount from line 10 . . . . **12**

13 20% of line 11 . . . . **13**

14 Total (add lines 12 and 13) **14**

15 Excess community income from line 8 . . . . **15**

16 Total (add lines 14 and 15) **16**

17 Tax on amount on line 16 . . . . **17**

18 Tax on amount on line 14 . . . . **18**

19 Tax on amount on line 12 . . . . **19**

20 Subtract line 19 from line 18 . . . . **20**

21 Multiply the amount on line 20 by 4 . . . . **21**

Note: *If no entry was made on line 6 above, skip lines 22 through 24 and go to line 25.*

22 Tax on amount on line 5 . . . . **22**

23 Tax on amount on line 7 . . . . **23**

24 Subtract line 23 from line 22 . . . . **24**

25 Tax (add lines 17, 21, and 24). Enter here and on Schedule TC (Form 1040), Part I, line 4. Also check Schedule G box on Schedule TC (Form 1040), Part I, line 4 . . . . **25**

There are some obvious tax reforms that could benefit the majority of Americans. By tax reform, we certainly don't mean the kind that Congress passes every few years; the Tax Reform Acts of 1969 and 1976 benefited lawyers and accountants, but just about everyone else lost out. The only meaningful way to talk about tax reform may be to disregard special-interest groups and do the following:

1 Eliminate all deductions except an absolute minimum number of *bona fide* business expenses.
2 Increase the exemption to, say, the poverty line of income; thus, the first $4,000 or $5,000 of income is not taxed at all.
3 Establish a uniform 15 to 20 percent straight (proportional) tax rate on all income, no matter who earns it or how.[3]

This approach is drastically different from what we have now. Notice, however, that the tax rate of 15 to 20 percent is lower than the actual taxes currently paid as a percentage of total income. Obviously, if you eliminate the high, complicated progressive tax system, you eliminate people's wasted efforts to avoid taxes. There would be a proportionately higher degree of work effort and higher national income on which to base our taxes. We actually could lower the overall tax rate and still take in as much revenue as we do now.

Oddly enough, many rich people would oppose lowering the tax rates; they know that, because of loopholes, they pay very few taxes anyway. Some pay much less than 15 or 20 percent of their total income.

If the existing tax system were simplified, the incentive for people to cheat would be reduced and the amount of work many of us want to do would increase because our tax rates would be lower. Since we don't have a progressive tax system anyway, it is difficult to argue against a nonprogressive (proportional) tax system.

Unfortunately, pure tax reform is a long way off. Until it is realized, you should know the ins and outs of tax reporting and tax payments. Incidentally, there's nothing wrong with taking advantage of every single legal way to avoid and reduce the taxes you owe your government. You have a right to spend what is legally yours. Income legally belongs to the individual, not the government.

---

[3]A proportional tax coupled with an exemption is called a *degressive system*.

HOW TO REDUCE YOUR TAX BURDEN

Supreme Court Judge Learned Hand once wrote, "Anyone may so arrange his affairs that his taxes shall be as low as possible; he is not bound to choose that pattern which will best pay the Treasury; there is not even a patriotic duty to increase one's taxes." In other words, you have every right to minimize the taxes you pay.

In this Practical Applications section, it won't be possible to discuss all the ways you can reduce your tax burden. The following books provide in-depth explanations of our tax system: Laser's *Tax Guide,* H&R Block's *Income Tax Workbook,* The Research Institute of America's *Individual Tax Return Guide,* the CCH *Master Tax Guide*—all published yearly. You can also get *Your Federal Income Tax* free from the IRS office in your area. Numerous other IRS booklets discuss different aspects of taxation. Furthermore, sophisticated tax lawyers and certified public accountants can, for a fee, elaborate on the subject.

THE DO'S AND DON'TS OF HIRING TAX HELP

Hundreds of thousands of individuals are in the business of preparing tax forms. Many of them work out of heavily advertised national franchises. As tax laws become more complicated, the tax preparation business is bound to grow. To avoid being deceived by professional tax preparers, follow these rules:

1. Be wary of tax preparers who promise to give you a check for your refund immediately. The preparer is probably offering you a loan on which you will pay interest.

2. Never sign a blank return.

3. Never sign a return prepared in pencil; it can be changed later.

4. Never allow your refund check to be mailed to the preparer.

5. Be wary of tax advisors who "guarantee" refunds, who want a percentage of the refund, or who supposedly know "all" the angles.

6. Avoid a tax preparer who advises you to overstate deductions, omit income, or claim fictitious dependents.

7. Make sure that the tax preparer signs the return he or she prepares and furnishes his or her address and tax identification number. (You, however, are legally responsible for virtually all errors on your return, no matter who fills it out, unless there is a blatant case of fraud brought against the tax preparer.)

8. Find out the educational background and experience of the preparer. Does the person have a degree in accounting?

9. Use only a preparer who has a permanent address so you can find that person easily if problems develop later.

10. Be wary of preparers who claim they will make good any amounts due because of a mistake on your return. Usually the preparer will pay only the penalty charges; you must pay any additional tax money due.

USING THE ZERO BRACKET AMOUNT

If you have no expenses or very few that qualify as legitimate deductions, you may wish to take advantage of the zero bracket amount (ZBA). If you use the ZBA, there is a flat $3,400 deduction for joint returns and a flat $2,300 deduction for single returns. Prior to 1977, the ZBA was called the standard deduction and was equal to 16 percent of adjusted gross income up to a maximum of $2,800 for a joint return and $2,400 for a single return.

If you determine that you are better off itemizing your deductions, then you must keep accurate records.

RECORD KEEPING

If you opt not to use the ZBA, you must keep acceptable records to support your deductions. If the IRS conducts a tax audit and you cannot adequately substantiate the deductions you have taken on your tax returns, they probably will be disallowed. And you may have to pay a penalty or, at a bare minimum, interest on the overdue taxes. You must keep your records for at least three years from the date your tax was paid or at least three years after the date your return was filed, whichever occurred later. Actually, it is advisable to keep them even longer, although they cannot be subpoenaed legally by the IRS after three years.

What Kinds of Records

When in doubt, keep a record. You should have records for all medical expenses, all business expenses, all taxes paid—for everything, that is, that could possibly reduce your effective tax burden. The best way to keep financial records is to write checks. If you do any amount of business for which the expenses are tax deductible, you also should keep a complete record of those expenses. If you move because of a change of job, you are allowed to deduct moving expenses, so keep records for all of those. When you sell your house or other major items, keep records of such transactions.

It's best to keep records on a regular basis. When you go through your check stubs each month to balance your statement, sort the checks and file them in envelopes marked "business expenses," "telephone," "medical expenses," and so on. If you can prove that you use part of your home as a place of business, you must keep records on all the expenses on your house: rental or mortgage payments, heating bills, light bills, telephone bills, electricity

bills, and others. Again, the best way to record these expenses is to pay for everything by check. The next best way is to keep a receipt for everything you pay for with cash. Charge cards also are helpful, because you get a receipt each time a charge is made on your card. If it is a receipt for a tax deductible item, you should keep it with your records.

Other Pointers on Record Keeping

Here are some other suggestions for record keeping:

1. Always identify your sources and amounts of income.

2. Keep adequate records in order to take advantage of capital gains and losses provisions. This applies to the purchase and sale of any assets, such as stocks and bonds.

3. Clarify for yourself, in writing, all the items reported on an income tax return, so you will be prepared for a possible audit.

4. Keep records indefinitely on the purchase, sale, and expenses of remodeling a home. If you sell a house and don't buy a new one, you may have to pay capital gains taxes. To reduce those capital gains taxes, you must be able to prove that you spent money remodeling or adding to your house.

5. Retain copies of your filed tax returns. They can help you prepare future returns, particularly if you engage in income averaging to reduce your taxes.

FIGURING OUT YOUR DEDUCTIONS

Remember, your goal is to reduce your taxable income by as much as possible using every legal device available. In the following chapter and Practical Applications section, we talk about legal tax shelters and loopholes. Here we will discuss legitimate

EXHIBIT 12-11.

**POSSIBLE INCOME
DEDUCTIONS THAT
CAN LOWER YOUR
TAX LIABILITY**

Accounting and auditing expenses for tax return preparation

Alimony

Alterations and repairs on business or income-producing property

Attending conventions (New laws only allow two conventions abroad a year. Travel must be coach class.)

Attorney's fees in connection with your trade or employment

Automobile expenses incurred during business trips, trips for charitable organizations, and trips for medical care

Automobile licenses

Business expense of employees in excess of amounts received as reimbursements

Campaign contributions

Casualty losses of all kinds that are uninsured and over $100 per loss

Charitable contributions (cannot exceed 50 percent of your income)

Child care expenses (this applies to divorced and separated people, as well as couples in which there is one full-time worker and the other is either a part-time worker, a full-time student, or seeking a job—a maximum of a $400 tax *credit,* $800 for two or more)

Condominium owners' interest and realty taxes

Depreciation of property used in business

Dues for professional societies and organized labor unions

Educational expenses if required to keep your employment or professional standards

Fees paid to secure employment

Fees paid for tax preparation and consultation

Fees paid for investment advisory services

Gambling losses (to be subtracted from gambling winnings only)

General sales taxes (state and local)

EXHIBIT 12-11 **CONTINUED**   Home office (only for individuals who have a separate place used only as an office and also a place where the individual *regularly* receives clients. Greatly restricted by the 1976 tax reform act.)

Income tax (state and city)

Interest you paid or finance charges for any loans or retail installment contracts

Medical expenses in excess of 3 percent of adjusted gross income

Moving expenses

Property taxes

Pro rata share of automobile expenses if used for business

Safe deposit box expenses

Union dues paid by the employee

---

deductions you may subtract from income before it becomes taxable.

A Partial Listing of Legitimate Deductions

Exhibit 12-11 lists some of the deductions the IRS allows.

Nonlegitimate Deductions

There are literally thousands of items that cannot be deducted legally from your income before you compute your taxes. Exhibit 12-12 lists some of those nonlegitimate items.

TAX FORMS

There is a multitude of forms to be filled out for different types of income. There are different forms for business profits and losses, capital gains, pension income, farm income, and so on. The basic form is the 1040, within which are schedules. Exhibit 12-13 shows the different schedules that can be attached to the form 1040, depending on the type of income you declare.

Other IRS forms are listed in Exhibit 12-14.

HOW TO AVOID A TAX AUDIT

Most, if not all, taxpayers wish to avoid being audited by the IRS. It is time-consuming, often traumatic, and may cost you more tax dollars. Thus, astute taxpayers try to minimize the chances of being audited when they fill out their returns. Exhibit 12-15 shows the percentage of individual returns that are audited, depending on income and whether deductions are itemized. That means that if you filled out a simple form 1040A with no itemized deductions and your income is less than $10,000, there are seven chances out of a thousand that your return will be audited.

What Prompts an Audit?

The most common reason an audit is made is unallowable items—deducting normal living expenses, for example. In fiscal 1975, 72 percent of all

IRS service center audits were made for this reason.

Audits also are made when an individual who is not qualified to do so uses head-of-household tax tables. For example, two formerly married individuals with joint custody of their children can't both claim to be the head of the household.

Individuals also are audited because:

1. Savings and loan associations, employers, and Social Security wage reports revealed information that did not agree with the tax return.

2. More than one return was filed under the same Social Security number.

3. There was a discrepancy between the state income tax return reported by state tax agencies and the federal income tax return.

4. The wrong tax table was used.

5. There were computation errors.

Beating the Computer

A large number of audits are triggered by computer scoring on audit potentials. The computer scores depend on the size of itemized deductions. If you claim a specific deduction that is much greater than the average for your income class, you can almost be certain of being audited. Exhibit 12-16 shows the figures for the average amount of deductions based on returns. These averages do not give you the right to deduct the specified amounts. You are only allowed to claim actual payments for taxes, contributions, interest, and so on. On the other hand, if your deductions are significantly less than the average, that may mean you are overlooking something (or are healthy and, perhaps, frugal).

Backing Up Your Deductions

The computer, of course, can't support material that you present for deductions, but the human classifiers at the IRS will spot it. If, for example, you have extremely high medical expenses one year, make a separate schedule of them, and attach copies of all the bills to your return. This will assist the classifier and perhaps save you a trip to the local field office. On the other hand, it's inappropriate to overdo the extra schedules. To reduce your chances of being audited, verify, when you file, anything that might stand out and raise questions.

EXHIBIT 12-12. **EXPENSES THAT CANNOT BE USED AS DEDUCTIONS**

- ☐ Commuting fees
- ☐ Food (unless prescribed for medical treatment)
- ☐ Funeral expenses
- ☐ Life insurance premiums
- ☐ Rent
- ☐ Social security tax paid for domestic employees
- ☐ Tax penalty payments
- ☐ Traffic fines
- ☐ Upkeep on car used only for pleasure or commuting

EXHIBIT 12-13.

SCHEDULE

A&B	Itemized deductions and interest and dividend income
C	Profit or loss from business or profession (sole proprietorship)
D	Capital gains and losses
E	Supplemental income schedule (pensions, annuities, rents, royalties, partnerships, estates, trusts, etc.)
F	Farm income and expenses
G	Income averaging
R & RP	Credit for the elderly
SE	Computation of Social Security self-employment tax
TC	Tax computation schedule for those who cannot use the tax tables and for certain taxpayers who must itemize deductions
2441	Credit for child and dependent care expenses

Human classifiers can quickly spot inconsistencies, so avoid them if possible. Your income after deductions must be enough to buy such essentials as food and clothing, so don't overdo the deductions. And employee or business expenses must be appropriate for your occupation.

HOW TO SURVIVE A TAX AUDIT

Should you receive in the mail a note from the IRS that says, "We are examining your federal income tax return for the above year(s) and we find we need additional information to verify your correct tax," don't despair. Many individuals are audited randomly even though their returns seem to be in order. Prior to your scheduled audit, remember that personal attitude helps in a successful negotiation with the auditor. Therefore, you should:

1. *Be prepared.* Know the facts in your case and, if possible, the law relating to the specific deductions being questioned.

2. *Be businesslike.* Answer the letter from the IRS promptly, and help the agent dispose of major issues quickly during the initial interview.

3. *Be cooperative.* Answer all questions. But *do not* volunteer unsolicited information, unless, of course, the agent has overlooked something that could alter things in your favor.

EXHIBIT 12-14

**OTHER IRS FORMS
OF INTEREST**

FORM	PURPOSE
843	Refund of excess Social Security taxes (FICA) paid
935	Power of attorney granted to another individual for a tax return
1040A	Short form using zero bracket amount
1040ES	Estimated tax
1040X	Amendment to already-filed return
1099	Income from banks, savings and loan associations, brokerage houses, rents, and royalties
2119	Sale or exchange of a residence
2333	A request for blank income tax forms
4070	The reporting of tips
4506	Request for a copy of a previously filed return
4868	Extension of time in which to file a return
SS-5	To obtain a Social Security number, replace a lost card, or a federal taxpayer identification number
W-4E	Exemption from withholding of no tax liabilities foreseen (primarily for retired persons and students)

Using Those Records

When you are audited, you realize how important record keeping is. An IRS auditor has the right to disallow completely unsubstantiated itemized deductions or to reduce them to what he or she might consider "reasonable." When you are asked to verify specific itemized deductions, provide only the information relating to those deductions, and provide it as completely as possible. You don't want to give the impression that you are hiding something.

For most individuals who are audited, negotiations with the IRS agent proceed smoothly. Once an agreement is reached, you will sign a form stating that you will pay the taxes you owe.

If You Disagree with the Agent

If you don't agree with the agent's proposal, you can take your dispute to a higher IRS level, either a

EXHIBIT 12-15.

PERCENTAGE OF AUDITED INDIVIDUAL RETURNS	NONBUSINESS INCOME	FIELD OR OFFICE AUDIT
	Under $10,000	Standard deduction, or ZBA, is used, 0.7 percent (7 out of 1000)
	Under $10,000	Itemized deductions are claimed, 4.3 percent (43 out of 1000)
	$10,000-$50,000	2.5 percent (25 out of 1000)
	$50,000 and up	12.4 percent (124 out of 1000)

district conference or an appellate division conference. Or you can ask that a ninety-day letter be issued and postpone settlement negotiations until it is issued.

Generally, when the amount of dispute is less than $2,500, a district conference is in order. If you aren't satisfied with the outcome of the district conference, you can go to the appellate division of the IRS.

The Next Step Is Tax Court

If you are still unsatisfied, you can request to go to the tax court. And if your dispute involves no more than $1,500 in additional taxes for any one year, you can go to the small tax case division of tax court. In these courts, tax cases are settled informally and as quickly as possible.

Small Tax Case Division. There are no formal rules of evidence or formal written opinions in this court. Consequently, there is no need for detailed findings of opinions and fact. Each case in the small tax case division is heard by commissioners rather than judges. You, the dissatisfied taxpayer, can petition the court: you can represent yourself, so you don't need the expensive services of an attorney.

Your chances of obtaining a decision in your

EXHIBIT 12-16. **AVERAGE DEDUCTIONS CLAIMED ON ADJUSTED GROSS INCOME, 1974**

TYPE	INCOME CLASS				
	$5-6,000	$9-10,000	$15-20,000	$30-50,000	$100,000 & Up
Medical expenses	671	435	305	402	654
Taxes	588	801	1,386	2,935	13,192
Contributions	277	298	412	945	10,825
Interest	570	800	1,178	1,799	9,423

favor are quite good. Latest data indicate that 72 percent of all cases were decided at least partially in favor of the taxpayer.

SHOULD YOU TAKE CHANCES?

If you're uncertain about the acceptability of a deduction, it's not necessarily unwise to take a chance. Many deductions are subject to interpretation by the IRS. So if you're audited, you stand a fair chance of winning your case. The act of taking deductions that aren't considered legitimate does not involve fraud. So even if you lose, you only pay an interest rate penalty on the taxes due. The interest rate is 1/2 of 1 percent per month, which, in many years, has been less than the rate of inflation.

GLOSSARY OF TERMS

TRANSFERS Payments—such as Social Security and unemployment—made to individuals by a government. These payments are not in exchange for goods or services provided by those individuals.

BENEFIT PRINCIPLE A principle of taxation in which people are charged taxes according to the benefits they receive from the government.

FREE RIDER PROBLEM Individuals attempt to get a "free ride" by not paying for the use of certain goods and services. For example, many people would rather let others pay for national defense; those who don't want to pay want a free ride.

PROPORTIONAL TAXATION A system of taxation in which the rate of taxation is uniform, no matter what the size of income. For example, proportional taxation of 20 percent would take 20 percent of an income of $100 and 20 percent of an income of $1 million.

PROGRESSIVE TAXATION A taxing system in which higher incomes are placed in higher tax brackets. In a progressive system, you pay a higher rate on the last dollar you earn than on the first dollar you earn.

REGRESSIVE TAXATION A system in which your tax rate falls as you earn more and more income.

MILLAGE The rate of property taxation expressed in mills; a mill equals 1/10 of one cent ($0.001).

TAX BRACKET The range of income subject to a specific tax rate.

CAPITAL GAIN The positive difference resulting when the selling price of an asset exceeds its purchase price.

CAPITAL LOSS   The negative difference resulting when the selling price of an asset is less than its purchase price.

DEDUCTIONS   Subtractions from income that can be made before taxes owed are computed.

ZERO BRACKET AMOUNT (ZBA)   The new name for a standard deduction. It is the amount of income on which no income taxes are assessed.

MINIMUM TAX   Taxes owed by individuals who have taken advantage of tax shelters and loopholes.

CHAPTER SUMMARY

1. More than 40 percent of every dollar goes to state, federal, and local governments. Part of these government revenues are returned to citizens in the form of transfers, such as Social Security and unemployment compensation.

2. There are three basic principles of taxation: benefit, ability to pay, and sacrifice.

3. There are three basic types of taxes: proportional, progressive, and regressive.

4. The property tax is a local tax assessed on real property.

5. The property tax is criticized because it isn't based on the ability-to-pay principle; it appears inequitable; it is regressive; and it is costly to administer.

6. The federal tax system consists of personal and corporate income taxes, Social Security contributions, excise taxes, and estate and gift taxes.

7. The federal personal income tax, the most important federal tax, is collected through withholding and estimated tax payments.

8. Taxable income consists of wages and salaries, interest, dividends, rents and royalties, profits, gambling winnings, alimony, and capital gains.

9. The IRS does not consider as taxable income accident and health insurance proceeds under $5,200 annually, workers' compensation payments, disability pension payments, Social Security benefits, life insurance proceeds, or veterans' disability payments.

10. Capital gains are often taxed at a lower rate than regular income.

11. For tax purposes, the difference between gross income and adjusted gross income is that the latter does not include legitimate business expenses and losses.

12. It is possible to reduce taxes by using income splitting and income averaging.

13. Individuals who take advantage of ways to reduce taxes often are subjected to a minimum tax of 15 percent on the total value of tax preference income when it exceeds $10,000 or on one-half of regular income taxes due for that year, whichever is greater.

14. Detailed information in filling out tax returns can be found in such books as Laser's *Tax Guide,* H&R Block's *Income Tax Workbook,* RIA's *Individual Tax Return Guide,* and the CCH *Master Tax Guide.* The IRS offers a free booklet called *Your Federal Income Tax.*

15. When hiring tax preparation help: (a) never sign a blank return, (b) never sign a return prepared in pencil, (c) never allow your refund check to be mailed to the tax preparer, and (d) make sure the tax preparer signs the return.

16. If you have few possible deductions, you may wish to take advantage of the ZBA and file a short form 1040A.

17. If you decide to itemize your deductions and fill out a long form 1040, you must have adequate records. They must be kept for at least three years from the date your tax was paid or at least three years from the date your return was filed, whichever occurred later.

18. The best way to keep records is to write checks or use credit cards for which you obtain receipts. To keep accurate records, file receipts and canceled checks in appropriately marked envelopes every month or so.

19. You should always identify your sources of income and keep adequate records on capital gains and losses. Tax audits most often occur because a taxpayer lists unallowable deductions, such as normal living expenses. The improper use of the head-of-household tax table also prompts audits.

20. Claiming deductions that grossly exceed average deductions also may prompt an audit.

21. If you have an unusually high deduction, it is advisable to attach substantiating documents to your tax return.

22. The best way to handle a tax audit is to be prepared, be businesslike, and be cooperative.

23. If you disagree with your auditor's conclusions, you can go to a district conference, an appellate division conference, or a regular court.

24. The small tax case division of the tax court handles cases involving no more than $1,500 in additional taxes for any one year.

25. Taking a chance on listing deductions is usually worthwhile because the IRS subjects deductions to various interpretations.

STUDY QUESTIONS

1. What are the principles of taxation? Which one do you think best justifies progressive taxation?

2. Would you prefer to have most taxes collected from individuals or from corporations?

3. Who really pays the corporate income tax?

4. When doesn't it pay to keep records for tax purposes?

5. When is it unadvisable to have a certified public accountant fill out your tax returns?

6. If a tax audit determines that you've taken a deduction that is not legitimate, what is your penalty?

7. "It is cheaper to give things to charity than to try to sell them." How could this be true?

8. What is the difference between progressive and regressive taxation?

9. What is the difference between gross earnings and take-home pay? What happens to the difference?

10. What is the difference between gross income and adjusted gross income?

11. When you itemize your deductions, which taxes can be included as deductions?

12. How can income averaging and income splitting reduce your taxes?

13. What is a zero bracket amount and when would it affect you?

CASE PROBLEMS

12-1 Property Tax Reform

Rose Quinn is a real estate broker and a member of the legislature in a rapidly growing southwestern state. Two plans for property tax reform are being discussed in the tax committee, and Rose is trying to decide which one to support. Currently, state law allows a maximum of fifty-five mills on property taxed at 30% of market value. Proposal 1 would set a maximum of fifteen mills and 100% of market value, and Proposal 2 would set a maximum of twenty-five mills and 75% of market value.

1. What would taxes be on a $50,000 house under the status quo and under each of the proposals?

2. Rose would like to keep property taxes as low as possible. Which plan do you think she would support?

Alice Wetherby, an accountant, and her husband, Josh, a recreation director, work in New York City. Their combined income is from $20,000 to $25,000 a year, which puts them in a 28% marginal tax bracket. Assuming that their income remains the same, what will be the tax effects of moving to Jackson Hole, Wyoming?

SELECTED REFERENCES

Audit of Returns, Appeals Rights, and Claims for Refund. Publication 556, Internal Revenue Service.

Carper, J. "How to Fight the I.R.S.—and Win." *American Home*, May 1977, p. 16.

Deutsch, R. W. "How Private is Your Tax Return?" *Nation's Business*, December 1973, pp. 66-67.

How to Prepare Your Personal Income Tax Return. Englewood Cliffs, N.J.: Prentice-Hall (published annually).

"If the IRS Calls You for a Tax Audit." *U.S. News*, April 11, 1977, pp. 96-98.

Janssen, Peter A. "Loosening the Grip of the IRS." *Money*, April 1977.

Lasser, J. K. *Your Income Tax.* New York: Simon and Schuster (published annually).

People and Taxes. Washington, D.C., Ralph Nader's Research Group (monthly newspaper).

"Time to Think about Next Year's Tax Return." *Changing Times*, April 1977.

"When the IRS Gets Your Tax Return," *U.S. News*, March 28, 1977, pp. 78-80.

"Where to Go for Tax Help." *Consumer Reports*, March 1976, pp. 130-137.

Your Federal Income Tax. Washington, D.C.: Superintendent of Documents (published annually).

Sheltering Your Income From Taxes

■ Few of us like to pay taxes. The more taxes we think we may have to pay the government, the more ways we'll seek to reduce that tax burden. Fortunately, there is a vast array of methods available to the taxpayer to reduce taxes owed. These methods are often called **tax loopholes** or **tax shelters,** because the income is sheltered from the grasping hands of the IRS. In this chapter, we will examine these legal means of reducing tax burdens.

A tax loophole is a legally available method of lowering taxes owed the government. The definition of a tax shelter is somewhat more restricted; generally, tax shelters involve specifically "protecting" income from assessed taxes. We will use the two terms interchangeably in this chapter.

AN OBVIOUS SHELTER—MUNICIPAL BONDS

One of the oldest and most obvious tax shelters is the income paid to the owners of municipal bonds, which are sold by local governments. The interest obtained on those bonds is not subject to federal and, in some cases, state income tax. Thus, it is possible for a wealthy person, who keeps all of his or her wealth in the form of municipal bonds, to pay no explicit federal taxes. For example, a person with $1 million worth of municipal bonds that yield 5 percent a year will attain $50,000 of income but won't have to report any of it on an income tax return.

The Benefits Derived Depend on Your Tax Bracket

The value of the tax-exempt status of income from municipal bonds is directly proportional to your marginal tax bracket. If you are in, say, the

333

22 percent bracket, the value of nontaxable income is certainly less than if you were in the 70 percent bracket. Consider the hypothetical case of two taxpayers obtaining $1,000 in interest-free income from municipal bonds. If one individual is in a 70 percent tax bracket, the tax savings is equal to $700; if the other is in a 22 percent tax bracket, the tax savings are equal to only $220.

This principle, in which the value of a tax shelter is in direct proportion to the person's marginal tax bracket, is illustrated in Exhibit 13-1. There we show equivalents between tax-free income from municipal bonds and taxable income from, say, corporate bonds, depending on the taxpayer's marginal tax rate. If a person in the 50 percent tax bracket has the choice between a tax-exempt bond yielding, say, 5 percent and a nontax-exempt bond yielding 9 percent, the former is a better deal. Why? Because the 50 percent bracket taxpayer must obtain at least 10

EXHIBIT 13-1.

THE VALUE OF TAX-FREE INCOME.

Locate your taxable income (after exemptions and any deductions) in the left-hand column. Then read across the table to find how much taxable return on an investment it would take to match the tax-free yields located at the top of the table.

TAXABLE INCOME joint return	TAXABLE INCOME single return	federal income tax bracket	4%	5%	5½%	6%	6½%	7%	8%
					TAX-EXEMPT YIELD				
					EQUIVALENT TAXABLE YIELD				
$ 8- 12,000		22%	5.13%	6.41%	7.05%	7.69%	8.33%	8.97%	10.26%
12- 16,000	$ 8-10,000	25	5.33	6.67	7.33	8.00	8.67	9.33	10.67
	10-12,000	27	5.48	6.85	7.53	8.22	8.90	9.59	10.96
16- 20,000		28	5.56	6.94	7.64	8.33	9.03	9.72	11.11
	12-14,000	29	5.63	7.04	7.75	8.45	9.15	9.86	11.27
	14-16,000	31	5.80	7.25	7.97	8.70	9.42	10.14	11.59
20- 24,000		32	5.88	7.34	8.09	8.82	9.56	10.29	11.76
	16-18,000	34	6.06	7.58	8.34	9.09	9.85	10.61	12.12
24- 28,000	18-20,000	36	6.25	7.81	8.59	9.38	10.16	10.94	12.50
	20-22,000	38	6.45	8.07	8.87	9.68	10.48	11.29	12.90
28- 32,000		39	6.56	8.20	9.02	9.84	10.66	11.48	13.11
	22-26,000	40	6.67	8.33	9.17	10.00	10.83	11.67	13.33
32- 36,000		42	6.90	8.62	9.48	10.34	11.21	12.07	13.79
36- 40,000	26-32,000	45	7.27	9.09	10.00	10.91	11.82	12.73	14.55
40- 44,000		48	7.69	9.62	10.58	11.54	12.50	13.46	15.38
44- 52,000	32-38,000	50	8.00	10.00	11.00	12.00	13.00	14.00	16.00
52- 64,000		53	8.51	10.64	11.70	12:77	13.83	14.89	17.02
64- 76,000	38-44,000	55	8.89	11.11	12.22	13.33	14.44	15.56	17.78
76- 88,000		58	9.52	11.90	13.09	14.29	15.48	16.67	19.05
88-100,000	44-50,000	60	10.00	12.50	13.75	15.00	16.25	17.50	20.00

percent on a taxable basis in order to match the 5 percent nontax yield on municipal bonds. The table shows that the higher the individual's tax bracket, the larger the benefit from nontaxed income.

The general formula. You can figure out the equivalent taxable yield if you know your marginal federal income tax bracket. The general formula is equal to:

$$\text{equivalent taxable yield} = \frac{\text{tax-exempt yield}}{1 - \text{your tax rate}}$$

Imagine, for example, that you are offered a tax-exempt municipal bond that yields 7 percent. If you're in the 22 percent bracket, you can figure out the equivalent taxable yield:

$$\text{equivalent taxable yield} = 7\% \div (1 - .22) = 0.07 \div 0.78 = 8.9744\%$$

In Exhibit 13-1, under the "7%" column and in the row for a 22 percent marginal tax bracket, is your taxable yield—8.97 percent.

Not All Interest Rates Are the Same

Before you rush out and trade in all your corporate bonds (the interest of which is taxable) for tax-exempt municipals, remember that those interest rates won't be the same. Those who most benefit from this particular tax shelter tend to accept a lower interest rate when they purchase municipal bonds than they would accept if they were purchasing a corporate bond issued by, say, General Motors. Therefore, we see a difference of approximately 35 to 40 percent between interest yields on municipals and interest yields on other types of bonds. Thus, if corporate bonds are yielding 10 percent, a municipal bond will be yielding only 6 to 7 percent. In effect, then, everyone who buys tax-exempt bonds implicitly pays a tax, which is the difference between the interest yield on a municipal bond and the interest yield on a corporate bond. Therefore, individuals who buy tax-exempt bonds don't escape paying federal income taxes completely. They do escape *explicit* taxation, but they pay a tax nonetheless.

Municipals Aren't for Everyone

Because tax-exempt municipals have lower interest yields than other bonds, not everyone will benefit by buying those tax exempts. Only if your marginal tax bracket is greater than that 35 to 40 percent differential is it worthwhile. Consider again the example of corporate bonds yielding 10 percent with tax exempts yielding, say, 6.5 percent. If you're in the 22 percent marginal tax bracket, you would have to pay 22 percent on the interest you earned from corporate bonds. That would reduce your rate of return to 7.8 percent [10 percent • (1-.22) = 7.8]. You would effectively be getting a higher after-tax rate of return than if you put your money in municipal bonds, so you would not benefit by buying the so-called tax shelter. Therefore, don't buy tax-exempt municipals unless your marginal tax rate exceeds at least 35 percent.

SHELTERING INCOME WITH PENSION PLANS

Most individuals save in order to have sufficient income for their retirement years. There are numerous private savings devices you can choose from to supplement Social Security, the retirement funds provided by the government.

A tax sheltered pension plan allows you to save *before*-tax—as opposed to *after*-tax—dollars. If, for example, you are in the 50 percent tax bracket, a pension tax shelter will allow you to save twice as many before-tax dollars as after-tax dollars.

A tax-exempt savings plan doesn't allow you to avoid paying taxes indefinitely on the savings you put into it. Eventually, you'll have to pay taxes on those savings dollars, but you pay them as you take them out, when you're retired. Thus, you save on taxes because you're usually in a lower tax bracket when you retire than when you are working. And you put off having to pay those taxes for many years, allowing your savings to grow at compounded rates.

Deferring Your Tax Payment

That last point is a key aspect of tax-exempt pension plans. By deferring taxes until a future date, you can earn interest on those deferred taxes while you aren't paying them. In other words, the government loans you that money—the taxes owed—for a number of years and doesn't charge you interest for that loan. You must repay it when you retire, but, in the mean time, you have made extra money.

Let us compare two possibilities—a regular savings program, in which the individual puts, say, $100 in a savings and loan account each year, and another program, in which the individual sets up a retirement pension plan containing money that is not taxed currently. To simplify the arithmetic, we'll assume that the individual is in the 50 percent tax bracket; thus, this individual can have the same after-tax income to spend during the year by putting away $200 in the tax-exempt pension plan. Let's assume further that the same rate of return is earned in the pension plan as in the savings and loan association.

As Exhibit 13-2 indicates, the individual with the pension plan will have more retirement dollars to spend than the individual without it, although they both have the same after-tax income during their working years. In our example, the tax-exempt savings plan would have yielded $14.34 more than the other plan after five years. This doesn't sound like a lot, but it is equivalent to an increase in total savings of 12.7 percent. That percentage figure would increase dramatically when comparing a tax sheltered plan to a nontax sheltered plan over a thirty-year period. Moreover, even 12.7 percent represents quite a difference if the sums of money involved are large. And they certainly would be greater than those in our example for the average American's retirement plan. To repeat, the benefit of the pension plan is that the payment of taxes is deferred until some later date. Moreover, with a tax-exempt pension plan, you don't pay taxes on the interest earned while it is being earned.

A Basic Saving Rule

As long as you plan to save a certain percentage of your income for retirement, you will almost always be better off if you can save through a qualified tax sheltered pension plan. In other words, if you are going to save anyway, let the government loan you money (taxes owed but *not* paid) on which you can earn interest over a number of years and don't have to repay until you retire.

Most qualified pension plans are offered by employers to employees. In this country, many individuals are covered under some form of an employer provided pension plan. In many cases, you have no choice about participating. And, with some plans, you may not be assured of receiving your retirement funds back if you leave the company before a specified number of years.

EXHIBIT 13-2. **THE BENEFITS OF A TAX SHELTERED SAVINGS PLAN**

	YEAR 1	YEAR 2	YEAR 3	YEAR 4	YEAR 5
PLAN 1					
Principal	$100.00	$102.50	$105.06	$107.69	$110.382
Interest	5.00	5.125	5.253	5.384	5.519
Taxes	−2.50	−2.5625	−2.627	−2.692	−2.7596
AFTER-TAX TOTAL	$102.50	$105.06	$107.69	$110.38	$113.14

NET AFTER-TAX SAVINGS, END OF 5 YEARS = $113.14

	YEAR 1	YEAR 2	YEAR 3	YEAR 4	YEAR 5
PLAN 2					
Principal	$200.00	$210.00	$220.50	$231.525	$242.826
Interest	10.00	10.50	11.025	11.57625	12.1413
TOTAL	$210.00	$220.50	$231.53	$242.83	$254.97

TAXES PAID AT 50% AT END OF YEAR 5 = .5 × $254.97 = 127.48
NET AFTER-TAX SAVINGS AT END OF 5 YEARS = $254.97 − 127.48 = $127.48

OTHER INDIVIDUAL RETIREMENT PLANS

There is a variety of other ways you can establish your own individual retirement plans in order to defer taxes on your savings. Basically, to qualify, you cannot be covered by an employer pension plan, or you must obtain some of your income by moonlighting—meaning income in addition to your regular salary.

Individual Pension Plans

There are basically two plans available to individuals whose employers don't provide pension plans or to those who are self-employed.

Keogh Plans. The Keogh Act of 1962 was passed to help self-employed individuals set up their own pension plans. Modified by the Employment Retirement Income Security Act (ERISA) of 1974, a Keogh Plan retirement program allows you to set aside 15 percent of your earned income up to $7,500 a year. In other words, you can put a maximum of $7,500 a year into your private pension plan. Unless you are totally disabled, you are penalized if you take the money out of the plan before you are fifty-nine and one-half years old. You must take money out of the plan when you reach seventy and one-half, even if you haven't retired and still receive income. Many insurance companies, mutual funds, and banks have developed master plans that simplify the establishment of a Keogh fund.

Individual Retirement Account (IRA). A newer retirement system is the IRA. You may contribute to an IRA account and deduct on your tax return $1,500, or 15 percent of your annual earnings, whichever is less. These contributions can be made in one lump sum or in installments. In principle, no contributions can be made to an IRA account in any year during which you participate in another pension program that qualifies for tax advantages; however, your existing IRA can continue and earn further taxes or dividends and interest. Like the Keogh plan, you must withdraw from the plan when you reach 70-½, and you pay a penalty on regular income taxes plus a 10 percent penalty on funds withdrawn before age 59-½. You can manage your own IRA account, deciding which investments to make or not to make; however, a number of financial institutions have already established IRA accounts to ease the management problem in record keeping.

Establishing a Spouse's Pension Plan

A spouse may now have a pension plan of his or her own. Under the 1976 Tax Reform Act, an employed husband or wife can set up either a jointly owned IRA and contribute 15 percent of income up to $1,750 or two separate IRAs, with up to $875 going to each. Previously, a nonemployed partner in a marriage was not eligible for an IRA. In the case of a divorce, the nonsalaried spouse will own his or her IRA.

Deferred Annuities

If you aren't qualified to start your own Keogh or IRA plan, then a deferred annuity may be the way to invest and save. With a deferred annuity, you invest income, which has already been taxed, in the annuity, deferring annual payments until you, the owner, decide you want them; or you can get the money in a lump sum. Essentially, you are sheltering the interest on your investment during the period you don't touch the money. There is no tax on withdrawals, up to the original amount invested. These annuities are sold mainly by stockbrokerage firms.

THE GLAMOUR SHELTERS—OIL DRILLING, CATTLE RAISING, MOVIES, AND REAL ESTATE

In the last couple of decades, the most publicized tax shelters have involved oil drilling funds, raising cattle, making movies, building apartments, and buying railroad tank cars. But the Tax Reform Act of 1976 severely restricted or eliminated completely the possible loopholes available to higher income investors in these glamour shelters.

THE VARIOUS TRUST TAX SHELTERS

It is possible to set up what are called trusts to reduce tax burdens. A **trust** is a legal arrangement whereby title to specific property is transferred by the creator of the trust to another person called the trustee, usually for the benefit of a third party called the beneficiary. This topic is treated in more detail in Chapter 20. Here, we will examine some of the various trust methods to reduce current taxes. Some of these, such as the so-called equipment trust, are available only to specialized groups.

Equipment Trust

If you are a dentist or a doctor, for example, you may be able to set up an **equipment trust** for your children. Such a trust gives control and, essentially, ownership of all your professional equipment and perhaps even your office building, if you own it, to your children. In return, your children charge you an annual rental fee. This fee becomes a business expense for you and income for them. The income to your children is now taxable, however, but at a much lower rate than it would have been had you received it. To benefit from this arrangement, you must now charge your children for some activity you normally would pay for, the most obvious being private education. If the education is legally required in your state, then this tax gimmick is permissible.

Take our example of the person in the 50 percent bracket. If that person is spending, say, $6,000 a year on private education for two children, the equipment trust conceivably could give that person $6,000 a year more spendable income. Without the equipment trust, he or she would have to earn $12,000 in order to have $6,000 to pay for private schooling. With the equipment trust, say, $6,000 can be paid to the children for renting the equipment; they then pay almost no taxes on that amount of money. In turn, they are charged $6,000 for their education, or they can pay it directly themselves.

Clifford Trust

A trust is actually a device that "gives birth to a new tax person," who pays a lower tax rate. This is the idea behind both the equipment trust and the Clifford trust. A Clifford trust is a legal device by which property is irrevocably given in trust to, say, a minor child in a low tax bracket for a predetermined period. In the case of the Clifford trust, the minimum is ten years and one day. The Clifford trust reduces your taxable income by shifting it to the beneficiary, who is in a lower tax bracket. The disadvantage of such a short-term irrevocable trust is that you cannot change the beneficiary or end the trust before the minimum time period.

If you own income-producing property already, such as stocks yielding dividends, bonds yielding interest, or any other such property, you have the first requirement for such a trust. You also must have a beneficiary who is in a lower tax bracket than you are. In most cases, short-term living trusts (that is, you are still alive) are set up for the benefit of one's children. If you're not concerned about touching the principal of the trust during the ten-year-one-day period, a Clifford trust may make sense for you.

Support Trust

A version of a short-term trust can be used to support elderly or dependent relatives. The beneficiary of such a support trust can receive all the income produced by the trust while she or he is alive. When the beneficiary dies, the trust reverts back to the donor (or to someone whom the donor has designated in the original trust agreement). This type of trust is feasible only if the beneficiary is in a lower tax bracket than the donor.

FRINGE BENEFITS

An increasingly important tax loophole, or shelter, available is fringe benefits. If an employer can offer you a fringe benefit that is a business deduction for the employer but not taxable income to you, then you come out ahead. For example, if you normally spend $200 a year on legal services that are not tax deductible, you will benefit if your employer is able to provide you a prepaid legal service for that same $200 a year. Why? Because $200 will be deducted from your salary before you are taxed. Again, if you are in the 50 percent tax bracket, that means that you won't have to pay $100 of taxes that you otherwise would have had to pay. In other words, in the 50 percent tax bracket, you must earn $400 in order to have $200 after taxes to buy those legal services. In fact, the 1976 Tax Reform Act did allow for employers to set up prepaid legal plans. They clearly are beneficial to employees who normally use after-tax dollars to purchase legal services that normally aren't tax deductible.

Of course, the employee only benefits to the extent that he or she normally would have purchased the fringe benefit in the absence of the employer's providing it. If you never use legal services, a prepaid legal service plan obviously isn't such a good deal.

There are numerous fringe benefits that constitute legitimate business expenses to the employer but aren't counted as taxable income to you. In addition to prepaid legal services, these are:

1   Health insurance
2   Dental insurance
3   Some forms of group life insurance
4   Prepaid psychiatric plans
5   Disability insurance (up to a limit)
6   Some forms of employee dependents' educational funds (although the IRS is restricting these).

Generally, it behooves you to take advantage of this legal tax loophole, which provides you with goods and services paid for with before-tax dollars. As tax rates have increased over time and as inflation has placed us in higher tax brackets, employers have offered more and more fringe benefits. This explosion of fringe benefits has been greatly, if not completely, a function of their tax advantages.

SOME LESS WELL-KNOWN TAX LOOPHOLES

As inflation pushes us into higher and higher tax brackets, we find ourselves faced with a difficult dilemma: the more we make, the more the government takes. It is not surprising, then, that individuals have responded by altering some of their behavior patterns and also by seeking ways to avoid higher taxes. We will look briefly at four relatively new such phenomena: (1) barter, (2) do-it-yourself activities, (3) buying consumer durables, and (4) leisure.

The New Barter Society

Barter has existed in America at least since Peter Minuit got the Indians to trade some blankets and beads for Manhattan Island in 1626. Actually, the Indians used barter for a least 5,000 years before that date. Because barter is an expensive way to make exchanges, it is more sensible to use money as a medium of exchange. Nonetheless, barter has been coming back in recent years because it represents a way to avoid paying income taxes.

Take a simple example. A dentist needs approximately $1,000 of legal services to set up a new pension plan; and a lawyer incidentally needs approximately $1,000 of gold inlays to replace silver fillings. Assume that both are in the 50 percent tax bracket. If they each purchased the needed services, each would have to earn $2,000 in order to have $1,000 after taxes to pay for those services. If, on the other hand, they make a trade, bartering legal services for dental care, no taxes will be paid—if the IRS is unaware of the deal. They each will save $1,000 in taxes but will obtain the services they wished to buy.

The IRS regards the new barter society with a wary eye. Of course, barter arrangements are difficult for the IRS to track down, but the law on this matter is clear; you are supposed to declare income realized in any form.

The number of barter groups throughout the nation is growing. Useful Services Exchange is a nonprofit clearinghouse in Reston, Virginia; Learning Exchange in Evanston, Illinois, has approximately 50,000 participants; Vacation Exchange Club allows people to barter houses for their vacations as does the Holiday Home Bureau. The Business Owners' Exchange in Minneapolis has about 500 members, including lawyers, dentists, and CPAs, each of whom pays a $150 membership fee. Members can trade their professional services, as well as material possessions, such as cars and boats. The Exchange issues checks, which look like commercial bank checks, and sends members monthly statements listing sales and purchases, but no real money is exchanged. United Trade Club in San Jose, California, has almost 2,000 members, also including doctors and lawyers.

Do-it-Yourself Activities

In Chapter 7, we explained the tax advantages of do-it-yourself activities to the homeowner. To repeat, rather than earning income, which is taxable, to hire someone to repair or maintain your home or car, you can provide the services yourself and avoid paying taxes by not declaring those do-it-yourself services as income. The do-it-yourself society has increased dramatically in the United States, partly because of rising repair and construction costs and partly because individuals in higher tax brackets realize these activities reduce their taxes.

Buying Consumer Durables

A less obvious effect of the high tax rate is the increased incentive for individuals to buy more consumer durable goods rather than to save or invest their money in more conventional outlets. Consider a numerical example. A family with $10,000 to save has a number of normal options for those savings—a savings and loan association account, a mutual fund, and so on. Let's assume that it can obtain a return before taxes of 10 percent per year. Let's also assume that the family is in a 50 percent tax bracket; thus, its after-tax rate of return on that $10,000 saving will be only 5 percent, or $500 a year. Now consider that it has the option of, say, installing a tennis court, which also will cost $10,000. A tennis court is a consumer durable item. And it's a form of investment because it yields a stream of (implicit) income in the future in the form of the pleasure derived from playing tennis on it. To duplicate the services from a tennis court on its property, the family would have to pay, say, $1,000 to a private club; thus, the implicit income stream, or yield on the investment in the tennis court, is approximately $1,000 a year. However, that income is not reported to the IRS. According to current IRS rulings and tax statutes, the implicit income or service flow from user-owned consumer durable goods, such as tennis courts, is nontaxable. The rate of return, then, from investing in a tennis court will be higher for this family than investing in bonds, for example. (To the extent that property taxes rise, the rate of return on the tennis court will be lower, however.)

Its not surprising, then, that individuals are buying more and bigger boats, more tennis courts, more expensive stereos, more luxury cars, and larger houses. This is particularly true for high-income individuals who face high tax rates.

The Leisure World

Finally, one of the easiest and perhaps most pleasant ways to avoid paying income taxes is to work less and, therefore, earn less income. Taking a longer vacation, choosing a job with fewer hours, quitting a second job, or retiring at an earlier age are all ways individuals can reduce their tax burden. Essentially, they substitute taxable income with leisure, which is a form of implicit income and, as yet, is nontaxed. We can predict that as more individuals are pushed into higher income tax brackets, work effort will decline accordingly.

PRACTICAL APPLICATIONS

HOW TO START YOUR OWN CORPORATION

There are numerous tax benefits available to individuals who incorporate. One of the major benefits is being able to set up a retirement plan that carries the benefits outlined in this chapter—deferring income taxes until you retire and thereby earning interest on the interest-free loan from the government, as well as implicitly paying a lower tax rate in the future. In this Practical Applications section we will describe a situation in which an individual might wish to incorporate and discuss the benefits from this incorporation.

SHOULD ONE INCORPORATE?

It is only possible to incorporate if you have nonsalaried income and can demonstrate that your corporation is engaged in a bona fide business activity. Thus, incorporation for individuals with regular jobs is limited to those who have *substantial* moonlighting income that can be funneled through the corporation. This income, by the way, cannot be salaried income; it must be in the form of payments that can go directly into a corporation. Thus, any checks you receive from which Social Security and federal withholding taxes have been deducted generally can't be deposited in your corporation as corporate income.

A family cannot incorporate simply because it is a family. It must be engaged in a bona fide business from which it receives nonsalaried income.

THE COSTS OF INCORPORATING

Virtually anyone in any state can start a corporation. But there are numerous legal and other expenses associated with starting and running such a venture. Consider the following expenses of starting and operating a corporation, as opposed to not funneling your income through this legal entity.

1. *Lawyers' setup fees.* These can range from a minimum of $250 to as much as $3,000.

2. *Accountants' setup fees.* It may cost several hundred dollars to set up a bookkeeping system for your corporation.

3. *Fees to the state.* You may pay an annual corporate fee to the state in which you are incorporated. This ranges from a few dollars to several hundred dollars, depending on the state.

4. *Unemployment insurance taxes.* Even if you are the only employee in your corporation and it is clearly set up for tax reasons only, you still must pay unemployment insurance taxes, either to the state in which you are registered or to the federal government.

5. *Employer's contribution to Social Security.* Even if you are a salaried employee of some other company, as an employee of your own corporation, you must pay an employer's "contribution" to Social Security. This "contribution" is nonrefundable and seems to be on the rise; it was $1070.85 in 1978 and is scheduled for big increases.

6. *Annual legal and accounting fees.* Many forms must be filled for corporations in different states. Typically, an accountant and/or a lawyer does this. Annual fees for such services can run into many hundreds of dollars. Numerous forms must be filled out every year for retirement funds in particular.

THE BENEFITS OF INCORPORATING

We've looked at the costs of incorporating. Now let's look at the benefits.

The Internal Revenue Service routinely allows pension plans consisting of two parts: a 10 percent retirement plan and a 15 percent profit-sharing plan. The 10 and 15 percent numbers refer to the percentage of the gross salary paid to the corporation's individual employees in any one year. Thus, if you had $50,000 of income funneled through your own corporation and paid to yourself as a salary, you could put $5,000 into your corporate pension plan and $7,500 into your corporate profit-sharing plan. There are specified maximums, but they're too high to affect most people.

Corporations can offer their employees larger pension plans than can the self-employed individual or the individual who is salaried but not covered by a private pension plan.

Fringe Benefits

When you start your own corporation, you can take advantage of a number of fringe benefits that provide you with items you might have bought otherwise with after-tax dollars. In other words, setting up the private corporation allows you to buy things with before-tax dollars. Let's look at some examples.

Term Life Insurance. You can, through your own corporation, purchase up to $50,000 of term life insurance every year with dollars out of the corporation. Because these dollars are a cost to the corporation, they aren't taxable. If you're in the 50 percent tax bracket, for example, that means that you are buying $50,000 of term insurance for "fifty-cent dollars." In our example, the cost of that insurance is implicitly one-half what it would have been had you purchased it outside the corporate structure.

A Medical Plan. You can set up a completely comprehensive medical plan to cover virtually all kinds of medical expenses. Thus, the corporation can reimburse you with before-tax dollars for any payments you make for medical insurance. The corporation can pay for all medicines, dental work, and anything that relates to your physical well-being. For someone with a large family, this comprehensive

medical plan can mean substantial savings every year. If, in general, you spend $2,000 more each year in medical expenses than your medical insurance covers and if you're in a 50 percent tax bracket, you get a "kickback" of $1,000.

The benefit of a medical plan is reduced by the availability of medical deductions that you alternatively could have taken off your income before figuring federal income taxes. Part of your medical insurance plus any medical expenses exceeding 3 percent of your adjusted gross income can be itemized as specific deductions on your personal federal income tax return. Essentially, then, a medical plan within the corporation for you and your dependents eliminates that part of your medical expenses that generally isn't deductible.

Leasing a Car. It is possible, as an unincorporated individual, to deduct the expenses of driving a car from your regular income tax form. But the IRS is less likely to bother you if you lease a car through your own corporation. Let's say you decide to buy a new car, and you find a firm that is willing to lease you one for $300 per month for three years. During that period of time, you can write off, as a business expense, $300 a month. If you are in the 50 percent tax bracket, you essentially are only paying $150. To make this arrangement legitimate, you must pay something into the corporation for personal use of the car—say, forty dollars per month. Thus, the tax benefit of leasing the car is reduced somewhat, but it still is substantial. Typically, when you lease a car through your corporation, you needn't be as careful about keeping a record of how you use the car, provided you don't use it excessively and you pay the corporation annually for personal use of the car.

Disability Insurance. You can purchase, with before-tax dollars, long-term disability insurance through the corporation. In other words, you can buy a salary continuation policy with before-tax dollars that you might otherwise have had to buy with after-tax dollars. Such policies pay you a certain amount of money every month if you become personally disabled and are, therefore, unable to work.

HOW TO MAKE FRINGE BENEFITS "STICK"

Fringe benefits are considered legitimate by the IRS only if you specify that they are available to all employees on a nondiscriminatory basis. That is, if you hire anyone else to work for the corporation, that person also must be eligible for such fringe benefits. Clearly, then, if you contemplate actually using a corporation for other than tax advantages, you might not want to be so generous in setting up, for example, a medical plan that covers everyone. It is extremely important that your lawyer include all the benefits just specified in the original employment agreement between your corporation and yourself, the sole employee. If they are randomly added later, an IRS auditor may exclude them. In such cases, the actual amount of the fringe benefit paid to you with corporate dollars becomes taxable income; and you, therefore, lose any tax savings.

GLOSSARY OF TERMS

TAX LOOPHOLES A method of legally lowering taxes owed to the government.

TAX SHELTER A way in which income is sheltered from all or part of federal state taxation.

TRUST A legal arrangement whereby title to specific property is transferred by the creator of the trust to another person, called the trustee, usually for the benefit of a third party, called a beneficiary.

EQUIPMENT TRUST A trust arrangement in which equipment, such as that in a dentist's office, is put into a trust for the benefit of a third party (for example, the dentist's children).

CLIFFORD TRUST A legal device by which property is irrevocably given in trust to, say, a minor child in a low tax bracket for a predetermined period, usually at least ten years plus one day.

SUPPORT TRUST A short-term trust set up to support elderly or dependent relatives. The beneficiary of the trust can receive all the income produced by it while the beneficiary is alive. When the beneficiary dies, the trust reverts back to the donor or another specified party.

CHAPTER SUMMARY

1. Municipal bonds are an obvious tax shelter because the income from them (interest) is not taxed by the federal government and, in some cases, not by state governments.

2. The benefit from the tax-exempt nature of the income yielded by a municipal bond is directly proportional to your marginal tax bracket: the higher your marginal tax bracket, the greater the benefit.

3. The yields on municipal bonds are bid down because people earning higher incomes are willing to pay more for the tax-free nature of the bonds' income. Thus, only if you are in a marginal tax bracket exceeding about 35 percent is it worthwhile to buy such bonds.

4. You can figure out the equivalent taxable yield with the following formula:

$$\text{equivalent taxable yield} = \frac{\text{tax exempt yield}}{1-(\text{your marginal tax rate})}$$

5. A tax-deferred pension plan allows you to save before-tax dollars. You receive an interest-free loan from the government on which you earn interest. And you aren't taxed until you take the retirement funds out of the plan; by then, you're generally in a lower marginal tax bracket.

6. A basic saving rule is: As long as you plan to save a certain percentage of your income, you will be better off if you can save by way of a qualified tax sheltered pension plan.

7. If you aren't covered by a pension plan by your employer, you can set up a Keogh Plan or an IRA.

8. You can reduce tax burdens by setting up such trust tax shelters as an equipment trust, a Clifford trust, or a support trust.

9. Nontaxable fringe benefits are advantageous if you would purchase the services anyway.

10. Fringe benefits include prepaid legal, medical, and dental insurance; some forms of group life insurance; prepaid psychiatric plans; disability insurance; and some forms of employee dependents' educational funds.

11. Some less well-known tax shelters are bartering, do-it-yourself activities, buying consumer durables, and increasing leisure.

12. Only if you have substantial nonsalaried income can you incorporate. And then you must demonstrate that you operate a bona fide business.

13. The costs of incorporation include: (a) lawyer's setup fees, (b) accountant's setup fees, (c) fees to the state, (d) unemployment insurance taxes, (e) employer's contribution to Social Security, and (f) annual legal and accounting fees.

14. The benefits of incorporating include being able to set up pension and profit sharing plans, as well as obtaining numerous fringe benefits that are paid for with before-tax dollars.

15. The fringe benefits you can obtain include, in one form or another, term life insurance, a medical plan, a leased car, and disability insurance.

STUDY QUESTIONS

1. Is a tax-free municipal bond a good investment for all individuals?

2. What is the general formula for expressing the equivalent taxable yield of a tax-exempt municipal bond?

3. Explain how a tax-deferred pension plan shelters income.

4. What is a Keogh Plan?

5. What is an individual retirement account (IRA)? How does it differ from a Keogh Plan?

6. How are fringe benefits a type of tax loophole?

7. List several unique ways of avoiding taxes that we have not yet discussed.

8. How is purchasing consumer durables a way to avoid taxes? Is leisure ever taxed?

9. Who should incorporate?

10. What are the costs of incorporation? What are the benefits?

CASE PROBLEMS

13-1   Investment Decisions

After the death of their father, Alton Jamison, a shipyard personnel manager in Bremerton, Washington, and his sister, Theresa Kempler, a city planner in Modesto, California, each received $10,000 from life insurance policies. They were discussing ways to invest the money. Alton was interested in buying an 11% corporate bond, and Theresa had heard that 6% municipal bonds were a good investment, but neither really knew which would be best for them. Alton, a bachelor, earns $33,000 in taxable income, and Theresa, who is married, has a taxable income of $27,000. What would you recommend for each of them?

31-2   Planning for Retirement

Bob and Marilyn Beaumont, a couple in their late forties, are planning for their retirement. They are in a 25% tax bracket. They have heard of IRAs and deferred annuities but don't clearly understand the difference between them. They want to put $1500 a year into one of these accounts. Explain to them the tax aspects of each of the plans.

SELECTED REFERENCES

"Despite New Law, You Can Still Find Tax Shelters." *U.S. News & World Report,* November 1976, pp. 83-85.

Edgerton, Terry, "A New Way to Shelter Income." *Money,* March 1977, pp. 77-78.

Josephus, Stuart R. *Tax Planning Techniques for Individuals.* New York: American Institute of Certified Public Accountants, 1971.

Pechman, Joseph A. and Okner, Benjamin A. *Who Bears the Tax Burden?* Washington, D.C.: The Brookings Institution, 1974.

Stern, Phillip M. *The Rape of the Taxpayer.* New York: Random House, 1973.

Investment

Saving and Saving Instruments

A man may, if he know not how to save, keep his nose to the Grindstone, and die not worth a Groat at last

Benjamin Franklin
Poor Richard's Almanac, January 1794

■ Almost two-thirds of all American families have savings accounts, and more than 30 million Americans have stocks or bonds. In total, the amount of savings in the United States in any one year may exceed $100 billion. Exhibit 14-1 shows the total amount of personal saving in the United States during the past eighty years.

WHY SAVE AT ALL?

You may want to save in order to leave a large estate to your heirs or to provide for yourself and your family during periods when your income is low relative to your expected expenditures. Those periods may occur when you are unemployed, disabled, or after you retire. Saving, then, enables you to spread out your consumption over your lifetime; your consumption remains consistent even when your income fluctuates or sometimes falls to zero, especially after you reach old age. You know that some time in the future you will no longer be able to work. You will either reach mandatory retirement age, or you will become so unproductive that no one will hire you. Your labor income stream will be cut off, and unless there are children, a benevolent government, or private charities to take care of you, you will face starvation—unless you have accumulated savings.

Therefore, you must decide today how much of your current income you want to set aside for the future. Unless you will literally starve if you reduce your current level of consumption even slightly, you probably will attempt to save a small amount out of your income. Most people are willing to reduce current consumption slightly in order to be able to exist when they no longer can work. Were they not to reduce

353

their current consumption at all, they might face certain starvation as soon as their income stream stopped.

Thus, saving is a method by which individuals can achieve an optimal consumption stream throughout their expected lifetime. Optimal here does not mean adequate or necessary but, rather, the most desirable from the individual's point of view. If you face the constraint of a low income for all your life, you probably still would want to provide some savings for those times when you can no longer work for an income.

WHAT DETERMINES HOW MUCH YOU SAVE?

Obviously, the more money (interest or yield) you can make on your savings, the more you will want to save (if nothing else changes). In other words, if a savings and loan association offered to give you 50 percent interest a year on anything you put into it, you probably would want to save more than you do now, when a savings and loan association gives you an interest rate of around 5 or 6 percent.

How Much Do You Value the Present?

To decide whether to save or how much to save, you should consider more than the interest rate on your savings. You also should look at how you value consumption today as opposed to consumption tomorrow. When you put off spending $100, you give up the pleasure from whatever you might have spent it on. In other words, you have to wait. If you

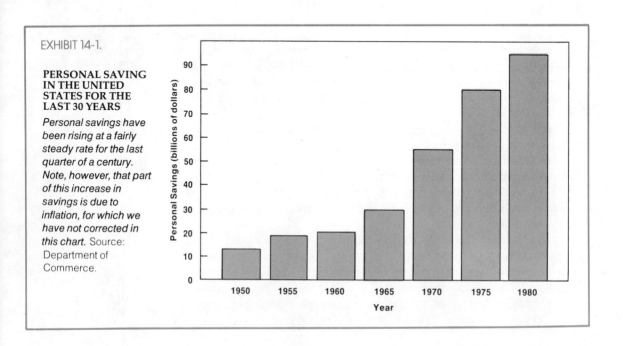

EXHIBIT 14-1.

PERSONAL SAVING IN THE UNITED STATES FOR THE LAST 30 YEARS

Personal savings have been rising at a fairly steady rate for the last quarter of a century. Note, however, that part of this increase in savings is due to inflation, for which we have not corrected in this chart. Source: Department of Commerce.

are impatient, even a high interest rate on savings may not induce you to save. Those who are less impatient about consuming may save more.

How Variable Is Your Income?

Another major determinant of how much you think you should save is how variable your income is. For example, people with stable incomes from secure government employment generally save a smaller percentage of their income than do people who are in business for themselves. Obviously, the more variable your income, the more likely you are to have years when your income is lower than usual. Hence, during the years when it is higher than usual, you generally save more.

How Much Retirement Income?

Moreover, how much you will save depends on how much future income you decide you should have when you're not working. To fully understand how much you will have in the future, you must understand **compound interest.** Obviously, if you earned no interest at all, your total savings at the end of a specific saving period—say, thirty years—would be exactly what you originally deposited. But that's not what usually happens: usually you earn interest on whatever you save.

THE NATURE OF COMPOUND INTEREST

If you decide to save by not consuming all your income, you can take what you save and invest it. You can put it in the stock market or buy bonds—that is, lend money to businesses. You also could put it in your own business. In any event, you might expect to make a profit or interest every year in the future for a certain period of time. To figure out how much you will have at the end of any specified time period, you must compound your savings, using a specified interest rate. Let's say you put $100 in a savings and loan association that yields 5 percent per year. At the end of one year, you have $105; at the end of two years, you have $105 plus 5 percent of $105, or $5.25, which gives you a total of $110.25. This same compounding occurs the third year, the fourth year, and so on.

The Power of Compounding

The impressive power of compound interest is shown in Exhibit 14-2.

Exhibit 14-3 shows one dollar compounded every year for fifty years at different interest rates. At an interest rate of 8 percent, one dollar will return $46.90 at the end of fifty years. Thus, if you inherited $20,000 when you were twenty years old and put it in an investment that paid 8 percent (after-tax) compounded annually, at age seventy you would have $938,000. It's not so difficult to understand how some people become millionaires. It doesn't take much business acumen to get an 8 percent rate of return in the long run. Someone who had invested in the stock market 50 years ago would have received much more than 8 percent. There are a number of people who inherit moderate amounts of money when they are young. If they put this money in the stock market and leave it there to compound itself, it increases enormously after thirty or forty years. Exhibit 14-4 shows what $1,000 can become in ten years at different interest rates and also what would happen if you deposited $1,000 a year, each year, for ten years.

Compound Interest and Investment Schemes

Many investment schemes succeed because of the power of compound interest. Take high-priced paintings. Art dealers claim that some paintings are good investments. They will cite, for example, a Picasso that someone purchased for only $5,000 and then sold for $15,000. You should find out, however, when it was purchased. Considering the length of time the painting was held, the actual gain in value might be very modest—say, only 3 percent a year. After all, if the painting cost $1,000 in 1955, at a 3 percent compound interest, it would be worth over $2,000 in 1980. The owner who sold it in 1980 probably could have done better in 1955 by investing the $1,000 in a savings account that yielded 4 or 5 percent. But because people get some consumption pleasure from having art work in their homes, they are willing to receive a lower rate of return than they expect from money in some other type of investment.

PRESENT VALUE CALCULATIONS—A DIGRESSION

Sometimes you have to figure out the reverse computation to compound interest. That is, you may want to know how much money you must put into savings today in order to have a specified amount, say, ten years from now. The amount you must put into savings today is called the present value, or discounted value, of the desired amount ten years hence.

If someone gave you a choice between receiving one dollar a year for the rest of your life or twenty dollars today, which would you prefer? You might be hard-pressed to decide which was the better deal. It's difficult to assess the value of dollars coming in at the end of each year, year in and year out. A dollar ten years from now certainly won't be as desirable as a dollar today. In fact, you might even be dead ten years from now, so the dollar would do you no good at all. The point is, dollars today are worth more than dollars tomorrow. You have to *discount* future dollars to figure out what they're worth to you today.

Discounting is a term we apply to the procedure of reducing *future* values to show how much they actually are worth today. We reduce them by a discount factor that depends on the discount rate we use, which is some interest rate. Let's say that you could take your money and put it in a savings and loan institution, where you might get a 5 percent rate of return. If you put in $1 today, you would have $1.05 a year from now. The discounted value of $1.05 to be received a year

EXHIBIT 14-2.

**THE DIFFERENCE
BETWEEN
COMPOUND AND
SIMPLE INTEREST**

At 5 percent simple interest, one cent would have become approximately one dollar if it had been invested at the birth of Christ at 5 percent simple interest.

On the other hand, 1,980 years later, the one cent invested at 5 percent compounded annual interest grows to about $90,120 followed by thirty-six zeros, or

$90,120,000,000,000,000,000,000,000,000,000,000,000,000

EXHIBIT 14-3.

ONE DOLLAR COMPOUNDED AT DIFFERENT INTEREST RATES FOR DIFFERENT PERIODS

Here we show the value of the dollar at the end of a specified period after it has been compounded at a specified interest rate. For example, if you took $1 today and invested it at 5 percent, it would yield $1.05 at the end of the year. At the end of ten years, it would be equal to $1.63, and at the end of fifty years, it would be equal to $11.50.

In this table, interest is compounded once a year at the end of every year. There are other ways of compounding interest, such as semiannually (once every six months), quarterly (once every three months), daily, and continuously. The actual compound factor in this table would have to be altered for each compounding scheme. Clearly, the more frequently a given interest percentage is compounded, the larger the return after a given period of time.

YEAR	3%	4%	5%	6%	8%	10%	20%	YEAR
1	1.03	1.04	1.05	1.06	1.08	1.10	1.20	1
2	1.06	1.08	1.10	1.12	1.17	1.21	1.44	2
3	1.09	1.12	1.16	1.19	1.26	1.33	1.73	3
4	1.13	1.17	1.22	1.26	1.36	1.46	2.07	4
5	1.16	1.22	1.28	1.34	1.47	1.61	2.49	5
6	1.19	1.27	1.34	1.41	1.59	1.77	2.99	6
7	1.23	1.32	1.41	1.50	1.71	1.94	3.58	7
8	1.27	1.37	1.48	1.59	1.85	2.14	4.30	8
9	1.30	1.42	1.55	1.68	2.00	2.35	5.16	9
10	1.34	1.48	1.63	1.79	2.16	2.59	6.19	10
11	1.38	1.54	1.71	1.89	2.33	2.85	7.43	11
12	1.43	1.60	1.80	2.01	2.52	3.13	8.92	12
13	1.47	1.67	1.89	2.13	2.72	3.45	10.7	13
14	1.51	1.73	1.98	2.26	2.94	3.79	12.8	14
15	1.56	1.80	2.08	2.39	3.17	4.17	15.4	15
16	1.60	1.87	2.18	2.54	3.43	4.59	18.5	16
17	1.65	1.95	2.29	2.69	3.70	5.05	22.2	17
18	1.70	2.03	2.41	2.85	4.00	5.55	26.6	18
19	1.75	2.11	2.53	3.02	4.32	6.11	31.9	19
20	1.81	2.19	2.65	3.20	4.66	6.72	38.3	20
25	2.09	2.67	3.39	4.29	6.85	10.8	95.4	25
30	2.43	3.24	4.32	5.74	10.0	17.4	237	30
40	3.26	4.80	7.04	10.3	21.7	45.3	1470	40
50	4.38	4.11	11.5	18.4	46.9	117	9100	50

hence, using a discount rate of 5 percent, is only $1. Or, put another way, the discounted value of one dollar one year from now at a 5 percent rate is about ninety-five cents. You could put your ninety-five cents in today and get about one dollar in a year. Two years from now, a dollar would be worth even less. You could put in about ninety-one cents today and have a dollar two years from now. The point is: *A dollar received in the future is worth less than a dollar received today.* Exhibit 14-5 shows various present values of future dollars at the end of specified years for particular interest rates. The higher the interest rate (that is, the higher the amount you actually could get by investing your savings), the lower the value of dollars in the future. Moreover, the further in the future you get those dollars, the smaller the present value.

TIME DEPOSITS

One of the major outlets of savings dollars in the United States is time deposits. Time deposits are defined as saving instruments which, in principle, cannot be turned into cash until a specified amount of time has passed after the request for cash is made. Additionally, the deposited money usually must remain deposited for a specific period of time in order for it to earn interest. The most common types of time deposits are savings accounts in commercial banks, savings and loan associations, and credit unions.

EXHIBIT 14-4.

**HOW COMPOUND
INTEREST HELPS
YOU BUILD A
NEST EGG**

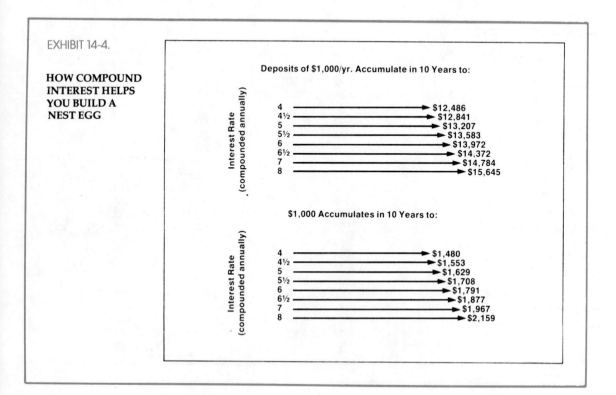

A major virtue of time deposits is their liquidity. A liquid asset is one that readily can be turned into buying power. Even though, in principle, you must wait a specified period of time before a time deposit can be turned into buying power, in practice, institutions offering time deposits rarely, if ever, require such a waiting period. Hence, the owners of time deposits can turn those time deposits into buying power rapidly.

Why Use Time Deposits?

Among the reasons time deposits are a popular form of savings for personal investment are the following:

Safe Investment. Since most time deposits up to $40,000 are insured in one way or another, the owner is virtually guaranteed that the **principal** will never be lost. Moreover, the value of the time deposit does not fluctuate as does, for example, the value of stocks purchased. The interest paid on time deposits is certain, and there is rarely, if ever, a default.

EXHIBIT 14-5.

PRESENT VALUES OF A FUTURE DOLLAR

Each column shows how much a dollar received at the end of a certain number of years in the future (identified on the extreme left-hand or right-hand column) is worth today. For example, at 5 percent a year, a dollar to be received 20 years in the future is worth only 37.7¢. At the end of 50 years, it isn't even worth a dime today. To find out how much $10,000 would be worth a certain number of years from now, just multiply the figures in the columns by 10,000. For example, $10,000 received at the end of 10 years discounted at a 5 percent rate of interest would be equal to $6,140.

NUMBER OF YEARS	3%	4%	5%	6%	8%	10%	20%	NUMBER OF YEARS
1	0.971	0.962	0.952	0.943	0.926	0.909	0.833	1
2	0.943	0.925	0.907	0.890	0.857	0.826	0.694	2
3	0.915	0.890	0.864	0.839	0.794	0.751	0.578	3
4	0.889	0.855	0.823	0.792	0.735	0.683	0.482	4
5	0.863	0.823	0.784	0.747	0.681	0.620	0.402	5
6	0.838	0.790	0.746	0.705	0.630	0.564	0.335	6
7	0.813	0.760	0.711	0.665	0.583	0.513	0.279	7
8	0.789	0.731	0.677	0.627	0.540	0.466	0.233	8
9	0.766	0.703	0.645	0.591	0.500	0.424	0.194	9
10	0.744	0.676	0.614	0.558	0.463	0.385	0.162	10
11	0.722	0.650	0.585	0.526	0.429	0.350	0.134	11
12	0.701	0.625	0.557	0.497	0.397	0.318	0.112	12
13	0.681	0.601	0.530	0.468	0.368	0.289	0.0935	13
14	0.661	0.577	0.505	0.442	0.340	0.263	0.0779	14
15	0.642	0.555	0.481	0.417	0.315	0.239	0.0649	15
16	0.623	0.534	0.458	0.393	0.292	0.217	0.0541	16
17	0.605	0.513	0.436	0.371	0.270	0.197	0.0451	17
18	0.587	0.494	0.416	0.350	0.250	0.179	0.0376	18
19	0.570	0.475	0.396	0.330	0.232	0.163	0.0313	19
20	0.554	0.456	0.377	0.311	0.215	0.148	0.0261	20
25	0.478	0.375	0.295	0.232	0.146	0.0923	0.0105	25
30	0.412	0.308	0.231	0.174	0.0994	0.0573	0.00421	30
40	0.307	0.208	0.142	0.0972	0.0460	0.0221	0.000680	40
50	0.228	0.141	0.087	0.0543	0.0213	0.00852	0.000109	50

Use As a Temporary Investment Outlet. It is easy to "get in and out" of time deposits, so many individuals use them to accumulate funds to transfer to another investment or to purchase a consumer durable good.

Saving for Emergencies. Since time deposits are highly liquid, the individual owner can **liquidate** for immediate buying power to cover unexpected doctor bills, casualty losses, or other emergencies.

Disadvantages of Time Deposits

Low Rate of Return. A major disadvantage of time deposits is their relatively low rate of return. Maximum time deposit rates of return generally are fixed by law and don't offer the average saver much to get excited about. Note, though, that one reason the rates of return on time deposits are so low is because the risk of losing one's money is low also. It is usually difficult, if not impossible, to obtain higher rates of return without incurring higher amounts of risk. Or, it is usually difficult to obtain higher rates of return without purchasing investment assets, which certainly are less liquid than time deposits.

Little Protection against Inflation. If the rate of inflation is 6 percent and the rate paid on a time deposit is 6 percent, then the real rate of return after inflation is accounted for is zero. Actually, it is even less than that. Federal and, sometimes, state income taxes must be paid on the earnings from time deposits before any account of inflation is taken. Thus, if a time deposit pays 6 percent per year and you are in the 50 percent tax bracket, your after-tax rate of return will be 3 percent. Again, if the rate of inflation was 6 percent, you get 3 percent minus 6 percent, which would equal a minus 3 percent. After paying taxes at the end of the year, you would have less purchasing power than when you started.

TIME DEPOSIT INSTITUTIONS AND THE INSTRUMENTS THEY OFFER

There are numerous institutions that offer time deposits in one form or another. Exhibit 14-6 shows how savers in America allocate their time deposits.

Commercial Banks

Commercial banks offer time deposit accounts in addition to checking accounts, which we discussed in Chapter 5. Time deposit accounts have different names at different commercial banks. The basic time deposit account is called a regular passbook savings account.

Passbook Savings Accounts. With such accounts, commercial banks give you a passbook in which your entries and withdrawals are indicated. Actually, some banks no longer have passbooks because all transactions are computerized.

Here are some of the possible savings accounts you can open:

1   *Individual*—owned by only one person, either an adult or a minor.

2   *Joint*—usually owned by two persons; usually a husband and wife.

3   *Voluntary Trust*—can be opened by an adult in trust for a child or another person. It is controlled by the trustee during his or her life. After the trustee's death, it is payable to the person named as beneficiary. Note, though, that the trustee can change the beneficiary at any time.

4   *Custodial*—similar to a trust account except that it is irrevocable and becomes the property of the minor for whom it was opened.

5   *Landlord Trust*—an account made for the benefit of tenants, whose lease security deposits must be placed in such accounts.

6   *Fiduciary*—accounts opened by administrators of an estate or a guardian for a minor or an incompetent person.

Club Accounts. There are several special types of savings accounts that enable customers to save for a specific goal. Thus, we find Chanukah, Christmas, and vacation club accounts in which you accumulate savings usually by depositing a fixed amount for fifty weeks. Often little or no interest is paid on these accounts, but they give you an incentive to save. If the bank does offer interest, you don't receive it unless you keep your money on deposit for a requisite number of months.

Bonus Savings Accounts. These are passbook-type accounts that pay a slightly higher interest rate if a minimum required balance is kept and/or a minimum holding period is used. The bonus-type account reverts to a regular account if any of the stipulations are violated.

EXHIBIT 14-6.

THE ALLOCATION OF SAVINGS ACCOUNTS, 1978

TYPE OF INSTITUTION	BILLIONS OF DOLLARS OF SAVINGS ACCOUNTS, 1978
Savings and loan associations	$469.7
Mutual savings banks	149.3
Credit unions	55.0
Commercial banks	556.9
Mutual funds	42.9
U.S. savings bonds, E and H Series, and freedom shares	80.1

Source: U.S. Federal Reserve, Board of Governors.

Certificates of Deposits. Many commercial banks offer what are called savings certificates, which are really small-scale certificates of deposits. They are issued in amounts ranging from $25 to $1,000; savers also can purchase multiples of $1,000. **Small-scale CDs,** as they are called, offer higher interest rates than do regular passbook accounts. The limitation is that you must not cash in the small CDs before a specified time period, from one to ten years. The longer the time period, the higher the interest rate offered. If you find you must cash them in sooner, you receive only the regular passbook account interest rate on the amount, and you lose ninety days interest.

If you have large sums of money to invest, you can purchase what are called **large-scale CDs.** These are sold in denominations of $100,000 and up. They are negotiable and do not carry any penalties for early cash-in (since you may resell them to a third party). Large-scale CDs often offer the highest interest rate available to bank savers.

Savings Banks

These banks accept deposits and lend them out for a long term to reliable borrowers at higher rates of interest than they had to pay depositors. Such banks provide a safe place in which to invest savings. As with commercial bank deposits, savings bank deposits often require that a notice be given before the money can be withdrawn. This provision is rarely put into effect, however. Although there are various types of saving banks, the main two are stock and mutual.

Stock Savings Banks. This savings bank is organized and conducted for profit by the owners of its capital stock. The greatest number of stock saving banks are located in the midwestern United States. These banks are regulated by the state in which they are chartered.

Mutual Savings Banks. These banks are owned by their depositors. In effect, their depositors pool their savings, which are invested by a board of trustees and a hired manager. Depositors are not paid a fixed rate of interest on their deposits; net earnings made from the bank's investments belong to the depositors and are divided among them in proportion to their deposits. Mutual savings banks are located primarily in the eastern United States, although there are a few in the northwest. The total amount that a single individual can invest in a mutual savings bank is limited.

As of the late 1970s, certain mutual savings banks in the New England area are offering the equivalent of checking account privileges. The instruments used are called negotiable orders or withdrawal, or NOWS. The customer is charged a small sum per check, but any remaining balance is allowed to earn interest. As we noted in Chapter 5, commercial banks have long been prevented by law from offering interest on checking accounts. NOW accounts are a way around this law and give mutual savings banks a competitive edge over commercial banks in the New England area.

Savings and Loan Associations

These thrift organizations, of which there are some 5,400, are designed to assist present and future homeowners. The names by which these associations are known vary in different parts of the country. Some are called cooperative banks or building and loan associations.

Generally, when you put your money into a savings and loan association, you get a passbook that indicates you are a shareholder in that organization. As a member, you are entitled to receive interest on your deposits. Savings and loan associations generally are not authorized to handle checking accounts.

Some savings and loan associations have tried to obtain the right to offer most of the same services of a commercial bank. That is, many savings and loan associations would like to compete with commercial banks by offering a form of checking account, safe deposit boxes, and other banking services. Actually, some states now allow their savings and loan associations to extend some of these services.

Credit Unions

One of the fastest growing savings institutions in the nation, credit unions are owned by their membership. They have four purposes:

1   To help their members save.
2   To enable their members to borrow money at lower-than-market interest rates.
3   To educate members in money management.
4   To provide opportunities for volunteer service.

As a member in a credit union, you usually buy shares, which are marked on your share booklet or passbook. In effect, credit unions are really cooperative small-loan banks that lend amounts to their members at "reasonable" rates of interest. Federal and state laws determine the maximum amount that may be loaned by the credit union. Because a credit union typically is set up for a particular group—teachers in a certain city or state, members of a specific labor union, and so on—you must be part of such an organization in order to join.

Credit union accounts are slightly more risky than other types of time deposit accounts. For example, during a three-year period in the late 1960s in California, 28 out of 600 some existing credit unions folded for various reasons. Most paid back the entire amount owed their members, but some were unable to do so. In any event, you should make sure that your account is insured by the National Credit Union Association (NCUA).

The Federal Government

The federal government offers two types of saving instruments, which are similar to some of those we have discussed. They are called Series E and Series H bonds.

Series E, or U.S., Savings Bonds. Originally, Series E bonds ran for ten years and paid 2.9 percent if held to maturity. As of the end of the

1970s, the maturity date was five years and the interest rate paid was 6 percent compounded semiannually. Note, though, that there is an implicit penalty for early withdrawal, or "cash-in" of a Series E savings bond. Because the interest rates are paid on a staggered basis that rises in later years, you have a financial incentive to keep them to maturity.

Series E bonds can be purchased at most banks (without fee) and are bought at 75 percent of the face value or the value that is paid to you on maturity. (They are, therefore, a type of discount bond.) They can be cashed in after two months without advance notice.

Series E bonds are issued in the following denominations: $25, $50, $75, $100, $200, $500, $1,000, and $10,000. To purchase them you pay 75 percent of that amount. For example, a $25 U.S. Savings Bond would cost you $18.75. In the following Practical Application, we will discuss whether or not Series E savings bonds are an advisable savings outlet.

Series H Savings Bonds. There are several differences between Series E and Series H bonds. The Series H bonds are offered only in denominations of $500, $1,000, and $5,000. They are not discount bonds; you pay the price stated on the bond itself. You receive an interest check from the government semiannually. Thus, if the current yield is 5 percent for the first year on a $1,000 bond, you will receive $25 at the end of six months and $25 at the end of the next six months. You can cash in a Series H bond at the face amount any time after six months from the issue date. As with Series E bonds, the interest rate yields are staggered, increasing the longer you hold them. As of 1978, for example, the interest yield for the first year was 5 percent, increased to 5.80 percent for the next four years, then for the last five years during a ten-year period, it was 6.5 percent. Again, there is an incentive to keep the bonds longer in order to benefit from this higher interest yield.

HOW MUCH TO SAVE?

In this chapter we have described why people save and some of their saving outlets. In the following three chapters, we will discuss other areas where saving dollars can go, such as stocks, bonds, art work, real estate, and the like. Remember, any money that is saved or invested is money that is not spent in the current year. Thus, every individual and/or family faces the decision of how much current income should be set aside for future consumption. The average rate of saving in the United States has remained around 8 to 10 percent. Therefore, you might want to save the average or, say, 10 percent.

No fixed rules can be made for everyone, however. When you're young, your rate of saving may be negative; that is, you may borrow in addition to spending all your year's income. When you're older, your rate of saving may hit the national average or even be greater. Then, of course, when you retire, your rate of saving may become negative again as you consume the fruits of your past saving.

HOW TO HAVE THE
BEST SAVINGS ACCOUNT

Since there are scores of time deposit institutions and even more saving instruments from which to choose, you must decide where to put your savings dollars. Before you decide, you may wish to figure out how much future income you will earn from a modest saving program. Exhibit 14-7 shows what monthly deposits you must put into a savings account bearing 6 percent interest compounded daily in order to have specific monthly withdrawals later. This table tells you, for example, that if you deposit as little as $32.41 every month for twenty years, you will be able to withdraw $107.59 each month for the following twenty years.

HOW OFTEN IS INTEREST
COMPOUNDED?

When you shop around for the highest possible interest rate on your savings, you must compare compounding periods, among other things. The more frequent the compounding period, the more interest you will receive. Exhibit 14-8 shows the difference between interest that is compounded semiannually, quarterly, monthly, weekly, daily, and continuously. For example, a savings account yielding 6 percent nominal interest will yield 6.09 percent if compounded semiannually, 6.1678 percent if compounded monthly, and 6.1837 percent if compounded continuously. Although these differences appear slight, they make impressive differences over long periods.

IS YOUR DEPOSIT INSURED?

When shopping among various time deposit institutions, you must find out if your deposit will be insured. In most savings banks and commercial banks, your deposit will be insured by the Federal Deposit Insurance Corporation, or FDIC. Deposits in savings and loan associations are most often insured by the Federal Savings and Loan Insurance Corporation, or FSLIC. Credit union deposits are usually insured by the National Credit Union Administration (NCUA), which supervises the National Credit Union Shareholders' Insurance Fund.

By the end of the 1970s, each depositor was protected to an upper limit of $40,000, should the covered savings institution fail. It is important to understand just how this $40,000 protection limits your potential loss.

Applies to a Single Depositor

The $40,000 protection applies to the total number of accounts a single depositor has under his or her name within a single bank. Thus, if you were to have a $36,000 savings account in one bank and also $6,000 in a checking account, you would be insured up to $40,000, not $42,000. Moreover, if you have accounts in the same name in a main office and in one or more branches of the insured bank, the accounts are added up together to determine your insurance.

Splitting Your Funds among Banks and Accounts

If you have so much of your savings in time deposits that you reach the maximum limitation on insurability, you either can split your funds among a number of banks or split your funds among a number of accounts. For example, if you are married, you can have an account, your spouse can have an account, and you both can have a joint account. Thus, your maximum insurability as a unit increases to $120,000. If you have children, you can set up guardian or trustee accounts, which are insured separately.

HOW INTEREST IS CALCULATED ON
YOUR SAVINGS DEPOSITS

We have discussed two variables among savings institutions—when interest is compounded and

EXHIBIT 14-7.

6 PERCENT INTEREST COMPOUNDED DAILY

DEPOSIT THESE AMOUNTS MONTHLY FOR THESE YEARS				FOR THESE MONTHLY WITHDRAWALS				TOTAL SAVED
5 yrs.	10 yrs.	15 yrs.	20 yrs.	5 yrs.	10 yrs.	15 yrs.	20 yrs.	
$ 71.64	$ 30.49	$ 17.17	$ 10.80	$ 96.69	$ 55.54	$ 42.23	$ 35.86	$ 5,000
107.46	45.73	25.76	16.20	145.04	83.32	63.34	53.79	7,500
143.27	60.97	34.34	21.61	193.39	111.09	84.46	71.72	10,000
179.09	76.22	42.93	27.01	241.74	138.86	105.58	89.65	12,500
214.91	91.46	51.51	32.41	290.09	166.64	126.69	107.59	15,000
250.73	106.70	60.10	37.81	338.44	194.41	147.81	125.52	17,500
286.55	121.94	68.69	43.21	386.79	222.18	168.92	143.45	20,000
322.37	137.19	77.27	48.61	435.14	249.96	190.04	161.38	22,500
358.19	152.43	85.86	54.01	483.48	277.73	211.16	179.31	25,000
394.00	167.67	94.44	59.42	531.83	305.51	232.28	197.25	27,500
429.82	182.92	103.03	64.82	580.18	333.28	253.39	215.18	30,000
465.65	198.16	111.62	70.22	628.53	361.05	274.51	233.11	32,500
501.46	213.40	120.20	75.62	676.88	388.82	295.62	251.04	35,000
537.28	228.65	128.79	81.02	725.23	416.60	316.74	268.97	37,500
573.10	243.89	137.37	86.42	773.58	444.37	337.85	286.90	40,000

EXHIBIT 14-8.

**EARNING MORE FOR
YOUR MONEY**

NOMINAL PERCENTAGE YIELD	ACTUAL YEARLY PERCENTAGE YIELD					
	Semiannually	Quarterly	Monthly	Weekly	Daily	Continuously
5¼%	5.3189	5.3543	5.3782	5.3875	5.3898	5.3903
5½	5,5756	5.6145	5.6408	5.6510	5.6536	5.6541
5¾	5.8327	5.8752	5.9040	5.9152	5.9180	5.9185
6	6.0900	6.1364	6.1678	6.1800	6.1831	6.1837
6¼	6.3476	6.3980	6.4322	6.4455	6.4488	6.4494
6½	6.6056	6.6602	6.6972	6.7116	6.7153	6.7159
6¾	6.8639	6.9228	6.9628	6.9783	6.9823	6.9830
7	7.1225	7.1859	7.2290	7.2458	6.2501	6.2508
7¼	7.3814	7.4495	7.4958	7.5138	7.5185	7.5193
7½	7.6406	7.7136	7.7633	7.7826	7.7876	7.7884
7¾	7.9002	7.9782	9.0313	8.0520	8.0573	8.0582

whether the deposit is insured. The third variable you must check is how interest is computed on your savings deposit. The American Bankers Association estimates that there are at least fifty-four ways of computing interest on passbook deposits. The San Francisco Consumer Action group maintains that there are about 200 different methods for figuring interest. Here we will examine the four basic interest calculation methods currently used:

1. **Low balance.**

2. **First-In, First-Out** (FIFO).

3. **Last-In, First-Out** (LIFO).

4. **Day of Deposit to Day of Withdrawal** (DD-DW).

Exhibit 14-9 shows that the variation in actual interest earned is dramatic, ranging in that example from $44.93 to $75.30 for the same nominal interest rate offered on the passbook savings account.

SOME RECOMMENDATIONS

A regular savings account is often considered the worst place possible you can put your savings dollars because it offers the lowest interest yields. But, people do need funds for emergencies, so you may wish to put two to three months' living expenses in a regular savings account.

Once you've decided to open a savings account, you'll probably want to put your money in other than commercial banks. You should consider thrift institutions, such as savings and loan associations, mutual savings banks, and credit unions. You will want to shop around for an institution that will give you the highest legal interest rate and the most liberal method of computing interest. Thus, you want a combination of the following:

1. Continuous or daily compounding and crediting of interest.

2. Day of deposit to day of withdrawal interest formula.

3. No withdrawal penalties—that is, no fees charged when you withdraw money.

4. No minimum balance required to earn interest.

5. Grace days for deposit and withdrawal.

There are few accounts available that would give you all of the above, but you can use this check list to find the best one available. Also, how you use your account will be important. If you rarely, if ever, take money from your savings account, then you can ignore penalties for withdrawal. On the other hand, if you take out funds routinely, then that will be an important consideration.

WHAT ABOUT THOSE CLAIMS OF 10 to 22 PERCENT INTEREST?

There are books on the market that claim to help you get unusually high interest rates, ranging up to 22 percent per annum. Can this really be done? Basically, the trick is to earn interest with the same dollars at two or more different bank accounts by taking advantage of the grace days that each account allows at the beginning and end of each quarter. For example, you open one account in a bank paying interest from day of deposit to day of withdrawal and another account in a bank paying interest only on money left on deposit for a full quarter. The last account will have grace days at the beginning and end of the quarter. You then deposit your money a few days late and withdraw it a few days early without losing any interest. You keep most of your money in this account but shift it to the daily interest account during grace periods. You can pick up a total of fifty-two days of double interest a year in savings

banks in some states. The result, however, is modest. A rise in an effective yield on a 5-¼ percent passbook goes only to 6.27 percent, and you must spend your time and possibly transportation getting this higher rate. The only way you can boost your return above 10 percent is by using the "float" in a checking account with overdraft privileges, and that's not a very sound financial practice.

SERIES E BONDS

These bonds are a type of time deposit instrument. While it may be advisable to have some U.S. Savings Bonds in your savings portfolio, they are not a very attractive savings instrument.

Today, if you purchase U.S. Savings Bonds, you are deprived of liquidity for sixty days, the interest yield is a modest 4.01 percent for the first year, and the rate increases very gradually thereafter. At maturity, a half percent bonus is added, raising the yield to 5-½ percent from the issue date to maturity. To determine what kind of return that is, let's look at your after-tax return. Assuming that you're in the 20 percent tax bracket, that 5-½ percent return nets you only 4.4 percent after taxes.

If you had received 4.4 percent in 1978 with a rate of inflation of approximately 8 percent, your real rate of return would have been minus 3.6 percent. That negative rate of return means that even though you got interest on your investment in U.S. Savings Bonds, at the end of the year your principal, plus the interest, minus your taxes, and minus the reduction in value of those dollars due to inflation, would have given you less (by a factor of 4 percent) purchasing power than you started with. In 1979, if the rate of inflation goes to, say, an average of 10.4 percent, your rate of return on U.S. Savings Bonds after taxes would be a minus 6 percent. Even if the rate of inflation were to remain at a steady 5 or 6 percent, anyone who buys U.S. Savings Bonds would, after taxes, have *less* purchasing power five years and ten months after the investment than at the time of the investment.

EXHIBIT 14-9.

THESE FOUR BANKS ALL PAY THE SAME INTEREST RATE—YET INTEREST PAYMENTS RANGE FROM $44.93 TO $75.30.
There are many ways of computing interest, as the text of our report indicates. Here are four passbooks showing the identical deposits and withdrawals (made on the same days), with explanations of how the interest has been computed under four common methods. All four assume a six per cent interest rate and quarterly crediting and compounding. Copyright 1975 by Consumers Union of United States, Inc., Mount Vernon, NY 10550. Excerpted by permission from Consumer Reports, February 1975.

**These four banks all pay the same interest rate—
yet interest payments range from $44.93 to $75.30.**

There are many ways of computing interest, as the text of our report indicates. Here are four passbooks showing the identical deposits and withdrawals (made on the same days), with explanations of how the interest has been computed under four common methods. All four assume a six per cent interest rate and quarterly crediting and compounding.

IN ACCOUNT WITH

	DATE	WITHDRAWAL	DEPOSIT	INTEREST	BALANCE	TELLER
1	JAN-1		**1,000.00		**1,000.00	
2	JAN 10		**2,000.00		**3,000.00	
3	FEB-6		**1,000.00		**4,000.00	
4	MAR-3	*1,000.00			**3,000.00	
5	MAR 20	**500.00			**2,500.00	
6	MAR 30	**500.00			**2,000.00	
7	APR-1			*14.79	**2,014.79	
8	JUL-1			*30.14	**2,044.93	
9						
10						

LOW BALANCE
Under this method, interest is paid only on the smallest amount of money that was in the account during the interest period. Despite a balance that reached $4000 during the first quarter, this account earned interest only on $1000—the lowest balance during that period. (There are no withdrawals during the second quarter, so the low-balance formula is not important there.) This method, which tends to discourage deposits, is the most punitive to savers. Yet 30 per cent of commercial banks still use it, according to a study last year by the American Bankers Association.
Interest: $44.93

IN ACCOUNT WITH

	DATE	WITHDRAWAL	DEPOSIT	INTEREST	BALANCE	TELLER
1						
2	JAN-1		**1,000.00		**1,000.00	
3	JAN 10		**2,000.00		**3,000.00	
4	FEB-6		**1,000.00		**4,000.00	
5	MAR-5	*1,000.00			**3,000.00	
6	MAR 20	**500.00			**2,500.00	
7	MAR 30	**500.00			**2,000.00	
8						
9	APR-1			*22.19	**2,022.19	
10	JUL-1			*30.25	**2,052.44	
11						

FIRST-IN, FIRST-OUT (FIFO)
With this method, withdrawals are deducted first from the starting balance of the interest period and then, if the balance isn't sufficient, from later deposits. This erodes the base on which your interest is figured and means you automatically lose interest on withdrawals from the start of the interest period rather than from the dates on which the withdrawals were actually made. Another variation of this method is to apply the first withdrawal to the first deposit, rather than to the beginning balance; this would earn $53.93. About 16 per cent of commercial banks use the FIFO methods, according to the ABA.
Interest: $52.44

IN ACCOUNT WITH

	DATE	WITHDRAWAL	DEPOSIT	INTEREST	BALANCE	TELLER
1						
2	JAN-1		**1,000.00		**1,000.00	
3	JAN 10		**2,000.00		**3,000.00	
4	FEB-6		**1,000.00		**4,000.00	
5						
6	MAR-5	*1,000.00			**3,000.00	
7	MAR 20	**500.00			**2,500.00	
8	MAR 30	**500.00			**2,000.00	
9						
10	APR-1			*28.10	**2,028.10	
11	JUL-1			*30.34	**2,058.44	
12						

LAST-IN, FIRST-OUT (LIFO)
Under this plan, withdrawals are deducted from the most recent deposits in the quarter and then from the next most recent ones. This method, which does not penalize savers as much as the two FIFO methods, is used by about 5 per cent of commercial banks.
Interest: $58.44

IN ACCOUNT WITH

	DATE	WITHDRAWAL	DEPOSIT	INTEREST	BALANCE	TELLER
1						
2	JAN-1		**1,000.00		**1,000.00	
3	JAN 10		**2,000.00		**3,000.00	
4	FEB-6		**1,000.00		**4,000.00	
5						
6	MAR-5	*1,000.00			**3,000.00	
7	MAR 20	**500.00			**2,500.00	
8	MAR 30	**500.00			**2,000.00	
9						
10	APR-1			*44.71	**2,044.71	
11	JUL-1			*30.59	**2,075.30	
12						

DAY-OF-DEPOSIT TO DAY-OF-WITHDRAWAL
Under this arrangement, the bank pays you interest for the actual number of days the money remains in the account. This method, which is sometimes called daily interest, instant interest, or day-in day-out, is the fairest to consumers. It is used by almost 50 per cent of commercial banks and 60 per cent of insured S&Ls (there are no industry figures for savings banks). It yields the greatest return.
Interest: $75.30

GLOSSARY OF TERMS

SAVING The nonconsumption of current income; the difference between income and consumption for any given time period, usually a year.

COMPOUND INTEREST Interest upon which interest is also paid. Sums earning compound interest increase at a geometric rate.

DISCOUNTING The procedure used to reduce future values to their present values. Discounting requires the use of a discount rate, which is the interest rate decided upon as appropriate for each particular case and depends on perceived risk.

TIME DEPOSITS Saving instruments which, in principle, cannot be converted into cash until a specified amount of time, such as sixty days, has passed after the request for cash is made.

PRINCIPAL The amount of money placed at interest or due as a debt. One earns interest on the principal of an investment. Typically, this applies to bonds.

LIQUIDATE To convert an asset into buying power or cash. The more rapidly an asset can be turned into cash without loss of value, the more liquid is the asset.

SMALL-SCALE CD'S Small denomination certificates of deposits issued in amounts ranging from $25 to $1,000. They cannot be cashed in before a specified time period, usually from one to ten years. If they are cashed in before their maturity date, there is an interest reduction penalty.

LARGE-SCALE CD'S Negotiable certificates of deposits sold in denominations of $100,000 and up.

LOW BALANCE A method of computing interest on a savings account; you receive interest only on the lowest balance in your account during the quarter, regardless of how much was deposited.

FIRST-IN, FIRST-OUT (FIFO) Using this method of computation, withdrawals during a period are deducted first from the beginning balance. If that balance isn't large enough from subsequent deposits, you lose interest on withdrawals from the *start* of the interest period or the earliest deposit dates, rather than from the time you actually made the withdrawals.

LAST-IN, FIRST-OUT (LIFO) In this method of interest computation, withdrawals are deducted from those funds most recently deposited within the interest period.

DATE OF DEPOSIT TO DATE OF WITHDRAWAL (DD-DW) All funds earn interest for the actual number of days they are on deposit.

CHAPTER SUMMARY

1. Individuals save—do not consume all of current income—in order to distribute their consumption evenly over a lifetime.

2. The determinants of the saving rate are: (a) the rate of return or interest earned on savings; (b) how much the individual values present over future consumption; (c) the variability of income earned; and (d) the desired amount of retirement income.

3. Small sums of money can grow to impressive amounts if interest on them is compounded over a number of years. Thus, investments may actually yield only modest rates of return even though they have grown to large sums after a certain period of time.

4. To figure out the value of a dollar at some time in the future, we must discount it back to the present. Discounting, therefore, allows us to figure out how much we must invest today in order to get a specified amount at some later date.

5. Individuals use time deposits as a form of saving because: (a) they are a safe investment, usually insured; (b) they can act as a temporary investment outlet; and (c) they are available for emergencies, such as illness and casualty losses.

6. The disadvantages of time deposits are that they often yield low rates of return, and they offer little protection against inflation.

7. There are several time deposit institutions, including: (a) commercial banks, (b) savings banks (both stock and mutual), (c) savings and loan associations, (d) credit unions, and (e) the federal government.

8. Commercial banks offer passbook savings accounts that can be taken out: (a) in the name of an individual (b) jointly, (c) as a voluntary trust, (d) as a custodial account, (e) as a landlord trust, and (f) as a fiduciary account.

9. Commercial banks also offer holiday and vacation club accounts, bonus savings accounts, and certificates of deposit.

10. Credit unions are owned by their membership and are dedicated to helping their members save, enabling their members to borrow at lower-than-market interest rates, and educating their members in money management.

11. The federal government offers Series E and Series H savings bonds.

12. It is important to note how often interest is compounded. Continuous compounding yields the highest real rate of return for any savings account.

13. The Federal Deposit Insurance Corporation (FDIC) insures deposits in commercial and savings banks.

14. The Federal Savings and Loan Insurance Corporation (FSLIC) insures deposits in savings and loan associations.

15. The National Credit Union Association (NCUA), using the National Credit Union Shareholders' Insurance Fund, insures credit union deposits.

16. Most insured deposits have a limit of $40,000 of protection.

17. It is possible to split up your funds among different banks and accounts in order to insure all time deposits.

18. In choosing a savings institution, it is important to check which type of interest calculation is used. The least favorable are low balance and FIFO. The most favorable are LIFO and DD-DW.

19. Additional things to check for in a savings institution are: (a) the extent of withdrawal penalties (if you plan to withdraw), (b) the necessity of a minimum balance to earn interest, and (c) the number of grace days for deposit and withdrawal.

20. It is generally difficult, if not impossible, to earn really high rates of interest on time deposits unless you are willing to spend time playing off grace periods and/or using (perhaps illegally) "float" from a checking account with overdraft privileges.

21. U.S. Savings Bonds are a relatively unattractive savings instrument for many savers and cannot be recommended except in special circumstances.

STUDY QUESTIONS

1. Why do people save?

2. What determines how much you save?

3. What is the difference between simple and compound interest?

4. If you put $100 in a savings institution that promises to give you back $320 in twenty years, what compound rate of interest will you be earning?

5. Why isn't a dollar received in the future worth as much as a dollar received today?

6. List some reasons for using time deposits. Are these reasons related to liquidity?

7. List some of the disadvantages of time deposits.

8. What are the advantages and disadvantages of so-called club accounts in banks and savings and loan associations?

9. What is a small-scale certificate of deposit, and who might purchase one?

10. What is the difference between a stock and a mutual savings bank?

11. What is the difference between a Series E and a Series H U.S. Savings Bond?

12. When might you want to buy Series E U.S. Savings Bonds?

13. Describe the four different methods for computing interest on saving account balances. Which method is the most advantageous?

CASE PROBLEMS

14-1 Inflation Affects Investments

Mack Sweeney, a twenty-year-old college student, entered a magazine sweepstakes and was one of the big winners. After he paid the taxes and set aside enough to pay for his college education, he had $25,000. Mack told his roommate, Jim, that he was going to invest the money at 10% and that he would be a millionaire by the time he was sixty. Jim thought he might be right, but he pointed out that if inflation continued at 8% a year, the money, in today's dollars, would only be worth about twice what it is now.

1. Was Mack right or wrong?

2. Was Jim right or wrong?

3. What major consideration in the growth of the money did they overlook?

14-2 Planning Ahead for Education

Ted and Marsha Ross of Wichita, Kansas, want to establish an educational fund for their three-year-old daughter, Betsy.

1. If the average state university education costs $5000 now and costs rise at 8% a year, what will it cost in fifteen years?

2. If they invest $1000 a year for ten years at 6% and then allow the fund to grow for another five years, will they have enough to pay for her education? (Hint: Use Exhibit 14-4 and then 14-3.)

3. How much would they have to invest now as a lump sum at 6% to achieve their goal in fifteen years?

SELECTED REFERENCES

"A Look at Some Ways People Are Saving Money." *U.S. News & World Report*, March 22, 1976, pp. 77-78.

Credit Union Statistics. National Credit Union Administration (NCUA), 2025 M Street, N.W., Washington, D.C. 20456, issued quarterly and annually.

Miller, Roger LeRoy. "Non-Disclosure: Red, White and Blue." *Business & Society Review*, Autumn 1974.

National Fact Book of Mutual Savings Banks. National Association of Mutual Savings Banks, Suite 200, 1709 New York Avenue, N.W., Washington, D.C. 20006, latest edition.

"Once-Meek Credit Unions Take On the Banking Industry." *U.S. News & World Report*, February 21, 1977, pp. 85-86.

Personal Money Management, American Bankers Association, 1120 Connecticut Avenue, N.W., Washington, D.C. 20036, latest edition.

Rudd, Nancy. *Selecting a Savings Account*. Agricultural Research Service (ARS), U.S. Department of Agriculture, Summer 1973.

Savings and Loan Fact Book. U.S. Savings and Loan League, 221 North LaSalle Street, Chicago, Illinois 60601, latest edition.

The Credit Union Yearbook. Credit Union National Association, Association of Filene House, 1617 Sherman Avenue, Madison, Wisconsin 53701, latest edition.

"Taking Another Look at U.S. Savings Bonds," *Changing Times*, March 1975, pp. 25-27.

"Things a Credit Union Can Do for You," *Changing Times*, January 1976, pp. 35-38.

Your Insured Deposit. Federal Deposit Insurance Corporation, 550 17th Street, N.W., Washington, D.C. 20429.

Your Savings and Investment Dollar. Chicago: Money Management Institute, Household Finance Corporation, 1973.

Investing in Securities

■ Millions of American families include securities in their investment portfolios. Different types of securities may be suitable for different families. And there are different strategies and procedures for buying and selling securities over time. Obviously, investing in securities is an interesting and complex activity—and certainly an important part of personal finance.

WHAT ARE SECURITIES?

Business firms and governments obtain necessary financing by selling securities to individuals (or families) and institutions. Securities are the tangible evidence of an investment by individuals and institutions in the affairs of business firms and governments. Bonds and stocks are the two major types of securities. Bonds represent the lending of money to firms and governments, while stocks represent the purchase of ownership in business firms. Options, mutual funds, and other types of securities are discussed in Chapter 16.

WHY INVEST IN SECURITIES?

If an individual or family has adequate cash reserves, retirement benefits, adequate life and other insurance coverage, and possibly an investment in a home, securities may be an appropriate way of investing additional available funds. Business firms and governments pay interest and dividends to investors for the use of their funds. In addition, the market prices of securities are subject to change, so investors can see their investments appreciate over time. But since security prices go

377

down as well as up, there is no guarantee that investors will benefit from appreciation. They may suffer capital losses instead of reaping capital gains.

Different Types of Risk in Securities Investments

The basic types of risks are business risk, financial risk, market risk, purchasing power risk, and interest rate risk.

Business Risk. The firm that issued the security may go out of business. When a business fails, stockholders often receive nothing. Bondholders are likely to receive at least part of the amount owed them on the bonds they purchased.

Financial Risk. This type of risk relates to the way the firm was financed. If a large amount of its financing was obtained by going into debt—issuing bonds—then the firm has a higher financial risk because it might be unable to meet its contractual interest payments. When that happens, it could be forced into bankruptcy, and the stockholders could lose everything.

Market Risk. This risk relates to the behavior of all investors in securities markets. Investors may change their minds about all securities, depending on social, political, and economic conditions. If the national mood is pessimistic, the price of all securities may fall.

Purchasing Power Risk. Because the price level of our economy has been inching upward, the purchasing power of the dollar has been declining. Certain securities with fixed nominal returns yield the investor lower and lower real returns after the drop in the purchasing power of the dollar is taken into account.

Interest Rate Risk. When the interest rate in the economy changes, the price of bonds, which offer a fixed periodic return, also changes. The market value, or price, of existing (old) bonds will fall every time the general, or average, interest rate in the economy rises. Hence, purchasers of bonds must consider the risk of interest rate increases that will lower the value of their bonds.

The Relationship between Risk and Rate of Return.

Suppose an individual buys, for $100, a security at the beginning of the year that promises to pay dividends of $4 during the year. If the security price increases to $108 by the end of the year, then the $100 investment is worth $112 ($100 principal plus $4 income plus $8 appreciation). However, if the security price decreases to $94 at the end of the year, the $100 investment is worth only $98 ($100 principal plus $4 income minus $6 loss in value). The investor's return is thus either 12 percent for the good year or 2 percent for the bad year. Expected return is a summary measure of possible return outcomes. If good and bad years each occur about 50 percent of the time, the individual's expected return would be an average 7 percent in this instance. The risk is that no one knows at the beginning of the year just which result (12 percent or -2 percent) will occur. A large expected return is clearly a desirable characteristic of a security, but risk is undesirable to most investors.

Exhibit 15-1 shows the usual way expected return and risk are related. Higher return usually is accompanied by higher risk. Savings in the form of time deposits are shown near the return axis of the diagram since they are a relatively safe investment. The two illustrative bonds are shown close together but at higher levels of both return and risk than time deposits. The three stocks have even greater return and risk and are not as close together. To better understand where and why particular bonds and stocks appear in such a pattern, we must examine more closely their distinctive characteristics.

Some individuals who include securities in their portfolios do so in order to learn more about such investments. Others do so because they

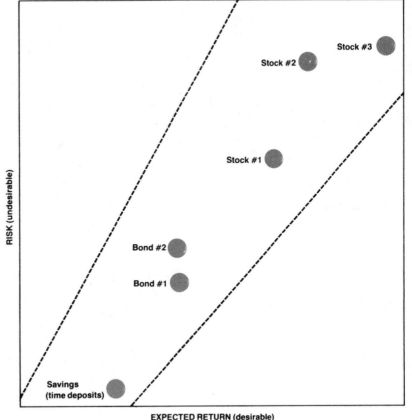

EXHIBIT 15-1

**EXPECTED RETURN
VERSUS RISK FOR
SECURITIES**

*To get a higher expected
rate of return, one must
incur more risk. Savings in
the form of time deposits
have a relatively low risk
but also a relatively low
expected rate of return.
Stocks and bonds yield
higher expected rates of
return but have higher
risks. Basically, you
cannot expect higher
returns without incurring
higher risk.*

RISK (undesirable)

Stock #3

Stock #2

Stock #1

Bond #2

Bond #1

Savings
(time deposits)

EXPECTED RETURN (desirable)

consider it a game. But the vast majority of individuals and families who own securities do so because they seek higher returns than are available from savings accounts (time deposits). If they achieve higher returns, future vacations, bigger homes, better educational opportunities, or larger estates to pass on to future generations, may be theirs.

Exhibit 15-2 shows the compounding effect of higher returns over longer horizons. We see that $100 placed in a 5 percent savings account (compounding annually) grows to $128 after five years and to $265 after twenty years. A 12 percent return causes $100 to grow to $965 after two decades, but a 2 percent loss causes $100 to decrease to $67 for the same horizon. Again, this is risk. Investors in securities apparently are willing to assume the higher risk that accompanies higher expected returns. Diversification, which may reduce risk, will be discussed in the following chapter.

CHARACTERISTICS OF BONDS

Bonds are issued by business firms and all levels of governments as evidence of the funds they are borrowing from investors. As with other types of loans, bonds almost always have a designated maturity date when the principal or face amount of the bond (or loan) is returned to the investor. Bonds sometimes are referred to as "senior securities" or "fixed income securities," because their owners receive a fixed dollar interest payment during each period of time until maturity.

EXHIBIT 15-2

COMPOUNDED EFFECT FOR SELECTED RETURNS AND HORIZONS FOR INVESTMENT OF $100

A savings account yielding 5 percent will produce $265 at the end of twenty years if $100 is invested. On the other hand, a stock yielding 12 percent will produce almost $1,000 after twenty years. If there is a 2 percent loss per year, the $100 will be reduced to only $67.

	HORIZON—NUMBER OF YEARS				
RETURN	1 year	2 years	5 years	10 years	20 years
15%	$115	$132	$201	$405	$1,637
12%	112	125	176	311	965
8%	108	117	147	216	466
5%	105	110	128	163	265
− 2%	98	96	90	82	67
−12%	88	77	53	28	8

In the bond trade, the word "bond" refers specifically to one with a face value of $1,000. Bonds may be sold below their face value, at a *discount*. They may be sold above their face value, at a *premium*. Bonds sold at premiums have yields that are less than their coupon, or stated, rates; bonds sold at a discount have yields that are greater.

Government Bonds

Government bonds are issued by the federal government, by various federal agencies, by states, and by municipal organizations. Bonds also are issued by foreign governments and municipalities. Government bonds differ in maturity, the method of paying interest to bondholders, risk, and the extent to which interest income is taxed. For example, the U.S. Treasury issues bills, certificates, notes, and bonds. Treasury bills, with maturities ranging from three months to one year, are sold through an auction process at a discount from their $10,000 face amount. No interest is paid. If you bought a six-month bill for $9,800, your dollar return would be $200 for the half-year horizon. Treasury certificates have a maturity of one full year, and buyers receive a single interest coupon that can be converted to cash. A 5 percent coupon on a $1,000 certificate would entitle you to a $50 interest payment. Treasury notes and bonds feature longer maturities and also have interest coupons attached. Income on all U.S. Treasury obligations are subject to federal income taxes but are exempt from state income taxes.

U.S. Treasury Issues. U.S. Treasury issues generally are considered to be the least risky of all securities because the taxing power of the United States government stands behind them. Bonds issued by various agencies of the federal government also are considered safe investments. Differences in yields for federal government and federal agency bonds are due largely to differences in maturities. Higher yields usually are associated with longer maturities. If you purchase federal government bonds, you might well require a higher return on a five-year bond than on a one-year certificate, simply because you must wait so much longer to get your $1,000 back.

State and Municipal Issues. State and municipal governments sell bonds to finance roads, schools, libraries, utilities, sewers, and fire and police stations. State bonds are issued by our fifty state governments, while municipal bonds are issued by cities, townships, and school districts and for special purposes, such as flood control. These bonds differ in their issue purpose and their maturity schedule. Certain types of revenue bonds issued by municipal governments provide for a fraction of the bonds to be retired each year. Interest received on municipal bonds is exempt from federal income taxes and, in some cases, from state taxes. As a result, municipal bonds often are desired securities for individuals and families in high federal income tax brackets. Note, though, that because the resources of state and local governments are not nearly as large as those of our federal government, there is greater risk associated with state and municipal bonds. Differences in yields among the bonds of state and local governments reflect risk differences as well as varying maturities.

Corporate Bonds

Corporations within the private sector differ from governmental units in that they sell both bonds and stocks to interested investors. Unlike government bonds, corporate bonds are available in a wide range of expected returns, risks, and other characteristics. That's because corporations differ greatly in their abilities to generate the earnings and cash flow necessary to make interest payments and to repay the principal amount of the bonds at maturity. Furthermore, corporate bonds are only part of the total debt and overall financial structure of corporate business.

Because debt financing represents a legal obligation on the part of the corporation, various features and terms of a particular bond issue are specified in a lending agreement called a bond indenture. A corporate trustee, often a commercial bank trust department, represents the collective well-being of all bondholders in ensuring that the terms of the bond issue are met by the corporation. The bond indenture specifies the maturity date of the bond and the pattern of interest payments until maturity. Most corporate bonds pay semiannually a coupon rate of interest on the $1,000 face amount of the bond. If you owned a 6 percent corporate bond, you would receive thirty dollars interest every six months. The indenture also indicates if any portion of the bond is to be retired each year in a series of so-called sinking fund payments. Any collateral for the bond issue, such as buildings or equipment, also is indicated. Additionally, the indenture indicates how you as a bondholder would fare—along with other creditors of the business firm—should the firm get into serious financial difficulty and not be able to meet all its legal obligations.

The following are different types of corporate bonds.

Debentures. No specific assets of the corporation are pledged as backing for this corporate bond. Rather, the general credit rating of the corporation is at stake, plus any assets that can be seized if the corporation allows the bonds to fall into default.

Mortgage Bonds. These corporate bonds are secured by a mortgage on all or part of the corporate-owned real property. There is a variety of mortgage bonds, including first, second, and even third mortgage types. The first mortgage bonds are the "senior" security: their owners have first claims to the assets of the company if it is liquidated.

Equipment Trust Bonds. The backing for the bond (loan) is a specific piece of equipment. The title of the equipment is vested in a trustee, who holds such title for the benefit of the owners of the bonds.

Collateral Trust Bonds. These corporate bonds are secured by nonreal estate collateral. Such collateral may be shares of stock in another corporation or accounts receivable.

Convertible Bonds. These bonds can be exchanged for a specified number of shares of common stock, when and if the bondholder so desires. The rate of conversion is determined when the convertible bond is issued.

Callable Bonds. Such bonds, which may be debentures or any other kind, can be called in and the principal repaid when the corporation so desires. The callable provision is put into the bond when it is issued.

Different Measures of Bond Yield

The expected return to a bondholder depends on the pattern of interest payments to be received, as well as on such characteristics as callability and convertibility. The current market price of the bond also is a factor. There are three different measures of return to a bond.

Nominal Yield. This is simply the annual coupon rate of interest expressed as a percentage of the face amount of the bond.

Current Yield. This is the dollar annual interest expressed as a percentage of the current market price. Thus, a 6 percent bond currently selling at $900 would have a nominal yield of 6 percent ($60 divided by $1,000) but a current yield of 6.67 percent ($60 divided by $900).

Yield-to-Maturity (or Effective Yield). This more complex calculation reflects the purchase price of the bond, the semiannual interest payments, and the face amount. It is also expressed as a percentage. A 6 percent bond that currently sells for $900 and matures in 7 ½ years has a yield-to-maturity of slightly under 7.8 percent. If you bought such a bond, your yield-to-maturity of 7.8 percent would be higher than the nominal yield of 6 percent because your $900 investment would grow to $1,000 at its maturity. (You would receive a capital gain of $100 after 7 ½ years.)

Yield-to-maturity is best determined with a calculator or by using a bond table. Exhibit 15-3, a portion of a page from a bond table, shows how the 7.8 percent value was obtained. The numbers in the figure are current market prices expressed as a percentage of face amount. The encircled "89.92" value means that a 6 percent coupon selling for $899.20 (quite close to $900) has a yield-to-maturity of 7.8 percent.

Step-by-Step Computation of Yield to Maturity

If you don't have a bond yield table available, you can figure out the yield-to-maturity, or effective yield, by using a four-step procedure. Consider the following example:

A bond sells at a $200 discount, or $800 (quoted at $80), and pays $50 annual interest. It matures in five years—that is, the company redeems the bond for $1,000 at the end of five years.

1 Compute its current yield by dividing the $50 annual interest by the current price: 6.25% current interest yield.

2 Calculate the capital gains yield that will be realized at the end of five years: 1.25%

3 Now turn to page 357 and look at Exhibit 14-3, which gives compound interest. Look in the row for five years. Approximately midway between 1.22 in the 4 percent column and 1.28 in the 5 percent column is 1.25 percent. Hence, the effective capital gains yield is approximately 4.5 percent.

4 When you add the results from the first three steps, you obtain the yield to maturity, or total effective yield, for this bond. It is 6.25 percent plus 4.5 percent, or 10.75 percent.

Of the three measures of return to a bond, yield-to-maturity (or simply *yield*) is the one most often used. It facilitates comparisons of bonds with other securities and investment opportunities. It also allows us to understand differences between various types of corporate and government bonds.

Exhibit 15-4 illustrates three important dimensions. First, bond

---

EXHIBIT 15-3

PORTION OF BOND TABLE FOR 6% NOMINAL YIELD

We are assuming that a bond purchased at approximately $900 matures in 7½ years. That is, the owner can cash it in for $1,000 at the end of that period. To find the yield-to-maturity, or total effective yield, we look for the number closest to 90.00 under the Years to Maturity column of 7½. That number is 89.92 or, in our case, is equivalent to $899.20, which is close to $900. In the extreme left-hand column, we see that the Yield-to-Maturity is 7.8 percent for a 6 percent coupon, or nominal, yield on a bond with a face value of $1,000.

YIELD TO MATURITY	YEARS TO MATURITY				
	6	6½	7	7½	8
7.00%	95.17	94.85	94.54	94.24	93.95
7.20%	94.24	93.86	93.49	93.14	92.80
7.40%	93.31	92.88	92.46	92.05	91.66
7.60%	92.40	91.91	91.44	90.98	90.54
7.80%	91.50	90.96	90.43	(89.92)	89.44
8.00%	90.61	90.01	89.44	88.88	88.35

yields vary over time because of changing economic conditions and the supply and demand for borrowed funds. Second, yields typically increase with longer maturities. Third, yields increase with risk. Risk ratings for corporate and state and local government bonds are provided by Moody's Investors Service and Standard and Poor's Corporation. U.S. government bonds, though not rated, are judged to be the least risky of all bonds. The Moody's ratings consist of nine different classes and grades ranging from Aaa (best quality) to Baa (lower medium quality) to Caa (poor standing) to C (extremely poor prospects). The ratings are based on detailed studies designed to assess the financial status of a particular corporation or government and to determine how risky their bonds are for investors. More precisely, the studies are designed to assess the ability of a government or corporation to make its interest and principal payments on schedule. Each corporate, state, and local issue is given a particular rating. An investor certainly should require a higher yield for bonds that are judged more risky.

CHARACTERISTICS OF STOCKS

Issuing stocks is another way corporations obtain financing. Stocks differ from bonds because they represent ownership in a business firm, whereas bonds represent borrowing by the firm. Governments do not issue stocks because there is no ownership of governments. Stocks are important because our private enterprise society rests upon the concept of private ownership of the business organizations that produce and distribute the countless products and services purchased by consumers.

A 1975 survey revealed that 25,270,000 individuals, representing

---

EXHIBIT 15-4

YIELD-TO-MATURITY FOR SELECTED BONDS OVER TIME
In this table we see that: (1) effective yields fluctuate over time; (2) the longer the maturity, the greater the effective yield on average; and (3) the greater the risk, the greater the effective yield.

BOND AND RATING	YIELD-TO-MATURITY (at year-end)					
	1972	1973	1974	1975	1976	1977
U.S. Treasury Bills (3 mo.)	5.06%	7.36%	7.01%	5.44%	4.35%	6.08%
U.S. Government (3-5 years)	6.00	6.70	7.20	7.40	5.90	7.33
State & Local Govts. (Aaa)	4.91	4.90	6.65	6.50	5.07	5.07
State & Local Govts. (Baa)	5.39	5.43	7.50	7.96	6.73	5.79
Corporate Bonds (Aaa)	7.08	7.68	8.89	8.79	7.98	8.54
Corporate Bonds (Baa)	7.93	8.48	10.63	10.56	9.12	8.99

11.8 percent of the total United States population, own corporate stock. The two major types of stock are preferred stock and common stock.

Preferred Stocks

From an investment standpoint, preferred stock is more similar to bonds than it is to common stock. It is not included among the liabilities of a business because there is no fixed maturity time when the preferred shares must be retired by the firm. As a preferred shareholder, you get your investment back by selling your shares to another investor rather than to the issuing firm. Occasionally, firms do retire preferred stock, but they are not legally obligated to do so. As a preferred shareholder, you also receive periodic dividend payments, usually established as a fixed percentage of the face amount of each preferred share. A 7 percent preferred stock with a face amount of $100 per share would pay its owner a $7 dividend each year. But again, this is not a legal obligation on the part of the firm as are the interest payments legally due to bondholders.

Stock is "preferred" in the sense that its owners must be paid their dividends before common shareholders may be paid a dividend and also because preferred shareholders have a higher claim on the assets of the corporation should the firm be liquidated. There are a number of different types of preferred stock, which we define here.

Cumulative Preferred Stock. For such a stock, any dividend payment not made in a given year must be made up before any dividends can be paid to owners of common stock. In other words, the corporation is liable to the preferred shareholders in this situation for past dividends that have not yet been paid. If, for example, a corporation fails to pay dividends for three years on a stock with a $100 par value and 5 percent interest rate, then the company must pay the cumulative preferred stockholders $15 per share at the end of the three years before any dividends can be paid to common stockholders. Sometimes there are limits to how far back dividends have to be paid—for example, three or five year cumulative limits.

Participating Preferred Stock. With this type of stock, the owner may share to some extent in additional dividends that are paid by the firm. Usually, the preferred stockholders are paid their agreed-upon rate of, say, five dollars per share, and then common stockholders are paid an equal percentage rate, after which all remaining corporation after-tax profits are distributed equally among preferred and common stockholders.

Convertible Preferred Stock. The owner of shares of this stock has the option of converting each of them into a specified number of common shares. Sometimes convertible preferred stocks can be exchanged for common stock in another company. In any event, the exchange ratio is determined when the convertible preferred shares of stock are issued. Hence, if there is an increase in the market value of the corporation's common stocks, the market value of the convertible preferred stock also rises.

Redeemable, or Callable, Preferred Stock. Such preferred stock is issued by a corporation under the explicit possibility that the corporation can, at some future time, buy back the shares of stock from the preferred stockholders. The terms of such a buy-back arrangement are specified when the preferred stock is issued. Corporations will issue callable preferred so they can call in the higher cost preferred stock and reissue lower cost shares if interest rates fall in the future.

Preferred shareholders are investors who have assumed a rather cautious position in their relationship to the corporation. They have a stronger position than common shareholders with respect to dividends and claims on assets. But, as a result, they do not share in the full prosperity of the firm if it grows successfully over time. A preferred shareholder receives fixed dividends periodically, and there may be changes in the market price of the shares. The return and risk for a share of preferred stock would be expected to lie somewhere between that of bonds and common stock and, thus, is consistent with the overall pattern shown in Exhibit 15-1. As a result, preferred stock is often categorized as a fixed income type of security, along with corporate bonds, even though the legal status is not the same. Some experts even contend that a preferred stock is more like a bond than a common stock, even though preferred stock appears in the ownership section of the firm's financial statements.

Common Stock

Common stock is the true ownership of a corporation. Each investor in a particular firm is entitled to one vote per common share held. Voting rights in a corporation apply to election of the firm's board of directors and to any proposed changes in the ownership structure of the firm. For example, as a common shareholder, you would be encouraged to vote in a decision on a proposed merger, since that possibly could change your proportional ownership. Many small investors in giant corporations probably feel, and rightfully so, that their small number of votes has little impact on the business firm—particularly when incumbent management owns a significant and often controlling proportion of the total votes. Still, voting rights are an important characteristic of common stock and one that some investors take seriously.

Because corporations are organized as ongoing entities, there is no intent to return a principal amount per share to each owner. No firm can ensure that the market price per share of its common stock won't go down over time. Neither does the issuing firm guarantee a dividend; indeed, some business firms never pay dividends. Considering these negative aspects, why would an individual even consider investing in common stock? The answer, of course, is that each owner is entitled to his proportional share of the after-tax earnings of the corporation. If, for example, you own 100 shares (.01 percent of one million shares outstanding) of a firm that earns $3 million after taxes, your proportional share is $300. Earnings are the key to the benefits that an investor receives from common stock.

The earnings of a corporation either are paid out in the form of cash dividends to common shareholders or are retained in the business for the expressed purpose of enhancing future earnings. If the board of directors of your firm (and it is *your* firm if you're a common shareholder) declares a dividend of $1.20 per share, then $120 of your $300 earnings is received now as a tangible benefit, with the other $180 retained. Your other tangible benefit is the market price per share that you receive when you ultimately sell part or all of your 100 common shares. But market price depends, among other things, on the recent earnings (and dividends) of the firm and, more importantly, on expectations for future earnings and dividends.

Common shareholders, then, are a group of investors who assume the *residual* position in the overall financial structure of a business. In terms of receiving payment for their investment, they are last in line. The earnings to which they are entitled also depend on all the other groups—suppliers, employees, managers, bankers, governments, bondholders, and preferred shareholders—first being paid what is due to them. Once those groups are paid, however, common shareholders are entitled to *all* the remaining earnings. This is the central feature of ownership in any business, be it a corner newsstand, a retail store, an architectural firm, or a giant international oil corporation. In each instance, the common stock owners occupy the riskiest position relative to all constituent groups. But, as a result, they logically expect a return on their investment that is greater than that accruing to the other groups. Again, we can see why the return and risk pattern of Exhibit 15-1 would be expected to hold. As one moves from savings accounts and U.S. government bonds, to corporate bonds with different ratings, to preferred stock, and, finally to common stock, expected returns increase to compensate for the higher risks that are undertaken.

Exhibit 15-5 is a comparison of stocks and bonds.

SECURITIES MARKETS

Securities are bought and sold at securities markets. These are the arenas and mechanisms that bring buyers and sellers of bonds and stocks together. Securities markets are important because they expedite securities transactions. They also are important because the market prices of completed transactions signal how buyers and sellers collectively view the current status and future prospects of particular governments and corporations.

Primary Securities Markets

This term refers to the ways in which governments and corporations sell securities to individuals and institutional investors. Occasionally, a firm will offer its existing common shareholders the opportunity to buy new securities directly from the firm. But, generally, distribution is done through financial intermediaries. Corporations, for example, use an investment banking firm or, frequently, a syndicate of investment bankers to help sell their securities to the investing public. In return for a dollar fee based on a small percentage of the total issue size, the investment banker advises the issuing firm on an appropriate issue price, the use of its sales network, and possible price support during the days following the sale. Sometimes, but not always, the investment banker is prepared to buy all securities not sold to the public. Naturally, the investment will charge a higher fee to assume that additional risk for the issuing firm.

Secondary Securities Markets

This refers to the ways in which investors trade securities. If a completed transaction consists of your selling fifty shares of a particular preferred stock to me for twenty-four dollars per share, then the number of pre-

EXHIBIT 15-5	Common Stocks	Bonds
HOW DO STOCKS AND BONDS DIFFER?	1. Stocks represent ownership.	1. Bonds represent owed debt.
	2. Stocks do not have a fixed dividend rate.	2. Interest on bonds must always be paid, whether or not any profit is earned.
	3. Stockholders can elect a board of directors, which control the corporation.	3. Bondholders usually have no voice in or control over management of the corporation.
	4. Stocks do not have a maturity date; the corporation does not usually repay the stockholder.	4. Bonds have a maturity date when the bondholder is to be repaid the face value of the bond.
	5. All corporations issue or offer to sell stocks. This is the usual definition of a corporation.	5. Corporations are not required to issue bonds.
	6. Stockholders have a claim against the property and income of a corporation after all creditors' claims have been met.	6. Bondholders have a claim against the property and income of a corporation that must be met before the claims of stockholders.

ferred shares outstanding to the given firm does not change. The twenty-four dollar market price per share tells the firm how you and I feel about the future prospects of that investment. Depending on the particular preferred stock, our transaction probably would be accomplished by our respective brokerage firms on one of the organized securities exchanges or on the over-the-counter market. We both would pay a brokerage commission to complete our transaction.

Organized Exchange

An organized stock exchange is a physical entity where trading is limited to members of the exchange and a prescribed list of stocks. An organized bond exchange is similar except that only bonds are traded. Membership on securities exchanges is purchased. While some individuals and families own memberships, most memberships belong to securities firms and other organizations in the business of providing execution, information (on securities), and other services to investors.

By far the largest organized exchange is the New York Stock Exchange (NYSE), which accounts for more than 70 percent of the total value of all stock trading on organized exchanges. Common and preferred stocks of most of the largest companies are listed on the New York Stock Exchange. To have its stock listed, a company must satisfy certain financial requirements of the exchange and also agree to keep the investing public informed about its affairs. The second largest stock exchange is the American Stock Exchange (AMEX), which handles stocks of companies that are somewhat smaller. Listing requirements for the American Stock Exchange are not as stringent as those for the New York Stock Exchange. Several regional stock exchanges also exist, but their listings often include stocks traded on the two largest exchanges. There also are a New York Bond Exchange and an American Bond Exchange.

Market Indicators. Much of what we hear and read about the securities markets is actually the New York Stock Exchange as portrayed by one or more of the popular market averages. The averages differ in the number of stocks included and in how the averages are constructed. The New York Stock Exchange Index includes all its listed stocks, the Standard and Poor's Composite Index includes 500 stocks, and the Dow Jones Industrial Average (DJIA) includes only 30. The DJIA is an unweighted average of the market prices of its stocks, while the other two indexes weight each stock price by the number of outstanding shares. The DJIA is the average mentioned most often in the financial news, but it is considered to be less representative of the total stock market because of its smaller composition.

Over-the-Counter Markets

Stocks and bonds not listed on organized securities exchanges are bought and sold on what is called the over-the-counter market (OTC).

This is really a complex communications network that transmits information about the prices at which securities firms scattered around the country are prepared to buy or sell securities for their customers. Price quotations currently are effected through a computer-based system known as NASDAQ. While most of the securities handled on the over-the-counter market are not listed on any organized stock exchanges, those that are sometimes are referred to as the third securities market. Most government and corporate bonds are traded over-the-counter.

The over-the-counter market differs from the organized stock exchanges in how the market for a given security is made. On an organized exchange, a particular member firm establishes an auction market for each security. That firm is referred to as the *specialist* in that security. It matches the buy and sell orders of *broker* firms, who represent the interests of the investing public without actually owning securities. Where necessary, the specialist also acts as a *dealer* and buys and sells the securities in order to maintain an orderly and continuous market. In contrast, the over-the-counter market consists of over 5,000 securities firms, acting both as brokers and dealers, in a decentralized, informal, negotiated market. No single member firm controls the consummation of transactions. Despite this important difference, you as an investor still place your buy and sell orders through a securities firm that serves as an intermediary and charges you a dollar fee for so doing.

Changes in Markets

Some changes are taking place in the United States securities markets. First, in May 1975, negotiated brokerage commissions replaced the fixed schedule of commissions that had existed for many years on the organized stock exchanges. Second, the securities industry is considering a composite transaction tape that would include bids from all buyers and sellers of each security, regardless of where the markets are being made. Third, there is a continuing trend away from the auction-type market of the organized exchanges toward a central market of brokers and dealers who collectively establish the trading arena for each security. Thus far, the impact of these changes mainly has been a reduction in brokerage fees paid by large institutional investors. But in the longer run, the changes are likely to affect the way we all buy execution, information, and other services from the securities industry.

THE RECORD FOR SECURITY INVESTMENTS

The procedures for buying and selling securities are important to potential investors. No less important, however, are the expected results of the various stocks and bonds that you may decide to purchase for your investment portfolio. A logical starting point for determining expected results is past achieved results. Fortunately, there is now available a rather comprehensive record of achieved investment results from different types of securities. Results for selected horizons are shown in Exhibit

15-6. Values are presented for "average" investments in U.S. Treasury bills, U.S. government bonds, corporate bonds, and common stocks. Over the total horizon—from 1926 to 1974—we see that riskier securities exhibited higher annual returns: bills (2.2 percent), government bonds (3.2 percent), corporate bonds (3.6 percent), and common stocks (8.5 percent). But we also see that just the opposite pattern was observed over the most recent five-year horizon from 1969 to 1974: bills (6.0 percent), government bonds (5.8 percent), corporate bonds (4.1 percent), and common stocks (-3.4 percent).

There is no guarantee that common stocks will generate the highest return just because they are the riskiest type of security. Still, as potential investors we need expectations for security returns in order to make investment decisions. The same two authors who calculated the historical returns in Exhibit 15-6 also dared to forecast returns for the period from 1976 to 2000. Their average annual results are: bills (6.8 percent), government bonds (8.0 percent), corporate bonds (8.2 percent), and common stocks (13.0 percent). Obviously, these conform to the pattern of higher risk accompanying higher expected return.

HOW TO SELECT SECURITIES

If you or your family have adequate cash reserves and life insurance, then it may be appropriate to invest these funds in securities. If so, you must decide which particular securities are appropriate for your investment portfolio. Security selection is a tough decision that should not be made casually. According to one school of thought, it requires a careful study of particular securities well beyond the general characteristics of bonds and stocks already discussed. It also necessitates a careful assessment of your personal financial status and future needs. For most individuals, security selection involves two steps: first, a decision on how your excess funds should be allocated to different types or categories of bonds and stocks; and second, decisions on particular bonds and particular stocks within each category.

The Necessity of Financial Planning

The first decision on appropriate categories should be based on your personal financial planning. That planning ought to reflect your future financial needs, such as education, vacations, gifts to children, and so on. You then can determine the return excess funds must achieve in order to meet your needs. If you have $4,000 to invest now and an expressed goal of a $5,000 vacation three years from now, then an annual return of 6.3 percent is required. This probably can be obtained in an extended savings account with almost no risk. But if your expressed need is $20,000 for your children's college education in fifteen years, then your $4,000 must earn an annual return of at least 11.3 percent. Among the securities we've discussed, only riskier common stocks might provide that return. You must decide if you are willing to assume

EXHIBIT 15-6

HISTORICAL RETURNS FOR BILLS, BONDS, AND COMMON STOCKS, SELECTED YEARS 1926-1974

SOURCE: R. G. Ibbotson and R. A. Sinquefield, "Stocks, Bonds, Bills and Inflation: Year-by-Year Historical Returns (1926-1974)," JOURNAL OF BUSINESS, January 1976.

Ending Year	Beginning Year					
	1926	1934	1944	1954	1964	1969
U.S. Treasury Bills						
1934	2.2%					
1944	1.1	0.2%				
1954	1.1	0.5	0.9%			
1964	1.4	1.2	1.7	2.4%		
1969	1.8	1.7	2.3	3.2	4.7%	
1974	2.2	2.2	2.9	3.8	5.2	6.0%
U.S. Government Bonds						
1934	5.5%					
1944	4.7	4.5%				
1954	3.9	3.5	2.5%			
1964	3.3	2.9	2.1	2.2%		
1969	2.7	2.2	1.3	0.8	−1.2%	
1974	3.2	2.9	2.4	2.5	2.9	5.8%
Corporate Bonds						
1934	6.8%					
1944	5.6	5.3%				
1954	4.4	3.8	2.5%			
1964	4.0	3.5	2.6	2.9%		
1969	3.2	2.7	1.6	1.3	−1.1%	
1974	3.6	3.1	2.4	2.5	2.4	4.1%
Corporate Stocks						
1934	2.0%					
1944	5.8	8.3%				
1954	9.6	12.4	17.4%			
1964	10.4	12.5	15.2	16.0%		
1969	9.8	11.5	13.1	12.4	6.8%	
1974	8.5	9.7	10.5	8.7	2.5	−3.4%

the risk of common stocks in order to accomplish your educational goal. Some may. But others may prefer to lower risk and invest in securities with a lower expected return. Your $4,000 invested in Aaa-rated corporate bonds yielding 8 percent would be expected to grow to $12,680 after fifteen years. Perhaps your children could work part-time to earn the remaining $7,320 to help you reach your $20,000 goal.

Risk Selection. The first decision, therefore, involves matching the *expected return* and *risk* characteristics of securities with your expressed needs. It may also involve additional characteristics. For example, we ignored *taxes* in the example and thus understated the return that really would be necessary. Protection against *inflation* is another characteristic that should be considered in your financial projections. *Liquidity* of your investment is another important characteristic, although most securities are considered quite liquid. Another characteristic is the extent to which you would need to monitor and *manage* certain investments; if the corporate bonds happened to be callable by the issuing firm and/or convertible by you, then you could not simply ignore the bonds for fifteen years.

Selecting Particular Stocks or Bonds. The second major decision involves selecting particular issues within each security type. *Security analysis* is the process of trying to understand the various securities of governments and corporations well enough to make sound judgments about which are suitable for a given portfolio. Literally thousands of books and articles have been written on security analysis. Viewpoints on how to analyze securities range from very specific, mechanical techniques to more general, intuitive approaches to a belief that few if any investors (especially individuals) are apt to be very successful, regardless of the method used. Most methods of security analysis can be categorized as either technical analysis or fundamental analysis.

Technical Analysis. Technical analysis is based on the belief that the securities markets quickly and accurately reflect all available information on a given security; but that information is not available to all investors simultaneously. So-called insiders and large institutional investors are presumed to receive certain types of information before it reaches individual investors. As a result, stock prices would be expected to follow certain patterns or formations as information eventually spreads to all investors. The purpose of technical analysis is to recognize recurring patterns as they develop and to base buy and sell decisions on those patterns and formations.

Those who practice technical analysis do not attempt to understand the economics behind the market price of a given security; they rely instead on carefully constructed charts of the security's price changes over time. There are countless patterns that "chartists" use to try and foresee future price changes that can be exploited profitably. Examples, shown in Exhibit 15-7, include resistance and support levels, head and shoulders, ascending bottoms, triangles, and triple tops. Unfortunately, a great deal of evidence on market efficiency, including careful study of various charting methods, almost totally refutes the validity of technical analysis. Some of that evidence will be reviewed in a later chapter.

Fundamental Analysis. The traditional version of **fundamental analysis** is based on the belief that, with careful study, one may discover a

EXHIBIT 15-7

CHARTING THE STOCK MARKET

Here we see an example of the so-called technical analysis for charting. Chartists believe that they can make some sense out of the ups and downs in the price of any particular stock or group of stocks. According to their theories, certain patterns can be recognized so that the future course of the price of a stock can be predicted. Can you make heads or tails of the diagram below?

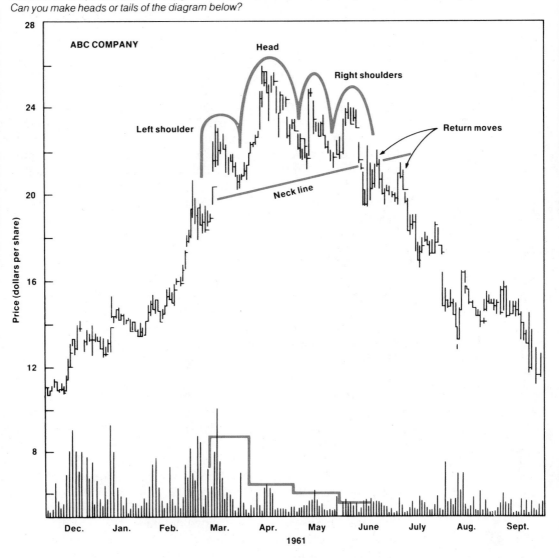

security whose current market price does not accurately reflect all available information about it. That could include a detailed understanding of the company or government whose security is being examined, as well as of the particular industry and overall economy. If such a belief is correct, and if the market itself eventually reaches the same conclusion, then it is possible to gain extra return by buying securities that are currently undervalued or to avoid extra loss by selling those issues that are overvalued. Extra gain or loss of return, of course, should be considered in addition to the longer-range trend of return that would be expected for the given security—even if the market price was always correct.

The modern version of investment theory is rather skeptical about anyone's ability to find overvalued or undervalued securities consistently. Thus, it is content to try and ascertain the longer-range trend of return for the total market, as well as an appropriate level of risk associated with the trend. While it has been stated that the growing evidence on efficient markets also refutes the usefulness of fundamental analysis, the more accepted logic is that careful fundamental analysis by many individuals and institutions is what makes securities markets efficient.

Investigating a Government Bond. How would you attempt a fundamental analysis of a given security? For a state or municipal bond, you might investigate the financial health of the issuing government, including its budgeting process, the ability of its management, and the status of labor demands by various services. The point is to determine the ability of that government to pay interest to bondholders and to retire its bonds at their maturity. A more cursory approach would be to rely on an independent summary appraisal of these and other factors as portrayed in the published ratings for a particular government bond.

Investigating a Corporate Bond. For corporate bonds, you again might choose to rely on the summary appraisals of others. Ratings of corporate bonds are similar to those of government bonds and generally are reliable. In particular, you should be aware of changes in bond ratings for a particular issue. For example, if a bond rating of Aaa is changed to Aa or A, that particular corporation has been judged less financially able to pay interest on its outstanding bonds or to retire maturing bonds.

Bond Prices and Interest Rates. In addition to bond ratings, you should familiarize yourself with changes in interest rates within the economy. An important relationship to remember, both for corporate and government bonds, is that as interest rates go up, bond prices go down. Conversely, as interest rates go down, bond prices go up. The reason for this inverse relationship is that the nominal (or coupon) yield on an existing bond remains fixed. If interest rates go up, then the existing bond pays less to investors than would a new bond of comparable risk at the higher rate. Hence, bond prices move downward so that the yield-to-maturity of the existing bond is comparable to a new bond that might be issued. In other words, the market for existing bonds serves to maintain a consistent relationship of expected return (yield-to-maturity) and associated risk. If you plan to hold your government or corporate bonds to maturity, then interest rate movements are less important since your yield-to-maturity is fixed. But if you contemplate selling some of your bonds prior to their maturity, interest rates are indeed important and should be followed closely.

Investigating Stocks. Summary appraisals also exist for preferred and common stocks. Various rating systems are used to indicate the relative risks of being a preferred or common shareholder. The ratings are based on the historical and forecasted growth of earnings dividends over time. Standard and Poor's has a rating system for preferred stocks of seven levels, ranging from AAA (prime quality) to A (sound) to B (speculative) to C (submarginal). Their rating system for common stocks, also of seven levels, ranges from A+ (excellent) to B+ (average) to C (lowest). You may find that the various rating systems for stocks do not agree nearly as much as do the ratings for bonds. As a result, rating systems for stocks probably are not used as extensively as are rating systems for bonds.

Doing a Complete Analysis. If you decide to go beyond summary appraisals, then you are into the real complexity of security analysis. The typical approach consists of an economic analysis, followed by an industry analysis and, finally, a company analysis. The ultimate purpose of these three complementary analyses is to focus on the likely dividends for a given stock issue and also on the likely changes in the market price of the preferred or common stock. While you might try to focus directly on earnings, dividends, and market prices, you probably would find that such an approach is not very rewarding.

Instead, you might decide to pursue the typical approach. *Economic analysis* or, better yet, a review of economic analysis done by various companies, agencies, and universities would be the first step. Such analyses provide an overall perspective of how our economy is expected to fare during the next year or more. They might include projections of the Gross National Produce (GNP), forecasts of personal income and interest rates, as well as prognoses for automobile sales, housing starts, and other key sectors of the economy. They might also include "guestimates" of the stock market during the next year. The term "guestimate" is used deliberately, because stock market projections typically are presented in rather broad ranges that are much less specific than other projections included in economic analyses.

Industry analyses comprise the next step. You should try to determine the key factors that are likely to affect the investment prospects of a given industry. For the paper industry, the availability of timber reserves may be central. For the heavy machinery industry, both energy and pollution effects are critical. For the automobile industry, pending labor contracts or possible governmental action to break up the larger corporations may be germane. For the integrated international oil industry, developments in the OPEC cartel are likely to be the dominant factor. Such factors should be logically pursued, where applicable, to their impact on industry demand, as well as on the cost and supply conditions of the industry. The relative attractiveness of a given industry within a total portfolio is another important factor and one that will be discussed further in the next chapter. One rationale for such analyses is that a clear and accurate understanding of a given industry can help you avoid errors that may be made in assessing a particular company within that industry.

The final step is *company analysis*. Here economic and industry analyses are used to provide a perspective for a detailed understanding of a given company and its securities. Try to establish how the demand for the company's products and services is likely to change during the next few months and years. This may involve consumer behavior (women's fashions). It may depend on research and technology (computers). Or it may rest on some external development beyond the control of the company (saccharine). You should assess the competition of the firm and how it may affect the demand facing your particular company. Evaluate the breadth and depth of company management. Try to determine how labor contracts and overall costs are likely to affect the potential earnings of the company. Estimate just how able the firm will be to pay interest on its outstanding debt and dividends to its preferred shareholders. And try to forecast future after-tax earnings as a basis both for projecting likely dividends to common shareholders and for attempting a valuation of the common stock.

Such an analysis is a big assignment. But it is necessary for making informed judgments about the expected return and risk characteristics of the bonds and stocks you are considering for your investment portfolio. Even if you rely heavily on summary appraisals, it still may be rewarding to take a careful look at a particular security to check on its suitability for your particular needs.

WHEN TO PURCHASE SECURITIES

In implementing your decisions about stocks and bonds, you must confront the question of timing. A popular recommendation is to "buy low and sell high." Unfortunately, you seldom know in advance just what is high or what is low. And, of course, not all security prices attain their relative high or relative low positions simultaneously. While some investment strategies emphasize selection and downplay the importance of timing, other strategies do just the opposite. Having just looked at security selection in some detail, it is now appropriate to consider timing.

Two Common Approaches

Suppose that you decide to invest $4,000 of your funds in common stocks. Suppose further that the $4,000 is presently in a savings account. One approach would be to buy immediately the common stocks of one or more corporations you have selected. In so doing, timing is dictated solely by your decision to invest. A second approach would be to delay action until you determine that the overall stock market is in the early stages of a broad market advance. Here timing is dictated by whatever method you use to make that assessment. You might rely on published market forecasts, utilize one or more of the many technical indicators (for example, the Dow Theory or Barron's Confidence Index), or just make a subjective judgment.

Formula Planning

A third approach is formula planning. This is a predetermined schedule for allocating your excess funds between common stocks (which offer greater returns during a rising market) and bonds or savings (which offer protection during a declining market). One version of formula planning utilizes a set of fixed proportions to which adjustments are made at each review point. Suppose that you decided on a 50 percent-50 percent mix for savings and common stocks, to be reviewed quarterly. Thus, you invest $2,000 of your funds in particular stocks and leave $2,000 in savings. The stock market does go up, and one quarter later, your $2,000 worth of stock (including dividends) has grown to $2,575, while your $2,000 savings (5 percent) has compounded to $2,025. Your funds total $4,600 at that point, so you sell $275 of stock ($2,300 remaining) and add to your savings ($2,300 total) in order to restore the 50 percent-50 percent mix. Had the stock market gone down instead, you would have shifted savings into common stocks in order to restore the mix. Notice that the formula plan causes you to sell stocks as the market goes up and purchase stocks as it goes down. The idea is to take advantage of market cycles as they materialize over time.

Another version of formula planning, which tries to take even greater advantage of market cycles, utilizes a set of variable proportions that vary with some market index. For example, as the market index (say, the DJIA) gets higher, the proportion for common stocks might decrease to 30 percent while that for savings would increase to 70 percent. In that way, you are better protected if the market eventually goes down. But if the market keeps going up instead, the formula plan has caused you, after the fact, to have made a poor decision. This, once again, is risk.

Dollar Cost Averaging

A fourth approach to timing, dollar cost averaging, is useful as part of a continuing program of purchasing securities. By investing a fixed amount at regular intervals, you effectively buy more shares at lower prices and fewer shares at higher prices. Suppose you decided to invest $1,000 in a particular common stock each year for four years. Your pattern of purchases might be as follows:

The average purchase price of the particular stock over the four years

YEAR	INVESTMENT	PURCHASE PRICE PER SHARE	SHARES PURCHASED
1	$1,000	$25	40.0
2	1,000	20	50.0
3	1,000	30	33.3
4	1,000	35	28.6
TOTALS	$4,000		151.9

was $27.50. But by using dollar cost averaging, your average cost per share was only $26.33.

Dollar cost averaging is like formula planning in that it provides a mechanical way to purchase securities. It differs from formula planning in that the success of dollar cost averaging is not tied to a prediction of future market cycles. You automatically buy more shares at lower prices and less shares at higher prices. However, if market price just keeps going down, dollar cost averaging, though successful, is clearly not useful. But, under that condition, neither is any other strategy that restricts itself to common stocks.

WHEN TO SELL SECURITIES

With the exception of formula planning, where funds are shifted between different types of securities, none of the approaches to timing deals with the question of when to sell securities. In fact, much less has been written about when to sell than when to buy. One explanation is that individuals sell securities in order to realize the goals and needs for which the investment program was undertaken in the first place. Ideally, in those instances, the market value of the securities sold is adequate to pay for the vacation, the education, or some other goal.

If the market prices of securities have risen, there may be a special reason why less attention is placed on selling. It has to do with the "locked-in" effect that results from capital gains. If you buy common stock A for twenty-four dollars per share and it eventually goes up to sixty dollars per share, then you have an unrealized capital gain of thirty-six dollars. Capital gains are often taxed at 40% the rate on regular income if the asset is held for one year or more. If your regular income tax rate is 40 percent (federal plus state), then you pay 16 percent on capital gains, and your potential tax liability on stock A is $7.20 per share. By not selling your shares of Stock A, you can postpone your tax liability indefinitely. Thus, there may well be a strong economic incentive not to sell securities for which you have a potential capital gain and tax liability. To sell common stock A in order to purchase stock B is to see your $60 market value per share drop immediately to $52.80. The drop is even greater if we include the two-way brokerage commissions required to switch from A to B.

An alternative explanation of why selling is often ignored is that it may indicate that an earlier decision to purchase securities has not measured up to one's expectations. How would you feel if common stock A, purchased for twenty-four dollars per share, gradually drops to seventeen dollars? It can be psychologically difficult to face up to poor investment results, even though we should not be terribly surprised by them.

One way to reduce the psychological anxiety associated with selling is to set up a selling plan before you implement the decision to purchase. For example, suppose your security analysis of common stock A convinced you that it is worth forty dollars per share, even though it currently sells for only twenty-four dollars. As part of your decision to buy shares of that stock, you might establish an upper limit of forty dollars and promise yourself to sell the stock if it reaches that level. At the same time, you might set nineteen dollars as a lower limit and promise to sell if it drops to that level. Sell limits are not perfect, of course. The price of stock A might increase past forty dollars and go on to sixty. Or it could fall to eighteen dollars, be sold, and then rise to seventy. Upper and lower selling limits, if established, should be committed to writing as part of your investment plan. Otherwise, you may be more inclined to second-guess yourself after common stock A is purchased and its market price changes over time. As we shall see in the Practical Applications section, it is possible to implement selling limits so there is no opportunity to second-guess yourself.

PRACTICAL APPLICATIONS

HOW TO MAKE DECISIONS ON BONDS AND STOCKS

Investing in securities is both risky and complex. While you may be able to minimize risk by keeping your funds in a savings account, you may not be able to attain certain financial goals that you set for yourself and/or your family. If you decide to invest in securities, you may be overwhelmed by the thousands of different bonds and stocks that are available and the sheer mass of existing information on the governments and business firms that issue those bonds and stocks. Here you will receive more specific tips on how to reach decisions on particular securities, as well as on how to implement those decisions.

GETTING STARTED

As with any decision, it is important to begin with a plan—in writing. In the context of investing, your plan should include a determination of the funds you appropriately can invest in securities. The plan also should include a specification of your financial goals. For example, to continue the illustration of the previous chapter, you have $4,000 to invest now toward a financial need of $20,000 for your children's education fifteen years hence. Your $4,000 would have to earn an annual rate of 11.3 percent in order for you to reach your goal.

The second part of your plan should compare different investment categories (securities) with those investment characteristics you consider important. The importance of expected return and risk have already been noted. So have inflation, liquidity, taxability, and manageability. Based upon what you've learned about bonds and stocks, you might construct a comparison such as in Exhibit 15-8. Relative comparisons are made within each column. As expected, higher expected return is accompanied by greater risk. There are also differences among the various investments in terms of hedges against inflation, taxability, and manageability.

While some individuals may be comfortable with simple comparisons such as in Exhibit 15-8, others may prefer more extensive descriptions. There is no magic formula for making the allocations. They should be based on your needs and your preferences, including your willingness to bear risk. In the illustration, the need for high return tends to preclude time deposits and the less risky government and corporate bonds. Suppose you decide to assume reasonable risk in order to achieve your goal. Accordingly, you place about half of your funds in common stocks and the other half in corporate bonds rated A or higher by purchasing two corporate bonds and two common stocks. Moreover, you plan to select and manage your securities yourself.

WHAT TO READ

No one could read all the available information on bonds and stocks, so you must narrow your reading to sources of information that are accurate, useful, and not too costly. If you wish to follow the suggestion of fundamental analysis described in this chapter, then your reading would consist of an economic analysis, an industry analysis, and a company analysis.

For Economic Analysis

An economic analysis provides a perspective for more detailed analyses of particular industries and companies. Overall economic news and developments, both national and international, appear regularly in the financial pages of newspapers. The most extensive coverage would be in *The Wall Street Journal, Barron's,* the *New York Times,* and other large metropolitan newspapers. Similar information, often with more statistical detail, is found in periodic magazines, such as *Business Week, Fortune,* and *Forbes.* There are also broad economic data in a variety of government publications *(Federal Reserve Bulletin* and *Survey of Current Business),* but many

EXHIBIT 15-8

**HYPOTHETICAL COMPARISON OF SAVINGS AND SELECTED SECURITIES
FOR FIVE INVESTMENT CHARACTERISTICS**

INVESTMENT CATEGORY	EXPECTED RETURN	RISK	INFLATION HEDGE	LIQUIDITY	TAX LIABILITIES	MGMT REQUIRED
Savings Account (Time Deposit)	7.7% (long term)	None (up to $40,000 per acct.)	None	Excellent	Federal & State	None
U.S. Treasury Bills	6.8%	None	None	Good	Federal	None
U.S. Treasury Bonds	8.0%	None	None	Good	Federal	None
Municipal Bonds (Aaa)	7.5%	Little	None	Good	State	None
Corporate Bonds (Aaa)	8.8%	Little	None	Good	Federal & State	None
Corporate Bonds (A)	9.5%	More	None	Good	Federal & State	None
Preferred Stock	10.5%	More	Some	Good	Federal & State	Some
Common Stock	13.0%	Greatest	Hopeful	Fair	Federal & State	Some

investors find that the regular coverage in two or three leading newspapers and magazines provides an adequate economic perspective. Newspapers are also a convenient source of recent price and volume information on many government bonds and corporate bonds and stocks.

Many of the leading brokerage firms and certain universities also prepare periodic economic forecasts. These typically include specific forecasts of the economy (the GNP, national income, etc.), the key sectors of the economy (autos, housing starts), interest rates on short-term and long-term bonds, and of the stock market (often via the DJIA). While certain economic forecasts are available only from the source itself, other sources are available in public libraries. These forecasts provide investors with added perspective for future investments.

For Industry Analysis

Industry analyses of varying depth also are available from brokerage firms on a regular basis and sporadically in financial newspapers and magazines, including *Forbes* and *Fortune.* Industry analyses also appear regularly as part of the Value Line Investment Service and the Industry Surveys of the Standard and Poor's Corporation. Both these services are expensive but usually are available in public libraries.

In addition to summary information on each firm, most industry analyses begin with a brief review of the national economy and then take a closer look at supply and demand conditions within a particular industry. Special attention may be paid to pending labor negotiations, availability of resources, governmental regulation, and foreign competition. Some of the analyses include mention of leading or troubled firms within the industry. It may not be necessary to read numerous surveys of the same industry since many overlap. The point is to find sources that are readable, provide an adequate but not excessive level of detail, and present viewpoints that coincide with your own thinking as developed from your research. As indicated and illustrated in this chapter, there are one or two key factors that tend to dominate in almost every industry. Your reading will help discover these.

For Company Analysis

A company analysis is the third step of a fundamental analysis. Probably the best source on how a particular business firm has evolved over time is *Moody's Manuals,* an annual series covering industrial firms (red volumes), transportation companies (green), public utilities (brown), banks and financial institutions (black), and various governments (blue). *Standard and Poor's Corporation Records* is similar in scope and coverage. Both are expensive publications, but many public libraries have them. The most comprehensive recent data on the organization and financing of a particular firm are found in the 10-K reports that each firm must file annually with the Securities and Exchange Corporation. These include a breakdown of the total business into products or divisions, changes in capital structure (all outstanding securities), as well as information on directors, management, executive compensation, property held, pending legal proceedings, and so on.

For many investors, a more readable summary of current information is the firm's annual report, a copy of which may be obtained from the firm upon request. Annual reports are of varying size, shape, color, and depth of coverage. There is no standard format, but the basic information is similar. Here are some tips for reading an annual report:

1. Have an open mind but skeptical eye toward unanswered questions and the "glossing over" of potential problems.

2. Examine data in the context of economic and industry analyses you have done.

3. Read it backwards. Assuming that you have an accounting background, you should begin with the auditor's statement to see if there are any qualifying opinions. Examine the numerous footnotes that usually accompany the financial statements to see if any accounting charges have been used to influence the continuity of firm earnings over time, read about the firm's products and developments, and, finally, read the inevitable, optimistic introductory letter from the firm's president and/or board chairperson.

Some of you may find the annual report and 10-K report pretty tough going. Fortunately, organizations with no financial or other vested interests publish summary reports on individual companies. Certain industry analyses conducted by securities firms include specific recommendations—that is, buy, hold, or sell—for firms within the industry. Other leading sources are *Standard and Poor's Stock Reports, Moody's Handbook of Widely Held Common Stock,* and *Value Line Ratings and Reports.* Brokers also will send you copies of such summary reports for particular stocks in which you contemplate investing.

While the various sources of company analyses discuss the business firm and its outstanding securities, the emphasis usually is on the common stock of the corporation. For investors interested in fixed-income securities, an excellent source is *Moody's Bond Record,* which most libraries have. Included for literally thousands of different bond issues is information on coupon rates, maturity, interest dates, bond ratings, current price and recent price range, yield-to-maturity, and call price.

WHOM TO LISTEN TO

Effective listening should supplement your reading. Of course, what you hear may well be less detailed than what you read. Still, it may reinforce what

EXHIBIT 15-9   **PARTIAL LIST OF NEW YORK STOCK EXCHANGE SECURITIES TRADED**

A	B	C	D	E	F	G	H	I	J	K
				Yld	P-E	Sales by				Net
High	Low	Stocks	Div.	%	Ratio	100s	High	Low	Close	Change
46⅛	37¼	Interco	2	4.6	8	2	43⅞	43⅞	43⅞	...
20½	7	IntDiv	8.11e	...	9	27	17¾	16¾	17¾	+1¼
34½	24⅝	Intrlk	2.20	7.8	11	60	28½	27¼	28⅜	+ ¾
23½	12¾	IntAlum	1	4.5	8	122	22⅞	22	22	− ⅝
275½	234¾	IBM	11.52	4.3	14	2125	267⅝	265	266	−1¼
25	18¾	IntFlav	.56	2.3	19	521	24⅞	24⅝	24⅞	...
37⅝	26	IntHarv	2.10	6.2	5	1612	34¼	32⅛	34	+1¼
44	35¼	IntMin	2.60	6.0	7	212	43½	43	43⅛	...
25¼	18⅛	IntMulti	1	4.0	9	335	25¼	24¾	25¼	+ ½
58	35⅛	IntPaper	2	4.6	8	589	44¾	43⅞	43⅞	− ⅜

The above stocks and prices are excerpted from a page in the *Wall Street Journal*. Below you will find definitions of the abbreviations used and explanations of the columns.

A. *High: This is the highest price paid for the stock to date this year.*
B. *Low: This is the lowest price paid for the stock to date this year.*
C. *Stocks: This is the name of the company, usually abbreviated.*
D. *Div.: This is the most recent annual dividend for each share*
E. *Yld %: The percentage of market price yielded by the dividend.*
F. *P-E Ratio: This is the ratio of the current selling price to the earnings per share.*
G. *Sales in 100s: This is the number of round lots (100 shares each) sold that day.
    The odd lots, which are less than 100 shares each, are not listed.*
H. *High:This is the highest price paid for the stock the day it is listed.*
I. *Low: This is the lowest price paid for the stock the day it is listed.*
J. *Close: This is the price of the stock at the end of the trading day.*
K. *Net Change: This is the difference between the closing price of the stock the
    day it is listed and the closing price of the stock at the end of the previous trading day.*

you have read; it may signal additional areas where you need to do more reading; or it may just serve as a further perspective to decide on particular bonds and stocks for your securities portfolio. There are three different sources for listening: radio and television, securities brokers, and friends and relatives.

The Mass Media

Many individuals regularly listen to the news on the radio or watch it on television. Recent developments in the national and international economies ultimately may affect the securities you hold. By listening to news reports, you may glean information on different industries or particular companies in which you are interested. News coverage is quite brief, and details often are lacking. But it may add perspective or alert you to potential problems with your investments. Seldom, however, should you decide to buy or sell a security just because you hear something on the news. There are specific programs on the radio and on television that relate to securities markets and investment. Perhaps the most widely known and viewed is *Wall Street Week,* which is aired on the public broadcast channel in most major cities.

Security Brokers

Brokers (sometimes called "account executives") are another source of information on particular industries and companies. Brokers will answer your questions over the phone. Some brokers respond only to your inquiries and questions, but others may call or send you pertinent information. Brokers seldom do security analyses themselves; instead, they serve to disseminate the research done by their firm or other Wall Street firms. Frequently, the stocks they mention are those that their brokerage firm currently is trying to sell. Brokers may call you more frequently when the stock market is rising than when it is falling. Because brokers usually are paid on commission, their interest in you is based on the size of your account and, especially, the volume of trading generated from your account. This is especially true today in an era of decreasing brokerage commissions.

The broker relationship is an important part of your investing plan. You should shop around for a broker just as you would for a new automobile or a family doctor. Try to find someone who will take the time to talk with you about your particular investment needs and your risk preferences. Select someone who will respond to your inquiries and perhaps make suggestions. Do not select someone who will try to influence the timing of your investment decisions; you should do that yourself.

Friends and Relatives

Friends and relatives are the poorest source of information. Because they may lack the time and resources to conduct thorough analyses, their information is likely to be more in the form of "hot tips"

about securities than informed judgments about particular stocks and bonds. Their financial situation may be quite different from yours, so a particular stock appropriate for them may be inappropriate for you. Business persons sometimes think — incorrectly — that success in their own company makes them experts in others as well. Our hot tip here is to watch out. Listening to friends and relatives won't hurt if their information is put into proper perspective. But ignore their advice if it hastens you toward decisions you might not reach by careful reasoning.

READING THE FINANCIAL NEWS

In order to get information on specific listed stocks and bonds, you must be able to interpret the data provided in your local newspaper and/or the *Wall Street Journal.* Exhibit 15-9 is a sample listing of New York Stock Exchange quotations. Below those quotations are explanations of each column.

Exhibit 15-10 shows a typical set of quotations on bonds listed by the New York Bond Exchange. As an example, consider Woolworth Bonds (Woolw). They yield a nominal interest of 9 percent; they are due in the year 1999; their current yield is 8.9 percent. On the trading day in the exhibit, 1,000 were sold. The high, the low, and the close were all $1,010.25.

HOW TO REACH DECISIONS

By reading and listening, you gather information about the economy, various industries, and particular bonds and stocks. It is up to you to put that information together with your final plan and investment preferences to reach specific decisions. You must decide exactly how many bonds (of a given government or corporation) to buy or sell, how many shares of preferred or common stock (of a given company) to buy or sell, and exactly when to do it. This isn't easy, and there's no set formula to help you. You must use your best judgment, based on a

EXHIBIT 15-10

**READING BOND
QUOTES**

A	B	C	D	E	F	G	H
Bonds		Cur Yld	Vol	High	Low	Close	Net Chg
WillR	4½92	cv	5	70	70	70	−1⅜
Wms	10¼83	9.7	25	106⅛	105⅝	105⅝	− ½
WiscTl	8s14	8.1	3	98¾	98⅝	98¾	+2¼
Witco	4½93	cv	1	73	73	73	−1
Womt	5½94	cv	6	84¾	84⅝	84⅝	− ⅛
Woolw	9s99	8.9	10	101⅛	101⅛	101⅛	...
WldAwy10s93		10.	55	98	98	98	+ ⅛
Wyly	7¼95f	cv	50	24¾	24⅜	24½	...
Xerox	6s95	cv	33	92½	92	92	− ½

A. Name of the company.
B. Coupon or nominal interest rate of the bond and its due or maturity date.
C. Current yield, or the coupon rate divided by the current selling price, where "cv" appears (This indicates that the bond is convertible into the company's stock. The price of the conversion is not given, however. Rather, a Standard and Poor's or a Moody's Bond Book or the financial statement of the corporation will give such information.)
D. Volume of sales in lots of 100.
E. Highest selling price of the bond that trading day. (Bonds are quoted in ⅛ points. A bond selling at 106⅛ has a price of $1061.25.)
F. Lowest price paid for that bond that trading day.
G. Closing price
H. Net change from the previous trading day's closing price.

careful reading and listening, to reach a logical decision.

To illustrate one such decision, we continue the example in which you have decided to purchase two bonds and two stocks in approximately equal proportions. Your selection, shown in Exhibit 15-11, would be based on the following logic. Beginning with common stocks, you have decided that resources will play an important role for many companies in the future. But uncertainty about the international economic and political scene pushes you away from oil and natural gas resources toward timber resources on a national scale. You are also convinced that continuing demand for housing will favor firms that are well managed and appear to have access to resources needed to develop their products. After reviewing several others, you choose Georgia-Pacific.

At the same time, you believe that the country and the vast majority of its citizens will prosper economically. To balance your first selection, you lean toward something in the broad area of consumer products. Further reading leads you to Revlon, for years a leader in the cosmetics industry. Say that both stocks are selling at price-earnings ratios [(earnings/price) = P–E ratio] of about fifteen, which is at the low end of their historical range. Neither is considered especially risky. Both also are well regarded in various stock surveys with a forecast of future appreciation. Among the thousands of possible corporate bonds, you select two issues whose yield-to-maturity is at the high end for their particular bond ratings. General Telephone of California is A-rated, while Ford Motor Credit is Aa-rated. Their 1993 and 1994 maturities are selected to coincide with the time your children will be entering college. In sum, your four selected securities are from firms in rather different kinds of business, and all are considered well managed. Each would seem to offer an attractive expected return at a reasonable risk.

Of course, you may not agree with such a logic. But it is a logic. And you should reason in a similar way before selecting stocks and bonds to meet your financial goals. It may be difficult to develop a logic in your choices without actually committing yourself. There are two possible sources of help. First, the monthly magazine, *Money,* has, in addition to its excellent articles on all aspects of investing, a regular feature titled "One Family's Finances." This case study of a family includes a discussion by a panel of experts of what the family should do financially. Occasionally, choosing stocks and bonds to meet expressed financial goals is included in the case study. Again, you need not agree with the experts' solution in order to benefit from reading the case study. Second, ask several friends, relatives, and acquaintances to outline the steps they followed in selecting their bonds and stocks. Here, the help may not be in the form of a particular logic. Individuals often make such decisions on the basis of a casual statement from another friend or their securities broker.

HOW TO IMPLEMENT DECISIONS

Once you reach a decision on particular stocks

and bonds, you must implement your decisions through your securities broker. If you already have selected a broker and opened an account at his or her firm, then you can call and describe the quantities of particular securities you wish to purchase. In doing so, you should be aware both of different types of accounts you may decide upon and different types of orders you may utilize.

Types of Brokerage Accounts

There are two types of accounts. A **cash account** is designed for investors who wish to buy securities and pay cash. Final payment for a cash purchase is due within five business days or seven calendar days of the trade date of your purchase. If you open a cash account, you may elect to have the bonds or stock certificates delivered to you and held by you, preferably in a safe deposit box. Alternatively, you may have the brokerage firm hold the bonds or stock certificates for you. Many investors prefer not to be bothered with physical possession of securities.

A **margin account** is designed for investors who wish to borrow a portion of the funds necessary to purchase securities from their brokerage firm. *Initial margin* refers to the percentage amount an investor must pay (typically 50 percent to 80 percent for stocks). *Maintenance margin* (a lower percentage, say, 25 percent) is the point at which the investor must pay additional funds if the market price of stocks bought on margin falls over time. Suppose initial margin were 50 percent and maintenance margin were 25 percent. Disregarding commissions, you would have to put up $2,000 in margin in order to buy $4,000 worth of stocks. If market price of those stocks fell to $2,500, then your margin would be only $500, which is only 20 percent of the market value of the stocks held. You would receive a **margin call** asking for a at least $125 to restore the 25 percent maintenance margin. Because margin calls during a depressed stock market are psychologically disturbing, most investors are advised to restrict their purchases of securities to a cash account.

In either case, your brokerage firm typically will send you a monthly statement of the securities you own, as well as your present cash balance. The cash balance reflects interest and dividends earned by your securities. For a margin account, the cash balance also reflects the funds borrowed, plus interest you must pay the brokerage firm for use of those funds. A positive cash balance does *not* earn interest, so you should not allow it to get very large before either investing it in additional securities or having it sent to you. You probably won't be reminded to do so by the brokerage firm.

Types of Orders

There are also different orders you may use to buy or sell securities. The simplest, **market order,** means that the broker is instructed to purchase or sell at the existing market price. In contrast, a **limit**

order means that the broker is to buy or sell only if market price reaches a designated amount. If you make a market order for twenty-five shares of Revlon Common, you will pay whatever the next transaction occurs at—say, $35.75. But if you make a limit order for twenty-five shares of Revlon at thirty-five dollars, then you buy the shares only if a transaction can be made at that price. Limit orders are also used by investors to "ensure" gains. They may be entered for a specific period of time, or they may be entered until the broker is otherwise notified, in which case the order is GTC, or good till canceled. A **stop-loss** or **stop order** is an order to sell stock when the market price hits or drops below a specified level. Presumably a stop-loss order protects the investor against a rapid decline in a stock price.

Costs of Buying and Selling Securities

Before entering your order to buy or sell, you

EXHIBIT 15-11

**ILLUSTRATION OF
SELECTED SECURITIES**

SECURITY	QUANTITY	RECENT PRICE	INVESTMENT
Bonds:			
General Telephone Company of California, 4⅝% coupon, 1993, A-rated, 9.8% yield-to-maturity	2 bonds	$ 560	$1,120
Ford Motor Credit Corp., 10½% coupon, 1994, Aa-rated, 10.4% yield-to-maturity	1 bond	$1,010	$1,010
Stocks:			
Georgia-Pacific Common	24 shares	$ 35	$ 840
Revlon, Inc. Common	25 shares	$ 40	$1,000
Total Investment			$3,970

should know what the transactions cost. In the mid 1970s, it would have been appropriate to include an exhibit showing the fixed schedule of brokerage commissions. But with the advent of negotiated commissions, there is no single commission schedule. Large institutions, whose transactions may involve thousands of shares, are able to bargain for commissions as much as 40 to 50 percent off any "fixed" schedule. Individuals usually cannot bargain as strongly because their transactions are smaller. Before selecting a brokerage firm and entering orders to buy common stocks, you should find out exactly how much commission you will pay. In so doing, you may find that some brokerage firms attempt to attract customers by offering discounted fees on even smaller orders. But you probably shouldn't by-pass a reputable and financially sound brokerage firm and/or a particular broker from whom you get useful advice and timely service just to save a few dollars on a transaction. The brokerage fee on bond transactions is smaller, as a percentage of the amount bought or sold, than it is for stock. Remember, when you sell securities, there may be federal and state taxes to pay on capital gains that have accrued.

The flow chart in Exhibit 15-12 shows all the procedures involved in purchasing bonds and stocks.

Setting Down Some Guidelines

The last step in implementing your decisions is to write down some tentative guidelines for selling your securities. Exhibit 15-13 shows the four securities included in the illustration. Bonds will be held until maturity unless their respective ratings are lowered. Stocks will be sold if their market price drops 20 percent. If prices rise considerably, you should reconsider your earlier analysis and perhaps switch to other stocks more suited to future growth. The selling rules should not be followed mechanically. They should be adapted to help reduce the uncertainty that can occur when the stock market goes through cycles. The rules obviously are not guaran-

teed to protect you against adverse market moves in the future. In fact, you may wish to change your selling rules eventually. By writing down your investment plan, analyzing available data, and establishing tentative selling rules, you more likely will be comfortable with the decisions you make about particular bonds and stocks. And, ultimately, you may be able to meet your financial goals through careful investment in securities.

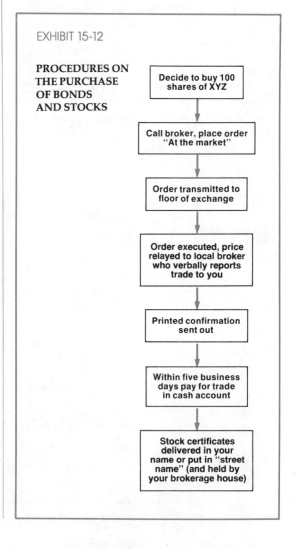

EXHIBIT 15-12

PROCEDURES ON THE PURCHASE OF BONDS AND STOCKS

Decide to buy 100 shares of XYZ

Call broker, place order "At the market"

Order transmitted to floor of exchange

Order executed, price relayed to local broker who verbally reports trade to you

Printed confirmation sent out

Within five business days pay for trade in cash account

Stock certificates delivered in your name or put in "street name" (and held by your brokerage house)

EXHIBIT 15-13	SECURITY	TENTATIVE SELLING PRICE
ILLUSTRATION OF TENTATIVE SELLING RULES	**Bonds:** General Telephone Company of California	Hold until maturity of A-rating continues. Sell if rating is lowered.
	Ford Motor Credit	Hold until maturity if Aa-rating continues. Sell if rating is lowered.
	Stocks: Georgia-Pacific Common	Sell if price drops below $28. Reconsider if price rises above $50.
	Revlon Common	Sell if price drops below $32. Reconsider if price rises above $44.

GLOSSARY OF TERMS

SECURITIES   Certificates issued by governments and business to obtain needed financing from investors.

BOND   An interest-bearing certificate issued by a government or corporation. The type of security that represents debt.

STOCK   A type of security that represents ownership. It does not guarantee interest.

RISK   A measure of the uncertainty associated with possible returns on a security or portfolio.

EXPECTED RETURN   An estimate of future return for a security or portfolio, including both income and appreciation, that is based on possible outcomes.

GOVERNMENT BOND   A security that indicates borrowing by federal, state, or local governments. A legal obligation on the part of the government that has a fixed maturity.

CORPORATE BOND   A security that indicates borrowing by a corporation. A legal obligation of the corporation that has a fixed maturity.

BOND INDENTURE   A document that specifies the legal provisions associated with a particular bond issue, including the timing of interest payments and the maturity of the bond.

NOMINAL YIELD   Sometimes called the coupon yield on a bond. It is calculated by dividing the par, or face, or maturity value (usually $1,000) by the annual interest payment guaranteed on the bond.

CURRENT YIELD   The bond yield calculated by dividing the annual interest payment by the current market price of the bond. If the current market price is par, then nominal yield and current yield are equal.

YIELD-TO-MATURITY   For government and corporate bonds, a measure of the effective annual return that the investor will earn if the bond is held to maturity. Also called effective yield.

PREFERRED STOCK   A security that indicates financing obtained from investors by a corporation. It is not a legal obligation for the firm and does not have a maturity but pays a fixed dividend each year. It has preferred position over common stock both for dividends and for assets in the event of firm liquidation.

COMMON STOCK   A security that indicates the real ownership in a corporation. It is not a legal obligation for the firm and does not have a maturity. It has the last claim on dividends each year and assets in the event of firm liquidation.

PRIMARY SECURITIES MARKETS   The procedure and financial intermediaries whereby corporations and governments sell their securities to investors.

SECONDARY SECURITIES MARKETS   The procedures and financial intermediaries whereby investors buy and sell securities that already have been issued by corporations and governments.

THIRD SECURITIES MARKET   A market in which large brokerage firms by-pass organized exchanges in order to buy and sell blocks of stock.

TECHNICAL ANALYSIS   A method by which investors process information about the recent market prices and trading volume of a given security in order to decide whether to buy, hold, or sell that security.

FUNDAMENTAL ANALYSIS   A method by which investors process information about the economy, an industry, and a particular firm in order to decide whether to buy, hold, or sell the securities of that firm.

FORMULA PLANNING   A predetermined schedule for switching investment funds between common stocks and fixed income securities as the stock market changes direction. The idea is to buy stocks at lower prices and sell stocks at higher prices.

DOLLAR COST AVERAGING   A predetermined schedule for purchasing over time a fixed amount of a given security each period. The idea is to buy more securities at lower prices and fewer securities at higher prices.

SECURITIES BROKER   An employee of a securities firm who provides information about various securities and handles the execution of all buy and sell orders by the investor. Sometimes called an account executive.

HOT TIPS   A colloquial expression referring to supposedly important and useful information about a security that one investor passes on to another. Usually of dubious value.

CASH ACCOUNT   An investor's account at a brokerage firm in which securities are purchased for cash only.

MARGIN ACCOUNT   An investor's account at a brokerage firm in which a portion of the necessary funds for purchasing securities is borrowed from the brokerage firm.

MARGIN CALL   Due to falling securities prices, an investor is informed by the brokerage firm that additional cash must be added to his margin account to bring it up to the margin requirement.

MARKET ORDER   An investor instructs his broker to buy or sell a security at the next available market price.

LIMIT ORDER   An investor instructs his broker to buy or sell a security at a specific market price.

STOP-LOSS ORDER   An order to sell a specified stock whenever the market price hits or falls below a specified price. Also called a stop order.

CHAPTER SUMMARY

1. If an individual or family has adequate cash reserves, life insurance, and retirement benefits, investment in securities, whether stocks or bonds, is a possible savings outlet.

2. In investing, expected return goes hand in hand with risk. Higher expected returns necessarily cause the investor to incur higher risk.

3. Bonds are issued by the U.S. government, state and municipal governments, and private corporations.

4. The Treasury issues bills, certificate notes, and bonds, which all have different maturity dates, ranging from three months to many years.

5. A bond issued by the U.S. Treasury is considered the least risky of all securities since it is backed by the taxing power of the United States government. Bonds issued by state and municipal governments are more risky.

6. There are many types of corporate bonds, including debentures,

mortgage, collateral trusts, equipment trusts, convertible, and callable. Convertibility and callability can be features of corporate bonds.

7. There are three different measures of bond yield: (a) nominal, (b) current, and (c) yield-to-maturity, or total effective yield.

8. Stocks may be common or preferred; the latter are a type of bond.

9. There are many types of preferred stocks, including cumulative, participating, convertible, and callable.

10. When firms don't pay out all their after-tax profits to stockholders, they keep what are called retained earnings. Such retained earnings presumably are used to increase the value of the corporation. Hence, the market price of that corporation's stock should rise because retained earnings have been reinvested.

11. There are many types of securities markets, including primary, secondary, third, and over-the-counter.

12. Of the numerous organized exchanges, both for stocks and bonds, the most well-known are the New York and American Stock and Bond Exchanges.

13. To determine how stocks are doing, you can look at several indexes, including the New York Stock Exchange Index of all its listed stocks; the Standard and Poors Composite Index, which includes 500 stocks; and the Dow Jones Industrial Average, which includes 30 blue chip stocks. The latter is an unweighted average of the market price of the thirty stocks.

14. Historically, short-term government bonds (bills) have yielded the lowest rate of return, followed by U.S. government bonds of longer duration, corporate bonds, and, finally, corporate stocks. These historical averages are often different, however, from rates of return for these types of securities over shorter time periods. For example, the rate of return to corporate stocks between 1969 and 1974 was -3.4 percent annually.

15. Financial planning is a necessary first step in deciding about investment and securities. Financial planning includes, but is not limited to, taking stock of the current and future resources of the financial unit, as well as current and future desires and needs, such as funds for education and other goals.

16. When choosing securities for investment, you must decide how much risk you can incur. Remember, risk and rate of return go hand in hand.

17. The process of selecting particular stocks or bonds involves security analysis, which may be of the technical or fundamental type.

18. A technical analysis includes analyzing the past price behavior of a particular stock or group of stocks.

19. A fundamental analysis examines the underlying features that will de-

termine the profitability of a company, a set of companies, or the economy in general. A complete fundamental analysis involves an economic, an industry, and a company analysis.

20. Since the coupon rate on a bond is fixed, bond prices fluctuate inversely with average interest rates in the economy. If, after you bought a bond for any particular price, the general interest rate in the economy rose, the market price of your bond would fall, and vice versa.

21. There are four ways to decide when to purchase securities: (a) buy a security as soon as you've selected it through a technical or fundamental analysis; (b) delay until you believe that the overall stock market is in the early stages of a broad market advance; (c) rely on formula planning, which uses a predetermined schedule and a set of fixed proportions of stocks and bonds; or (d) employ dollar-cost averaging.

22. The decision when to sell securities can be based on technical analysis, fundamental analysis, tax considerations, and financial necessity.

23. Risk and rate of return are closely related. You must decide how much risk you can afford to take before you undertake an investment program. In doing a fundamental analysis, you can obtain economic information from the *Wall Street Journal, Barron's,* the *New York Times, Business Week, Fortune, Forbes, U.S. News & World Report,* the *Federal Reserve Bulletin,* and the *Survey of Current Business.*

24. Excellent materials for industry analysis can be obtained from *Forbes* and *Fortune* magazines, from the Value Line Investment Service, and from the industry surveys of the Standard and Poor's Corporation.

25. Company analysis information can be obtained from *Moody's Manuals, Standard and Poor's Corporation Records,* Form 10-K, and annual reports provided by corporations.

26. Annual reports are often aimed at "selling" the company; thus, they must be read critically. Investors with accounting backgrounds can benefit from reading the auditor's comments.

27. Additional information on companies can be obtained from *Standard and Poor's Stock Reports, Moody's Handbook of Widely Held Common Stock,* and *Value Line Ratings and Reports.*

28. For information on which stocks to buy, you can listen to the mass media, security brokers, and friends and relatives.

29. Friends, relatives, and brokers often give potential investors hot tips, which may not be the same thing as informed judgments.

30. The two types of brokerage accounts are cash and margin.

31. You may receive a margin call if the value of a stock purchased on margin falls sufficiently to impair the ability of the brokerage house to recover the money implicitly loaned to you.

32. Two types of brokerage orders are market and limit. When you buy or sell "at the market," you expect to get the best price possible at that time. A limit order, however, specifically indicates a maximum price you will pay or a minimum price at which you will sell your shares.

33. Because different brokerage houses offer different rates for buying and selling stocks and bonds, it is often difficult to compare commissions.

STUDY QUESTIONS

1. "Risk and rate of return are positively related." Do you agree with this statement? Why or why not?

2. Which do you think are a better investment—stocks or bonds? Why?

3. What is a preferred stock? Do preferred stockholders have specific claims on the assets of a bankrupt firm?

4. What is the difference between a cumulative and noncumulative preferred stock?

5. What is the difference between participating and nonparticipating preferred stocks?

6. What does it mean when a preferred stock is callable?

7. Explain the system of bond ratings that Standard and Poor's and Moody's use.

8. How does a change in the average interest rate in the economy affect the price of old or existing bonds?

9. Describe the various securities markets.

10. Name and describe the three basic types of orders.

11. What is a margin requirement?

12. List the steps that you would follow when purchasing a stock on the New York Stock Exchange.

13. What is the difference between a company analysis and an industry analysis? When would you want to use one instead of the other?

CASE PROBLEMS

15-1 Dart Throw Leads to Bond Selection

Nancy Yarborough received $850 from her grandparents when she graduated from college. Using the only bond selection method she could recall from her personal finance book, she threw two darts at the *Wall Street Journal* and pierced two corporate bond listings. Nancy wants to purchase the one with the greatest yield-to-maturity. Bond A paid fifty dollars annual interest and matured in four years. Bond B paid sixty dollars annually and matured in six years.

What would you advise her to do?

15-2 Stock Selling Decisions

The Waltons, a couple from Phoenix, Arizona, purchased two issues of stock seven years ago. They now want to sell one of them to pay for a second honeymoon. To minimize the tax effects, they would like to sell the stock that has the least capital gain. They also want to know which one has shown the greatest effective yield. Please help them.

SELECTED REFERENCES

Branch, Ben. *Fundamentals of Investing.* Santa Barbara, CA: Wiley-Hamilton, 1976.

D'Ambrosio, C. A. *A Guide to Successful Investing.* Englewood Cliffs, NJ: Prentice-Hall, latest edition, 1970.

Engle, L. *How to Buy Stocks.* New York: Bantam Books, 1971.

Farrell, Maurice L. *Dow Jones Investor's Handbook.* Princeton, NJ: Dow Jones Books, 1975.

Fisher, P. A. *Conservative Investors Sleep Well.* New York: Harper & Row, 1975.

Graham, B. *The Intelligent Investor.* New York: Harper & Row, 3rd revised edition, 1965.

Lorie, J. H. and Hamilton, M. T. *The Stock Market.* Homewood, IL: Richard D. Irwin, 1973.

Malkiel, B. G. *A Random Walk Down Wall Street.* New York: W. W. Norton & Company, 1973.

Mr. Dollar Investor. *My Stockbroker Is A Bum.* Jericho, NY: Exposition Press, 1971.

New York Stock Exchange Fact Book. New York: New York Stock Exchange, annually.

Smith, A. *The Money Game.* New York: Random House, 1968.

Smith, K. V. and Eiteman, D. K. *Essentials of Investing.* Homewood, IL: Richard D. Irwin, 1974.

"The Right Way to Read the Stock Market Averages." *Changing Times,* April 1977, pp. 39-41.

Alternative Strategies
for Securities*

SIXTEEN

■ The previous chapter dealt with characteristics of securities and with the relationship between risk and return as it pertains to various government bonds and corporate bonds and stocks. Investing becomes even more complex when we consider the expected returns and risks of a portfolio of securities. Various concepts of diversification lead us to alternative strategies for investing in securities.

RETURN AND RISK OF PORTFOLIOS

A portfolio of securities is a collection of one or more stocks and bonds owned by an individual, family, or organization in an attempt to meet certain expressed investment goals. A family's total portfolio is a collection of its cash reserves, cash value of life insurance, retirement benefits, equity in a home, securities, and all other investments. It can be argued that all investment decisions are really portfolio decisions, since a particular security or other investment is always bought or sold relative to a total portfolio. Just as bonds and stocks have return and risk characteristics, so do portfolios of bonds and stocks.

Portfolio Relationships

Four important relationships concerning the returns and risks of securities and portfolios are depicted in Exhibit 16-1. They are presented for a portfolio consisting of three securities (A, B, and C). Were the relation-

---

*This is an optional chapter for those with a particular interest in securities investment.

419

ships extended to larger portfolios, the situation would become more complex.

Relationship #1 reiterates the definition of a portfolio as a collection of securities. In other words, the portfolio is just the sum of its component parts. Relationship #2 tells us that the expected return of a portfolio is the sum of the expected returns of its component securities. More precisely, *expected portfolio return* is a weighted average of the expected returns of the component securities. If you decide to split your $4,000 of excess funds equally between a 5 percent savings account and a particular common stock with expected return of 12 percent, then the expected return of your portfolio is 8.5 percent (50 percent times 5 percent *plus* 50 percent times 12 percent). But if you decide to put two-thirds

EXHIBIT 16-1.

RETURN AND RISK RELATIONSHIPS FOR SECURITIES AND PORTFOLIOS

These four relationships show how we can analyze different aspects of a portfolio. Relationship #1 tells us that this particular portfolio consists of three securities. Relationship #2 indicates that the expected portfolio rate of return is the sum of the expected returns of each individual security. Relationship #3 indicates that the risk of a particular portfolio is the sum of the risks of the individual securities plus additional risk factors that take account of each pair of securities within the portfolio. Relationship #4 restates relationship #3; we consider the unique risk to each security plus one market-related risk for the entire security market under scrutiny.

RELATIONSHIP #1

| **Portfolio** | = | Security A | *plus* | Security B | *plus* | Security C |

RELATIONSHIP #2

| **Expected Portfolio Return** | = | Expected Return of Security A | *plus* | Expected Return of Security B | *plus* | Expected Return of Security C |

RELATIONSHIP #3

| **Portfolio Risk** | = | Risk of Security A | *plus* | Risk of Security B | *plus* | Risk of Security C |

plus Correlation Risk AB
plus Correlation Risk AC
plus Correlation Risk BC

RELATIONSHIP #4

| **Portfolio Risk** | = | Unique Risk of Security A | *plus* | Unique Risk of Security B | *plus* | Unique Risk of Security C |

plus Market-Related Risk of Portfolio

of your funds in the riskier stock, your expected portfolio return is 9.7 percent (33 percent times 5 percent *plus* 67 percent times 12 percent).

The increase in expected portfolio return from 8.5 percent to 9.7 percent is, of course, possible only if you are willing to take an added portfolio risk. Relationship #3 suggests that portfolio risk is the sum of the risks of the three securities *plus* an additional risk component for *each pair* of securities included in the portfolio. This **correlation risk** between securities A and B is a measure of how future returns to A are expected to relate to the future returns of B. The more *closely* the returns of securities A and B are expected to move together in the future, the *greater* is the correlation risk that that pair of securities adds to the overall portfolio. The same is true for all pairs of securities held.

As a practical matter, correlation risk is complex. But, conceptually, it is *most* important to all investors, small or large. Relationship #3 tells us that the total risk for a portfolio is more than just the sum of its parts because of interrelationships. In other words, if a portfolio consists of three stocks, the total risk of the portfolio is not the sum of the individual risks of the three stocks. Rather, we must add an interrelationship risk, or correlation risk. Selection of stocks in a portfolio may be done with an eye to reducing total portfolio risk, meaning that the correlation factor, or correlation risk, must be made smaller. This can be done by having securities whose respective price movements will not be related.

As an example, consider picking three stocks, all in the automobile industry. The correlation risk for each of the pairs will be relatively high since changes in the industry as a whole will probably affect each of the companies in a similar way. On the other hand, if one stock is chosen from the automobile industry, one from the agricultural sector, and one from the medical sector, their correlation risks may be lower; hence, the total risk of the portfolio would decrease.

It is difficult to reduce the correlation risk for large portfolios. An alternative is illustrated in relationship #4, which is based on the assumption that the future return of any security can be related to the future return of the securities markets. That assumption really should be stated in terms of either bonds or stocks, since measures of the overall securities markets are really measures either of the bond market or the stock market. Let us consider stocks. Relationship #4 states that the risk of a portfolio of *three* common stocks consists of *four* components: one component of *unique risk* for each of the common stocks, plus one *market-related risk* component for the stock market as a whole. For a portfolio of twenty stocks, there would be a total of twenty-one components (twenty individual plus one market-related). Portfolios of twenty or more securities are not at all uncommon; the simplification accorded by relationship #4 is, therefore, attractive.

An Example of Risk Calculation

Suppose that, after careful analysis, future returns during a planning horizon for common stock A and the stock market are provided and plotted, as in Exhibit 16-2. Each of the seven points plotted in the exhibit might be based on a different economic and market scenario for the planning horizon. The best line, fitted through those points, is sometimes called the characteristic line for the given stock or security. The dispersion of plotted points about a characteristic line is a measure of the "unique risk" of the particular security. The characteristic line itself subjectively depicts the most likely relationship between individual stock return and stock market return during the planning horizon. The *slope* of the characteristic line is a measure of "responsiveness" of the particular

EXHIBIT 16-2.

ILLUSTRATIVE CHARACTERISTIC LINE FOR COMMON STOCK A

On the horizontal axis, we measure future market return for the stock market in general. On the vertical axis, we measure the expected future return for stock A. Each point represents where the stock's return would be relative to the entire market under uniquely different economic conditions for the planning period. The line that fits these points is called a characteristic line. Its slope is called the beta. If the beta is one, the stock under study will follow exactly the entire stock market. If the beta is greater than one, the stock will have a higher rate of return when the market goes up, and vice versa. If the slope is less than one, it will react less than in proportion to changes in the entire stock market. The beta, therefore, is a measure of risk relative to the market in general.

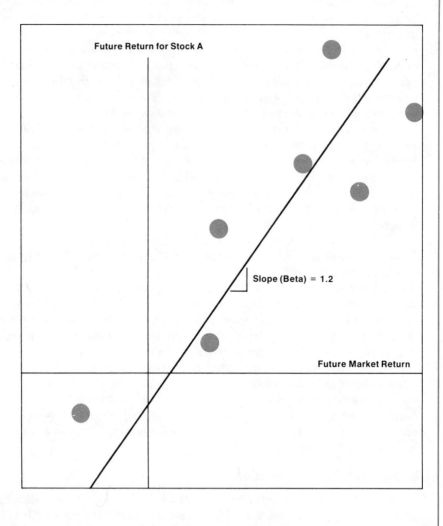

security (here common stock A) to the overall stock market. This has become known as beta in the financial literature and is often used as a surrogate for the risk of a given security.

If an individual stock return is likely to follow market returns rather closely, then the estimate of beta would be 1.0 (unity). In the illustration of common stock A, the estimated slope is 1.2; this means that if the stock market return goes up 10 percent stock A return should go up 12 percent. Or if stock market return goes down 5 percent, stock A return probably will go down 6 percent. If a security has an estimated beta less than unity, it is referred to as a "defensive" security. If, instead, a security has a beta greater than unity, it is termed an "aggressive" security. According to this definition, common stock A is aggressive. Intuitively this makes sense, since the higher the beta, the wider the range of possible return outcomes and, hence, the greater the risk to the investor.

The concept of a characteristic line helps us understand relationship #4 in Exhibit 16-1. As a particular security is added to a portfolio, there are two risk considerations. The first is the unique risk of the security as given by the dispersion about its characteristic line. The second is how that security contributes to market-related risk. But market-related risk is just market risk multiplied by the beta of the portfolio. And the beta of any portfolio is a simple weighted average of the betas of its component securities. Suppose that your portfolio consisted of three stocks equally held, whose estimated betas were 1.2, 1.3 and 0.8, respectively. The portfolio beta would be $\frac{1}{3}[1.2 + 1.3 + 0.8] = 1.1$; hence, market-related risk would be 110% of stock market return. This is a much simpler procedure than estimating the correlation risks needed in relationship #3. While correlation risk between any two securities is useful conceptually, our subsequent discussion of portfolios will lean extensively on relationship #4.

CONCEPTS OF DIVERSIFICATION

If we assume that investors prefer less risk to greater risk, then it is appropriate to consider ways of reducing risk. *Diversification* is an attempt to do so. A simple solution is for an investor to place funds in a savings account or invest in U.S. Treasury bills, both of which are virtually without risk. The problem with that solution is that expected return would then be lower than that from stocks and bonds, for example. As a result, the investor may not meet expressed investment goals. The alternative solution is to add risky securities to the portfolio in order to diversify against risk but without undue sacrifice of expected return. In this context, there are three concepts of diversification.

Random Diversification

The first concept is random diversification. You may recall reading about the U.S. Senator who threw darts at the financial page listing all NYSE common stocks; he suggested that a portfolio so chosen probably would outperform many professionally managed portfolios. But what would happen to the risk of the portfolio as more darts hit the newspaper? Recall relationship #4 from Exhibit 16-1. As more stocks are randomly selected, there will be one unique risk component for each stock, plus one market-related component that is the portfolio beta multiplied by the overall market risk. But random selection should cause portfolio beta to approach unity and the market-related risk component in relationship #4 to become just total market risk. The unique risk components of individual stocks also will tend to offset one another so that the total unique risk becomes smaller and smaller relative to total market risk. The result is that *portfolio risk gradually approaches total market risk* (and so, too, does the portfolio's rate of return).

Consider the characteristic line of a portfolio constructed by random selection. As more stocks are added, the future portfolio return points move closer and closer toward a straight line, which has a slope closer and closer to unity. No attention is given to expected portfolio return in this concept of diversification, though it is clear that it moves closer and closer to expected market return as more stocks are added randomly. Quite simply, the portfolio return eventually becomes the market return when stocks are selected randomly.

Risk-Reducing Diversification

The idea here is to add *dissimilar* securities to the portfolio in order to reduce risk, without concern for the resulting expected return. This can be accomplished (according to relationship #4) by adding securities with low betas, since that reduces the market related component of total portfolio risk. Putting your excess funds into savings accounts or U.S. Treasury bills is really an example of this concept of diversification since the beta associated with either savings accounts or bills would be zero. The betas of most government and corporate bonds also are quite small; thus, fixed income securities are appropriate for **risk-reducing diversification.** In contrast, the betas of common stocks vary considerably. Exhibit 16-3 shows industry betas ranging from 2.36 (leisure time) to .35 (gold mining). Betas for most common stocks and industries are within the range from 1.5 to 0.5. The estimated betas in Exhibit 16-3 are based on historical quarterly returns over the five-year period from 1972 to 1976. The industries are defined by Standard and Poor's Corporation, and the market used in estimating characteristic lines is represented by the *Standard and Poor's Composite Index.*

Alternatively, risk-reducing diversification can be accomplished (according to relationship #3) by adding pairs of securities with low correlation risk. Among fixed-income securities, this suggests bonds with different maturity dates or bonds from firms and governments that are dispersed geographically. Among more risky securities, this suggests common stocks from different industries, since correlations among securities in a given industry are usually higher than the correlations between securities from different industries. It also suggests why everyone should always consider each potential investment relative to his or her total portfolio of securities, savings accounts, retirement funds, and other investment holdings.

Efficient Diversification

Here the idea is to consider how securities added to a portfolio affect both its expected return and risk characteristic. Because it considers return as well as risk, efficient diversification is a riskier action than either random diversification or risk-reducing diversification. It also is a more difficult concept since it necessitates return-risk trade-offs. An *efficient portfolio* has either highest attainable expected return for a given level of risk or lowest attainable risk for a given level of expected return. Efficient portfolios can be calculated only with sophisticated computer algorithms that require input that includes explicit assessment of expected return and risk for each security being considered, as well as of correlation risk between all pairs of securities.

Comparison of Diversification Concepts

Now let's compare the three concepts of diversification. Efficient diversification has the greatest conceptual appeal but is the most difficult to implement because you need a computer. Random diversification is the easiest to implement but is not very satisfying psychologically. How many of your friends, for example, would be willing to base their total investment program on the throw of darts or dice? Risk-reducing diversification, which falls between the other two concepts in terms of difficulty, suffers because it ignores expected return, which is a primary motive for many investors. We are thus left with disadvantages for all three concepts. Many institutional investors (pension plans, insurance companies, etc.) profess expertise in making return-risk trade-offs, but

EXHIBIT 16-3.	INDUSTRY	ESTIMATED BETA
ESTIMATED HISTORICAL BETAS FOR COMMON STOCKS IN SELECTED INDUSTRIES, QUARTERLY 1972-1976	Leisure Time	2.36
	Shoes	1.86
	Aerospace	1.67
	Publishing	1.39
	Office and Business Equipment	1.08
	Tire and Rubber	1.01
	Truckers	.89
	Drugs	.80
	Industrial Machinery	.69
	Telephone	.65
	Gold Mining	.35

few of them utilize efficient diversification fully in practice. Individual investors should be aware of the four relationships of Exhibit 16-1 and try to reflect the notions of diversification as portfolios are constructed and managed over time.

HOW MANY SECURITIES TO HOLD

A critical question about diversification is: How many securities should you hold? Should the number be different for individuals and institutions? Is it possible to have too many securities in a portfolio? We cannot answer these questions precisely, but we can observe what individuals and institutions seem to do and see how that squares with some recent studies of diversification and risk reduction.

For Institutions

Let's begin with institutional portfolios. Because of the huge sums of money under management, many institutional portfolios include 50 to 100 or even more bonds and stocks. To do otherwise would be to concentrate large amounts of total portfolio wealth in single securities and to have a significant effect on security prices as particular issues are bought and sold for the portfolio. Furthermore, the holdings of some institutional portfolios are legally constrained from having any single security with more than a prescribed percentage of the total portfolio wealth. If a common stock fund is restricted from having more than five percent invested in any one issue, then a lower limit of at least twenty stocks must be held. The recently enacted pension legislation, with its emphasis on diversification, may cause many pension funds to increase the number of securities held. Only the costs of properly monitoring all securities in the portfolio would result in an upper limit on the number of issues held.

For Individuals

Individual portfolios are much smaller, both in total portfolio value and number of issues held. Neither legal constraints nor market effects place lower limits on number of issues held by individuals. As a result, it has been estimated that the individual family that owns securities has an average of four or five stocks and even fewer bonds. Individuals could hold greater numbers of securities, but the individual investor's transaction and monitoring costs would increase.

Diversification in Practice

Several studies have been made of risk reduction in portfolios of randomly selected common stocks. Findings suggest that with fifteen to twenty stocks, most of the unique risk, *on average*, is eliminated, and only market-related risk remains. It might seem, then, that institutional portfolios have too many holdings, while individual portfolios have too few. However, the fiduciary responsibility of professional money managers is such that the "on average" finding is not good enough. Indeed, some money managers contend that at least 200 stocks would have to be held in order for the portfolio to consistently follow a market average, such as the *Standard and Poor's Composite Index*. Large institutional portfolios, with bond holdings limited to the higher ratings and spread across different maturities and with stocks spread across a wide range of industry groupings, would appear to be reasonably diversified in a risk-reducing sense.

Many individual portfolios would appear to be poorly diversified, especially if one looks only at the bonds and stocks held. A better way to view an individual's diversification would be to examine securities in light of other parts of his or her total wealth. But that data are often not available. In any event, individuals with limited funds available for bonds and stocks are not apt to be as well diversified as are those who can afford to own fifteen to twenty different securities. If you have decided to invest $4,000 in common stocks, then presumably you could allocate $200 to each of twenty different stocks. Because fractional shares cannot be purchased and because a higher percentage brokerage fee would have to be paid on orders of only a few shares, such a tactic would not be recommended. Alternative tactics that offer some diversification would range from $400 allotments in ten stocks to $1,000 allotments in four stocks. As a practical matter, experts advise you to lean toward the latter. Regardless of your choice, it is clear that you ought to select particular stocks that are in different industries or in different economic sectors. You also should be aware of the risk level (perhaps using beta) of the stocks you select, so that the risk level of your securities portfolio is consistent with the risk you are willing to assume for risky investments.

CHARACTERISTICS OF MUTUAL FUNDS

Investment companies provide an alternative way for individuals to achieve diversification in their securities portfolio. An investment company is a large portfolio of investments—usually securities—that is managed professionally on behalf of many smaller investors. In return for a management fee, the professional manager buys and sells securities toward some expressed portfolio goal. The two services being offered are professional investment management and diversification. Professional investment management relieves the individual of economic, industry, and company analyses that are considered necessary to manage portfolios properly. The effectiveness of professional management is best judged by the performance of the portfolio over time. Diversification is made possible because the funds of many investors add up to a large pool of wealth that can be spread across a large number of securities.

Types of Investment Companies

There are two different types of investment companies—closed-end and open-end—which differ in their ownership structure.

Closed-End. A closed-end investment company resembles other corporations in that there is a fixed number of shares outstanding. These shares are traded on the organized stock exchanges or over-the-counter, just as shares of corporate common stock are. Shares of a closed-end investment company are bought or sold in the secondary securities market. Portfolios of some closed-end investment companies are specialized in terms of their investments, while others attempt to diversify broadly. Certain closed-end companies are discussed later in this chapter.

Open-end. Open-end investment companies are mutual funds. A large part of total wealth in investment companies is in mutual funds. Mutual funds do not have a fixed capitalization or a fixed number of issued securities, but instead are prepared to buy and sell ownerships shares from investors directly. Mutual fund shares are traded in primary securities markets instead of on the organized exchanges or over-the-counter. Numbers of outstanding shares of mutual funds are subject to greater change over time than are those of closed-end companies, because individual investors are constantly buying and selling shares from the company. In fact, many individuals tend to sell their mutual fund shares in years that show bad portfolio results. While certain studies have questioned the ability of mutual fund managers to perform as well as the stock market averages, it is doubtful that mutual fund portfolios have fared any better or worse than other individual and institutional portfolios.

When you purchase or sell mutual fund shares in a so-called no-load fund, the transaction is made at the fund's *net asset value* (NAV)—the total market value of its securities portfolio divided by the current number of outstanding shares. The net asset value of a fund per share is called the bid price of the fund. This price is computed daily and appears in the newspapers. The ask price of a fund is the bid price plus the commission or sales charge, if it exists.

As an owner of mutual fund shares, you receive your return from three sources: distributions of dividends and interest earned by the securities in the fund; distributions of capital gains realized by the fund; and changes in the net asset value of the fund, which reflects unrealized capital gains. If you buy a mutual fund share at ten dollars and, during the year, it pays dividends of forty cents and distributes thirty cents of capital gains, then your income yield is 7 percent. If the net asset value rises to $10.50 by the end of the year, your total annual return is 12 percent.

As an owner, you have a risk similar to that of a large securities portfolio. Because of the diversification provided, your risk typically is smaller than if you held bonds and stocks directly. An examination of the characteristic lines of mutual funds reveals that, as expected, unique risk is diversified away to a great extent, and future return points fit close to the characteristic line. It also reveals that the average slope or beta for mutual funds is about .8; hence, mutual funds are "defensive," at least on average.

Categories of Mutual Funds

Mutual funds are categorized in several ways. One method is by the type of securities held. There are common stock funds, preferred stock funds, and bond funds. A balanced fund holds both bonds and stocks. Because most mutual funds are common stock funds, a further categorization is by portfolio objective. There are growth funds, income funds, growth (primary goal) with income (secondary goal), and income with growth. Mutual funds are sometimes categorized by size and risk level as well. For example, one grouping is "smaller growth funds: long-term growth of capital and income, above-average volatility." There are also funds that specialize in particular types of investments, such as insurance and bank stocks, international issues, and convertible securities. A recent development in the industry is money market funds that invest in U.S. government bills and other short-term investments with a primary goal of high percentage yield at very low risk.

Mutual funds are also divided into load and no-load funds. A *load fund* is one for which a percentage fee is paid when you buy mutual fund shares. A load is not paid when you sell mutual fund shares. The load charge is a percentage of the total investment; it can be as high as 9 percent and frequently is 8 percent or 8.5 percent. If you pay an 8.5 percent load on a $1,000 investment in mutual fund shares, then the $85 load is subtracted from $1,000 to give $915 as your effective investment. Hence, you really pay 9.3 percent on the fund shares you purchase. The load is intended as compensation for the organization that sells the mutual fund shares to you. While it may be tempting to view the load charge as a payment for diversification, there are *no-load funds* with no sales force and no load fees.

The load charge, if it exists, is in addition to a management fee paid to the professional portfolio manager. It also is in addition to all brokerage commissions that are incurred as the professional manager buys and sells securities for the mutual fund portfolio. Because brokerage commissions and management fees are paid from the total portfolio value of the fund, they reduce the net asset value per share. If you decide to invest in securities via a mutual fund, you will have rather high transaction costs. It is not surprising that many investment experts recommend that you limit your attention to no-load funds, particularly if their achieved performance is comparable to that of the load funds. If there is a particular no-load fund whose expressed investment objective coincides with your particular financial needs, there would seem to be no reason to pay a loading charge.

WHAT ARE INDEX FUNDS?

The stock market has not done well in the last decade or so. Given our understanding of risk as the variability of future returns, we shouldn't be too surprised. Still, countless individuals have become disillusioned with the stock market and switched their investment funds back into savings accounts. There has also been disillusionment with the portfolio results achieved by professional money managers. Much has been written about the inability of pension funds, mutual funds, and other managed portfolios to do any better than—or even as well as—the overall stock market.

If a managed portfolio can't outperform an unmanaged market average, then why not just invest in a portfolio that closely resembles the market average? An index fund is a portfolio designed to do just that. The returns achieved on such a portfolio over time should be similar to market returns over time; thus, your achieved performance should be no worse (nor any better) than market performance. Portfolio risk should also be equal to market risk for an index fund. The idea of an index fund is simple, but there are some implementation problems. For example, what market average is to be matched? How many stocks should be included? How close must the index fund follow the market average? What is to be done with the dividends that are earned over time? What happens when additional funds are added? What management fee should be charged for an index fund?

Because index funds are a relatively new phenomenon, there are only preliminary answers to these questions. The market average to be followed appears likely to be the *Standard and Poor's Composite Index,* since it is the comparison standard in most performance studies. The number of stocks used is likely to range between 200 and the 500 stocks actually included in the *Composite Index.* The proportional weight of each stock held in the index fund is set equal to the proportional weight of that stock relative to the market average. Managers of index funds state a goal of returns that is within a fraction of one percent of market returns. Periodically—say, monthly—accumulated dividends and new funds are distributed across the stocks in the index fund in the appropriate proportions. And the management fee charged is significantly lower than that for more actively managed portfolios because not nearly as much is spent on security analysis.

There has been substantial opposition to index funds. Critics argue that indexing is a cop-out or that it is a fad that eventually will fade away. Others fear that if all investors turn to index funds, there will be no need for security analysis and the stock market will become inefficient. We disagree with both extremes, believing instead that there will be some increased demand for index funds, particularly if they can be managed at lower costs. The initial motivation for index funds came from pension funds, a highly competitive and performance-oriented segment of professional money management. But now index funds are being offered to investors as a type of mutual fund. For those individuals who seek diversification, for whom a portfolio beta of unity is acceptable, and for whom expected market return is suitable for their financial needs, index funds would seem to be an appropriate investment possibility.

INVESTING IN REIT'S

Real estate has been considered a sensible hedge against inflation in recent years. By owning homes, millions of families include real estate in their total portfolio. And, for the vast majority, that investment probably has exhibited the highest rate of appreciation within the portfolio. Positive experience with real estate suggests the possibility of additional real estate investments beyond home ownership. Real estate investment trusts (REITs) are a recent development that facilitates real estate investments by individuals.

To understand the popularity of REITs, we should review the characteristics of real estate in general. In one sense, real estate resembles bonds and stocks because it offers the owner the possibility of appreciation in market value over time. It may also offer the owner a periodic cash flow analogous to interest on bonds or dividends on stocks. Periodic cash flow does not arise from home or land ownership. It does arise from other real estate investments, usually from the renting of residential or commercial property. The periodic cash flow to investors may be fairly constant over time (resembling bond interest), or it may fluctuate (resembling dividends). There also may be certain cash outflows associated with managing the real estate property. As a result, the cash flow in a given year may be either an inflow to the investor or an outflow from the investor.

The market price of the real estate investment clearly is more like that of common stock since there is no maturity date (as there is with bonds) when the principal is returned to the investor. But there is one vital difference: real estate investments (except REITs) do not sell on organized stock exchanges, over-the-counter, or in any kind of secondary market for which there is a chronological record of buy and sell offers and completed transaction prices. There are, of course, markets for real estate, but information about such markets is scarce. One might know the purchase price of a real estate property and its sales price some time later, but it is unlikely that interim market prices would be known. This precludes measuring the variability of returns over time, calculating a characteristic line for a given investment, or comparing its return and risk characteristics with other real estate investments, common stocks, or other assets.

Liquidity, taxability, and manageability are also rather important features. Real estate is considered to be much less liquid than securities, because there are no secondary markets and also because investment is typically quite large. There are special tax considerations associated with real estate. The depreciation of buildings and improvements are tax deductible, as are the interest payments if the real estate investment involves borrowing. Along with operating expenses, those deductible items determine the applicable taxes and, therefore, the cash flow to the investor. Real estate is probably the most popular and widely used tax shelter, mainly because depreciation and interest are deductible for tax purposes. A real estate investment also requires management, particularly if facilities are rented. The investor can hire someone to manage the operation, or he or she may decide to operate it alone. Either way, this consideration also makes real estate investments different from bond and stock investments.

Size of Real Estate Investments

The size of real estate investments precludes most individual investors. Shopping centers, apartment complexes, and office buildings may cost hundreds of thousands or millions of dollars. Even a duplex or single-family residence may cost more than the total portfolio wealth of many investors. While small investors can't afford to buy large businesses, such as General Motors and Eastman Kodak, corporate ownership in the form of common stock allows you to buy a few shares of these giant companies. In other words, common stock is a way of packaging the ownership of a large business so that individuals and families can participate. And as we have seen, an investment company is a way of further packaging the ownership of common stocks so that individuals and families can have diversification as well as ownership.

A Special Type of Investment Company

A real estate investment trust (REIT) is an investment company specializing in real estate. It packages investments in real estate so that individuals and families can participate in this type of asset beyond mere home ownership. A REIT is a closed-end company (not open-ended, as a mutual fund is), and its shares are traded in the secondary securities markets. There are two types of REITs you might consider: mortgage and equity. A *mortgage real estate investment trust* specializes in the mortgage financing aspect of real estate. Large banks and other institutions have offered to the public mortgage REITs that pay attractive yields compared with other fixed income securities. In contrast, an *equity real estate investment trust* specializes in the residual ownership of real estate. The appeal of an equity REIT is that it provides ownership in properties that ought to hedge against inflation, as well as diversification via a portfolio of different types and locations of properties.

Unfortunately, several mortgage REITs have encountered financial difficulty in some years because certain banks have selected poor real estate investments. As a result, returns to owners of some mortgage REITs have been poor if not disastrous. This bad experience also has been attributed, perhaps unfairly, to the equity REITs as well. A limited but growing body of data reveals that achieved returns and variability of returns over time of the equity REITs compare to those of managed common stock portfolios. As a result, it would seem that the equity REITs have served a useful role. There are only a few equity REITs now in existence, but we would expect more to form because of the useful way they package real estate for individual investors.

INVESTING IN DUAL FUNDS

A dual fund is a special way of packaging the income and appreciation characteristics of a portfolio of common stock. Suppose you and a friend have different portfolio needs, and you each want to invest $4,000. Your friend wants income from common stock, and you want appreciation from the same source. By pooling your funds, you can purchase a portfolio of stocks totaling $8,000. It is agreed that your friend will receive all the dividends earned by an $8,000 portfolio for only a $4,000 investment. You, in turn, are entitled to all the appreciation on the $8,000 portfolio. You have created a dual fund in which one is the "income owner" and the other the "capital owner." You *both* accomplish your goals on the basis of *twice* the funds you invested. More specifically, a dual fund is a closed-end investment company with dual ownership. The small investments of many investors are pooled to purchase a portfolio of common stocks. An equal number of income shares and capital shares are issued. Owners of the *income shares* receive the dividends from the portfolio, while owners of the *capital shares* are entitled to any capital gains.

Few dual funds currently exist; the original ones were created in about 1967. Both the income shares and the capital shares of the existing dual funds are traded in the secondary securities markets. The income shares have a maturity, or call date, when the owners are scheduled to receive a certain call value per share. The call dates range from mid-1979 (American Dualvest) to mid-1985 (Hemisphere Fund). The income shares of a dual fund are similar to those of a bond. Moreover, most of the income shares sell at a market price below the call value per share. If you buy an income share and hold it to maturity, you are entitled to the appreciation that must occur. When that appreciation is added to the dividend yield, the total expected return may be attractive. For example, at one time Putnam Duofund sold for $17.50 per share. Its income shares pay $1.28 (7.3 percent yield) and have a call value of $19.75 in January 1983 (hence 1.6 percent annual appreciation). Thus, the total return on an income share of Putnam Duofund is 8.9 percent with a relatively low risk.

The capital shares of dual funds are similar to regular closed-end investment companies because there is an underlying net asset value per share that may differ from their market price per share. The net asset value of a regular closed-end fund, as with a mutual fund, is the total portfolio value divided by the number of outstanding shares. But mutual funds do not sell in secondary markets, and there is no market price per share. Investors who buy and sell mutual fund shares do so at the net asset value; investors in closed-end funds do so at the market value per share. One would expect the market price of closed-end funds and dual funds, whose portfolios both consist of highly liquid securities, to be close to their respective net asset values. That has not, however, been observed. Over the last ten to fifteen years, the existing fifteen to twenty regular closed-end investment companies have sold in secondary markets at an average discount from net asset value of just over 5 percent. Some shares occasionally have sold at a premium above the underlying net asset value. Meanwhile, the capital shares of dual funds have sold at an average discount of over 15 percent. (Incidentally, it is not clear if equity REITs sell at a discount or not, since there are difficulties determining a net asset value and an absence of a market price over time.)

INVESTING IN OPTIONS

REITs and dual funds represent only a small proportion of the total securities markets. *Options,* in contrast, represent a rapidly growing area of investor activity. They are not securities per se but a sort of derived security whose future results depend on what happens to particular common stocks. Options represent additional opportunities or alternative strategies that may be suitable for certain investors.

An option is a right or power to do something. *Stock options,* sometimes given to managers of a business firm as a performance incentive, give the recipients the right to purchase the common stock of the firm for which they work. *Warrants* are another type of option occasionally used by a firm to obtain its financing; they are issued along with bonds or preferred stock and give the owners of those securities a right to purchase shares of the same firm at some designated price. Stock options and warrants both are used by a firm to accomplish its stated objective. Neither is of any value unless the market price of the firm's common stock rises above some particular level. Warrants are traded in the secondary markets, but stock options are not.

Calls and Puts

The options most often referred to are calls and puts. They have nothing to do with the firm and its activities directly. A **call option** is a negotiable contract that gives its owner the right to *buy* 100 shares of a given common stock at a predetermined "striking price" within a prescribed period of time. A **put option** is similar except that its owner is given the right to *sell* 100 shares of a given common stock. Call and put options are purchased from an **option writer,** who is another investor willing to sell the right to buy (call) or the right to sell (put) in return for an *option premium.* Call and put options are typically "written" for 30, 60, 90, or 180 days (six months). They do not affect the underlying company and its common stock. For those familiar with gambling terminology, options may be likened to "side bets" at a craps table.

Suppose, for example, that you have been following the common stock of Wind-up Widgets, and you believe that its price will rise during the next few months. It currently sells for $40 per share, so one alternative is to purchase 100 shares with your $4,000. Assuming that Wind-up doesn't pay dividends and ignoring transaction costs, your possible dollar profit (or loss) and percentage return on investment is shown on the left-hand side of column 2 in Exhibit 16-4. Your profit (or loss) depends on what happens to the market price of the stock. You might lose your entire investment, or you could double it or more.

Suppose that a six-month call option on Wind-up also is available for a premium of $450. An alternative strategy for you would be to buy the call and leave the remaining $3,550 of your funds in a savings account. Possible outcomes of profit and return on investment are shown in column 3 of Exhibit 16-4. If the price of Wind-up does not change or goes down, then you'll lose your $450 investment (plus commissions). But if the price of Wind-up does go up, your possible dollar returns are only $450 less than had you bought the 100 shares outright. The market price of Wind-up would have to rise four and one-half points, to $44.50 per share, for you to break even on the purchase of a call option.

Your percentage return (not annualized) on investment for the option is considerably higher than for owning the stock. The possibility of earning a much higher return on investment, coupled with a maximum possible loss equal to the call premium, is the feature that attracts many investors to options. Clearly, it is a risky strategy since those high returns are only possible if the market price of the common stock moves extensively in a relatively short period of time.

The right-hand side of column 4 in Exhibit 16-4 includes the possible outcome of buying a put option. The premium paid for the put also is $450. Obviously, a put is the opposite of a call. Certainly you would not buy a put option unless you thought that the market price of Wind-up Widgets was likely to fall.

In order for you to buy a put or a call, someone must be willing to sell (or "write") such options. The option writer receives the option premium at the time of the transaction. Further action occurs only if the market price of the underlying stock moves in a way that causes you to exercise the particular option you purchased from the writer. If the price goes up and you exercise a call, the writer must deliver 100 shares at the striking price. If the price goes down, and you exercise a put, then the writer must buy the 100 shares at the striking price. If the price moves in the wrong direction or remains constant, then your option expires and the option writer does nothing.

Probably less than half the options written are eventually exercised. Option writers essentially bet on relatively stable prices, while option buyers bet on significant price movements. Option writers seek additional income for their portfolios, while option buyers seek appreciation. One popular strategy of option writers is to sell calls on stocks already held in the portfolio—that is, to sell "covered calls." In so doing, they receive immediate income via the call premium. If the calls eventually are exercised, the writers already possess the stock to sell to the owner of the call. Thus, these are called **covered options;** an uncovered one is called a naked option.

For many years, the small volume of option transactions was conducted by a handful of securities dealers who made markets in particular put and call options. In 1973, the Chicago Board Options Exchange (CBOE) was established as a secondary market for call options. If you purchase a call option and the underlying common stock price goes up, there are two ways you can realize your profit: either you can exercise the option at the striking price and sell the 100 shares at the higher market price, or you simply can sell your option in the secondary market, where its market price would be higher to reflect the rise in common stock price. Initial response to the CBOE was favorable, and the number of call options listed has increased over time. The American Stock Exchange began trading call options in 1975. Put options began trading on the CBOE in 1977.

Other, more complicated strategies involve combinations of put and call options. There are ways to reduce risk in which options can be combined with securities in certain hedging strategies. Options also can be used to help ensure profits that already have been made but not realized. And there are certain tax implications that may make certain option strategies useful for some investors. For many investors, the complexity of options may be intimidating. But for others, option writing (using covered calls) or the occasional purchase of options may be appropriate—*if* such strategies are considered within the context of the total portfolio and the investor's long-range goals.

EXHIBIT 16-4.

HYPOTHETICAL OUTCOMES OF CALL AND PUT OPTIONS FOR WIND-UP WIDGETS

MARKET PRICE OF WIND-UP	PURCHASE 100 SHARES		PURCHASE 1 CALL		PURCHASE 1 PUT	
	$ PROFIT	RETURN ON INVESTMENT	$ PROFIT	RETURN ON INVESTMENT	$ PROFIT	RETURN ON INVESTMENT
(1)	(2)		(3)		(4)	
80	$4000	100%	$3550	789%	$ (450)	(100%)
70	3000	75	2550	567	(450)	(100)
60	2000	50	1550	344	(450)	(100)
50	1000	25	550	122	(450)	(100)
45	500	12.5	50	11	(450)	(100)
40 (purchase price)	0	0	(450)	(100)	(450)	(100)
35	(500)	(12.5)	(450)	(100)	50	11
30	(1000)	(25)	(450)	(100)	550	122
20	(2000)	(50)	(450)	(100)	1550	344
10	(3000)	(75)	(450)	(100)	2550	567
0	(4000)	(100)	(450)	(100)	3550	789

HOW TO MANAGE YOUR PORTFOLIO

Complexities arise when one considers an entire portfolio of securities rather than just individual issues. Managing securities and other investments should be done within the larger context of your total portfolio. You must decide whether you will manage them yourself or pay someone else to oversee your portfolio. In this Practical Applications section, we will offer tips on how to plan, monitor, and evaluate your total portfolio.

PLANNING YOUR TOTAL PORTFOLIO

In Chapter 15, we suggested that you should begin your securities investing with a written plan, which will help you determine which bonds and stocks are appropriate for meeting your financial goals. You should also prepare a written plan for your total portfolio. This plan will include not only your bonds, but your cash reserves, your life insurance, your retirement benefits, your home, and any other investments you own or contemplate owning. The plan will be quite extensive because you presumably have several financial goals. For example, you may wish to take an extensive vacation once your children are in college. You may wish to continue your current standard of living after you retire. And you may wish to accumulate enough wealth so you can make a sizable contribution to some charitable cause or perhaps to your alma mater. In sum, your portfolio plan should help tie together many different aspects of your personal finances.

Exhibit 16-5 is an example of how you might decide to allocate your total investment wealth. During your college days, you have only cash reserves. Your home equity increases during your working career, but at retirement you don't want to have maintenance and upkeep responsibilities. Bonds are most prevalent during the retirement years. During mid-career, when your income and ability to withstand risk are greatest, stocks are desirable. Riskier ventures, such as investment real estate, options, or investment hobbies, also are more appropriate during mid-career. Again, you may not fully agree with such logic. And the sample allocations may change if your income is considerable or if you are heir to a large fortune. The important thing, of course, is to try and develop a logic that is suitable for you, your chosen career, and your lifetime financial goals.

SHOULD YOU MANAGE YOUR OWN PORTFOLIO?

As part of your financial plan, you must decide how to manage your securities. The Practical Applications section of Chapter 15 included a number of tips on how to process information for specific buy or sell decisions. We also discussed how mutual funds, other investment companies, and options provide alternative strategies for investing in bonds and stocks. At some point, you must decide whether you will invest directly or indirectly in securities. The factors on which that decision should be based are diversification, management cost, and your desire for personal involvment.

We already have seen that the expected return on a portfolio of securities (or of a total portfolio) is just a weighted average of the component securities (or investments). But the risks of a portfolio include not only a component of risk unique to each security held but also a market-related component of risk that reflects the contribution of each security to the portfolio (see p. 409). Diversification in a portfolio is desirable because it helps reduce risk exposure. Mutual funds and other managed portfolios achieve considerable diversification because they hold a larger number of securities. The relevant question to ask is whether or not you can achieve ample diversification by yourself. Clearly, the portfolio on p. 409 (the $4,000 illustration) is not nearly as well diversified as a mutual fund would be, even though its four securities were chosen deliberately from different

EXHIBIT 16-5.   **SAMPLE LIFETIME INVESTMENT ALLOCATIONS**

INVESTMENT CATEGORY	AGE AND SCENARIO				
	20 (College)	30 (Early Career)	40 (Mid-Career)	50 (Late Career)	60 (Retirement)
Cash Reserves (Savings & Cash Value of Insurance)	100%	30%	10%	10%	10%
Equity in Home	0	20%	30%	40%	0
Bonds	0	20%	10%	20%	70%
Stocks (or Mutual Funds)	0	30%	40%	30%	20%
Riskier Ventures	0	0	10%	0	0
TOTAL	100%	100%	100%	100%	100%

industries and types of securities. From a source such as Value Line, you can learn the beta of any given stock (1.00 for Georgia-Pacific and .85 for Revlon) and thus calculate the portfolio beta of your stock holdings. But betas are not available for bonds or other investments and neither are estimates of correlation risk between pairs of securities. As a result, your overall risk assessment for your holdings of securities necessarily must be done subjectively. Diversification improves when you assess your securities within the context of the larger portfolio. But you still may decide it is too risky to spread your excess funds across so few issues.

Management of your portfolio involves the entire process of planning, analyzing, and implementing your investment selections. If you select a professional manager, full-time, experienced individuals will watch your securities. It would seem, then, that professional management would be preferable to your own personal management, although this may not always be the case.

There are costs associated with professional management. The loading charge by most mutual funds would seem to be an unnecessary evil, so it is often suggested that you restrict your attention to no-load funds whenever possible. If you decide on a professional manager, then you must pay a management fee for the services. The annual fee for a mutual fund typically would be a fraction of one percent of the assets under management. Fees charged by trust departments and other investment advisory firms are comparable, although they may have a minimum account size (often $50,000 or more) that may preclude the smaller amount you can allocate to securities. Balanced against the dollar fee you pay each year for professional management should be the value of your time spent in planning, analyzing, and implementing your own investment decisions. Also, don't forget the higher percentage brokerage commissions that you pay on your smaller transactions.

The last factor to consider is your personal interest in managing your securities. It is not unreasonable to want to do it yourself. After all, it's your wealth and your financial goals. And you may learn things about the economy and various industries that will help you in your occupation. Even if diversification favors professional management (as it clearly does) and its costs slightly favor the use of a professional (as we suspect it does, on balance), you still may decide to do it yourself. The final decision involves highly personal factors. The important thing is to make that decision just as carefully as you would try to execute each part of your total financial plan.

WHAT TO LEARN ABOUT MUTUAL FUNDS

Suppose you decide to place all or a portion of your $4,000 into mutual funds and thereby avoid the problems of selecting and managing bonds and stocks for your portfolio. But soon you discover that you haven't avoided all the problems. You must select from among some 500 funds of all sizes, types, and objectives. You must keep a watchful eye on your selection to see that your financial goals are met. Still, this is a comparatively small search problem. While some people might argue that you should divide your assets between two mutual funds for additional diversification, let's assume that you plan to select just one fund. Your primary goal is the growth of your investment.

A Place to Start

A good place to begin is with *Investment Companies,* the most comprehensive reference on mutual funds (and other investment companies), which is published annually by Wiesenberger Financial Services. This source, usually available in public libraries, contains the name, address, brief history, objective, and extensive performance data for every mutual fund. In addition, the first part of this reference provides an extensive description of the mutual industry, its growth, and myriad other useful details. After reading the general information, you should focus on that smaller set of mutual funds for which capital growth is the primary goal, assuming that your objective is investment growth as opposed to current income. The Wiesenberger source reveals that there are nine categories for the 556 funds it covers. There is one category (119 funds) whose objective is "maximum capital gains." "Growth of total capital" is the objective of another category (153 funds). Because the latter category uses more conventional investment and somewhat less risky strategies, you may decide to limit your search to it.

To check your choice, you should review the historical performance of the different categories. You also should review the performance of particular funds within your chosen category to try to spot likely candidates for your investment. Because hundreds of securities are held in the typical mutual fund, it is not feasible for you to go through the steps of fundamental analysis recommended in Chapter 15. Instead, you must rely on achieved (historical) performance as a possible indication of further performance. Unfortunately, this resembles technical analysis, a procedure frowned upon by many. The process of selecting a mutual fund is twofold: a matching of their expressed objectives with your financial goals and a check on how well mutual fund management has accomplished their objectives in the past.

Checking Performance Rankings

Wiesenberger calculates, for each mutual fund, a percentage return for each year and also for selected periods within the most recent decade. Each return is *not* annualized—put in terms of a one-year period—in the usual manner. The Wiesenberger method is to assume a $10,000 investment at the beginning of each period and to add the sum of all dividends and capital gains distribution during the period to the final value of the fund shares purchased. The results may be considered **performance rankings.**

EXHIBIT 16-6.   **ILLUSTRATION OF WIESENBERGER PERFORMANCE RANKINGS**

MUTUAL FUND	1967	1970	Single Years 1973	1975	2 Years 1974-75	4 Years 1972-75	7 Years 1969-75	10 Years 1966-75
Load:								
Chemical Fund	30.7%	−6.4%	−14.6%	21.2%	− 9.5%	1.3%	20.6%	62.9%
Dreyfus Fund	26.5	−6.4	−18.8	31.2	4.6	− 9.3	−12.7	25.3
Keystone S-3	32.2	−1.9	−26.8	46.8	− 2.4	−18.7	−13.8	23.8
National Investors Corp.	31.6	−9.0	−25.6	33.6	− 9.7	−16.0	2.4	42.9
Windsor Fund	31.4	6.0	−24.6	54.1	26.5	4.1	13.6	71.9
No-Load:								
David Balson Investment Fund	21.0%	− .4%	−10.0%	21.9%	−10.6%	− .4%	15.2%	53.6%
deVegh Mutual Fund	26.1	2.8	−17.6	34.1	5.6	−12.2	− 8.0	30.6
Johnston Mutual Fund	30.1	−5.5	−21.0	31.6	−10.0	−10.8	6.6	57.2
T. Rowe Price Growth Stock	26.8	−8.0	−25.0	34.9	− 9.7	−21.5	− 1.4	33.6
Stein Roe & Farnham Stock Fund	27.0	−6.6	−17.8	31.8	− 9.4	− 9.2	− 4.9	32.1

Exhibit 16-6 is a sample of such returns during the decade from 1966 to 1975 for ten funds in your chosen category. The ten funds generally are considered to be among the better performers in recent years. Five are load funds and five are no-load. There are considerable differences in fund performance from year to year: the rankings range from 54.1 percent to 21.2 percent in 1975. There are even greater differences in fund performance over the decade. Windsor Fund was the best performer over the decade, due largely to its outstanding performance in 1975. But remember, there is no guarantee that the leading performers will continue to be so during the next decade or beyond. Still, you may be more comfortable selecting a "good" performer rather than a "poor" performer. As always in invest-ing, there is no guarantee of success if you seek higher expected returns than those available from a riskless savings account.

Using *Forbes*

Yet another check on achieved performance is offered in the annual August 15 issue of *Forbes* magazine, which includes **performance ratings** for most of the available mutual funds. The *Forbes* classification scheme differs from Wiesenberger, but you still can trace their assessment of any given set of funds. Performance is based on appreciation in net asset value, plus all dividend and capital gains distributions. Their past horizon, again different from that of Wiesenberger, is divided, after the fact, into rising markets and declining markets. For example, the August 15, 1976, *Forbes* ratings utilized the total period from February 1966 through June 1976 and divided it into three rising markets (October 1974 to June 1976 being the most recent) and three declining markets (January 1973 to October 1974 the most recent). Performance for each mutual fund is averaged both for the three rising and the three declining markets. The following letter ratings (à la the grade curve in college) are assigned to each fund based on its ranking against other funds: A+ for the top 12.5 percent, A for the next 12.5 percent, B for the next 25 percent, C for the next 25 percent, and D for the lowest 25 percent. The F rating is reserved for funds that did especially poorly during a down market. The total stock market automatically receives a "C" in both rising and declining markets since it reflects average performance of all funds.

Exhibit 16-7 includes the *Forbes* performance ratings for the same sample of mutual funds whose objective is closest to your financial goal. We again see the differences in performance among the selected firms. There is also a striking contrast for most funds between performance during rising markets and performance during declining markets. Most funds that perform above average during rising markets also perform below average during declining markets, and vice versa. The reason for this pattern, which persists across virtually all available mutual funds, is that their size precludes a large-scale change in portfolio holdings every time a new part of the market cycle begins. Moreover, mutual fund managers seldom can tell when the market is about to change direction. The result is that mutual fund portfolios tend to be rather stable over time, and few, if any, are rated A or A+ during both types of markets. If a fund is rated A or better for both types of markets, it probably is a small fund that hasn't existed for long. Regrettably, outstanding performance in all markets seldom persists.

After reviewing performance rankings and ratings, you should be able to narrow your search for a mutual fund down to three or four leading candidates. One additional criterion is whether the fund is load or no-load. As suggested before, the loading charge seems unnecessary. So you decide to restrict yourself to those five funds, even though Windsor Fund (a load fund) was the best performer of the sample over the decade. The next step is to find out more about those particular funds in order to reach a decision. The Wiesenberger source includes one page of concise description on each fund, including more detail on its portfolio objectives, a cursory review of its investment holdings, and some of the investment options available to investors.

Obtaining A Prospectus

Now you should write to the fund under consideration and request a copy of its latest prospectus. A **prospectus** is a document required by the Securities and Exchange Commission (SEC) of any business firm or investment company that intends to sell securities to the public. For mutual funds, it identifies the investment objective and policies of the fund as well as any existing restrictions. For example, most mutual funds cannot buy securities on margin, they cannot deal in securities options, and they cannot place large proportions of their assets in single securities. There also are restrictions on the activities of the mutual fund officers that are designed to protect investors. The prospectus also explains the loading charge (if one exists) and the management fee. Also included are the number of procedures whereby investors can systematically invest in mutual fund shares over time or systematically withdraw funds from their investment. Often, several mutual funds are managed in a group, and the investor may be allowed to switch periodically from one fund to another at minimal cost.

After carefully reading the prospectuses for those few mutual funds that seem suited to your financial plan, you should be able to make a final choice. If you select a load fund, then your securities broker can assist you in purchasing shares. If you select a no-load fund, then you should contact the fund directly about your desire to invest.

EXHIBIT 16-7.

ILLUSTRATION OF FORBES PERFORMANCE RATINGS

MUTUAL FUND	RISING MARKETS	DECLINING MARKETS	ASSET SIZE
Load:			
Chemical Fund	C	B	$ 940 million
Dreyfus Fund	C	C	1,598 million
Keystone S-3	A+	D	116 million
National Investors Corp.	A	D	742 million
Windsor Fund	B	B	524 million
No-Load:			
David Balson Investment Fund	C	B	$ 225 million
deVegh Mutual Fund	B	C	84 million
Johnston Mutual Fund	A	D	295 million
T. Rowe Price Growth Stock	B	D	1,210 million
Stein Roe & Farnham Stock Fund	B	D	182 million

LEARNING ABOUT OTHER ALTERNATIVES

Chapter 15 discussed several strategies in addition to mutual funds. For closed-end funds, dual funds, real estate investment trusts, and mutual funds specializing in bonds and short-term investments, the suggested procedures to follow are similar to those for mutual funds. Namely, you should compare their investment objectives against your financial goals and try to find a suitable match. You should review historical performance to narrow the list of possibilities. And then you should examine prospectuses for detailed information that enables you to make a final choice. Except for real estate investment trusts, coverage of the other alternatives are found in both *Investment Companies* and *Forbes.* Exhibit 16-8, a listing of most of the closed-end investment companies, dual funds, and equity REITs, should also prove useful.

EVALUATING YOUR TOTAL PORTFOLIO

It is not enough to carefully plan and construct a portfolio. You must continue to monitor the portfolio to ensure that your investment selections remain appropriate toward meeting your financial goals. If you manage your own securities, you must continue to follow the companies involved and their respective industries. You must be alert to significant changes in the financial status of given business firms and governments and their abilities to continue paying interest and dividends. Similarly, you must be alert to how consumer tastes, competition, regulation, and other factors are likely to influence the market prices of

EXHIBIT 16-8. **LISTING OF SELECTED ALTERNATIVES FOR INVESTING**

CLOSED-END INVESTMENT COMPANIES	DUAL FUNDS	EQUITY REAL ESTATE INVESTMENT TRUSTS
Adams Express	American Dualvest	American Realty Trust
Advance Investors	Gemini Fund	Denver Real Estate Investors
Carriers & General	Hemisphere Fund	First Fidelity Investment Trust
Consolidated Investment Trust	Income & Capital Shares	First Union Real Estate Investment
General American Investors	Leverage Fund of Boston	Franklin Realty & Mortgage Trust
Lehman Corporation	Pegasus Income & Capital Fund	General Growth Properties
Madison Fund	Petnam Duofund	GREIT Realty Trust
Niagara Share Corporation	Scudder Duo-Vest	Hubbard Real Estate Investment
Tri-Continental Corporation		Pennsylvania REIT
U.S. & Foreign Securities		Realty Income Trust
		REIT of America
		Riviera Realty Trust
		U.S. Leasing Real Estate Investors
		U.S. Realty Investments
		Washington REIT
		Wisconsin REIT

your securities. In other words, you must continue to process information and form judgments just as you did when you first made selections for your portfolio.

Here are some additional tips. First, be prepared to change your financial plan if necessary. Suppose you invest $4,000 in a group of common stocks with the goal of reaching $20,000 in fifteen years. That would require an annual return of 11.3 percent. If your investment (with dividends reinvested) has grown to only $6,000 after six years (an annual growth of 7.0 percent), then it will have to grow at a rate of 14.3 percent during the next nine years. But 14.3 percent is well beyond the return you expect from the common stocks you own. One alternative is to switch your holdings to stocks with higher expected return. Of course, that means you must assume higher risk. Or perhaps you'd rather just admit

that you may not reach your $20,000 goal, and make the best of it.

Second, always be prepared to reduce risk where possible. Suppose that your $4,000 grows instead to $10,000 after six years (16.5 percent annual rate). Now you only need an annual growth of 8.0 percent for the remaining nine years in order to reach $20,000. You probably should sell your riskier stocks and invest in the highest-rated corporate bonds that have a yield-to-maturity of 8 percent. Resist the temptation to believe that you will continue to earn 16.5 percent and thus have over $39,000 at the end of nine more years. You were probably more lucky than wise, and you now should minimize the risk of reaching that particular goal.

Third, a portfolio should be evaluated by investment categories rather than in total. If your portfolio consists of cash reserves, bonds, stocks, and a mutual fund, then you should evaluate each of those four categories separately. Otherwise, you will be comparing apples with oranges. Your bonds should be checked for yield and such special features as imminent callability or convertibility. Your stocks should be compared with overall trends in the stock market. And your mutual fund should be compared with other mutual funds having similar objectives. And you always should include all relevant transaction costs—especially loading charges and taxes—in your performance evaluation.

When evaluating bonds, stocks and mutual funds, you should pay particular attention to risk as well as investment objectives. A common stock with beta of 1.3 should not be expected to perform the same as another stock whose beta is 0.8. The same is true of mutual funds. Suppose you own a mutual fund with a portfolio beta of .8 that achieved a return of 9 percent in a year when the *Standard and Poor Corporate Index* had a return of 10 percent. Rather than concluding that your mutual fund "underperformed" the market, you should realize that you ac-

tually did better than the 8 percent (.8 times 10 percent) you would expect for that particular risk level. In other words, you actually "outperformed" the market on a *risk-adjusted* basis. Stock betas are available from Value Line and other advisory services, while mutual fund betas are available from Wiesenberger. Use them to evaluate performance. For bonds, probably the best way to reflect risk in your performance comparisons is by using bond ratings.

Finally, your evaluations should properly reflect different types of securities markets. Just because a stock performs poorly during one three-year period doesn't mean we should expect the same during all periods. In fact for mutual funds, we saw a persistent pattern of inconsistent mutual fund performance during rising and declining markets. Where possible, you should evaluate over different periods in order to have a more complete picture of achieved performance. Thus, you should become more confident of the ability of particular securities and other assets within your portfolio to contribute toward your financial goals.

GLOSSARY OF TERMS

PORTFOLIO   A collection of securities and other assets held by an investor.

CORRELATION RISK   A component of total portfolio risk that concerns the interrelationship of future returns for two securities.

CHARACTERISTIC LINE   Depicts the responsiveness of return on a security or portfolio to the return on the overall securities market.

BETA   The slope of the characteristic line for a security or portfolio that measures the contribution of that security to the total portfolio.

UNIQUE RISK   A component of total portfolio risk that is not related to the overall securities market.

MARKET-RELATED RISK   A component of total portfolio risk that can be related to the overall securities market. Equals the beta of the security or portfolio times the risk of the market.

RANDOM DIVERSIFICATION   An attempt to reduce portfolio risk by randomly adding securities to the portfolio.

RISK-REDUCING DIVERSIFICATION   An attempt to reduce portfolio risk by adding dissimilar securities to the portfolio.

EFFICIENT DIVERSIFICATION   An attempt to reduce portfolio risk for a given level of expected portfolio return or to increase expected portfolio return for a given level of portfolio risk.

INVESTMENT COMPANY   A large portfolio of securities managed professionally on behalf of many smaller investor/owners.

CLOSED-END FUND   An investment company with a fixed ownership structure. Investors buy and sell shares in the secondary market.

MUTUAL FUND   An investment company that continually buys or sells to investors shares of ownership in the portfolio.

INDEX FUND   A portfolio whose holdings and future performance are designed to resemble closely that of the overall stock market.

REAL ESTATE INVESTMENT TRUST (REIT)   A closed-end company whose portfolio consists of real estate investments.

DUAL FUND   A closed-end company with two types of ownership. Income shares receive all income from the portfolio, and capital shares receive all the capital gains.

CALL OPTION   An investor buys, for a certain premium, the right to purchase 100 shares of a particular common stock at a specified price within a specified period of time.

PUT OPTION   An investor buys, for a certain premium, the right to sell 100 shares of a particular common stock at a specified price within a specified period of time.

OPTION WRITER   An investor who sells call and put options.

COVERED OPTION   A call option whose stocks are held by the writer to cover if the buyer of the option exercises his or her right.

NAKED OPTION   A call option whose necessary stocks are not in the portfolio of the writer.

PERFORMANCE RANKINGS   Numerical values of achieved performance used to rank a group of mutual funds or other portfolios.

PERFORMANCE RATINGS   Letter grades used to rate the achieved performance of a group of mutual funds or other portfolios.

PROSPECTUS   A publication describing the securities a business firm or investment company intends to sell to the public.

CHAPTER SUMMARY

1. Expected portfolio return equals the sum of the expected returns of the individual securities.

2. Total portfolio risk equals the sum of the risks of individual securities, plus the sum of the correlation risks between pairs of securities.

3. Total portfolio risk also can be considered the sum of unique risk of each individual security plus market-related risk of the entire portfolio.

4. The more closely the returns of two securities are expected to move together, the greater is their correlation risk, which suggests that overall portfolio risk can be reduced by using securities whose returns (and/or prices) do not vary together. One way to measure the riskiness of a stock is to compute its beta, which equals the slope of a line that best fits the estimated association between the return for a particular stock and the return for the market in general.

5. When individual stocks perfectly match movements in the markets as a whole, their beta is equal to one. If a stock's beta exceeds one, it is termed "aggressive." If its beta is less than one, it is termed a "defensive" security.

6. There are three concepts of portfolio diversification: (a) random, (b) risk reducing, and (c) efficient.

7. As the number of individual securities in a portfolio increases, portfolio risk gradually approaches market risk.

8. Risk-reducing diversification requires adding dissimilar securities to a portfolio. However, such procedures ignore expected rate of return.

9. Efficient diversification requires computing, with electronic computers, the trade-off between expected rate of return and risk reduction.

10. While institutional investors, such as insurance companies and pension funds, may wish to hold large numbers of securities, this is often impossible for individuals with a more limited total portfolio value.

11. An alternative to purchasing individual securities is to purchase shares in an investment company, which pools many investors' resources to buy a large portfolio of investments. Investment companies may be closed-end, with a fixed number of shares, or open-end, with a flexible number of shares.

12. Mutual funds are open-end investment companies whose outstanding shares fluctuate over time. Shares in a mutual fund are purchased at the asked price, which is equal to the net asset value of the fund per share plus any loading or selling charges.

13. When a loading or selling charge is applicable, it is a load fund; when it is not applicable, it is a no-load fund.

14. Different categories of mutual funds may buy only common stocks,

only preferred stocks, or only bonds. Some mutual funds have a combination of stocks and bonds. And some purchase securities for growth as opposed to income, and vice versa.

15. Investors pay an annual management fee to the professional portfolio manager for both load and no-load mutual funds.

16. The concept of an index fund became more popular in the 1970s. This fund purchases a large variety of stocks so that the fund's performance will duplicate some broad market average, such as *Standard & Poor's Composite Index*. Because index funds do no research analysis, management fees are lower.

17. Individuals may purchase shares in mortgage or equity real estate investment trusts (REITs). REITs are closed-end investment companies; their shares are traded in the secondary securities markets.

18. An investment in a dual fund allows individuals to choose between income or appreciation on their investment. Few such funds exist.

19. The trading in put and call options involves a fixed possible absolute loss—the price of the option—along with high possible return on investment. Here, again, expected rate of return and risk go hand in hand.

20. Sellers of options predict stable prices, whereas buyers of options predict unstable prices in the future.

21. Planning a total portfolio is similar to making out a budget, but it is more long-range.

22. Typical lifetime investment allocations often dictate large cash reserves, during youth; some purchase of stocks, bonds, and real estate in the form of a home in early career; a shift toward more stocks or mutual funds in midcareer; and, finally, more bonds during retirement.

23. Factors determining your decision whether or not to manage your own portfolio are: (a) diversification, (b) management costs, and (c) your personal interest in being involved. You can learn about all the different types of mutual funds by reading *Investment Companies*, published annually by Wiesenberger Financial Services; *Forbes* annual August 15th issue; or Fundscope's *Mutual Fund Guide* every April.

24. The Weisenberger Financial Services provide performance rankings and the Forbe's services provide performance ratings of mutual funds.

25. After narrowing your choice to several alternative mutual funds, you can request a prospectus for each.

STUDY QUESTIONS

1. What is a portfolio?

2. How do you calculate the expected return for a portfolio consisting of three securities?

3. Is portfolio risk merely the sum of the risk of each of the securities in the portfolio?

4. What does a beta of one mean? What happens when the beta is greater than one? Less than one?

5. What is diversification?

6. What is risk reduction diversification?

7. What is a mutual fund?

8. What is the difference between a load and a no-load mutual fund?

9. Explain the nature of a real estate investment trust (REIT).

10. What is the difference between a call option and a put option?

11. What is the difference between a covered option and a naked option?

CASE PROBLEMS

16-1   The Wisdom of Diversification

Ed and Joan Carlton, a couple in their early fifties, inherited 500 shares of RHO, Inc., from Joan's father, who had accumulated them on a profit-sharing plan. RHO, Inc., stock has fluctuated greatly in price during the last ten years. It currently sells for sixty dollars per share, which is 15 percent lower than last year at this time but is still above the ten-year average. The Carltons are not sure if it is wise to hold only one stock, and would like information on ways to diversify. Please explain the different methods of portfolio diversification to them.

16-2   Making Diversification Decisions

After hearing your explanation, the Carltons decided to diversify. They have $30,000 in three-year certificates of deposit yielding 7 percent a year; one $10,000 certificate matures each year. Ed has a $50,000 term policy paid by his employer and a $25,000 whole life policy with a cash value of $8500. They also have $3500 in a 6 percent savings account and $45,000 equity in their $55,000 home.

Assuming that they would like to have a balanced investment plan consistent with their ages and lifestyle, what distribution would you recommend?

Ehrbar, A. F. "Index Funds: An Idea Whose Time Has Come." *Fortune,* June 1976.

Ehrbar, A. F. "The Mythology of the Option Market." *Fortune,* October 1976.

"Forbes Mutual Fund Survey," *Forbes,* annual August 15 issue.

Mead, S. B. *Mutual Funds: A Guide for the Lay Investor.* Braintree, MA: D. H. Mark Publishing, 1971.

Mutual Fund Fact Book. Washington: Investment Company Institute, annually.

"Mutual Fund Guide." Fundscope, annual April issue.

Rugg, D. O. and Hale, N. B. *The Dow Jones-Irwin Guide to Mutual Funds.* Homewood, IL: Dow Jones-Irwin, 1976.

Sauvain, H. C. *Investment Management* Englewood Cliffs, NJ: Prentice-Hall, 1973.

Shelton, J. P., Brigham, E. F.; and Hofflander, A. E. "An Evaluation of Dual Funds." *Financial Analysts Journal,* May-June 1976.

Smith, K. V. and Eiteman, D. K. *Essentials of Investing.* Homewood, IL: Richard D. Irwin, 1974.

Smith, K. V. and Shulman, D. "Institutions Beware: The Performance of Equity Real Estate Investment Trusts." *Financial Analysts Journal,* September-October 1976.

Wiesenberger, A. *Investment Companies.* New York: Arthur Wiesenberger & Company, annually.

Market Competition and Alternative Investments*

SEVENTEEN

■In the last two chapters, we outlined many, but not all, of the various ways you can invest in the stock and bond markets. There are numerous theories on how to get rich in those markets. And there are countless more on how to get rich in other financial markets, some of which we will discuss later in this chapter. The business and economics sections of bookstores abound with "get rich quick" theories in the form of books with such titles as *How I Made $2 Million in the Stock Market* or *How You, Too, Can Become a Millionaire Overnight.* Admittedly, many individuals do make fortunes by "wheeling and dealing" in investment markets. Each investor must ask whether he or she, as an individual actually can duplicate the money-making activities of others who have gotten rich. In the fields of business, economics, and investment, one school of thought maintains that most investors *cannot* and do not get rich quick. The most they can hope for is a normal or competitive rate of return. This school of thought uses, in one form or another, a theory called either the random walk hypothesis or the efficient market hypothesis.

A RANDOM WALK DOWN WALL STREET

To understand this theory, we must understand what random walk means and the best way to do so is by analogy. Suppose that a drunk person—too drunk to "see straight"—was put in a large auditorium. Now, would you be able to predict where this person would end up after two seconds of walking? Four seconds? Ten seconds? Probably not,

*This is an optional chapter for those with special interests in investments.

451

because the person's walking would be so completely random; where he or she was two seconds ago gives you no information about where he or she would go. Thus, when something takes a random walk, it is impossible to predict its next position by its present position. This is not unlike the physicist's notion of Brownian motion. Because the movement of very small particles suspended in solutions is random, you can't predict the future course of a suspended small particle by knowing its current location.

Thus, the random walk hypothesis asserts that the future course of stock prices, for example, is independent of prices today or yesterday. According to this theory, then, it is impossible to predict what stock prices will be tomorrow by knowing what they are today or at any time in the past. This theory also has been called the efficient market hypothesis.

FORMS OF THE EFFICIENT MARKET HYPOTHESIS

What was just described as the random walk theory is now called the weak form of the efficient market hypothesis. There is also the semistrong form and the strong form.

Weak Form of Hypothesis

To repeat, the weak form of the efficient market hypothesis asserts that the current prices of assets (in our examples, the price of common stocks) fully reflect the information available in the historical record of past prices. In other words, an investor, according to this form of the hypothesis, cannot hope to improve his or her ability to select "correct" stocks by knowing the history of prices. Osborne presented this theory in 1959.[1] He looked at the numbers representing stock prices to see whether they conformed to certain laws governing the motion of physical bodies and he discovered a high degree of conformity between the movements of stock prices and the laws governing Brownian motion. If you believe in the weak form of the efficient market hypothesis, or random walk theory, you won't put much faith in so-called technical analysis, which charts the past prices of stocks. The technical analyst attempts to predict future stock prices by such charting techniques.

There were many attacks on Osborne's initial research. A number of other researchers attempted to derive so-called filter rules, which might go as follows: "Wait until stock prices have advanced by x percent from some trough and then buy stock; next, hold stocks until they have declined y percent from some subsequent peak and then sell them or sell them short. Continue this process until bankrupt or satisfied." At first, these researchers showed that the filter technique could yield extremely

[1]M.F.M. Osborne, "Brownian Motion in the Stock Market," *Operations Research*, Vol. 7, March/April 1959, pp. 145-73.

high rates of return. Unfortunately, that research was flawed because the costs of going in and out of the market were not included in the calculations. In other words, brokers' commissions were ignored. There were other problems with the filter technique research, and, ultimately, the random walk hypothesis remained intact. It was (and is) not possible to use a simple rule of when to buy and sell in order to realize higher-than-competitive rates of return.

Semi-Strong Forms of Hypothesis

This form of the efficient market hypothesis asserts that current prices of stocks not only fully reflect all information inherent in past prices but also all public knowledge about underlying companies and the economy in general. The semi-strong form of this hypothesis implies that it is fruitless to acquire and analyze knowledge about what companies are doing. Basically, this is an assertion that investment markets are efficient. When a market is efficient, all the facts that are knowable about companies whose stocks are being traded is already fully discounted in the current price of stocks. In other words, there is no such thing as an undervalued or overvalued stock at any moment in time. Stock prices are always correct.

Rates of return in the stock market are positive; thus, in an efficient market, current prices are what we might call unbiased estimates of future prices. But they also provide a rate of return that, on average, will be positive and "normal" after taking into account brokerage commissions, taxes, and so on.

Competition in the Market. Information flows rapidly in the stock market. If you read in *The Wall Street Journal* that, say, International Chemical and Nuclear (ICN) has just discovered a cure for cancer, you might be tempted to run out and buy ICN stock. But you will be no better off (according to the efficient market hypothesis) than you would be buying any other stock. By the time you read about ICN's discovery (which may mean increased profits in the future for the company), thousands and thousands of other people will have read it, too. Once information about a company's profitability is generally known, that information has no useful value for predicting the future price of the stock. Information that becomes public is capitalized upon almost immediately. People consider what it means for future profits and bid up the price of the stock to a level that reflects the future expected increase in profits.

If you believe in the weak form of the efficient market hypothesis, technical analysis is out of the picture. If you believe in the semi-strong form of this theory, then so-called fundamental analysis won't be considered useful either.

Strong Form of Hypothesis

The strong form of the efficient market hypothesis asserts that even

453

*Market
Competition
and
Alternative
Investments*

those with privileged or inside information cannot always use that information to obtain higher-than-normal rates of return.

Inside Information. Suppose you're the janitor at International Chemical and Nuclear, and you often look at some of the memos thrown in the wastepaper baskets. You've noticed recently that there have been several memos about some miracle drug. Last night, you saw a memo that said: "Success! We've done it." Now you have inside information. Assuming that the scientists and corporation officers who knew about this discovery didn't tell anyone else, you have some very valuable information that no one outside the company knows about. You should go out and buy as many shares of ICN as you possibly can. Borrow on your house; borrow on your car; borrow on your life insurance and anything else, because you're going to strike it rich. When other investors hear the good news later, they'll bid up the price of ICN, and, theoretically, you'll be able to sell out at a big profit.

Testing the Strong Form. The strong form of the efficient market hypothesis has been tested by looking at the performance of portfolios managed by groups that might have inside or special information. One such group is mutual funds with professional managers, who spend many resources to obtain special information. Nonetheless, studies of mutual funds have shown that, after transactions costs were taken into account, such funds did no better than the market in general. This has been offered as support of the strong form of the efficient market hypothesis.

A PARADOX IN THE EFFICIENT MARKET HYPOTHESIS

If the hypothesis is true, paradoxically it must also be true that many investors do not believe it. In other words, if market prices of stocks are to fully and immediately reflect what is known about companies whose shares are traded, then there must be a large group of investors who conscientiously attempt to learn about companies whose securities are traded. That is, there must be many people who undertake, at a minimum, fundamental analysis. If that effort was abandoned, the market's efficiency would diminish quite readily. Note, though, that this is not really a paradox. It is true for all competitive markets. Individual investors will compete until it is no longer worth competing. Large amounts of resources will go into attempting to find out information that might conceivably help an individual investor or a group of investors "make a killing." And that competition makes the market efficient. We might say that investing and seeking out information in investment markets is a game worth winning, although it may not be a game worth playing. Hope for the large killing is what causes so many people to enter the game and make the market efficient.

IMPLICATIONS OF THE EFFICIENT MARKET HYPOTHESIS

If you believe in this theory, you can draw a number of implications from it.

Economies of Scale

To search for undervalued and overvalued securities costs about the same, whether the investor has $1,000 or $10 billion. We presume, then, that there are possible economies of scale in security analysis and portfolio management. Thus, the search for under and overvalued stocks would seem to make more sense for large financial institutions, such as pension plans and mutual funds, than it does for the individual investor.

Can't Get Superior Profits

If the hypothesis is correct, the chance is small that an individual investor will make a killing in the stock market by analyzing public information in the usual way. The only possible way to make a killing is by searching out unique ways to form expectations—that is, have better judgment—about the future prospects for individual companies. You must have a new technique for analyzing public information, and, of course, that technique must work. And, when it does, you must keep it a secret.

Mutual Funds Okay

Even if studies show that mutual funds, after transactions costs are taken into account, can do no better than the market in general, mutual funds still serve a useful function. Individuals of modest wealth are convinced by mutual fund advertising that common stocks are an appropriate investment. Moreover, mutual funds provide an extremely efficient way for a relatively small investor to obtain diversification. Finally, mutual funds provide useful custodial services and bookkeeping. And, given the existence of the third market and negotiable brokerage commissions, mutual funds can buy brokerage services on relatively favorable terms.

INVESTMENT PLANS

Investment plans and sophisticated investment counselors abound. In their advertising, they sometimes promise a higher rate of return on stock dollars than is available elsewhere. A typical ad might show, for example, the average rate of return for investing in all the stocks on the New York Stock Exchange. An investment counselor would claim that his or her stock portfolio makes 15 percent a year rather than the average 8 percent earned by buying all stocks together. However, these investment counselors usually neglect to say that the 15 percent rate of return doesn't include the investment counseling fees nor the trading costs—that is, brokers' commissions—for buying and selling stocks.

Investment services usually do considerable trading: they go in and out of the market—buying today, selling tomorrow. Each time someone buys or sells a stock, that person pays a commission to the broker. Thus, the more trading your investment counselor does, the more trading costs you incur. In almost all cases studied, however, investments made through counselors do no better than the general market averages, because any profits they make are absorbed by brokerage and counseling fees. Thus, you would be better off paying brokerage fees and not using the services of an investment counselor.

In the following Practical Applications section, we will present rules for investing that are consistent with the efficient market hypothesis. But, first, let's look at some alternative forms of investment other than stocks and bonds.

ALTERNATIVE FORMS OF INVESTMENT

Even though the stock and bond markets get the most coverage in the financial press, there are literally hundreds of alternative outlets for your investment and savings dollars. Among others, they are: (1) the commodity futures market, (2) real estate, (3) precious metals, (4) antiques, (5) art work, (6) jewelry, and (7) other assets. We will look at these investment possibilities in general here and then discuss investing in them in the following Practical Applications section.

The Commodity Futures Market

Many of us engage in contracting when we order a product that is to be delivered at a future date. I may order next year's model of a Chevrolet from my local dealer two months before the car is scheduled to arrive on the premises. You may order a book from a bookstore that won't be delivered to you for three weeks. A farmer may make a contract to deliver a million bushels of grain to a grain elevator operator at a specific month in the future at a price that both parties agree upon today. All such contracts are called **forward contracts.**

A forward contract is not, strictly speaking, the same as a **futures contract,** which applies only to those commodities executed in *formal* commodities exchange markets, such as the Chicago Board of Trade, the Chicago Mercantile Exchange, the New York Coffee and Sugar Exchange, and others throughout the world. There are organized open futures markets for frozen orange juice concentrate; oats; soy beans; wheat; corn; cotton; sorghum; sugar; barley; lard; hides; soybean oil; frozen, powdered, and shelled eggs; frozen chickens; potatoes; silver; rubber; cocoa; pepper; flax seed; copper; wool; pork bellies; platinum; foreign exchange; and government insured mortgages. Moreover, futures contracts are made for standard qualities and quantities of a commodity. In the futures market for frozen orange juice concentrate, for example, a standard contract is for 15,000 pounds of concentrate. It is necessary for the futures contract to call for delivery at a standard time during the year. And, finally, futures contracts can be entered into only through a broker.

The difference between a forward and a futures contract is, however, more profound than this simple explanation indicates. In a futures market, the dealings are strictly impersonal: buyers and sellers know nothing but the contract price, the time, a few attributes of the product, and the place of delivery. In other words, a futures contract might state that 40,000 bushels of Minnesota #2 red wheat will be delivered in Winnipeg on November 3 through 10, 1979. Because there are lots of economies of transactions here, the transactions costs are relatively low in a futures market. Comparatively speaking, few futures markets actually exist; there are many more unorganized forward markets. Perhaps that's because forward markets, in contrast to futures markets, permit more "custom-made" contracting. The buyer and seller engage in personal, rather than impersonal, dealing and can specify many more aspects of the transaction than is possible in an organized futures market.

If you *buy* a futures contract today, you agree to accept delivery of a specified amount of wheat at a specified future date at a specified place. You also agree to pay the price specified in the futures contract. The specified price in the futures contract is called the futures price. You might look in the newspaper today and find out that the futures price of wheat to be delivered three months from now is so many dollars per bushel. You can compare the futures price with today's spot price, which is the price of wheat bought "on the spot." It is also called today's cash price. People who trade in the spot, or cash, market are the actual producers, processors, and distributors of the commodity.

On the other side of the exchange, it is possible to *sell* a futures contract. When you do, you agree to deliver a specified amount of a commodity on a specified date at a specified price. Those who have agreed to deliver commodities in the future at a stated price are said to have a short position or to be or to go short. (Short selling, incidentally, is also possible in the stock market.) They have sold futures contracts. Those who agree to buy in the future have a long position, or they are, or have gone, long. They have bought futures contracts; they have some commodities coming to them.

Futures contracts are not generally settled at maturity by actual physical delivery of the commodity to a warehouse, for which the purchaser obtains the warehouse receipt. Rather, more than 95 percent of futures contracts are either closed out before their maturity date or settled by payment of the difference between the price stipulated in the contract and the spot price of the commodity at the date of maturity. Hence, if the futures price for a bushel of wheat was $5 when the contract was written and, at the date of maturity, the spot price was $5.10, the owner of the futures contract would merely pay the purchaser of the futures contract 10¢ times the number of bushels specified. Note that the volume of futures contracts is not tied to volume of physical product or even constrained by it.

If you read certain ads paid for by commodity brokerage firms, you may conclude that it's possible to make a killing in the commodities market. Indeed, some people do, but most do not. This is consistent with the efficient market hypothesis. We must be skeptical of ads that tell us it is possible to earn large gains (profits) with a very small downside risk. Although, presumably, this could be done by placing a sell order that is automatically initiated whenever the price of futures contracts for the commodity you are dealing in falls by a certain amount.

Real Estate

Will Rogers once said, "It's easy to make money. Just figure out where people are going, and then buy the land before they get there." Obviously, investment experts are aware of this precept, too. And, if you believe in the efficient market hypothesis, such information has a zero value when it becomes public. It is not necessarily true that "land is always a safe investment." The value of land can fall the way the value of anything else can. The fact that the average price of land has been rising for a long time doesn't necessarily mean you will make more than you could by investing money in, say, a savings and loan association.

In the last few years, real estate has been a good investment. Exhibit 17-1 shows what has happened to stocks, houses, and the CPI. Stock values have not kept up with inflation since 1967. Housing values have and, at times, have surpassed it. In other words, the rate of return to investing in a house has been positive, even after accounting for inflation.

First and Second Mortgages. Usually, first mortgages are issued by savings and loan associations and banks. Sometimes it is possible for an individual to invest in them by means of a mortgage pool. A savings and loan association, for example, may offer investment shares in the pool at $10,000 each. These shares usually offer an interest rate of one to two percentage points above what you can obtain on a federally insured savings deposit. Another quite popular alternative is the second mortgage market. With a second mortgage, you must wait, upon de-

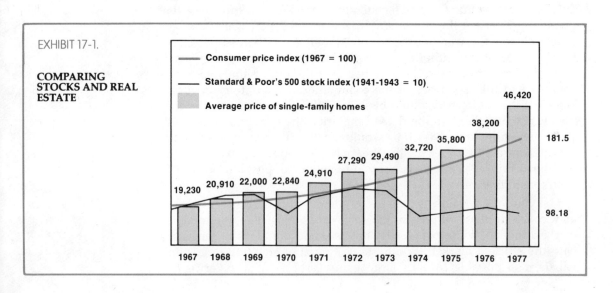

EXHIBIT 17-1.

COMPARING STOCKS AND REAL ESTATE

— Consumer price index (1967 = 100)

— Standard & Poor's 500 stock index (1941–1943 = 10)

▢ Average price of single-family homes

fault, until the owner of the first mortgage has collected. Thus, the investor in a second mortgage is less protected, unless the first mortgage represents a relatively small amount of the total market value of the real estate. Since second mortgages are riskier than first mortgages, they usually offer higher rates of return. One problem with a second mortgage is that there is no standard procedure in case of a default. An attorney must initiate foreclosure proceedings, which may take six to twelve months.

Limited Partnerships. Real estate syndicates offer a large number of limited partnerships. A syndicate is a group of people joined together under one management. The participants are called the partners; the management is called a general partner. The real estate investment syndicate will buy and manage a property, such as an apartment house, undeveloped raw land, and so on. As an individual partner, you will buy a certain percentage of the total package and be responsible for your pro rata share of expenses. When the investment is sold, you receive a pro rata share of the sale minus what is owed on the mortgage, to the general partners, and so on.

Precious Metals

It is possible to buy and sell precious metals for investment purposes. For many years, a tremendous amount of mythology has surrounded one precious metal—gold. It was thought that gold was an appropriate investment because it had an inherent stable and/or rising value. If we look at the market price of gold in Exhibit 17-2, we find that it once did offer high rates of return to investors. However, look at what has happened to the market price of gold during the period from 1973 to 1978. It has been extremely volatile, which means that it, like many other investments, does not guarantee an extraordinary (or even positive) rate of return. According to the efficient market hypothesis, the price of gold at any one time reflects all the information available about its future prices and its past prices. Thus, the notion that gold has some *inherent* quality that will keep its price high has little validity. Consider, for example, the possibility of Russia and South Africa deciding to sell and mine ten times more gold than they have over the past decade. The only way this increased supply can be sold is if the price falls while the demand is stable. If this were to happen, the market price of gold would fall, common mythology notwithstanding.

Other precious metals include silver and platinum, which is more expensive than gold. Many people have made lots of money by buying silver when it was cheap and selling it when it was dear. But that doesn't necessarily mean this is a sure-fire way to get rich quick. There also have been periods when the price of silver has fallen.

Antiques

Some investors are avid antique collectors. They can recount tales of finding incredibly rare and valuable antiques in small, out-of-the-way

459
*Market
Competition
and
Alternative
Investments*

stores. Of course, they picked up those antiques for a song, resold them, and made a killing. Or so they say. Investing in antiques requires a knowledge of what is authentic and what isn't. As with all other investments, it also involves being able to predict which antiques will be more valuable in the future than others.

During the late 1960s and throughout the 1970s, antiques were a relatively good investment. That is to say, the average price of all antiques rose at a faster rate than, say, the average price of common stocks or of all precious metals taken together. We might point out, though, that the antique market is not as liquid as, say, the market for common stocks. If you purchase an antique today, you may not be able to sell it readily tomorrow without incurring high transactions costs. One virtue of liquid markets is that you can buy and sell at a moment's notice without incurring high transactions costs in the form of brokerage commissions or fees for information concerning the price at which the asset you wish to buy or sell is actually trading. If you have a rare antique, obviously there aren't many others like it around. To find out the appropriate, or market, trading price takes time and effort and

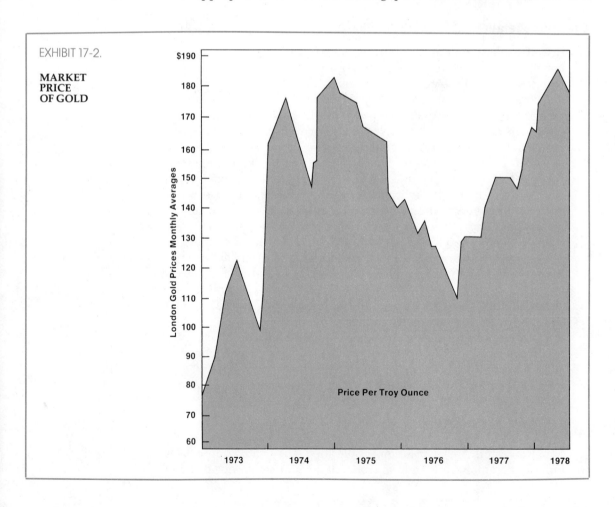

EXHIBIT 17-2.

MARKET PRICE OF GOLD

maybe even money. You would expect, then, that the average rate of return on antiques would have to be higher to take account of the illiquidity in the market.

A countervailing force that tends to lower antique prices concerns the pleasure individuals derive from owning, using, and seeing antiques in their own homes. Let's assume you have $1,000. If you put it in a savings and loan association, you may earn, say, 6 percent over a one-year period. If you buy an antique desk, which you look at, use, and enjoy, you may be willing to receive less than 6 percent rate of return on that investment because of the consumption, or use, value you derive throughout the year. You might be willing to accept only 3 percent rate of return because you get an implicit 3 percent worth of services from the antique desk for that year.

Art Work

Exhibit 17-3 is an index of art prices over a 200 year period. On average, an investment in paintings will have paid off a much higher rate of return than an investment in common stocks. Again, this doesn't necessarily mean that paintings are a superior investment. If you believe in the efficient market hypothesis, what has happened in the past is no

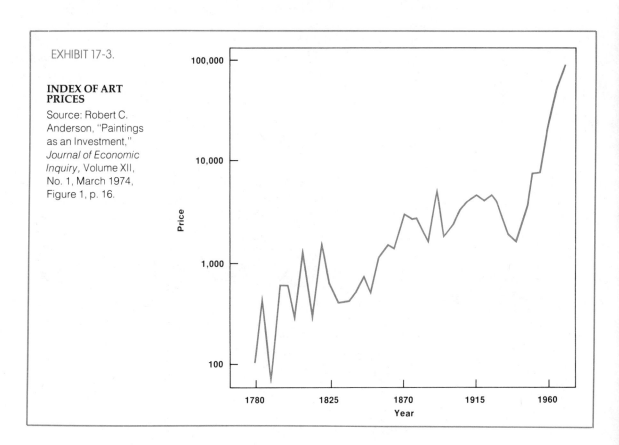

EXHIBIT 17-3.

INDEX OF ART PRICES
Source: Robert C. Anderson, "Paintings as an Investment," *Journal of Economic Inquiry*, Volume XII, No. 1, March 1974, Figure 1, p. 16.

predictor of what will happen in the future. Public information already will be fully discounted in the price of a new painting you buy today, whether it's by Picasso, Rembrandt, or an unknown painter who lives in your community. To have the requisite information for investing in art, you need: (1) a detailed knowledge of fine art, (2) the ability to spot authentics and fakes, and (3) the ability to predict which painters will be in demand in the future and which will not.

An additional cost you incur when investing in paintings but not in most other investments involves insurance. Usually you have to insure fine art separately. But you don't have to do this if, for example, you purchase savings and loan association shares. Your savings are generally insured by some agency associated with the government. You don't have to worry about loss of your savings in a savings account through theft. But you do have that worry if you have expensive paintings or jewels in your house.

Jewelry

Many investors believe diamonds are their best friends. Jewelry with diamonds—as well as jade, sapphires, emeralds, and so on—has been considered a good investment outlet by many for many years. But, to repeat, if you believe in the efficient market hypothesis, jewelry should be no better or no worse an investment than any other asset. Moreover, you must know something about jewelry before you can be certain you are getting an authentic jewel. You can rely on experts to help you, but that costs additional fees and thus reduces your total possible investment. And you must consider loss, so the jewels must either be heavily insured, carefully guarded, or kept in a safe deposit box.

CONCLUSION

By now, you should have a general idea of the major features of different investment markets. None of them should be ruled out a priori. Nor should one of them be singled out a priori as *the* best investment for you. As you obtain a larger and larger portfolio, diversification requires that you at least "dabble" in a variety of investment outlets.

PRACTICAL APPLICATIONS

463
*Market
Competition
and
Alternative
Investments*

HOW TO APPLY THE EFFICIENT MARKET HYPOTHESIS

The efficient market hypothesis contends that most security analysis is logically incomplete and of little value. The analyst must determine whether the price of the stock already reflects the substance of any technical or fundamental analysis. There must be a significant difference between the opinion of the analyst and the opinion of other investors who determine the current price of the stock. And the analyst must have some valid and objective reason why his or her opinion is different.

HOT TIPS

What about your broker's hot tips? Actually, it is highly unlikely that any broker will have real inside information. After all, if it's really inside information, why would that individual share it with you? Why wouldn't the broker take advantage of it to get rich quickly? Brokers often get this information from the research department of their firms. Almost all stockbrokerage companies have large research staffs that investigate different industries, different companies, and the future of the general economy and issue research statements on their findings. Often, they recommend which stocks should be bought because they are underpriced.

Actually, this research information is of little value to an investor. You will do no better by following the advice of research branches of your stockbrokerage company than you will by randomly selecting stocks, particularly those listed on the New York Stock Exchange and the American Stock Exchange. Nevertheless, the amount of research by firms, individuals, organizations, and governments on companies offering stocks is enormous. Such information flows freely; by the time you receive the results of research on a particular company, you can be sure that thousands and thousands of other people already have them, too. And since so many brokerage firms employ research analysts, you can be sure that there are numerous analysts investigating every company in the open stock market.

RISK TAKING

The greater the risk, the greater the expected rate of return. Thus, when an investment with an expected high rate of return is offered, the investor must pay for that high expected yield by incurring more risk. The rational risk-averse investor will seek to diversify in order to reduce investment risk. Diversification, even in the stock market alone, is not particularly difficult.

Actually, it's quite amazing how quickly one can obtain sufficient diversification in the stock market. A portfolio consisting of only sixteen stocks on the New York Stock Exchange will mirror price changes in all listed stocks extremely closely. Stated technically, 90 percent of all possible reduction in relative dispersion is achieved with sixteen stocks. Thus, having sixteen stocks in your portfolio will yield the same rate of return 90 percent of the time as having all the New York Stock Exchange listed companies.

Don't Specialize

In order to increase diversification and, thereby, reduce risk, the individual investor should not specialize when purchasing shares of stock. Investment counselors can provide information on the relative risk of virtually every traded share of stock. This relative risk is based upon past price changes relative to the average of all stock price changes. Or, alternatively, the individual investor can purchase shares in unspecialized mutual funds. These unspecialized mutual funds generally have, by definition, large diversified portfolios. Rates of return of mutual funds vary consistently because of differences in risk. If, as an individual investor, you decide that maintenance of initial capital is highly desirable, then you will pick neither a specialized fund or one

464

Investment

advertising higher-than-normal rates of return. In both cases, you would incur greater-than-normal degrees of risk.

USING INVESTMENT COUNSELORS

Based on the efficient market hypothesis, the use of an investment counseling firm is imperative. Investment counseling can be defined as advising investors on their investment policies, as opposed to telling them which stocks to buy and when.[2] An investment counselor determines the degree of risk you wish to take. After that degree of risk is determined, the counselor assembles a portfolio that yields the desired level of risk. That portfolio is then changed or controlled in order to maintain the level of risk. The investment counselor does not engage in security analysis, which would be inconsistent with the efficient market hypothesis.

AN ALTERNATIVE—INDEX FUNDS

Growing belief that the stock market is efficient has fostered index funds, which are mutual funds that purchase a portfolio designed to match exactly the movements in the sum of stock market averages. At this time, few such funds are available to the small investor. Only relatively large pension plans can invest in such instruments. We predict that index funds eventually will be available to small investors. They will be appropriate assets, provided that such funds don't have loading charges (high sales charges) and that their yearly management fee indicates that no management is involved (only a computer program). Index funds would appear to be an ideal way to follow the efficient market hypothesis to the letter.

THE COMMODITY FUTURES MARKET

If you are interested in commodity futures trading, it is relatively easy to set up an account with an established brokerage house, such as Merrill Lynch, Pierce, Fenner & Smith, Inc. (commodity division); Cargill Investor Services, Inc.; Loeb Rhodes, Hornblower and Company; Conti-Commodity Services, and others.

Reading the Price of Futures

Virtually every major newspaper in the United States carries some information on futures prices. Exhibit 17-4 is a sample of futures prices for wheat, corn, oats, and soybeans traded on the Chicago Board of Trade. Each column is explained in the exhibit.

Exhibit 17-5 lists where major commodities are traded, the size of the contract, the minimum margin per contract, the minimum per transaction, and the daily trading limit (the maximum amount the price is allowed to change before trading is stopped).

The Margin per Contract

To trade in commodities futures, you don't have to put up the full purchase price of the desired futures contracts. Rather, you put up a margin or a percentage of the total price. If, however, the value of the purchased futures contracts changes adversely by more than your margin, your broker will require you to put up additional money to cover your potential losses.

Rules for Speculating in Commodities

Experts in the commodities field have formulated the following rules for speculating in commodities.

1. Determine in advance how much you can afford to lose. Make that your limit for commodities speculation.

2. Before you invest, study the commodities market in general and then individual commodities.

3. Stay with commodities you know something about—for example, those relating specifically to your work or business.

[2]Portfolio management is usually defined as the execution of policy. Security analysis is the provision of information traditionally required for portfolio management.

465

*Market
Competition
and
Alternative
Investments*

EXHIBIT 17-4.

**HOW TO READ
FUTURES PRICE
QUOTATIONS**

CHICAGO (AP)

FUTURES TRADING ON THE CHICAGO BOARD OF TRADE WEDNESDAY:

WHEAT (5,000 bu)

	(1)	(2)	(3)	SETTLE (4)	(5)
Dec	2.68	2.69	2.64¾	2.65¾	+.04½
Mar	2.77	2.78	2.74	2.75¾	+.05¼
May	2.83	2.83	2.79¾	2.81½	+.05½
Jul	2.84½	2.86½	2.83½	2.85½	+.05¼
Sep	2.90	2.91	2.88½	2.90	+.04½
Dec	3.00	3.00	2.97½	3.00	+.05½

CORN (5,000 bu)

Dec	2.22½	2.25	2.20¼	2.21¼	+.03
Mar	2.33	2.33	2.28¼	2.29¾	+.02¾
May	2.37	2.37	2.32½	2.33¾	+.02
Jul	2.39	2.39	2.34¾	2.36¼	+.02½
Sep	2.37	2.37¾	2.34¼	2.35¼	+.02¼
Dec	2.37	2.37½	2.34¾	2.36½	+.01¾

OATS (5,000 bu)

Dec	1.31	1.33¼	1.29½	1.32½	+.04
Mar	1.35½	1.36½	1.33¼	1.36¼	+.03
May	1.37½	1.38	1.35½	1.37½	+.01¾
Jul	1.38½	1.38½	1.36	1.37¾	+.01¼
Sep	1.39	1.39	1.36½	1.38	+.01¼

SOYBEANS (5,000 bu)

Nov	5.82	5.92	5.79½	5.83¾	+.14½
Jan	5.9p	5.98	5.86	5.90½	+.13¾
Mar	6.09	6.10	5.93½	5.98¼	+.12¾
May	6.13	6.15	6.01	6.06½	+.14¾
Jul	6.10	6.19	6.06	6.12½	+.17
Aug	6.12	6.17½	6.07	6.13½	+.16
Sep	6.03	6.05	5.96	6.03	+.15½
Nov	6.03	6.06	5.94	6.00½	+.14½
Legend:	(1)	(2)	(3)	(4)	(5)

Legend:

(1) *Open.* This is the price at which the first transaction of the day took place.

(2) *High.* The highest price at which transactions were made during the day.

(3) *Low.* The lowest price at which transactions were made during the day.

(4) *Close.* This is sometimes given as two prices and unless they are marked as bid and asked, trading was taking place at both prices or a range between those prices as the closing bell sounded.

(5) *Change.* This is the change in price from the time of the first transaction until the time of the last transaction.

4. Before you invest, formulate a trading plan that includes how long you want your money tied up, how much you are willing to lose, and so on. Once you have made the plan, stick to it.

5. Don't put more than 25 percent of your available capital into commodity positions at any one time.

6. Don't diversify into more commodities that you can follow at one time.

7. Because commodity markets can turn overnight, stay in close touch with your market and your broker. When you travel, make sure your broker can always reach you.

REAL ESTATE

The real estate market is so vast that it would be difficult to present here all the details concerning investing in that market. If you wish to purchase raw land, it is important to obtain the services of a qualified and honest real estate agent in the area where you wish to purchase. And, remember, even a good agent can sell you land that may not rise in value. In fact, its value could even fall.

Limited Partnerships

If you decide to invest in a limited partnership via a real estate syndicate, make sure you evaluate the following risks:

1. If the syndicate is buying a building, will it be fully rented at the proposed rates?

2. Will the IRS challenge some of the proferred tax deductions? Only a check with a tax attorney or a qualified CPA will tell you that. And, even then, no one may know for sure until the IRS actually makes a ruling.

3. Will the general partners remain solvent and stand behind their investment? You would lose quite a bit if the general partners went bankrupt. The property management would decline while the limited partners decided whom they should sue and who should be the new manager.

For information on potential real estate syndicates, check ads in the financial pages of your newspaper. Large real estate brokerage houses will tell you if they have put together any syndicates. There are several directories listing syndicate management groups. Take a look at the *Real Estate Syndication Digest* published each year and available from 235 Montgomery Street, San Francisco, California 94104. It costs eighty-five dollars, so you may wish to find a copy in your local library. A check with the Better Business Bureau and the Chamber of Commerce on the proposed general partners for a syndicate also would be advisable.

HOW TO INVEST IN PRECIOUS GEMS

There are some rules to follow if you are interested in precious gems as a part of your diversified portfolio. Remember at the outset that there is no guarantee that prices of top-quality precious gems will appreciate in the future.

Buy from Reputable Jewelers

Buying gems is a tricky business. Therefore, you shouldn't risk dealing with a fly-by-night jeweler. Some of the top jewelers in the country are Cartier in New York, Shreve, Crump and Low Company in Boston, and Gump's in San Francisco. Even with reputable jewelers, it is possible to negotiate or bargain on investment-quality gems.

An outside appraisal. Before you buy, it is always necessary to get an outside appraisal, either from another jeweler or from an appraiser. An appraiser generally will charge you a commission of 1.5 percent of the gem's value. Local jewelers will identify appraisers in your area.

Certification. Every stone you buy should be

467

*Market
Competition
and
Alternative
Investments*

certified by the Gemological Institute of America, which has offices in Los Angeles and New York. If a stone you wish to purchase has not been certified, you can send it to the institute's offices by registered mail. To authenticate a one-carat diamond, they may charge thirty dollars.

Insuring Gems

Gems must be insured against theft or loss. Rates depend on where you live and from whom you purchase the insurance. A rough rule of thumb is an annual premium of $2 to $4 per $100 of the stone's value. On the other hand, if you put your gems in a safe deposit box, the vault insurance will only cost you 20¢ per $100 of the gem's value.

More Information on Gems

By going to auctions and museums to view gem collections, you can learn more about stones. There are a number of good books on the subject; one of the best is *How to Invest in Gems* by Benjamin Zucker (New York Times Book Company, 1976).

INVESTING IN GOLD

For several years, it has been legal for Americans to own gold in any form. The current price of gold, which can be found in the financial pages of newspapers, is usually stated on a per ounce basis at specific gold exchanges, such as London.

Buying Gold Bullion Coins

A number of countries have minted gold bullion coins. Their value rises and falls in relation to the London spot price of gold, which is posted twice daily at the London Gold Exchange. In the United States, the most popular gold coin for investment purposes is the Krugerrand, which is minted regularly in South Africa and weighs exactly one troy ounce of gold. It sells for a premium of anywhere from 2 to 5 percent over the simple gold bullion price. Thus, if an ounce of gold sells for $150 on the London Gold Exchange, you might have to pay $158 for a Krugerrand. If the Krugerrand you buy comes with a loop, bezzle, and chain attached, it is then coin jewelry, and you must add 30 to 100 percent or more to its price.

Where Can You Buy Gold?

Your stockbroker may be able to sell you gold on account. If you do not take possession of the gold, you pay nothing for assaying its correct weight, delivery insurance, and sales tax. You may even get free storage for six months and then pay a tax-deductible fee of ten cents per ounce each month.

There are several precious-metals exchange companies, such as Premex, Inc., in Detroit and Monex International, Ltd., in Newport Beach, California. These companies sell gold on margin accounts. For 20 to 33⅓ percent down, you can invest in gold on a ten-year contract, which can be renewed once. The minimum amount of gold that can be purchased on such a contract, however, is one kilobar or 32.15 ounces of gold. You pay the "going" rate of interest on the amount of money loaned to you by the exchange company. Additionally, you must pay a loading expense of about 6 percent of the spot price of gold. Finally, a typical buy and sell commission may total 3½ percent.

OTHER INVESTMENTS

It would take several books to describe the intricacies of investing in other assets that might make up your diversified portfolio. Suffice it to say that the more specialized the investment area, the more time you must spend learning about it. To become a skilled investor in art and antiques, for instance, is not something that can be done in a matter of days. Those who consistently make a higher-than-normal rate of return in such activities are usually experts, who receive part of that return for all the time they spent acquiring information about the particular assets.

EXHIBIT 17-5. **WHERE COMMODITIES ARE TRADED**

COMMODITY	EXCHANGES TRADING*	SIZE OF CONTRACT	MINIMUM MARGIN PER CONTRACT**	MINIMUM COMMISSION PER TRANSACTION	DAILY TRADING LIMIT
Cattle (live)	Chicago Mercantile	40,000 lb.	$ 900	$40.00	1.5¢ per lb.
Corn	Chicago Board of Trade, MidAmerica Commodity	5,000 bu.	1,000	30.00	10¢ per bu.
Cotton #2	New York Cotton	50,000 lb.	2,500	60.00	2¢ per lb.
Ginnie Mae certificates	Chicago Board of Trade	$100,000 principal amount (8% certificates)	1,500	60.00	$750 per contract
Gold	Commodity Exchange, Chicago Mercantile, Chicago Board of Trade, MidAmerica Commodity, New York Mercantile	100 troy oz.	300	45.00	$10 per oz.
Hogs (live)	Chicago Mercantile, MidAmerica Commodity	30,000 lb.	900	35.00	1.5¢ per lb.
Pork bellies (frozen)	Chicago Mercantile	36,000 lb.	1,500	45.00	2¢ per lb.
Silver	Commodity Exchange, Chicago Board of Trade, MidAmerica Commodity	5,000 troy oz.	1,000	22.50	20¢ per oz.
Soybeans	Chicago Board of Trade, MidAmerica Commodity	5,000 bu.	3,000	30.00	20¢ per bu.
Sugar #11	New York Coffee & Sugar	112,000 lb.	2,000	62.00	1¢ per lb.
Treasury bills (90-day)	Chicago Mercantile	$1 million (face value at maturity)	1,500	60.00	½ of 1% per $1 million

469
*Market
Competition
and
Alternative
Investments*

EXHIBIT 17-5 **CONTINUED**

Wheat	Chicago Board of Trade, Kansas City, MidAmerica Commodity, Minneapolis	5,000 bu.	1,250	30.00	20¢ per bu.

*The first exchange listed is the primary market for the commodity.

**Although minimum margins and commissions are established by the trading exchange, brokerage houses can set higher margins and commissions. Transaction commissions cover both purchase and sale of contract.

GLOSSARY OF TERMS

RANDOM WALK HYPOTHESIS   A theory of stock price movements that asserts that no information is contained in the past behavior of those prices for predicting future behavior.

EFFICIENT MARKET HYPOTHESIS   In its weakest form, this is synonymous with the random walk theory of the stock market. In stronger forms, it asserts that all information is properly discounted into the current price of stocks. In other words, stock prices are correct, neither being undervalued or overvalued at any time.

FILTER RULE   An investing rule that tells you how long to keep stocks and when to sell them. For example, one set filter rule is to wait until stock prices have advanced by 10 percent from their trough and then buy the stocks, hold them until they have declined 2 percent from a subsequent peak, and then sell them.

INSIDE INFORMATION   Information obtained by insiders in a corporation before the public obtains it.

FORWARD CONTRACT   A contract in which delivery of an asset is promised at a future date and for which payment is decided upon now.

FUTURES CONTRACT   Basically a forward contract on an organized futures market, such as that for wheat, corn, and the like.

FUTURES PRICE   The price specified in the futures contract that must be paid per unit of the commodity in question at some future date.

SPOT PRICE   The actual price paid for the commodity today.

CASH PRICE   Synonymous with spot price.

SHORT POSITION   The position of one who has agreed to deliver commodities in the future at a stated price.

LONG POSITION   The position of one who has agreed to buy commodities in the future at a stated price.

SECOND MORTGAGE   A loan for which a house or other real estate is put up as collateral. However, the holder of the first mortgage has first claim to the proceeds of the sale of the house in the case of default. Whatever is left over pays off what is owed on the second mortgage.

LIMITED PARTNERSHIP   A partnership in which the limited partners are only liable for the investment dollars in which they have invested.

SYNDICATE   A group of individuals banded together for the purpose of engaging in an investment.

INVESTMENT COUNSELING   The process of advising investors on their investment policies according to risk and preferences and picking a portfolio consistent with that level of desired risk.

CHAPTER SUMMARY

1. If the stock market is highly competitive and information flows freely, then the efficient market hypothesis in its weakest form predicts that information on past prices generally will yield no useful guidelines for picking stocks or assets for purchase.

2. The semi-strong form of the efficient market hypothesis asserts that the current prices of stocks reflect all information from the past and all present public knowledge.

3. The strong form of the hypothesis asserts that even those with privilege or inside information cannot make a higher-than-normal rate of return in the investment market.

4. Playing the stock market is a game that may not be worth playing, but it is worth winning. That's why individuals continue to seek "winners" when, in fact, the probability of winning is very low.

5. One implication of the efficient market hypothesis is that you would have to search out unique ways of forming expectations about the future prospects for an individual company. In other words, you must have a new technique for analyzing public information; that technique must work; and it must be kept secret.

6. There are numerous alternative investments besides stock and bond markets. They include the futures market, real estate, precious metals, antiques, paintings, and jewelry.

471

*Market
Competition
and
Alternative
Investments*

7. The futures market is an organized market in which one buys and sells commitments to sell or buy a specified amount of a specified commodity at a specified price at a specified time in the future.

8. When you buy a futures contract today, you agree to accept delivery of a specified amount of the commodity in the future at a particular price. The opposite occurs when you sell a futures contract.

9. Most futures contracts are settled before maturity. Less than 5 percent of such contracts actually are fulfilled.

10. Real estate prices can go down. And, even if they go up, they may still yield a lower rate of return than could have been obtained in other investments.

11. One can invest in REITs, first and second mortgages, and limited partnerships in the real estate industry.

12. Precious metals have, during certain periods in time, offered high rates of return. These high rates are not guaranteed, however. The price of gold, for example, has fluctuated greatly, and many people who bought and sold at the wrong time have lost money investing in it.

13. Antiques, paintings, and jewelry have offered relatively high rates of return in the last decade. But these relative high rates are not guaranteed in the future.

14. If you believe in the efficient market hypothesis, hot tips from brokers have little value.

15. According to this hypothesis, research information provided to the investor is generally of little value.

16. In order to reduce risk, it is necessary to diversify, even in the stock market.

17. Diversification in the stock market requires holding as few as eight stocks. But the more stocks that are held, the lower the amount of risk.

18. The efficient market hypothesis suggests that investment counseling is more appropriate than security analysis.

19. Even though index funds make sense according to the efficient market hypothesis, they generally are unavailable to the small investor.

20. Among the rules for speculating in commodities are: (a) determining in advance how much you can afford to lose, (b) studying general commodities in which you are interested, (c) remaining informed about those commodities, (d) making a trading plan, (e) not putting more than 25 percent of your available capital into a position, and (f) diversifying only when you can follow all the commodities in which you have invested.

21. One way to invest in real estate is through a limited partnership in which a syndicate buys a building, undeveloped land, and so on. For

information on potential real estate syndicates, consult the *Real Estate Syndication Digest*, which is available at your local library.

22. If you decide to invest in precious gems, buy only from reputable dealers, have an outside appraisal, and make sure the stone is certified and insured.

23. If you decide to invest in gold, you can purchase South African Krugerrands through numerous dealers and perhaps even your stock broker.

STUDY QUESTIONS

1. Do stockbrokers have more information than you have about which stocks to buy?

2. What is the justification for the random walk theory of stock price movements?

3. The value of land has always gone up. If that's true, why don't investors put all their investment funds in land?

4. The rate of return on the stock market is basically the rate of return to American business. As long as American business continues to make a rate of return of around 10 percent, so, too, should investors in the stock market. Do you agree or disagree?

5. Why is there so little agreement about appropriate investments?

6. What is a filter rule?

7. What does it mean to say that stock prices are correct?

8. How can you obtain inside information?

9. What is the difference between a forward and a futures contract?

10. What is the difference between a short and a long position?

CASE PROBLEMS

17-1   Which Real Estate Investment and Why

The Wilson brothers wish to invest $600,000 in some area of real estate. They have been trying to decide which area would be best for them, but they don't really know enough about any of them to make a decision. They are considering first mortgages, second mortgages, undeveloped land, commercial buildings, or real estate trusts.

Explain the advantages and disadvantages of each and draw up a recommendation for them.

17-2   Investing Money Instead of Time

Michael Wendover, forty, is an extremely busy real estate broker and land developer. He earns a good deal of money and already has

473

*Market
Competition
and
Alternative
Investments*

substantial real estate holdings. He would like to invest his future profits in other areas and has mentioned commodities, antiques (his mother made a killing by buying junk at auctions), or perhaps common stock. Michael does not want to spend time managing his investment. He would like both a "sure thing" and some high-risk investment for the sake of "excitement." In the long run, he would be satisfied with a rate of return just a "little bit higher" than average.

1. Explain some of the ways he could invest and not have to spend a great deal of time managing the investment.

2. Assuming that he wants 50% of his total investments in real estate, which he will manage himself, what distribution would you recommend for the other 50%? Support your answer.

SELECTED REFERENCES

Chestnutt, George A., Jr. *Stock Market Analysis: Facts and Figures.* Greenwich, Conn.,: Chestnutt Corporation, latest edition.

Friend, Irwin, et al. *Mutual Funds and Other Institutional Investors: A New Perspective.* New York: McGraw-Hill, 1970.

Lorie, James H. and Hamilton, Mary T. *The Stock Market.* Homewood, Ill., Richard D. Irwin, 1973.

Tomorrow's Concerns

GIVE YOURSELF
A TAX BREAK...
You may be eligible for
the IRA
ACCOUNT
which allows you to deduct up to
$1750*
before taxes
Ask about the details.
*Maximum deduction for husband and nonworking spouse.

Annuities and Pensions

EIGHTEEN

■Planning for retirement involves comparing your expected retirement living expenses with what you can expect to receive from the government in the form of Social Security payments (to be discussed in the following chapter), private pension plans, and any private streams of income you have purchased. These private streams of income, called **annuities,** generally are sold by insurance companies. You can specify different types of annuity, or income, streams as the payoff to a whole life insurance policy. In this chapter, we first will discuss the various aspects of private annuities and then look at private pension plans.

An annuity pays the policy holder for living; it generally provides for periodic payments—yearly, monthly, or weekly—of a fixed sum of money. Certain kinds of annuities provide for partial retirement income and, therefore, eliminate the need to pay, for example, large life insurance premiums. Annuities can provide for a safe retirement and also can provide tax advantages by deferring income-tax payments until a later date, when most individuals are in a lower marginal tax bracket.

Annuities are sometimes given in the form of contracts for periodic payments of money for a specified period of time. Sometimes, however, the annuity is specified for the life of the **annuitant**—that is, the person to whom payments will be made.[1] The contractual annuity obligates the issuer of the annuity, usually an insurance company, to pay a fixed number of dollars per time period for a specified time or for life.

About 75 percent of annuities are group annuities set up through

---

[1]In the insurance industry, annuity almost automatically means a lifetime income stream.

employee-employer retirement programs. Individuals purchase about 20 percent of all annuities outstanding. The remainder are programs set up by insurance companies as alternatives to a lump sum payment for death.

WHY PEOPLE BUY ANNUITIES

There are at least three reasons why an individual may wish to purchase an annuity contract: (1) to provide for retirement income, (2) to free up capital, and (3) to lower taxes.

Providing Retirement Income

The most obvious reason to purchase an annuity is to ensure that there will be sufficient income during retirement years. According to most people's tastes, Social Security payments generally don't provide an adequate income. Therefore, many people set aside additional retirement funds by purchasing an annuity.

Freeing Up Capital

It is possible to purchase, in one lump sum, a life annuity guaranteeing, say, $10,000 a year until death. A relatively wealthy person, who has decided upon that specified level of income, may have to pay, say, $100,000 for that annuity at age sixty-five. All of his or her capital in excess of $100,000 now may be used however the person desires for other investment purposes. Thus, if the person makes bad investments with the remaining part of his or her wealth, he or she is still guaranteed $100,000 on which to live until death.

Reducing Taxes

Individuals may be offered annuity contracts in exchange for capital assets they own. An individual who owns large holdings of land may wish to sell them upon retirement in order to live off the proceeds. If that land has appreciated greatly, however, the individual immediately would be subject to capital gains taxes. To avoid capital gains taxation, the owner of the land might accept an annuity contract in exchange for the property. The individual owner of the annuity contract will have to pay some taxes on the annual income received. But such income is taxed under what the IRS calls an **exclusion ratio**,[2] a formula that greatly

---

[2]The exclusion ratio is determined by dividing the amount invested in the contract by the expected return from the contract. Suppose, for example, that $10,000 is the amount invested in the contract and that the annuitant is supposed to receive monthly $100 for life. Further suppose that his or her expected lifetime is twenty years. One hundred dollars per month times twelve months times twenty years equals $24,000. Then the exclusion ratio is $10,000/$24,000, which equals $41\frac{2}{3}\%$. This means that the annuitant can exclude $41\frac{2}{3}\%$ from each $100 per month received from the annuity. Taxes are reduced by the marginal tax rate times this exclusion.

reduces taxes owed on annuity income. Additionally, the tax is payable over a period of time, rather than in a lump sum, thus making it even more advantageous.

TYPES OF ANNUITIES

As Exhibit 18-1 illustrates, several different kinds of annuities can be purchased.

Fixed Annuities

The most common type of annuity is a **fixed annuity.** Insurance experts give two main advantages for these annuities: they provide freedom from investment worry and protection against a depression. The two general kinds of fixed annuities are named according to the time at which the income starts.

1   *Deferred life annuity:* This type most often is purchased a number of years before retirement. It can be purchased either by making annual premium payments over a number of years or by paying a lump sum some years before the annuity income would begin. Either way, payment is made well before the date when you wish to receive the income.

2   *Immediate annuity:* This type usually is purchased just before retirement, often in place of or in exchange for a level-payment whole life policy. Its premium must be paid in a single lump sum.

Whether you choose a deferred or an immediate annuity, you have

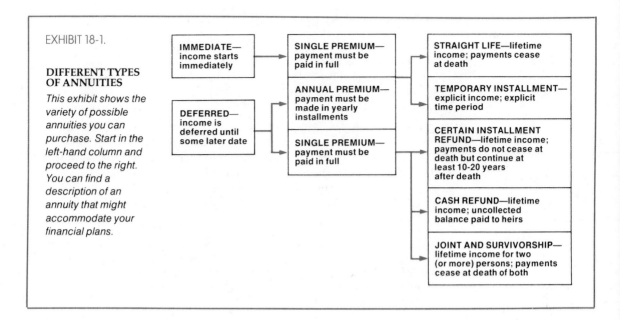

EXHIBIT 18-1.

DIFFERENT TYPES OF ANNUITIES

This exhibit shows the variety of possible annuities you can purchase. Start in the left-hand column and proceed to the right. You can find a description of an annuity that might accommodate your financial plans.

IMMEDIATE—income starts immediately

DEFERRED—income is deferred until some later date

SINGLE PREMIUM—payment must be paid in full

ANNUAL PREMIUM—payment must be made in yearly installments

SINGLE PREMIUM—payment must be paid in full

STRAIGHT LIFE—lifetime income; payments cease at death

TEMPORARY INSTALLMENT—explicit income; explicit time period

CERTAIN INSTALLMENT REFUND—lifetime income; payments do not cease at death but continue at least 10-20 years after death

CASH REFUND—lifetime income; uncollected balance paid to heirs

JOINT AND SURVIVORSHIP—lifetime income for two (or more) persons; payments cease at death of both several choices, at different prices, of the kinds of payments you can receive.

1   *Straight life:* You are guaranteed a fixed income for life, but all payments cease at your death. (In this case, the company providing the annuity is clearly betting on your death.)

2   *Temporary:* You are guaranteed a specified income for a certain length of time only (not sold commercially).

3   *Installments certain:* You are guaranteed income for the remainder of your life; in addition, you are guaranteed payments for a certain period—say, ten or twenty years—even if you don't live that long. If you die before the end of the guaranteed period, your beneficiary collects. If you live longer than the guaranteed period, you still receive income, since this payment plan guarantees that period in addition to income for the length of your life.

4   *Installment refund:* You are again guaranteed payments for life. In addition, your heirs are guaranteed installment payments until the balance on what you paid is returned.

5   *Cash refund:* This plan resembles the installment refund, except that, at your death, the balance is paid to your heirs in a lump sum.

6   *Joint and survivorship:* Two or more persons (usually husband and wife) are guaranteed an income for life as long as either is living. This type of payment plan most clearly eliminates the need for life insurance.

ANNUITIES ARE NOT CHEAP

Annuities are a relatively expensive investment; that is, they yield a relatively low rate of return. Exhibit 18-2 shows some average costs of annuities. And Exhibit 18-3 indicates how annuities compare with other types of investments. As with whole life insurance, an important factor to consider when thinking about annuities is how well you could invest in alternative income-producing assets; this includes considering the forced savings nature of annuities. In most cases, younger persons should invest in some form of life insurance before considering annuities. And it is perhaps best to diversify your investments anyway; there is no ideal investment designed to meet every individual's needs.[3]

---

[3]There is, however, a tax advantage to annuities that is important to high-income individuals with high marginal tax brackets. The interest credited to annuity cash values is not taxable as income until you begin to receive your annuity income. Generally, this income annuity is obtained during the retirement years, when you will be in a lower tax bracket.

A LOOK AT VARIABLE ANNUITIES

With a **variable annuity**, you can either pay small sums into a plan over a period of years or pay a large sum shortly before retirement to provide retirement income. This is the only type of annuity that *may* be "inflation-proof," because the sum you receive on a fixed regular basis is not in itself fixed; since the money you pay in is invested in the stock market, it varies with the stock market return. Your payments depend on the market value of the common stocks in your account.

Variable annuities often yield a greater return than fixed annuities. Of course, this is partly due to the greater risk involved; if the stock market declines during the period when you are collecting against your variable annuity, so, too, does the amount you receive in payments.

How Variable Annuities Developed

Apparently, the modern form of a variable annuity was developed by the Teachers Insurance and Annuity Association of America, which established the College Retirement Equities Fund (CREF) in 1952. This fund enables college teachers contributing to TIAA retirement systems

---

EXHIBIT 18-2. **COMPARISON OF COSTS OF TWO KINDS OF ANNUITIES**

IMMEDIATE SINGLE PREMIUM ANNUITY (Income to begin at once)

AGE		MONTHLY INCOME PER $1,000			COST OF $10 OF MONTHLY INCOME		
Male	Female	Straight Life	10 Years Certain	Installment Refund	Straight Life	10 Years Certain	Installment Refund
50	55	$4.93	$4.88	$4.73	$2030	$2050	$2110
55	60	5.51	5.41	5.20	1838	1847	1920
60	65	6.30	6.08	5.81	1605	1644	1721
65	70	7.36	6.87	6.56	1375	1455	1524
70	75	8.80	7.73	7.50	1145	1293	1331

DEFERRED ANNUAL PREMIUM ANNUITY (For men age 65 when it starts*)

	MONTHLY INCOME PER $100 A YEAR PURCHASE			COST PER YEAR OF $10 OF MONTHLY		
Age at Issue	Straight Life	10 Years Certain	Installment Refund	Straight Life	10 Years Certain	Installment Refund
30	$33.17	$31.33	$30.39	$ 30.15	$ 31.92	$ 32.92
35	26.49	25.01	24.50	37.73	39.98	40.82
40	20.57	19.42	19.03	48.61	51.49	52.55
45	15.34	14.49	14.20	65.19	69.01	70.42
50	10.71	10.12	9.92	93.37	98.81	100.81
55	6.62	6.26	6.13	151.06	159.74	163.13

*A woman would receive 15 to 20 percent less in annuity income per $100 of annual premium than a man of comparable age at issue.

to direct part or all of their contributions toward a CREF variable annuity. There are approximately 400,000 college teachers making contributions to CREF. Most major insurance companies offer variable annuities in addition to fixed annuities. A balanced annuity combines a variable annuity and a fixed annuity; members of TIAA, for example, can purchase balanced annuities.

How Well Do Variable Annuities Pay Off?

Since the payment of a variable annuity depends on the performance of the stock market or some other fluctuating investment, how you do depends on how the stock market does. Over a long period of years, the stock market has done well. But over any short period of time, it can do moderately well or extremely poorly. Variable annuities purchased during the last decade will show an extremely poor rate of return, especially correcting for inflationary erosion of the dollars to be paid back.

PRIVATE PENSION PLANS

The first pension plan was started in the United States in 1875. By the middle of the Great Depression (1934-35), less than 15 percent of the U.S. labor force was covered by private pension plans. By 1980, it is estimated that more than 90 percent of the labor force will be covered by

---

EXHIBIT 18-3.

COMPARISON OF ANNUITY WITH SAVINGS OR INVESTMENT

COST OF AN ANNUITY			RETURNS ON INVESTING OR SAVING THE SAME AMOUNT TO YIELD $100 A MONTH TO LIVE ON		
Purchaser	Life expectancy	$100 a month guaranteed for life costs:	You can live on dividends or interest only if your money earns:	With lower earnings, you can tap interest and principal; your money will last:	And still living, your life expectancy then will be:
A woman age 62	19.5 years (49% live at least 20 yrs.)	$17,300	7%	at 3%, 19 yrs. at 4%, 22 yrs.	at 81, 9 years at 84, 7.5 years
A man age 65	14.5 years (27% live at least 20 yrs.)	$13,750	8.75%	at 3%, 14 yrs. at 4%, 16 yrs.	at 79, 7.5 years at 81, 0 years

either public or private pension plans or a combination of both. Exhibit 18-4 shows the number of people covered by major pension retirement programs in the United States.

The big impetus to *private* pension plans was an insertion in the Internal Revenue Code in 1939 that makes contributions to qualified pension plans nontaxable. In Chapter 13, we presented a numerical example of the tax savings possible from putting savings into a pension plan. Basically, you earn interest on the taxes you would have paid the government had you not used the pension plan; and, further, you postpone paying those taxes until you retire.

Pension plans got a big boost during World War II when they were used as a way to increase workers' salaries legally. During the war, there were government-mandated freezes on many wages and salaries. Employers could bid away employees from competing firms, however, by offering them an implicit increase in their salary in the form of a pension plan paid for, in part or wholly, by the employer.

KINDS OF PENSION PLANS

The major public pension plan today is Social Security, or Old Age Survivor Insurance, which we discuss in the following chapter. Other forms of public pension plans are the Railroad Retirement Plan, Civil Service, and the various state and local government retirement plans for their employees. In this chapter, we will discuss only private pension plans, which fall into two categories—insured and uninsured.

Insured Plans

Insurance companies offer insured pension plans. In return for payments to the company, annuity and life insurance contracts are issued. These contracts involve a specific type of insurance program that takes the form of a group plan. The funds are collected from individual employees through payroll withholdings or are paid directly by the employer or both.

Insurance companies offer four basic types of group plans.

Deposit Administration Plan. A single fund is set up for all employees. The employer makes contributions, which go into a fund that accumulates interest. An annuity is purchased only when an individual employee retires.

Deferred Group Annuity. This is also called a conventional group annuity plan. Each year, the employer purchases a paid-up annuity for member employees; the annuity income, however, is deferred until retirement of the employee covered by the plan. Upon retirement, each yearly annuity is added up to reach a gross figure that is "owed" the employee. An employee then chooses a specific retirement option.

Group Annuities and Permanent Life Insurance. This plan provides each employee with whole life insurance during his or her working years. At retirement, an automatic annuity option converts to retirement income for the individual. If the covered employee dies before reaching retirement age, his or her beneficiaries receive the face value of the whole life insurance policy.

Individual Policy Pension Plan. Under this system, the employer makes yearly payments into a fund on behalf of his or her employees. The fund is managed by an insurance company. Interest earned is credited to the fund; management expenses are subtracted from it. When the employee retires, a single premium paid-up life insurance policy or an annuity is then purchased out of the fund for the employee.

Noninsured Private Pension Plans

With **noninsured pension plans**, the employer makes contributions to a chosen trustee. The trustee, typically a trust department of a large commercial bank, then invests the money and distributes it to the retired employee at the appropriate time. The noninsured pension plan offers no guarantee of fixed dollars to a retired individual. Thus, if the trustee is unsuccessful in managing the fund, the employee might receive less money than he or she would have had contributions been made to an insured retirement plan. On the other hand, if the trustee is successful, the employee will receive more dollars for retirement or the cost to the employer will be less.

EXHIBIT 18-4.

NUMBER OF PEOPLE COVERED BY PRIVATE PENSION PLANS FUNDED WITH LIFE INSURANCE COMPANIES

| | YEAR ESTABLISHED | |
| | 1971 | 1976 |
TYPE OF PLAN	# Persons Covered	# Persons Covered
Individual Policy Pension Trust	115,000	1,975,000
Group Permanent Life Insurance	10,000	
Tax Sheltered Annuities	55,000	1,105,000
Deferred Annuity Group Annuities	45,000	165,000
Deposit Administration Group Annuities	60,000	11,810,000
Keogh Plans	25,000	460,000
Other Plans	25,000	785,000

Perhaps the two most important concepts relating to pension plans are
funding and **vesting**.

Funding

The concept of funding concerns whether the pension plan's
liabilities—retirement payments—can be met from a fund set up to do
so. Thus, with a *fully funded plan* the accumulated assets each year are
equal to the future pension benefits owed to employees that year. When
pension plans are fully funded, every participant can be paid off completely at any time.

At the other extreme, zero funding means that the employer pays
pension benefits to retired employees out of current revenues. This is
typically known as a pay-as-you-go plan; the Social Security system is a
zero-funded, pay-as-you-go plan.

Vesting

Vesting refers to the degree to which an individual legally will own his
or her share of a pension plan if he or she should leave the company
prior to the specified retirement age. In a *fully vested pension plan*, the
individual legally owns his or her pro rata portion of the plan; thus, if he
or she leaves the company prior to retirement, payment is made in cash.
Some plans allow employees to keep their funds in the plan even after
leaving the company's employ. In many cases, employees' contributions
have been fully vested, whereas employers' contributions have not.
Thus, leaving the company results in a loss in the value of the employer's contribution to the pension plan.

REGULATING PENSION PLANS

The Employee Retirement Income Security Act (ERISA) was passed in
1974. The act (also called the Pension Reform Act), which changed the
make-up of literally millions of retirement plans throughout the United
States, did the following:

1   Established minimum requirements for funding and for vest-
    ing.
2   Imposed regulations on the management of pension funds,
    such as:
    a. No more than 10 percent of the assets of the fund can be in
    the form of stock of the employing firm.
    b. Managers cannot buy fund property that they own per-
    sonally.
    c. An annual report must be made to the Secretary of Labor.
    d. Each year employees must receive full information regard-
    ing benefits.

3   Established the Pension Benefit Guarantee Corporation (PBGC), which guarantees pension rights and makes up deficits incurred by funds that collapse. Eligible retirees can be paid up to $750 a month from the PBGC. It is financed by premiums collected from the employer.

4   It changed the rules relating to individual retirement programs, such as the Keogh Plan and the Individual Retirement Account.

Portability

In the United States, nearly 5 percent of civilian employees leave their jobs every year. When an employee leaves a job, he or she also may have to leave the private pension plan if it isn't portable. Portability refers to the ability of employees to take their pension accounts wherever they go. In other words, your rights accrue to your numbered account even if you leave a particular job. The Pension Reform Act of 1974 encouraged portability without making it mandatory. Basically, it provides a method for transferring pension credits into an individual retirement account for a worker who leaves a job before retirement. Then, if the worker's new employer is willing, these credits can be transferred into the new employer's pension plan.

The Act further requires that the employer advise a departing employee of any vested rights that have accumulated. The employer then must report these to the Social Security Administration, which keeps a record of them along with the worker's Social Security account. Later, when the worker applies for Social Security retirement benefits, the Social Security Administration will indicate that there are certain private pension benefits available as well.

HOW TO SET UP YOUR OWN RETIREMENT PLAN

Every individual should have a savings program to provide for those years when he or she won't be earning income. We pointed out the benefits of saving via a pension plan in Chapter 13, when we looked at so-called tax loopholes. Clearly, if you are eligible for an individual retirement plan, you should take advantage of the laws governing such plans. In this Application, we will look at who is eligible for these pension programs and how they operate. We discussed the Keogh Plan and the IRA in Chapter 13; here we will give more specifics on how they operate.

THE KEOGH PLAN

The Keogh Plan, you will remember, is made available to self-employed individuals under provisions of the Self-Employed Individuals Tax Retirement Act of 1962, also known as the Keogh Act. This act was amended by the Pension Reform Act of 1974.

Who is Eligible for a Keogh Plan?

All self-employed individuals, such as accountants, architects, authors, doctors, farmers, and lawyers, are eligible. Any owner or partner in an unincorporated business also is eligible. And anyone who receives self-employment income from personal services can set up a Keogh Plan.

Maximum Contributions

By the late 1970s, the maximum contribution to a Keogh Plan was $7,500 or 15 percent of earned income, whichever is less. Thus, if your self-employment income was $10,000, you would be able to set aside only $1,500 in a Keogh Plan. On the other hand, if your self-employed income was $100,000, you would not be able to set aside 15 percent of that but, rather, only $7,500.

When Do You Make Contributions?

Contributions to the Keogh Plan can be made until April 15 of the year after they are to be deducted from earned income before taxes are calculated. Note, however, that the Keogh Plan must be set up legally during the year in which you are going to subtract Keogh Plan payments from earned income before computing federal taxes. Thus, you must set up a plan during 1982 in order to get benefits from that plan, even though payments to it may not be made until April 15, 1983.

When Can You Get Your Money?

You cannot remove retirement funds paid into a Keogh Plan prior to age fifty-nine and one-half, unless you suffer permanent disability. Administrators of Keogh Plans, however, frequently distribute Keogh assets to the beneficiary before the law allows and are not penalized.

What Taxes Do You Pay on Keogh Plan Funds?

Keogh Plan funds are taxed as ordinary income. However, if you take out all your funds as a lump sum at age fifty-nine and one-half or later, you may use what is called a special ten-year averaging method. Thus, if you receive $100,000 from your Keogh Plan at age fifty-nine and one-half, you calculate the taxes owed as if you were paying on ten annual incomes of $10,000. No other income is included in this annual average when figuring what you owe.

Investing Keogh Funds

The IRS requires that the Keogh Plan be set up as a trust and managed by a trustee, usually a bank or some other administrator. But that doesn't mean it's impossible to switch from one investment plan to another with any Keogh Plan trust. You are not committed to the investments you originally made.

As long as the new plan with new investments meets IRS trusteeship requirements, it is valid. Typical Keogh investment strategies involve purchasing mutual fund accounts, time deposit accounts in bank or savings associations, and U.S. retirement plan bonds, which are sold by the U.S. government in denominations of $50, $100, and $500 and pay 6 percent a year compounded twice a year. You can buy them, without having to choose a trustee, directly from the Federal Reserve Banks or branches throughout the country or from the Bureau of the Public Debt, Securities Transactions Branch, Washington, D.C. 20226.

Keogh Plan funds should not include tax-exempt municipal bonds. Since income taken out of a Keogh Plan at retirement is taxed as income, it makes no sense to get the lower yields from tax-exempt municipals, when you ultimately must pay tax on that yield anyway. Thus, avoid tax exempts for a Keogh Plan.

What Forms Must Be Filled Out?

What happens to a Keogh Plan must be reported each year on Form 5500-K. And there are numerous other schedules that may be required. If, though, you are engaged in a one-person plan, no separate schedules are needed. Form 5500-K merely requires the name of the person covered by the plan, the trustee, and a few other items.

INDIVIDUAL RETIREMENT ACCOUNTS (IRAs)

The 1974 Tax Reform Act set up individual retirement accounts, which are similar to Keogh Plans.

Who Is Eligible?

All individuals who are not self-employed but are not covered by a private pension plan are eligible to set up their own IRA. Self-employed individuals can also set up IRAs in addition to Keogh Plans. But salaried workers cannot set up both.

What Is The Maximum Contribution?

For an individual, the maximum is 15 percent of earnings or $1,500, whichever is smaller. As of 1977, however, a married individual could make a maximum contribution of $1,750, provided that the other member of the couple was unemployed. The contributions for the individual and spouse must be equal to qualify for this higher maximum.

When Can You Get Your Money?

Usually, you can take your money out at age fifty-nine and one-half or after. Unlike the Keogh Plan, which strictly forbids taking money out except for disability, an IRA permits you to take it out any time. But you are then subject to a penalty that is 10 percent of the money you withdraw.

How Much Tax Do You Pay?

Payment of taxes on monies taken out after age fifty-nine and one-half is exactly the same as with Keogh Plans.

What Forms Do You Fill Out?

Each year, you must file Forms 5329 and 5498 with your regular tax return. If these forms are not submitted by April 15, the IRS can, in principle, collect $10 for each day they are late up to a maximum of $5,000. They must be submitted every year, even if a contribution was *not* made to the IRA plan during that year.

Investment Strategies for IRAs

Investments in IRAs are similar to those in a Keogh Plan. They can consist of time deposit accounts, mutual funds, and so on. Additionally, an IRA can invest in U.S. individual retirement bonds available from the government. These resemble the U.S. retirement plan bonds that are appropriate only for Keogh investors. IRAs are routinely approved by the government with the individual as the manager trustee of the account. In other words, with an IRA, you need not satisfy the strict trusteeship requirements that the IRS imposes on Keogh Plans.

ANNUITY   A stream of income payments, usually received monthly for a definite period or for the lifetime of the annuitant.

ANNUITANT   The person who receives the stream of income from the annuity.

EXCLUSION RATIO   The formula by which the IRS computes taxes owed on an annuity income stream.

FIXED ANNUITY   A stream of income that is guaranteed for a period or lifetime and is fixed in the dollar amount received during each payment period.

VARIABLE ANNUITY   An annuity whose income stream is a function of how well the investment portfolio of the issuing company performs.

INSURED PENSION PLANS   Pension plans offered by insurance companies.

NONINSURED PENSION PLANS   Pension plans for whom the trustee typically is a trust department of a large commercial bank. A noninsured pension plan offers no guarantee of fixed dollars to a retired individual.

FUNDING   A concept relating to pension plans. When a plan is fully funded, the pension plan's liability can be met out of the available fund.

VESTING   A feature of a pension plan that refers to the degree to which an individual legally owns his or her share of such a plan even after leaving a company prior to retirement.

PORTABILITY   The ability of the worker to take a pension account wherever he or she goes.

CHAPTER SUMMARY

1. An annuity, which pays the policy holder during his or her entire lifetime, is issued on the bet that the policy holder will live less than expected.

2. Annuities can provide safe retirement income (ignoring inflation) and also can offer tax advantages by deferring income-tax payments until a time when most individuals are in a lower marginal tax bracket. People buy annuities to: (a) provide retirement income, (b) free up capital, and (c) lower taxes.

3. There are several types of fixed annuities, including deferred life and immediate.

4. When you choose either an immediate or deferred annuity, you have several choices of the kind of payment you will receive: (a) straight life, (b) temporary, (c) installment certain, (d) installment refund, (e) cash refund, and (f) joint and survivorship.

5. Variable annuities may be more inflation-proof than fixed annuities. Historically, they have yielded a greater return than fixed annuities, but they offer more risk.

6. During years when the stock market does poorly, the payments from a variable annuity also are poor.

7. Most of the numerous private pension plans in the United States are insured and offered through a group set up by an employer.

8. Insurance companies offer four basic types of group pension plans: (a) deposit administration, (b) deferred group annuity, (c) group annuity and permanent life insurance, and (d) individual policy pension plan.

9. Pension plans that are zero funded are essentially pay-as-you-go. The Social Security system is an example.

10. Fully vested pension plans give you full property rights in your account even if you leave the company prior to retirement.

11. All self-employed individuals are eligible for a Keogh Plan, as are owners or partners in unincorporated businesses.

12. Maximum contributions to a Keogh Plan are $7,500 or 15 percent of earned income, whichever is less.

13. You cannot remove your retirement funds from a Keogh Plan before age fifty-nine and one-half unless you suffer a permanent disability. But apparently some Keogh Plan administrators have given out Keogh assets before the law allows.

14. Keogh funds usually are put into a trust and managed by a trustee, usually a bank or some other administrator. Keogh investments involve mutual funds, time deposits, and U.S. retirement bonds.

15. All individuals who are not self-employed and not covered by a private pension plan are eligible to set up their own individual retirement accounts (IRAs).

16. The maximum contribution to an IRA is 15 percent of your earnings or $1,500, whichever is smaller. A married individual can contribute $1,750 provided the other member of the couple is unemployed.

17. In principle, you cannot take your money out of an IRA before age fifty-nine and one-half. If you do, you are subject to a penalty of 10 percent of the money you withdraw.

STUDY QUESTIONS

1. How does an annuity differ from a life insurance policy?

2. What is the difference between a single premium annuity contract and an installment premium annuity contract?

3. Explain and differentiate among annuities that are (a) immediate, (b) deferred, (c) joint and last survivorship, (d) fixed dollar, and (e) variable.

4. What is the difference between a funded pension plan and an insured pension plan?

CASE PROBLEMS

18-1   Investing for Retirement

Sherman Perez, sixty-five, and his wife, Meg, fifty-five, have $150,000 that they wish to invest for their retirement years. Sherman estimates that, in addition to income from Social Security, his pension, and mutual funds, they will need between $600 and $650 per month. Meg will need $550 per month after Sherman's death. They want to spend minimal time managing their retirement fund. Sherman wants to purchase an annuity for himself but is not sure which kind to buy. He also wants to provide an annuity for Meg, but, again, he's not sure of what type or when to buy it. Any money not currently invested in annuities will be invested in bonds with a net compounded income of 6%.

What advice would you give them? (Ignore the tax aspects.)

18-2   Cold Cash or a Straight Life Annuity?

Andrew Beresford, sixty, has been owner-manager of an apartment complex for the past twenty years. Now he wants to sell out and retire to Phoenix. He has had an offer of $450,000 cash and wants to accept it. His accountant has suggested that, instead of selling property, he accept a straight life annuity.

1. Why would his accountant suggest this?

2. How much monthly income would he receive from the annuity?

3. Assuming he has a life expectancy of fifteen years, what would be his exclusion ratio?

SELECTED REFERENCES

American Institute for Economic Research. *Annuities from the Buyer's Point of View.* Economic Education Bulletin Number 10-7, August 1970.
Collins, Thomas. *The Complete Guide to Retirement.* Englewood Cliffs, NJ: Prentice-Hall, 1972.
Corrick, Frank. *Planning Your Retirement Years.* New York: Pilot Books, 1972.
"How to Build a Pension Fund with an IRA." *Changing Times,* November 1976, pp. 39-42.

Social Security

■ During the Depression, it was evident that many people had not provided for themselves in case of emergencies. An especially large percentage of the elderly population, which could not rely on its children for support, became destitute. To prevent a recurrence of so much pain and suffering by elderly people, Congress passed the Social Security Act of 1935. By January 1940, when the first monthly benefit started, only 22,000 people received payments. Today, however, well over 90 percent of people sixty-five or older receive Social Security benefits—or *could* receive them if they weren't still working. If our population growth continues to slow down, the average age of the population will continue to rise. Hence, the total number of people eligible for and receiving Social Security will increase as a percentage of the total population. Exhibit 19-1 shows the current and projected percentage of the adult population aged 62 and over.

The Social Security system is basically an *involuntary* benefit program; that is, if we work, we *must* participate in the Social Security program. Even self-employed people must pay self-employment Social Security taxes. If you work for someone else and earn over fifty dollars in any quarter, your employer must file Social Security taxes for you. Of the people earning money in the United States, 95 percent contribute to Social Security. According to supporters of the program, Social Security is obligatory in order to ensure that all older Americans will have at least a basic living income and won't need welfare payments.

PROVISIONS OF THE SOCIAL SECURITY ACT

The Social Security Act, sometimes called the OASDHI, provides benefits for old-age retirement, survivors, disability, and health insurance.

493

It is essentially an income transfer program, financed by compulsory payroll taxes levied on both employers and employees; those who are employed transfer income to those who are retired or disabled. One pays for Social Security for others while working and usually receives benefits after retirement. The benefit payments usually are made to those reaching retirement age. Also, when an insured worker dies, benefits accrue to his or her survivors. Special benefits provide for disabled workers. Additionally, Social Security now provides for Medicare, which we described in Chapter 10. The Social Security Act of 1935 also provided for the establishment of an unemployment insurance system.

BASIC BENEFITS OF SOCIAL SECURITY

In the following Practical Applications section you will learn where to get information with which to figure, tentatively, the benefits you are allowed under Social Security. (The predictions must be tentative because Congress frequently changes the benefits.) Here is what you currently can expect from Social Security:

1 Medicare payments in the future.
2 Should you die prematurely, payments to your beneficiary.
3 Should you die prematurely, payments to your children until they complete college.

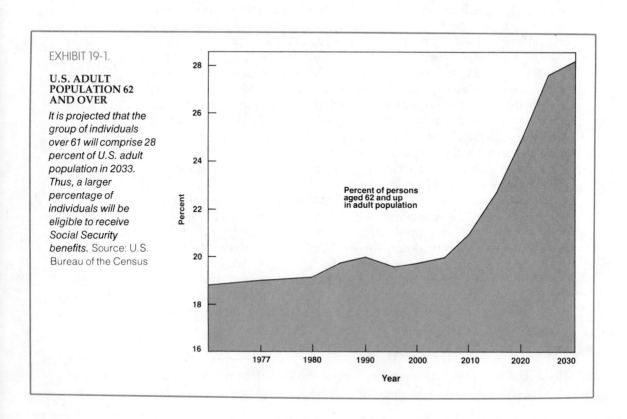

EXHIBIT 19-1.

U.S. ADULT POPULATION 62 AND OVER

It is projected that the group of individuals over 61 will comprise 28 percent of U.S. adult population in 2033. Thus, a larger percentage of individuals will be eligible to receive Social Security benefits. Source: U.S. Bureau of the Census

Percent of persons aged 62 and up in adult population

Percent

Year

4   Payments to you and your dependents if you are totally disabled and unable to work.

5   A retirement annuity—that is, payment of a certain amount
of money every month after you retire until you die. This
payment is legislated, and can be changed, by Congress.

6   If you die, a modest lump sum, presumably to pay for burial
expenses.

Whenever you calculate your insurance needs, you first must consider the basic coverage you will receive from Social Security.

PROBLEMS WITH SOCIAL SECURITY

A number of respected researchers have studied Social Security and
reached some pretty depressing conclusions. In the first place, you must
remember that Social Security is not really an insurance policy in the
sense that you are guaranteed a certain amount of money. Your beneficiaries receive that amount of money only if you die, just as with a
regular insurance policy; but if you live, you get retirement payments
that depend upon what Congress legislates, not on how much money
you have put in. Future Congresses may not be as kind as past Congresses, so you may find yourself with a very small retirement income if you
rely only on Social Security. And the greater your pre-retirement income
(say, $45,000 versus $11,000 yearly), the smaller will be the proportion
replaced by Social Security upon your retirement.

How Social Security Is Paid

In theory, Social Security is supported by a tax on a portion of the
employee's income that is matched by the employer. However, you
must realize that generally you, the employee, pay for much or all because your wages would be that much higher if the employer did not
have to "contribute." The combined Social Security and Medicare tax for
1979 was 6.13 percent of every worker's income; therefore, the employer

EXHIBIT 19-2.

FEDERAL INSURANCE TAX RATES—PERCENT OF COVERED EARNINGS	YEARS	SOCIAL SECURITY AND MEDICARE TOTAL
Source: U.S. Department of Health, Education, and Welfare.	1977	5.85
	1978	6.05
	1979	6.13
	1981	6.65
	1982	6.70
	1985	7.05
	1986	7.15

paid an equal amount. This tax applies only to the first $22,900 earned a year.[1] After that, it no longer is applicable. Hence, the Social Security contribution, otherwise known as payroll tax, and indicated on your payroll receipt as FICA (Federal Insurance Contributions Act), is highly regressive. Because benefits are proportionally greater for low income earners than high income earners, the regressive nature of the tax is compensated for. The tax rates, moreover, have been increasing rapidly and have more than doubled since 1967. Nonetheless, few seem to recognize the regressive nature of this particular income tax and the fact that, for the majority of taxpayers, it is greater than the income taxes they pay. In Exhibit 19-2, we show the legislated increases in Social Security and Medicare (hospital insurance) tax rates from 1977 to 1986.

IF YOU WORK AFTER SIXTY-FIVE, YOU MAY NOT GET PAID

As it currently stands, the Social Security Act penalizes you tremendously if you decide to remain working past the retirement age of sixty-five: in 1978 you could earn only $4,000, after which your Social Security check is reduced. If your earned, or services, income exceeds that figure, Social Security benefits are reduced one dollar for every two dollars earned. "Earned" here strictly means income that is made by a wage earner, *not* as dividends, interest, or pensions. If you decide to invest lots of money, you could make millions of dollars and still get full Social Security. But if you decide to work hard and continue earning wages, you may lose all your Social Security payments. It is conceivable that you could work till seventy and never get a penny of Social Security benefits, even though you were forced to pay for them all your working life. Your decision to work after age sixty-five certainly will be influenced by this highly regressive taxation system. We say "taxation system" because you obviously are taxed if, for every dollar you earn, you lose fifty cents in Social Security benefits; that is equivalent to a tax rate of 50 percent. This seems a bit steep considering that under the federal personal income-tax system, the 50 percent marginal tax rate applies only to individuals making well over $30,000 a year. But for people over sixty-five, this 50 percent rate started at $4,000 in 1978. It stays in effect until the worker reaches age seventy-two. After that, you can earn any amount without loss of benefits.

Many observers feel that this aspect of the Social Security program is quite unfair. It penalizes older people who work. Professor Carolyn Shaw Bell, of Wellesley College, also points out that the Social Security system is not insurance but, rather, a transfer. People who work pay Social Security taxes. People who get Social Security benefits receive the income that is taxed away. Essentially, it is a subsidy by younger workers for older, retired people. There is also a transfer from those who

[1] By law, this tax base automatically rises whenever the rate of inflation reaches specified levels.

continue to work after age sixty-five to their peers who don't work. At the beginning of this decade, for example, there were 3 million people over sixty-five in the labor force, a full 22 percent of older men and 10 percent of older women. According to Professor Shaw Bell, these 3 million people are "unjustly hemmed in between bleak job market prospects, on the one hand, and the necessity, on the other, of paying out of their meager earnings to support not only themselves but others of their own age."[2] Remember, these 3 million working people continue to pay Social Security taxes.

Supporters of Social Security point out that its benefits are meant to replace lost earnings. Hence, if a person continues to earn above the minimum amount after age sixty-five, his or her earnings have not been lost. Therefore, the insurance—Social Security—does not pay the benefits, just as a fire insurance policy does not pay if a fire hasn't occurred.

OTHER FACTS ABOUT SOCIAL SECURITY

As Carolyn Shaw Bell points out, Social Security is not truly an insurance program: "contributions" don't go into a trust fund that is used to pay you an annuity when you retire.

Not Actuarially Sound

Those who view the payroll tax as a contribution to a trust fund would have trouble understanding how Social Security actually works. In 1974, the trust fund was approximately $50 billion, enough to cover perhaps one year of benefits. A private insurance program or pension fund must, by law, have a trust fund that, at any moment, could finance all the benefits promised to its members. But the benefits owed members of Social Security are valued at more than $2.5 trillion! Those who suggest that individuals be allowed to withdraw voluntarily from the system have been criticized by such supporters of Social Security as former Vice President Nelson Rockefeller and the late President Johnson; Rockefeller predicted that such withdrawal would lead to the collapse of the Social Security system.

Apparently, then, the system is not actuarially sound, as trust funds are legally required to be. Rockefeller's prediction is unquestionably correct. When the system began in 1935, it was hoped that it would be actuarially sound around 1960. This hope has not been realized.

Original System was Sound

FICA collections started in 1937, but benefits were delayed until 1940. The starting tax was 2 percent—1 percent each on employer and em-

---

[2]Carolyn Shaw Bell, *Challenge*, July/August 1973, p. 22.

ployee on the first $3,000 of income. Since no one received any benefits for three years, the trust fund became sizable. Thus, although the Social Security tax was to increase in 1940, it did not. In fact, it wasn't until 1950 that it rose to 3 percent (1.5 percent on each party). Since then, coverage has expanded greatly. We can surmise that the politics of Social Security are the cause of both increased coverage and greater benefits, for these two campaign promises win votes. Social, economic, and political pressures have escalated benefits to levels undreamed of in 1940. Checks then were as little as $10 per month, $41.20 at most. By the mid-1970s, the minimum was $100 and the maximum close to $400 per month for a man retiring at age sixty-five. On the other side of the coin, taxes paid in have skyrocketed. When the system started, collections were $30; by 1965, the maximum any worker could pay was only $174; by 1977, the maximum had jumped to $965.25.

A Transfer System

Those who are working today are paying taxes to finance retirement payments to those who are no longer working. Each year, there has been a slight surplus, which has been put into the relatively small trust. With those "surplus" Social Security contributions, the trust purchases U.S. Government Bonds.

If you contribute to a private insurance or pension plan, what you ultimately receive depends on how much you put in. And you pay income taxes on the benefits. But this is not the case with Social Security.

What You Put In vs. What You Get Out

There is, to be sure, a relationship between how much you put into Social Security and how much you get out, but it is a tenuous relationship at best. In the mid 1970s the maximum wage-related benefit was about three times the minimum, whereas the maximum so-called average monthly wage on which benefits were based was eighty times the minimum sufficient to qualify. But the range would be even greater if account were taken of the total number of years the worker paid into Social Security. In truth, the benefits received are much more closely related to your marital status or the number of children in your family than to how much money you have contributed.

There are other anomalies in the benefit payment system that could not be justified if Social Security were truly an insurance system. For example, the later you enter the system, the better off you are: as long as you worked the minimum number of quarters, you will receive the same benefits as someone who has worked many more. Generally, the wealthier in our society profit by this because they start work later. What's more, people with higher incomes generally have longer life expectancies and will, therefore, receive payments for a longer period. Blacks are discriminated against doubly because they go to work sooner and die earlier on average. It is not surprising that Social Security has been labeled the poor man's welfare payment to the middle class.

Clearly, then, Social Security pays differently to individuals who have paid in identical "contributions." On the other hand, Social Security will pay exactly the same benefits to individuals who have paid in vastly different "contributions."

Insurance Principle Not Upheld

The government occasionally has contradicted itself when referring to the insurance principle of Social Security. More precisely, it has been selective in its invocation of that principle. For example, in a court test of the constitutionality of the rule prohibiting benefit payments to persons deported for subversive activities, the Social Security Administration rejected entirely the insurance concept: "The OASI (Old Age, Survivors Insurance) is in no sense a federally administered 'insurance program' under which each worker pays 'premiums' over the years and acquires at retirement an indefeasible right to receive for life a fixed monthly benefit, irrespective of the conditions which Congress has chosen to impose from time to time." There we have it. The insurance principle officially is endorsed in support of all Social Security *taxes* and rejected when benefits are denied.

SPECIAL ASPECTS OF THE SOCIAL SECURITY SYSTEM

Now let's look at a number of special aspects of the Social Security system.

Benefiting Students

We noted earlier that benefits of Social Security included those for a recipient's children's college education. Thus, Social Security is not just a retirement system. Over 95 percent of all children under eighteen and their mothers would receive monthly cash benefits if the working father died. In such families, unmarried children up to age twenty-two can collect benefits based on a parent's earnings. Basically, if you are between the ages of eighteen and twenty-two, you are eligible for Social Security payments if one of your parents is receiving retirement benefits or Social Security disability payments, provided that you are unmarried and a full-time student at a qualified educational institution. While attending college, you can receive checks through the end of the term in which you become twenty-two. If you stop attending school, become a part-time student, or marry, your checks automatically stop (and so do those to your widowed parent until he or she reaches retirement age).

What Is a Qualified Educational Institution? Under the Social Security Act, a school, college, or university is considered an educational institution if it meets one of these three criteria:

1   It is operated or directly supported by the United States, by a state or local government, or by a political subdivision of the government unit.

2   It has been approved by a state or accredited by a state—recognized or nationally recognized accrediting agency.

3   It is unaccredited, but credits are accepted on transfer by at least three accredited institutions on the same basis as if the credits had been transferred from an accredited institution.

Under this broad definition, virtually all public and private high schools, trade or vocational schools, and colleges and universities qualify.

Who Is a Full-Time Student? Under the act, a full-time student attends an educational institution full-time. And he or she carries a subject load considered full-time for day students under the standards and practices of the educational institution. However, a student will *not* be considered in full-time attendance if:

1   He or she is enrolled in a junior college, college, or university in a course of study of less than thirteen school weeks' duration.

2   He or she is enrolled in any other educational institution and either the course of study is less than thirteen school weeks' duration or his or her schedule attendance is less than twenty hours a week.

Who Is Fully Insured?

In order for monthly benefits to be payable to you and/or your spouse in old age and/or your widow or widower or family and/or your aged dependent parents if you die, you must be "fully insured." This means that you have worked and paid Social Security taxes for a minimum number of quarters. The minimum depends on the year in which you reach sixty-two or the date of your disability or death, if that happens before age sixty-two.

Basically, a worker becomes fully insured if one of the following is satisfied:

1   Ten years (forty quarters of coverage) acquired any time after 1936. (You get one quarter of coverage for each calendar quarter in which you are paid total wages of fifty dollars or more.)

2   At least one quarter of coverage for each calendar year elapsing after 1950 or, if later, after the year the person attained age twenty-one and prior to the year that person attains age sixty-two or dies.

3   A person is fully covered with fewer than six quarters of coverage if:

a. he or she attained age 72 before 1969, and

b. he or she had at least one quarter of coverage required for each calendar year elapsing after 1950 and after the year he attained age sixty-five or she attained age sixty-two, and

c. he or she has a minimum of three quarters of coverage.

It is interesting to note that the contributions to the Social Security system are compulsory, yet extensive requirements must be met before you qualify to collect benefits.

COLLECTING DISABILITY PAYMENTS

Nearly all people who pay into the Social Security system are eligible to collect disability payments before age sixty-five. There are, of course, a number of rules and qualifications that must be met before the Social Security Administration will pay disability benefits.

Minimum Pay-In Period

Under most circumstances, you must have been paying Social Security contributions for at least five years in the ten-year period just prior to your disability. This rule applies to individuals who become disabled at age thirty-one or older. If you become disabled prior to that age, you must have had Social Security credit for one and a half years of work prior to your disability, subject to a six-quarter minimum. And, finally, a disabled person under the age of twenty-two often can get disability Social Security payments based on the earnings of a parent or even a grandparent.

The Necessary Degree of Disability

There is no clear-cut requirement for the degree of disability necessary to obtain disability benefits. Rather, the law states that your disability must render you unable to "engage in any substantial gainful activity." This disability must be expected to last for at least one year or longer. Your payments will start in the sixth month after the disability occurred.

When you apply for disability insurance benefits, your doctor or other personnel at the hospital or clinic where you have been treated must complete a medical report provided by your local Social Security office.

How Much Do You Get?

Monthly disability insurance payments basically are the same as the old age benefits you would receive if you were retired. Figure out your average earnings as if you had reached age sixty-two when you became disabled.

PRACTICAL APPLICATIONS

HOW TO CALCULATE YOUR SOCIAL SECURITY BENEFITS

To understand what Social Security might mean for you, you should figure out your potential Social Security benefits. To get an idea of current benefits, write your Social Security office for the latest figures for individuals receiving Social Security payments.

GETTING A CURRENT REPORT

One of the first things you should do is write the Social Security Administration and give them your Social Security number and the name on your Social Security card. Ask for a current report of your account. In fact, you can request such a Statement of Earnings annually. It is best to do this at least once every three years because there is a time limit within which errors can be corrected. You can obtain a number of addressed Requests for Statements of Earnings cards, such as that in Exhibit 19-3 from your local Social Security office.

HOW TO FIGURE SOCIAL SECURITY PAYMENTS

To begin collecting benefits from Social Security, you must have accumulated a certain number of work credits during your lifetime. Exhibit 19-4 shows just how much credit you need at age sixty-two. Should you stop working before you have the required number of work credits, you can't receive Social Security benefits. But the credit you already have earned will remain on your Social Security record. And you can add additional work credits if you return to work in a job covered by Social Security.

Basically, your Social Security check is based on your average earnings over a number of years. The amount of the check can vary from person to person. Just because you always have earned the maximum amount covered by Social Security doesn't necessarily mean you will get the highest benefits. In January 1978, the maximum a man reaching sixty-five could get was $5,876.40, because the maximum amount of earnings covered by Social Security was lower in past years than it is now. In figuring out your average earnings, use both lower and higher amounts.

In future years, though, Social Security benefits will be increased automatically to reflect changes in the cost of living. To figure your benefits, follow steps one through eight in Exhibit 19-5.

WHEN YOU SHOULD TAKE ACTION

When one of the following occurs, you should consult your Social Security office:

1. You become disabled.

2. A worker in your family dies.

3. You approach retirement age, either sixty-two or sixty-five.

4. You reach seventy-two (because you will receive benefits, no matter how much you are earning).

EXHIBIT 19-3.

REQUEST FOR STATEMENT OF EARNINGS CARD

REQUEST FOR STATEMENT OF EARNINGS

SOCIAL SECURITY → NUMBER

DATE OF BIRTH →

MONTH	DAY	YEAR

Please send a statement of my social security earnings to:

NAME _____

STREET & NUMBER _____

CITY & STATE _____ ZIP CODE _____

Print Name and Address In Ink Or Use Typewriter

SIGN YOUR NAME HERE (DO NOT PRINT) _____

Sign your own name only. Under the law, information in your social security record is confidential and anyone who signs another person's name can be prosecuted.
If you have changed your name from that shown on your social security card, please copy your name below exactly as it appears on your card.

EXHIBIT 19-4.

AMOUNT OF WORK CREDITS REQUIRED BY SOCIAL SECURITY

IF YOU REACH 62 IN	YOU NEED CREDIT FOR THIS MUCH WORK
1977	6½ years
1978	6¾
1979	7
1980	7¼
1981	7½
1983	8
1987	9
1991 or later	10

EXHIBIT 19-5.

HOW TO FIGURE YOUR SOCIAL SECURITY BENEFITS

Source: Social Security Administration

STEP 1

Your retirement check depends on your average earnings over a period of years. Based on the year you were born, pick the number of years you need to count from Chart #1. Write the number of years here:

_____

STEP 2

Complete the worksheet that is Chart #2. Column "A" shows maximum earnings covered by Social Security. In Column "B," list your earnings, beginning with 1951. Write "0" for each year with no earnings. If you earned more than the maximum in any year, list only the maximum. Estimate your earnings for future years, including any years you plan to work past sixty-five. Stop with the year *before* you retire.

STEP 3

Cross off your list the years of your *lowest* earnings until the number of years left is the same as your answer to Step 1. (You may have to leave some years of "0" earnings on your list.)

STEP 4

Add up the earnings for the years left on your list. Write this figure in the space marked "TOTAL" at the bottom of the worksheet and here.

$_____

STEP 5

Divide this total by the number you wrote for Step 1. The result is your average yearly earnings covered by Social Security. Write the figure here.

$_____

STEP 6

Look at the benefit chart in Exhibit 19-3. Under the heading, "For Workers," find the average yearly earnings figure *closest* to your own. Look at the column listing your age at retirement to see about how much you can expect to get. Write the figure here.

$_____

STEP 7

If you have an eligible spouse or child or both, look under the heading "For Dependents" to find about how much they can get, based on the same average yearly earnings you used to figure your check. Write the amount of any dependents' benefits here.

$_____

STEP 8

Finally, add the figures you wrote for Steps 6 and 7 to see how much your total family retirement benefit will be under Social Security. Write the figure here.

$_____

The total cannot exceed the amount in the "Family benefits" column.

CHART #1

YEAR YOU WERE BORN	YEARS NEEDED
1913	19 years
1914	20
1915	21
1916	22
1918	24
1920	26
1925	31
1930 or later	35*

*Maximum number of years that count

EXHIBIT 19-5. **CONTINUED**

CHART #2

WORKSHEET

YEAR	A	B
1951	$3,600	$_____
1952	3,600	_____
1953	3,600	_____
1954	3,600	_____
1955	4,200	_____
1956	4,200	_____
1957	4,200	_____
1958	4,200	_____
1959	4,800	_____
1960	4,800	_____
1961	4,800	_____
1962	4,800	_____
1963	4,800	_____
1964	4,800	_____
1965	4,800	_____
1966	6,600	_____
1967	6,600	_____
1968	7,800	_____
1969	7,800	_____

WORKSHEET (cont.)

YEAR	A	B
1970	7,800	_____
1971	7,800	_____
1972	9,000	_____
1973	10,800	_____
1974	13,200	_____
1975	14,100	_____
1976	15,300	_____
1977	16,500	_____
1978	17,700	_____
1979	22,900	_____
1980	22,900*	_____
TOTAL		$_____

*The maximum amount of annual earnings that count for social security will rise automatically in future years as earnings levels increase. Because of this, the base in 1980 and later may be higher than $22,900.

CHAPTER SUMMARY

1. The Social Security system is an involuntary benefit program. All individuals, including the self-employed, must contribute to it if they earn over fifty dollars in any quarter. Over 95 percent of the working population in the United States contributes to Social Security.

2. Social Security provides for: (a) Medicare; (b) payments to a surviving beneficiary; (c) if the insured dies, payments to children until they have completed college; (d) payments to you or your dependents if you are totally disabled; and (e) a retirement annuity.

3. The retirement annuity depends on Congressional legislation.

4. The worker and the employer "contribute" to Social Security. The rate

at which the tax is paid and the base on which it is levied depend upon what Congress legislates.

5. Social Security recipients between the ages of sixty-two and sixty-five could earn up to $3,240 in 1978 without losing any benefits. Recipients between the ages of sixty-five and seventy-two could earn up to $4,000 in 1978 before they forfeited any benefits. After reaching those maximum limits, a Social Security recipient loses one dollar of benefits for each one dollar of earnings above the earnings limit. This 50 percent tax does not apply to anyone over the age of seventy-two or to income earned from investments and bonds, for example.

6. The Social Security system is not like a private pension plan. Because it has zero funding, it is a pay-as-you-go system.

7. The Social Security system depends upon the general taxing ability of the U.S. government.

8. Basically, Social Security is a transfer system from those who work to those who don't.

9. The Social Security system will provide for payments to college-age students if their insured parent dies.

10. You must be a full-time student, however, to receive such payments from the Social Security Administration. That means you must be enrolled in a junior college, college, or university in a course of study of more than thirteen school weeks' duration.

11. To be fully insured by the Social Security Administration, you must have worked and paid in for ten years (forty quarters of coverage) at some time after 1936 or have been covered for at least one quarter for each calendar year since 1950.

12. You can obtain a current Social Security status report by submitting a Request for Statement of Earnings. You can obtain these cards from your local Social Security Administration office or post office.

13. You can use the worksheet in the Application to figure out Social Security benefits that might be coming to you or to a parent or relative who is about to retire.

14. You should contact the Social Security Administration when: (a) you become disabled, (b) a worker in your family dies, (c) you are near retirement age, and (d) you reach age seventy-two.

STUDY QUESTIONS

1. Why is the Social Security system called an involuntary benefit program?

2. List the basic benefits from Social Security.

3. Both the employee and the employer are assessed a "contribution" for

Social Security. But some people say that the employee ends up paying it all. What do they mean?

4. Could the Social Security system ever go bankrupt?

CASE PROBLEMS

19-1 The Vagaries of Social Security

Harold Schultz, a former professor of English at Southern University, retired in 1977 at age sixty-five. He had been covered by Social Security twenty-five years prior to his retirement and earned more than the maximum salary each year. He has three dependents, his wife, Gladys, forty-five, and two children, ages eleven and nine. He has been offered a part-time job at Southern, where he would be teaching Geriatric Poetry and Modern Grammar for one semester. This would pay $1600 over the amount allowed by Social Security for retired people.

1. What is the base benefit he is now receiving from Social Security? (His Chart 2 total is $144,600.)

2. How much additional money is he receiving for his dependents?

3. What are his total benefits?

4. If he accepts the teaching job, will this change his benefits? By how much?

19-2 Retirement Benefits

Marlene, Harold's first wife, returned to school after their divorce in 1963. She has been employed in the university business office since 1964, has earned enough to be fully covered each year, and will retire in 1980 at age sixty-five. She has two dependents, Steve and Myra, who will be twenty-one and nineteen in 1980.

1. What will her base benefit be at retirement? (Her Chart 2 total is $168,300.)

2. What will be the total benefit for Marlene and the two children?

3. If Steve marries in June, 1979, what will Marlene's total benefit be when she retires?

SELECTED REFERENCES

Brittain, J.A., "The Social Security System Is Not Perfect, But It's Not Bankrupt." *Challenge,* January/February 1975.

Henle, P., "Social Security Reform: A Look at the Problems." *Monthly Labor Review,* February 1977, pp. 55-58.

Hopp, M.A. and Sommerstad, C.R., "Social Security Reform: A Look at the Problems," *Monthly Labor Review,* February 1977.

Pechman, Joseph A., et al. *Social Security: Perspectives for Reform.* Washington, D.C.: The Brookings Institution, 1968.

"Will Social Security Be There When You Need It?" *Changing Times,* February 1977.

Wills, Trusts, and Estate Planning

TWENTY

■ Most individuals accumulate wealth throughout their lifetimes. At some point in their lives, they have more assets than liabilities. Thus, their net worth is positive. For this reason, setting up wills, providing trusts, and engaging in careful estate planning are important to virtually everyone. In this chapter, we will examine why it is necessary to draw up a will. Then we will look at some of the more important trusts that can be created and the benefits and costs of doing so. Finally, we'll discuss the elements of estate planning and indicate ways in which federal and state estate taxes can be minimized. The Practical Applications section contains salient points about wills.

WHAT IS A WILL

A **will** is a legal document through which you dispose of your property or estate. Your **estate** consists of the difference between all your assets and all your liabilities. In addition, your will gives directions for the distribution of your estate; it specifies who shall receive what and how it should be used.

Generally, a will is ineffective prior to the death of the writer of the will. A will can be destroyed, canceled, or modified at any time by its writer. The person who makes out the will is called a **testator**, if a male, and a **testatrix**, if a female. Thus, if a person dies leaving a will, he or she is said to have died **testate**. On the other hand, if he or she dies without a will, that person is said to have died **intestate**.

WHY SHOULD YOU MAKE OUT A WILL?

If you should die intestate, the following things will occur, and each is

509

an additional reason why everyone should make out at least a simple will.

1 You cannot name the person who will oversee the distribution of your estate. That person is called the **executor**, if a male, or the **executrix**, if a female.

2 You generally cannot name a guardian for your minor children or other dependents. This is particularly critical if both you and your spouse should die at the same time.

3 You lose the ability to direct the disposal of your property in order to maximize its benefit to your heirs.

4 Your family and/or heirs will become unnecessarily involved in court procedures, which could have been avoided with a valid will.

5 If you have no immediate family, persons in whom you have no particular interest may receive the bulk of your property.

6 The possibility of minimizing inheritance and state taxes is eliminated.

7 Even if you have immediate family, the state will decide which percentage of your estate each individual will receive. You may have two offspring, one of whom is immensely rich, the other abysmally poor. Both may receive equal parts of your estate when you die if you do not have a will.

8 You cannot prevent your property from reverting to the state if you haven't named a person or persons legally qualified to inherit or claim it. (This is called escheat.)

What a Will Allows You to Do

Basically, a will allows you to decide the following:

1 Who gets your property.
2 How much each person or institution gets.
3 When that property will be received.
4 How the property can be safeguarded.
5 Who will handle its disposition.

Limitations on Disposition of Property by the Will

A person cannot do just anything he or she wants in a will. For example, it is generally impossible to eliminate completely a person's spouse from a will. In most states, the surviving spouse can elect to take the amount granted by state statutes for intestate situations. In other words, if state law says that the surviving spouse shall receive at least one-third of the estate and the will indicates that the spouse shall receive nothing, the surviving spouse usually will get the one-third amount. In a number of situations, however, it is possible to disinherit children.

Provisions in a will that are deemed against "public policy" can be invalidated by the courts. For example, a provision in a person's will to spend $20 million to erect a 300-foot statue of that person in place of an existing house in a suburban neighborhood would certainly not be held valid, even if it didn't violate local zoning ordinances. Provisions providing for bequests of property to individuals only if they remain unmarried throughout their lifetimes usually are held invalid since marriage is considered a "socially desirable" institution.

A Will Disposes Only of Certain Property

A will disposes of property that is not otherwise taken care of. There may be a large amount of property in a person's estate that does not pass to heirs through disposition of the will. For example, in most cases, life insurance proceeds automatically go to the beneficiary. If certain property is owned by two persons as joint tenants with the right of survivorship, then the survivor becomes sole owner of the property, no matter what the deceased's will states.

WHAT IS PROBATE?

Even though you have set up a will that explicitly states who should get what, how, when, and where, the will and your property must be **probated.** That is to say, it must be taken before a probate court in the appropriate jurisdiction. The court will make sure that the will has a genuine signature on it and that its execution will carry out your intent as precisely as possible. The person who has been named executor or executrix must satisfy what is usually called the Surrogate's Court in your area that all debts have been paid and that state and federal taxes also have been paid. Additionally, anyone who might have a claim on the estate supposedly has to have been notified before your will can be executed properly.

The procedure generally followed involves your attorney admitting the will to a probate court. Your attorney then issues letters testamentary to the executor or executrix named in the will. All proper parties are notified, and the required proof is submitted by the witnesses to the will to satisfy the court that the will is valid.

Because creditors usually have from four months to a year to make a claim, estates remain in the probate court for some time. The executor or executrix may attempt to settle federal estate taxes within nine months after your death; however, the IRS and state taxing authorities can take additional time to indicate their acceptance. Generally, it is only after all these things are completed that the distributions can be made from your estate. Furthermore, if any provision in the will is contested, it may remain in probate for many months, if not years. Medium-sized estates of $50,000 or so often take at least a year to be probated. It is possible to reduce the amount of your assets that go through probate. But, unless you have virtually no net worth, it is impossible to avoid probate altogether.

JOINT OWNERSHIP

Two individuals, usually husband and wife, can own many of their
assets jointly. Joint ownership can assume the following forms: (1) **joint
tenancy**, (2) **tenancy by the entirety**, and (3) **tenancy in common**.

Joint Tenancy

In a joint tenancy ownership arrangement, there are two or more
owners. Each owns a percentage of an asset but not a specific part of it.
Each joint owner can dispose of his or her share without the permission
of other owners. When one owner dies, his or her share goes to the
surviving owners.

Tenancy by the Entirety

This type of joint ownership is available only to husbands and wives. In
an arrangement involving tenancy by the entirety, neither husband nor
wife can dispose of his or her share of the asset without the permission
of the other. When one spouse dies, entire ownership of the property is
automatically assumed by the surviving spouse.

Tenancy in Common

In this arrangement, there may be two or more owners. Each may dispose of his or her share without the permission of the other owners.
Unlike joint tenancy, tenancy in common has the share of a deceased
owner going to his or her heirs. These heirs may or may not be the other
owner or owners.

Why Is a Will Necessary?

In all these forms of joint ownership, it would appear that the deceased
person's assets would pass on to the appropriate individuals without
having to be probated. Note, though, that it is still necessary to have a
will for the following reasons:

1   It is virtually impossible to put *all* property in joint ownership.
     All property not in joint ownership may not be dispersed upon
     its owner's death as he or she would have wanted. In other
     words, local intestacy law may disperse the property other-
     wise.
2   Without a will, property goes to the survivor outright in a joint
     ownership arrangement. A will, however, makes distribution
     more flexible. It can put "brakes" on surviving beneficiaries so
     they cannot spend their inheritance immediately.
3   If two co-owners die simultaneously and both lack wills, then
     property can be distributed under local intestacy law to heirs in
     a way that the deceased individuals may not have wished.

4   There may be no funds set aside for the payment of estate taxes or other debts if there is no will. Trouble may result when surviving co-owners refuse to cooperate.

TRUSTS

Generally, a trust is an arrangement whereby you leave your property to an individual, a bank, or a trust company to manage for the benefit of your heirs. Most trusts are set up because there are minor children surviving a parent or parents. The funds are usually invested by the **trustee** (the designated holder of the trust) in order to support and educate the children. After a period of time designated in the will or trust agreement, the remaining assets are distributed, usually to the beneficiaries of the trust.

The trustee has two principle responsibilities: to execute his or her fiduciary (or trust) responsibility in good faith and prudently and to preserve the principal in the trust and invest it so that the beneficiaries receive at least a reasonable rate of return. If beneficiaries are dissatisfied with a trustee's performance, they usually can petition a state court for a change in the trust agreement or for a change in trustees. Since the trustee is responsible for managing the assets in the trust, care must be taken in selecting the trustee. Friends or relatives obviously will take a more personal interest in your trust than will an institution. Nonetheless, a professional trust company can offer you investment competence and continuity for the life of the trust. Perhaps it might be best to have co-trustees—a professional company, such as a trust department of a bank, or your lawyer and a close friend or relative.

Trusts can be created for anyone's benefit, including a spouse or a charity, and are not necessarily designed for the protection of children. For example, a surviving spouse may not have the interest or ability to manage the deceased spouse's estate; therefore, a trust agreement may be the most desirable method of arranging for use of the assets. Trusts also can be established while you are still living, and these can provide at least as many benefits as a trust created at death.

Life Insurance Trust

A life insurance trust is administered by a bank or any other trustee but not an insurance company. The trustee is named to manage the insurance proceeds after death for any heirs inexperienced in handling large sums of money.

Living Trust

A living trust permits you to make the income from your assets payable to yourself while you are alive or have them reinvested for your future benefit. This type of trust is not subject to probate. But if the living trust can be revocable—that is, altered or canceled at any time—then it will be subject to estate taxes.

Funded Trusts

With the funded trust, funds or assets other than life insurance can be put under the same expert management as the life insurance trust. This reduces estate administrative expenses and averts taxation. That is, taxes do not have to be paid first by a surviving spouse and then by the children who would inherit the same funds from her or him.

Testamentary Trust

A **testamentary trust** is tailor-made for you. In your will, for example, you can create a testamentary trust that makes certain your property will be managed expertly and used as you desire. The trustee, usually a bank, is given broad investment powers.

THE TAXATION OF ESTATES

Prior to 1976, this section on estate taxes would have included methods by which those taxes could have been minimized. However, the Tax Reform Act of 1976 virtually rewrote the estate and gift tax code. Specifically, the deductions and credits granted in the 1976 Tax Reform Act exempt all but the extremely rich from federal estate taxes. Thus, one basic reason for setting up trusts has been eliminated for almost all individuals in the United States. In the past, gift taxes (those imposed on the grantor of the gift) were less than estate taxes. Thus, it was beneficial for older individuals to make parts of their estates gifts to their future heirs to reduce the total taxes on the estate. This is often not the case now. The tax rate, which is the same for gifts and estates, is given in the unified rate schedule in Exhibit 20-1.

Comparing the Old Law with the New

It is interesting to compare the old federal estate tax laws with the new one. Under the old law, you could leave half your estate to your spouse, tax-free; then an additional $60,000 was exempt from taxes. Now you have the option of leaving half your estate *or* up to $250,000 (whichever is *greater*) to your spouse, tax-free. The $60,000 additional exemption is increased by means of a tax credit to $175,000 by 1981. Exhibit 20-2 shows taxes due at the first partner's death, which includes the marital deduction. These figures are for 1981 and beyond; the taxes due were slightly more in 1979 and 1980. We also show the taxes due on the estate of a single person.

THE NUMBERS ARE SMALL

In 1981, 98 percent of all estates will have paid no federal estate tax. That isn't surprising when you realize that estates up to $425,000 can be passed onto heirs free of any estate and gift taxes. For a person who has yet to accumulate significant wealth, it hardly pays to try to grasp the intricacies of estate taxation.

EXHIBIT 20-1.

**UNIFIED RATE
SCHEDULE**

UNIFIED RATE SCHEDULE

If the amount with respect to which the tentative tax is to be computed is:	The tentative tax is:
Not over $10,000	18% of such amount.
Over $10,000 but not over $20,000	$1,800, plus 20% of the excess of such amount over $10,000.
Over $20,000 but not over $40,000	$3,800, plus 22% of the excess of such amount over $20,000.
Over $40,000 but not over $60,000	$8,200, plus 24% of the excess of such amount over $40,000.
Over $60,000 but not over $80,000	$13,000, plus 26% of the excess of such amount over $60,000.
Over $80,000 but not over $100,000	$18,200, plus 28% of the excess of such amount over $80,000.
Over $100,000 but not over $150,000	$23,800, plus 30% of the excess of such amount over $100,000.
Over $150,000 but not over $250,000	$38,800, plus 32% of the excess of such amount over $150,000.
Over $250,000 but not over $500,000	$70,800, plus 34% of the excess of such amount over $250,000.
Over $500,000 but not over $750,000	$155,800, plus 37% of the excess of such amount over $500,000.
Over $750,000 but not over $1,000,000	$248,300, plus 39% of the excess of such amount over $750,000.
Over $1,000,000 but not over $1,250,000	$345,800, plus 41% of the excess of such amount over $1,000,000.
Over $1,250,000 but not over $1,500,000	$448,300, plus 43% of the excess of such amount over $1,250,000.
Over $1,500,000 but not over $2,000,000	$555,800, plus 45% of the excess of such amount over $1,500,000.
Over $2,000,000 but not over $2,500,000	$780,800, plus 49% of the excess of such amount over $2,000,000.
Over $2,500,000 but not over $3,000,000	$1,025,800, plus 53% of the excess of such amount over $2,500,000.
Over $3,000,000 but not over $3,500,000	$1,290,800, plus 57% of the excess of such amount over $3,000,000.
Over $3,500,000 but not over $4,000,000	$1,575,800, plus 61% of the excess of such amount over $3,500,000.
Over $4,000,000 but not over $4,500,000	$1,880,800, plus 65% of the excess of such amount over $4,000,000.
Over $4,500,000 but not over $5,000,000	$2,205,800, plus 69% of the excess of such amount over $4,500,000.
Over $5,000,000	$2,550,800, plus 70% of the excess of such amount over $5,000,000.

STATE INHERITANCE AND ESTATE TAXES

An inheritance tax is paid by those who receive the property; an estate tax is paid by the estate. Most states impose an inheritance tax, but some impose an estate tax instead. Others impose both. The state inheritance tax (or estate tax, if that is the case) usually is set at a lower rate than the federal estate tax. Note, though, that state exemptions usually are smaller than federal exemptions. Thus, the actual state tax due can be, and often is, considerably higher than the federal tax due.

State inheritance taxes are based on the value of the assets inherited by the individual. They are owed to the state in which the inherited assets are located rather than the state in which the person inheriting them lives. In many cases, the state tax rate varies not only with the value of the assets but also with the relationship of the recipient to the deceased. Exhibit 20-3 lists state inheritance taxes.

The "Pick Up" Tax

Most states have an added estate tax, which usually is called a "pick up" tax. This tax is designed to ensure that an amount at least equal to the maximum allowable federal estate tax credit is charged. This tax does not, however, increase the *total* death taxes paid; it applies only when the amount due from other state death taxes is less than the allowable federal estate credit.

EXHIBIT 20-2.

FEDERAL ESTATE
TAXES IN 1981
AND AFTER

ADJUSTED GROSS ESTATE	TAXES DUE AT FIRST PARTNER'S DEATH	TAXES DUE AT DEATH
(after subtracting debts, funeral expenses, administrative costs, etc.)	(includes marital deduction)	(single persons)
$ 60,000	$ 0	$ 0
80,000	0	0
100,000	0	0
200,000	0	6,600
300,000	0	37,200
400,000	0	68,000
500,000	21,400	98,900
1,000,000	98,800	265,600

EXHIBIT 20-3.
**STATE
INHERITANCE TAX
RATES**
Source: Commerce Clearing House

SELECTED CATEGORIES OF HEIRS AS OF SEPTEMBER 1, 1976

State	Rate (percent)			Maximum rate applies above (thousands)
	Spouse, child or parent	Brother or sister	Other than relative	
California	3—14	6—20	10—24	$ 400
Colorado	2—8	3—10	10—19	500
Connecticut	2—8	4—10	8—14	1,000
Delaware	1—6	5—10	10—16	200
Hawaii	1.5—7.5	3.5—9	3.5—9	250
Idaho	2—15	.4—20	8—30	500
Illinois	2—14	2—14	10—30	500
Indiana	1—10	5—15	7—20	1,500
Iowa	1—8	5—10	10—15	150
Kansas	.5—5	3—12.5	10—15	500
Kentucky	2—10	4—16	6—16	500
Louisiana	2—3	5—7	5—10	25
Maine	5—10	8—14	14—18	250
Maryland	1	10	10	
Massachusetts	1.8—11.8	5.5—19.3	8—19.3	1,000
Michigan	2—8	2—8	10—15	750
Minnesota	1.5—10	6—25	8—30	1,000
Missouri	1—6	3—18	5—30	400
Montana	2—8	4—16	8—32	100
Nebraska	1	1	6—18	60
New Hampshire		15	15	
New Jersey	1—16	11—16	15—16	3,200
North Carolina	1—12	4—16	8—17	3,000
Oregon	3—12	3—12	3—12	500
Pennsylvania	6	15	15	
Rhode Island	2—9	3—10	8—15	1,000
South Dakota		4—16	6—24	100
Tennessee	5.5—9.5	6.5—20	6.5—20	500
Texas	1—6	3—10	5—20	1,000
Virginia	1—5	2—10	5—15	1,000
Washington	1—10	3—20	10—25	500
West Virginia	3—13	4—18	10—30	1,000
Wisconsin	1.25—12.5	5—25	10—30	500
Wyoming	2	2	6	
District of Columbia	1—8	5—23	5—23	1,000

PRACTICAL APPLICATIONS

HOW TO MAKE
OUT YOUR WILL

THE COMPOSITION OF A WILL

When you reach your state's legal age and if you have many assets, you should make out a will. While each will is different, most have at least five principle sections.

1. The opening recitation.

2. The dispositive clauses.

3. The administrative clauses.

4. A testamonium clause.

5. An attestation clause.

Opening Recitation

This part of a will indicates who you are, where you live, and that you are of sound mind and competent to make a will. In addition, this section may revoke all previous wills, indicate that all debts and funeral expenses should be paid, and, sometimes, give instructions as to how you should be buried.

Dispositive Clauses

This section indicates who should get what. In other words, it indicates legacies, of which there are four types: (1) specific, (2) general, (3) demonstrative, and (4) residuary.

Specific legacy. A particular piece of property in the estate is given to a particular person or institution; for example, you give your dog to your daughter.

General legacy. You give a specific amount of money to an individual or institution. Such a cash bequest is paid out of the general assets in the estate.

Demonstrative legacy. A specific amount of money is bequeathed, along with the source of its payment; for example, $5,000 a year will go to the deceased's mother to be paid out of royalties on books he has written.

Residuary legacy. This bequest is payable out of the remainder of the estate after everything else has been paid, including the preceding three types of legacies and all debts and administrative expenses.

Administrative Clauses

The section of the will containing administrative clauses sets up the machinery for making sure your instructions are followed. In this section, you name your executors and the guardians for any minor children you have. Shortly, we will describe the duties of an executor or executrix.

Testamonium Clause

The testamonium clause concludes the will and indicates that you are signing your name to approve it. The will should not, however, be signed unless witnesses are present. An unwitnessed will may be no better than a blank piece of paper.

Attestation Clause

The attestation clause is signed by witnesses. It indicates that they know you signed the will of your own free will and were of sound mind when you did it. Witnesses must sign in the presence of each other, as well as in your presence.

THE IMPORTANT JOB OF THE EXECUTOR

In every will, you must indicate who shall carry out your instructions. The persons or institutions who carry out your instructions are called your executors. Choosing an executor is a difficult task. You must be able to trust that person or institution and believe that he, she, or it will take a personal interest in seeing that your estate is properly handled after your death. Many states have limitations on who can be an executor. For example, Florida requires that the executor either be a blood relative or a resident of the state of Florida; if you live in Florida, you could not name as executor for your estate a close friend who lived in California.

The Executor's Duties

It would be impossible to indicate all the duties the executor must perform, but here are some.

1. Managing the estate until it is settled, including
    a. Collecting debts due the estate.
    b. Managing real estate; arranging for maintenance and repairs.
    c. Registering securities in the name of the estate.
    d. Collecting insurance proceeds.
    e. Running family business, if necessary.
    f. Arranging for the family's support during probate.
    g. Properly insurancing assets.

2. Collecting all assets and necessary records, including
    a. Locating the will, insurance policies, real estate papers, car registrations, and birth certificates.
    b. Filing claims for pension, Social Security, profit sharing and veterans benefits.
    c. Taking possession of bank accounts, real estate, personal effects, and safe deposit boxes.
    d. Obtaining names, addresses, and Social Security numbers of all heirs.
    e. Making an inventory of all assets.
    f. Setting up records and books.

3. Determining the estate's obligations, including
    a. Determining which claims are legally due.
    b. Obtaining receipts for all claims paid.
    c. Checking on mortgages and other loans

4. Computing and then paying all death taxes due, which requires
    a. Selecting the most beneficial tax alternatives.
    b. Deciding which assets to sell to provide necessary funds.
    c. Paying taxes on time to avoid penalties.
    d. Opposing what you think are unfair evaluations established by governmental taxing authorities.

5. Computing beneficiaries' shares and then distributing the estate, which includes
    a. Determining who gets particular items and settling family disputes.
    b. Transferring title to real estate and other property.
    c. Selling off assets to pay cash legacies.
    d. Paying final estate costs.
    e. Preparing accountings for the court's approval.

Given the amount of work involved in executing a will, one would hope that the executor or executrix would take a personal interest. A friend or relative might; but such a person might lack the necessary financial training to do so properly. That's why some people make a close relative or personal friend one co-executor and name a professional trust company as another co-executor.

AVOIDING COMMON MISTAKES

Lawyers who handle estates and wills frequently encounter a number of related mistakes. Here are some of those mistakes and suggestions for avoiding them.

Writing Your Will Yourself

Handwritten wills (officially called holographic) are legal in less than 50 percent of the states. Even in states where they are legal, it is difficult to establish their validity. Oral wills are generally accepted only during combat, although some states recognize oral wills made during a final illness.

Disinheritance

If you desire to disinherit a particular family member (where it is possible to do so), you must be explicit in your will. Otherwise, the disinherited person may be able to persuade a court that you were not competent to make the will. You might want to write the following:

After careful thought and introspection, I have decided and hence determined that it is better not to include a bequest to my niece, Martha.

Misunderstanding State Requirements

Each state has different requirements for a valid will. When you die, your permanent residence determines which state's laws apply. If you retire to California, make sure that the will you had made in Minnesota is valid.

Not Keeping Your Will Up-to-Date

In many states, a will becomes invalid if it was drawn up before you either married or had children. Any change in civil status or family should dictate that a new will is in order with new specifications about dividing your estate.

Not Reappraising Your Executor or Executrix Regularly

What if you named as an executor a person who since has become mentally incompetent? What if you named as an executrix a woman who died? It will take much longer than usual to wind up an estate when such an event occurs. In any case, it is generally wise to name an alternate executor or executrix in case the first person you chose cannot or will not serve.

Not Specifying What Happens If an Heir Dies before You Do or Simultaneously

Air and automobile travel have increased the likelihood that several members of the same family may die in the same accident. If this happens, it is necessary that a second or even third beneficiary be listed in the will in case the previous one or ones are already dead. You might put a "delay clause" in all insurance policies and in the will; it would specify that the first listed beneficiary must survive you by at least thirty days, or the money will go to other heirs on the list.

Keeping Your Will in a Safe Deposit Box

In many states, your safe deposit box is sealed at your death and cannot be opened without a court order, which may require time and expense.

Not Destroying an Old Will after Making a New One

A new will does not automatically invalidate an old one. The new one must specify that the person making the will revokes all former wills.

Omitting Too Much

Essentially, a will should get rid of the entire estate. In other words, wills should have a clause directing the disposal of residue and remainder.

A LETTER OF LAST INSTRUCTION

In addition to your will, you should have a separate letter of last instruction. The letter, which is opened at death, should contain the following information:

1. The location of your will.
2. Instructions about your burial.
3. The location of all your relevant documents, such as your Social Security card, marriage certificate, and birth certificate.
4. The location of all safe deposit boxes.
5. A list of your life insurance policies and where they are deposited.
6. Pension statements.
7. A list of all stocks and bonds, real and other property, and bank accounts and their locations.

8. Any instructions concerning a business in which you might have been engaged.

9. A statement of reasons for not giving part of your estate to someone who normally would be expected to receive it.

A letter of last instruction is not a legal document. It does not replace a will and should not be considered a substitute for a valid will, which would be accepted by a probate court in the state of residence.

WHERE SHOULD YOU PUT YOUR WILL?

A will should be readily available upon the death of its maker. Therefore, once your will has been written, you should do at least one of the following:

1. Leave the original copy of the will with the attorney who drew it up. The attorney then will put it in a safe deposit box in the law offices or in a financial institution.

2. If you have a safe deposit box at home, you may keep the original copy of the will in it. But this is not often recommended.

3. You can keep the original copy of the will in your own safe deposit box in a financial institution. Many experts object to this placement, however, because a court order may be necessary for the box to be opened after your death.

4. If a professional trust company or financial institution has been named as an executor of the estate, that institution may keep the original copy of the will.

5. Some financial experts suggest that the husband's will be put in the wife's safe deposit box and the wife's will be put in the husband's safe deposit box.

GLOSSARY OF TERMS

WILL   A written document that allows a person to determine the disposition of his or her property at death.

ESTATE   The total property of whatever kind that is owned by a decedent prior to the distribution of that property in accordance with the terms of a will (or, when there is no will, by the laws of inheritance in the state of domicile of the decedent).

TESTATOR/TESTATRIX   A person who has made and/or left a will.

TESTATE   To have died and left a will.

INTESTATE   To have died without leaving a valid will.

EXECUTOR/EXECUTRIX   The personal representative of the person who made a will. The executor takes charge of the estate, pays the debts, and so on.

PROBATE   Proving a will before a court having jurisdiction over the administration of the estate.

JOINT TENANCY   Two or more people own a percentage but not a specific piece of some form of property. When one owner dies, the surviving owner(s) assumes full ownership of the property.

TENANCY BY THE ENTIRETY   Joint owners of property are husband and wife.

TENANCY IN COMMON   Because there are two or more owners of property, transactions involving the property are not legal unless all the owners give their signed permission.

TRUSTEE   The person holding legal title to trust property.

TESTAMENTARY TRUST   A will or trust that bestows specific rights to specific individuals after the death of the person who created the will or trust.

INHERITANCE TAX   A tax assessed by the federal government or the state government (or both) on a certain portion of an estate upon the death of its owner.

LEGACY   A gift of property by will, usually a specific gift for a specific person.

ADMINISTRATIVE CLAUSES   Those clauses in a will that ensure that the instructions are carried out.

TESTAMONIUM CLAUSE   The concluding clause of a will that indicates you are signing your name to approve it.

ATTESTATION CLAUSE   The clause that witnesses sign to validate a will.

CHAPTER SUMMARY

1. Virtually everyone with any assets should have a will prepared; otherwise a person will die intestate.

2. When you die intestate, you have no control over who oversees the distribution of your estate; who will be the guardian for minor children, if your spouse is no longer living; or who will get what percentage of your estate.

3. A will allows you to designate: (a) who gets your property, (b) how much each person or institution gets, (c) when the property will be received, (d) how the property can be safeguarded, and (e) who will handle its disposition.

4. A will disposes of only certain amounts of property; for example, life insurance proceeds automatically go to the stated beneficiary.

5. A will must be probated—that is, taken to the appropriate court to demonstrate that all debts and taxes have been paid and that the will is valid.

6. Probate takes from four months to a year for relatively simple estates and wills and longer for more complicated and contested wills.

7. Joint ownership can assume the following forms: joint tenancy, tenancy by the entirety, and tenancy in common.

8. Even though property is held in common, a will is still necessary.

9. Many wills provide for at least part of the estate to go into a trust that will be administered by a trustee for the benefit of the heirs of the deceased.

10. The trustee has two principal responsibilities: to execute his or her trust responsibility in good faith and to preserve the principal in the trust and invest that principal wisely.

11. There are numerous types of trusts, including life insurance, living, funded, and testamentary.

12. The Tax Reform Act of 1976 greatly reduced and simplified the taxation of estates. All estate and gift taxes are now unified, and there are large credits for married individuals.

13. In addition to federal estate taxes, state inheritance and estate taxes must be paid in certain states.

14. A will usually consists of: (a) an opening recitation, (b) dispositive clauses, (c) administrative clauses, (d) a testamonium clause, and (e) an attestation clause.

15. The dispositive clauses usually indicate the legacies in the will, which can be of four types: (a) specific, (b) general, (c) demonstrative, and (d) residuary.

16. The executor or executrix of a will has numerous duties, including: (a) managing the estate until it is settled, (b) collecting all assets and necessary records, (c) determining the state's obligations, (d) computing and paying all death taxes due, and (e) computing beneficiaries' shares and distributing them.

17. When making out a will, you should: (a) have someone else prepare it, (b) make sure that you specifically disinherit a close relative if you wish to do so, (c) make sure that your current will meets requirements of your current state of residence, (d) make sure your will is changed when your family and financial circumstances change, (e) reappraise your executor/executrix regularly to avoid having an incompetent administer your estate, (f) make sure you specify what happens if an heir dies before you do or at the same time, (g) not leave your *only* copy of the will in a safe deposit box, and (h) make sure you destroy an old will if you have a new one.

18. A letter of last instruction is a document that is opened at death and gives information about the location of your will, your assets, pension statements, and how to run your business.

STUDY QUESTIONS

1. What are the goals of estate planning?

2. Explain the major purpose of a will.

3. What happens when one dies intestate?

4. List and describe the basic parts of a will.

5. How can one legally change the provisions of a will?

6. What is the probate process?

7. What are the three forms of joint ownership? How do they differ from one another?

CASE PROBLEMS

20-1 Wily Waldo's Will

Waldo Ritter was a stubborn, cantankerous, wealthy man of seventy-two years when he took unto himself a beautiful bride some forty years younger than he. His five sons were scandalized and, of course, worried about their inheritance. Waldo assured them that they had nothing to worry about. He held all of his assets as sole owner, and his new wife would inherit only the house (valued at $85,000) and $340,000 in other assets, all of which were specified in his will. His children would then have $6,250,000 to divide equally among themselves. Waldo had to hire—and fire—three attorneys until he found one who would write his will the way he wanted it. Waldo died, smiling, seven years later.

1. What would be each son's share of the gross estate? (Ignore the taxation aspects.)

2. Assuming the state allowed the surviving spouse the right of election, what would be the disposition of the estate if his widow did not like the terms of the will?

3. Assume that Waldo was smiling because he had just been informed of the birth of his second daughter. How would this affect the distribution of the estate?

4. Describe some other ways that Waldo could have arranged for the distribution of his wealth that might have avoided some of the problems and minimized tax effects.

20-2 Zeb Doles Out His Dough

Zebulon Kingston, your great-uncle, has asked you to review his will before he has it witnessed. It reads as follows:

I want to leave my property to my kinfolk. Don't nobody try to change this after I'm gone, or I'll come back and haunt you. Ellie, my wife, gets the house and $80,000 right off the top and anything what's left over after the rest get theirs and the bills are all paid and I'm buried and paid for. Don't want no big funeral, but buy a couple of rounds of drinks for the boys at Don's Bar and Grill on the day you put me under. Give $25,000 to the Salvation Army and $15,000 to Cattleman U. for kids that want to study that personal finance. Also want to give $100,000 to my kids Tom and Dick and $15 and my busted shotgun to my no-good son Harry, so as he can get it fixed and blow his greedy brains out. Got some Xerox and IBM stocks somewhere, cause these pay out about $25,000 a year. Give $5000 a year to Ellie and $20,000 a year to my secretary Madge until she dies, and then the whole thing what's left goes to Ellie. And Ellie, you take care of getting all this done for me, you hear?

Zeb tells you that the estate will be "in the neighborhood" of $700,000 and that he owes $50,000, "give or take a few thousand."

Rearrange Zeb's will in a more acceptable style, and identify the appropriate clauses and the types of legacies.

SELECTED REFERENCES

Ashley, Paul P. *You and Your Will*. New York: McGraw-Hill, 1975.

Consadine, Millie and Pool, Ruth. *Wills: A Dead Give-Away*. New York: Doubleday, 1974.

Freilincher, Morton. *Estate Planning Handbook—with Forms* Englewood Cliffs, NJ: Prentice-Hall, latest edition.

"Maybe Joint Ownership Is Right for You, Maybe Not." *Changing Times*, June 1975, pp. 51-53.

"What If You Were Asked to Be an Executor?" *Changing Times*, October 1970, pp. 37-39.

"Why Estate Planning Makes So Much Sense." *Better Homes & Gardens*, May 1976, pp. 36-40.

Ziegler, Richard S. and Flaherty, P.F. *Estate Planning for Everyone—The Whole Truth from Planning to Probate*. New York: Funk & Wagnalls, 1974.

APPENDIX C

How to Arrange for a Funeral

Here are some suggestions for arranging for a funeral.

1.   Contact the funeral director and, when appropriate, the clergyperson preferred by the family.

2.   Notify the attorney who handled affairs of the deceased.

3.   Secure personal data and any special requests or instructions of the deceased regarding funeral services.

4.   Contact the local newspaper for the obituary.

5. Make necessary arrangements with a cemetery.

6. Cooperate with the funeral director and attorney in securing forms for filing claims with insurance companies, banks, fraternal groups, veteran or military organizations, governmental offices, and others.

KEEPING FUNERAL COSTS REASONABLE

Once you have selected a funeral director, you should obtain a written statement of the charges. The statement should include the following:

1. Services, including merchandise selected, and the total price.

2. The supplemental items of service and merchandise requested and the price of each item.

3. The terms of payment.

4. The items for which the funeral director will advance his or her cash, such as flowers, long distance calls, and so on.

Funeral directors often quote a single amount for "standard" services, including the casket and the use of the funeral home facilities and a hearse. They do not, however, include the cemetery plot (which may have been chosen earlier), the burial or crematory fees, and such items as flowers, obituary notices, and the clergyperson's honorarium.

In addition to the type of funeral service, you will have to decide on at least some of the following four items:

1. Casket.

2. Cemetery space.

3. Grave.

4. Cremation.

After the funeral, a number of legal items which are covered in detail in Chapter 20, have to be dealt with immediately.

INDEX

†